Law and Philosophy

AN INTRODUCTION WITH READINGS

Thomas W. Simon
Illinois State University

McGraw Hill

Boston   Burr Ridge, IL   Dubuque, IA   Madison, WI   New York   San Francisco   St. Louis
Bangkok   Bogotá   Caracas   Lisbon   London   Madrid
Mexico City   Milan   New Delhi   Seoul   Singapore   Sydney   Taipei   Toronto

McGraw-Hill Higher Education

A Division of The McGraw-Hill Companies

LAW AND PHILOSOPHY: AN INTRODUCTION WITH READINGS

1 2 3 4 5 6 7 8 9 0 QPF/QPF 0 9 8 7 6 5 4 3 2 1 0

ISBN 0-07-027587-4

Vice president and editor-in-chief: *Thalia Dorwick*
Editorial director: *Jane E. Vaicunas*
Sponsoring editor: *Monica Eckman*
Editorial coordinator: *Hannah Glover*
Project manager: *Christine Walker*
Production supervisor: *Kara Kudronowicz*
Coordinator of freelance design: *David W. Hash*
Freelance cover design: *Joshua Van Drake*
Senior photo research coordinator: *Carrie K. Burger*
Compositor: *Carlisle Communications, Ltd.*
Typeface: *10/12 New Century Schoolbook*
Printer: *Quebecor Printing Book Group/Fairfield, PA*

Library of Congress Cataloging-in-Publication Data

Simon, Thomas W., 1945–
    Law and philosophy : an introduction with readings / Thomas W. Simon.—1st ed.
        p.   cm.
    Includes bibliographical references and index.
    ISBN 0-07-027587-4
    1. Law—Philosophy.   I. Title.

K235 .S57   2001
340'.1—dc21   00-024792
                                                          CIP

www.mhhe.com

For

Sylvia E. Simon
—who lived to see some things "put on good paper"

Eva Emmalien Visscher-Simon
—who matured faster than the book and the author

Frank Michelman, Harvard Law School
—who exemplifies the best in law and teaching

William Banner, Howard University
—who exemplifies the best in philosophy and teaching

And in Memory of

Isabel Hollands
—who wanted me to become a lawyer sooner

Summary of Contents

Table of Contents

Acknowledgments

Since this textbook was written for students, I gratefully acknowledge the critical role Illinois State University students played in creating this work. Ann Vybiral, with admirable organizational skills and unrewarded dedication, guided the project through its initial stages. Jason Heinrich excelled as a critic and commentator. Dylan Burch ably and energetically commanded the project through rough waters. Scott Berends worked laboriously compiling materials. Amy Hoch adeptly moved from teaching assistant to teacher's teacher. Jeff Bricker, Beth Ferrara, Jinell Gordon, Alexis Kapf, Mollie Monroe, Eddie O'Kelly, Jeanine Sabanas, Rachel Tulle and many others lent helpful (and greatly appreciated) hands. For most of these students, the project became a labor of love. My thanks also go to the many other students at Illinois State University who field-tested the material.

David Adams (California State University, Pomona), editor of a leading anthology in legal philosophy, deserves special mention. We began a project together that became different from the original conception. David's professional standards and accomplishments set goals that I continually strive to reach. Raymond Belliotti (SUNY at Fredonia) gave crucial doses of helpful suggestions and enthusiastic encouragement. Any high-quality marks for the text should go to him. Any shortcomings can probably be attributed to not taking his advice or that of many others who read portions of the manuscript, including: Marcia Baron (University of Illinois, Champaign-Urbana), Tom Digby (New England College), Pat Franken (Illinois State University), Mark Gould (Haverford), Richard Haynes (University of Florida), Michael Howard (University of Maine, Orono), Walter Probert (University of Florida), David Schuman (University of Oregon), and Carl Wellman (Washington University). Every work I have managed to produce has benefitted from the encouragement of Sandra Bartky (University of Illinois, Chicago Circle) and Elizabeth Bartholet (Harvard Law School).

I gratefully acknowledge the support from the National Endowment for the Humanities, including seminar directors Jules Coleman (Yale Law School), Donald Kommers (University of Notre Dame School of Law), and Crawford Young (University of Wisconsin). Special mention must go to Donald Kommers whose support often helped me through difficult times. A Fulbright Fellowship enabled me to teach materials from the book at the Law Faculty of the University of Ljubljana in Slovenia throughout the trying times of the Kosovo crisis. Dean Kranz and Professor Pavcic did their utmost to make this possible. I also acknowledge the support of Harvard Law School's Liberal Arts Fellowship program, where the project began, as well as the Oregon Humanities Center. Finally, and certainly not least, I wish to acknowledge the generous support of Illinois State University, including the dean, Paul Schollaert. Without the steady and helpful guidance of Julie Gowan, chair of the Department of Philosophy, the anthology would never have been published. The chair's assistant, Iris Baird, and the departmental secretary, Donna Larsen, rendered services, again, far beyond the call of duty.

Sarah Moyers, the first editor from McGraw-Hill, believed in the project and patiently gave excellent professional advice and unending support. Monica Eckman, the current editor, has done an outstanding job taking over the project midstream.

Nora Visscher-Simon, Eva Emmalien Visscher-Simon, and Petra Visscher again stood steadfast in putting their lives on hold so that this work could be completed. Many apologies and many thanks.

Preface

Although students in philosophy of law will make up the primary audience for this text, the work should appeal to a broad audience, including those studying jurisprudence in law school and political theory in political science. Students and teachers will find a diverse selection of readings. The work serves as an introduction to law as well as an introduction to philosophy. The readings include many of the classics from the history of political philosophy; Plato, Aristotle, Aquinas, Hobbes, Rousseau, and Locke who regain their prominent places in philosophy of law. By providing basic introductory and historical information, students receive a solid grounding in the law as well. They will attain a greater appreciation for issues through a familiarity with basic legal concepts and with legal history. The introductory materials in chapter 1 provide an overview of common and civil law as well as regional and international systems. Students also receive a solid grounding in legal reasoning in chapter 3, and constitutional interpretation in chapter 4. They benefit from knowing how to apply the analyses to concrete situations. The anthology contains a broad selection of cases, extensively edited to exclude technical legal issues and other extraneous materials. With a few exceptions, case citations and footnotes have been deleted from the selections to facilitate reading. Commentaries and analyses follow many of the cases. Along with case excerpts, the introductory material and Discussion Issues sections contain descriptions of many more cases. For ease of exposition, a simplified and somewhat idiosyncratic reference form has been adopted within the body of the text. Cases and scholarly works are cited by name, date, and page numbers. Case citations and an extensive bibliography appear at the end of the book.

The text makes complex legal and philosophical concepts understandable and accessible. Central concepts, the names of key writers, and technical terms appear throughout the text in bold face type. In place of a glossary, technical terms are explained, wherever possible, within the text. Although the text errs on the side of inclusion, it still leaves out important material and bypasses noteworthy authors. Space limitations have precluded giving more attention to important areas of the law, such as environmental law, and to the new intellectual movements (postmodernism, pragmatism) that have recently experienced a growth spurt in law schools. To do justice to these issues requires another volume. Representative voices from contemporary legal theories (communitarianism, critical legal studies, feminist jurisprudence, critical race theory, and law and economics) appear throughout the text. The challenge of balancing breadth with depth has been difficult enough for the wide scope of issues already included. Readers will find the coverage extensive. Constitutional law receives the most attention with international and criminal law having a considerable share as well. Diverse global perspectives inform each issue and legal subject. Discussion Issues, for example, include case materials from Canada, France, Iran, Japan, and South Africa.

Philosophy of law is a story with many common themes. The text roughly traces a time line from law's beginnings in ancient times to current trends in international law. Similarly, it tracks the history of legal theory from its natural law roots to its contemporary, contested realist and moral theory branches. No one theme ties all of this together, but a number of threads give the work continuity. The text, for example, follows issues of responsibility (legal and moral) for violence as they recur throughout history. The themes give a unity and a noteworthy seriousness to the anthology. Issues surrounding war crimes tribunals (the Nuremberg trials) occur near the beginning of the text (chapter 2), and the anthology ends (chapter 8) with an assessment of the newly formed International Criminal Court. Some theorists make their voices heard in a number of chapters. For example, the modern works of Hobbes, Locke, and Kant and contemporary ones from H. L. A. Hart and Ronald Dworkin provide continuity. The contrasts between Hart's and Dworkin's philosophies become more marked as their theories are applied to new issues throughout the text. The opinions of some U.S. Supreme Court justices (Blackmun, Brennan, Marshall, Rehnquist, and Scalia) receive more than their fair share of coverage in the pages that follow. The redundancy has a purpose. Issues will begin to converge. Students will see, for example, how Justice Brennan applies his philosophical approach to a wide variety of cases, including those dealing with child abuse and the death penalty. Brennan's approach becomes more pronounced when compared to the theoretical perspective adopted by Justice Rehnquist on the same issues. These legal disputes have profound implications for the nature of law.

A text in philosophy of law should challenge students. A number of mechanisms help compensate for excluded areas. Undergraduate students want to find out about law schools, and in this anthology, they will have a window into academic disputes raging in law schools. They also read about debates concerning legal education, including the controversy over affirmative action as it affects law schools. Questions do not appear only in the designated Discussion Issues section, but rather appear throughout the text. The questions do not simply interrogate the readings. They also help extend the breadth and depth of coverage in the main body of each chapter.

The anthology has the advantage of giving instructors considerable flexibility. The units and selections, preceded by appropriate introductory material, are self-contained. This gives instructors more freedom to design an organizational structure that best suits their students' needs. For example, while a single section focuses on free speech, cases and materials relating to this issue are included throughout the anthology. Instructors will find it difficult to include all the materials in a single semester course. They may, for example, choose to focus solely on constitutional issues, covered in chapters 4–6 (constitutional law per se, Bill of Rights, privacy, and equality). The chapters break down into distinct areas of law (international, constitutional, and criminal) and into different philosophical concepts (values, reasoning, liberalism, freedom, rights, equality, responsibility, and punishment).

Introduction

Philosophy and law make odd companions. Philosophers use abstract principles that seem to have little or nothing to do with the real world. Lawyers work on concrete issues that appear far removed from the abstract world of philosophers. Philosophy students learn about theories that try to provide some degree of unity and coherence to a subject matter. Law students study many different types of laws that seem to have little or nothing to do with one another. Philosophy of law offers to help make sense of law. Armed with abstract principles, it unifies "the scraps and fragments" of law.

> I will venture to affirm, that no other body of Law, obtaining in a civilized community, has so little of consistency and symmetry as our own [English law]. Hence its enormous bulk; and (what is infinitely worst than its bulk) the utter impossibility of conceiving it with distinctness and precision. If you would know the English Law, you must know all the details that make up the mess. For it has none of those large coherent principles which are a sure index to details. And, since details are infinite, it is manifest that no man (let his industry be what it may) can encompass the whole system.
>
> Consequently, the knowledge of an English Lawyer, is nothing but a beggarly [inadequate] account of scraps and fragments. His memory may be stored with numerous particulars, but of the Law as a whole, and of the mutual relations of its parts, he has not a conception. . . .
>
> To the student who begins the study of the English law, without some previous knowledge of the rationale of law in general, it naturally appears an assemblage of arbitrary and unconnected rules. But if he approached it with a well-grounded knowledge of the general principles of jurisprudence, and with the map of a body of law distinctly impressed upon his mind, he might obtain a clear conception of it (as a system or organic whole) with comparative ease and rapidity.
>
> With comparative ease and rapidity, he might perceive the various relations of its various parts; the dependence of its minuter rules on general principles;

and the subordination of such of these principles as are less general or extensive, to such of them as are more general, and run through the whole of its structure (Austin, *Lectures on Jurisprudence* [1869], Vol. II, pp. 1117–18).

Further, philosophy of law brings to the surface moral and other philosophical issues that often remain hidden within law's technicalities. A study of philosophy and law has mutual benefits. Philosophy attains a degree of relevance through its study of law, and law achieves greater clarity through philosophy.

> Philosophy needs an interest in the law to recover for itself the motivation that belongs only to matters of felt importance, and the respect that is accorded only to those who are making a contribution to the life of their times. The law needs philosophy to restore to itself that direction, clarification, and background, which it appears to have lost (E. T. Mitchell [1937], p. 113).

Since law has a close—although not always happy—relationship with politics, **political philosophy** plays a crucial role in law. The chapters that follow focus on different areas of law and on different philosophers and philosophies. A classical political philosopher anchors each area of the law covered: **Thomas Hobbes** (law of "primitive" cultures), **Immanuel Kant** (international law), **John Locke** (constitutional law), and **Friedrich Nietzsche** (criminal law). The philosophers offer distinct perspectives on law and on human nature. Some political philosophers talk about the **state of nature,** in which humans live without all the rules, laws, and institutions that define civil society. The seventeenth-century English philosopher Thomas Hobbes found the natural state an unpleasant one, in which life became "solitary, poor, nasty, brutish, and short" (*Leviathan* 1651). The bleak image of a Hobbesian state of nature, "where every man is Enemy to every man," made a lasting impact on political philosophy and on law. Hobbes's analysis brings to the surface fundamental and sometimes disturbing questions about humans, society, and law. Are humans, by nature, nasty, greedy, and aggressive? Can governments tame those natural instincts only through authoritarian means? Does the law play a key role in the authoritarian state?

A reading from Hobbes begins chapter I. Hobbes plays a central role in the analysis, as evidenced by the many references to him throughout the text. Like the Hobbesian image, which still sets the framework for debates over international law, fundamental questions reappear throughout the study. Those who take a pragmatic, realistic view, for example, believe self-interested states in the world of international politics operate in the same way that Hobbes's individuals do in the state of nature. On a realist's view, international law has little or no moral content, since it arises out of contracts among independent nation-states. In contrast to the realist, the Enlightenment philosopher, Immanuel Kant, has inspired a moral approach to international law. In *Perpetual Peace* (1795), he envisioned "moral states" evolving to a point at which they would agree to denounce war. Kant, far ahead of his time in his thinking about international law, found hope in the idea of nations moving from a state where the threat of war is constant to a state of perpetual peace. A reading from Kant begins chapter 2.

Moral philosophy comes to the forefront in chapter 3 in the context of **Ronald Dworkin's** highly influential work on judicial decision making.

The focus then turns more explicitly to constitutional law in chapter 4. Many scholars credit John Locke, a seventeenth-century English philosopher, with laying the intellectual foundation for the U.S. Constitution. Locke painted a far more benign picture of the state of nature than Hobbes did. His philosophy set the foundation for a limited government. His **liberalism** and its associated constitutional solutions to social problems, however, have come under attack from proponents of **communitarianism** and **critical legal studies.** The writings of the nineteenth-century philosopher **John Stuart Mill** plays a critical role in chapter 5 on freedom (liberty). Chapter 6 pits Dworkin and other proponents of rights against their critics, including **Richard Rorty** and **Michael Sandel. Aristotle** sets the terms of the debate on equality in chapter 7. Finally, chapter 8 examines responsibility and punishment within criminal law. The chapter highlights **Nietzsche,** who raised provocative questions about human irrationality and state brutality. With questions on human nature, we come, full circle, back to Hobbes. The final section, on international criminal law, also brings the discussion back to Kant. Although law has a natural affinity with political philosophy, other branches of philosophy receive ample attention. Chapter 1 provides a brief introduction to philosophy. **Ethics** plays a key role in almost every philosophical analysis of law. Different ethical theories—for example, **deontology** (basing ethics on duty) and **utilitarianism** (basing ethics on overall goodness)—provide radically different assessments of law. **Epistemology** (study of knowledge) and **logic** (study of correct reasoning) also receive their due, particularly in chapter 3.

As noted, this textbook serves as an introduction to law as well as an introduction to philosophy. Chapter 1 surveys different legal systems and branches of law, highlighting international, constitutional, and criminal law. In chapter 2 on **international law,** war crimes and slavery cases receive considerable attention since they raise issues of cultural relativists' challenges to a universal ethics. Chapter 3 includes examples from **private law,** particularly **contracts** and **torts.** Chapter 4 traces the development of the philosophical foundations of **constitutional law.** Separate chapters cover the different constitutional issues of freedom, rights, and equality. Chapter 5 deals with **freedom,** especially the freedoms of speech and religion guaranteed by the Bill of Rights of the U.S. Constitution. Chapter 6 highlights fundamental **rights,** primarily privacy rights revolving around abortion and the right to die. Chapter 7 turns the focus to **equality** particularly, the equal protection issues of discrimination and affirmative action. Finally, chapter 8, on **criminal law,** examines responsibility and punishment, especially as they apply to the insanity defense and to the death penalty.

The book thoroughly covers classical and contemporary versions of the following legal theories: **natural law, legal positivism, formalism, legal realism,** and **constructivism.** The text traces these through the history of jurisprudence. It begins with natural law in ancient Greece and ends with natural law's reformulation in contemporary jurisprudence. The reader will have ample exposure to leading figures in the history of jurisprudence: natural law theorist **St. Thomas Aquinas,** legal positivists **John Austin** and **H. L. A. Hart,** and constructivist **Ronald Dworkin.** Lesser known figures— formalist Christopher Columbus Langdell, pragmatist Oliver Wendell Holmes, realist Felix Cohen, and many more—will also become familiar. Despite the breadth of coverage, the demands of depth require excluding a thorough treatment of the most recent legal theories. Space does not permit doing full justice to recent approaches to jurisprudence, including **critical legal studies, feminist jurisprudence, critical race theory,** and **law and economics.** However, brief introductions to the new perspectives appear in their invaluable role as critics of traditional jurisprudence.

Lively cases and heated debates, reprinted throughout the text, challenge preconceptions on controversial issues. The text takes a novel approach to **applied ethics,** with moral issues becoming more concrete in their legal setting. Also, since many moral issues in the United States take on a legal framework, "applied ethics in law" represents a realistic approach to these issues. A wide variety of accessible philosophical readings should sharpen critical faculties to assess the issues. Introductions that describe the authors and their positions provide a context for each reading and include questions to guide the reader. The Discussion Issues in each chapter take the reader beyond the readings by posing informative and provocative questions for discussion and research. Each chapter includes one or more Controversies sections, which throw the philosophical analyses and legal formulations into the heat of the political fires. The success of the journey has no exact measure. Philosophers may not make better lawyers, but they probably make better law students because law schools are dominated by appellate arguments which appear in abundance in this text. In any event, readers should come away better informed about philosophy and about law. The questions raised, however, may prove more valuable than the answers given. Minimally, the journey should provide a sense of how philosophy and law enrich one another.

CHAPTER 1

Law and Philosophy

PRELIMINARY INQUIRIES

". . . and the life of man, solitary, poor, nasty, brutish, and short."
THOMAS HOBBES (1651), *Leviathan*, ch. XIII.

Individuals often bring prejudices, biases, opinions, and distorted images to a subject. For whatever reasons, law and philosophy seem particularly vulnerable to common misrepresentations. For example, in *Henry VI,* Shakespeare said, "The first thing we do, let's kill all the lawyers." On the other hand, Plato said, ". . . the human race will not be free of evils until either the stock of those who rightly and truly follow philosophy acquire political authority or the class who have power in the cities be led by some dispensation of providence to become real philosophers" (*Epistles* 7, 325d6–326b4. Did Shakespeare really want to kill all the lawyers? Did Plato want to make all philosophers rulers? What do professional lawyers and professional philosophers do?

Page 2 of this chapter includes materials that explore various opinions and images about law and philosophy. The selections on page 4 raise broad questions, not only about law, but also about society and human nature. Different views about the **nature of humans** and about the basis for society lead to different ideas about law. The issue of law's relationship to morality unfolds on page 13 with questions about **civil disobedience.** The materials included in these three sections begin to raise questions that recur throughout the study of law and philosophy. The chapter provides brief introductions to **philosophy** on page 23, to **law** on page 25, and to varieties of **legal systems** on page 28.

Please note that citations to philosophical and other scholarly works appear within the text in the following order: author, publication date, and page number. Bibliographic sources appear at the end of the text. To economize, most footnotes, including case citations, have been deleted from the readings. Footnotes, when used, and article sections have been renumbered.

"The first thing we do, let's kill all the lawyers."
WILLIAM SHAKESPEARE, 2 *Henry VI,* 4.2.78

Lawyers have seldom won any popularity contests. In "The Lawyers Know Too Much," a poem by Carl Sandburg, the speaker praises the bricklayer, the mason, the farmer, and others whose work outlives them. The speaker then wonders "why a hearse horse snickers, hauling a lawyer's bones away" (Llewellyn 1930, p. 170). This illustrates a long-held public attitude toward lawyers. Before we consider the views of others about law and lawyers, though, we need to examine our own preconceptions. Images have a powerful hold on our thinking. What visual image do you have of law and lawyers? Benjamin Sells invites us to consider law's image in Reading 1-1 from *Psychoanalyzing Law.* After reading the selection, imagine yourself as a psychotherapist. "Law" makes an appointment to visit. What does "Law" look like? Is it old? Male? Conservative? What would it say to you?

READING 1-1

Psychoanalyzing Law
"What Does the Law Want?" (1994)

Benjamin Sells

The most important first step in understanding anything psychologically is to get an image. Images are more complete, more fertile, than concepts because they have a broader range of expression and are therefore more precise. Also, images allow our personal perspectives to coalesce with more enduring psychic patterns. So, in turning a psychological eye to the Law, we first need an *image* of what we are talking about.

I ask the reader to conduct the following experiment:

Imagine you are a psychotherapist. It's mid-afternoon on a Wednesday in October. You're sitting in your office, catching up on some mail. Your next session isn't for a couple of hours, and you're just getting ready to start a letter to a colleague when a knock comes on your door. You quickly double-check your appointment book to make sure you haven't forgotten someone, but no, the blank lines confirm that no one is due until four. You open the door and a person is standing there whom you have never seen before, but who bears a certain distant familiarity.

"Hello," says the person, "I'm the Law. I want to talk with you about some things."

"Come in, come in," you say, not really sure what to make out of this.

"I'm sorry to show up without an appointment," says the Law. "But I just happened to be walking down the street and saw your sign out front. I hadn't really thought about coming to a therapist until about five minutes ago, but then I decided what the hell, I might as well give it a shot. Do you have some time to talk?"

"Sure," you say. "My next appointment isn't for a while yet. Here, let me take your coat. Would you like some coffee? Tea?"

Question One: What does the person who has just walked into your office look like? Be very precise, and try to imagine this person in detail. Is the Law male or female? Old, young, middle-aged? How is the Law dressed? What kind of coat did you take from the Law? Is the Law carrying anything? Does the Law prefer coffee or tea? How does the Law speak, move, sit? Can you see the Law's eyes? What are they like? Try to imagine the Law as clearly as you can, getting as full-fledged an image as possible. Concentrate on the details, and be as accurate as you can.

"So," you say as you both sit down, "what brings you here?"

"Like I said, I was just walking down the street and saw your sign."

"Was there anything in particular you wanted to talk about?"

The Law sits silently for a moment, and appears to be staring at something on the floor halfway between the two of you. Then the Law looks up and says "Yes, I guess there is something bothering me."

Question Two: What does the Law say? What's bothering the Law?

From Sells (1994) *The Soul of the Law.* Rockport, MA: Element Books, Inc., pp. 23–24. Reprinted with permission.

DISCUSSION ISSUES

1. *Lawyer Jokes.* In William Shakespeare's *Henry VI,* Dick the Butcher speaks the line that appears at the beginning of the chapter about killing all the lawyers. This may qualify as one of the most recited lines from Shakespeare—often quoted after the telling of a lawyer joke. A more charitable reading came from U.S. Supreme Court Justice John Paul Stevens, who countered the common anti-lawyer interpretation of the passage when he said, "As a careful reading of that text will reveal, Shakespeare insightfully realized that disposing of lawyers is a step in the direction of a totalitarian form of government" (*Walter v. National Ass'n of Radiation Survivors,* p. 371, n. 24, Stevens, J. dissenting). Daniel J. Kornstein (1994), a lawyer, proposed the following three possible interpretations: (1) Common rebel leader Cade had just finished a speech to the common folk concerning what he would do when he became king. His campaign promises included abolishing money and making it a felony to drink small beer. Dick's charge may have amounted to a joke blurted out in response to Cade's speech. (2) Dick's claim may have been a serious political charge. He was from the uneducated peasant class, and lawyers protected the English upper class. Soon after Dick's line was spoken, Cade executed a clerk because he could write. Cade associated the clerk with the literate rulers and oppressors, which included lawyers. (3) Dick may not have been attacking all law, but only its perverted forms. The Duke of Gloucester had implemented the law in a fair and humane manner during the infancy of King Henry VI. The peasants rebelled after Gloucester's murder.

   Collect some lawyer jokes and then consider these questions. Do the jokes convey serious charges against lawyers and the law? Do lawyers train to avoid the truth? Do philosophers study to find the truth?

2. *The Power of Images.* Just as you visualized Law, now try to visualize "Crime." What are the first images, words, and associations that come to your mind when you think about crime? Do you imagine darkness? Does the image include a non-white male hurting someone or stealing something? Do the associations include corporations?

   Do the same experiment for "Rape." Do you imagine a stranger attacking at night? Most rapes are committed by someone the victim knows. Does the name of the protest day to counter violence against women, "Take Back the Night," convey a misleading image? Should the name be changed to "Take Back the Day"?

3. *False Images of Philosophers.* Do philosophers deserve the title "Great Thinkers"? Should the study of philosophy consist of the study of great thinkers such as Socrates, who, in his search for knowledge and the good life, continually asked questions? According to Socrates, "Those who really apply themselves in the right way to philosophy are preparing themselves for dying and death" (Plato, *Phaedo,* 640a, p. 116). Plato viewed Socrates as "truly the wisest and justest, and best of all the men I have ever known" (Epistle VII). He has become the model philosopher. Has the cult of Socrates created a false image of philosophers?

4. *Philosophical Lawyers.* Philosophical discussions often seem neverending, and philosophical questions seem never to have a right answer. Philosophy poses a nuisance to lawyers who face pressing practical problems. However Martha Nussbaum, a philosopher who teaches at a law school, urges law teachers to encourage students to philosophize more, not less (Nussbaum 1993). She challenges law students to wonder more, and approvingly quotes the following passage:

   > Philosophy does not stand outside the world any more than man's brain is outside him because it is not in his stomach. But philosophy, to be sure, is in the world with its brain before it stands on the earth with its feet, while many other human spheres have long been rooted in the earth and pluck the fruits of the world long before they realize that the "head" also belongs to this world or that this world is the world of the head.

Does this view from Karl Marx (1882), then a young doctoral student, undermine the picture of the impractical, other-worldly philosopher?

B. NATURAL STATE OF WAR: HOBBES

"Man was not created governed."

A. M. HOCART, *KINGS AND COUNCILLORS*

Law pervades much of what we do and governs many human interactions. The law shapes some relationships—child-parent, wife-husband, student-teacher, employer-employee, and landlord-tenant—and creates other relationships, such as a corporation's board of directors and its shareholders. Laws place limits on behavior and establish boundaries. They mark an individual's private space, set limits on noise levels from neighbors, and provide ways to enforce property lot lines. Warning signs on commercial products are often the result of a lawsuit. For example, McDonald's Restaurants serve coffee a particular way because a jury awarded eighty-one-year-old Stella Liebeck $2.9 million (reduced by the judge to $640,000) for injuries suffered when she spilled scalding coffee on herself. It may prove difficult to find areas of life that are untouched by law.

Imagine a society without any laws or legal rules. How would survivors on a deserted island deal with their former institutional structures? Would the validity of marriages from the old society be recognized in the new society? Does it even make sense to speak about marriage without laws? How would the inhabitants enforce rights to private possessions? How would they establish territorial boundaries? What would they do about noisy neighbors? Would the inhabitants turn on each other to gather whatever they could for themselves? Would they allow brute force to rule? If humans are by nature aggressive, and if they are motivated primarily by self-preservation, then an authoritarian government would be an attractive escape from the turbulent natural state. Alternatively, a more idyllic and peaceful natural state might lead to the rejection or at least the questioning of the more violent and repressive "civilized" state left behind. Would humans cooperate with one another and share resources once they had recognized their common plight?

Philosophers conceptualize a prepolitical stage before civilization called a **state of nature.** When they imaginatively lift the constraints of the civilized world, does the resulting state of nature look like a forced march through a battlefield? Or does it seem more like a pleasant stroll through the woods? Historians associate the brutal battlefield image with **Thomas Hobbes** (1558–1679) and the serene, natural image with **Jean-Jacques Rousseau** (1712–1778). Between these two extremes lies a conception developed by **John Locke** (1632–1704). In a Lockean state of nature, individuals neither inevitably fall into a state of war against one another, nor do they establish a blissful state of peace and harmony. Individuals coexist without the need of a higher authority to establish order, but a state of war becomes a threat and a reality. Lockeans establish a government and laws to preserve rights found in the state of nature. Unlike Hobbesian individuals, however, they refuse to give up all of their rights, including the right to abolish the government. Hobbes and his views of human nature will be covered in this chapter, while Locke's views will be presented in chapter 4 on liberalism and constitutional law. Rousseau's views provide a counterbalance throughout the text.

Philosophers have imagined a state of nature in order to probe more deeply into questions about law, human nature, and the origins of society. Hobbes provided a classical description of a hypothetical state of nature—of life without civil authority. Individuals caught in this state of constant conflict would have a way out of their predicament. They could enter an agreement to establish order, but they would have to pay a price for this security. That is, they would have to give up the liberty they enjoyed in the state of nature. By handing over their natural rights and liberties to an absolute sovereign, the law would become whatever the sovereign said it was. Hobbes saw law as the command of the sovereign (see section on legal positivism, chapter 2). Because the sovereign—the political authority—makes laws, Hobbes forged a tight link between law and authority. Without legal authority vested in an absolute sovereign, do societies revert to a Hobbesian state of nature? Does only the fear of a coercive power restrain humans?

1. Hypothetical State of Nature

Views about human nature and society influence theories about law. Hobbes's *Leviathan* (1651), in Reading 1-2, provides an excellent place to begin thinking about the role of law in society. Hobbes said that he and fear were twins. When a civil war in 1640 began to turn England upside down, he fled to France, where he tutored the future Charles II in exile. Hobbes set out to defend the crown against attack, and in speculating on what humans would be like without any civil authority to govern them, he found that humans in a state of nature would be in a "continual fear, and danger of violent death." To escape the continual war, humans had to hand over their natural rights to the sovereign. Is Hobbes's vision of the state of nature simply a philosophical device? Do some individuals still live in a Hobbesian state?

2. Real State of Nature?

In his first book, *The Forest People,* anthropologist Colin Turnbull described the Pygmies of Zaire. He presented them as an example of humans who live peacefully without the need of law, as we know it. Pygmies live uncorrupted by the worst and most advanced forms of civilization. They symbolize a peaceful state of nature and show the world how to counterbalance the urge for self-preservation with an inner feeling of compassion. Perhaps, though, outsiders romanticize them.

Those who, like Rousseau, have a positive view of the state of nature, have had some influence on legal theory, but Hobbes's bleaker vision has had a more powerful influence on legal philosophy. In *The Mountain People* (Reading 1-3), Turnbull turned to the Ik of Uganda. The Ik lost their sense of humanity and became a scattered band of hostile people whose only goal was individual survival. Do the Ik personify a Hobbesian state of nature? Does the Ik "society" mirror our own, as Turnbull suggests?

Turnbull describes a band of individuals who may exemplify many features of a Hobbesian state of nature. While Hobbes presents a hypothetical state of nature, Turnbull, perhaps, gives a real description of human nature.

READING 1-2

Human Nature as Anti-Social

"Of the Natural Condition of Mankind as Concerning Their Felicity and Misery" (1651)

Thomas Hobbes

Nature has made men so equal in the faculties of the body and mind as that though there be found one man sometimes manifestly stronger in body or of quicker mind than another, yet, when all is reckoned together, the difference between man and man is not so considerable as that one man can thereupon claim to himself any benefit to which another may not pretend as well as he.

For as to the strength of body, the weakest has strength enough to kill the strongest, either by secret machination or by confederacy with others that are in the same danger with himself.

And as to the faculties of the mind, setting aside the arts grounded upon words and especially that skill of proceeding upon general and infallible rules called science, which very few have and but in few things, as being not a native faculty born with us, nor attained, as prudence, while we look after somewhat else, I find yet a greater equality among men than that of strength. For prudence is but experience, which equal time equally bestows on all men in those things they equally apply themselves unto. That which may perhaps make such equality incredible is but a vain conceit of one's own wisdom, which almost all men think they have in a greater degree than the vulgar; that is, than all men but themselves and a few others whom by fame, or for concurring with themselves, they approve. For such is the nature of men that howsoever they may acknowledge many others to be more witty or more eloquent or more learned, yet they will hardly believe there be many so wise as themselves, for they see their own wit at hand and other men's at a distance. But this proves rather that men are in that point equal than unequal. For there is not ordinarily a greater sign of the equal distribution of anything than that every man is contented with his share.

From this equality of ability arises equality of hope in the attaining of our ends. And therefore if any two men desire the same thing, which nevertheless they cannot both enjoy, they become enemies; and in the way to their end, which is principally their own conservation, and sometimes their delectation only, endeavour to destroy or subdue one another. And from hence it comes to pass that where an invader has no more to fear than another man's single power, if one plant, sow, build, or possess a convenient seat, others may probably be expected to come prepared with forces united to dispossess and deprive him not only of the fruit of his labour, but also of his life or liberty. And the invader again is in the like danger of another.

And from this diffidence of one another there is no way for any man to secure himself so reasonable as anticipation; that is, by force or wiles to master the persons of all men he can so long till he see no other power great enough to endanger him, and this is no more than his own conservation requires and is generally allowed. Also because there be some that taking pleasure in contemplating their own power in the acts of conquest, which they pursue farther than their security requires, if others that otherwise would be glad to be at ease within modest bounds should not by invasion increase their power, they would not be able, long time, by standing only on their defense, to subsist. And by consequence, such augmentation of dominion over men being necessary to a man's conservation, it ought to be allowed him.

Again, men have no pleasure, but on the contrary a great deal of grief in keeping company where there is no power able to over-awe them all. For every man looks that his companion should value him at the same rate he sets upon himself; and, upon all signs of contempt or undervaluing, naturally endeavours as far as he dares (which among them that have no common power to keep them in quiet is far enough to make them destroy each other) to extort a greater value from his contemners by damage, and from others by the example.

So that in the nature of man we find three principal causes of quarrel. First, competition; secondly, diffidence; thirdly, glory.

The first makes men invade for gain; the second for safety; and the third for reputation. The first use violence to make themselves masters of other men's persons, wives, children, and cattle; the second to defend them; the third for trifles, as a word, a smile, a different opinion, and any other sign of undervalue, either direct in their persons or by reflection in their kindred, their friends, their nation, their profession, or their name.

Hereby it is manifest that during the time men live without a common power to keep them all in awe, they are in that condition which is called war; and such a war as is of every man against every man. For WAR consists not in battle only, or the act of fighting, but in a tract of time wherein the will to contend by battle is sufficiently known; and therefore the notion of *time* is to be considered in the nature of war as it is in the nature of weather. For as the nature of foul weather lies not in a shower or two of rain but in an inclination thereto of many days together, so the nature of war consists not in actual fighting but in the known disposition thereto during all the time there is no assurance to the contrary. All other time is PEACE.

Whatsoever therefore is consequent to a time of war, where every man is enemy to every man, the same is consequent to the time wherein men live without other security than what their own strength and their own invention shall furnish them withal. In such condition there is no place for industry, because the fruit thereof is uncertain; and consequently no culture of the earth; no navigation nor use of the commodities that may be imported by sea; no commodious building; no instruments of moving and removing such things as require much force; no knowledge of the face of the earth; no account of time; no arts; no letters; no society; and which is worst of all, continual fear and danger of violent death; and the life of man, solitary, poor, nasty, brutish, and short.

It may seem strange to some man that has not well weighed these things that nature should thus dissociate and render men apt to invade and destroy one another; and he may therefore, not trusting to this inference made from the passions, desire perhaps to have the same confirmed by experience. Let him therefore consider with himself, when taking a journey he arms himself and seeks to go well accompanied; when going to sleep he locks his doors; when even in his house he locks his chests; and this when he knows there be laws and public officers armed to revenge all injuries shall be done him; what opinion he has of his fellow-subjects when he rides armed; of his fellow citizens when he locks his doors; and of his children and servants when he locks his chests. Does he not there as much accuse mankind by his actions as I do by my words? But neither of us accuse man's nature in it. The desires and other passions of man are in themselves no sin. No more are the actions that proceed from those passions till they know a law that forbids them, which till laws be made they cannot know, nor can any law be made till they have agreed upon the person that shall make it.

It may peradventure be thought there was never such a time nor condition of war as this, and I believe it was never generally so over all the world, but there are many places where they live so now. For the savage people in many places of America, except the government of small families, the concord whereof depends on natural lust, have no government at all and live at this day in that brutish manner, as I said before. Howsoever, it may be perceived what manner of life there would be where there were no common power to fear, by the manner of life which men that have formerly lived under a peaceful government use to degenerate into, in a civil war.

But though there had never been any time wherein particular men were in a condition of war one against another, yet in all times, kings and persons of sovereign authority, because of their independency, are in continual jealousies and in the state and posture of gladiators, having their weapons pointing and their eyes fixed on one another; that is, their forts, garrisons, and guns upon the frontiers of their kingdoms; and continual spies upon their neighbours, which is a posture of war. But because they uphold thereby the industry of their subjects, there does not follow from it that misery which accompanies the liberty of particular men.

To this war of every man against every man this also is consequent, that nothing can be unjust. The notions of right and wrong, justice and injustice, have there no place. Where there is no common power, there is no law; where no law, no injustice. Force and fraud are in war the two cardinal virtues. Justice and injustice are none of the faculties neither of the body nor mind. If they were, they might be in a man that were alone in the world as well as his senses and passions. They are qualities that relate to men in society, not in solitude. It is consequent also to the same condition that there be no propriety, no dominion, no *mine* and *thine* distinct; but only that to be every man's that he can get, and for so long as he can keep it. And thus much for the ill condition, which man by mere nature is actually placed in though with a possibility to come out of it, consisting partly in the passions, partly in his reason.

The passions that incline men to peace are fear of death, desire of such things as are necessary to commodious living, and a hope by their industry to obtain them. And reason suggests convenient articles of peace upon which men may be drawn to agreement. These articles are they, which otherwise are called the Laws of Nature. . . .

From Hobbes (1651), *Leviathan*. Reprinted in (1990) *Society and the Individual*. Richard T. Garner and Andrew Oldenquist, editors. Belmont, CA: Wadsworth, pp. 105–107.

READING 1-3
Human Nature as Selfish
"Man Without Law" (1972)

Colin M. Turnbull

There seemed to be increasingly little among the Ik that could by any stretch of the imagination be called social life, let alone social organization. Yet such small-scale societies usually offer a shining example of how man can live sociably with his neighbors, often in the most difficult of circumstances. He even does this without the need for "law" as we know it, and without the physical coercion that accompanies it to force us to behave in the accepted manner. In such societies judgment as to what is right and wrong, good and bad, is based not so much on the nature of the action in question as on the circumstances in which the action took place, and on the sociality of the motivations.

The Congo Pygmies are only one example of this, for among them there is neither any law backed by the threat and possibility of physical coercion nor any centralized authority. The Mbuti Pygmies do not even have a council of elders, and anyone who has influence today may be without it tomorrow. Yet it is not hard to see what holds that society together, for they have all those things the Ik seemingly lack. They have a vital family life and a concept of family that can be expanded to include the band or even larger units. They have an economy that demands cooperation, cutting across differences of age and sex, involving the whole band. It reinforces and is reinforced by the familial ideal. This alone would seem to be enough, but beyond this they have a communal spirit that is difficult to define without either seeming like a woolly-minded romantic or reducing it to terms that are both unromantic and inadequate. It is, let us say, centered on a love for and devotion of their forest world, and results in their wholehearted, unquestioning identification with it. And what more powerful force toward social unity and cohesion can there be than such a deep-rooted sense of identity? All this the Ik lack, and more besides.

When the Pygmies, who are no angels, become involved in disputes, they manage to settle them without stigmatizing anyone as a criminal, without resort to punitive measures, without even passing judgment on the individuals concerned. Settlement is reached with one goal in mind, and that is the restoration of harmony within the band, for the good of the whole. If there is one thing that is surely wrong in their eyes, it is that the dispute should have taken place to begin with, and to this extent both disputants are to blame and are held in temporary disfavor. All this, too, the Ik lack, for while their disputes rarely reach the stage of physical violence, their violence is there, deep and smoldering, scarring each man and woman, making life even more disagreeable and dividing man against his neighbor even further. There is simply no community of interest, familial or economic, social or spiritual.

With the Ik the family does not even hold itself together, much less serve as a model for a wider social brotherhood of Ik. Economic interest is centered on as many individual stomachs as there are people, and cooperation is merely a device for furthering an interest that is consciously selfish. We often do the same thing in our so-called "altruistic" practices, but we tell ourselves it is for the good of others; the Ik have dispensed with the myth of altruism, but they have also largely dispensed with acts that in reality served at least mutual interests. They too have no centralized leadership, nor the means of physical coercion, yet they do undeniably hold together with remarkable tenacity, and I had thought I might uncover something in the realm of law and custom, power and authority, that would offer the explanation. In some instances of transition from tribe to nation the central government supplants custom with law, and authority with power, by the use of the vast technology and armory at its disposal and by its sophisticated techniques of coercion. The Uganda government had the power, and it had supplied a law that was fair and equal to all, but it was unwilling to use the power to enforce the law in any but the most perfunctory manner . . . . To compel the Ik to accept any law or form of government that they did not want to accept would have been a vastly expensive project, and would have involved the open use of brute, and perhaps brutal, force. Coupled with understanding, this might not have been such a bad thing. . . .

In evidence, too, of how recently the Ik knew goodness, and of how rapidly we could lose it, are not only the stories told by the old who remembered it, but their lives. . . . [Many Ik] died without complaint, long before their time, because of the end of goodness; and goodness died with them. They died without complaint because the chill dispassion that is the Ik's new weapon against the world, their world, had touched them. . . . [T]here can be no mistaking the direction in which those facts point, and that is the most important thing of all, for it may affect the rest of mankind as it has affected the Ik. The Ik have "progressed," one might say, since the change that has come to them has come with the advent of civilization to Africa and is therefore a part of that phenomenon we so blandly and unthinkingly refer to as progress. They have made of a world that was alive a world that is dead, a cold, dispassionate world that is without ugliness because it is without beauty, without hate because it is without love, and is without any realization of truth even, because it simply is. And the symptoms of change in our own society indicate that we are heading in precisely the same direction.

If we grant, as the evidence indicates we should, that the Ik were not always as they are, and that they once possessed in full measure those values that we all hold to be basic to humanity, indispensable for both survival and sanity, then what the Ik are telling us is that these qualities are not inherent in humanity at all, they are not a necessary part of human nature. Those values which we cherish so highly and which some use to point to our infinite superiority over other forms of animal life may indeed be basic to human society, but not to humanity, and that means that the Ik clearly show that society itself is not indispensable for man's survival, that man is not the social animal he has always thought himself to be, and that he is perfectly capable of associating for purposes of survival without being social. The Ik have successfully abandoned useless appendages, by which I refer to those "basic" qualities such as family, cooperative sociality, belief, love, hope and so forth, for the very good reason that in their context these militated against survival. By showing that man can do without these appendages the Ik show that man can do without society in the sense we mostly mean by the word (implying those qualities), for they have replaced human society with a mere survival system that does not take human emotion into account. . . .

Such interaction as there is within this system is one of mutual exploitation. That is the relationship between all, old and young, parent and child, brother and sister, husband and wife, friend and friend. That is how it already is with the Ik. They are brought together by self-interest alone, and the system takes care that such association is of a temporary nature and cannot flourish into anything as dysfunctional as affection or trust. Does that sound so very different from our own society? In our own world the very mainstays of a society based on a truly social sense of mutuality are breaking down, indicating that perhaps society itself as we know it has outworn its usefulness, and that by clinging to an outworn system more proper to the neolithic age we are bringing about our own destruction. We have tinkered with society, patching it up to cope with two thousand years of change, but it shows signs of collapse almost everywhere, and the signs are the more violent where the society is more "advanced." It is only to the "backward societies" that this new violence has not yet come. Family, economy, government and religion, the basic categories of social activity and behavior, despite our tinkering, are no longer structured in a way that makes them compatible with each other or with us, for they are no longer structured in such a way as to create any sense of social unity involving a shared and mutual responsibility between all members of our society. At the best they are structured so as to enable the individual to survive as an individual, with as little demand as possible that any vestigial remains of mutual responsibility should be expressed in mutuality of action. It is the world of the individual, as is the world of the Ik. . . .

"Man Without Law," reprinted with the permission of Simon & Schuster, from *The Mountain People* by Colin M. Turnbull. Copyright © (1972) by Colin M. Turnbull.

DISCUSSION ISSUES

1. *Degenerate Human Nature and the Purpose of Morality.* In William Golding's *Lord of the Flies* (1954), English schoolboys from six to twelve years of age are cast adrift in the Pacific after being evacuated during the next world war. On an uninhabited island, they must create their own social system without the veneer of civilization. Things quickly degenerate into a war between Jack's warrior tribe and Ralph's more "civilized" group. Before their rescue, the warriors kill Simon, murder Piggy, and hunt Ralph as if he were a pig. Golding writes:

   > The theme is an attempt to trace the defects of society back to the defects of human nature. The moral is that the shape of a society must depend on the ethical nature of the individual and not on any political system however apparently logical or respectable. The whole book is symbolic in nature except the rescue in the end where adult life appears, dignified and capable, but in reality enmeshed in the same evil as the symbolic life of the children on the island. The officer, having interrupted the manhunt [of Ralph], prepares to take the children off the island in a cruiser which will presently be hunting its enemy in the same implacable way. And who will rescue the adult and his cruiser?

   Do you agree that morality "formed over the ages and internalized within us hold us back and hopefully defeat the 'Lord of the Flies' in society, whether [it is] inherent in us individually or an emergent property of corporate existence" (Pojman 2000, p. 39)?

2. *Knowing Human Nature.* What is human nature? How do we know anything about it? Hobbes and Turnbull make similar claims about human nature. How would a philosopher, using reason, and an anthropologist, using empirical data, justify their claims about human nature?

3. *Law and Order.* Is law necessary to tame barbaric human nature? Consider the phrase "law and order." In a speech dedicating what was to become Northwest-

ern University School of Law, David Dudley Field praised the virtues of law, claiming that "[w]ithout it there could be no civilization and no order. Where there is no law, there can be no order, since order is but another name for regularity, or conformity to rule. Without order, society would relapse into barbarism." Do law and order go hand in hand? Alternatively, is the excessive use of law a sign of a society that cannot govern itself? For Grant Gilmore, "[t]he better the society, the less law there will be. In heaven there will be no law, and the lion will lie down with the lamb" (quoted from selections reprinted in Presser and Zainaldin 1989, pp. 712–718).

C. LAW AND OBEDIENCE

"In the law courts nobody cares a rap for the truth about what is just or good, but only about what is plausible"
—(PLATO, PHAEDRUS, 272D).

Hobbes tried to separate the question of "What is law?" from the question "On what grounds should the law be obeyed or disobeyed?" However, the issues about disobeying the law do raise questions about the nature of law. Civil disobedience often poses fundamental challenges to law. If law is more than raw authority, what justifies our obedience to it? Does law have a connection to morality? Do individuals have a moral obligation to obey law? Is disobeying a law ever morally justified? The following examination of the famous trial of Socrates sets the stage for these questions.

1. Duty to Obey the Law

During Socrates' time, Athenian citizens, age thirty or older, volunteered for jury service and received a small compensation when chosen. Criminal cases appeared before a jury only after a preliminary screening and hearing by a magistrate. A 501-member jury would hear, in one day, a complete case on any charge, except homicide. A guilty verdict, which could not be appealed, required only a simple majority. Any citizen could bring a charge. Plaintiffs paid full costs if they lost and a heavy fine if one-fifth of the jurors did not support the charge. The accuser could name the penalty, but the defendant could propose an alternative.

The leaders of the restored democracy in Athens brought Socrates, at the age of seventy, to trial. The indictment read, according to Diogenes Laertius in *Lives of the Philosophers,* "Socrates is guilty (i) of not worshipping the gods whom the State worships, but introducing new and unfamiliar religious practices; (ii) and, further, of corrupting the young. The Prosecutor demands the death penalty" (Copleston 1962, vol. 1, pt. 1, p. 135). The second charge was an oblique reference to two of Socrates' best students, Alcibiades and Critias (a cousin of Plato's mother), who had plotted and carried out deeds against Athenian democracy. Alcibiades had previously had an intimate relationship with Socrates. He became a leader in Sparta after fleeing Athens when he was accused of being a traitor. Critias played a prominent role in a former nondemocratic Athenian government. During the trial, various charges were brought against Socrates. Meletus claimed that Socrates' speculations about the physical sciences amounted to impiety, while Lycon cited previous cases of impiety. Anytus, whose son studied with Socrates, accused him of teaching the young to disrespect their parents. He also charged Socrates with violating his duty as an Athenian citizen by refusing to participate in public functions.

Socrates, as recorded by his pupil Plato in the *Apology,* defended himself against the charges. For example, Socrates exposed an inconsistency in Meletus' formal charges. He noted that Meletus had accused him of introducing gods other than those recognized by the state, but, in response to Socrates' questions, Meletus charged that Socrates did not believe in any god. Apparently, then, Socrates stood charged with both polytheism (belief in many gods) and atheism (belief in no god). Socrates' arrogant displays at "logic chopping" did not sit well with the jurors. By a vote of 281 to 220, the jury found him guilty. When Socrates refused to propose a reasonable alternative penalty, such as exile, the jury, by an even greater margin, sentenced him to death. Socrates responded: "Death must be one of two things: either he who is dead becomes naught, and has no consciousness of anything; or else, as men say, there is a certain change and removal of the soul from one place to another." In Plato's dialogue, Crito tries to persuade Socrates to save his life by escaping into exile (see Reading 1-4), but Socrates does not find civil disobedience justified. Illegal acts harm law, society, and citizens, including the wrongdoer. Do citizens have a moral obligation to obey the law?

2. Right to Disobey the Law

Civil disobedience has a long and noble history, as evidenced by the works and deeds of Henry David Thoreau, Mahatma Gandhi, Martin Luther King, Jr., and others. For example, in 1872, police arrested Susan B. Anthony for committing the illegal act of registering and voting in an election. In 1972, Russell Means and Dennis Banks led a group of Native American protesters to take over the District of Columbia offices of the Bureau of Indian Affairs.

What does civil disobedience mean? The question of what it means takes priority over attempts to justify civil disobedience. We must have a clear idea of what requires justification before we can attempt to justify it. According to contemporary philosopher John Rawls in Reading 1-5, civil disobedience must be motivated by conscience, and it must be political, public, and nonviolent. Rawls defines civil disobedience and then proposes the following conditions needed to justify it. The act, which should have a reasonable likelihood of success, must be a last resort attempt to oppose a clear and substantial injustice, and it must appeal to the community's sense of justice. Why should someone exhaust all normal political channels before engaging in civil disobedience? Should civil disobedience also challenge the community's sense of justice? Does the protester have an appeal to a higher, moral law? Does this higher (natural) law enable someone to determine which state laws are unjust?

Justifying Obedience to the Law
The Crito

Plato

CRITO: But look here, Socrates, it is still not too late to take my advice and escape. Your death means a double calamity for me: quite apart from losing a friend whom I can never possibly replace, I'll have this additional problem, that a great many people who don't know you and me very well will think that I let you down, saying that I could have saved you if I had been willing to spend the money; and what could be more shameful than to get a name for thinking more of money than of your friends? Most people will never believe that it was you who refused to leave this place when we tried our hardest to persuade you.

SOCRATES: But my dear Crito, why should we pay so much attention to what 'most people' think? The most sensible people, who have more claim to be considered, will believe that things have been done exactly as they have.

CRITO: As you can see for yourself, Socrates, one is obliged to bear in mind popular opinion as well. Present circumstances are quite enough to show that the capacity of ordinary people for doing one harm is not confined to petty annoyances, but has hardly any limits if you once get a bad name with them.

SOCRATES: I only wish that ordinary people had an unlimited capacity for doing harm; that would mean they had an unlimited power for doing good, which would be a splendid thing. In actual fact they have neither. They cannot make a man wise or foolish; they achieve whatever luck would have it.

CRITO: Have it that way if you like; but tell me this, Socrates. I hope that you aren't worrying about the possible effects on me and the rest of your friends, and thinking that if you escape we shall have trouble with informers for having helped you to get away, and have to forfeit all our property or pay an enormous fine, or even incur some further punishment? If any idea like that is troubling you, dismiss it altogether. It's surely right for us to run that risk in saving you, and even worse, if necessary. Take my advice, and do as I bid.

SOCRATES: All that you say is very much in my mind, Crito, and a great deal more besides.

CRITO: . . . So as I say, you mustn't let any fears like this make you dispirited about escaping; and you mustn't feel any misgivings like those you mentioned at your trial, that you wouldn't know what to do with yourself if you left this country. Wherever you go, there are plenty of places where you will find a welcome, particularly if you choose to go to Thessaly—I have friends there who will make much of you and give you complete protection, so that no one in Thessaly can interfere with you.

Besides, Socrates, I don't even feel that it is just for you to do what you are doing, throwing away your life when you might save it. You are doing your best to treat yourself in exactly the same way as your enemies would, or rather did, when they wanted to ruin you. What is more, it seems to me that you are betraying your sons too. You have it in your power to finish bringing them up and educating them, and instead of that you're proposing to go off and desert them, and so far as you are concerned they'll be left to get along as the whim of fortune determines. They will probably have the kind of luck that usually comes to orphans when they lose their parents. Either one ought not to have children at all, or one ought to see their upbringing and education through to the end, but it strikes me that you are taking the most irresponsible course. You ought to make the choice of a good man and a brave one, considering that you profess to have made goodness your principal concern all through life. Really, I am ashamed, both on your account and on ours your friends'; it will look as though we had played something like a coward's part all through this affair of yours. First there was the way you came into court when it was quite unnecessary—that was the first act; then there was the conduct of the defence—that was the second; and finally, to complete the farce, we get this situation, which makes it appear that we have let you slip out of our hands through some lack of courage and enterprise on our part, because we didn't save you, and you didn't save yourself, when it would have been quite possible and practicable, if we had been any use at all.

There, Socrates; if you aren't careful, besides the harm there will be all this disgrace for you and us to bear. Come, make your plans. Really it's past the time for that now; the decision should have been made already. There is only one plan—the whole thing must be carried through during this coming night. If we lose any more time, it can't be done, it will be too late. I appeal to you, Socrates, on every ground; take my advice and please do as I say! . . .

SOCRATES: . . . we must consider whether or not it is just for me to try to get away without being released by the Athenians. If it turns out to be just, we must make the attempt; if not, we must drop it. As for the considerations you raise about expense and reputation and bringing up children, I am afraid, Crito, that these are the concerns of the ordinary public, who think nothing of putting people to death, and would bring them back to life if they could, with equal indifference to reason. Our real task, I fancy, since the argument leads that way, is to consider one question only, the one which we raised just now: shall we be acting justly in paying money and showing gratitude to these people who are going to rescue me, and in escaping or arranging the escape ourselves, or shall we really be acting unjustly in doing all this? If it becomes clear that such conduct is unjust, I cannot help thinking that the question whether we are sure to die, or to suffer any other ill-effect for that matter, if we stand our ground and take no action, ought not to weigh with us at all in comparison with the risk of acting unjustly.

CRITO: I agree with what you say, Socrates; now consider what we are to do. . . .

SOCRATES: Do we say that there is no way that one must ever willingly commit injustice, or does it depend upon circumstance? Is it true, as we have often agreed before, that there is no sense in which an act of injustice is good or honourable? Or have we jettisoned [abandoned] all our former convictions in these last few days? Can you and I at our age, Crito, have spent all these years in serious discussions without realizing that we were no better than a pair of children? Surely the truth is just what we have always said. Whatever the popular view is, and whether the consequence is pleasanter than this or even tougher, the fact remains that to commit injustice is in every case bad and dishonourable for the person who does it. Is that our view, or not?

CRITO: Yes, it is.

SOCRATES: Then in no circumstances must one do wrong.

CRITO: No.

SOCRATES: In that case one must not even return injustice when one is wronged, which most people regard as the natural course.

CRITO: Apparently not.

SOCRATES: Tell me another thing, Crito: ought one to inflict injuries or not?

CRITO: Surely not, Socrates.

SOCRATES: And tell me: is it right to inflict an injury in retaliation, as most people believe, or not?

CRITO: No, never.

SOCRATES: Because, I suppose, there is no difference between injuring people and doing them an injustice.

CRITO: Exactly.

SOCRATES: So one ought not to return an injustice or an injury to any person, whatever the provocation. . . .

CRITO: Yes, I stand by it and agree with you. Go on.

SOCRATES: Well, here is my next point, or rather question. Ought one to fulfil all one's agreements, provided that they are just, or break them?

CRITO: One ought to fulfil them.

SOCRATES: Then consider the logical consequence. If we leave this place without first persuading the state to let us go, are we or are we not doing an injury, and doing it to those we've least excuse for injuring? Are we or are we not abiding by our just agreements?

CRITO: I can't answer your question, Socrates; I am not clear in my mind. . . .

SOCRATES: Look at it in this way. Suppose that while we were preparing to run away from here (or however one should describe it) the Laws and communal interest of Athens were to come and confront us with this question: 'Now, Socrates, what are you proposing to do? Can you deny that by this act which you are contemplating you intend, so far as you have the power, to destroy us, the Laws, and the whole State as well? Do you imagine that a city can continue to exist and not be turned upside down, if the legal judgements which are pronounced in it have no force but are nullified and destroyed by private persons?'—How shall we answer this question, Crito, and others of the same kind? There is much that could be said, especially by an orator, to protest at the abolition of this law which requires that judgements once pronounced shall be binding. Shall we say, 'Yes: the State is guilty of an injustice against me, you see, by passing a faulty judgement at my trial'? Is this to be our answer, or what?

CRITO: What you have said, certainly, Socrates.

SOCRATES: Then what if the Laws say, 'Was there provision for this in the agreement between you and us, Socrates? Or did you undertake to abide by whatever judgements the State pronounced?' If we expressed surprise at such language, they would probably say: 'Don't be surprised at what we say, Socrates, but answer our questions; after all, you are accustomed to the method of question and answer. Come now, what charge do you bring against us and the State, that you are trying to destroy us? Did we not give you life in the first place? Was it not through us that your father married your mother and brought you into this world? Tell us, have you any complaint against those of us Laws that deal with marriage?' 'No, none,' I should say. 'Well, have you any against the Laws which deal with children's upbringing and education, such as you had yourself? Are you not grateful to those of us Laws which were put in control of this, for requiring your father to give you an education in music and gymnastics?' 'Yes', I should say. 'Very good. Then since you have been born and brought up and educated, can you deny, in the first place, that you were our child and slave, both you and your ancestors? And if this is so, do you imagine that your rights and ours are on a par, and that whatever we try to do to you, you are justified in retaliating? Though you did not have equality of rights with your father, or master if you had one, to enable you to retaliate, and you were not allowed to answer back when you were scolded nor to hit back when you were beaten, nor to do a great many other things of the same kind, will you be permitted to do it to your country and its Laws, so that if we try to put you to death in the belief that it is just to do so, you on your part will try your hardest to destroy your country and us its Laws in return? And will you, the true devotee of goodness, claim that you are justified in doing so? Are you so wise as to have forgotten that compared with your mother and father and all the rest of your ancestors your country is something far more precious, more venerable, more sacred, and held in greater honour both among gods and among all reasonable men? Do you not realize that you are even more bound to respect and placate the anger of your country than your father's anger? That you must either persuade your country or do whatever it orders, and patiently submit to any punishment that it imposes, whether it be flogging or imprisonment? And if it leads you out to war, to be wounded or killed, you must comply, and it is just that this should be so—you must not give way or retreat or abandon your position. Both in war and in the lawcourts and everywhere else you must do whatever your city and your country commands, or else persuade it that justice is on your side; but violence against mother or father is an unholy act, and it is a far greater sin against your country.'—What shall we say to this, Crito? That what the Laws say is true, or not?

CRITO: Yes, I think so. . . .

Justifying Disobedience to the Law
"Duty and Obligation" (1971)

John Rawls

THE DEFINITION OF CIVIL DISOBEDIENCE

. . . The problem of civil disobedience, as I shall interpret it, arises only within a more or less just democratic state for those citizens who recognize and accept the legitimacy of the constitution. The difficulty is one of a conflict of duties. At what point does the duty to comply with laws enacted by a legislative majority (or with executive acts supported by such a majority) cease to be binding in view of the right to defend one's liberties and the duty to oppose injustice? This question involves the nature and limits of majority rule. For this reason the problem of civil disobedience is a crucial test case for any theory of the moral basis of democracy. . . .

I shall begin by defining civil disobedience as a public, nonviolent, conscientious yet political act contrary to law usually done with the aim of bringing about a change in the law or policies of the government. By acting in this way one addresses the sense of justice of the majority of the community and declares that in one's considered opinion the principles of social cooperation among free and equal men are not being respected. A preliminary gloss on this definition is that it does not require that the civilly disobedient act breach the same law that is being protested. It allows for what some have called indirect as well as direct civil disobedience. And this a definition should do, as there are sometimes strong reasons for not infringing on the law or policy held to be unjust. Instead, one may disobey traffic ordinances or laws of trespass as a way of presenting one's case. Thus, if the government enacts a vague and harsh statute against treason, it would not be appropriate to commit treason as a way of objecting to it, and in any event, the penalty might be far more than one should reasonably be ready to accept. In other cases there is no way to violate the government's policy directly, as when it concerns foreign affairs, or affects another part of the country. A second gloss is that the civilly disobedient act is indeed thought to be contrary to law, at least in the sense that those engaged in it are not simply presenting a test case for a constitutional decision; they are prepared to oppose the statute even if it should be upheld. To be sure, in a constitutional regime, the courts may finally side with the dissenters and declare the law or policy objected to unconstitutional. It often happens, then, that there is some uncertainty as to whether the dissenters' action will be held illegal or not. But this is merely a complicating element. Those who use civil disobedience to protest unjust laws are not prepared to desist should the courts eventually disagree with them, however pleased they might have been with the opposite decision.

It should also be noted that civil disobedience is a political act not only in the sense that it is addressed to the majority that holds political power, but also because it is an act guided and justified by political principles, that is, by the principles of justice which regulate the constitution and social institutions generally. In justifying civil disobedience one does not appeal to principles of personal morality or to religious doctrines, though these may coincide with and support one's claims; and it goes without saying that civil disobedience cannot be grounded solely on group or self-interest. Instead one invokes the commonly shared conception of justice that underlies the political order. It is assumed that in a reasonably just democratic regime there is a public conception of justice by reference to which citizens regulate their political affairs and interpret the constitution. The persistent and deliberate violation of the basic principles of this conception over any extended period of time, especially the infringement of the fundamental equal liberties, invites either submission or resistance. By engaging in civil disobedience a minority forces the majority to consider whether it wishes to have its actions construed in this way, or whether, in view of the common sense of justice, it wishes to acknowledge the legitimate claims of the minority.

A further point is that civil disobedience is a public act. Not only is it addressed to public principles, it is done in public. It is engaged in openly with fair notice; it is not covert or secretive. One may compare it to public speech, and being a form of address, an expression of profound and conscientious political conviction, it takes place in the public forum. For this reason, among others, civil disobedience is nonviolent. It tries to avoid the use of violence, especially against persons, not from the abhorrence of the use of force in principle, but because it is a final expression of one's case. To engage in violent acts likely to injure and to hurt is incompatible with civil disobedience as a mode of address. Indeed, any interference with the civil liberties of others tends to obscure the civilly disobedient quality of one's act. Sometimes if the appeal fails in its purpose, forceful resistance may later be entertained. Yet civil disobedience is giving voice to conscientious and deeply held convictions; while it may warn and admonish, it is not itself a threat.

Civil disobedience is nonviolent for another reason. It expresses disobedience to law within the limits of fidelity to law, although it is at the outer edge thereof. The law is broken, but fidelity to law is expressed by the public and nonviolent nature of the act, by the willingness to accept the legal consequences of one's conduct. This fidelity to law helps to establish to the majority that the act is indeed politically conscientious and sincere, and that it is intended to address the public's sense of justice. To be completely open and nonviolent is to give bond of one's sincerity, for it is not easy to convince another that one's acts are conscientious, or even to be sure of this before oneself. No doubt it is possible to imagine a legal system in which conscientious belief that the law is unjust is accepted as a defense for noncompliance. Men of great honesty with full confidence in one another might make such a system work. But as things are, such a scheme would presumably be unstable even in a state of near justice. We must pay a certain price to convince others that our actions have, in our carefully considered view, a sufficient moral basis in the political convictions of the community.

Civil disobedience has been defined so that it falls between legal protest and the raising of test cases on the one side, and conscientious refusal and the various forms of resistance on the other. In this range of possibilities it stands for that form of dissent at the boundary of fidelity to law. Civil disobedience, so understood, is clearly distinct from militant action and obstruction; it is far removed from organized forcible resistance. The militant, for example, is much more deeply opposed to the existing political system. He does not accept it as one which is nearly just or reasonably so; he believes either that it departs widely from its professed principles or that it pursues a mistaken conception of justice altogether. While his action is conscientious in its own terms, he does not appeal to the sense of justice of the majority (or those having effective political power), since he thinks that their sense of justice is erroneous, or else without effect. Instead, he seeks by well-framed militant acts of disruption and resistance, and the like, to attack the prevalent view of justice or to force a movement in the desired direction. Thus the militant may try to evade the penalty, since he is not prepared to accept the legal consequences of his violation of the law; this would not only be to play into the hands of forces that he believes cannot be trusted, but also to express a recognition of the legitimacy of the constitution to which he is opposed. In this sense militant action is not within the bounds of fidelity to law, but represents a more profound opposition to the legal order. The basic structure is thought to be so unjust or else to depart so widely from its own professed ideals that one must try to prepare the way for radical or even revolutionary change. And this is to be done by trying to arouse the public to an awareness of the fundamental reforms that need to be made. Now in certain circumstances militant action and other kinds of resistance are surely justified. I shall not, however, consider these cases. As I have said, my aim here is the limited one of defining a concept of civil disobedience and understanding its role in a nearly just constitutional regime. . . .

57. THE JUSTIFICATION OF CIVIL DISOBEDIENCE

With these various distinctions in mind, I shall consider the circumstances under which civil disobedience is justified. For simplicity I shall limit the discussion to domestic institutions and so to injustices internal to a given society. The somewhat narrow nature of this restriction will be mitigated a bit by taking up the contrasting problem of conscientious refusal in connection with the moral law as it applies to war. I shall begin by setting out what seem to be reasonable conditions for engaging in civil disobedience, and then later connect these conditions more systematically with the place of civil disobedience in a state of near justice. Of course, the conditions enumerated should be taken as presumptions; no doubt there will be situations when they do not hold, and other arguments could be given for civil disobedience.

The first point concerns the kinds of wrongs that are appropriate objects of civil disobedience. Now if one views such disobedience as a political act addressed to the sense of justice of the community, then it seems reasonable, other things equal, to limit it to instances of substantial and clear injustice, and preferably to those which obstruct the path to removing other injustices. For this reason there is a presumption in favor of restricting civil disobedience to serious infringements of the first principle of justice, the principle of equal liberty, and to blatant violations of the second part of the second principle, the principle of fair equality of opportunity. Of course, it is not always easy to tell whether these principles are satisfied. Still, if we think of them as guaranteeing the basic liberties, it is often clear that these freedoms are not being honored. After all, they impose certain strict requirements that must be visibly expressed in institutions. Thus when certain minorities are denied the right to vote or to hold office, or to own property and to move from place to place, or when certain religious groups are repressed and others denied various opportunities, these injustices may be obvious to all. They are publicly incorporated into the recognized practice, if not the letter, of social arrangements. The establishment of these wrongs does not presuppose an informed examination of institutional effects. . . .

A further condition for civil disobedience is the following. We may suppose that the normal appeals to the political majority have already been made in good faith and that they have failed. The legal means of redress have proved of no avail. Thus, for example, the existing political parties have shown themselves indifferent to the claims of the minority or have proved unwilling to accommodate them. Attempts to have the laws repealed have been ignored and legal protests and demonstrations have had no success. Since civil disobedience is a last resort, we should be sure that it is necessary. Note that it has not been said, however, that legal means have been exhausted. At any rate, further normal appeals can be repeated; free speech is always possible. But if past actions have shown the majority immovable or apathetic, further attempts may reasonably be thought fruitless, and a second condition for justified civil disobedience is met. This condition is, however, a presumption. Some cases may be so extreme that there may be no duty to use first only legal means of political opposition. If, for example, the legislature were to enact some outrageous violation of equal liberty, say by forbidding the religion of a weak and defenseless minority, we surely could not expect that sect to oppose the law by normal political procedures. Indeed, even civil disobedience might be much too mild, the majority having already convicted itself of wantonly unjust and overtly hostile aims. . . .

DISCUSSION ISSUES

1. *Degrees of Obedience.* Distinguish among phrases such as "absolute," "prima facie," and "in general." How do these phrases change the issues at stake as posed in the following questions? Is there an absolute obligation to obey the law? Is there a prima facie obligation to obey the law—that is, only acts of disobedience must be justified? Is it, in general, obligatory to obey the law? (See Wasserstrom 1963.)

2. *Conscientious Objection.* Henry David Thoreau refused to pay a poll tax in protest of the U.S. government's war with Mexico, its support of slavery in the South, and its violation of the rights of Native Americans. In "On the Duty of Civil Disobedience" (1849), he claimed that he had a duty to follow his moral conscience, which supplied a higher law than the law of the land. Did Thoreau have an adequate moral justification for disobeying the law? How can an appeal to an individual conscience support an appeal to a universal moral law?

3. *Disobeying the Courts.* In a "Letter from Birmingham City Jail," Martin Luther King, Jr., argued for a moral obligation to break unjust laws nonviolently (King 1964, pp. 76–95). The U.S. Supreme Court invalidated a conviction of the Freedom Marchers, led by Dr. King, for violation of a parade permit ordinance (*Shuttlesworth v. City of Birmingham* 1969). However, the Court also upheld a conviction of the Birmingham marchers for violating a state court injunction (*Walker v. Birmingham* 1966). The Court stated that it could "not hold that the petitioners [marchers] were constitutionally free to ignore all the procedures of the law and carry their battle to the streets. One may sympathize with the petitioners' impatient commitment to their cause. But respect for judicial process is a small price to pay for the civilizing hand of law, which alone can give abiding meaning to constitutional freedom." Should it be easier to justify disobedience to a legislative statute or executive order than to a judicial command?

4. *Approaches to Civil Disobedience.* In evaluating civil disobedience, it is more important, at this stage, to think about the kinds of questions asked than about the answers. Should we look at the consequences of acts of civil disobedience? Do these acts lead to beneficial or harmful results? Does civil disobedience set a bad example, thereby undermining the moral force of law? Alternatively, should we evaluate civil disobedience according to some principles? Should we ask those who advocate civil disobedience to generalize (universalize) their principle? What if everyone disobeyed the law?

5. *Approaches to Revolution.* Compare and contrast these views on revolution:
   a. Immanuel Kant wrote, "There can . . . be no legitimate resistance of the people to the legislative chief of state; for juridical status, legitimacy, is possible only through subjection to the general legislative Will of the people. Accordingly, there is no right of sedition, much less a right of revolution" (Kant 1797, p. 86). Is there ever a right to a violent revolution?
   b. Thomas Jefferson wrote that "a little rebellion now and then is a good thing, and as necessary in the political world as storms in the physical" (Jefferson 1955, p. 92). Does each generation have a right to rebel against the previous one? Why should the rules of one generation bind another?
   c. A contemporary philosopher distinguished among three types of violent rebellion: (1) radical rebellion, in which a group wants to change intolerable oppressive conditions; (2) rebellion for self-determination, in which a group seeks independence; and (3) conservative rebellion, in which a group wants to maintain the status quo against the forces of radical change (Honoré 1988). Do any of these goals have a justification if carried out by violent means? Herbert Marcuse issued the following caution: "There are forms of violence and suppression which no revolutionary situation can justify." Do the ends ever justify the means?

D. PHILOSOPHY: AN INTRODUCTION

The word *philosophy* comes from the ancient Greek words *philos,* meaning love, and *sophia,* meaning wisdom. Etymologically (from the origins of the words), philosophy is the love of wisdom. Note that the definition uses the word *wisdom* and not *knowledge* or *information.* How does wisdom differ from opinion, knowledge, and understanding? What is wisdom? Do philosophers attain a special state of mind called *wisdom?* A former teacher jokingly called two contemporary philosophers who both had the last name of Wisdom, "the Lesser Wisdom" and "the Greater Wisdom." We could not seriously define *wisdom* as "professional philosophers by the name Wisdom," of course, but the elimination of one of many possibilities still does not provide a definition of wisdom. So, we are back to the original question, "What is wisdom?" Perhaps we should first examine the question itself. In trying to define wisdom, we are searching for the meaning of a word or term, but what is meaning? We have only begun to examine wisdom—that is, one part of the phrase "love of wisdom." Even more questions will arise about love.

The previous paragraph contains many questions, each one designed to probe at a more fundamental level than the one before. This process provides a clue to a certain kind of philosophizing—namely, the activity of asking fundamental questions.

Some cultures equate age with wisdom. British philosopher Bertrand Russell, who lived a long life (1872–1970), offered the following sage advice about philosophizing:

> Philosophy is to be studied, not so much for the sake of any definite answers to its questions, since no definite answers can, as a rule, be known to be true; but rather for the sake of the questions themselves; because these questions enlarge our conception of what is possible, enrich our intellectual imagination, and diminish the dogmatic assurance which closes the mind against speculation; but above all because, through the greatness of the universe which philosophy contemplates, the mind also is rendered great, and becomes capable of that union with the universe which constitutes its highest good (Russell 1959, p. 161).

Philosophy begins in wonder, continues with questions, proposes answers, leaves more questions, and ends in wonder.

Like any discipline, philosophy has its subcategories. Different areas of philosophy, such as logic, epistemology, ethics, and political philosophy, aid in the analysis of law. **Logic,** the study of formal and informal reasoning, plays a critical role in law. One group of legal theorists, **formalists,** see law as a rational, logical system. A formalist judge makes decisions deductively—that is, by drawing conclusions from premises according to formal rules of reasoning. Another group of legal theorists, the **realists,** view law as an all-too-human activity. Realists find judges making pragmatic, and often illogical, decisions. The study of law also draws upon **epistemology**—that is, on theories of knowledge. For example, what epistemological status do stories, or narrative, have in law? At each stage of the legal process, an account of events is transformed. A client tells a story to a lawyer, who molds it into a legal claim, which a judge eventually renders into yet another account in a written opinion. Do the different story tellers retain the objective facts of a case throughout the process? Do legal theorists ignore reason and facts when they introduce stories about their lives into their theories? Chapter 3 focuses on logic and epistemology.

Ethics is the study of basic principles and concepts used to evaluate conduct. Is ethics, in determining whether conduct is right or wrong, higher than law? **Legal positivists** draw a sharp distinction between ethics and law. **Natural law theorists** use ethical principles to evaluate law. As with all philosophical subfields, ethical issues appear throughout the text, but they receive special attention in chapter 2.

Political philosophy, commonly thought of as a branch of ethics, examines the nature and justification of political institutions. What role does law have within a political philosophy? Fundamental questions about law quickly become entangled in questions about justifications of the state and its institutions, which, in turn, relate to questions about human nature. Views about the political and legal order may vary, for example, according to whether a theorist takes a negative view of human nature, as Hobbes does; a positive view, such as Rousseau's; or a middle-of-the-road view like Locke's. It seems easier to justify an authoritarian political order with a pessimistic view of human nature than with an optimistic one. While chapter 4 discusses political philosophy in depth, the subject plays a prominent role throughout the text. Chapters 5 through 8 address specific political concepts, with a focus on freedom in chapter 5, rights in chapter 6, equality in chapter 7, and responsibility in chapter 8. It is obvious, then, that philosophy of law encompasses all branches of philosophy, including logic, epistemology, ethics, and political philosophy.

> Literary critic F.C.S. Northrop wrote, "To be sure, there are lawyers, judges, and even law professors who tell us they have no legal philosophy. In law, as in other things, we shall find that the only difference between a person 'without a philosophy' and someone with a philosophy is that the latter knows what his philosophy is. . . ." (Northrop, 1959, p.6)

Philosophy may seem like a remote and peripheral subject when it comes to the study of law. However, asking philosophical questions about law is far from a leisure activity. Philosophers do not ask random questions about law. They ask fundamental or basic questions. Given the impact of law on people's lives and on the political order, it is essential to pose philosophical questions such as, "What should be the role of law in society?" Philosophical inquiry should have an informed basis. Philosophical questions about law have a greater impact when they reflect an understanding of different types of law. Philosophical analyses of law in the United States use American law, especially American constitutional law. Philosophical issues, however, arise in many other areas of law as well.

E. AREAS OF LAW

Since the law does not fall neatly into natural divisions, what justifies dividing law in one way as opposed to another? Do value judgments affect the way laws are divided into subcategories? The Romans divided law into two categories—the law of persons *(in personam),* which sought judgments against individuals, and the law of things *(in rem),* which were actions against a thing or property without regard to the person or owner. **William Blackstone** (1723–1780), who is considered the most influential writer on British common law, divided law into (1) rights of persons, (2) rights of property, (3) private wrongs (torts), and (4) public wrongs (criminal law) (Abadinsky 1991, p. 43). Today, the areas of law have multiplied far beyond a few distinct categories, which makes the task of dividing law into discrete areas all the more difficult. Generally speaking, the law breaks down into the following areas: international, constitutional, private, public, and criminal (Friedman 1998, pp. 163–179).

International law was once called "law of nations," but philosopher Jeremy Bentham (1789) renamed it "international law." It includes public international law, which covers relations among states, and private international law, which deals with relations among individuals and businesses from different nations. As the world has become increasingly interdependent, international law has taken on increased importance (see chapter 2 for more information about international law).

Most philosophical discussions, however, have revolved around **constitutional law** issues. With their interest in fundamental questions, American philosophers have turned to the constitution, since it incorporates the fundamental principles underlying their legal system (see chapters 4, 5, 6, and 7 for more coverage of constitutional law). Two basic types of law operate within this constitutional framework that can be loosely designated as **private law** and **public law.** Private law, including property, contracts, and torts, focuses for the most part on economic issues (see chapter 3 for examples from private law). Public law, including education, employment, and family law, places more emphasis on social welfare issues.

The study of private law, which includes property, contract, and tort law, lies at the core of American legal education. These three subjects comprise a substantial portion of the first-year law school curriculum. Law schools limit the scope of **property law** to real property, that is, to real estate, or land. **Contract law** involves issues surrounding voluntary agreements that parties make. **Tort law** covers civil—that is, noncriminal, private—wrongs that do not arise out of contractual relations.

The subject areas of public law have, themselves, changed over time. **Family law,** while having a long history as a separate area within law, has changed dramatically. Originally it was governed primarily by state law, but family law has now become an area riddled with federal constitutional issues that overlap with criminal and other areas of law. **Employment law** has also changed. It began, in the first part of the nineteenth century, as a field dominated by contract law, but it was influenced by tort law later in that century. Labor law left its mark early in the twentieth century, and today, civil rights issues prevail in employment law. **Education law,** still a fledgling area, has become more prominent due, in part, to recent civil rights legislation.

Criminal law, which needs little or no introduction at this stage, receives in-depth coverage in chapter 8.

While almost every American law school requires courses in property, contracts, and torts, students take education, employment, or family law as electives. Except for constitutional law, schools commonly require only one other public law related course—namely, criminal law. Why do law schools require mostly private law subjects and few public law ones? Are there economic reasons, such as future employment concerns, for requiring one set over another? Do these questions fall far from their mark? Those with a career orientation argue that law teachers should know what law students need to know to become professional lawyers. Law schools, and not philosophical inquiry, should address controversies over what subjects to require.

However, consider that professional law schools proliferate mainly in the United States. European countries treat legal education as a liberal arts undergraduate study. Blackstone's appointment in 1758 to an Oxford University chair of jurisprudence marked the beginning of English legal education as a university subject rather than as an apprenticeship at the Inns of Court (Berman et al. 1996, pp. 2–3). American legal education took a radically different course with the founding of Harvard Law School in 1817 as a professional law school. Should legal education be part of the general education of every citizen or at least of every college student? A critical legal studies scholar has made the controversial claim that professional law schools help legitimate the *status quo* social and economic order (Kennedy 1982).

As noted in the introduction, each area of law lends itself to certain types of philosophical questions. A few more details will help to further illustrate the link between philosophical issues and types of law. A discussion of international law raises fundamental questions about law, while its global scope has stimulated theorists to seek universal principles, or natural laws, that provide the norms for all types of laws. American constitutional law operates within a political order dominated by the political philosophy of liberalism. Liberalism and associated political ideas, such as freedom, rights, and equality, set the background for legal and moral issues, or what philosophers call "applied ethics," including abortion, affirmative action, and euthanasia, which arise within constitutional law.

Contemporary American legal theorists have launched challenges to liberalism and constitutionalism. In addition to mirroring changes in society and elsewhere in the academy, "outsider jurisprudence," a loose mixture of theories, critiques, and movements, arose out of a dissatisfaction with liberalism and constitutionalism. The outsiders accused the insiders of having failed to address the problems of the disenfranchised. The insiders—that is, proponents of constitutional liberalism—professed a commitment to both liberty and equality. However, from the outsiders' perspective, liberty took priority for insiders, thereby causing equality to be sacrificed. In the final analysis, constitutional liberalism did not live up to its promises. It failed to include those who were largely excluded from the legal system and from legal theory.

Outsider theorists turned to political philosophies such as Marxism, as alternatives to liberalism, and to different political concepts, such as power, duties, and community. Outsider jurisprudence includes **critical legal studies (CLS), feminist jurisprudence,** and **critical race theory,** with the three perspectives spinning off one another on certain issues. The outsiders never fully functioned as a unified movement. All three movements gave central importance to political concepts, but each perspective placed a different emphasis on what aspects of the political they found crucial. Critical legal studies began the charge against liberalism in the 1970s and focused on the politics found beneath the surface of the seemingly rational doctrinal legal analyses. Feminists charged that CLS largely ignored the role of gender. Critical race theorists, in turn, found that CLS and feminist jurisprudence underplayed the role of race.

Another new jurisprudence, **law and economics,** also became the object of CLS criticism. CLS took up the radical left of the political spectrum and placed law and economics on the conservative right. Law and economics, focusing largely on private law, uses economic analyses to resolve legal issues. A study of property, torts, and contracts generates issues within an economic framework of market capitalism and poses questions about public, nongovernmental, human interactions. Law and economics has become dominant in private law areas.

F. LEGAL SYSTEMS

Claims about the law's connection to authority and to morality may hold across all legal systems or only apply to some. History and the social sciences reveal a variety of legal systems. This section highlights only two types, civil and common, and then focuses almost exclusively on the common law system. Regrettably, this leaves out a great deal. For example, many African nations have **customary law,** which reflects traditional cultural values (see Barton et al. 1983). Although students seldom learn about them, many different kinds of legal systems, with a variety of permutations and combinations within and among each, have flourished and still flourish throughout the world.

Comparative law has begun to play a more important role in legal education (Glendon et al. 1994; Schlesinger et al. 1998). An examination of other legal systems often sheds light on ethical issues within the American legal system. The abortion debate, for example, takes place within a legal framework constructed around American constitutional law. Does a change in the legal framework change the abortion debate? Do courts within the European nations approach the abortion issue differently than American courts? The landmark decision, *Roe v. Wade,* in the United States would be unthinkable in France. The French frame the abortion controversy, not in legal terms, but largely in political and ethical ones. Another example is the different roles that common law and civil law judges play in criminal proceedings. These differences pose challenges to the formation of international courts, such as the *ad hoc* war crimes' tribunals and proposed permanent international criminal court.

Historically, the **common law** began in England, following the Norman conquest. In 1086, William I (aptly called "William the Conqueror") sent out his Norman census-takers to survey the newly conquered population and study their customs and norms. The common law evolved as the King's judges, over the centuries, molded local customs into a national system of common rules or laws. When judges relied on previous judicial decisions to rule in a new case, they helped to unify the common law. A doctrine evolved that held judicial judgments final *(res judicata)* and barred subsequent suits on the same issues with the same parties. Previous judgments set **precedents,** which served as the basis for future decisions dealing with similar facts *(stare decisis).* Common law courts dealt with money damages, and equity courts evolved to fill the gaps not covered by the common law. Subjects who could not find justice in the common law courts petitioned the king, who referred the matter to separate courts of equity or chancery courts. Common law courts had jurisdiction over things *(in rem)* and provided money damages. Equity courts had jurisdiction over individuals *(in per-*

sonam) and could command, or enjoin, a person to perform a specific act, called an injunction. Equity courts also relied on precedent, or previous decisions, in devising a set of legal principles to govern cases.

Today, the common law has a difficult and unusual vocabulary, but with historical roots. The 1086 Norman conquest made French the language of the royal courts, but they retained Latin for formal written records. The English legal profession adopted a dialect known as "law French," which includes such terms as *plaintiff, defendant,* and *the seisin of freehold,* for their legal concepts.

Legislators play the same central role in **civil law systems** that judges do in common law countries. While judges make common law as general rules and principles, the executive and the legislature oversee or sanction the design of the civil law as a body of detailed codes, designed to cover, in advance, all areas of potential legal dispute. Hammurabi's Code (see chapter 8), in ancient Babylon (1745–1702 B.C.), dealt with almost all aspects of public life, including marriage and divorce, trade and commerce, property and crime. Civil law countries follow Hammurabi's strategy in creating comprehensive codes. The idea of a comprehensive legal code stemmed, in part, from the eighteenth-century Enlightenment project of developing detailed rational systems to show the inherent order in nature. Napoleon, in 1804, provided the political drive needed to devise detailed laws that everyone could understand. The Napoleonic Code, which became the model for civil law systems, still survives largely intact in France. Legal scholars, rather than judges, often take the primary responsibility for designing codes, and the civil law systems they design leave little or no room for filling in the code's gaps with judicial interpretations. Civil law judges, largely recruited from the civil service, apply the codes to cases, but unlike their common law counterparts, they do not rely on precedent. Within a case, civil law judges play an active role, particularly when compared with the passive role taken by common law judges.

In civil law **inquisitorial systems,** such as those found in continental Europe and Latin America, judges, trained separately from lawyers within the civil service, conduct investigations into the facts of a case. Judges, not attorneys (as in common law systems), call and question witnesses.

In common law **adversarial systems,** judges, often elected or politically appointed, referee the opposing lawyers, who engage in active combat. Judges and lawyers, especially in the United States, have the same basic professional training. Judges in the United States typically come from the ranks of practicing attorneys, while judges in continental Europe are career bureaucrats who have not practiced law and generally issue unsigned court opinions without dissent. Because of the differences in structure and function, relatively strong judiciaries often arise within common law systems, and weak court systems operate in civil law systems. A political philosophy dedicated to a "government of individuals" underlies civil law systems. The French, for example, in promoting the virtues of legislative supremacy, envision laws created by representative assemblies, not by courts. A philosophy of a "government of laws" dominates common law systems. Americans see the judiciary as a coequal branch to the legislative and the executive branches of government. However, diversity prevails even within the civil and common law systems.

1. Common Law Systems

England and the United States have common law systems, but they differ greatly, just as the legal professions of England and the United States contrast sharply (Jacobs et al. 1996). England has two types of lawyers—**solicitors** and **barristers.** At the risk of oversimplifying, solicitors generally act as office lawyers who often initiate legal actions, while barristers serve as courtroom lawyers, advocating before prestigious courts on either side of a legal case. Solicitors come mainly from the lower middle and working classes; barristers rise from upper middle class and the aristocracy (Jacobs et al. 1996, p. 86). Solicitors generally fill the ranks of appointed judges for lower courts; barristers, the higher appeal courts. Also, nonlawyers (accountants and Citizens' Advice Bureaux, the largest provider of legal assistance) play a much more prominent role in England than they do in the United States.

The two common law systems differ most in the role and power of the judiciary. The judiciary has a secondary role within the English system and a primary role in the United States. In England, the judiciary functions within the legislative branch, falling under the jurisdiction of the upper house of Parliament, called the House of Lords. English philosophers, such as John Locke, echo the long-standing doctrine of parliamentary supremacy. The Judicial Committee of the House of Lords, or Law Lords, serves as the highest court, the court of last resort. The House of Lords does not have elected members. Rather, the Lord Chancellor administers the court system and plays a key role in most judicial appointments. English judiciary cannot exert its muscle by appealing to a basic law, such as the U.S. Constitution, that sets the outer limits for all other laws, because England does not have a written constitution. Further, it does not have judicial review in the sense of constitutional review. However, English courts have increasingly exercised administrative control over other governmental agencies. Still, England has a wealth of judge-made law, since English judges, over a period of many centuries, made law when Parliament did not act. Criminal and property matters are two examples of areas in which judges, particularly in the earlier stages, made the law. The modern English legislature has sought to restrain the judiciary "by very detailed drafting, which attempts however unsuccessfully to envisage all the situations which the legislator intends to be covered, and by the doctrine that the courts must apply only the words of the statute, and cannot apply them by analogy to new cases not explicitly covered by these words" (Freeman 1994, pp. 1283–1284). So, while English judges have more power than their continental European counterparts, English courts play a relatively subservient role in contrast to American courts.

The United States inherited a common law system from its former ruler, England, but the system grew in peculiarly American soil. The United States' written constitution, which incorporated crucial doctrines (federalism, the separation of powers, and checks and balances), transformed English common law. These structures set the framework for a strong judiciary to develop "a government of laws, and not of men" (John Adams, in the 1776 draft of the Constitution of the Commonwealth of Massachusetts). While the law plays a central role in the United States, it remains debatable whether the culture is excessively litigious or more legally oriented than those of other countries. Alexis de Tocqueville said, "Scarcely any political question arises in the United States that is not resolved, sooner or later into a judicial question" (1956, p. 280). The sheer number of lawyers lends support to the law-focused thesis. Harvard Law School graduates more lawyers each year than the entire country of Japan produces (Jacobs et al. 1996). The United States has 1 lawyer for every 350 inhabitants. That one lawyer would serve 900 citizens in the United Kingdom, 1,800 in France, and 9,200 in Japan (Oda 1992, p. 102, appendix 2). The United States boasts a 70 percent pass rate for combination (state and national) bar examinations, while Japan has about a 2 percent pass rate (Jacobs et al. 1996, pp. 320–321). American citizens file a high volume of legal claims, but the Japanese rarely litigate. However, this may say more about the unavailability of alternative dispute avenues in the United States and more about Japanese governmental policies that discourage court litigation than it does about the two cultures.

Under federalism, the United States has federal courts and fifty independent state-court "systems," ranging from Illinois' unitary court system to New York's largely decentralized model. Each state has its constitution, a supreme court (although not always called that), and an independent judicial system, which operates alongside the federal system. The federal system consists of a hierarchy of judges and courts, including 300 full-time and 150 part-time magistrates; district courts (94 trial courts in every state) with about 600 judges; courts of appeals (11 circuits and the District of Columbia); and the Supreme Court. The federal system also has specialized courts: the Court of Claims, the Tax Court, the Court of Military Appeals, and the Special District Court (three-judge panels that include two district court judges and one circuit court judge). The major sources of law governing the United States include the Constitution (the supreme law of the land), legislation (statutory laws), and appellate court decisions (case law).

The Supreme Court had a humble start. It began operating in New York City in 1790 and then moved to the basement of the Senate chambers in Washington, DC. At first, the Supreme Court—referred to as the Court—heard few cases. Many politicians refused appointments to the Court, regarding it as the least important branch of government. The Court's prestige and power changed, however, soon after John Adams, just before leaving office, appointed his secretary of state, John Marshall, as chief justice. Adams wanted to save the constitution from the radical, newly elected president, Thomas Jefferson. In *Marbury v. Madison* (1803), which is discussed at length in chapter 4, Chief Justice Marshall issued a decision that established judicial review. Only three of six justices showed up to hear arguments in what became the Court's most famous case. In *Marbury*, Marshall established the Court's authority to rule on the constitutionality of executive acts and congressional enactments. Although the Supreme Court did not use this power to invalidate a federal statute until 1857 *(Dred Scott v. Sandford)*, it quickly claimed the power to invalidate state laws *(Fletcher v. Peck,* 1810), helping to establish the Court as equal to the other two branches of the federal government. The major impact of judicial review, even on state courts, came much later. While the Marshall court (1801–1835) overturned more than twelve state laws, the Court's most active period came during the Lochner Era

(1898–1938). During that period, it invalidated far more federal and state laws than during any previous span.

The Supreme Court rarely uses its jurisdiction to hear cases of the first instance, or **original jurisdiction**—that is, most cases that go to the Supreme Court do not originate there. A party may petition the Court for *certiorari,* meaning "to be made more certain" (discretionary review), which the Court may grant at its discretion. With "cert," the Court decides which cases to hear. A party may also request an appeal when a federal or state court strikes down a federal law. Finally, a U.S. Court of Appeals may issue a certification seeking instructions on deciding a question of law. Judges, some more strictly than others, rely on *stare decisis* (stand by the decision), that is, its own previous decisions and those of higher courts. Two distinct schools of judicial review have emerged (see chapter 4). **Interpretavists** admonish judges to enforce only those norms found explicitly or implicitly in the Constitution, while **noninterpretavists** urge judges to go beyond the Constitution.

Finally, we need to be familiar with some bibliographic peculiarities of the law. United States Supreme Court opinions can be found in an official report, *United States Supreme Court Reports* (US), and in two private reports, *Supreme Court Reporter* (S.Ct.) and *Lawyer's Edition* (L.Ed.). Courts cite *Brown v. Board of Education,* for example, as 347 US 483 (1954), which translates as volume 347 of the *United States Supreme Court Reports,* page number 483, which is the beginning page number for the case that was decided in 1954. (The form is modified in this text by placing the date first and omitting periods in some abbreviations. Full citations appear at the end of the book.) The first-named party, Brown, lost in the lower court and appealed to the Supreme Court. The opinion is also found in the other two reports as 74 S.Ct. 686 and 98 L.Ed. 873. The Brown case was taken to the Supreme Court on appeal from one of the thirteen circuit courts, which, in turn, heard the appeal from one of the ninety-four trial-level district courts. Citations of Brown from district courts appear in the form 98 F.Supp. 797. State court opinions are published in a National Reporter System, divided into regional volumes such as Pacific ("P.2d," for *Pacific Reporter, Second Series*), Southeastern (S.E.), and so forth. The United States Code Annotated (U.S.C.A.) has commentary on judicial decisions relating to federal statutes. The Internet provides easy access to court opinions and law review articles. Most law-related websites—for example http://jurist.law.pitt.edu/—have links to all other important sites. Previously inaccessible and costly legal search engines, such as LEXIS and Westlaw, have become increasingly available to undergraduate students and to the general public.

2. Civil Law Systems

Civil law systems vary widely. For example, the judiciary has a subordinate position in the French civil law system, and French judges traditionally limit their decisions to the cases before them. France adheres to the idea of legislative supremacy and maintains a system of review of governmental administration, which is headed by the Council of State and is completely separate from the courts. The Council of State, not the courts, deals with complaints against government bureaucrats. Historically, France has had a long-standing hostility toward the idea of judicial review, and its highest court of appeals, the Court of Cassation, has limited review powers. However, the Constitutional Council, begun in 1958, has played an increasingly prominent role in subjecting proposed legislation to constitutional review.

Constitutional courts, devoted solely to ruling on general constitutional issues, have played an even more active role in other civil law countries. Austria adopted a constitutional court in 1919, largely at the urging of the philosopher **Hans Kelsen** (1881–1973), who ranks as the twentieth century's most prominent continental legal philosopher (Freeman 1994). He served on the Austrian Constitutional Commission that proposed a constitutional court and became one of its first judges (1920–1928). Kelsen's theories also had a major influence on legal debates in many countries, including Pakistan and Uganda, during their postrevolutionary periods. For Kelsen, legal systems consist of a pyramid of norms that specify how individuals should behave. Each norm rests on the validity of a higher norm, with a basic nonlegal norm that governs all others at the top. All legal acts must derive from a single basic norm, which, in turn, legitimizes the first positive norm, the constitution. Judges have some discretion in shaping the norms. Kelsen's model has spread throughout Europe, most markedly through the many newly formed states of Eastern and Central Europe.

In 1950, the German Federal Republic (West Germany) established a constitutional court of sixteen justices elected by both houses of the legislature to enforce the basic norms of the German Constitution. The Bundesverfassungsgericht has the power of **anticipatory judicial review.** This means that the court rules on some legislation before it is passed if a certain percentage of the federal or state legislators request it. In addition, individual citizens may bring constitutional questions to the court. In contrast, federal courts in the United States may not issue advisory opinions.

The Hungarian constitutional court (1989), perhaps the strongest to date, may hear any constitutional challenge to a law, even those brought by foreigners. A group of law professors, for example, successfully challenged Hungary's capital punishment statute. The court found that it violated the basic norm (Kelsen), or core value, of human dignity. Litigants in U.S. courts must have an actual **case and controversy** before they can even consider the constitutional issues looming in their cases. However, in the United States, once a federal court has a case before it, any judge can rule on constitutional issues as they arise during a case's litigation. In civil law systems, only a specialized court may rule on constitutional issues. While Europe contains a wide variety of court systems, all of them have had to face the increasing power of regional courts.

3. Regional Law

Since World War II, a variety of supranational regional legal systems have developed. Great Britain, France, and most Western and some Eastern European countries now fall under the jurisdiction of the European Court of Justice (the ECJ in Luxembourg), which deals with economic issues among member states, and the European Court of Human Rights (the ECHR in

Strasbourg, France). The ECHR conducts its proceedings using a civil law inquisitorial rather than an adversarial approach like Great Britain's. Great Britain has had many cases before the ECHR. It is not treaty bound to accept the decisions of the Court. However, by *de facto* abiding by the Court's decisions, Great Britain now has a constitutional court located in France. As an example of its judicial authority, the European Court ruled that the United Kingdom did not have a right to stop the *Sunday Times* from publishing an article about the legal proceedings brought on behalf of children born with physical defects resulting from the drug thalidomide. Likewise, French citizens have successfully won human rights protections, unavailable to them at the national level, through the ECHR. The European Convention on the Rights of Man has the status of constitutional law in Austria, and most of the convention's provisions take authority over the Constitution in the Netherlands. Should the United States submit to the authority of a regional system of law in the same way that some European countries have?

In addition, a number of other regional human rights systems exist. For example, the Organization of American States (OAS) adopted the American Convention on Human Rights (1978), which established a Commission on Human Rights and an Inter-American Court of Human Rights. The commission reviews reports for state parties in their human rights progress, and the court also hears human rights cases. The Organization of African Unity (OAU) adopted the African Charter on Human and People's Rights, which has been in force since 1986. The OAU established a commission that functions primarily as a promotional and reporting entity. The charter did not provide for a court or any other means of adjudicating claims of human rights violations, but rather became the first human rights treaty to give attention to the duties of states, groups, and individuals and not simply to their rights (see chapter 6). However, the OAU has recently adopted an African Court of Human Rights. Does it make sense to talk about regions having different approaches to rights? Are rights relative to a regional culture, such as African, American, Asian, or European?

4. International Law

Some commentators have questioned whether Germany under the Nazis really had a system worthy of the name "law" (see chapter 2 on war crimes' issues). By any plausible standard, however, present day Germany has a legal system, and few would doubt that other nations had or have systems of laws, called "municipal law." Differences of opinion reach a fever pitch, however, when it comes to international law. Is there a law of nations or an international law?

John Austin, a nineteenth-century English jurist (see chapter 2, on legal positivism), refused to put international law in the category of positive law, instead categorizing it as positive morality. According to Austin, law is a series of commands issued by a sovereign and backed by sanctions. International law seems to lack all three ingredients—commands, a sovereign, and sanctions—and consists, instead, of state practice and state consent, not commands. Austin's analysis also casts doubt on the international sovereign's existence, such as the United Nations, since it derives its authority from the states. States do not give their obedience to a superior international body. Further, international organizations owe their existence to nation-states. Finally, international law remains largely unenforceable, although it may have some moral or political force.

Austin and others who are skeptical about international law rely heavily on a questionable analogy between municipal law and international law. While the United Nations Security Council has power to use force granted to it by the United Nations Charter, the General Assembly is not fully akin to a legislature. Resolutions from the General Assembly, except those dealing with the internal operation of the organization, are not binding. However, resolutions and other examples of "soft law" can have considerable impact on nation-states. Even though international law does not have formal institutions that create law, it does have a number of methods for establishing laws, including conventions (treaties), custom (practice among states), general principles (rules and principles common to all legal systems), and subsidiary means (judicial opinions and writings of jurists).

The Jay Treaty of 1794, designed to settle an ongoing dispute between Great Britain and the United States, ushered in a century marked by the establishment of more than two hundred international arbitral tribunals, culminating in the establishment of the Permanent Court of Arbitration (PCA). Nineteenth-century jurists had high expectations for public international arbitration as an alternative to war. In the aftermath of World War I, the first permanent international law court was established. In 1920, the Permanent Court of International Justice (PCIJ) came under the control of the League of Nations. Andrew Carnegie built a home for the PCA and the PCIJ in The Hague (The Netherlands), but the prediction that nations would settle their difference less on the battlefield and more in The Hague proved false. The aftermath of World War II brought about a continuation of the PCIJ with the establishment of the International Court of Justice (ICJ), but under a radically different international organization—the United Nations.

The PCIJ and the ICJ, collectively known as the World Court, have averaged about three opinions per year. The ICJ consists of fifteen members elected by a complicated procedure. Ironically, before nineteenth-century philosopher Jeremy Bentham successfully lobbied to replace "the law of nations" with "international law," the law of nations allowed suits with individuals as parties. Now, only states may be parties before the ICJ. Any state party may appoint a national as a judge to the ICJ for the duration of a case, if the state does not already have a national sitting as a judge. The ICJ has compulsory jurisdiction over state parties only if the state parties to the dispute have previously agreed to it. States, however, can issue reservations to the ICJ's general compulsory jurisdiction. Some states, such as France and the United States, have withdrawn their consent to compulsory jurisdiction. Practically speaking, then, the ICJ has limited jurisdiction over cases. Many ICJ cases deal with jurisdictional disputes among states, and a few cases have involved the use of force by one state against another. In 1928, sixty-three states, including Germany, signed the Kellogg-Briand Pact for the Renunciation of War, except in cases of self-defense. The United Nations Charter (Article 2[4]) prohibits the use of force except in the case of self-defense or as part of a UN-authorized contingent (see chapter 2). Some jurists have charged that NATO's recent bombing campaign in Kosovo violated international law by not falling under either exception in the Charter.

The Universal Declaration of Human Rights, adopted without opposition in 1948, placed human rights high on international law's agenda. The International Covenant on Civil and Political Rights (1976) established, as the name implies, a code of civil and political rights. Individual complaints of violations of these first-generation rights may be heard by the Human Rights Committee. Second-generation rights, social and economic rights, became codified in the International Covenant on Economic, Social and Cultural Rights, which have also been in force since 1976. Both conventions include a system in which each state-party presents reports on the status of rights in their country. Third-generation rights include rights of development, the right to a protected environment, rights of peace, and the right of self-determination.

CHAPTER 2

International Law

VALUES

The peoples of the earth have thus entered in varying degree into a universal community, and it has developed to the point where a violation of rights in one part of the world is felt everywhere.
— IMMANUEL KANT (1795), *Perpetual Peace,* Third Definitive Article

Despite some efforts to sever law from morality, legal judgments often overlap with moral ones. Chapter 3 allows for a narrower focus on these judgments, but here, instead of particular judgments, we will examine the most general aspects of law and morality by asking two related questions: First, is there an international law? Second, is there a universal ethics? Both questions receive affirmative replies from eighteenth-century philosopher **Immanuel Kant.** Page 38 of this chapter includes an examination of Kant's political and ethical proposals. The term *Kantianism* has become a label for the most influential ethical theory based on duty. Page 49 uses imaginary judicial opinions from a famous hypothetical case, the Speluncean Explorers, to introduce four legal theories. Pages 58–79 take up the rivalry, introduced earlier, between **natural law** and **legal positivism.** The controversy revolves around whether law operates separately from morality. The dispute between **formalists** and **realists** will be deferred until chapter 3.

Should morality place limits on a judge's obligation to implement the law? Should a Nazi judge carry out a legal obligation to verify an individual's eligibility for extermination based on her or his Jewishness (Lyons 1984, p. 85)? Should a northern U.S. judge rely on a legally valid statute to return runaway slaves to their southern owners (see chapter 3)? Philosophy and law merge most dramatically over value issues. Ask the question "What is the nature of law?" and an associated question soon follows: "What is the relationship between law and morality?" Although related, law and morality are not identical. Some laws, such as those governing automobile registration, seem to have little to do with morality. Likewise, the law does not capture every ethical principle. It would prove to be an insurmountable task to try to derive all moral rules from laws, but, despite being separate, legal and ethical questions often intermingle. The issues surrounding war crimes, covered at the end of this chapter, offer a difficult challenge to natural law and positivism.

1. Universal Ethics and International Law

In 1868, the U.S. House of Representatives voted to impeach then-president of the United States, Andrew Johnson. When it came time to vote in the Senate, Senator Edmund G. Ross had to decide whether to cast his vote concerning Johnson's impeachment according to principles or out of self-interest (see Reading 2-1). The House impeached William Jefferson Clinton in 1998 for lying before a Grand Jury. Is it always wrong to lie?

Immanuel Kant (1724–1804), who tried to demonstrate that lying is always wrong, developed a deontological ethical theory. **Deontology** comes from the Greek word *deon,* which means duty. Kant provided a rational foundation for an ethics of duty. For him, ethical questions required rational answers. He began with a puzzle about scientific knowledge and human freedom. If deterministic and universal scientific laws govern the world, how can individuals act freely? Kant proposed a resolution to the clash between scientific determinism ("every event has a cause") and human freedom. He did not find any incompatibility between **determinism** and **free will,** and he found order compatible with human freedom. Universal laws captured the idea of order. Kant argued that order has an intimate connection to freedom and that humans have freedom and autonomy only if universal moral laws govern them. Because individuals act freely and independently only when they act according to universal moral laws, free will depends on universal laws.

Universal moral laws have a common form, which Kant called "the **categorical imperative.**" It has two versions. The first version deals with the universality of moral laws: "Act only on that maxim through which you can at the same time will that it should become a universal law" *(Groundwork for the Metaphysics of Morals).* Kant maintained that universal principles should guide morality, and that ethical standards do not hold for only certain people at a given time and place. Lying does not pass the universalizing test, since a person cannot consistently will that everyone should make false promises. A world of liars would undermine the practice of promising. Kant remains steadfast in insisting on the universal character of a moral imperative against lying. Therefore, lying proves to be morally wrong, even under the rare circumstance when it seems to save a life, as suggested in the following excerpt:

> "After you have honestly answered the murderer's question as to whether his intended victim is at home, it may be that he has slipped out so that he does not come in the way of the murderer, and thus that the murder may not be committed. But if you had lied and said he was not at home when he had really gone out without your knowing it, and if the murderer had then met him as he went away and murdered him, you might be justly accused as the cause of his death. For if you had told the truth as far as you knew it, perhaps the murderer might have been apprehended by the neighbors while he searched that house and thus the deed might have been prevented. Therefore, whoever tells a lie, however well intentioned he might be, must answer for the consequences, however, unforeseeable they were, and pay the penalty for them." (Kant 1788 in Beck 1959, p. 348).

The second version of the categorical imperative focuses on the **autonomy**—the ability to choose freely—and the intrinsic worth of each human being: "Act in such a way that you always treat humanity, whether in your own person or in the person of any other, never simply as a means but always at the same time as an end." Should a German citizen have lied to Nazi officials—legally sanctioned agents of the German government—to protect Jews in hiding (Bok 1978)? Humans have a value that does not depend on other values. In Kantian ethics, individuals should never use other individuals merely as a means to an end. Of course, humans often use other humans, and Kant does not condemn every slight incident of one person using another. But he does condemn acts in which one person ignores another's autonomy and uses that person only instrumentally, merely as a means.

If universal ethical principles apply to all humans, the laws of the states should reflect these ethical principles. Governments, according to Kant, exist to protect individual freedom and autonomy. He recognized republican states (parliamentary democracies), which have constitutions based on ethical principles that demonstrate a commitment to individual freedom and autonomy, as those governed by the rule of law. States must respect their citizens' freedom to become part of the international community. In one of his last writings, *Perpetual Peace* (1795), Kant envisioned a federation of nations governed by an ethical international law based on a compact between republican states (Reiss 1991). He believed that a perpetual peace would become a reality only among a federation of republican states.

Kant's approach to international law and order stands in stark contrast to that of Hobbes. According to Hobbes, each state stands as separate and autonomous, as does each individual in Hobbes's state of nature. The 1648 Peace of Westphalia, which ended the bloody Thirty Years War and the medieval period, also marked the rise of the sovereign state. Hobbes celebrated the sovereign state as "that great Leviathan, or rather (to speak more reverently) of that Mortall God, to which we owe under the Immortal God, our peace and defense" (Hobbes in 1987, p. 89).

> The only way to erect such a Common Power, as may defend them from the invasions of Foreigners, and the injuries of one another, and thereby to secure them in such sort, as that by their own industry, and by the fruits of the Earth, they may nourish themselves and live contentedly; is, to confer all their power and strength upon one Man, or upon one Assembly of men, that may reduce all their Wills, by plurality of voices, unto one Will: which is to say, to appoint one Man, or Assembly of men, to bear their Person; and every one to own, and acknowledge himself to be Author of whatsoever he that so beareth their Person, shall Act, or cause to be Acted, in those things which concern the Common Peace and Safety; and therein to submit their Wills, everyone to his Will, and their Judgments, to his Judgments. (Hobbes in 1987, p. 89)

A Hobbesian realist keeps violence in check by balancing power among states.

Hobbes and Kant both accepted the idea of sovereign nations. French theorist **Jean Bodin** (1530–1596) introduced the word *sovereign* into political theory (Donner 1994, p. 2). Bodin searched for a concept to show how to avoid anarchy (disorder) with absolute authority. The term *souverain* described those French courts, such as the Parlement of Paris and the Cour des Aides, from which there was no appeal. Thus, a sovereign state avoids chaos with its absolute power, and a state exerts its sovereignty by having absolute authority over its internal affairs:

> [I]t is the distinguishing mark of the sovereign that he cannot in any way be subject to the commands of another, for it is he who makes law for the subject, abrogates law already made, and amends obsolete law. (Bodin 1955, p. 28).

International law adopted Bodin's formal concept of a state and concerned itself only with the formal structure of a purported state. It did not substantively assess a state's internal operations. "According to international law, every actual power which has asserted itself, in whatever way, as the supreme juridical organization of a country, must be acknowledged as the legal power, and therefore as the legitimate authority of that country. Hence international law is interested only in the effectiveness of the basis of the organization in question, and not in what it contains" (Pitamic 1933, p. 9).

Each state, then, has sovereignty, so no higher law governs a state without its consent. In a Hobbesian view, all states are equally legitimate as long as they qualify as states. If an effective government has control over a specified territory and a designated population, then it qualifies, formally, as a sovereign state. According to Kant, not all states stand equally legitimate, and he proposed to evaluate states morally. He accepted the idea of state sovereignty, however he conditioned the attainment of global justice on nations qualifying as **constitutional republics.** Kant's "First Definitive Article of a Perpetual Peace" says, "The Civil Constitution of Every State shall be Republican." Kant rejected the idea of a world government as a "soulless despotism," instead favoring a federation of externally equal and inwardly republican states. Each free and independent state would enter a treaty to renounce war. Along similar lines, Fernando R. Tesón (1998), a contemporary legal theorist, advocates amending the United Nations Charter to accept only republican states as new members.

Kant's approach to ethics, law, and world politics raises critical questions. After you have read Reading 2-2, consider the following questions: Should each state have the ultimate legal authority over its citizens? When, if ever, do other nations or external organizations have a duty to interfere in the internal affairs of another nation? Does global justice require a supreme authority with the power to settle disputes? Does ethics have a role to play in international law and politics? Is there a way to reconcile **Kantian idealism** with **Hobbesian realism?**

Ethics of Duty
"Duty in Life: Edmund G. Ross" (1998)

Lawrence M. Hinman

After Abraham Lincoln's assassination, Andrew Johnson succeeded to the presidency, pursuing Lincoln's policy of reconciliation and rebuilding in the South. Radical Republicans, disliking Johnson personally and committed to pursuing a much more punitive policy toward southern states, barely had the two-thirds majority necessary to consistently override presidential vetoes. With the appointment of Edmund G. Ross, long an ardent opponent of Johnson and his policies, to finish out the Senate term of the deceased Jim Lane (a Johnson supporter), it looked as though the radical Republicans would at last have their solid two-thirds majority, enabling them not only to override vetoes but also even to impeach the president.

The bill of impeachment was passed by the House early in 1868 and went quickly to the Senate for a vote. Public sentiment was strongly against Johnson, and especially strong in Kansas, Ross's home state. Ross knew well that he would probably lose his political career and any further opportunities for success in public life if he failed to vote against Johnson. He opposed Johnson's policies and disliked him personally. Yet despite all of this and in the face of intense pressure and threats to his life and reputation, Ross took seriously his oath "to do impartial justice." His was the deciding vote on the floor of the Senate, and his decision was clear: Andrew Johnson did not deserve to be removed from office. To remove him for what were essentially partisan political considerations would be equivalent to degrading the presidency itself and turning the United States *de facto* into a purely congressional government.

Ross was never elected to political office again. When he returned to his native Kansas, he was shunned by his former friends and sentenced to a life of isolation and relative poverty. Ross anticipated all of this, yet he voted the way in which he did because he believed that it was the right thing to do. He did it despite the personal consequences, and he did it despite his personal feelings about Johnson and his policies. This is what Kant means by *acting for the sake of duty,* doing something because it is the right thing to do. If any moral philosopher is able to truly appreciate Edmund Ross's decision, it is Immanuel Kant. . . .

His ethical theory rests on three central insights. The first two of these insights state the conditions for a morally good action:

- An action has moral worth if it is done for the sake of duty.
- An action is morally correct if its maxim can be willed as a universal law.

Actions that have both moral worth and moral correctness are morally good actions. In addition to these two insights, Kant develops a third claim about the way in which we ought to act in order to respect both ourselves and other people:

- We should always treat humanity, whether in ourselves or other people, as an end in itself and never merely as a means to an end.

These are the three pillars on which Kant's ethics rests: duty, universalizability, and respect. . . .

One of the morally admirable characteristics of Edmund Ross's decision is that he not only did the right thing, but also he did it for the right reason. Ross did not act out of any self-centered motives. Indeed, if Ross had been an ethical egoist, he would have acted quite differently. There were plenty of factors pushing him in the other direction. He did not like Johnson, he disagreed with Johnson's policies, his political career would be ruined by a vote in Johnson's favor, and even his family's fortunes would be adversely affected. The only reason for voting against removing Johnson from office was that it was the right thing to do.

Contrast this actual case to a hypothetical variant. Imagine that the same events were unfolding today, but that Ross's motivation was somewhat different. Imagine that he was tired of politics, feeling that his political career had reached a dead end. Imagine, further, that he saw the crucial vote on Johnson as an excellent career possibility. By skillfully manipulating the media, he could focus attention on himself and the agony of his decision. Media coverage would increase dramatically. A best-selling book, talk shows, the lecture circuit, and perhaps even a miniseries beckon in the future. "Integrity," our hypothetical Ross says to himself, "is a big thing with the voters today. If I vote against removing Johnson from office, I might even have a good chance at the presidency myself in a few years." Buoyed by these prospects, our imaginary Ross casts his vote against removing the president from office. . . .

Which action, Kant would ask, do we think is morally the better action? . . .

READING 2-2
Universal Principles of Law and Morality
The Theory of Right (1797)

Immanuel Kant

POLITICAL RIGHT

It is futile to hunt for *historical documentation* of the origins of this mechanism. That is, we cannot reach back to the time at which civil society first emerged (for savages do not set up any formal instruments in submitting themselves to the law, and it can easily be gathered from the nature of un-civilised man that they must have initially used violent means). But it would be quite culpable to undertake such researches with a view to forcibly changing the constitution at present in existence. For this sort of change could only be effected by the people by means of revolutionary conspiracy, and not by the legislature. But revolution under an already existing constitution means the destruction of all relationships governed by civil right, and thus of right altogether. And this is not a change but a dissolution of the civil constitution; and the transition to a better one would not then be a metamorphosis but a palingenesis, for it would require a new social contract on which the previous one (which is now dissolved) could have no influence. But it must still be possible for the sovereign to alter the existing constitution if it cannot readily be reconciled with the idea of the original contract, and yet in so doing to leave untouched that basic form which is essential if the people are to constitute a state. This alteration cannot be such that the state abandons one of the three fundamental forms and reconstitutes itself in accordance with one of the two remaining ones, as would happen, for example, if the aristocrats agreed to submit to an autocracy or to disband and create a democracy or vice versa. This would imply that it depended on the sovereign's own free choice and discretion to subject the people to whatever constitution he wished. For even if the sovereign decided to go over to democracy, he might still be doing the people an injustice; for they might themselves detest this form of constitution and find one of the two others more congenial.

The three forms of state are merely the *letter* . . . of the original legislation within civil society, and they may therefore remain as part of the mechanism of the constitution for as long as they are considered necessary by old and long established custom (i.e. purely subjectively). But the *spirit* of the original contract . . . contains an obligation on the part of the constitutive power to make the *mode of government* conform to the original idea, and thus to alter the mode of government by a gradual and continuous process (if it cannot be done at once) until it accords *in its effects* with the only rightful constitution, that of a pure republic. The old empirical (and statutory) forms, which serve only to effect the *subjection* of the people, should accordingly resolve themselves into the original (rational) form which alone makes *freedom* the principle and indeed the condition of all *coercion*. For coercion is required for a just political constitution in the truest sense, and this will eventually be realised in letter as well as in spirit. [*Freedom depends upon a coercive order,* Editor]

This, then, is the only lasting political constitution in which the *law* is the sole ruler, independent of all particular persons; it is the ultimate end of all public right, and the only condition in which each individual can be given his due *peremptorily*. But as long as the various forms of the state are supposed to be represented literally by an equivalent number of distinct moral persons invested with supreme power, only a *provisional* internal right instead of an absolute condition of right can obtain within civil society.

Any true republic, however, is and cannot be anything other than a *representative system* of the people whereby the people's rights are looked after on their behalf by deputies who represent the united will of the citizens. But as soon as a head of state in person (whether this head of state be a king, a nobility, or the whole populace as a democratic association) also allows himself to be represented, the united people then does not merely represent the sovereign, but actually *is* the sovereign itself. For the supreme power originally rests with the people, and all the rights of individuals as mere subjects (and particularly as state officials) must be derived from this supreme power. Once it has been established, the republic will therefore no longer need to release the reins of government from its own hands and to give them back to those who previously held them, for they might then destroy all the new institutions again by their absolute and arbitrary will. . . .

INTERNATIONAL RIGHT

§ 53

The human beings who make up a nation can, as natives of the country, be represented as analogous to descendants from a common ancestry . . . even if this is not in fact the case. But in an intellectual sense or for the purposes of right, they can be thought of as the offspring of a common mother (the republic), constituting, as it were, a single family *(gens, natio)* whose members (the citizens) are all equal by birth. These citizens will not intermix with any neighbouring people who live in a state of nature, but will consider them ignoble, even though such savages for their own part may regard themselves as superior on account of the lawless freedom they have chosen. The latter likewise constitute national groups, but they do not constitute states.

What we are now about to consider under the name of international right or the right of nations is the right of *states* in relation to one another (although it is not strictly correct to speak, as we usually do, of the *right of nations;* it should rather be called the *right of states*. The situation in question is that in which one state, as a moral person, is considered as existing in a state of nature in relation to another state, hence in a condition of constant war. International right is thus concerned partly with the right to make war, partly with the right of war itself, and partly with questions of right after a war, i.e. with the right of states to compel each other to abandon their warlike condition and to create a constitution which will establish an enduring peace. A state of nature among individuals or families (in their relations with one another) is different from a state of nature among entire nations, because international right involves not only the relationship between one state and another within a larger whole, but also the relationship between individual persons in one state and individuals in the other or between such individuals and the other state as a whole. But this difference between international right and the right of individuals in a mere state of nature is easily deducible from the latter concept without need of any further definitions.

§ 54

The elements of international right are as follows. Firstly, in their external relationships with one another, states, like lawless savages, exist in a condition devoid of right. Secondly, this *condition* is one of war (the right of the stronger), even if there is no actual war or continuous active fighting (i.e. hostilities). But even although neither of two states is done any injustice by the other in this condition, it is nevertheless in the highest degree unjust in itself, for it implies that neither wishes to experience anything better. Adjacent states are thus bound to abandon such a condition. Thirdly, it is necessary to establish a federation of peoples in accordance with the idea of an original social contract, so that states will protect one another against external aggression while refraining from interference in one another's internal disagreements. And fourthly, this association must not embody a sovereign power as in a civil constitution, but only a partnership or *confederation*. It must therefore be an alliance which can be terminated at any time, so that it has to be renewed periodically. This right is derived from another original right, that of preventing oneself from lapsing into a state of actual war with one's partners in the confederation. . . .

§ 55

If we consider the original right of free states in the state of nature to make war upon one another (for example, in order to bring about a condition closer to that governed by right), we must first ask what right the state has *as against its own subjects* to employ them in a war on other states, and to expend or hazard their possessions or even their lives in the process. Does it not then depend upon their own judgement whether they wish to go to war or not? May they simply be sent thither at the sovereign's supreme command?

This right might seem an obvious consequence of the right to do what one wishes with one's own property. Whatever someone has himself substantially *made* is his own undisputed property. These are the premises from which a mere jurist would deduce the right in question. . . .

But while this legal argument (of which monarchs are no doubt dimly aware) is certainly valid in the case of animals, which can be the *property* of human beings, it is absolutely impermissible to apply it to human beings themselves, particularly in their capacity as citizens. For a citizen must always be regarded as a co-legislative member of the state (i.e. *not just as a means, but also as an end in himself*), and he must therefore give his free consent through his representatives not only to the waging of war in general, but also to every particular declaration of war. Only under this limiting condition may the state put him to service in dangerous enterprises.

We shall therefore have to derive the right under discussion from the *duty* of the sovereign towards the people, not vice versa. The people must be seen to have given their consent to military action, and although they remain passive in this capacity (for they allow themselves to be directed), they are still acting spontaneously and they represent the sovereign himself.

§ 56

In the state of nature, the *right to make war* (i.e. to enter into hostilities) is the permitted means by which one state prosecutes its rights against another. Thus if a state believes that it has been injured by another state, it is entitled to resort to violence, for it cannot in the state of nature gain satisfaction through *legal proceedings,* the only means of settling disputes in a state governed by right. Apart from an actively inflicted injury (the first aggression, as distinct from the first hostilities), a state may be subjected to *threats.* Such threats may arise either if another state is the first to make *military preparations,* on which the right of *anticipatory attack* . . . is based, or simply if there is an alarming increase of power . . . in another state which has acquired new territories. This is an injury to the less powerful state by the mere fact that the other state, even without offering any active offence, is *more powerful;* and any attack upon it is legitimate in the state of nature. On this is based the right to maintain a balance of power among all states which have active contact with one another.

Those *active injuries* which give a state the *right to make war* on another state include any unilateral attempt to gain satisfaction for an affront which the people of one state have offered to the people of the other. Such an act of *retribution* . . . without any attempt to obtain compensation from the other state by peaceful means is similar in form to starting war without prior declaration. For if one wishes to find any rights in wartime, one must assume the existence of something analogous to a contract; in other words, one must assume that the other party has *accepted* the declaration of war and that both parties therefore wish to prosecute their rights in this manner.

§ 57

The most problematic task in international right is that of determining rights in wartime. For it is very difficult to form any conception at all of such rights and to imagine any law whatsoever in this lawless state without involving oneself in contradictions . . . The only possible solution would be to conduct the war in accordance with principles which would still leave the states with the possibility of abandoning the state of nature in their external relations and of entering a state of right.

No war between independent states can be a *punitive* one. For a punishment can only occur in a relationship between a superior . . . and a subject . . ., and this is not the relationship which exists between states. Nor can there be a *war of extermination* . . . or a *war of subjugation* . . .; for these would involve the moral annihilation of a state, and its people would either merge with those of the victorious state or be reduced to bondage. Not that this expedient, to which a state might resort in order to obtain peace, would in itself contradict the rights of a state. But the fact remains that the only concept of antagonism which the idea of international right includes is that of an antagonism regulated by principles of external freedom. This requires that violence be used only to preserve one's existing property, but not as a method of further acquisition; for the latter procedure would create a threat to one state by augmenting the power of another. . . .

§ 61

Since the state of nature among nations (as among individual human beings) is a state which one ought to abandon in order to enter a state governed by law, all international rights, as well as all the external property of states such as can be acquired or preserved by war, are purely *provisional* until the state of nature has been abandoned. Only within a universal *union of states* (analogous to the union through which a nation becomes a state) can such rights and property acquire *peremptory* validity and a true *state of peace* be attained. But if an international state of this kind extends over too wide an area of land, it will eventually become impossible to govern it and thence to protect each of its members, and the multitude of corporations this would require must again lead to a state of war. It naturally follows that *perpetual peace,* the ultimate end of all international right, is an idea incapable of realisation. But the political principles which have this aim, i.e. those principles which encourage the formation of international alliances designed to *approach* the idea itself by a continual process, are not impracticable. For this is a project based upon duty, hence also upon the rights of man and of states, and it can indeed be put into execution. . . .

In the present context, however, a *congress* merely signifies a voluntary gathering of various states which can be *dissolved* at any time, not an association which, like that of the American states, is based on a political constitution and is therefore indissoluble. For this is the only means of realising the idea of public international right as it ought to be instituted, thereby enabling the nations to settle their disputes in a civilised manner by legal proceedings, not in a barbaric manner (like that of the savages) by acts of war.

COSMOPOLITAN RIGHT

§ 62

The rational idea, as discussed above, of a *peaceful* (if not exactly amicable) international community of all those of the earth's peoples who can enter into active relations with one another, is not a philanthropic principle of ethics, but a principle of *right*. Through the spherical shape of the planet they inhabit . . . , nature has confined them all within an area of definite limits. Accordingly, the only conceivable way in which anyone can possess habitable land on earth is by possessing a part within a determinate whole in which everyone has an original right to share. Thus all nations are *originally* members of a community of the land. But this is not a *legal community* of possession . . . and utilisation of the land, nor a community of ownership. It is a community of reciprocal action . . ., which is physically possible, and each member of it accordingly has constant relations with all the others. Each may *offer* to have commerce with the rest, and they all have a right to make such overtures without being treated by foreigners as enemies. This right, in so far as it affords the prospect that all nations may unite for the purpose of creating certain universal laws to regulate the intercourse they may have with one another, may be termed *cosmopolitan*. . . .

CONCLUSION

If a person cannot prove that a thing exists, he may attempt to prove that it does not exist. If neither approach succeeds (as often happens), he may still ask whether it is *in his interest to assume* one or other possibility as a hypothesis, either from theoretical or from practical considerations. In other words, he may wish on the one hand simply to explain a certain phenomenon (as the astronomer, for example, may wish to explain the sporadic movements of the planets), or on the other, to achieve a certain end which may itself be either *pragmatic* (purely technical) or *moral* (i.e. an end which it is our duty to take as a maxim). It is, of course, self-evident that no-one is duty-bound to make an *assumption* . . . that the end in question can be realised, since this would involve a purely theoretical and indeed problematic judgement; for no-one can be obliged to accept a given belief. But we can have a duty to act in accordance with the idea of such an end, even if there is not the slightest theoretical probability of its realisation, provided that there is no means of demonstrating that it cannot be realised either.

Now, moral-practical reason within us pronounces the following irresistible veto: *There shall be no war,* either between individual human beings in the state of nature, or between separate states, which, although internally law-governed, still live in a lawless condition in their external relationships with one another. For war is not the way in which anyone should pursue his rights. Thus it is no longer a question of whether perpetual peace is really possible or not, or whether we are not perhaps mistaken in our theoretical judgement if we assume that it is. On the contrary, we must simply act as if it could really come about (which is perhaps impossible), and turn our efforts towards realising it and towards establishing that constitution which seems most suitable for this purpose (perhaps that of republicanism in all states, individually and collectively). By working towards this end, we may hope to terminate the disastrous practice of war, which up till now has been the main object to which all states, without exception, have accommodated their internal institutions. And even if the fulfillment of this pacific intention were forever to remain a pious hope, we should still not be deceiving ourselves if we made it our maxim to work unceasingly towards it, for it is our duty to do so. To assume, on the other hand, that the moral law within us might be misleading, would give rise to the execrable wish to dispense with all reason and to regard ourselves, along with our principles, as subject to the same mechanism of nature as the other animal species.

It can indeed be said that this task of establishing a universal and lasting peace is not just a part of the theory of right within the limits of pure reason, but its entire ultimate purpose. For the condition of peace is the only state in which the property of a large number of people living together as neighbours under a single constitution can be guaranteed by *laws*. The rule on which this constitution is based must not simply be derived from the experience of those who have hitherto fared best under it, and then set up as a norm for others. On the contrary, it should be derived *a priori* by reason from the absolute ideal of a rightful association of men under public laws. For all particular examples are deceptive (an example can only illustrate a point, but does not prove anything), so that one must have recourse to metaphysics. And even those who scorn metaphysics admit its necessity involuntarily when they say, for example (as they often do): 'The best constitution is that in which the power rests with laws instead of with men.' For what can be more metaphysically sublime than this idea, although by the admission of those who express it, it also has a well-authenticated objective reality which can easily be demonstrated from particular instances as they arise. But no attempt should be made to put it into practice overnight by revolution, i.e. by forcibly overthrowing a defective constitution which has existed in the past; for there would then be an interval of time during which the condition of right would be nullified. If we try instead to give it reality by means of gradual reforms carried out in accordance with definite principles, we shall see that it is the only means of continually approaching the supreme political good—perpetual peace.

From Kant (1797), *The Metaphysics of Morals.* In *Kant: Political Writings.* Hans Reiss, ed. Cambridge: Cambridge University Press, pp. 162–175. Reprinted with the permission of Cambridge University Press.

B. APPROACHES TO LAW: AN OVERVIEW

Law and philosophy instructors sometimes use hypotheticals for teaching purposes. Lon Fuller's (1902–1978) classical hypothetical case, the Speluncean Explorers, provides the background for a discussion of universal justice and a comparison of various theories of law (see Reading 2-3). Explorers trapped in a cave decide to kill and eat one of their own in order to survive. They choose the victim randomly and, thereby, violate a state statute (positive law): "Whoever, shall willfully take the life of another shall be punishable by death." After their rescue, the state prosecutes them for murder. Should the judges appeal to moral principles outside the positive law and dismiss the murder charge? Should the judges fulfill their legal duty and enforce the letter of the law, which demands upholding the explorers' conviction for murder? Should the judges take into account the political situation in which the public demands acquittal and the chief executive indicates an unwillingness to pardon the accused? The judges approach the case from different theoretical perspectives, including **natural law, legal positivism, formalism,** and **realism.** Fuller's imaginary judges write opinions that serve as introductions to different legal theories.

READING 2-3

The Greatest Fictional Case of All Time
"The Case of the Speluncean Explorers" (1949)

Lon L. Fuller

OPINION OF CHIEF JUSTICE TRUEPENNY

The four defendants are members of the Speluncean Society, an organization of amateurs interested in the exploration of caves. Early in May of 4299 they, in the company of Roger Whetmore, then also a member of the Society, penetrated into the interior of a limestone cavern of the type found in the Central Plateau of this Commonwealth. While they were in a position remote from the entrance to the cave, a landslide occurred. Heavy boulders fell in such a manner as to block completely the only known opening to the cave. When the men discovered their predicament, they settled themselves near the obstructed entrance to wait until a rescue party should remove the detritus that prevented them from leaving their underground prison. On the failure of Whetmore and the defendants to return to their homes, the Secretary of the Society was notified by their families. It appears that the explorers had left indications at the headquarters of the Society concerning the location of the cave they proposed to visit. A rescue party was promptly dispatched to the spot.

The task of rescue proved one of overwhelming difficulty. It was necessary to supplement the forces of the original party by repeated increments of men and machines, which had to be conveyed at great expense to the remote and isolated region in which the cave was located. A huge temporary camp of workmen, engineers, geologists, and other experts was established. The work of removing the obstruction was several times frustrated by fresh landslides. In one of these, ten of the workmen engaged in clearing the entrance were killed. The treasury of the Speluncean Society was soon exhausted in the rescue effort, and the sum of eight hundred thousand frelars, raised partly by popular subscription and partly by legislative grant, was expended before the imprisoned men were rescued. Success was finally achieved on the thirty-second day after the men entered the cave.

Since it was known that the explorers had carried with them only scant provisions, and since it was also known that there was no animal or vegetable matter within the cave on which they might subsist, anxiety was early felt that they might meet death by starvation before access to them could be obtained. On the twentieth day of their imprisonment it was learned for the first time that they had taken with them into the cave a portable wireless machine capable of both sending and receiving messages. A similar machine was promptly installed in the rescue camp and oral communication established with the unfortunate men within the mountain. They asked to be informed how long a time would be required to release them. The engineers in charge of the project answered that at least ten days would be required even if no new landslides occurred. The explorers then asked if any physicians were present, and were placed in communication with a committee of medical experts. The imprisoned men described their condition and the rations they had taken with them, and asked for a medical opinion whether they would be likely to live without food for ten days longer. The chairman of the committee of physicians told them that there was little possibility of this. The wireless machine within the cave then remained silent for eight hours. When communication was re-established, the men asked to speak again with the physicians. The chairman of the physicians' committee was placed before the apparatus, and Whetmore, speaking on behalf of himself and the defendants, asked whether they would be able to survive for ten days longer if they consumed the flesh of one of their number. The physicians' chairman reluctantly answered this question in the affirmative. Whetmore asked whether it would be advisable for them to cast lots to determine which of them should be eaten. None of the physicians present was willing to answer the question. Whetmore then asked if there were among the party a judge or other official of the government who would answer this question. None of those attached to the rescue camp was willing to assume the role of advisor in this matter. He then asked if any minister or priest would answer their question, and none was found who would do so. Thereafter no further messages were received from within the cave, and it was assumed (erroneously, it later appeared) that the electric batteries of the explorers' wireless machine had become exhausted. When the imprisoned men were finally released, it was learned that on the twenty-third day after their entrance into the cave Whetmore had been killed and eaten by his companions.

From the testimony of the defendants, which was accepted by the jury, it appears that it was Whetmore who first proposed that they might find the nutriment without which survival was impossible in the flesh of one of their own number. It was also Whetmore who first proposed the use of some method of casting lots, calling the attention of the defendants to a pair of dice he happened to have with him. The defendants were at first reluctant to adopt so desperate a procedure, but after the conversations by wireless related above, they finally agreed on the plan proposed by Whetmore. After much discussion of the mathematical problems involved, agreement was finally reached on a method of determining the issue by the use of the dice.

Before the dice were cast, however, Whetmore declared that he withdrew from the arrangement, as he had decided on reflection to wait for another week before embracing an expedient so frightful and odious. The others charged him with a breach of faith and proceeded to cast the dice. When it came Whetmore's turn, the dice were cast for him by one of the defendants, and he was asked to declare any objections he might have to the fairness of the throw. He stated that he had no such objections. The throw went against him, and he was then put to death and eaten by his companions.

After the rescue of the defendants, and after they had completed a stay in a hospital where they underwent a course of treatment for malnutrition and shock, they were indicted for the murder of Roger Whetmore. At the trial, after the testimony had been concluded, the foreman of the jury (a lawyer by profession) inquired of the court whether the jury might not find a special verdict, leaving it to the court to say whether on the facts as found the defendants were guilty. After some discussion, both the Prosecutor and counsel for the defendants indicated their acceptance of this procedure, and it was adopted by the court. In a lengthy special verdict the jury found the facts as I have related them above, and found further that if on these facts the defendants were guilty of the crime charged against them, then they found the defendants guilty. On the basis of this verdict, the trial judge ruled that the defendants were guilty of murdering Roger Whetmore. The judge then sentenced them to be hanged, the law of our Commonwealth permitting him no discretion with respect to the penalty to be imposed. After the release of the jury, its members joined in communication to the Chief Executive asking that the sentence be commuted to an imprisonment of six months. The trial judge addressed a similar communication of the Chief Executive. As yet no action with respect to these pleas has been taken, as the Chief Executive is apparently awaiting our disposition of this petition of error.

It seems to me that in dealing with this extraordinary case the jury and the trial judge followed a course that was not only fair and wise, but the only course that was open to them under the law. The language of our statute is well known: "Whoever shall willfully take the life of another shall be punished by death," N.C.S.A. (N.S.) § 12-A. This statute permits of no exception applicable to this case, however, our sympathies may incline us to make allowance for the tragic situation in which these men found themselves.

In a case like this the principle of executive clemency seems admirably suited to mitigate the rigors of the law, and I propose to my colleagues that we follow the example of the jury and the trial judge by joining in the communications they have addressed to the Chief Executive. There is every reason to believe that these requests for clemency will be heeded, coming as they do from those who have studied the case and had an opportunity to become thoroughly acquainted with all its circumstances. It is highly improbable that the Chief Executive would deny these requests unless he were himself to hold hearings at least as extensive as those involved in the trial below, which lasted for three months. The holding of such hearings (which would virtually amount to a retrial of the case) would scarcely be compatible with the function of the Executive as it is usually conceived. I think we may therefore assume that some form of clemency will be extended to these defendants. If this is done, then justice will be accomplished without impairing either the letter or spirit of our statutes and without offering any encouragement for the disregard of law.

OPINION OF JUSTICE FOSTER

I am shocked that the Chief Justice, in an effort to escape the embarrassments of this tragic case, should have adopted, and should have proposed to his colleagues, an expedient at once so sordid and so obvious. I believe something more is on trial in this case than the fate of these unfortunate explorers; that is the law of our Commonwealth. If this Court declares that under our law these men have committed a crime, then our law is itself convicted in the tribunal of common sense, no matter what happens to the individuals involved in this petition of error. For us to assert that the law we uphold and expound compels us to a conclusion we are ashamed of, and from which we can only escape by appealing to a dispensation resting within the personal whim of the Executive, seems to me to amount to an admission that the law of this Commonwealth no longer pretends to incorporate justice.

For myself, I do not believe that our law compels the monstrous conclusion that these men are murderers. I believe, on the contrary, that it declares them to be innocent of any crime. I rest this conclusion on two independent grounds, either of which is of itself sufficient to justify the acquittal of these defendants.

The first of these grounds rests on a premise that may arouse opposition until it has been examined candidly. I take the view that the enacted or positive law of this Commonwealth, including all of its statutes and precedents, is inapplicable to this case, and that the case is governed instead by what ancient writers in Europe and America called "the law of nature."

This conclusion rests on the proposition that our positive law is predicated on the possibility of men's coexistence in society. When a situation arises in which the coexistence of men becomes impossible, then a condition that underlies all of our precedents and statutes has ceased to exist. . . .

I conclude, therefore, that at the time Roger Whetmore's life was ended by these defendants, they were, to use the quaint language of nineteenth-century writers, not in a "state of civil society" but in a "state of nature." This has the consequence that the law applicable to them is not the enacted and established law of this Commonwealth, but the law derived from those principles that were appropriate to their condition. I have no hesitancy in saying that under those principles they were guiltless of any crime.

What these men did was done in pursuance of an agreement accepted by all of them and first proposed by Whetmore himself. Since it was apparent that their extraordinary predicament made inapplicable the usual principles that regulate men's relations with one another, it was necessary for them to draw, as it were, a new charter of government appropriate to the situation in which they found themselves.

It has from antiquity been recognized that the most basic principle of law or government is to be found in the notion of contract or agreement. Ancient thinkers, especially during the period from 1600 to 1900, used to base government itself on a supposed original social compact. Skeptics pointed out that this theory contradicted the known facts of history, and that there was no scientific evidence to support the notion that any government was ever founded in the manner supposed by the theory. . . . Moralists replied that, if the compact was a fiction from a historical point of view, the notion of compact or agreement furnished the only ethical justification on which the powers of government which include that of taking life, could be rested. The powers of government can only be justified morally on the ground that these are powers that reasonable men would agree upon and accept if they were faced with the necessity of constructing anew some order to make their life in common possible.

Fortunately, our Commonwealth is not bothered by the perplexities that beset the ancients. We know as a matter of historical truth that our government was founded upon a contract or free accord of men. The archeological proof is conclusive that in the first period following the Great Spiral the survivors of that holocaust voluntarily came together and drew up a charter of government. Sophistical writers have raised questions as to the power of those remote contractors to bind future generations, but the fact remains that our government traces itself back in an unbroken line to that original charter.

If, therefore, our hangmen have the power to end men's lives, if our sheriffs have the power to put delinquent tenants in the street, if our police have the power to incarcerate the inebriated reveler, these powers find their moral justification in that original compact of our forefathers. If we can find no higher source for our legal order, what higher source should we expect these starving unfortunates to find for the order they adopted for themselves? . . .

This concludes the exposition of the first ground of my decision. My second ground proceeds by rejecting hypothetically all the premises on which I have so far proceeded. I concede for purposes of argument that I am wrong in saying that the situation of these men removed them from the effect of our positive law, and I assume that the Consolidated Statutes have the power to penetrate 500 feet of rock and to impose themselves upon these starving men huddled in their underground prison.

Now it is, of course, perfectly clear that these men did an act that violates the literal wording of the statute which declares that he who "shall willfully take the life of another" is a murderer. But one of the most ancient bits of legal wisdom is the saying that a man may break the letter of the law without breaking the law itself. Every proposition of positive law, whether contained in a statute or a judicial precedent, is to be interpreted reasonably, in the light of its evident purpose. . . .

The statute before us for interpretation has never been applied literally. Centuries ago it was established that a killing in self-defense is excused. There is nothing in the wording of the statute that suggests this exception. Various attempts have been made to reconcile the legal treatment of self-defense with the words of the statute, but in my opinion these are all merely ingenious sophistries. The truth is that the exception in favor of self-defense cannot be reconciled with the *words* of the statute, but only with its *purpose*.

The true reconciliation of the excuse of self-defense with the statute making it a crime to kill another is to be found in the following line of reasoning. One of the principal objects underlying any criminal legislation is that of deterring men from crime. Now it is apparent that if it were declared to be the law that a killing in self-defense is murder such a rule could not operate in a deterrent manner. A man whose life is threatened will repel his aggressor, whatever the law may say. Looking therefore to the broad purposes of criminal legislation, we may safely declare that this statute was not intended to apply to cases of self-defense.

When the rationale of the excuse of self-defense is thus explained, it becomes apparent that precisely the same reasoning is applicable to the case at bar. If in the future any group of men ever find themselves in the tragic predicament of these defendants, we may be sure that their decision whether to live or die will not be controlled by the contents of our criminal code. Accordingly, if we read this statute intelligently, it is apparent that it does not apply to this case. The withdrawal of this situation from the effect of the statute is justified by precisely the same considerations that were applied by our predecessors in office centuries ago to the case of self-defense. . . .

I therefore conclude that on any aspect under which this case may be viewed these defendants are innocent of the crime of murdering Roger Whetmore, and that the conviction should be set aside.

OPINION OF JUSTICE TATTING

In the discharge of my duties as a justice of this Court, I am usually able to dissociate the emotional and intellectual sides of my reactions, and to decide the case before me entirely on the basis of the latter. In passing on this tragic case I find that my usual resources fail me. On the emotional side I find myself torn between sympathy for these men and a feeling of abhorrence and disgust at the monstrous act they committed. I had hoped that I would be able to put these contradictory emotions to one side as irrelevant, and to decide the case on the basis of a convincing and logical demonstration of the result demanded by our law. Unfortunately, this deliverance has not been vouchsafed me.

As I analyze the opinion just rendered by my brother Foster, I find that it is shot through with contradictions and fallacies. Let us begin with his first proposition: these men were not subject to our law because they were not in a "state of civil society" but in a "state of nature." I am not clear why this is so, whether it is because of the thickness of the rock that imprisoned them, or because they were hungry, or because they had set up a "new charter of government" by which the usual rules of law were to be supplanted by a throw of the dice. Other difficulties intrude themselves. If these men passed from the jurisdiction of our law to that of "the law of nature," at what moment did this occur? Was it when the entrance to the cave was blocked, or when the threat of starvation reached a certain undefined degree of intensity, or when the agreement for the throwing of the dice was made? These uncertainties in the doctrine proposed by my brother are capable of producing real difficulties. Suppose, for example, one of these men had had his twenty-first birthday while he was imprisoned within the mountain. On what date would we have to consider that he had attained his majority—when he reached the age of twenty-one, at which time he was, by hypothesis, removed from the effects of our law, or only when he was released from the cave and became again subject to what my brother calls our "positive law"? These difficulties may seem fanciful, yet they only serve to reveal the fanciful nature of the doctrine that is capable of giving rise to them.

But it is not necessary to explore these niceties further to demonstrate the absurdity of my brother's position. Mr. Justice Foster and I are the appointed judges of a court of the Commonwealth of Newgarth, sworn and empowered to administer the laws of that Commonwealth. By what authority do we resolve ourselves into a Court of Nature? If these men were indeed under the law of nature, whence comes our authority to expound and apply that law? Certainly *we* are not in a state of nature.

Let us look at the contents of this code of nature that my brother proposes we adopt as our own and apply to this case. What a topsy-turvy and odious code it is! It is a code in which the law of contracts is more fundamental than the law of murder. It is a code under which a man may make a valid agreement empowering his fellows to eat his own body. Under the provisions of this code, furthermore, such an agreement once made is irrevocable, and if one of the parties attempts to withdraw, the others may take the law into their own hands and enforce the contract by violence—for though my brother passes over in convenient silence the effect of Whetmore's withdrawal, this is the necessary implication of his argument.

The principles my brother expounds contain other implications that cannot be tolerated. He argues that when the defendants set upon Whetmore and killed him (we know not how, perhaps by pounding him with stones) they were only exercising the rights conferred upon them by their bargain. Suppose, however, that Whetmore had had concealed upon his person a revolver, and that when he saw the defendants about to slaughter him he had shot them to death in order to save his own life. My brother's reasoning applied to these facts would make Whetmore out to be a murderer, since the excuse of self-defense would have to be denied to him. If his assailants were acting rightfully in seeking to bring about his death, then of course he could no more plead the excuse that he was defending his own life than could a condemned prisoner who struck down the executioner lawfully attempting to place the noose about his neck. . . .

Since I have been wholly unable to resolve the doubts that beset me about the law of this case, I am with regret announcing a step that is, I believe, unprecedented in the history of this tribunal. I declare my withdrawal from the decision of this case.

OPINION OF JUSTICE HANDY

. . . The problem before us is what we, as officers of the government, ought to do with these defendants. That is a question of practical wisdom, to be exercised in a context, not of abstract theory, but of human realities. When the case is approached in this light, it becomes, I think, one of the easiest to decide that has ever been argued before this Court. . . .

I have never been able to make my brothers see that government is a human affair, and that men are ruled, not by words on paper or by abstract theories, but by other men. They are ruled well when their rulers understand the feelings and conceptions of the masses. They are ruled badly when that understanding is lacking.

Of all branches of the government, the judiciary is the most likely to lose its contact with the common man. . . .

But outside of these fields I believe that all government officials, including judges, will do their jobs best if they treat forms and abstract concepts as instruments. We should take as our model, I think, the good administrator, who accommodates procedures and principles to the case at hand, selecting from among the available forms those most suited to reach the proper result.

The most obvious advantage of this method of government is that it permits us to go about our daily tasks with efficiency and common sense. . . .

I come now to the most crucial fact in this case, a fact known to all of us on this Court, though one that my brothers have seen fit to keep under the cover of their judicial robes. This is the frightening likelihood that if the issue is left to him, the Chief Executive will refuse to pardon these men or commute their sentence. As we all know, our Chief Executive is a man now well advanced in years, of very stiff notions. Public clamor usually operates on him with the reverse of the effect intended. As I have told my brothers, it happens that my wife's niece is an intimate friend of his secretary. I have learned in this indirect, but, I think, wholly reliable way, that he is firmly determined not to commute the sentence if these men are found to have violated the law. . . .

. . . I conclude that the defendants are innocent of the crime charged, and that the conviction and sentence should be set aside.

1. *Contrasting Legal Theories.* Try to determine which, if any, of the Spelluncean judicial opinions in Reading 2-3 fall into the following categories:

   a. *Natural Law.* Does the law compel "the monstrous conclusion" that these men are murderers? Did these explorers act outside civil society and in a state of nature, where no laws, except survival of the fittest, apply? Are there higher laws or ethical principles that should apply to this case? Even if the explorers violated the letter of their nation's law, should the court judge them by the spirit of the law? Would it be better to appeal to the purpose of a law rather than to its "spirit" (whatever that means)?

   b. *Positivism.* Should a judge cast aside a personal sense of morality in deciding this case? Should a judge stay true to the written law and stick to the statute's plain meaning?

   c. *Formalism.* Does the case turn on drawing conclusions from a formal theory, such as probability theory? Anthony D'Amato (1980, p. 467) has constructed an analysis of the case in which a judge calculates the probabilities for surviving if the explorers included and if they did not include the victim, Whetmore, in throwing the dice. By including Whetmore, their chances of dying were one in five, or 20 percent. If they had excluded Whetmore, their chances of dying would have increased to one in four, or 25 percent. Does it follow, then, that the defendants willfully murdered Whetmore since they acted to advance their self-interests at the expense of another's life?

   d. *Realism.* Is there any objective way to decide this case? Are judicial decisions largely subjective? Is it realistic to think that judges can avoid taking account of public opinion and acknowledging the realities of the administration of criminal law?

2. *Do Numbers Count?* Should it matter, legally or morally, how many lives the accused saved and how many lives the accused sacrificed? Consider the following: "Edward is the driver of a trolley, whose brakes have failed. On the track ahead of him are five people; the banks are so steep that they will not be able to get off the track in time. The track has a spur leading off to the right, and Edward can turn the trolley onto it. Unfortunately, there is one person on the right hand track. Edward can turn the trolley, killing the one; or he can refrain from turning the trolley" (Thompson 1986, p. 71).

3. *States of Nature at Sea.* Imagine that a yacht sets out to sea with four friends on board, three older and one younger. A terrible storm sweeps the yacht away and capsizes it 1,600 miles from shore. All four manage to climb into an open boat. The boat does not have any water except rainwater. Two tins of turnips last for three days, and on the fourth day, the crew catches a small turtle that lasts until the twelfth day. Five days follow without water and seven without food. On the eighteenth day, two of the older men propose to draw lots to determine who should die to save the rest. The other older crew member refuses. The two conspire, with the other's knowledge but without his explicit consent. They decide to kill the youngest, assuming that he would probably die first from famine. The three survivors live off the blood and body of the youngest, who was killed by the oldest. Without this sustenance, the members of the crew would not survive the next four days until their rescue. Should the court find the elder crew members guilty of murder or excuse them because of the necessity of their acts? Does the law, or even morality, apply in this case? Far from being a fanciful case like the Speluncean Explorers, this description comes from an actual British case, *The Queen v. Dudley and Stephens* (1884–1885).

4. *Deciding Who Should Die.* An American ship left Liverpool, England for Philadelphia. Two-hundred fifty miles from the shores of Newfoundland, the

vessel struck an iceberg and sank. Before thirty-one of the passengers perished, the crew launched a jolly boat and a longboat. The captain, seven crew members, and one passenger went into the jolly boat. Nine from the crew (including one mate and a cook) and thirty-two passengers got into the longboat. Before the boats parted company, the captain put the mate in charge.

According to testimony, the longboat leaked and would have sunk or otherwise been in great peril if it had kept the load it had. Before the boats parted, the mate indicated to the captain that, unless the jolly boat took some of the longboat's passengers, the mate would have to cast lots and throw some overboard. The captain refused to heed the warning. One day later, with the boat sinking, the mate directed the crew to throw overboard all male passengers, except two married men and one small boy. The mate and the crew threw fourteen male passengers overboard. Two women also perished, but testimony differed concerning who decided what. On the second day, the remaining people on the longboat were rescued, and, after six days at sea, the jolly boat was also rescued.

The prosecution argued that the seamen had a duty to the passengers and that they should have consulted with the passengers and used a lot system for selection. Counsel for the defense countered that the whole company had been reduced to a "state of nature" where "all became their own lawgivers." The court stated that the phrase "law of nature" only meant that "there are certain great and fundamental principles of justice which, in the constitution of nature, lie at the foundation and make part of all civil law, independently of express adoption or enactment." The court found the mate guilty of homicide but mitigated the sentence (*United States v. Holmes* 1842). Analyze the prosecution and defense arguments. How do they use the word "nature"?

C. NATURAL LAW

The tension between "sticking to the law" and "reaching outside law to morality" informs many contemporary disputes in the philosophy of law. The conflict between natural law and legal positivism turns on determining the relationship between law and morality. Neither side wants to sever law completely from morality. Natural law proponents see a necessary connection between law and morality. Legal positivists find a useful conceptual separation between law and morality. War crimes and genocide provide challenges to these seemingly abstract theories.

Is there a way to morally assess our laws? The ancient Roman **Cicero** (106–43 B.C.) saw natural law as "the standard by which Justice and Injustice are measured" in the written law. Natural law has served as a means of evaluating whether positive laws qualify as just or unjust. The ancient Greeks provided the most famous appeal to natural law in literature. Antigone, in Sophocles' play by the same name, used natural law in her battle with the legal authority. King Creon refused to grant burial rights for her brother Polyneices. Antigone admitted that Creon, the embodiment of the state, made the positive law, but she proclaimed that a higher, "unwritten and unfailing" natural law governed the state. "Much of jurisprudence simply rings changes on the disagreement between Creon and Antigone" (Posner 1990, p. 10). Throughout history, individuals of conscience have used natural law to justify condemnation of and disobedience to a state's positive law.

Martin Luther King, Jr. strove to change discriminatory laws, while Robert Jackson, at the Nuremberg War Trials, condemned an entire system of laws. However, questions remain. Who determines the injustices of positive law? On what basis does a law fail the test? Natural law theorists base morality on nature and not on the positive law, and they disagree over the origins of natural law. According to St. Thomas Aquinas, a thirteenth-century Roman Catholic theologian, natural law had a religious origin, while Hugo Grotius, the sixteenth-century father of international law, believed it had a secular origin. Aquinas and Grotius adopted a substantive approach to natural law, seeing it as making substantive assessments of municipal law.

1. Religious Natural Law

Thomas Aquinas (1225–1274), born of Italian nobility, chose a clerical life over a secular one. After Thomas entered the Dominican Order, his family, favoring the Benedictine Order, kidnapped and imprisoned him for one year. Determined to remain a Dominican, Thomas returned to his studies. His fellow students called him a "dumb ox," but his teacher, Albert the Great, responded, "The bellowing of that ox will be heard throughout the world" (Sigmund 1988, p. xv). While studying at the University of Paris, Aquinas successfully defended himself against charges brought by the Bishop of Paris for his excessively rational, Aristotelian views. His teacher proved correct and his accusers wrong. Aquinas served as personal advisor to Pope Urban IV and became canonized a century after his death (1323). His teachings were declared to be the basis of Roman Catholicism.

Aquinas distinguished four kinds of law: eternal, divine, natural, and human (positive). Eternal law governs the universe according to Divine Reason and establishes an objective order to the physical world and a reality to the moral world. Divine law is God's law revealed through the Scriptures. Humans make positive laws for the purpose of leading them gradually to virtue. Natural law serves as a bridge for rational creatures between eternal and human law. It enables humans to distinguish, through the natural light of reason, good from evil. Thus, natural law is "nothing else than the rational creature's participation in the eternal laws" (*Summa Theologiae* [1266–1273] Question 91, Second Article, in Sigmund 1988). Reason can guide individuals to derive positive law from natural law: "That one must not kill may be derived as a conclusion from the [natural law] principle that one should do harm to no man." (*Summa Theologiae* [1266–1273] Question 95, Second Article, in Sigmund 1988). According to Aquinas, humans must adjust positive law to the natural law. If they fail to do this, then they do not produce laws "but a perversion of law." Aquinas seems to agree with Augustine that "a law that is not just, seems to be no law at all":

> [L]aws may be unjust in two ways: first, by being contrary to human good . . . either in respect of the end, as when an authority imposes on his subjects burdensome laws, conducive, not to the common good, but rather to his own cupidity or vainglory;—or in respect to the author, as when a man makes a law that goes beyond the power committed to him;—or in respect to form, as when burdens are imposed unequally on the community, although with a view to the common good. . . . Secondly, laws may be unjust through being opposed to the Divine good: such are the laws of tyrants inducing to idolatry, or to anything else contrary to the Divine law." (Aquinas, *Summa Theologica,* Part II, First Part. Qua. 96[4], in Sigmund 1988, p. 53)

A problem arises in determining which laws qualify as unjust, particularly if natural law is open to interpretation and subject to change. Martin Luther King, Jr., for example, appealed to natural law when he proclaimed that segregation laws were no law at all since they were out of harmony with the moral law or the law of God. However, historically, natural law theory has also been used to justify slavery. Does Nazi law qualify as law according to natural law theory? Theorists continue to dispute whether Aquinas wanted to establish criteria for law or to make a claim about the moral force of law (see Soper 1992, p. 2393). He laid the foundation for discussions of natural law up to and including the present.

French philosopher **Jacques Maritain** (1882–1973) chaired a human rights committee, whose members included Aldous Huxley and Teilhard de Chardin (Schall 1998, p. 223). The committee's reports formed the basis of the United Nations Declaration of Rights (1948). Maritain applied a neo-Thomistic account of natural law to international law (see Reading 2-4).

2. Secular Natural Law

Dutch jurist **Hugo Grotius** (1583–1645) constructed a largely secular approach to natural law. He found the source of natural law in the social and rational nature of humans and received a prison sentence for favoring free will over the Calvinist doctrine of predestination. He wrote his most famous works while exiled in France. The Dutch East India Company had commissioned him for advice on the lawfulness of capturing merchant vessels. Grotius used his consulting work as the basis for his classic study, *On the Law of War and Peace* (1625), which is his response to the devastation of the Thirty Years War. He explored the use of reason and ethics as a means of judging the laws of nations, and he derived his thirteen precepts of law from nine general concepts of law. Rousseau attacked Grotius for his defense of slavery and absolutism in *On the Social Contract* (1756). However, Grotius had defended these practices as rare exceptions, justified only under certain circumstances. "Grotius's natural law bars only clear, positive injustices, acts that are unambiguously destructive of society" (Forde 1998, p. 640). Grotius placed a minimum of clear justices under natural law and rejected a Christian natural law approach that attempted to place everything virtuous within natural law. Grotius, in contrast to Kant, gave priority to peace over justice. Like Hobbes, however, he thought that individuals surrendered their right to revolt by opting for security within a nation state. Grotius is considered to be the founder of international law.

Do we face a "normatively empty but empirically overflowing world" where "there is today no way of 'proving' that napalming babies is bad except by asserting it (in a louder and louder voice), or by defining it as so, early in one's game, and then later slipping it through, in a whisper, as a conclusion" (Leff 1974, as reprinted in Dau-Schmidt and Ulen, 1998, p. 39)? It makes sense to have normative standards to evaluate national legal systems and state laws. Some evaluations appear to be noncontroversial. Intuitively, a legal system that supports slavery, apartheid, or genocide has no moral justification. But what arguments support these ethical intuitions? What happens when we consider more debatable positive laws? What arguments support assessing polygamy laws as unjust? Do natural law justifications disguise attempts of one culture to impose its values on another? For example, after World War II, the Allies accused the Germans and the Japanese of having violated natural law. Did these accusations amount to nothing more than victor's justice? Disturbed by these questions, some theorists have abandoned the quest to find universal moral values (a substantive approach) in favor of universal procedural norms.

3. Procedural Natural Law

After teaching in Oregon and Illinois, **Lon Fuller** (1902–1978) succeeded Roscoe Pound as the Carter Professor of General Jurisprudence at Harvard (1939–1972). He practiced labor law for the famous Boston firm of Ropes and Gray and wrote important works in contract law. In his jurisprudential work known as "Eunomics," a term he coined meaning the science of social ordering, he rejected the distinction between fact and value in debates with philosophers Ernest Nagel and Willard van Orman Quine. Fuller constructed an allegory about the unhappy reign of a new monarch named Rex to illustrate the need for a procedural natural law (see Reading 2-5). Rex decided to reform the legal system after wiping the slate clean from the previous monarch—but Rex never got it right. First, he did not publish his rulings, and then he published his rulings but failed to give reasons for them and neglected to publish the rules in advance. He issued contradictory commands and incomprehensible rules. After correcting all previous procedural problems, Rex made up a legal code that demanded impossible conditions of compliance. The code allowed only ten seconds to answer a summons from the throne and made it illegal to fall down or to hiccup. Rex's final revision failed to keep abreast of the changing times, and he finally cast the revisions to the wind, deciding each case that came before him on an *ad hoc* basis. After Rex's death, Rex II took the power away from the lawyers and gave it to the psychiatrists so that people could be happy without rules. The reader can draw several lessons from the fable. Rex had failed to abide by the general procedural purposes of any legal system, violating what Fuller called "the internal morality of law." Fuller, thereby, proposed a procedural natural law theory. If a society failed to institute procedural principles, the society stood rightfully accused of not having a legal system. Does it make sense to rely on purely procedural norms? Assume that Rex had gotten all the procedures right. Does procedural compliance guarantee that there will not be any substantive legal failings? Commentators question what Fuller's procedural failures have to do with morality (see Golding 1986).

So, Fuller adopted a proceduralist approach to natural law. He did not concern himself "with the substantive aims of legal rules, but with the ways in which a system of rules for governing human conduct must be constructed and administered if it is to be efficacious and at the same time remain what it purports to be" (Fuller 1964, p. 97). Fuller, who refused to separate law from morality, demanded that law have an internal morality (procedural fairness) to qualify as law. However, he did not completely disregard substantive natural law. He took procedural morality as conducive to substantive morality. If a system violates a basic procedural sense of justice and fairness, it does not qualify as a legal system. According to Fuller (1959), the

Nazis used legislation, retroactively, to transform murder into lawful execution. Nazi law included the following: "Whoever commits an action which is deserving of punishment according to the sound principles of the people shall be punished. If no determinate penal law is applicable to the action, it shall be punished according to whatever law fits it best" (Nazi law, 1935). Further, they made wholesale killings in concentration camps lawful by secret enactment. These procedural shortcomings, as well as their failure to obey their own enactments, provide ample evidence of the Nazis' disregard for the inner morality of law. Therefore, according to Fuller, Nazi "law" should not qualify as law.

READING 2-4

Modern Natural Law Theory
"The Rights of Man" (1950)

Jacques Maritain

The First Element (Ontological) in Natural Law

Since I have not time here to discuss nonsense (we can always find very intelligent philosophers, not to quote Mr. Bertrand Russell, to defend it most brilliantly) I am taking it for granted that we admit that there is a human nature, and that this human nature is the same in all men. I am taking it for granted that we also admit that man is a being gifted with intelligence, and who, as such, acts with an understanding of what he is doing, and therefore with the power to determine for himself the ends which he pursues. On the other hand, possessed of a nature, or an ontologic structure which is a locus of intelligible necessities, man possesses ends which necessarily correspond to his essential constitution and which are the same for all—as all pianos, for instance, whatever their particular type and in whatever spot they may be, have as their end the production of certain attuned sounds. If they do not produce these sounds they must be tuned, or discarded as worthless. But since man is endowed with intelligence and determines his own ends, it is up to him to put himself in tune with the ends necessarily demanded by his nature. This means that there is, by the very virtue of human nature, an order or a disposition which human reason can discover and according to which the human will must act in order to attune itself to the essential and necessary ends of the human being. The unwritten law, or natural law, is nothing more than that. . . .

What I am emphasizing is the first basic element to be recognized in natural law, namely the *ontological* element; I mean the *normality of functioning* which is grounded on the essence of that being: man. Natural law in general, as we have just seen, is the ideal formula of development of a given being; it might be compared with an algebraical equation according to which a curve develops in space, yet with man the curve has freely to conform to the equation. Let us say, then, that in its ontological aspect, natural law is an *ideal order* relating to human actions, a *divide* between the suitable and the unsuitable, the proper and the improper, which depends on human nature or essence and the unchangeable necessities rooted in it. I do not mean that the proper regulation for each possible human situation is contained in the human essence, as Leibniz believed that every event in the life of Caesar was contained beforehand in the idea of Caesar. Human situations are something existential. Neither they nor their appropriate regulations are contained in the essence of man. I would say that they ask questions of that essence. Any given situation, for instance the situation of Cain with regard to Abel, implies a relation to the essence of man, and the possible murder of the one by the other is incompatible with the general ends and innermost dynamic structure of that rational essence. It is rejected by it. Hence the prohibition of murder is grounded on or required by the essence of man. The precept: thou shalt do no murder, is a precept of natural law. Because a primordial and most general end of human nature is to preserve being—the being of that existent who is a person, and a universe unto himself; and because man insofar as he is man has a right to live.

Suppose a completely new case or situation, unheard of in human history: suppose, for instance, that what we now call *genocide* were as new as that very name. In the fashion that I just explained, that possible behaviour will face the human essence as incompatible with its general ends and innermost dynamic structure: that is to say, as prohibited by natural law. The condemnation of genocide by the General Assembly of United Nations has sanctioned the prohibition of the crime in question by natural law—which does not mean that that prohibition was part of the essence of man as I know not what metaphysical feature eternally inscribed in it—nor that it was a notion recognized from the start by the conscience of humanity. . . .

The Second Element (Gnoseological) in Natural Law

Thus we arrive at the *second* basic element to be recognized in natural law, namely natural law *as known,* and thus as measuring in actual fact human practical reason, which is the measure of human acts. . . .

Natural law is an unwritten law. Man's knowledge of it has increased little by little as man's moral conscience has developed. The latter was at first in a twilight state. Anthropologists have taught us within what structures of tribal life and in the midst of what half-awakened magic it was primitively formed. This proves merely that the knowledge men have had of the unwritten law has passed through more diverse forms and stages than certain philosophers or theologians have believed. The knowledge which our own moral conscience has of this law is doubtless still imperfect, and very likely it will continue to develop and to become more refined as long as humanity exists. Only when the Gospel has penetrated to the very depth of human substance will natural law appear in its flower and its perfection.

HUMAN RIGHTS AND NATURAL LAW

I need not apologize for having dwelt so long on the subject of natural law. How could we understand human rights if we had not a sufficiently adequate notion of natural law? The same natural law which lays down our most fundamental duties, and by virtue of which every law is binding, is the very law which assigns to us our fundamental rights. . . .

At this point we see that a positivistic philosophy recognizing Fact alone—as well as either an idealistic or a materialistic philosophy of absolute Immanence—is powerless to establish the existence of rights which are naturally possessed by the human being, prior and superior to written legislation and to agreements between governments, rights which the civil society does not have to *grant* but to *recognize* and sanction as universally valid, and which no social necessity can authorize us even momentarily to abolish or disregard. Logically, the concept of such rights can seem only a superstition to these philosophies. . . .

For a philosophy which recognizes Fact alone, the notion of Value,—I mean Value objectively true in itself—is not conceivable. How, then, can one claim rights if one does not believe in values? If the affirmation of the intrinsic value and dignity of man is nonsense, the affirmation of the natural rights of man is nonsense also.

ABOUT HUMAN RIGHTS IN GENERAL

Let us now discuss further some problems which deal with human rights in general. My first point will relate to the distinction between Natural Law and Positive Law. One of the main errors of the rationalist philosophy of human rights has been to regard positive law as a mere transcript traced off from natural law, which would supposedly prescribe in the name of Nature all that which positive law prescribes in the name of society. They forgot the immense field of human things which depend on the variable conditions of social life and on the free initiative of human reason, and which natural law leaves undetermined.

As I have pointed out, *natural law* deals with the rights and the duties which are connected in a *necessary* manner with the first principle: "Do good and avoid evil." This is why the precepts of the unwritten law are in themselves or in the nature of things (I am not saying in man's knowledge of them) universal and invariable.

Jus gentium, or the *Law of Nations,* is difficult to define exactly, because it is intermediary between natural law and positive law. Let us say that in its deepest and most genuine meaning, such as put forward by Thomas Aquinas, the law of nations, or better to say, the common law of civilization, differs from natural law because it is *known,* not through inclination, but through the *conceptual exercise of reason,* or through rational knowledge; in this sense it pertains to positive law, and formally constitutes a juridical order (though not necessarily written in a code). But as concerns its content, *jus gentium* comprises both things which belong also to natural law (insofar as they are not only known as rationally inferred, but also known through inclination) and things which—though obligatory in a universal manner, since concluded from a principle of natural law—are beyond the content of natural law (because they are *only* rationally inferred, and not known through inclination). In both cases *jus gentium* or the common law of civilization deals, like natural law, with rights and duties which are connected with the first principle in a *necessary* manner. And precisely because it is known through rational knowledge, and is itself a work of reason, it is more especially concerned with such rights and duties as exist in the realm of the basic natural work achieved by human reason, that is, the state of civil life.

Positive Law, or the body of laws (either customary law or statute law) in force in a given social group, deals with the rights and the duties which are connected with the first principle, but in a *contingent* manner, by virtue of the determinate ways of conduct set down by the reason and the will of man when they institute the laws or give birth to the customs of a particular society, thus stating of themselves that in the particular group in question certain things will be good and permissible, certain other things bad and not permissible.

But it is by virtue of natural law that the law of Nations and positive law take on the force of law, and impose themselves upon the conscience. They are a prolongation or an extension of natural law, passing into objective zones which can less and less be sufficiently determined by the essential inclinations of human nature. For it is *natural law itself which requires that whatever it leaves undetermined shall subsequently be determined,* either as a right or a duty existing for all men, and of which they are made aware, not by knowledge through inclination, but by conceptual reason—that's for *jus gentium*—or—this is for positive law—as a right or a duty existing for certain men by reason of the human and contingent regulations proper to the social group of which they are a part. Thus there are imperceptible transitions (at least from the point of view of historical experience) between Natural Law, the Law of Nations, and Positive Law. There is a dynamism which impels the unwritten law to flower forth in human law, and to render the latter ever more perfect and just in the very field of its contingent determinations. It is in accordance with this dynamism that the rights of the human person take political and social form in the community. . . .

READING 2-5

Law's Inner Morality
The Morality of Law (1964)

Lon L. Fuller

THE MORALITY THAT MAKES LAW POSSIBLE

The Consequences of Failure

Rex's bungling career as legislator and judge illustrates that the attempt to create and maintain a system of legal rules may miscarry in at least eight ways; there are in this enterprise, if you will, eight distinct routes to disaster. The first and most obvious lies in a failure to achieve rules at all, so that every issue must be decided on an ad hoc basis. The other routes are: (2) a failure to publicize, or at least to make available to the affected party, the rules he is expected to observe; (3) the abuse of retroactive legislation, which not only cannot itself guide action, but undercuts the integrity of rules prospective in effect, since it puts them under the threat of retrospective change; (4) a failure to make rules understandable; (5) the enactment of contradictory rules or (6) rules that require conduct beyond the powers of the affected party; (7) introducing such frequent changes in the rules that the subject cannot orient his action by them; and, finally, (8) a failure of congruence between the rules as announced and their actual administration.

A total failure in any one of these eight directions does not simply result in a bad system of law; it results in something that is not properly called a legal system at all, except perhaps in the Pickwickian sense in which a void contract can still be said to be one kind of contract. Certainly there can be no rational ground for asserting that a man can have a moral obligation to obey a legal rule that does not exist, or is kept secret from him, or that came into existence only after he had acted, or was unintelligible, or was contradicted by another rule of the same system, or commanded the impossible, or changed every minute. It may not be impossible for a man to obey a rule that is disregarded by those charged with its administration, but at some point obedience becomes futile—as futile, in fact, as casting a vote that will never be counted. As the sociologist Simmel has observed, there is a kind of reciprocity between government and the citizen with respect to the observance of rules. Government says to the citizen in effect, "These are the rules we expect you to follow. If you follow them, you have our assurance that they are the rules that will be applied to your conduct." When this bond of reciprocity is finally and completely ruptured by government, nothing is left on which to ground the citizen's duty to observe the rules.

The citizen's predicament becomes more difficult when, though there is no total failure in any direction, there is a general and drastic deterioration in legality, such as occurred in Germany under Hitler.[1] A situation begins to develop, for example, in which though some laws are published, others, including the most important, are not. Though most laws are prospective in effect, so free a use is made of retrospective legislation that no law is immune to change ex post facto if it suits the convenience of those in power. For the trial of criminal cases concerned with loyalty to the regime, special military tribunals are established and these tribunals disregard, whenever it suits their convenience,

---

[1] I have discussed some of the features of this deterioration in my article, "Positivism and Fidelity to Law," 71 *Harvard Law Review* 630, 648–57 (1958). This article makes no attempt at a comprehensive survey of all the postwar judicial decisions in Germany concerned with events occurring during the Hitler regime. Some of the later decisions rested the nullity of judgments rendered by the courts under Hitler not on the ground that the statutes applied were void, but on the ground that the Nazi judges misinterpreted the statutes of their own government. See Pappe, "On the Validity of Judicial Decisions in the Nazi Era," 23 *Modern Law Review* 260–74 (1960). Dr. Pappe makes more of this distinction than seems to me appropriate. After all, the meaning of a statute depends in part on accepted modes of interpretation. Can it be said that the postwar German courts gave full effect to Nazi laws when they interpreted them by their own standards instead of the quite different standards current during the Nazi regime? Moreover, with statutes of the kind involved, filled as they were with vague phrases and unrestricted delegations of power, it seems a little out of place to strain over questions of their proper interpretation.

the rules that are supposed to control their decisions. Increasingly the principal object of government seems to be, not that of giving the citizen rules by which to shape his conduct, but to frighten him into impotence. As such a situation develops, the problem faced by the citizen is not so simple as that of a voter who knows with certainty that his ballot will not be counted. It is more like that of the voter who knows that the odds are against his ballot being counted at all, and that if it is counted, there is a good chance that it will be counted for the side against which he actually voted. A citizen in this predicament has to decide for himself whether to stay with the system and cast his ballot as a kind of symbolic act expressing the hope of a better day. So it was with the German citizen under Hitler faced with deciding whether he had an obligation to obey such portions of the laws as the Nazi terror had left intact.

In situations like these there can be no simple principle by which to test the citizen's obligation of fidelity to law, any more than there can be such a principle for testing his right to engage in a general revolution. One thing is, however, clear. A mere respect for constituted authority must not be confused with fidelity to law. Rex's subjects, for example, remained faithful to him as king throughout his long and inept reign. They were not faithful to his law, for he never made any. . . .

THE CONCEPT OF LAW

Legal Morality and Natural Law

Proceeding with that exposition, then, the first task is to relate what I have called the internal morality of the law to the ages-old tradition of natural law. Do the principles expounded in my second chapter represent some variety of natural law? The answer is an emphatic, though qualified, yes.

What I have tried to do is to discern and articulate the natural laws of a particular kind of human undertaking, which I have described as "the enterprise of subjecting human conduct to the governance of rules." These natural laws have nothing to do with any "brooding omnipresence in the skies." Nor have they the slightest affinity with any such proposition as that the practice of contraception is a violation of God's law. They remain entirely terrestrial in origin and application. They are not "higher" laws; if any metaphor of elevation is appropriate they should be called "lower" laws. They are like the natural laws of carpentry, or at least those laws respected by a carpenter who wants the house he builds to remain standing and serve the purpose of those who live in it.

Though these natural laws touch one of the most vital of human activities they obviously do not exhaust the whole of man's moral life. They have nothing to say on such topics as polygamy, the study of Marx, the worship of God, the progressive income tax, or the subjugation of women. If the question be raised whether any of these subjects, or others like them, should be taken as objects of legislation, that question relates to what I have called the external morality of law.

As a convenient (though not wholly satisfactory) way of describing the distinction being taken we may speak of a procedural, as distinguished from a substantive natural law. What I have called the internal morality of law is in this sense a procedural version of natural law, though to avoid misunderstanding the word "procedural" should be assigned a special and expanded sense so that it would include, for example, a substantive accord between official action and enacted law. The term "procedural" is, however, broadly appropriate as indicating that we are concerned, not with the substantive aims of legal rules, but with the ways in which a system of rules for governing human conduct must be constructed and administered if it is to be efficacious and at the same time remain what it purports to be.

D. LEGAL POSITIVISM

Legal positivists reject the natural law condition that for something to qualify as law it must be "required of morality." Natural law theorists assert and legal positivists deny any necessary connection between law and morality. Instead, positivists regard law as artificial, not natural, and as a social fact made, or *posited,* by humans. By separating laws and morals, positivists do not deny an interplay between the two, but they issue a caution. They urge us to remember the distinction between descriptive statements that tell "what is" and prescriptive statements that proclaim "what ought to be." Eighteenth-century British philosopher David Hume (1711–1776) first brought this seemingly elementary distinction between "is" and "ought" into the philosophical spotlight. Hume defied his family's wishes and refused to continue his law studies at the University of Edinburgh. Instead, he chose to study philosophy on his own, but he never attained an academic appointment. He wrote:

> I cannot forbear adding to these reasonings an observation, which may, perhaps, be found of some importance. In every system of morality, which I have hitherto met with, I have always remarked, that the author proceeds for some time in the ordinary way of reasoning, and establishes the being of God, or makes observations concerning human affairs; when of a sudden I am surprised to find that instead of the usual copulations of propositions, *is* and *is not,* I meet with no proposition that is not connected with an *ought* or an *ought not.* This change is imperceptible; but is, however, of the last consequence. For as this *ought,* or *ought not,* expresses some new relation or affirmation, 'tis necessary that it should be observed and explained; and at the same time that a reason should be given, for what seems altogether inconceivable, how this new relation can be a deduction from others [that is, follows logically], which are entirely different from it. But as authors do not commonly use this precaution, I shall presume to recommend it to the readers; and am persuaded, that this small attention would subvert all the vulgar systems of morality, and let us see, that the distinction of vice and virtue is not founded merely on the relations of objects, nor is perceived by reason" (Hume 1777, *Treatise of Human Nature*).

Therefore, Nazi law, while morally repugnant, still qualifies descriptively as law for the positivists. This separation thesis marks legal positivism as a distinct philosophy of law.

Positivists developed sophisticated answers to questions about the nature of law. The concepts of **sovereignty, command, sanctions,** and **rules** have played key roles in the development of legal positivism. These ideas, although criticized and rejected by many contemporary positivists, still influence legal thought. In the discussion that follows, each concept pairs with a particular philosopher and a specific model. Legal philosophers use other disciplines (mathematics for Hobbes) as well as exemplary areas of the law (criminal law for Austin and civil law for Hart) as models for constructing their theories. Hobbes admired the order and precision of geometry and called his method an "ordered approach." He presented his philosophy in the form of exact definitions, similar in form to those found in mathematics. Hobbes, in dramatic fashion, attempted to unite law and order. He modeled his sovereign on Order, which was prompted by a fear of Disorder. Often, theorists call on the force of Law to subdue Disorder. And frequently a law-and-order position goes in a Hobbesian direction, where, to paraphrase Hobbes, "not laws but humans rule." Philosophers of law sometimes model their theories on different types of law (Murphy and Coleman 1990). John Austin saw law as "the command of the sovereign backed-up by sanctions." His focus on commands and penalties fit a criminal law model. H. L. A. Hart, in contrast, conceived of law as not only an Austinian enforcer but also as a facilitator. A civil law (especially contract law) model fits best with Hart's tempered authoritarian and mildly punitive view of law.

To complete the picture, a constitutional law model lends itself to a murkier picture, shunned by legal positivists. Students and practitioners, with an eye to precision and clarity, often find constitutional law confusing. To them, reading cases in constitutional law seems more like reading a disjointed novel or a philosophy text than a well-reasoned and clear text in science or social science. Ronald Dworkin (highlighted in chapter 3) makes a virtue out of this vice by offering an account that treats law as literature. Dworkin uses an analogy to writing a chain novel to help tie together the loose ends of constitutional law into a relatively unified moral theory. Dworkin's use of the novel as a model contrasts sharply with more scientifically oriented models, especially Hobbes's "ordered approach." But let us return to some key ingredients in the positivist model, namely, sovereignty, commands, sanctions, and rules.

1. Sovereignty: The Ordered Approach

Thomas Hobbes (1588–1679) represents a bridge between natural law and positivism, because his writings contain elements of each. Hobbes became a prominent political thinker largely as a result of his *Leviathan* (1652). As discussed previously (see pages 6–9), Hobbes put forth a pessimistic view of human nature, solved only by individuals agreeing to submit to absolute authority. He had few illusions about human goodness, believing that any civil society had the potential to lapse into a state of nature, a state of war in which all are against all. According to Hobbes, when government and order break down, chaos reigns. Human nature makes it impossible for any government to be effective without absolute power. Therefore, in order to avoid a state of affairs where everyone's life is "solitary, poor, nasty, brutish and short," individuals living in a state of nature should form a contract to give simple obedience to an absolute sovereign (see page 39).

As noted in chapter 1, Hobbes said he had been born in fear, having faced political turmoil in England. One historian described this period of England's civil war as "the world turned upside down" (Hill 1975). Members of various political movements, from the rabble to the respectable, questioned, through word and deed, all establishment institutions—the army, the church, science, royalty. The chaos and disorder that reigned in 1640s England had a lasting influence on Hobbes. He believed that only the force of an absolute sovereign, Leviathan, could tame the monstrous rebellion, Behemoth.

Hobbes accepted certain "laws of nature," such as the general rule "by which a man is forbidden to do that, which is destructive of his life, or taketh away the means of preserving the same" (*Leviathan,* chapter 14). Individuals who submitted to the authority of the state followed the dictates of natural law to protect themselves. Hobbes saw laws as commands, backed by threats and sanctions, of the sovereign and, therefore, identified law with its source, the sovereign. He sided with "government by men" and not of laws, believing an effective sovereign must function above the law and must not operate in the disguise of a judicial interpreter of the law. He rejected judge-made or common law and thought that judges should not follow the judgments of unlearned and ignorant men in precedent cases. Instead, Hobbes favored codification—that is, the enactment of clear, precise legislative statutes.

2. Commands and Sanctions: The Criminal Law Model

John Austin (1790–1859) served for five years in the British Army. Some commentators think Austin's military service influenced his fascination with command and other military ideas. After leaving an unsuccessful law practice, he turned to teaching and received an appointment as chair of Jurisprudence at the University of London. Austin's lectures were well received but not well attended. As a result, he experienced financial difficulties, since lecturers earned their living from paid attendance. He published his lectures as *The Province of Jurisprudence Determined* (1832). In London, Austin lived near utilitarian legal reformer, **Jeremy Bentham** (1748–1832) and had, as a student, noted utilitarian, **John Stuart Mill** (1806–1873). Austin became a disciple of Bentham's. He sympathized with Bentham's crusade to achieve clarity in the law through careful codification and shared many of his legal reform efforts. Most importantly, Austin agreed with Bentham's **utilitarian** philosophy. Utilitarians focus on consequences, evaluating acts or rules according to their ability to bring about the best overall balance of good over bad consequences. Bentham used the quantity of pleasure and pain to measure consequences. Austin, however, took a less evaluative, and less reform route than Bentham. He saw his primary task as describing and not prescribing law. He strove for systematic clarity and carefully examined key ingredients needed to understand law. For Austin, as for Hobbes, the key to law lay in the concepts of command, duty, and sanction. Austin identified law with general commands issued by a sovereign that, in turn, created obligations in citizens. Positive law exists *by the position* (hence, positivist) of the sovereign, who can issue sanctions. *Law is a "general command of the sovereign to govern the conduct of society's members."* Most importantly, the sovereign must back up the commands and needs the threat of a sanction for noncompliance. Austin sees the sovereign as a gunman who can threaten others with evil or harm if they fail to carry out the commands—but, Austin's sovereign is not just any gunman. Austin's "legal gunman" has a certain pedigree. Austin's armed sovereign has a history of the people's habitual obedience. The sovereign acts as the sheriff, but he is not subject to the law. According to Austin, the law flows ultimately from power, so the sovereign, defined in terms of power, sits above the law. The Austinian terms *command, sanction,* and *threat* resonate with the criminal law. Perhaps, however, law operates in a quieter, less forceful manner, more akin to the civil law. After Austin, legal positivism developed in a more moderate direction.

3. Rules: The Civil or Private Law Model

Like Austin, **Herbert Lionel Adolphus Hart** (1907–1992) also practiced law before taking on an academic career. At Oxford University, in 1952, he became Professor of Jurisprudence. He worked closely with linguistic philosopher John L. Austin (not to be confused with the legal theorist John Austin, without the middle initial *L*). Analytic philosopher John L. Austin helped Hart develop conceptual analyses of legal terms. Because of Hart's work, **analytic philosophy** and Hart himself have had a strong influence on philosophy of law. His *Concept of Law* "is universally regarded the most significant contribution to legal philosophy" (Murphy and Coleman 1990, p. 26). His *Causation in Law* (1959), co-authored with A. M. Honoré, still ranks as the definitive work on legal causation. Although influenced greatly by jurist John Austin, Hart attacked Austin's core notion of a sovereign issuing coercive commands. He did not think that all laws fit Austin's model. Rather, he believed that some laws, particularly those in criminal law, fit Austin's "commands-backed-by-sanctions" model. Criminal law threatens punishment, but other laws facilitate action rather than threaten penalties. Contract law, for example, describes conditions someone must fulfill in order to enter into a legally enforceable agreement. Many types of laws confer powers without commanding anyone to do anything. Hart added power-conferring, **secondary rules** to Austin's **primary rules** or commands.

Hart imagined that a primitive society needs more than a sovereign's commands to thrive (see Reading 2-6). Primitive societies operate according to primary rules of obligation—therefore, they have laws. However, a system of primary rules has drawbacks. Primary rules are uncertain, static, and inefficient, but secondary rules, which govern primary rules, offer a cure for a defective system of primary rules. In other words, each primary rule defect has a secondary rule cure. Secondary rules come in three varieties: rules of recognition, change, and adjudication. **Rules of recognition** cure the uncertainty problem by specifying criteria used to determine the validity of legal rules. A rule of recognition is whatever a legal system uses as its final authority for determining whether something is a law. The rule might simply state that a particular book contains the society's laws. **Rules of change** overcome the static defect by setting down procedures for making laws. **Rules of adjudication** provide efficiency. They confer competence upon judicial officials to judge and enforce the law. Since a legal system combines primary and secondary rules, Hart defined *law as a union of primary rules and secondary* *rules*. Primary rules create duties; secondary rules confer powers. The distinction between the two enabled Hart to resolve a troubling aspect of Austin's theory. Because Austin's sovereign stands above the law, Austin leaves one sheriff (the sovereign) outside the law. According to Hart, though, laws (secondary rules) govern all the rulers (the governmental officials). Secondary rules enrich Austin's simple model of social control. They explain ways to determine valid laws from among the primary rules. A legal system exists (1) if citizens generally abide by the secondary rules and (2) if the officials accept, from an internal point of view, the rules of recognition. Legislation and judicial decisions have the force of law because officials fully accept that the validity of primary rules depends on criteria determined by secondary rules.

Hart accepted a minimal part of natural law—for example, survival as a common human goal. Sociologically speaking, Hart found that basic facts about the human condition (vulnerability; approximate equality among humans; limited altruism, resources, and understanding; strength of will) limit law's content. However, Hart refused to draw any conclusions from these sociological observations. Unlike natural law theorists, he did not propose them as a higher basis for positive law. He also retained the most characteristic ingredient of legal positivism, namely, the **separation of law from morality** (see Reading 2-7). According to Hart, unjust legal systems still qualified as having law. Hart considered himself to be a critical moralist and thought that the separation of law from morality should encourage unrelenting moral criticism of law. He believed the separation thesis should prevent the uncritical acceptance of a law as moral simply because it was law (MacCormick 1981). Hart claimed that primitive law (see Turnbull Reading 1-3) and international law have the same structure. Primary rules impose obligations on members of the international community and on a primitive society. International law and primitive societies both have primary rules that impose obligations on their members. However, neither international law nor primitive societies have secondary rules that provide the general criteria of validity for laws—that is, "ways in which the primary rules may be conclusively ascertained, introduced, eliminated, varied, and the fact of their violation conclusively determined" (Hart 1994).

READING 2-6

Importance of Rules for Law
"Law as the Union of Primary and Secondary Rules" (1994)

H. L. A. Hart

THE ELEMENTS OF LAW

It is, of course, possible to imagine a society without a legislature, courts, or officials of any kind. Indeed, there are many studies of primitive communities which not only claim that this possibility is realized but depict in detail the

life of a society where the only means of social control is that general attitude
of the group towards its own standard modes of behaviour in terms of which
we have characterized rules of obligation. A social structure of this kind is often referred to as one of 'custom'; but we shall not use this term, because it often implies that the customary rules are very old and supported with less social pressure than other rules. To avoid these implications we shall refer to
such a social structure as one of primary rules of obligation. If a society is to
live by such primary rules alone, there are certain conditions which, granted
a few of the most obvious truisms about human nature and the world we live
in, must clearly be satisfied. The first of these conditions is that the rules
must contain in some form restrictions on the free use of violence, theft, and
deception to which human beings are tempted but which they must, in general, repress, if they are to coexist in close proximity to each other. Such rules
are in fact always found in the primitive societies of which we have knowledge, together with a variety of others imposing on individuals various positive duties to perform services or make contributions to the common life (compare Turnbull, Reading 1-3). Secondly, though such a society may exhibit the
tension, already described, between those who accept the rules and those who
reject the rules except where fear of social pressure induces them to conform,
it is plain that the latter cannot be more than a minority, if so loosely organized a society of persons, approximately equal in physical strength, is to endure: for otherwise those who reject the rules would have too little social pressure to fear. This too is confirmed by what we know of primitive communities
where, though there are dissidents and malefactors, the majority live by the
rules seen from the internal point of view.

More important for our present purpose is the following consideration. It
is plain that only a small community closely knit by ties of kinship, common
sentiment, and belief, and placed in a stable environment, could live successfully by such a regime of unofficial rules. In any other conditions such a
simple form of social control must prove defective and will require supple-
mentation in different ways. In the first place, the rules by which the group
lives will not form a system, but will simply be a set of separate standards,
without any identifying or common mark, except of course that they are the
rules which a particular group of human beings accepts. They will in this respect resemble our own rules of etiquette. Hence if doubts arise as to what
the rules are or as to the precise scope of some given rule, there will be no procedure for settling this doubt, either by reference to an authoritative text or
to an official whose declarations on this point are authoritative. For, plainly,
such a procedure and the acknowledgement of either authoritative text or
persons involve the existence of rules of a type different from the rules of obligation or duty which *ex hypothesi* are all that the group has. This defect in
the simple social structure of primary rules we may call its *uncertainty*.

A second defect is the *static* character of the rules. The only mode of change
in the rules known to such a society will be the slow process of growth, whereby
courses of conduct once thought optional become first habitual or usual, and
then obligatory, and the converse process of decay, when deviations, once severely dealt with, are first tolerated and then pass unnoticed. There will be no
means, in such a society, of deliberately adapting the rules to changing circumstances, either by eliminating old rules or introducing new ones: for, again,

the possibility of doing this presupposes the existence of rules of a different type from the primary rules of obligation by which alone the society lives. . . .

The third defect of this simple form of social life is the *inefficiency* of the diffuse social pressure by which the rules are maintained. Disputes as to whether an admitted rule has or has not been violated will always occur and will, in any but the smallest societies, continue interminably, if there is no agency specially empowered to ascertain finally, and authoritatively, the fact of violation. . . .

The remedy for each of these three main defects in this simplest form of social structure consists in supplementing the *primary* rules of obligation with *secondary* rules which are rules of a different kind. The introduction of the remedy for each defect might, in itself, be considered a step from the prelegal into the legal world; since each remedy brings with it many elements that permeate law: certainly all three remedies together are enough to convert the regime of primary rules into what is indisputably a legal system. We shall consider in turn each of these remedies and show why law may most illuminatingly be characterized as a union of primary rules of obligation with such secondary rules. Before we do this, however, the following general points should be noted. Though the remedies consist in the introduction of rules which are certainly different from each other, as well as from the primary rules of obligation which they supplement, they have important features in common and are connected in various ways. Thus they may all be said to be on a different level from the primary rules, for they are all *about* such rules; in the sense that while primary rules are concerned with the actions that individuals must or must not do, these secondary rules are all concerned with the primary rules themselves. They specify the ways in which primary rules may be conclusively ascertained, introduced, eliminated, varied, and the fact of their violation conclusively determined.

The simplest form of remedy for the *uncertainty* of the regime of primary rules is the introduction of what we shall call a 'rule of recognition'. This will specify some feature or features possession of which by a suggested rule is taken as a conclusive affirmative indication that it is a rule of the group to be supported by the social pressure it exerts. . . .

The remedy for the *static* quality of the regime of primary rules consists in the introduction of what we shall call 'rules of change'. The simplest form of such a rule is that which empowers an individual or body of persons to introduce new primary rules for the conduct of the life of the group, or of some class within it, and to eliminate old rules. . . .

The third supplement to the simple regime of primary rules, intended to remedy the *inefficiency* of its diffused social pressure, consists of secondary rules empowering individuals to make authoritative determinations of the question whether, on a particular occasion, a primary rule has been broken. The minimal form of adjudication consists in such determinations, and we shall call the secondary rules which confer the power to make them 'rules of adjudication'. Besides identifying the individuals who are to adjudicate, such rules will also define the procedure to be followed. . . .

Hart, H.L.A.: "The Elements of Law," from *The Concepts of Law* (2nd edition, 1994) reprinted by permission of Oxford University Press.

Law Distinguished from Morality
"Positivism and the Separation of Laws and Morals" Part I (1983)

H. L. A. Hart

Contemporary voices tell us we must recognize something obscured by the legal 'positivists' whose day is now over: that there is a 'point of intersection between law and morals', or that what *is* and what *ought* to be are somehow indissolubly fused or inseparable, though the positivists denied it. What do these phrases mean? Or rather which of the many things that they *could* mean, *do* they mean? Which of them do 'positivists' deny and why is it wrong to do so?

I

I shall present the subject as part of the history of an idea. At the close of the eighteenth century and the beginning of the nineteenth the most earnest thinkers in England about legal and social problems and the architects of great reforms were the great Utilitarians. Two of them, Bentham and Austin, constantly insisted on the need to distinguish, firmly and with the maximum of clarity, law as it is from law as it ought to be. This theme haunts their work, and they condemned the natural-law thinkers precisely because they had blurred this apparently simple but vital distinction. By contrast, at the present time in this country and to a lesser extent in England, this separation between law and morals is held to be superficial and wrong. Some critics have thought that it blinds men to the true nature of law and its roots in social life. Others have thought it not only intellectually misleading but corrupting in practice, at its worst apt to weaken resistance to state tyranny or absolutism, and at its best apt to bring law into disrespect. The now pejorative name 'Legal Positivism', like most terms which are used as missiles in intellectual battles, has come to stand for a baffling multitude of different sins. One of them is the sin, real or alleged, of insisting, as Austin and Bentham did, on the separation of law as it is and law as it ought to be. . . .

Bentham and Austin were not dry analysts fiddling with verbal distinctions while cities burned, but were the vanguard of a movement which laboured with passionate intensity and much success to bring about a better society and better laws. Why then did they insist on the separation of law as it is and law as it ought to be? What did they mean? Let us first see what they said. Austin formulated the doctrine:

> The existence of law is one thing; its merit or demerit is another. Whether it be or be not is one enquiry; whether it be or be not conformable to an assumed standard, is a different enquiry. A law, which actually exists, is a law, though we happen to dislike it, or though it vary from the text, by which we regulate our approbation and disapprobation. This truth, when formally announced as an abstract proposition, is so simple and glaring that it seems

idle to insist upon it. But simple and glaring as it is, when enunciated in abstract expressions the enumeration of the instances in which it has been forgotten would fill a volume.

Sir William Blackstone, for example, says in his 'Commentaries', that the laws of God are superior in obligation to all other laws; that no human laws should be suffered to contradict them; that human laws are of no validity if contrary to them; and that all valid laws derive their force from that Divine original.

Now, he *may* mean that all human laws ought to conform to the Divine laws. If this be his meaning, I assent to it without hesitation. . . . Perhaps, again, he means that human lawgivers are themselves obliged by the Divine laws to fashion the laws which they impose by that ultimate standard, because if they do not, God will punish them. To this also I entirely assent. . . .

But the meaning of this passage of Blackstone, if it has a meaning, seems rather to be this: that no human law which conflicts with the Divine law is obligatory or binding; in other words, that no human law which conflicts with the Divine law *is a law*. . . .[1]

Austin's protest against blurring the distinction between what law is and what it ought to be is quite general: it is a mistake, whatever our standard of what ought to be, whatever 'the text by which we regulate our approbation or disapprobation'. . . .

[His] prime reason for this insistence was to enable men to see steadily the precise issues posed by the existence of morally bad laws, and to understand the specific character of the authority of a legal order. . . .

In view of later criticisms it is also important to distinguish several things that the Utilitarians did not mean by insisting on their separation of law and morals. They certainly accepted many of the things that might be called 'the intersection of law and morals'. [He] never denied that, as a matter of historical fact, the development of legal systems had been powerfully influenced by moral opinion, and, conversely, that moral standards had been profoundly influenced by law, so that the content of many legal rules mirrored moral rules or principles. . . .

Secondly, neither Bentham nor his followers denied that by explicit legal provisions moral principles might at different points be brought into a legal system and form part of its rules, or that courts might be legally bound to decide in accordance with what they thought just or best. Bentham indeed recognized, as Austin did not, that even the supreme legislative power might be subjected to legal restraints by a constitution and would not have denied that moral principles, like those of the Fifth Amendment, might form the content of such legal constitutional restraints. Austin differed in thinking that restraints on the supreme legislative power could not have the force of law, but would remain merely political or moral checks; but of course he would have recognized that a statute, for example, might confer a delegated legislative power and restrict the area of its exercise by reference to moral principles.

What both Bentham and Austin were anxious to assert were the following two simple things: first, in the absence of an expressed constitutional or legal provision, it could not follow from the mere fact that a rule violated

---

[1]Austin, *The Province of Jurisprudence Determined* 184–5 (Library of Ideas edn. 1954).

standards of morality that it was not a rule of law; and, conversely, it could not follow from the mere fact that a rule was morally desirable that it was a rule of law. . . .

DISCUSSION ISSUES

1. *Universal Values.* Do the values of one historical period or one culture differ radically from those of another? Do universal, basic value judgments underlie the wide diversity of cultures? John Finnis has written the most influential contemporary version of natural law theory titled *Natural Law and Natural Rights.* He proposed the following "self-evident" universal values: (1) concern for the value of human life, (2) procreation of human life, (3) sexual activity restrictions, (4) concern for truth, (5) values of cooperation, (6) friendship, (7) property rights, (8) value of play, (9) respect for the dead, and (10) concern for superhuman principles or powers (Finnis 1980, pp. 83–84). Do these values qualify as universal? What should Finnis add or subtract from the list? Should universal values be grounded in religion?

2. *Constitutional Natural Law.* Excerpts from the case of *Calder v. Bull* (1798) (actually titled *Calder et Wife v. Bull et Wife,* since wives did not need proper names then) appear in constitutional law textbooks. The case involved the question of whether a legislative demand for a new hearing in a probate case was *ex post facto* ("after the fact"—that is, a law passed after the action that the law regulates). The case became part of constitutional lore, not because of the issue, but because of the stark contrast between the approaches taken by the justices. Justice Chase labeled his "beyond-the-Constitution" position as a natural law perspective. Justice Iredell took a positivist approach, insisting that the court enforce only those limits on the legislature found explicitly in the constitution. Chase's political foes saw his antipositivism and willingness to go beyond the letter of the law as a disguise for inappropriately stating and imposing his political views. The House of Representatives impeached Chase primarily for his improper conduct, including political partisanship, at criminal trials. For example, during a charge to a jury, he had voiced his fear that universal suffrage would lead to mobocracy ("rule by the mob"). Chase proclaimed that improper conduct hardly constituted the "high crimes and misdemeanors" required for impeachment, and the Senate failed to convict him.

   Some commentators see the history of constitutional law as the interplay between the Chase and the Iredell forces. Since few jurists today talk about natural law, it seems that positivist Iredell won the battle against higher law theorist, Chase. Judicial opinions, at least in the United States, seldom contain direct references to natural law, however, some exceptions do appear. For example, the Louisiana Supreme Court invoked natural law when it permitted parents to recover damages for prenatal injury to a fetus born dead because of an injury (*Danos v. St. Pierre* 1981). Today, however, Chase's position has resurfaced under the guise of what has become known as **substantive due process.** This is the judicial protection not only of fair procedures but also of certain values. Since chapter 4 includes a detailed discussion of the development of Supreme Court appeals to "fundamental values" and the like, a few general questions will suffice at this stage. What is the relationship between natural law and constitutional law?

As "the fundamental law of the land," a constitution sets the normative, or value, standards for all other laws. Do basic constitutional principles have a basis in natural law, or should they?

3. *Cultural Relativism.* Universal values may exist across cultures but perhaps only at vague levels of generality. While every culture, even the Ik described in chapter 1 (see Turnbull, Reading 1-3), accepts the command, "Do good; avoid evil," each culture interprets the command differently, as is shown in the following excerpt:

> [I]f we turn to the more general natural moral laws, we find that they are so vague that they hide all sorts of differences that both parties would regard as crucial. As anthropologists . . . have pointed out, all cultures have a concept of murder. But if we try to give the concept of murder some specific content which would cover its uses in all cultures, we run into difficulty. While all cultures agree that murder is wrong, this is completely compatible with the Eskimos' killing members of their family if they do not feel they can make it through the winter; or with infanticide [killing infants] in Polynesia and Greece; or with the old Scandinavian habit of clubbing one's older ancestors to death so that they might go to Valhalla. But for these people this killing is not murder which is by implicit definition wrong. Just what will count as murder in a given culture varies radically. (Nielsen 1959, p. 1).

What justifies one culture's condemning the moral values and practices of another culture? Should only those living within a culture evaluate that culture's morality?

4. *Cultural Defense.* Cultures do not remain isolated from one another. If two or more cultures clash, which one's morality should predominate? Should the dominant culture allow members of nondominant cultures to defend their acts on the basis of their culture? Does it make sense for the law to recognize a cultural defense? Should the law give some force to a nondominant culture's acceptance of, for example, group suicide as described in the following passage?

> On 29 January, 1985, Fumiko Kimura waded into the Pacific Ocean from a Santa Monica beach, with her two children. Hours later, doctors would unsuccessfully try to revive four-year-old Kazutaka and his six-month-old sister, Yuri. Their mother, though close to death, was successfully resuscitated and survived to face two charges of first-degree murder. In disclosing the reasons for her actions, the 32-year-old Kimura mentioned an unfaithful husband, a previously failed marriage, and the perception that she herself had failed as a wife. By Japanese custom, she had tried to commit *oyako-shinju* or "parent-child suicide" an act, while illegal in her native Japan, allegedly follows a Japanese custom as a way of escaping certain intolerable situations." (Woo 1989, pp. 403–404)

Should the courts permit cultural defenses that negate criminal responsibility (see *People v. Sherwood* [1936], chapter 8)? Should the courts accept cultural factors only as mitigating factors during sentencing? Does suicide, as Aquinas thought, violate natural law? Is there a moral difference between individual suicide (for example, the practice of hara-kiri in Japanese traditional culture) and group suicide *(oyako-shinju)*?

5. *Universal Norms and Jurisdiction.* "Isn't it bad to napalm babies, wicked to starve the poor, depraved to buy and sell each other" (Leff 1979, p. 1249)? Are there certain kinds of wrongs so outrageous that every culture or nation should

condemn them? Should civilized nations condemn only heinous crimes that "shock the conscience"? Should they attempt to punish those individuals (and nations) that commit these crimes? If a citizen of one country has committed a grave crime, such as genocide, should other nations bring charges and try that individual in their courts? Should a United States court try an individual charged with genocide in Rwanda if the individual visits, resides, or has any other dealings in the United States (a relatively recent, 1992, ratifier of the 1948 Genocide Convention)?

The Judiciary Act of 1789 states, "The district courts shall have original jurisdiction of any civil action by an alien for a tort only, committed in violation of the law of nations or a treaty of the United States." Dr. Joel Filartiga filed an alien tort action against Americo Norberto Pena-Irala, former Inspector General of Police in Asuncion, Paraguay. He accused Pena-Irala of the severe torture and murder of his son, Joelito, allegedly killed in retaliation for his father's political activities against the government. When Filartiga learned of Pena's visit to the United States, he filed suit asking for compensatory and punitive damages. Finding torture prohibited by all nations, the court granted jurisdiction (*Filartiga v. Pena-Irala* 1980; Claude 1983, pp. 275–295). Should courts in the United States take jurisdiction over Bosnian-Serb leaders for rape committed in the former Yugoslavia? In a U.S. federal court, Bosnian Muslim women sued a former Bosnian Serb leader for rapes committed during the Bosnian War (*Doe v. Karadzic* 1994).

6. *Grudge Informer.*

> In 1944, a woman, wishing to be rid of her husband, denounced him to the authorities for insulting remarks he had made about Hitler while home on leave from the German army. The wife was under no legal duty to report his acts, though what he had said was apparently in violation of [the 1934] statutes making it illegal to make statements detrimental to the government of the Third Reich or to impair by any means the military defense of the German people. The husband was arrested and sentenced to death, apparently pursuant to the statutes, though he was not executed but was sent to the front. In 1949, the wife was prosecuted in a West German court for the offense we would describe as illegally depriving a person of his freedom. This was punishable as a crime under the German Criminal Code of 1871 which had remained in force since its enactment. The wife pleaded that her husband's imprisonment was pursuant to the Nazi statutes and hence that she had committed no crime. The court of appeal to which the case ultimately came held that the wife was guilty of procuring the deprivation of her husband's liberty by denouncing him to the German courts, even though he had been sentenced by the court for having violated a statute, since, to quote the words of the court, the statute "was contrary to the sound conscience and sense of justice of all decent human beings." This reasoning was followed in many cases which have been hailed as a triumph of the doctrines of natural law and as signaling the overthrow of positivism. (Fuller 1969, pp. 245–253)

Should the court have rejected the wife's reliance on Nazi law? The 1934 law she cited was invalid, since it contravened fundamental principles of morality (natural law). Should the court have admitted that the 1934 Nazi statutes did have the force of law and contended that only a retrospective law would punish the wife? How do retrospective laws violate natural law? How would a legal positivist, such as Hart (see Hart [1958] for his discussion of the case) analyze this case?

The twentieth century may have ended with the dubious distinction of having been the most violent century in recorded history. After the Holocaust, which included the extermination of five to six million Jews, world leaders vowed that it would never happen again. However, during the past three decades, the world has witnessed mass killings in Cambodia, Bosnia, and Rwanda—to name only the better known ones. The persistence of these mass killings provides a stark challenge to natural law and positivism. The atrocities that have occurred and that continue to occur on such a great scale call into question the very foundations of law and morality. The increasing frequency of genocide raises doubts about the force of decency and about the strength of civilization's inner fabric. How has law dealt with and how should it confront genocide and war crimes? To have a viable universal judiciary, one must justify international laws and international legal institutions. What justifications, if any, do natural law theory and legal positivism offer?

Natural law theorists must confront positivist challenges to their defense of international law. Debates over the positivists' concepts of sovereignty, command, and rules have their counterparts in disputes over whether international law qualifies as positive law. First, if law involves a higher authority, a sovereign, is the sovereign above the law? Hobbes considered the law of nations to be a state of nature. If nation-states represent today's sovereigns, what laws, if any, rule over the states? Second, does law need commands backed up by sanctions? In short, does law necessitate the use of force? Does international law require an institutionalized force behind it to qualify as law? Third, is the international community like a primitive society—that is, without laws in the fullest sense (see Hart, Reading 2-7)? These questions become more than academic when posed in the context of war crimes.

After World War II, the international community did not have legal structures in place for addressing genocide and war crimes. The legal lexicon did not have a generally accepted word to cover atrocities on the scale of the Holocaust. The victorious Allies established temporary *(ad hoc)* military tribunals to deal with crimes committed by the Nazi and Japanese governments. The London Agreement (1945) established the International Military Tribunals at Nuremberg, and the Allies established a similar tribunal for Tokyo in 1946. The Nuremberg Tribunal convicted nineteen of the twenty-two indicted defendants and sentenced twelve of them to death. The Tokyo Tribunal convicted all twenty-five defendants and sentenced seven, including one civilian, to death. In 1948, the United Nations passed the Convention on the Prevention and Punishment of the Crime of Genocide. In 1992, the Security Council established war crimes' tribunals for the former Yugoslavia and for Rwanda, however these *ad hoc* tribunals cannot invoke the death penalty. The current, primary international judicial institution, the International Court of Justice (ICJ), does not have jurisdiction over international crimes committed by individuals on behalf of states (see page 34). On July 17, 1998, the world community moved a step closer to creating a global justice structure. More than one-hundred nations signed the Rome Statute of the International Criminal Court (ICC). Once it is established, the ICC, unlike the ICJ, will have jurisdiction over individuals for genocide, crimes against humanity, and war crimes. The United States, fearing that its personnel would be too vulnerable to ICC jurisdiction, refused to sign the Rome Treaty, along with only a handful of other nations.

Again, natural law theorists face positivist challenges regarding these newly created international legal structures. Within legal positivism, important questions arise concerning international criminal tribunals. First, consider the international character of these courts. How do these tribunals enforce or expect to enforce their rulings? Austin would point to the lack of an international sovereign with the power to issue commands backed by sanctions. Second, consider the fragile positive law base of these tribunals. Legitimate courts operating within a state apply and interpret laws passed by legislatures, but international tribunals do not have analogous legislative bodies. The military character and Allied composition of the Nuremberg and Tokyo tribunals gave some support to the charge of "victor's justice." Third, consider the authority by which these tribunals make judgments. In Hart's terms, what secondary rules operate on an international tribunal? Interestingly, Stanley Paulsen, in Reading 2-8, tries to turn the tables on the Austinian version, at least, of legal positivism, making it the culprit and not the critical voice.

International criminal courts do not appear to fare well within a proceduralist version of natural law. Consider the tribunals from the standpoint of due process or procedural fairness. Fuller charged the Nazi system with departing from the ideal of rule of law. How do the Nuremberg trials fare concerning Fuller's inner morality of law? Does Nuremberg stand justly accused of failing to use basic principles of fairness that demand public notice of understandable laws? Does Nuremberg stand guilty of making something unlawful after the fact? Exactly what positive laws did the Nazi defendants violate? The charter that created the tribunal included the following crimes:

Crimes Against Peace: namely, planning, preparation, initiation or waging of a war of aggression, or a war in violation of international treaties, agreements or assurances, or participation in a Common Plan or Conspiracy for the accomplishment of any of the foregoing.

War Crimes: namely, violations of the laws or customs of war. Such violations shall include, but not be limited to, murder, ill-treatment or deportation to slave labor or for any other purpose of civilian population of or in occupied territory, murder or ill-treatment of prisoners of war or persons on the seas, killing of hostages, plunder of public or private property, wanton destruction of cities, towns, or villages, or devastation not justified by military necessity.

Crimes Against Humanity: namely, murder, extermination, enslavement, deportation, and other inhumane acts committed against any civilian population, before or during the war, or persecutions on political, racial, or religious grounds in the execution of or in the connection with any crimes within the jurisdiction of the Tribunal, whether or not in violation of domestic law of the country where perpetrated.

The tribunal, then, applied these to past acts, perhaps thereby making illegal something that was not illegal when it was done *(ex post facto)*. Were the Nuremberg trials a victory for the rule of law or a political show? The Nuremberg trials dramatically illustrate the clash between positivism and substantive natural law theory. Robert Jackson's plea for the prosecution of Nazi war criminals rests, ultimately, on moral grounds (see Reading 2-9). Did morality, and not necessarily law, demand punishment of those responsible for the atrocities that included the slaughter of Jews as well as many Roma (Gypsies), homosexuals, and disabled people? If so, what morality? And whose morality? Does H. L. A. Hart successfully justify his rejection of natural law and defend the positivist's separation of law and morality charge in Reading 2-10?

The Holocaust raises questions not only of individual legal guilt but also of collective guilt. Karl Jaspers resigned from his post at Heidelberg University in 1937 but continued to live, with his Jewish wife, under the Third Reich. In 1948, Jaspers (Kritz 1995) addressed the issue of German responsibility and guilt after the war. He distinguished four kinds of guilt: criminal, political, moral, and metaphysical. A. Zvie Bar-on, a professor of philosophy at Hebrew University in Israel, explores Jaspers' position and discusses Adolf Eichmann in Reading 2-11. The Israelis abducted Eichmann in Argentina and took him to Israel, where the Israeli government tried, convicted, and executed Eichmann for active and significant participation in the Final Solution, that is, the Nazi policy that led to the extermination of more than six million European Jews. As his defense, Eichmann claimed to have followed Kant. He said he formulated his Categorical Imperative as "Be loyal to the laws, be a disciplined person, live an orderly life, do not come in conflict with laws." Does Eichmann correctly interpret Kant as charging individuals to obey orders? Zvie Bar-on asks whether Kant could save Eichmann. Does Kantian ethics provide an ethical excuse not for Eichmann's actions but for Jaspers' indifference?

READING 2-8

Classical Positivism and the Nazi State
"Classical Legal Positivism at Nuremberg"
(1975)

Stanley Paulsen

I

Of the three principal criminal defenses raised at the Nuremberg Trials—the defenses of act of state, superior orders, and ex post facto law—two were expressly rejected in the Nuremberg Charter, and all three were rejected in the prosecution's arguments and later in the Tribunal's Judgment. To those skeptical of the legitimacy of the trials, the rejection of the defenses can be explained in terms of parochial political considerations ("Allied policy") but cannot be justified on either legal or philosophical grounds.

Is the skeptic's position on the rejection of the defenses warranted? I argue that it is not. The skeptic fails to take account of an underlying dispute between defense counsel on the one hand and the prosecution and Tribunal on the other—a dispute over the applicability of doctrines of classical legal positivism to the Nuremberg Trials that reflects radically different philosophical persuasions about the nature of law. Specifically, drawing on material from the proceedings of the International Military Tribunal at Nuremberg, I show that, as understood and presented by defense counsel, the defenses of act of state and superior orders presuppose the doctrine of absolute sovereignty, one of two fundamental doctrines of classical legal positivism. And I offer an interpretation of the defense of ex post facto law in terms of the other fundamental doctrine of classical legal positivism, the doctrine that laws are commands. Given my contention that there are noncontingent links between the doctrines of classical legal positivism and the Nuremberg criminal defenses, the Tribunal's grounds for rejecting the doctrines apply as well to its rejection of the defenses. Although my concern here is to show that the noncontingent links exist, I believe it could also be shown that the Tribunal was justified in rejecting classical legal positivism, a theory of law that precludes the very possibility of international law. To demonstrate the latter, however, would require a developed philosophy of international law, something well beyond the scope of this paper.

I begin by sketching the two fundamental doctrines of classical legal positivism as they are set out by the most historically influential proponent of that theory, John Austin. Then, after introducing the law of the Nuremberg Charter, I examine the defenses of act of state, [and] superior orders. . . .

II

Jean Bodin's *Six Books of the Commonwealth* (1576) is a convenient mark of the transition from a medieval world, which regarded law as prior to and more fundamental than the institutions of politics, to a modern world, which regards law as an instrument of the state. . . .

John Austin's sovereign, on the other hand, is a thoroughly modern figure. In *The Province of Jurisprudence Determined* (1832), Austin distinguishes between "*natural* law" and "the aggregate of the rules, established by political superiors, [that] is frequently styled *positive* law, or law existing *by position*," and he confines "the term *law,* as used simply and strictly," to positive law. The ensuing theory, classical legal positivism, rests on two fundamental doctrines, the command doctrine and the doctrine of absolute sovereignty. The command doctrine is itself to be understood in terms of the components of the legal norm.

Austin speaks of three such components: the commander's intention that a party act (or forbear from acting) in a particular way, the commander's expression of his intention to the party, and—central to the command doctrine—

the commander's power to impose a sanction if the commanded party fails to comply with the directive. . . .

The other fundamental doctrine of classical legal positivism is that of absolute sovereignty. Austin understands sovereignty, in the language of the command doctrine, as an instance of the power relation of superior to inferior, with the critical qualification that the superior member of the power relation in this instance is not the inferior member in some other instance. What is perhaps the most distinctive feature of sovereignty in Austin is that it issues from a factual state of affairs. To underline this feature we may ask: Who has the right in a society to issue directives, to delegate authority, to be in a word the sovereign power? The answer of James Bryce is representative: "The person or body to whom in the last resort the law attributes this right is the logically supreme power, or Sovereign, in the State." For Austin, however, the identity of the sovereign is not a question of legal right, but a question of who satisfies certain factual conditions. As he puts it in a well-known passage:

> The superiority which is styled sovereignty . . . is distinguished from other superiority . . . by the following marks or characters:—1. The *bulk* of the given society are in a *habit* of obedience or submission to a *determinate* and *common* superior. . . . 2. That certain individual, or that certain body of individuals, is *not* in a habit of obedience to a determinate human superior.

The sharp contrast between Austin's view and that represented here by Bryce is in the end a difference between a sovereign power above the law and one subject to the law. Austin's sovereign, having unlimited legal power to enforce his commands, is himself "incapable of *legal* limitation."

Several corollaries of the doctrine of absolute sovereignty are of special interest in connection with the defenses at Nuremberg. One corollary, pertaining to the act of state defense, is the notion of a positive legal right as a triadic relation, or a relation among duty-bearer, right-holder, and sovereign. . . . Austin uses this notion to demonstrate, by way of reductio ad absurdum arguments [showing the absurd conclusions these arguments lead to], that the sovereign cannot be either a duty-bearer or a right-holder. Another corollary, this one with an impact on the defense of superior orders, is the requirement of unconditional obedience. Given the sovereign's legally unlimited power, subjects cannot legally condition their obedience to the sovereign on, for example, moral grounds. As the legal positivist cliché has it, there is no necessary connection between positive law and morality.

Given the doctrines of command and absolute sovereignty, it is not surprising that classical legal positivism has no place for international law. . . .

IV

The defense of act of state, providing for imputation to the state of an individual's act as an "act of state" and thereby precluding adjudication before a foreign or international forum, was expressly rejected in article 7 of the Nuremberg Charter:

The official position of defendants, whether as Heads of State or responsible officials in Government departments, shall not be considered as freeing them from responsibility or mitigating punishment.

Notwithstanding the Charter provision, counsel for the defense at a number of points raised the act of state defense and, with it, the doctrine of absolute sovereignty. How, exactly, is the defense related to absolute sovereignty?

Acts of state are "acts performed by individuals in their capacity as organs of the State and therefore acts imputed to the State." Imputation of an individual's act to the state might be thought not only to shield the actor from a claim by an injured party but also to deprive the injured party of his claim altogether, for he cannot have, as a matter of positive law, any claim against a sovereign state. Or so it could be argued, as Austin's concept of a positive legal right as a triadic relation illustrates. Assume, as members of Austin's triadic relation, a sovereign *(A)* who sets the positive law, an individual *(B)* on whom a right is conferred, and another *(C)* on whom a duty is imposed. By the method of reductio ad absurdum it can be demonstrated that *A,* the sovereign, cannot stand in either of the positions occupied by *B* and *C.* If, for example, *A* rather than *C* owed a duty to *B,* what would the result be? The supposition that *A* is a duty-bearer implies in Austin's scheme a "superior sovereign" setting the positive law from which *A*'s duty and *B*'s right emanate, contrary to the hypothesis that *A* is sovereign. Similarly for the supposition that *A* is a right-holder.

One qualification to the act of state defense, as stated above, is essential. An individual performs "acts of state" in his capacity as an "organ of the state," but it is not enough that *he,* an official rather than a private individual, acts. The individual acts in an official capacity only if his acts are "performed at the government's command or with its authorization." The requirement that the individual's acts be authorized by his government establishes a distinction, in the conduct of officials, between lawful (authorized) and unlawful (unauthorized) acts. Whether an official's act is lawful may be determined through citizens' claims against the official. And such claims are allowed by Austin's analysis of a legal right as a triadic relation. If an official acts in excess of the powers of his office, he is personally liable; and the relation here between duty-bearer (the official) and right-holder (the citizen) emanates from, and is enforced by, the third party to the relation, the sovereign. This way around the act of state defense, preserving the dogma of absolute sovereignty while at the same time avoiding a grant of license to officials, is well established in English domestic law.

The situation is different in the international context, where to invoke the Austinian doctrine of absolute sovereignty and its corollary regarding positive legal rights is tantamount to raising the act of state defense. Suppose that sovereign state *A* brings a claim, either in its courts or before an international forum, against sovereign state *B* or against an individual for an act imputed to state *B* as an act of state. The claim implies a "superior sovereign," the third member of the legal relation, who sets the positive law from which *A*'s right and *B*'s duty emanate. But this is contrary to the hypothesis that *A* and *B* are themselves sovereign powers. The doctrine of sovereignty means inter alia that positive law always emanates from a superior power. Between *A* and *B,* which are equal powers, there can be no positive law. It was this doctrine that counsel for the defense at Nuremberg invoked in the course of raising the act of state defense, and this doctrine that the prosecution and Tribunal rejected in denying that defense.

The arguments of Professor Hermann Jahrreiss, associate defense counsel, are prominent here. In his statement concerning juridical aspects of the trial, Jahrreiss raised the act of state defense and, with it, the doctrine of absolute sovereignty. He began by asking the Tribunal to suppose, contrary to fact, that there had existed in the 1930s not the ineffectual Kellogg-Briand Pact of 1928 but "a general and unambiguous [peace] pact . . . accepted and applied by the contracting parties in fundamental and factual agreement." Given this supposition, "Would the liability of individuals to punishment for the breach of such a treaty be founded in international law?" Jahrreiss answered that "not even the liability of the state to punishment, let alone that of individuals," would be so founded. For although a state could be said to have committed an offense against "international law," a violation, that is, of an obligation incurred by consent, the offending state would not be subject to punishment under international criminal law. And what is more, individuals could not be said to have committed any offense whatever under international law. Jahrreiss appealed directly to the doctrine of absolute sovereignty to support the immunity of individuals from prosecution by an international forum. The prosecution of individuals, he asserted, "cannot take place as long as the sovereignty of states is the organizational basic principle of interstate order."

What does Jahrreiss' appeal to the doctrine of absolute sovereignty amount to? He assumed that the acts of the defendants were within the scope of the powers delegated to them and could be imputed to the state as acts of state, thereby granting the individual defendants legal immunity. He then used this assumption in the international context, arguing that it would be contrary to the doctrine of absolute sovereignty to grant a foreign or international forum the power to hold an individual legally liable for acts imputed to the individual's state as acts of state. If liability under positive law could be imposed by a foreign or international forum, that would set limits on what is by definition unlimited, the legal power of the sovereign state. The upshot of the argument is clear. If an individual has no legal liability for a breach of the ideal peace pact of Jahrreiss' supposition, the same conclusion holds a fortiori [with even greater force] for a breach of the existing Kellogg-Briand Pact.

Moreover, the doctrine of absolute sovereignty gave Jahrreiss a means of denying the applicability of nonpositivist criteria for the identification of law—consent, perhaps, or consonance with morality. For Jahrreiss to have allowed such criteria would have left open the possibility that a legal order other than the positive legal order, for example, international law, had the better claim to legitimacy and might therefore prevail over positive law in cases where norms from each order conflicted. The prosecution and Tribunal clearly rejected Jahrreiss' presupposition of absolute sovereignty but were less clear on the matter of the applicability of nonpositivist criteria for the identification of law.

Sir Hartley Shawcross, chief prosecutor for the United Kingdom, directly attacked the classical legal positivist doctrine of absolute sovereignty in his reply to Jahrreiss, arguing that the doctrine is incompatible with commonplace obligations of governments. According to the classical legal positivist, only individuals have legal obligations, and only because the state has power to secure compliance by imposing sanctions. Shawcross argued that states also have legal obligations, but a state's obligations cannot be said to be conditioned on the state's power. Classical legal positivism, restricting as it does the scope of legal obligation to the extent of state power, must be rejected in any system of law that recognizes the legal validity of a state's obligations. As Shawcross put it, referring expressly to the classical legal positivists, "Legal purists may contend that nothing is law which is not imposed from above by a sovereign body having the power to compel obedience. That idea of the analytical jurists has never been applicable to International Law. If it had, the undoubted obligation of States in matters of contract and tort could not exist."

In its Judgment, the Tribunal reaffirmed article 7 of the Charter and rejected the classical legal positivist doctrine of absolute sovereignty. Speaking directly to article 7, the Tribunal contended that "the very essence of the Charter is that individuals have international duties which transcend the national obligations of obedience imposed by the individual state." Having rejected the doctrine of absolute sovereignty as it applied to acts of the defendants, the Tribunal likewise rejected the act of state defense as it applied to these same acts. As the Tribunal put it, "He who violates the laws of war cannot obtain immunity while acting in pursuance of the authority of the state if the state in authorizing action moves outside its competence under international law."

The viability of the defense of act of state as understood and presented by defense counsel at Nuremberg presupposes the applicability of the doctrine of absolute sovereignty. A parallel presupposition is at work in connection with the defense of superior orders.

V

The defense of superior orders, according to which the accused is not criminally liable for committing an act ordered by his superior, was rejected in article 8 of the Nuremberg Charter although allowed as a factor in mitigation of punishment. In the words of the Charter:

> The fact that the defendant acted pursuant to order of his Government or of a superior shall not free him from responsibility, but may be considered in mitigation of punishment if the Tribunal determines that justice so requires.

The Charter's rejection of an unqualified defense of superior orders reflected the German Military Code and also the newly revised law of war manuals of Great Britain and the United States. Nevertheless, counsel for the defense at a number of points raised the defense of superior orders and, with it, the classical legal positivist doctrine of absolute sovereignty and its corollary, the requirement of unconditional obedience. In considering the relation of the defense to the doctrine of absolute sovereignty, it will be useful to begin with a fairly typical case, that of a foot soldier who is issued iniquitous orders.

Imagine that a soldier in the field has just been ordered by his commanding officer to kill prisoners of war and that the order reflects the will of the military command structure and the policies of the state. The soldier sees himself faced with a genuine moral dilemma posed by the consequences of obedience to the order on the one hand and disobedience on the other. If he obeys, the consequences for the prisoners are clear; and if he disobeys, he is virtually assured of prosecution before a court-martial for a serious violation of military law. The soldier, desiring both to preserve the prisoners' lives and to avoid prosecution, hopes to challenge successfully his commanding officer's order.

One challenge available to him speaks to the morality of the order. Can the soldier legally justify disobedience on grounds that the act in question is immoral? According to the doctrine of absolute sovereignty, he cannot; to contend otherwise is to allow a legal obligation to be overturned on extra-legal grounds—here, on moral grounds. As an expression of the sovereign, the commanding officer's order, coupled with legally unlimited power to enforce obedience, is sufficient to establish a legal obligation, and the obligation is unconditional. If the obligation can be overturned at all, it can be done only by successfully challenging it *qua* legal obligation. One challenge directed to the legal validity of the order is based on the incompatibility of the order with international law, specifically, with the law of war. Can the soldier legally justify disobedience on grounds that the order is contrary to the law of war? Again, according to the doctrine of absolute sovereignty, he cannot; to hold otherwise is to introduce just another "extra-legal" ground. Since the sovereign is incapable of legal limitation, there cannot be, as defense counsel Hans Laternser put it, "any question of a crime if the order requires action which is not directed against the authority of the State, but on the contrary is demanded by that authority."

When associate defense counsel Jahrreiss raised the defense of superior orders, it was not, however, in the familiar context of a foot soldier's orders from his superior, but in the extraordinary context of the Nazi defendants, policy-makers in Hitler's Germany. That Jahrreiss presupposed the doctrine of absolute sovereignty is evident throughout his argument, and nowhere more so than in his reification of the absolute sovereign in the person of Hitler. Jahrreiss first addressed the moral and international legal challenges to orders given by a superior, challenges we have looked at in connection with the foot soldier. Observing that orders "can always be measured . . . against the rules of international law, morality, and religion," Jahrreiss argued that to allow officials to use such rules to determine for themselves whether orders are lawful and to "decide accordingly whether to obey or refuse" would be to undermine the sovereignty of the state. Unilateral decisions made by officials on the legal validity of orders would in the end imperil the state's "supreme orders, which must be binding on the hierarchy if the authority of the state is to subsist at all." Having dismissed the moral and international legal standards, Jahrreiss asked whether an order could be measured "against the existing written and unwritten law of the state concerned." He addressed himself here specifically to challenges to orders defective in legal form. For example, could an official challenge the legal validity of an order if "the person giving the order has exceeded his competency or made a mistake in form"? Again resting his case on the doctrine of absolute sovereignty, Jahrreiss denied officials this right of challenge, maintaining that "there must under every government exist orders that are binding on the members of the hierarchy under all circumstances, and therefore represent law to the officials concerned, even though outsiders may find that they are defective as regards content or form. . . ."

Jahrreiss' primary interest, however, was in the legal status of the orders of Hitler himself. These directives, decisions, instructions, and the like were defective if judged by traditional standards, the standards, for example, of the Weimar Constitution. But the so-called Enabling Act of 24 March 1933 swept away the old standards. The Act in effect authorized Hitler to change statutory and even constitutional law by decree, thereby giving legal credence to the abolition of the separation of powers in Germany. The result, Jahrreiss argued, was a doctrine of absolute sovereignty personified in Hitler. "Now in a state in which the entire power to make final decisions is concentrated in the hands of a single individual, the orders of this one man are absolutely binding on the members of the hierarchy. This individual is their sovereign, their *legibus solutus.*" In offering this characterization of Hitler, Jahrreiss suggests that the Nazi defendants' duty of unconditional obedience to Hitler was not unlike that of the foot soldier's to his commanding officer.

Sir Hartley Shawcross, replying to Jahrreiss' effort to raise the defense of superior orders, expressly rejected the classical legal positivist requirement of unconditional obedience, arguing that "no rule of international law . . . provides immunity for those who obey orders which—whether legal or not in the country where they are issued—are manifestly contrary to the very law of nature from which international law has grown" and are illegal by "every test of international law, of common conscience, [and] of elementary humanity." International law "must consider the legality of what is done by international and not by municipal tests."

Robert H. Jackson, chief of counsel for the United States, argued that the joint use of the defense of superior orders and the defense of act of state generates an absurdity. If individual *A* is not legally responsible for an act because his superior, *B,* ordered him to perform that act, then according to the converse of the defense of superior orders, the doctrine of respondeat superior, *B* is responsible. Now suppose that *B* is head of state. He cannot invoke the defense of superior orders to free himself of responsibility, but he can impute his act to the state as an "act of state." "Those in lower ranks were protected against liability by the orders of their superiors. The superiors were protected because their orders were called acts of state." As Jackson observed, "the combination of these two doctrines means that nobody is responsible."

In its Judgment, the Tribunal reaffirmed article 8 of the Charter, holding its provisions to be "in conformity with the law of all nations." And the Tribunal dismissed the arguments of defense counsel.

That a soldier was ordered to kill or torture in violation of the international law of war has never been recognized as a defense to such acts of brutality . . . The true test, which is found in varying degrees in the criminal law of most nations, is not the existence of the order, but whether moral choice was in fact possible.

The Tribunal's "test" conditions the availability of a defense on the possibility of a moral choice, but what was meant by "moral choice" is not obvious. The "choice" may be understood in genuinely moral terms, inviting serious reflection on the propriety of harming or killing innocent persons to avoid one's own punishment or death. On this interpretation, the soldier has a "moral choice" even when faced with death. But "choice" may also be understood simply as ruling out a situation in which, as Brigadier General Telford Taylor expressed it, "opportunity for reflection, choice, and the exercise of responsibility is non-existent or limited." Given either interpretation, what is significant is that the Tribunal based its test on this "choice." For the possibility of a choice to obey runs directly counter to the classical legal positivist requirement of unconditional obedience to state law and involves a rejection of the doctrine underlying that requirement, namely the doctrine of absolute sovereignty.

That the defense of superior orders presupposes sovereignty is not surprising, for the defense plays its primary role in military law, a body of law in which such concepts as authority and orders predominate. As one theorist puts it, a paradigm of "unconditional obedience to an external, norm-establishing authority" is "a military formation, where a host of people are subjected in their movements to a military order to which they all conform." Unlike the superior orders defense, however, the defense of ex post facto law has no obvious connection to the doctrines of classical legal positivism.

READING 2-9
Higher Justice and Nazi Crimes
The Case Against the Nazi War Criminals, (1946)

Robert H. Jackson

The privilege of opening the first trial in history for crimes against the peace of the world imposes a grave responsibility. The wrongs which we seek to condemn and punish have been so calculated, so malignant and so devastating, that civilization cannot tolerate their being ignored because it cannot survive their being repeated. That four great nations, flushed with victory and stung with injury stay the hand of vengeance and voluntarily submit their captive enemies to the judgment of the law is one of the most significant tributes that Power ever has paid to Reason.

This Tribunal, while it is novel and experimental, is not the product of abstract speculations nor is it created to vindicate legalistic theories. This inquest represents the practical effort of four of the most mighty of nations, with the support of fifteen more, to utilize International Law to meet the greatest menace of our times—aggressive war. The common sense of mankind demands that law shall not stop with the punishment of petty crimes by little people. It must also reach men who possess themselves of great power and make deliberate and concerted use of it to set in motion evils which leave no home in the world untouched. It is a cause of this magnitude that the United Nations will lay before Your Honors. . . .

When I say that we do not ask for convictions unless we prove crime, I do not mean mere technical or incidental transgression of international conventions. We charge guilt on planned and intended conduct that involves moral as well as legal wrong. And we do not mean conduct that is a natural and human, even if illegal, cutting of corners, such as many of us might well have committed had we been in the defendants' positions. It is not because they yielded to the normal frailties of human beings that we accuse them. It is their abnormal and inhuman conduct which brings them to this bar.

We will not ask you to convict these men on the testimony of their foes. There is no count of the Indictment that cannot be proved by books and records. The Germans were always meticulous record keepers, and these defendants had their share of the Teutonic passion for thoroughness in putting things on paper. Nor were they without vanity. They arranged frequently to be photographed in action. We will show you their own films. You will see their own conduct and hear their own voices as these defendants re-enact for you, from the screen, some of the events in the course of the conspiracy.

We would also make clear that we have no purpose to incriminate the whole German people. We know that the Nazi Party was not put in power by a majority of the German vote. We know it came to power by an evil alliance between the most extreme of the Nazi revolutionists, the most unrestrained of the German reactionaries, and the most aggressive of the German militarists. If the German populace had willingly accepted the Nazi program, no Stormtroopers would have been needed in the early days of the Party and there would have been no need for concentration camps or the Gestapo, both of which institutions were inaugurated as soon as the Nazis gained control of the German state. Only after these lawless innovations proved successful at home were they taken abroad. . . .

While the defendants and the prosecutors stand before you as individuals, it is not the triumph of either group alone that is committed to your judgment. Above all personalities there are anonymous and impersonal forces whose conflict makes up much of human history. It is yours to throw the strength of the law back of either the one or the other of these forces for at least another generation. What are the real forces that are contending before you?

No charity can disguise the fact that the forces which these defendants represent, the forces that would advantage and delight in their acquittal, are the darkest and most sinister forces in society—dictatorship and oppression, malevolence and passion, militarism and lawlessness. By their fruits we best know them. Their acts have bathed the world in blood and set civilization back a century. They have subjected their European neighbors to every outrage and torture, every spoliation and deprivation that insolence, cruelty, and greed could inflict. They have brought the German people to the lowest pitch of wretchedness, from which they can entertain no hope of early deliverance. They have stirred hatreds and incited domestic violence on every continent. These are the things that stand in the dock shoulder to shoulder with these prisoners.

The real complaining party at your bar is Civilization. In all our countries it is still a struggling and imperfect thing. It does not plead that the United States, or any other country, has been blameless of the conditions which made the German people easy victims to the blandishments and intimidations of the Nazi conspirators.

But it points to the dreadful sequence of aggressions and crimes I have recited, it points to the weariness of flesh, the exhaustion of resources, and the destruction of all that was beautiful or useful in so much of the world, and to greater potentialities for destruction in the days to come. It is not necessary among the ruins of this ancient and beautiful city, with untold members of its civilian inhabitants still buried in its rubble, to argue the proposition that to start or wage an aggressive war has the moral qualities of the worst of crimes. The refuge of the defendants can be only then hope that International Law will lag so far behind the moral sense of mankind that conduct which is crime in the moral sense must be regarded as innocent in law.

Civilization asks whether law is so laggard as to be utterly helpless to deal with crimes of this magnitude by criminals of this order of importance. It does not expect that you can make war impossible. It does expect that your juridical action will put the forces of International Law, its precepts, its prohibitions and, most of all, its sanctions, on the side of peace, so that men and women of good will in all countries may have "leave to live by no man's leave, underneath the law."

From Jackson (1946) "Opening Address for the United States, Nuremberg Trials," *The Case Against the Nazi War Criminals.* New York: Knopf, pp. 3–10, 88–91.

READING 2-10

Nazi Law Supplanting Morality
"Positivism and the Separation of Laws and Morals" Part II (1983)

H. L. A. Hart

IV

[Another] criticism of the separation of law and morals is of a very different character; it certainly is less an intellectual argument against the utilitarian distinction than a passionate appeal supported not by detailed reasoning but by reminders of a terrible experience. For it consists of the testimony of those who have descended into Hell, and, like Ulysses or Dante, brought back a message for human beings. Only in this case the Hell was not beneath or beyond earth, but on it; it was a Hell created on earth by men for other men.

This appeal comes from those German thinkers who lived through the Nazi regime and reflected upon its evil manifestations in the legal system. One of these thinkers, Gustav Radbruch, had himself shared the 'positivist' doctrine until the Nazi tyranny, but he was converted by this experience and so his appeal to other men to discard the doctrine of the separation of law and morals has the special poignancy of a recantation. What is important about this criticism is that it really does confront the particular point which Bentham and Austin had in mind in urging the separation of law as it is and as it ought to be. These German thinkers put their insistence on the need to join together what the Utilitarians separated just where this separation was of most importance in the eyes of the Utilitarians; for they were concerned with the problem posed by the existence of morally evil laws.

Before his conversion Radbruch held that resistance to law was a matter for the personal conscience, to be thought out by the individual as a moral problem, and the validity of a law could not be disproved by showing that its requirements were morally evil or even by showing that the effect of compliance with the law would be more evil than the effect of disobedience. Austin, it may be recalled, was emphatic in condemning those who said that if human laws conflicted with the fundamental principles of morality then they cease to be laws, as talking 'stark nonsense'.

> The most pernicious laws, and therefore those which are most opposed to the will of God, have been and are continually enforced as laws by judicial tribunals. Suppose an act innocuous, or positively beneficial, be prohibited by the sovereign under the penalty of death; if I commit this act, I shall be tried and condemned, and if I object to the sentence, that it is contrary to the law of God . . . the court of justice will demonstrate the inconclusiveness of my reasoning by hanging me up, in pursuance of the law of which I have impugned the validity. An exception, demurrer, or plea, founded on the law of God was never heard in a Court of Justice, from the creation of the world down to the present moment. (Austin 1832 in (1954), p. 185)

These are strong, indeed brutal words, but we must remember that they went along—in the case of Austin and, of course, Bentham—with the conviction that if laws reached a certain degree of iniquity then there would be a plain moral obligation to resist them and to withhold obedience. We shall see, when we consider the alternatives, that this simple presentation of the human dilemma which may arise has much to be said for it.

Radbruch, however, had concluded from the ease with which the Nazi regime had exploited subservience to mere law—expressed, as he thought, in the 'positivist' slogan 'law as law' . . .—and from the failure of the German legal profession to protest against the enormities which they were required to perpetrate in the name of law, that 'positivism' (meaning here the insistence on the separation of law as it is from law as it ought to be) had powerfully contributed to the horrors. His considered reflections led him to the doctrine that the fundamental principles of humanitarian morality were part of the very concept of *Recht* or Legality and that no positive enactment or statute, however clearly it was expressed and however clearly it conformed with the formal criteria of validity of a given legal system, could be valid if it contravened basic principles of morality. This doctrine can be appreciated fully only if the nuances imported by the German word *Recht* are grasped. But it is clear that the doctrine meant that every lawyer and judge should denounce statutes that transgressed the fundamental principles not as merely immoral or wrong but as having no legal character, and enactments which on this ground lack the quality of law should not be taken into account in working out the legal position of any given individual in particular circumstances. The striking recantation of his previous doctrine is unfortunately omitted from the translation of his works, but it should be read by all who wish to think afresh on the question of the interconnection of law and morals.

It is impossible to read without sympathy Radbruch's passionate demand that the German legal conscience should be open to the demands of morality and his complaint that this has been too little the case in the German tradition. On the other hand there is an extraordinary naïvety in the view that insensitiveness to the demands of morality and subservience to state power in a people like the Germans should have arisen from the belief that law might be law though it failed to conform with the minimum requirements of morality. Rather this terrible history prompts inquiry into why emphasis on the slogan 'law is law', and the distinction between law and morals, acquired a sinister character in Germany, but elsewhere, as with the Utilitarians themselves, went along with the most enlightened liberal attitudes. But something more disturbing than naïvety is latent in Radbruch's whole presentation of the issues to which the existence of morally iniquitous laws give rise. It is not, I think, uncharitable to say that we can see in his argument that he has only half digested the spiritual message of liberalism which he is seeking to convey to the legal profession. For everything that he says is really dependent upon an enormous overvaluation of the importance of the bare fact that a rule may be said to be a valid rule of law, as if this, once declared, was conclusive of the final moral question: 'Ought this rule of law to be obeyed?' Surely the truly liberal answer to any sinister use of the slogan 'law is law' or of the distinction between law and morals is, 'Very well, but that does not conclude the question. Law is not morality; do not let it supplant morality.'. . .

"Positivism and the Separation of Laws and Morals," *Essays in Jurisprudence and Philosophy.*
© (1983) by the Harvard Law Review Association for Harvard Law Review.

Could Kant Save Eichmann?
Measuring Responsibility (1985)

A. Zvie Bar-on

"Collective guilt" is a nasty phrase. We recoil instinctively from the concept expressed by it. Collective indictment appears, at least *prima facie,* synonymous with injustice, vindictiveness, blurring of distinctions.

For all that, history has recorded quite a few cases of communities and even whole nations being condemned collectively. In recent years, moreover, we witnessed (in Vatican pronouncements) a significant act in the opposite direction: a people was acquitted of the collective guilt of deicide, of which it was accused nearly 2,000 years ago, this accusation having brought in its wake senseless hatred between nations and innumerable crimes against the people on whose forehead the mark of Cain had been set for no good reason. Were this the only case throughout history in which collective guilt had been imposed on innocent people, it would be sufficient to make its concept repugnant to us. All the more so, as it is one case among many. Did the Nazis not make collective indictment into a method, a constant component in their refined technique of oppression and destruction?

It is thus obvious that when dealing with the problem of guilt for the enormous crime of the Final Solution, we must be extremely cautious. And yet, the question has to be formulated in terms of collective guilt: is the whole German people guilty, and if so, what is the nature of that guilt? If not, who is to blame for the murder of six million European Jews during the period between 1939 (or perhaps 1933) and 1945? Who is to blame for converting an entire state into a well-oiled machine for executing this murder? A machine which was supposed to go on with the job until the last Jew in the world had been killed. Who then is guilty and what is the nature of the guilt? Trying to answer this question, I have no illusions; it is very complex and I may hope to contribute only partially to its solution. . . .

COULD KANT SAVE EICHMANN?

[Eichmann's tale in Jerusalem] is open to criticism on several counts. First of all, prior to the Wannsee Conference, did he really act according to his later version of the Categorical Imperative, which we have accepted as its approximately correct interpretation? Of course not. It would be simply ludicrous to describe his Nazi activity up to 1942 as compatible with Categorical Imperative, in particular if we recall one of Kant's alternative formulations of it, according to which a moral person must relate to his fellow-man, be he Christian or Jew, Gypsy or Negro, man or woman, not merely as to a means for his own plans and ambitions, but as to an end in itself. There is hardly any action of Eichmann's party, even before gaining power, there is no law it had initiated, no order its leaders had issued, which does not contradict directly the Kantian conception of ethics in its letter and spirit. It is also beyond doubt that while working out methods and policies for the implementation of the discriminatory laws and orders of the Nazi government, Eichmann showed wholehearted identification with their contents and spirit. He could therefore maintain that he was acting them out as if he were their legislator. But that, on its own, is far from being a sufficient condition for an action to accord with Kant's moral law. Moreover, there is in Kant's philosophy no trace of support for the contention that a man is allowed to forego the Categorical Imperative when pressed to do something against his will and sense of justice. Quite the contrary. Consider, for instance, the parable told in the *Kritik der praktischen Vernunft* (2nd ed., p. 54), where a vassal is ordered by his prince under the threat of death to bear false witness against an honest man whom the prince wishes to destroy. The moral of it is that a man's duty is to refuse to do anything which would harm his fellow man, even if he thereby endangers his future and his life. That, according to Kant, is the measure of a man's true freedom.

Until now we have assumed that Eichmann told the truth in the courtroom. However, the facts established at the trial contradict this assumption. It is clear that Eichmann's activity in the framework of the Final Solution was not against his will, as shown by his enthusiasm, initiative and diligence in carrying out his functions. The strongest evidence is provided by his behavior during the second half of 1944, when it was obvious that the fate of Germany had been sealed, yet Eichmann was feverishly continuing the deportations. Were the whole program contrary to his will, he would certainly have taken advantage of the tendency then prevailing among the leaders of the SS (apparently endorsed by Himmler) to stop the bloodbath, and have thereby returned to a state of "harmony" between himself and the Categorical Imperative. Instead, he continued his Final Solution activities; only that now *he defied the orders of his superiors.*

We are left with the following conclusions. There is no reason to assume that, throughout his Nazi career, Eichmann was at any time acting against his will and convictions. His identification with the Nazi ideology was complete throughout and his actions followed directly from it. There is also no argument to show that these actions were at any time compatible with the principles of Kantian ethics.

There was not and there could not be anything in his "Kantian argumentation" to strengthen his main line of defense, which sought, as we saw, to transmit all the guilt up the ladder of command to its very top, to Hitler alone, or at most to him and the group of his closest associates. This response, which in effect clears the whole German people of guilt, except for one or a few individuals, is not unique to Eichmann. It has been offered by many Germans and non-Germans; but a legion of arguers will not add a whit of validity to the argument. . . .

CONCLUSIONS

. . . To the question: "Is it justified to apply in this case the notion of collective guilt?", we should give a qualified affirmative answer. It must be qualified because we do not wish to have the very notion of collective guilt white-washed from its pejorative meaning, whether in the law, in morality, or in the political realm. We plead for an exceptional application in our case because of the entirely exceptional character of the crime, which can be brought under the two headings:

(a) the initiation, planning, and execution of the genocide of the Jewish people within the context of the Rosenberg style "biological reshuffle" of the population of Europe (and later, presumably, of the whole world);
(b) the transformation, for the sake of (a), of the German state, all its economic, juridical, and technical resources included, into a criminal state.

The crime is exceptional, entirely new, without precedent in the history of mankind, and this fact justifies the use of the concept of collective guilt when trying to measure the responsibility for the crime. The application is however qualified. We use for this purpose two cross-distinctions, one between the direct and the indirect, the other between the personal and impersonal responsibility. The first of Karl Jaspers' *kinds* of guilt—the "criminal guilt"—is both personal and direct; the second, the "political guilt," is indirect and impersonal; while the remaining two—the "moral" and the "metaphysical" (whether they should be separated will be subsequently questioned)—are personal but indirect.

The clearest case is obviously the first one, that of the criminal guilt. It should be imputed—as Jaspers rightly urges—to every German (indeed, to every human being) who had participated in the initiation, planning, and execution of the Final Solution. The determination of the exact dimension of this kind of guilt, and of the punishment for it, is in the hands of the judiciary authority. Jaspers thinks, we remember, that for punishing this kind of crime—and only for it—the death penalty should be reintroduced (if it was revoked previously). I prefer to leave this question open. I consider proper the maximal penalty allowed by the state, but "death penalty or not"—is a very difficult question which deserves a separate analysis. Anyhow, the responsibility here is personal and direct, the heaviest known in the history of the law, I presume.

At the other end of the spectrum I would place the "political guilt" which is, as mentioned above, impersonal and indirect. But it is very real because of the fact that a whole state was transformed into an instrument of crime. Jaspers says: "Every citizen of a modern state is responsible for the actions of its government and administration, unless he speaks and acts openly against them." He says "modern state," not just "state." What he probably has in mind is that unlike previous times, in the modern state the relationship of a citizen with the state is such that he *nolens volens* has his share in keeping this state alive, even if he is not involved in what is commonly called "political life," does not belong to any political party, does not even bother to leave his house on the general elections day. Even such a person is responsible for the body politic. There is however no good reason available for considering this responsibility a personal one. And since the guilt is not personal, neither is the punishment. The state as a whole is punished and its citizens are affected only so far as their well-being depends upon the state.

We may accept Jaspers' view that in accordance with the nature of political reality the factor which was supposed to punish the guilty in this case was the victor, *i.e.,* the Allied Powers. But Jaspers also ruled that the victorious powers were justified in treating occupied Germany as they liked, in accordance with their own political interests; the Germans had no basis for complaints of injustice. If this means that the policy of the Allied Powers could have been completely arbitrary and not subject to any general criteria of evaluation and criticism, then this stand cannot be accepted. Such a conception would offend the sense of justice of us all, and not only of the Germans. I would therefore modify Jaspers' formula to the effect that the Allies should have acted in accordance with the interests of the whole mankind, or of the family of nations.

This implies that the occupation authorities should have done everything possible to eradicate from Germany—from its institutional and cultural structures—all that could reasonably be identified with roots of totalitarianism, and this includes the simplified "earlier" Eichmannian conception of the Categorical Imperative. Was this accomplished in postwar Germany? In West Germany, denazification proceeded to quite a considerable extent, while in East Germany it seems not to have materialized at all. The new regime there remained totalitarian. This totalitarianism may be different from that of the Nazi regime; it seems however, to be in several respects more dangerous than the Soviet variety.

Problems of a different nature are bound to arise in connection with the other two kinds of guilt. As Jaspers presents the moral guilt of the Germans, a certain incompatibility is revealed within the very concept of moral duty. The line of reasoning runs as follows: the source of the moral guilt of the Germans is any action or forbearance of action, that implied support, in any form, of the Nazi regime. Specifically, this guilt meant responsibility for the lot of the victims of that regime, including of course the victims of the Final Solution. But, asks Jaspers, did this responsibility impose on every German the moral duty of endangering his own life in an effort to save those victims? This question is answered with an unqualified "no." Such an answer is, we should say, not self evident. It requires reasons, justification. That is to say, the limit that Jaspers puts to the moral responsibility of the Germans is theory-dependent. And what theory will justify Jaspers' stand?

This question brings us back to the same ethical theory which Eichmann tried to use for his defense: the Kantian doctrine. According to it one has the moral duty to respect his fellow man, to refrain from offending him, never to treat him only as a means to further one's goals or ambitions. Thus, as we have seen, this theory could not possibly help Eichmann in the hour of his predicament. But alas, this same theory does not make everyone duty-bound to endanger one's own life in order to save one's fellow man from destruction.

Kant's ethical theory can be criticized on this account. It could even be argued that in the conditions of the Nazi terror such an ethical thesis must have played into the hands of the Nazis, providing an ethical excuse for the indifference to the fate of the victims. However, a person who had adopted the Kantian ethics before the Nazis seized power, could have felt it difficult to depart from it when with the change of regime it became inadequate. Should this person have proposed *ad hoc* an altogether new ethics?

This might have been Jaspers' dilemma which he attempted to solve by means of the distinction between the "moral" and the "metaphysical" guilt. If the guilt imputed to every German who did not do his utmost to save his fellow man from destruction did not follow from his moral duty, there is an alternative way of proving it real—by making it follow from the metaphysical fact of human solidarity. Nevertheless, the overall result of Jaspers' argument is unequivocal: every German who lived in Germany during the Nazi rule and did not actively oppose the regime, bears responsibility for the lot of the victims of that regime.

I think that Jaspers' dilemma would be avoided if we did not interpret the moral duty of man in terms of Kantian ethics which leaves outside of morality the (metaphysical) fact of basic human solidarity and co-responsibility. It seems to me more reasonable to combine moral duty with human co-responsibility from the outset and to interpret the one in terms of the other. Still, whichever way we treat these basic assumptions, Jaspers' final conclusion appears to be inevitable.

Baron, A. Zvie (1985) "Measuring Responsibility," from *Philosophical Forum*, reprinted in 1991 *Collective Responsibility*. Copyright © 1985 Philosophical Library, New York. Reprinted with permission of Philosophical Library.

DISCUSSION ISSUES

1. *Superior Orders Defense.* Consider the following: "A German soldier is guilty of murder if, in order that he may not be shot for disobedience and his wife tortured in a concentration camp, he shoots a Catholic priest" (Wyzanski 1946, pp. 66–70). When, if ever, should soldiers disobey their superiors on moral grounds? How would natural law theorists and positivists analyze a defense of superior orders? Do soldiers, as was suggested at Nuremberg, hide behind the letter of commands to avoid facing moral dilemmas? Should international tribunals refuse to allow the plea that a defendant was merely carrying out orders as a defense to the commission of an international crime but allow a superior orders claim as a mitigation of punishment? (See Discussion Issues on cultural relativism on page 78 that raise the same question about a cultural defense.)

2. *Orders, Duty, and Responsibility.* The Israeli trial court (1961) found Eichmann, head of the German Gestapo's Jewish Office, responsible for the mass extermination of Jews, even though Eichmann had never killed or ordered another to kill any other human being. Consider the following defense of the Israeli court's decision:

   Eichmann . . . certainly bears responsibility for persecuting Jews, because of his substantial contributions to Nazi objectives. Eichmann advised the collecting centers on how to meet their "quotas." He ensured that adequate trains were available to transport Jews to death camps . . . he knew the fate of the Jews he sent to "the East." It is unnecessary to show that someone like Eichmann personally participated in acts of persecution to explain his moral responsibility for the death of countless Jews. (Kritz 1995, p. 215, fn. 271)

3. *Unjustified Obedience to Orders.* During the Korean conflict, U.S. airman Kinder apprehended a Korean man in a bomb dump and turned him over to his superior officers. They proceeded, without provocation, to pistol whip the man. The officers ordered the airman, although not directly, to take the "oriental male

human being" to the most conspicuous place, where a sentry would shoot him. The airman shot the man. Many countries do not regard a "defense of superior orders" as a complete defense, but the *United States Military Manual* considers it a complete excuse. Although the rules governing court martials recognized a superior orders justification, it noted that "the justification does not exist . . . when the order is such that a man of ordinary sense and understanding would know it to be illegal." In *United States v. Kinder* (1954), the Military Board of Review found airman Kinder guilty of premeditated murder. The board stated that "where one obeys an order to kill a severely injured, defenseless human being who is not resorting to violence, for the apparent reason of making his death an example to others," then, given the evidence in this case, "the accused complied with a palpably unlawful order fully aware of its unlawful character." Is Kinder guilty of premeditated murder?

4. *Open-Ended Laws.* Consider the following: Orders, regulations, and laws—by their open-ended nature—always remain subject to interpretation in a particular circumstance. However, soldiers should not interpret orders. Does the open-ended nature of law, then, provide a defense for soldiers who simply follow commands, since military orders never cover all situations that might arise in practice (Christopher 1994, p. 148)? Plato writes on the subject:

> Laws can never issue an injunction binding on all which really embodies what is best for each; it cannot prescribe with perfect accuracy what is good and right for each member of the community at any one time. The difference of human personality, the variety of man's activities, and the inevitable unsettlement attending all human experience make it impossible for any art whatsoever to issue unqualified rules holding good on all questions at all times. But we find practically always that the law tends to issue just this invariable kind of rule. It is like a self-willed, ignorant man who lets no one do anything but what he has ordered and forbids all subsequent questioning of his orders even if the situation has shown some marked improvement on the one for which he originally legislated. (Plato, *The Statesman,* 294b–c in Hamilton and Cairns 1982)

5. *Retroactive Laws.* Prior to the Nuremberg trials, international law failed to make individuals liable for wars of aggression. Consider a Nazi defense based on the claim that Nazi officials did not violate any international law at the time:

> It would fly straight in the face of the most fundamental rules of criminal justice—that criminal laws shall not be *ex post facto* and that there shall be *nullen crimen et nulla poena sine lege*—no crime and no penalty without an antecedent law. . . . The feeling against a law evolved after the commission of an offense is deeply rooted. . . . The antagonism to *ex post facto* laws is not based on a lawyer's prejudice encased in a Latin maxim. It rests on the political truth that if a law can be created after an offense, then power is to that extent absolute and arbitrary. To allow retroactive legislation is to disparage the principle of constitutional limitation. It is to abandon what is usually regarded as one of the essential values at the core of our democratic faith. (Wyzanski 1946, pp. 66–70)

Was Justice Jackson correct to argue (in Reading 2-9) that nations, nevertheless, have a right to develop, retroactively, newer and stronger international laws?

6. *Nazi Law?* Can a state have a system of laws without a moral foundation? Hart argued that immoral rules still retain their claim to legal status; "laws may be laws but too evil to be obeyed" (Hart 1958, pp. 593–629). Lon Fuller responded that immoral rules do not deserve the title "law." "To me there is nothing shocking in saying that a dictatorship which clothes itself with the tinsel of legal form can so depart from the morality of order, from the inner morality of law itself, that it ceases to be a legal system" (Fuller 1959, p. 660). Was Nazi law "law"?

7. *Whose law?* East German (German Democratic Republic[GDR]) border guards shot and killed citizens attempting to flee the GDR. After East Germany's reunification with West Germany in 1990, the government prosecuted these guards. The guards claimed that they had followed the operating rule of law in East Germany. The West Germans countered that these rules violated international law. Which view should prevail? (For a discussion, see Fletcher 1996, pp. 20–21.)

Legal Reasoning

PRIVATE LAW, PUBLIC CHALLENGES

The rule of law is a nobler ideal than the rule of legal texts.
—DWORKIN (1978), *Taking Rights Seriously*

Throughout the history of jurisprudence, **natural law theorists** and **legal positivists** have disputed broad issues, such as the question of law's relationship to morality. **Formalism** and **realism** represent a largely more recent division among legal theorists. The battle between formalists and realists centers less on the broader questions of law's relationship to morality and more on how judges make decisions. Still, fundamental questions regarding the nature of law and morality never stay far below the surface, particularly with a subject such as judicial decision making. Formalists view judges as reinforcing and uncovering fundamental legal rules and principles to decide cases. Realists counter that judges do not merely consult legal rules, but actually find legal rules that suit their interests. Formalists opt for clear-cut "black-letter" or "bright line" rules, untainted by a judge's personal and political tastes, while realists assess the personal and political context of judicial decision making. Page 103, on formalism, includes discussions of legal education and **deductive science.** The exposition of realism on page 107 discusses associated movements, namely **skepticism, scientism,** and **pragmatism.** The clash between formalism and realism raises important questions concerning the nature of **logic** and the role of **fact** and **fiction** in law. The formalism versus realism discussion ends with a look at **Social Darwinism** and **eugenics.**

These ethical concerns serve as a bridge to the examination on pages 138–140 of the role of moral philosophy in judicial decision making. Ronald Dworkin's approach, labeled as **constructivism,** provides a connection between the natural law versus positivist controversy and the formalist versus realist dispute. Dworkin has offered strong critiques of positivism and has shifted the philosophical debate about law to a focus on adjudication. However, unlike formalists and realists, Dworkin finds an explicit role for moral philosophy in judicial decision making. At one point, he acknowledged an affinity between his moral-philosophy approach and natural law.

The issues of **slavery** and **apartheid** that are raised at the end of the chapter, place the debates over legal theory into a concrete and challenging context.

During the twentieth century, rival legal theorists often fought their battles on law school turf—with formalists and realists disagreeing about how to teach law. Law schools did not always dominate legal education, though. In the nineteenth century, when law was a vocation and not a profession, most lawyers trained themselves in private law offices. However, **Christopher Columbus Langdell's** appointment as dean of Harvard Law School in 1870 marked a new beginning for legal education in the United States (see Friedman 1973). He made it more difficult for students to be accepted into law school (requiring a college degree or a passing score on an examination) and more difficult for them to graduate (increasing the length of stay from one to three years). Langdell's introduction of the case book method of study, which provided students with a neatly ordered series of judicial opinions, revolutionized legal education. Under Langdell, judge-made law or **common law** (see page 29) attained high stature, and statutory law was shunned. Economic, political, and social questions took a back seat in the law school curriculum, while the more formal aspects of law became central. Langdell's formalist model began to play a key role in legal education and in legal thought. In Reading 3-1, Thomas C. Grey provides an example from contract law that illustrates Langdell's formalist approach.

At first, other law schools greeted Langdell's revolution with derision. For example, "Boston University Law School was founded in 1872 as an alternative to the Harvard insanity" (Friedman 1973, p. 533). However, the case book method soon spread to other law schools, including Northwestern, Iowa, Cincinnati, and Columbia, and law schools began to attract more students from the upper strata of society. The American Bar Association, founded in 1878, instituted bar examinations, and the Association of American Law Schools, formed in 1900, began to accredit law schools. Night school and part-time law schools that followed vocational models and catered to the working class lost battles over bar admittance standards and accreditation standards. This marked, at the turn of the twentieth century, the demise of law as a vocation and the rise of law as a profession. What was this formalist model that became so influential? Law schools began to teach law as a deductive science.

1. Deductive Science

Langdell promoted law as a science, but not a science as we normally think of it (see Reading 3-2). "To Langdell, law was a science, the library was its laboratory, and cases were its natural elements" (Auerbach 1976, p. 75). Langdell tried to deduce principles of law from judicial opinions. He believed that printed books contained the materials of legal science, just as laboratories held the materials for physics and chemistry. By contemporary standards, Langdell had an outdated and distorted view of science—but his views fit his times. The idea that science centers on testing theories through controlled experimentation has not always prevailed. For centuries, Euclid's mathematical system (*Elements of Geometry,* 300 B.C.) served as a model for science. In the seventeenth century, theorists of music (Mersenne's *Harmonie Universelle,* 1636), politics (Hobbes's *Leviathan,* 1651), and ethics (Spinoza's *Ethics,* 1674) presented their arguments in deductive form. They derived theorems from definitions, axioms, and postulates. The deductive model, although eventually supplanted, held its ground throughout the nineteenth century, so Christopher Langdell's promotion of law as a deductive science of law coincided with the beliefs of his time. Even more important is that the formalist quest, begun by Langdell, continues to attract legal scholars. The growing strength of a movement called **law and economics** attests to the power of a formalist approach to law. Scholars will undoubtedly continue to struggle to put law on a solid, rational basis.

2. A Realist Critique

Oliver Wendell Holmes (1841–1935), a controversial and influential longtime justice on the U.S. Supreme Court, served as a transitional figure. He straddled the fence between legal formalists and realists. One commentator called Holmes "the most illustrious figure in the history of American law" (Posner 1992a, p. ix). He was wounded three times during the Civil War, attended and taught briefly at Harvard Law School, and served for twenty years on the Supreme Judicial Court of Massachusetts. President Theodore Roosevelt appointed Holmes to the United States Supreme Court at the age of sixty-two, where he served for almost thirty years. Holmes launched the first salvo that legal realists hurled at formalists. His response to Langdell's formalism has become a classic (see Reading 3-3). Although he recognized Langdell as "the greatest living legal theologian," Holmes saw logic as an "evening dress which the newcomer puts on to make itself presentable"; the "important phenomenon is the man underneath it, not the coat" (Friedman 1973, p. 544). For Holmes, the removed world of Langdell's logic differed from the real world of law. After all, law was a practice.

READING 3-1

Formalism Exemplified
"Langdell's Orthodoxy" (1983)

Thomas C. Grey

Langdell was mainly a doctrinal writer rather than a philosopher, and to get a sense of his legal theory it is best to begin by looking at his treatment of a doctrinal problem. When someone accepts a contractual offer by mail, does the contract become binding when the acceptance is mailed or when it is received? There are practical arguments on both sides of the question, but most modern writers have agreed that the balance of convenience favors making the acceptance binding when mailed—the so-called "mailbox rule." And modern writers, thinking it more important to have the question settled than to worry endlessly over whether it is settled right, have agreed to treat the mailbox rule as established law.

When Langdell confronted it, the question had not yet been settled. The courts of England and New York had adopted the mailbox rule, but those of Massachusetts had rejected it. According to Langdell, the issue between the alternatives was not merely a practical one. In his view, fundamental principles dictated that the acceptance must be received before the contract could be formed. This followed from the doctrine that a promise could not be binding unless it was supported by consideration. The consideration for the offer was the offeree's return promise. But a promise by its nature is not complete until communicated; a "promise" into the air is no promise at all. Since there was no promise, there was no consideration and could be no contract, until the letter of acceptance was received and read. The mailbox rule could not be good law.

Langdell took note of the argument that the mailbox rule would best serve "the purposes of substantial justice, and the interests of the contracting parties, as understood by themselves," and responded that this was "irrelevant"—a claim that has ever since been taken to express the wretched essence of his kind of legal thinking. . . .

From Grey (1983), "Langdell's Orthodoxy," *University of Pittsburgh Law Review* 1. Reprinted by permission.

READING 3-2

The Formal Science of Law
Introduction to the Law of Contracts (1871)

Christopher Columbus Langdell

. . . Law, considered as a science, consists of certain principles or doctrines. To have such a mastery of these as to be able to apply them with constant facility and certainty to the ever-tangled skein of human affairs, is what constitutes a true lawyer; and hence to acquire that mastery should be the business of every earnest student of law. Each of these doctrines has arrived at its present state by slow degrees; in other words, it is a growth, extending in many cases through centuries. This growth is to be traced in the main through a series of cases; and much the shortest and best, if not the only way of mastering the doctrine effectually is by studying the cases in which it is embodied. But the cases which are useful and necessary for this purpose at the present day bear an exceedingly small proportion to all that have been reported. The vast majority are useless, and worse than useless, for any purpose of systematic study. Moreover, the number of fundamental legal doctrines is much less than is commonly supposed; the many different guises in which the same doctrine is constantly making its appearance, and the great extent to which legal treatises are a repetition of each other, being the cause of much misapprehension. If these doctrines could be so classified and arranged that each should be found in its proper place, and nowhere else, they would cease to be formidable from their number. It seemed to me, therefore, to be possible to take such a branch of the law as Contracts, for example, and, without exceeding comparatively moderate limits, to select, classify, and arrange all the cases which had contributed in any important degree to the growth, development, or establishment of any of its essential doctrines; and that such a work could not fail to be of material service to all who desire to study that branch of law systematically and in its original sources. . . .

From Langdell (1871), *Selection of Cases on the Law of Contracts.* Reprinted (1983) Birmingham, AL.: The Legal Classics Library, pp. v–vii.

READING 3-3

The Path to Realism
"Book Review of Langdell's Casebook" (1880)

Oliver Wendell Holmes, Jr.

It is hard to know where to begin in dealing with this extraordinary production,—equally extraordinary in its merits and its limitations. No man competent to judge can read a page of it without at once recognizing the hand of a great master. Every line is compact of ingenious and original thought. Decisions are reconciled which those who gave them meant to be opposed, and drawn together by subtle lines which never were dreamed of before Mr. Langdell wrote. It may be said without exaggeration that there cannot be found in the legal literature of this country, such a *tour de force* of patient and profound intellect working out original theory through a mass of detail, and evolving consistency out of what seemed a chaos of conflicting atoms. But in this word "consistency" we touch what some of us at least must deem the weak point in Mr. Langdell's habit of mind. Mr. Langdell's ideal in the law, the end of all his striving, is the *elegantia juris,* or *logical* integrity of the system as a system. He is, perhaps, the greatest living legal theologian. But as a theologian he is less concerned with his postulates than to show that the conclusions from them hang together. A single phrase will illustrate what is meant. "It has been claimed that the purposes of substantial justice and the interests of contracting parties as understood by themselves will be best served by holding &c., . . . and cases have been put to show that the contrary view would produce not only unjust but absurd results. *The true answer to this argument is that it is irrelevant;* but" &c. (pp. 995, 996, pl. 15). The reader will perceive that the language is only incidental, but it reveals a mode of thought which becomes conspicuous to a careful student.

If Mr. Langdell could be suspected of ever having troubled himself about Hegel, we might call him a Hegelian in disguise, so entirely is he interested in the formal connection of things, or logic, as distinguished from the feelings which make the content of logic, and which have actually shaped the substance of the law. *The life of the law has not been logic: it has been experience.* The seed of every new growth within its sphere has been a felt necessity. The form of continuity has been kept up by reasonings purporting to reduce every thing to a logical sequence; but that form is nothing but the evening dress which the new-comer puts on to make itself presentable according to conventional requirements. The important phenomenon is the man underneath it, not the coat; the justice and reasonableness of a decision, not its consistency with previously held views. No one will ever have a truly philosophic mastery over the law who does not habitually consider the forces outside of it which have made it what it is. More than that, he must remember that as it embodies the story of a nation's development through many centuries, the law finds its philosophy not in self-consistency, which it must always fail in so long as it continues to grow, but in history and the nature of human needs. As a branch of anthropology, law is an object of science; the theory of legislation is a scientific study; but the effort to reduce the concrete details of an existing system to the merely logical consequence of simple postulates is always in danger of becoming unscientific, and of leading to a misapprehension of the nature of the problem and the data.

. . . But it is to be remembered that the book is published for use at a law school, and that for that purpose dogmatic teaching is a necessity, if any thing is to be taught within the limited time of a student's course. A professor must start with a system as an arbitrary fact, and the most which can be hoped for is to make the student see how it hangs together, and thus to send him into practice with something more than a rag-bag of details. For this purpose it is believed that Mr. Langdell's teachings, published and unpublished, have been of unequalled value. . . .

From Holmes (1880), "Book Review of Langdell's Casebook," 14 *American Law Review* 233, pp. 233–235.

B. REALISM: JUDGES AS POLICY MAKERS

Formalism thrived from 1870 to 1920, while legal realism had its strongest following from 1920 to 1940. Holmes had anticipated some realist themes—skepticism, scientism, and pragmatism—at the turn of the century. He stated what became a central slogan for realists: "The life of law has not been logic; it has been experience" (Posner 1992b, p. 1). Holmes saw judges as neither logicians nor moralists. He believed that to understand law we must divorce law from morals and examine what judges do—they face the practical problems involved in resolving disputes.

1. Skepticism

Holmes had a deep-seated skepticism toward the moral posturing of natural law theorists. His doubting attitude typified a realist one:

> It is enough for the knight of romance that you agree that this lady is a very nice girl—if you do not admit that she is the best that God ever made or will make, you must fight. There is in all men a demand for the superlative, so much so that the poor devil who has no other way of reaching it attains it by getting drunk. It seems to me that this demand is at the bottom of the philosopher's efforts to

prove that truth is absolute and the jurist's search for criteria of universal validity which he collects under the head of natural law. (Holmes 1918, p. 40)

Skepticism (originally from the Greek *skeptiko,* meaning inquirers) has a long history in philosophy. Philosophers often regard skepticism as an irritant that refuses to go away, and many agree with David Hume who noted that a skeptical argument "admits of no answer, and produces no conviction." Nevertheless, skepticism has survived and thrived in philosophy and in law as an attitude to counter **dogmatism.** A dogmatist refuses to yield on a position, despite reasoning and evidence to the contrary.

> [Skepticism] has been like an anonymous letter received by a dogmatic philosopher who does not hold a position. The letter raises fundamental problems for the recipient by questioning whether he has adequate grounds for his assertions and assumptions or whether his system is free from contradictions or absurdities. The recipient may try to fend off the attack by challenging whether any philosopher could write the letter without opening himself to similar attacks. By imputing an author, the dogmatist may show the problem involved in consistently stating skepticism, but he does not thereby reply to the arguments in the letter. Skeptical arguments are usually parasitical, in that they assume the premises of the dogmatist and show problems that ensue, on the standards of reasoning of the dogmatist. (Popkin 1967, pp. 459–460)

2. Scientism

Holmes proposed a **"bad man" theory of law.** He looked at law "as a bad man, who cares only for the material consequences" and yet who obeys law (Holmes in 1897, p. 457). According to Holmes, the study of law is the study of predictions and prophecies of what courts will do. The law, therefore, does not exist in the Kantian realm of moral ideals. Rather, it operates in the realm of predictable consequences of the bad man. The bad man wants only to know what he can do without getting in trouble, therefore he needs to predict the legal system's actions and reactions. Holmes urges legal scholars to do something similar.

> Take the fundamental question, What constitutes the law? You will find some text writers [formalists such as Langdell] telling you that it is something different from what is decided by the courts of Massachusetts or England, that it is a system of reason, that it is a deduction from principles of ethics or admitted axioms or what not, which may or may not coincide with the decisions. But if we take the view of our friend the bad man we shall find that he does not care two straws for the axioms or deductions, but that he does not want to know what the Massachusetts or English courts are likely to do in fact. I am much of his mind. *The prophecies of what the courts will do in fact, and nothing more pretentious, are what I mean by the law.* (Holmes 1897, pp. 460–461)

Louis Brandeis (1856–1941) developed what Holmes had begun. Although Brandeis had studied law under Langdell, he turned away from Langdell's abstract formalism and toward law's social and economic context. When Brandeis submitted a brief to the U.S. Supreme Court in *Mueller v. Oregon* (1908), he helped turn realists to inductive or empirical science. Oregon had passed a law establishing a maximum ten-hour workday for women employed in manufacturing, mechanical establishments, and laundries. Brandeis argued the case before the same Supreme Court where he would later distinguish himself as a Justice. His **Brandeis Brief** was only two pages long, but it included a 113-page appendix containing citations of many social facts. It was compiled largely by Josephine Goldmark, Brandeis' sister-in-law. The brief was designed to demonstrate the adverse effects of working conditions on women. Brandeis believed that lawyers should not only argue the legal rules but should also educate courts about economic and social facts.

3. Pragmatism

The Brandeis Brief illustrated the increasingly important role of law in the social sciences as they rose in status at the turn of the twentieth century. A scientific attitude that was focused on experimentation had combined with a new philosophy—**pragmatism.** "By the beginning of the twentieth century the pragmatism of William James and John Dewey had provided a broad philosophy that attempted to explain the human and social meaning of science and that suggested how the scientific method could be employed to understand and resolve human problems on all levels" (Purcell 1973, p. 10). To understand legal realism, we need to look briefly at pragmatism, a quintessential American school of philosophy that flourished from the late 1800s to the early 1900s. Two of pragmatism's most prominent members, **Charles Sanders Peirce** (1839–1914) and **William James** (1842–1910) joined scientists and jurists in The Metaphysics Club. Holmes met with this new breed of intellectuals upstairs in his room in Cambridge "under flaring gas lamp" for intense intellectual debate. When Peirce, who was trained as a chemist, and James, a trained biologist, set out to establish a scientific philosophy, they focused less on the practical and more on the pragmatic. They sought to explore ways that knowledge related to human action and conduct. According to James, "The truth of an idea is not a stagnant property inherent in it. It becomes true, is made true by events. Its verity is in fact an event, a process: the process namely of its verifying itself, its verification. Its validity is the process of its valid-ation" (James 1910, p. 201). A pragmatist will test a claim by its consequences, that is, by the differences it makes.

> The pragmatic method . . . is to try to interpret each notion by tracing its respective practical consequences. What difference would it practically make to say if this notion rather than that notion were true? If no practical difference whatever can be traced, then the alternative means practically the same thing, and all dispute is idle.
> *Theories thus become instruments, not answers to enigmas, in which we can rest.* . . . It [pragmatism] agrees with nominalism . . . in always appealing to particulars; with utilitarianism in emphasizing practical aspects; with positivism in its disdain for verbal solutions, useless questions and metaphysical abstractions. (James 1925, pp. 45, 53)

Pragmatism paved the way for Holmes and the legal realists who vowed to take law and its philosophies out of Langdell's library and into society.

Realists, however, did not go as far as pragmatist **John Dewey's** (1859–1952) scientism. Dewey thought that even the values found in law could be verified scientifically. Recently, pragmatism has had a revival in legal theory (see, for example, Brint and Weaver 1991). Even theorists from opposing perspectives (such as critical legal studies, and law and economics) now call themselves pragmatists.

The increased focus on the legal practitioner and on what judges do, as well as the more prominent role of the social sciences, helped to change legal education. According to a view shared by Supreme Court Justices Louis Brandeis and Felix Frankfurter, law schools should not be divorced from social issues, but should, instead, participate in public service. Unlike formalist law teachers, a new generation of realist law teachers "were the scientists who gathered, sorted, and evaluated data to produce legal solutions for social malfunctions" (Auerbach 1976, p. 77).

Realism grew out of a reorientation toward what judges do. Formalists saw judges as engaged in a respectable and logical intellectual discourse about rules and precedents, but when realists looked beneath the formalist "methods," they found judges using rules as rationalizations. Legal realists did not agree about which factors influenced judicial decision making the most. Harvard Law Dean **Roscoe Pound** (1870–1964), who labeled formalism as mechanical jurisprudence, proposed a new **sociological jurisprudence.** He lobbied for less formalism and more instrumentalism in law, and criticized the formalist orientation of law as leading to a "government of the living by the dead" (Pound 1906, p. 729). He urged lawyers to "think of legal principles as instruments rather than as eternal pigeonholes." Justice **Benjamin N. Cardozo** explicitly rejected "mechanical jurisprudence" that follows the dictates of logic irrespective of where it leads, instead arguing in favor of a legal realist interpretation (see Reading 3-4).

4. Logical Positivism

Other realists gave more extra-legal explanations than Pound for the problems with the judicial system. The New Deal realists accepted the empirical orientation of their predecessors but promoted **moral relativism**—a view that denies the existence of objective transcultural moral values. They wanted to strip the law of its artificial coverings. For example, **Jerome Frank** (1889–1957) used neo-Freudian psychoanalysis to uncover the psychological influences of judges. Realists also challenged the ideological assumptions of the formalists. **Morris Cohen** (1880–1947), for example, found the idea of "freedom of contract" illusory since it ignored the unequal bargaining power between worker and industrial owner.

However diverse their opinions, realists shared a disdain for metaphysics with logical positivists (not to be confused with legal positivists). **Logical positivism** in philosophy is split geographically much like civil and common law is split. Continental European countries adopted a variety of civil law systems (see chapter 1), while Great Britain and the United States developed common law systems. Although logical positivism has clear continental European roots, most of its members fled to the United States with the rise of Nazism. Philosophy became geographically divided between the grander metaphysical theories on continental Europe and the more scientifically oriented analyses in Great Britain and the United States. Logical positivism grew out of the **Vienna Circle** (1922–1938), a group of scientists, mathematicians, and philosophers who met periodically in Vienna, Austria. The logical positivists issued harsh critiques of Hegelian metaphysics, which dominated continental European philosophy. Metaphysicians used transcendental concepts to study the nature of reality. Otto Neurath, a member of the Vienna Circle, set out to destroy transcendental metaphysics, which he saw as supporting conservative politics, particularly in Germany. When Hitler and the Third Reich banned publications of all logical positivists' writings in 1938, members of the Vienna Circle fled to the United States, where they had a major influence on philosophy. The logical positivists found metaphysical concepts meaningless, since they did not fit into the category of logical (or mathematical) concepts or of scientific concepts, which could be empirically verified. The logical positivist found metaphysical statements, such as "The Absolute is beyond time," neither true nor false but meaningless. Legal realists, such as **Felix Cohen,** dismissed similar concepts in law (see Reading 3-5). Cohen recommended that realists cleanse law of its supernatural concepts. Some logical positivists took the analysis one step further and found ethical concepts to be in the same category as metaphysical concepts. For **emotivists,** ethical judgments have no empirical validity and ethical claims, accordingly, do little more than serve as expressions of emotions and feelings. Saying "Lying is wrong" stands on the same epistemological footing as saying "Yuck!" after being served peach-caramel-marshmallow ice cream. Like many of the realists, Cohen adopted a scientific attitude toward law, but the realists did not systematically examine where ethics fit into their scientific perspective. Cohen saw that the study of law had two aspects—an empirical aspect and a prescriptive (ethical) one. By asking "How do courts decide cases?" legal researchers should empirically examine the cause and effect of judicial decisions. By asking "How should judges decide cases?" realists should ethically assess the social values at stake in judicial opinions. Should realists have given a scientific assessment of social values?

The law contains many fictions as well as facts. Fictions provide ways to give new authority to old rules. In ancient Rome, an adoptive mother would simulate birth pangs to "give birth" to the adopted child, who was brought out from under the mother's skirts. The fictional birth gave new authority to the old rule that only blood relationships could create family ties (Berman and Greiner 1996, pp. 441–447). The corporation-as-a-person represents one of the most famous fictions. Realists (see Reading 3-5) find legal fictions nonsensical. They ask rhetorically, "Do corporations have rights?" Contrary to the realist inclination to deny rights to corporations, courts have extended some constitutional rights to these legal fictions, such as equal protection, due process, freedom of the press, freedom from self-incrimination, and freedom from unreasonable searches. The realist would remain puzzled and ask: "Where are these corporations?"

READING 3-4

Mechanical Jurisprudence Debunked

Hynes v. New York Central Railroad (1921)

JUDGE BENJAMIN CARDOZO

On July 8, 1916, Harvey Hynes, a lad of 16, swam with two companions from the Manhattan to the Bronx side of the Harlem River, or United States Ship Canal, a navigable stream. Along the Bronx side of the river was the right of way of the defendant, the New York Central Railroad, which operated its trains at that point by high-tension wires, strung on poles and cross-arms. Projecting from the defendant's bulkhead above the waters of the river was a plank or springboard, from which boys of the neighborhood used to dive. One end of the board had been placed under a rock on the defendant's land, and nails had been driven at its point of contact with the bulkhead. Measured from this point of contact the length behind was 5 feet; the length in front 11. The bulkhead itself was about 3½ feet back of the pier line as located by the government. From this it follows that for 7½ feet the springboard was beyond the line of the defendant's property and above the public waterway. Its height measured from the stream was 3 feet at the bulkhead, and 5 feet at its outermost extremity. For more than five years swimmers had used it as a diving board without protest or obstruction. . . .

In climbing on the board, they became trespassers and outlaws. The conclusion is defended with much subtlety of reasoning, with much insistence upon its inevitableness as a merely logical deduction. A majority of the court are unable to accept it as the conclusion of the law.

We assume, without deciding, that the springboard was a fixture, a permanent improvement of the defendant's right of way. Much might be said in favor of another view. We do not press the inquiry for we are persuaded that the rights of bathers do not depend upon these nice distinctions. Liability would not be doubtful, we are told, had the boy been diving from a pole, if the pole had been vertical. The diver in such a situation would have been separated from the defendant's freehold. Liability, it is said has been escaped because the pole was horizontal. The plank when projected lengthwise was an extension of the soil. We are to concentrate our gaze on the private ownership of the board. We are to ignore the public ownership of the circumambient spaces of water and of air. Jumping from a boat or a barrel, the boy would have been a bather in the river. Jumping from the end of a springboard, he was no longer, it is said, a bather, but a trespasser on a right of way.

Rights and duties in systems of living law are not built upon such quicksands.

Bathers in the Harlem River on the day of this disaster were in the enjoyment of a public highway, entitled to reasonable protection against destruction by the defendant's wires. They did not cease to be bathers entitled to the same protection while they were diving from encroaching objects or engaging in the sports that are common among swimmers. . . .

The truth is that every act of Hynes from his first plunge into the river until the moment of his death was in the enjoyment of the public waters, and under cover of the protection which his presence in those waters gave him. The use of the springboard was not an abandonment of his rights as bather. It was a mere by-play, an incident, subordinate and ancillary to the execution of his primary purpose, the enjoyment of the highway. The by-play, the incident, was not the cause of the disaster. Hynes would have gone to his death if he had been below the springboard or beside it. . . . The wires were not stayed by the presence of the plank. They followed the boy in his fall, and overwhelmed him in the waters. . . .

[3] This case is a striking instance of the dangers of "a jurisprudence of conceptions" (Pound, Mechanical Jurisprudence 8 *Columbia Law Review,* pp. 605, 608, 610), the extension of a maxim or a definition with relentless disregard of consequences to "a dryly logical extreme." The approximate and relative become the definite and absolute. Landowners are not bound to regulate their conduct in contemplation of the presence of trespassers intruding upon private structures. Landowners are not bound to regulate their conduct in contemplation of the presence of travelers upon the adjacent public ways. There are times when there is little trouble in marking off the field of exemption and immunity from that of liability and duty. Here structures and ways are so united and commingled, superimposed upon each other, that the fields are brought together. In such circumstances, there is little help in pursuing general maxims to ultimate conclusions. They have been framed alio intuitu [from a different point-of-view]. They must be reformulated and readapted to meet exceptional conditions. Rules appropriate to spheres which are conceived of as separate and distinct cannot both be enforced when the spheres become concentric. There must then be readjustment or collision. In one sense, and that a highly technical and artificial one, the diver at the end of the springboard is an intruder on the adjoining lands. In another sense, and one that realists will accept more readily, he is still on public waters in the exercise of public rights. The law must say whether it will subject him to the rule of the one field or of the other, of this sphere or of that. We think that considerations of analogy, of convenience, of policy, and of justice, exclude him from the field of the defendant's immunity and exemption, and place him in the field of liability and duty. . . .

From *Hynes v. New York Central Rail Road* (1921) 131 NE 898.

READING 3-5

Supernaturalism in Law
"Transcendental Nonsense and the Functional Approach" (1935)

Felix S. Cohen

I. THE HEAVEN OF LEGAL CONCEPTS

Some fifty years ago a great German jurist [Rudolf von Ihering (1818–1892), who promoted a sociological theory of law] had a curious dream. He dreamed that he died and was taken to a special heaven reserved for the theoreticians of the law. In this heaven one met, face to face, the many concepts of jurisprudence in their absolute purity, freed from all entangling alliances with human life. Here were the disembodied spirits of good faith and bad faith, property, possession, *laches* [neglect to assert a claim in time], and rights *in rem* [legal action against a thing, not a person]. Here were all the logical instruments needed to manipulate and transform these legal concepts and thus to create and to solve the most beautiful of legal problems. Here one found a dialectic-hydraulic-interpretation press, which could press an indefinite number of meanings out of any text or statute, an apparatus for constructing fictions, and a hair-splitting machine that could divide a single hair into 999,999 equal parts and, when operated by the most expert jurists, could split each of these parts again into 999,999 equal parts. The boundless opportunities of this heaven of legal concepts were open to all properly qualified jurists, provided only they drank the Lethean [a river in Hades from ancient Greek mythology] draught which induced forgetfulness of terrestrial human affairs. But for the most accomplished jurists the Lethean draught was entirely superfluous. They had nothing to forget.

Von Jhering's dream has been retold, in recent years, in the chapels of sociological, functional, institutional, scientific, experimental, realistic, and neo-realistic jurisprudence. The question is raised, "How much of contemporary legal thought moves in the pure ether of Von Jhering's heaven of legal concepts?" One turns to our leading legal textbooks and to the opinions of our courts for answer. May the Shade of Von Jhering be our guide.

1. Where Is a Corporation?

... Clearly the question of *where a corporation is,* when it incorporates in one state and has agents transacting corporate business in another state, is not a question that can be answered by empirical observation. Nor is it a question that demands for its solution any analysis of political considerations or social ideals. It is, in fact, a question identical in metaphysical status with the question which scholastic theologians are supposed to have argued at great length, "How many angels can stand on the point of a needle?" Now it is extremely doubtful whether any of the scholastics ever actually discussed this question. Yet the question has become, for us, a symbol of an age in which thought without roots in reality was an object of high esteem.

Will future historians deal more charitably with such legal questions as "Where is a corporation?" Nobody has ever seen a corporation. What right have we to believe in corporations if we don't believe in angels? To be sure, some of us have seen corporate funds, corporate transactions, etc. (just as some of us have seen angelic deeds, angelic countenances, etc.). But this does not give us the right to hypostatize, to "thingify," the corporation, and to assume that it travels about from State to State as mortal men travel. Surely we are qualifying as inmates of Von Jhering's heaven of legal concepts when we approach a legal problem in these essentially supernatural terms. . . .

Of course, it would be captious [overly critical] to criticize courts for delivering their opinions in the language of transcendental nonsense. Logicians sometimes talk as if the only function of language were to convey ideas. But anthropologists know better and assure us that "language is primarily a pre-rational function." Certain words and phrases are useful for the purpose of releasing pent-up emotions, or putting babies to sleep, or inducing certain emotions and attitudes in a political or a judicial audience. The law is not a science but a practical activity, and myths may impress the imagination and memory where more exact discourse would leave minds cold.

Valuable as is the language of transcendental nonsense for many practical legal purposes, it is entirely useless when we come to study, describe, predict, and criticize legal phenomena. And although judges and lawyers need not be legal scientists, it is of some practical importance that they should recognize that the traditional language of argument and opinion neither explains nor justifies court decisions. When the vivid fictions and metaphors of traditional jurisprudence are thought of as reasons for decisions, rather than poetical or mnemonic devices for formulating decisions reached on other grounds, then the author, as well as the reader, of the opinion or argument, is apt to forget the social forces which mold the law and the social ideals by which the law is to be judged. Thus it is that the most intelligent judges in America can deal with a concrete practical problem of procedural law and corporate responsibility without any appreciation of the economic, social, and ethical issues which it involves. . . .

6. The Nature of Legal Nonsense

It would be tedious to prolong our survey; in every field of law we should find the same habit of ignoring practical questions of value or of positive fact and taking refuge in "legal problems" which can always be answered by manipulating legal concepts in certain approved ways. In every field of law we should find peculiar concepts which are not defined either in terms of empirical fact or in terms of ethics, but which are used to answer empirical and ethical questions alike, and thus bar the way to intelligent investigation of social fact and social policy. *Corporate entity, property rights, fair value,* and *due process* are such concepts. So too are *title, contract, conspiracy, malice, proximate cause,* and all the rest of the magic "solving words" of traditional jurisprudence. Legal arguments couched in these terms are necessarily circular, since these terms are themselves creations of law, and such arguments add precisely as much to our knowledge as Moliere's physician's discovery that opium puts men to sleep because it contains a dormitive principle.

Now the proposition that opium puts men to sleep *because* it contains a dormitive principle is scientifically useful if "dormitive principle" is defined physically or chemically. Otherwise it serves only to obstruct the path of understanding with the pretense of knowledge. So, too, the proposition that a law is unconstitutional *because* it deprives persons of property without due process of law would be scientifically useful if "property" and "due process" were defined in non-legal terms; otherwise such a statement simply obstructs study of the relevant facts.

If the foregoing instances of legal reasoning are typical, we may summarize the basic assumptions of traditional legal theory in the following terms:

Legal concepts (for example, *corporations* or *property rights*) are supernatural entities which do not have a verifiable existence except to the eyes of faith. *Rules of law,* which refer to these legal concepts, are not descriptions of empirical social facts (such as the customs of men or the customs of judges) nor yet statements of moral ideals, but are rather theorems in an independent system. It follows that a *legal argument* can never be refuted by a moral principle nor yet by any empirical fact. *Jurisprudence,* then, as an autonomous system of legal concepts, rules, and arguments, must be independent both of ethics and of such positive sciences as economics or psychology. In effect, it is a special branch of the science of transcendental nonsense. . . .

2. The Abatement of Meaningless Questions

It is a consequence of the functional attack upon unverifiable concepts that many of the traditional problems of science, law, and philosophy are revealed as pseudo-problems devoid of meaning. As the protagonist of logical positivism, Wittgenstein, says of the traditional problems of philosophy:

> "Most propositions and questions, that have been written about philosophical matters, are not false, but senseless. We cannot, therefore, answer questions of this kind at all, but only state their senselessness. Most questions and propositions of the philosophers result from the fact that we do not understand the logic of our language. (They are of the same kind as the question whether the Good is more or less identical than the Beautiful.) And so it is not to be wondered at that the deepest problems are really no problems."[1]

The same thing may be said of the problems of traditional jurisprudence. As commonly formulated, such "problems" as, "What is the holding or *ratio decidendi* of a case?" or "Which came first,—the law or the state?" or "What is the essential distinction between a crime and a tort?" or "Where is a corporation?" are in fact meaningless, and can serve only as invitations to equally meaningless displays of conceptual acrobatics.

[1]WITTGENSTEIN, TRACTATUS LOGICO-PHILOSOPHICUS (1922) prop. 4.003. And *cf.* JAMES, PRAGMATISM (1908): "The pragmatic method is primarily a method of settling metaphysical disputes that otherwise might be interminable. . . . The pragmatic method in such cases is to try to interpret each notion by tracing its respective practical consequences. . . . If no practical differences whatever can be traced then the alternatives mean practically the same thing, and all dispute is idle. It is astonishing to see how many philosophical disputes collapse into insignificance the moment you subject them to this simple test of tracing a practical consequence (pp. 45–49.)

Fundamentally there are only two significant questions in the field of law. One is, "How do courts actually decide cases of a given kind?" The other is, "How ought they to decide cases of a given kind?" Unless a legal "problem" can be subsumed under one of these forms, it is not a meaningful question and any answer to it must be nonsense.

3. The Redefinition of Concepts

. . . In brief, Holmes . . . [has] offered a logical basis for the redefinition of every legal concept in empirical terms, *i.e.* in terms of judicial decisions. The ghost-world of supernatural legal entities to whom courts delegate the moral responsibility of deciding cases vanishes; in its place we see legal concepts as patterns of judicial behavior, behavior which affects human lives for better or worse and is therefore subject to moral criticism. . . .

The age of the classical jurists is over, I think. The "Restatement of the Law" by the American Law Institute is the last long-drawn-out gasp of a dying tradition. The more intelligent of our younger law teachers and students are not interested in "restating" the dogmas of legal theology. There will, of course, be imitators and followers of the classical jurists, in the years ahead. But I think that the really creative legal thinkers of the future will not devote themselves, in the manner of [Langdell] Williston, Wigmore, and their fellow masters, to the taxonomy of legal concepts and to the systematic explication of principles of "justice" and "reason," buttressed by "correct" cases. Creative legal thought will more and more look behind the pretty array of "correct" cases to the actual facts of judicial behavior, will make increasing use of statistical methods in the scientific description and prediction of judicial behavior, will more and more seek to map the hidden springs of judicial decision and to weigh the social forces which are represented on the bench. And on the critical side, I think that creative legal thought will more and more look behind the traditionally accepted principles of "justice" and "reason" to appraise in ethical terms the social values at stake in any choice between two precedents. . . .

A truly realistic theory of judicial decisions must conceive every decision as something more than an expression of individual personality, as concomitantly and even more importantly a function of social forces, that is to say, as a product of social determinants and an index of social consequences. A judicial decision is a social event. Like the enactment of a Federal statute, or the equipping of police cars with radios, a judicial decision is an intersection of social forces: Behind the decision are social forces that play upon it to give it a resultant momentum and direction; beyond the decision are human activities affected by it. The decision is without significant social dimensions when it is viewed simply at the moment in which it is rendered. Only by probing behind the decision to the forces which it reflects, or projecting beyond the decision the lines of its force upon the future, do we come to an understanding of the meaning of the decision itself. . . .

Cohen, Felix S. "Transcendental Nonsense and the Functional Approach." This article originally appeared in 35 *Columbia Law Review* 809 © (1935). Reprinted by permission.

C. CONTROVERSIES: LOGIC, FACT, AND FICTION

1. Legal Logic

When Holmes said that "the actual life of law has not been logic: it has been experience," he meant **syllogistic logic,** also known as classical **Aristotelian logic.** The standard syllogism contains a major premise, a minor premise, and a conclusion. For example, if "All A are B" (major premise) and "All B are C" (minor premise), then it follows necessarily that "All A are C" (conclusion). In classical legal thought, the major premise was thought of as a general legal rule, and the minor premise, a factual claim regarding the specific case. Lawyers and judges, then, would infer a necessary conclusion from the relationship between the legal rule (major premise) and the facts (minor premise). Pragmatist philosopher **John Dewey** (1859–1952) took Holmes to task for his narrow view of logic (see Reading 3-6). Dewey called for a more general sense of logic than formal logic, in which validity is determined by strict **rules of inference,** and for a **logic of inquiry,** in which validity is shown by its success. A broader, informal sense of logic seems more in keeping with the way lawyers and judges reason. While formal logic helps with precision, it has limited applications. Judges, then, reason by interpreting words, drawing analogies, citing rules, and finding principles.

2. Legal Facts

The law has seen an explosion of facts in law as noted by the anthropologist **Clifford Geertz** (see Reading 3-7), but how does the legal system categorize facts? Classifying an item as a fact proves important, as indicated by the legal realist **Kurt Llewellyn** (1893–1962) in Reading 3-8, however the law may place too much importance on facts as philosopher J.R. Lucas tries to show (Reading 3-9). In any event, the law places importance on the distinction between **issues of fact** and **issues of law.** Criminal trials often hinge on questions of fact, while civil trials focus more on questions of law. The distinction between fact and law determines, in part, the distribution of responsibilities between judge and jury. In Reading 3-10, we see what distinguishes issues of fact from those of law.

3. Legal Fictions

"[L]aw . . . is part of a distinctive manner of imagining the real. At base, it is not what happened, but what happens, that law sees" (Geertz 1973, p. 173). The law often does not keep pace with events. Contract law, for example, governed liability for product defects (see Reading 3-11). A manufacturer's liability for a defective product extended to those who had a contract relationship with the manufacturer or **privity of contract.** Manufacturers had contract relationships with automobile sellers but not with automobile consumers, since consumers stood too far removed from manufacturers to establish typical contract relationships. Because dealers and buyers did not include automobile makers in their contracts, manufacturers could use the defense of an absence of privity of contract to avoid liability. **Implied war-**

ranty provided the fiction needed to achieve a more equitable result: "[A] warranty 'implied in law' presupposes a fictitious promise by the seller of goods to be liable for losses resulting from defects in the goods, and in certain matters the legal implications cannot be defeated even by an express disclaimer by the seller" (Berman 1996, p. 443). Legal fictions, then, may give "new law the authority of old law" (Berman 1996, p. 443). The debates among formalists and realists have not ended; they continue to shape disputes over the nature of legal education and legal philosophy. Langdell's case book method, based on abstract rules, still prevails. Today, however, reflecting a realist influence, case books include statutory materials, law review articles, law professors' notes, questions, and problems. As a theory or approach to law, realism has influenced an exciting new array of perspectives on law, including critical legal studies, feminist jurisprudence, and critical race theory, as well as law and economics.

READING 3-6
The Logic of Inquiry
"Logical Method and Law" (1924)

John Dewey

. . . Justice Holmes says, "The language of judicial decision is mainly the language of logic. And the logical method and form flatter that longing for certainty and for repose [harmony of everything fitting together] which is in every human mind. But certainty generally is an illusion." From the view of logicalmethods here set forth, however, the undoubted facts which Justice Holmes has in mind do not concern logic but rather certain tendencies of the human creatures who use logic; tendencies which a sound logic will guard against. For they spring from the momentum of habit once forced, and express the effect of habit upon our feelings of ease and stability—feelings which have little to do with the actual facts of the case.

However this is only part of the story. The rest of the story is brought to light in some other passages of Justice Holmes. "The actual life of the law has not been logic: it has been experience. The felt necessities of the times, the prevalent moral and political theories, intuitions of public policy, avowed or unconscious, even the prejudices which judges share with their fellow-men, have had a good deal more to do than the syllogism in determining the rules by which men should be governed." In other words, Justice Holmes is thinking of logic as equivalent with the syllogism, as he is quite entitled to do in accord with the orthodox tradition. From the standpoint of the syllogism as the logical model which was made current by scholasticism there *is* an antithesis between experience and logic, between logic and good sense. For the philosophy embodied in the formal theory of the syllogism asserted that thought or reason has fixed forms of its own, anterior to and independent of concrete subject-matters, and to which the latter have to be adapted whether or no. This defines the negative aspect of this discussion; and it shows by contrast the need of another kind of logic which shall reduce the influence of habit, and shall facilitate the use of good sense regarding matters of social consequence.

In other words, there are different logics in use. One of these, the one which has had greatest historic currency and exercised greatest influence on legal decisions, is that of the syllogism. To this logic the strictures of Justice Holmes apply in full force. For it purports to be a logic of rigid demonstration, not of search and discovery. . . .

It thus implies that for every possible case which may arise, there is a fixed antecedent rule already at hand; that the case in question is either simple and unambiguous, or is resolvable by direct inspection into a collection of simple and indubitable facts, such as Socrates is a man. It thus tends, when it is accepted, to produce and confirm what Professor Pound has called mechanical jurisprudence; it flatters that longing for certainty of which Justice Holmes speaks; it reinforces those inert factors in human nature which make me hug as long as possible any idea which has once gained lodgment in the mind. . . .

If we trust to an experimental logic, we find that general principles emerge as statements of generic ways in which it has been found helpful to treat concrete cases. The real force of the proposition that all men are mortal is found in the expectancy tables of insurance companies, which with their accompanying rates show how it is prudent and socially useful to deal with human mortality. The universal stated in the major premise is not outside of and antecedent to particular cases; neither is it a selection of something found in a variety of cases. It is an indication of a single way of treating cases for certain purposes or consequences in spite of their diversity. Hence its meaning and worth are subject to inquiry and revision in view of what happens, what the consequences are, when it is used as a method of treatment.

As a matter of fact, men do not begin thinking with premises. They begin with some complicated and confused case, apparently admitting of alternative modes of treatment and solution. Premises only gradually emerge from analysis of the total situation. The problem is not to draw a conclusion from given premises; that can best be done by a piece of inanimate machinery by fingering a keyboard. The problem is to *find* statements, of general principle and of particular fact, which are worthy to serve as premises. As matter of actual fact, we generally begin with some vague anticipation of a conclusion (or at least of alternative conclusions), and then we look around for principles and data which will substantiate it or which will enable us to choose intelligently between rival conclusions. No lawyer ever thought out the case of a client in terms of the syllogism. He begins with a conclusion which he intends to reach, favorable to his client of course, and then analyzes the facts of the situation to find material out of which to construct a favorable statement of facts, to *form* a minor premise. At the same time he goes over recorded cases to find rules of law employed in cases which can be presented as similar, rules which will substantiate a certain way of looking at and interpreting the facts. And as his acquaintance with rules of law judged applicable widens, he probably alters perspective and emphasis in selection of the facts which are to form his evidential data. And as he learns more of the facts of the case he may modify his selection of rules of law upon which he bases his case. . . .

Failure to recognize that general legal rules and principles are working hypotheses, needing to be constantly tested by the way in which they work out in application to concrete situations, explains the otherwise paradoxical fact that the slogans of the liberalism of one period often become the bulwarks of reaction in a subsequent era. There was a time in the eighteenth century when the great social need was emancipation of industry and trade from a multitude of restrictions which held over from the feudal estate of Europe. Adapted well enough to the localized and fixed conditions of that earlier age, they become hindrances and annoyances as the effects of methods, use of coal and steam, showed themselves. The movement of emancipation expressed itself in principles of liberty in use of property, and freedom of contract, which were embodied in a mass of legal decisions. But the absolutistic logic of rigid syllogistic forms infected these ideas. It was soon forgotten that they were relative to analysis of existing situations in order to secure orderly methods in behalf of economic social welfare. Thus these principles became in turn so rigid as to be almost as socially obstructive as "immutable" feudal laws had been in their day. . . .

If we recur then to our introductory conception that logic is really a theory about empirical phenomena, subject to growth and improvement like any other empirical discipline, we recur to it with an added conviction: namely, that the issue is not a purely speculative one, but implies consequences vastly significant for practise. I should indeed not hesitate to assert that the sanctification of ready-made antecedent universal principles as methods of thinking is the chief obstacle to the kind of thinking which is the indispensable prerequisite of steady, secure and intelligent social reforms in general and social advance by means of law in particular. If this be so infiltration into law of a more experimental and flexible logic is a social as well as an intellectual need. . . .

From Dewey (1924), "Logical Method and Law," *Cornell Law Quarterly.* 17, pp. 20–21, 22–23, 26–27.

READING 3-7

Fact Explosions

"Local Knowledge: Fact and Law in Comparative Perspective" (1973)

Clifford Geertz

. . . Explosion of fact, fear of fact, and, in response to these, sterilization of fact confound increasingly both the practice of law and reflection upon it.

The explosion of fact can be seen on all sides. There are the discovery procedures that produce paper warriors dispatching documents to each other in wheelbarrows and taking depositions from anyone capable of talking into a tape recorder. There is the enormous intricacy of commercial cases through which not even the treasurer of IBM much less a poor judge or juror could find his way. There is the vast increase in the use of expert witnesses; not just the icy pathologist and bubbling psychiatrist of long acquaintance but people who are supposed to know all about Indian burial grounds, Bayesian probability, the literary quality of erotic novels, the settlement history of Cape Cod, Filipino speech styles, or the conceptual mysteries—"What is a chicken? Anything that is not a duck, a turkey, or a goose"—of the poultry trade. There is the growth of public law litigation—class action, institutional advocacy, *amicus* [friend-of-the-court] pleading, special masters, and so on—which has gotten judges involved in knowing more about mental hospitals in Alabama, real estate in Chicago, police in Philadelphia, or anthropology departments in Providence than they might care to know. There is the technological restlessness, a sort of rage to invent, of contemporary life which brings such uncertain sciences as electronic bugging, voice printing, public opinion polling, intelligence testing, lie detecting and, in a famous instance, doll play under juridical scrutiny alongside the more settled ones of ballistics and fingerprinting. But most of all there is the general revolution of rising expectations as to the possibilities of fact determination and its power to settle intractable issues that the general culture of scientism has induced in us all; the sort of thing that perhaps led Mr. Justice Blackmun into the labyrinths of embryology (and now following him with less dispassionate intent, various congressmen) in search of an answer to the question of abortion.

The fear of fact that all this has stimulated in the law and its guardians is no less apparent. . . .

From Geertz (1973), *The Interpretation of Cultures.* New York: Basic Books, p. 171.

READING 3-8
Facts?
"What Are the Facts?" (1951)

Karl N. Llewellyn

What are *the facts?* The plaintiff's name is Atkinson and the defendant's Walpole. The defendant, despite his name, is an Italian by extraction, but the plaintiff's ancestors came over with the Pilgrims. The defendant has a schnautzer-dog named Walter, red hair, and $30,000 worth of life insurance. All these are facts. The case, however, does not deal with life insurance. It is about an auto accident. The defendant's auto was a Buick painted pale magenta. He is married. His wife was in the back seat, an irritable, somewhat faded blonde. She was attempting back-seat driving when the accident occurred. He had turned around to make objection. In the process the car swerved and hit the plaintiff. The sun was shining; there was a rather lovely dappled sky low to the West. The time was late October on a Tuesday. The road was smooth, concrete. It had been put in by the McCarthy Road Work

Company. How many of these facts are important to the decision? How many of these facts are, as we say, legally relevant? Is it relevant that the road was in the country or the city; that it was concrete or tarmac or of dirt; that it was a private or a public way? Is it relevant that the defendant was driving a Buick, or a motor car, or a vehicle? Is it important that he looked around as the car swerved? Is it crucial? Would it have been the same if he had been drunk, or had swerved for fun, to see how close he could run by the plaintiff, but had missed his guess?

Is it not obvious that as soon as you pick up this statement of the facts to find its legal bearings you must discard some as of no interest whatsoever, discard others as dramatic but as legal nothings? And is it not clear, further, that when you pick up the facts which are left and which do seem relevant, you suddenly cease to deal with them in the concrete and deal with them instead in *categories* which you, for one reason or another, deem significant? It is not the road between Pottsville and Arlington; it is "a highway." It is not a particular pale magenta Buick eight, by number 732507, but "a motor car," and perhaps even "a vehicle." It is not a turning around to look at Adorée Walpole, but a lapse from the supposedly proper procedure of careful drivers, with which you are concerned. Each concrete fact of the case arranges itself, I say, as the *representative* of a much wider abstract *category* of facts, and it is not in itself but as a member of the category that you attribute significance to it. But what is to tell you whether to make your category "Buicks" or "motor cars" or "vehicles"? What is to tell you to make your category "road" or "public highway"? The court may tell you. But the precise point that you have up for study is how far is it safe to trust what the court says. The precise issue which you are attempting to solve is whether the court's language can be taken as it stands, or must be amplified, or must be whittled down....

From Llewellyn (1951), *The Bramble Bush.* New York: Oceana, pp. 47–48.

READING 3-9

Fact Worship
"On Not Worshipping Facts" (1958)

J. R. Lucas

My sights in this paper are trained on facts. Most people think that they know what facts are; that while their friends often, and themselves occasionally, are ignorant of the facts, at least they know what sort of things facts are—they can recognise a fact when they see it. Facts, in the popular philosophy of today, are good, simple souls; there is no guile in them, nor any room for subjective bias, and once we have made ourselves acquainted with them, we have reached the beginning and summit of all wisdom.

This view is false; and not only false, but dangerously false. Facts are not at all what people think they are; they are not the simple solid elements out of which the whole fabric of our knowledge is constructed, and the belief that they are is responsible for many of the obsessions which afflict academics, not least the historians.

. . . We should be chary of making facts the cornerstone of our thinking, since at the higher levels of abstraction where philosophers talk about Acquaintance with Facts, and discuss the relations between True Propositions and Facts, too little context remains for any determinate meaning to survive. There are other words better suited to be philosophical specimens, which can stand being isolated and examined *in vacuo,* without losing their sense: it is in terms of these that a philosopher, when tempted to say something about Facts, should rephrase what he has to say, since then he is less likely to be misled.

That the meaning of the word "fact" is not the same in all cases can be brought out by Aristotle's Method of Opposites. We ask "What is it being contrasted with? Is it a fact as opposed to a fiction? Or as opposed to a theory? Or as opposed to an interpretation? Or a question of fact as opposed to a question of law?" This in itself is enough to show that there is no one unitary concept of fact, but rather a whole sheaf of concepts, bound together indeed, but distinct. More formal proofs can be produced: the fact/nonfact contrast may be used twice in the same sentence to make different distinctions; so that what are correctly described as facts according to one contrast are equally correctly not described as facts according to the other. . . .

To explain my first crude version of [the] meaning [of "fact"], I shall need to set it in the context of a *dialogue,* a *discussion,* or a *dispute. . . .*

In a dispute there is always some point at issue: but in any discussion that is to continue, there must also be many points which are common ground. It is fruitless to argue if we do not disagree about something: it is fruitless, too, to argue if we disagree about everything. We must start with some points of agreement if our discussion is to get us anywhere, and only by taking them as agreed and unquestionably true can we hope to reach agreement over the point at issue. These points of agreement we call *the facts.* On the basis of these we argue and may succeed in reaching a conclusion. If we do reach a conclusion, then this point now agreed between us will be *a fact* in any further dispute the pair of us may have. That is to say, a fact is a fact relative to a given dispute, or relative to two or more persons at a given time arguing about a given point. The points that both sides accept as true, each side will describe by the word "fact": points whose truth one side would challenge should not be called facts, unless their truth can be established on the basis of other facts, premises, that is, which are conceded as unquestionably true. The word "fact" is an incomplete symbol; the complete locution being "facts in respect of such and such a dispute." Before we can answer the question "What are the facts?" we need to know, either from the context or by being told explicitly, with respect to what dispute the question is being asked. This is the fundamental reason why we cannot talk of Facts with a big F: the word "fact" is an incomplete symbol, and as the issue in dispute varies, so also will the facts.

Let me take some examples. In a court of law there may be two sorts of issue in dispute: issues of fact and issues of law. In most criminal cases, it is a question only of determining what actually happened—a question of fact; while in many civil cases, the sole difficulty is to determine the correct interpretation of the law—a question of law; and there are yet other cases in

which the court has to decide both a question of fact and a question of law.
There will be rival accounts of what happened, but some things, different in
each case, will not be contested by either party: both plaintiff and defendant,
for example, might agree that plaintiff had chartered a ship from the defendants upon certain terms, and the ship had taken a cargo on board at Buenos
Aires and discharged it at Pembroke Dock. They disagree on other points—
the condition of the cargo before it was taken on board, whether it was properly examined in South America, when the deterioration took place, and
what was the cause; but there are some points they do agree about; and on
the basis of these and other facts, the court reaches a conclusion about what
actually happened. This question having been settled, it is no longer a point
in issue but becomes a *fact* with respect to the next question the court has to
address itself to, namely what the legal consequences are; that is to say, how
the law lays it down that cases like this are to be treated. . . .

A similar variableness appears in value-judgments. Very seldom is the
distinction between facts and values either as sharp as philosophers like to
think, or drawn where they think it ought to be drawn. Often the facts which
we adduce to support an evaluative conclusion, are not absolutely non-
evaluative themselves. In a dispute about a man's moral worth we claim,
and it will be conceded to us, that at least *this* action was generous and that
just, and it will be claimed against us, and we shall concede, that some other
deed was inexcusable and yet another difficult to defend. Again, in discussing the morality of euthanasia, we do not begin from facts purely "descriptive"; our starting point will be a mixture of "factual" facts—that there
are some painful diseases that are known to be incurable, some general
moral principles—that it is wrong to kill and wrong not to alleviate unnecessary suffering, (these are sometimes called "moral facts"), and some more
specific common moral judgments—that to kill a person in such and such
circumstances would be to murder him, and all these are usually described
by non-philosophers as facts. Only in the abstract examples invented by
philosophers is the sense of the word "fact" fixed, and only there can it be
equated to that which "descriptive" statements describe.

Even scientists determine what constitutes a fact by reference to the
questions in dispute. The Theory of Evolution, the Theory of Special Relativity, and Quantum Mechanics, started by being speculations, then became hypotheses, then were well-founded theories, and now can be described as facts.
They are the starting point for further discussion. . . .

In most cases where the word "fact" is used of a definite type of statement, an epistemological distinction between the more and the less certain
is being made, with the facts being those that are more certain and less dis-
putable than statements of some other, less favoured, type. . . .

. . . One weakness alone attaches to the method: as there are few facts, if
any, that we cannot in our metaphysical moments be uncertain of, our concept of truth is *regressive;* our criterion grows progressively and indefinitely
more stringent. At first we exclude those propositions of morals, theology and
metaphysics, whose elimination is welcome to many of the enlightened; but
the more we think, the more nice we become as to what are unquestionable
truths; and so the truths of logic, mathematics, and natural science, of common sense and everyday life, join the procession to the guillotine.

For there are no basic facts: there are only facts relative to a dispute. Since there is nothing that cannot on some occasion be reasonably doubted, there can be no truths established beyond doubt to all comers, no elemental facts which we just have to accept and on which all else is based. Nothing is never doubtful, though this is not to say that everything is always doubtful. In every dispute we have to start somewhere, though there is nowhere that is the starting point for every dispute.

This is a little too strong: though there is nothing we *cannot* doubt, there are many things that, apart from our metaphysical moments, we *do not* doubt: there is a core of accepted truths that are unquestioned by all people living at a given time, and unquestionable by any reasonable man at that time, not engaged in philosophy; and on these established platitudes, accepted by the many though not by the philosophers, we can base all our reasonable and practical contentions. These facts, adequate for our non-philosophical constructions, prove, however, shifting sands when we try to build a theory of knowledge or theory of truth upon them: because then we try to have our facts as basic facts, neutral elemental atoms, facts not with regard to this or that specifiable issue, but with regard to any conceivable issue; facts not in the context of a dispute between two actual or likely disputants, but in the context of any argument between any possible disputants whatsoever, or rather, facts in no context at all. We think too much of facts as hard, brute facts, existing independently of us and ineluctable, as things that are what they are, and whose consequences will be what they will be, and about which we must not seek to be deceived. Having hypostatised them, we bow down to them, and prostrate ourselves before them. It is unnecessary. It is impossible. Facts are not sacred: they are not worth worshipping: they do not exist: they are not even things.

READING 3-10

Issues of Fact Versus Issues of Law
Matters of Fact / Matters of Law (1972)

William R. Bishin and Christopher D. Stone

The matter of fact/matter of law dichotomy comes up in many contexts. . . . What are the differences; how does one distinguish a matter of fact from a matter of law? Is what people want to express by this dichotomy translatable into respectively different relationships the two classes of statement bear to "reality" and to "the law," so that the one is simply a report of what exists and the other a report of what a body of legal rules decrees?

Consider, for example, the two statements S(a) "defendant had a gun in his possession," and S(b) "defendant is guilty" (uttered by a duly appointed judge after a trial consistent with the authoritative procedures, etc.). The latter is, as clearly as can be, a statement of law, in the sense that its meaning cannot be understood independently of a body of rules and rituals; clearly S(b) involves far more than a report of "reality." But is the meaning of S(a) uninvolved in these same rules? Is the evidence on which a witness will utter S(a) to a policeman the same evidence, and does it require the same state of mind on his part, as that on which he will utter S(a) on the witness stand in a murder trial? Is it possible he might believe S(a) "true" for the first purpose (where the "rules" say that what he is saying will amount to the policeman's investigating Defendant's involvement a little more deeply) but not "true" for the second purpose (where the "rules" say that what he is saying will amount to increasing the probability of the jury bringing back a verdict of "guilty")? If so, does not the reason have to do with the fact that, in the second context, the meaning of S(a) is involved, albeit in a very complex way, with a statement of law? That is, can any statement of "fact" (ostensibly a report of reality) ever be wholly dissociated from a statement of "law" (ostensibly a report of the legal rules) when the "fact" will have "legal" consequences?

If there is some such complex involvement, how can "fact" and "law" be distinguished? Will the distinction always be the same? Are people always trying to attach the same consequences to a fact-law dichotomy in each context in which the dichotomy is invoked? Can we ever make an adequate general distinction between fact and law in epistemological terms, or do we have to look at particular types of cases, and include reference to institutional aims and rules? . . .

From Bishin and Stone (1972), *Law, Language, and Ethics.* Mineola, New York: The Foundation Press, p. 359.

READING 3-11

Legal Fictions at Work

Henningsen v. Bloomfield Motors, Inc., and Chrysler Corporation (1960)

Judge Benjamin Cardozo

The new Plymouth was turned over to the Henningsens on May 9, 1955. No proof was adduced by the dealer to show precisely what was done in the way of mechanical or road testing beyond testimony that the manufacturer's instructions were probably followed. Mr. Henningsen drove it from the dealer's place of business in Bloomfield to their home in Keansburg. On the trip nothing unusual appeared in the way in which it operated. Thereafter, it was used for short trips on paved streets about the town. It had no servicing and no mishaps of any kind before the event of May 19. That day, Mrs. Henningsen drove to Asbury Park. On the way down and in returning the car performed in normal fashion until the accident occurred. She was proceeding north on Route 36 in Highlands, New Jersey, at 20–22 miles per hour. The highway was paved and smooth, and contained two lanes for northbound travel. She was riding in the right-hand lane. Suddenly she heard a loud noise "from the bottom, by the hood." It "felt as if something cracked." The steering-wheel spun in her hands; the car veered sharply to the right and crashed into a highway sign and a brick wall. No other vehicle was in any way involved. A bus operator driving in the left-hand lane testified that he observed plaintiffs' car approaching in normal fashion in the opposite direction; "all of a sudden [it] veered at 90 degrees . . . and right into this wall." As a result of the impact, the front of the car was so badly damaged that it was impossible to determine if any of the parts of the steering wheel mechanism or workmanship or assembly were defective or improper prior to the accident. The condition was such that the collision insurance carrier, after inspection, declared the vehicle a total loss. It had 468 miles on the speedometer at the time.

The insurance carrier's inspector and appraiser of damaged cars, with 11 years of experience, advanced the opinion, based on the history and his examination, that something definitely went "wrong from the steering wheel down to the front wheels" and that the untoward happening must have been due to mechanical defect or failure; "something down there had to drop off or break loose to cause the car" to act in the manner described. . . .

Chrysler points out that an implied warranty of merchantability is an incident of a contract of sale. It concedes, of course, the making of the original sale to Bloomfield Motors, Inc., but maintains that this transaction marked the terminal point of its contractual connection with the car. Then Chrysler urges that since it was not a party to the sale by the dealer to Henningsen, there is no privity of contract between it and the plaintiffs, and the absence of this privity eliminates any such implied warranty.

There is no doubt that under early common-law concepts of contractual liability only those persons who were parties to the bargain could sue for a breach of it. In more recent times a noticeable disposition has appeared in a number of jurisdictions to break through the narrow barrier of privity when dealing with sales of goods in order to give realistic recognition to a universally accepted fact. The fact is that the dealer and the ordinary buyer do not, and are not expected to, buy goods, whether they be foodstuffs or automobiles, exclusively for their own consumption or use. Makers and manufacturers know this and advertise and market their products on that assumption; witness, the "family" car, the baby foods, etc. The limitations of privity in contracts for the sale of goods developed their place in the law when marketing conditions were simple, when maker and buyer frequently met face to face on an equal bargaining plane and when many of the products were relatively uncomplicated and conducive to inspection by a buyer competent to evaluate their quality. . . . With the advent of mass marketing, the manufacturer became remote from the purchaser, sales were accomplished through intermediaries, and the demand for the product was created by advertising media. In such an economy it became obvious that the consumer was the person being cultivated. Manifestly, the connotation of "consumer" was broader than that of "buyer." He signified such a person who, in the reasonable contemplation of the parties to the sale, might be expected to use the product. Thus, where the commodities sold are such that if defectively manufactured they will be dangerous to life or limb, then society's interests can only be protected by eliminating the requirement of privity between the maker and his dealers and the reasonably expected ultimate consumer. In that way the burden of losses consequent upon use of defective articles is borne by those who are in a position to either control the danger or make an equitable distribution of the losses when they do occur. . . .

Under modern conditions the ordinary layman, on responding to the importuning of colorful advertising, has neither the opportunity nor the capacity to inspect or to determine the fitness of an automobile for use; he must rely on the manufacturer who has control of its construction, and to some degree on the dealer who, to the limited extent called for by the manufacturer's instructions, inspects and services it before delivery. In such a marketing milieu his remedies and those of persons who properly claim through him should not depend "upon the intricacies of the law of sales. The obligation of the manufacturer should not be based alone on privity of contract. It should rest, as was once said, upon 'the demands of social justice.' " "If privity of contract is required," then, under the circumstances of modern merchandising, "privity of contract exists in the consciousness and understanding of all right-thinking persons."

Accordingly, we hold that under modern marketing conditions, when a manufacturer puts a new automobile in the stream of trade and promotes its purchase by the public, an implied warranty that it is reasonably suitable for use as such accompanies it into the hands of the ultimate purchaser. Absence of agency between the manufacturer and the dealer who makes the ultimate sale is immaterial.

From *Henningsen v. Bloomfield Motors, Inc., and Chrysler Corporation* (1960)161 A.2d 69.

DISCUSSION ISSUES

1. *Defense of Formalism.* A formalist might admonish a judge to strictly follow the rules laid out in the law. This advice has the advantages of (1) limiting judicial discretion, and (2) making the law more certain and predictable. The following is also true:

   > To be formalistic as a decisionmaker is to say that something is not my concern, no matter how compelling it may seem. When this attitude is applied to the budget crisis or to eviction of the starving, it seems objectionable. But when the same attitude of formalism requires judges to ignore the moral squalor of the Nazis or the Ku Klux Klan in the First Amendment cases, or the wealth of the plaintiff who seeks to recover for medical expenses occasioned by the defendant's negligence, it is no longer clear that refusal to take all factors into account is condemnible. (Schauer 1989, pp. 509)

   Should judges ignore these other factors?
2. *A Dilemma for Sophists.* Plato and Aristotle gave the term "sophist" a bad name. Aristotle described Sophists as those "who make money by sham wisdom" (Aristotle, *Sophistical Refutations* 165a22). Traveling from place to place, Sophists taught Greek citizens how to win lawsuits, among other things. Protagoras, the

first of the Sophists in Athens, posed the following dilemma involving two seemingly equally problematic choices:

> A law professor made a contract with a pupil on a contingent basis. The professor was not to be paid until his pupil won his first case as a lawyer. When the professor thought he had taught the pupil enough, he asked for his fee, but the pupil refused because he had not won his first case. The shrewd professor sued the pupil, since he thought he could not lose. If the professor won he would get a judgment against the pupil and thus get paid, whereas if he lost the pupil will have won his first case and the professor would be entitled to be paid, under the terms of the contract. At the trial, the pupil, in his first case ever, moved that there is a non-suit. The pupil explained that he could not lose because if he won the case he would not have to pay the professor, whereas if he lost he would not have won his first case and therefore would not have to pay, under the terms of the contract. (Harvey 1988)

Analyze the arguments.

3. *Logic and Meaning.* Analyze the following: "He who harms another should be punished. He who communicates an infectious disease to another person harms him. Therefore he who communicates an infectious disease to another person should be punished" (example from Paul E. Treusch *The Syllogism* as reprinted in Hall 1938, p. 552). Does the analysis turn on the logical structure or on the meaning of ambiguous terms such as *harms*?

4. *Logical Citizenship.* Kurt Gödel, called the greatest logician of all times, fled to the United States when the Nazis took over Austria. He had discovered a proof that no logical system could ever express all the truths of mathematics. While studying for his citizenship examination for the United States, Gödel notified his close friend Albert Einstein, the founder of relativity theory, that he had discovered a logical flaw in the Constitution. Gödel thought that the Constitution permitted the possibility that an evil dictatorship could arise in America. Einstein succeeded in quieting Gödel when he tried to bring this to the attention of the hearing judge. Harvard Law Professor Lawrence Tribe thinks that Gödel was perplexed by Article V (describing procedures for amending the Constitution), which does not place substantive constraints on how to amend the Constitution. If the proper procedures were followed, could an amendment eliminate the essential features of a democratic (republican) form of government and dissolve all protections of rights? (As adapted from Holt 1998, p. 92.) Was Gödel's worry a purely logical one?

5. *Facts and Values.* Geertz states that law is "part of a distinctive manner of imagining the real" (1973, p. 173). Is the law based, not on what happened, but on what the law sees as having happened? Geertz also says that "legal representation is normative from the start" (1973, p. 174). The law filters facts through rules of procedure, laws of evidence, and so forth. Does the law impose its values on the facts?

6. *Racism and Scientific Facts.* Sociologist James Davis described the widespread use of the one-drop rule to determine racial classifications (Davis 1991). In light of the following cases, is race a scientific fact? First, *Plessy v. Ferguson* (1896) established the "separate but equal" doctrine that governed race relations until 1954. A blond-haired, blue-eyed Homer Adolph Plessy denied that the statute barring Negroes from trains applied to him because he claimed not to be a Negro. As evidence, he cited the fact that he only had a black great-grandmother. His genealogy made him, at most, one-eighth Negro. The Court noted: "The pe-

tition for the writ of prohibition averred that petitioner was seven-eighths Caucasian and one-eighth African blood; that the mixture of colored blood was not discernible in him; and that he was entitled to every right, privilege, and immunity secured to citizens of the United States of the white race." However, the Court took judicial notice of the fact that a Negro was any person with any black ancestry (the one-drop rule).

Second, Mrs. Susie Phipps, was denied a passport since she had designated her color as "white." She asked the Louisiana courts to change the color designation on her deceased parents' birth certificates. The state presented genealogical evidence of her great-great-great-great-grandmother's black race. According to the state, "black" meant "having more than one-thirty-second black ancestry." Should the courts refuse to disturb the parents' racial designation? Should the courts reassert Phipps's legally black classification (see *Jane Doe v. Louisiana* 1986)?

7. *Anti-Racism and Social Science Facts.* Critics charged that the U.S. Supreme Court opinion in *Brown v. Board of Education* issued a decision based on issues of fact and not on issues of law. The Court had cited data and authorities from the social sciences to show that racial segregation had a particularly devastating effect on black persons. This led one lower court to conclude that "the existence or non-existence of injury to white or black children from integrated or segregated schooling is a matter of fact for judicial inquiry and was so treated in Brown" (*Stell v. Savannah-Chatham County Board of Education* 1963). If the evidence showed that black children suffered from integration, this would presumably favor a segregated school system. The appeals court rejected the claim that the decision in *Brown* turned on issues of fact. It found that the *Brown* court prohibited segregated schools on grounds of their inherent inequality (*Jackson Municipal School District v. Evers* 1966). Today, opponents of affirmative action charge that racial preferences make blacks feel inferior. Should cases dealing with segregation and affirmative action turn on issues of fact?

D. CONTROVERSIES: SOCIAL DARWINISM AND EUGENICS

1. Social Darwinism

Pragmatism was not the only turn-of-the-century philosophy that had a major and lasting impact on legal theory. British philosopher **Herbert Spencer** (1820–1903) saw all developmental processes as going through the same evolutionary stages of progression. He had an enormous influence on a group of American philosophers who were called Social Darwinists by their critics. Critics caricatured Social Darwinists as advocating a survival of the fittest in society, just as Darwin had for nature. Social Darwinism had little connection to Darwin's theory of evolution. Spencer defended the idea of ***laissez-faire,*** which opposes government intervention in economic affairs. He argued that individuals should be permitted to pursue their private interests without interference from the state. An economic sense of liberty pervaded the U.S. Supreme Court until the Court-packing crisis in 1937. Although the Court does not impose serious restraints on economic regulation today, understanding the 1905 *Lochner* case (see Reading 3-12) will aid in understanding contemporary debates about cases involving contraception (*Griswold* 1965) and abortion (*Roe* 1973, see chapter 6, p. 326). Should the Court give special protection to noneconomic values, such as autonomy and privacy? Is there a justification for the sharp decline in judicial protection of economic liberties and the dramatic rise in judicial intervention on behalf of noneconomic personal rights? The Court uses substantive due process to construct a policy position that protects economic freedoms in Lochner.

READING 3-12

Economic Freedom
Lochner v. New York (1905)

JUSTICE RUFUS PECKHAM, Opinion of the Court

... The mandate of the statute that "no employé shall be required or permitted to work," is the substantial equivalent of an enactment that "no employé shall contract or agree to work," more than ten hours per day, and as there is no provision for special emergencies the statute is mandatory in all cases. It is not an act merely fixing the number of hours which shall constitute a legal day's work, but an absolute prohibition upon the employer, permitting, under any circumstances, more than ten hours work to be done in his establishment. The employé may desire to earn the extra money, which would arise from his working more than the prescribed time, but this statute forbids the employer from permitting the employé to earn it.

The statute necessarily interferes with the right of contract between the employer and employés, concerning the number of hours in which the latter may labor in the bakery of the employer. The general right to make a contract in relation to his business is part of the liberty of the individual protected by the Fourteenth Amendment of the Federal Constitution.... Under that provision no State can deprive any person of life, liberty or property without due process of law. The right to purchase or to sell labor is part of the liberty protected by this amendment, unless there are circumstances which exclude the right. There are, however, certain powers, existing in the sovereignty of each State in the Union, somewhat vaguely termed police powers, the exact description and limitation of which have not been attempted by the courts. Those powers, broadly stated and without, at present, any attempt at a more specific limitation, relate to the safety, health, morals and general welfare of the public. Both property and liberty are held on such reasonable conditions as may be imposed by the governing power of the State in the exercise of those powers, and with such conditions the Fourteenth Amendment was not designed to interfere....

The State, therefore, has power to prevent the individual from making certain kinds of contracts, and in regard to them the Federal Constitution offers no protection. If the contract be one which the State, in the legitimate exercise of its police power, has the right to prohibit, it is not prevented from prohibiting it by the Fourteenth Amendment. Contracts in violation of a statute, either of the Federal or state government, or a contract to let one's property for immoral purposes, or to do any other unlawful act, could obtain no protection from the Federal Constitution, as coming under the liberty of person or of free contract. Therefore, when the State, by its legislature, in the assumed exercise of its police powers, has passed an act which seriously limits the right to labor or the right of contract in regard to their means of livelihood between persons who are *sui juris* (both employer and employé), it becomes of great importance to determine which shall prevail—the right of the individual to labor for such time as he may choose, or the right of the State to prevent the individual from laboring or from entering into any contract to labor, beyond a certain time prescribed by the State. . . .

The question whether this act is valid as a labor law, pure and simple, may be dismissed in a few words. There is no reasonable ground for interfering with the liberty of person or the right of free contract, by determining the hours of labor, in the occupation of a baker. There is no contention that bakers as a class are not equal in intelligence and capacity to men in other trades or manual occupations, or that they are not able to assert their rights and care for themselves without the protecting arm of the State, interfering with their independence of judgment and of action. They are in no sense wards of the State. Viewed in the light of a purely labor law, with no reference whatever to the question of health, we think that a law like the one before us involves neither the safety, the morals nor the welfare of the public, and that the interest of the public is not in the slightest degree affected by such an act. The law must be upheld, if at all, as a law pertaining to the health of the individual engaged in the occupation of a baker. It does not affect any other portion of the public than those who are engaged in that occupation. Clean and wholesome bread does not depend upon whether the baker works but ten hours per day or only sixty hours a week. The limitation of the hours of labor does not come within the police power on that ground. . . .

JUSTICE OLIVER WENDELL HOLMES, Dissenting

This case is decided upon an economic theory which a large part of the country does not entertain. If it were a question whether I agreed with that theory, I should desire to study it further and long before making up my mind. But I do not conceive that to be my duty, because I strongly believe that my agreement or disagreement has nothing to do with the right of a majority to embody their opinions in law. It is settled by various decisions of this court that state constitutions and state laws may regulate life in many ways which we as legislators might think as injudicious or if you like as tyrannical as this, and which equally with this interfere with the liberty to contract. Sunday laws and usury laws are ancient examples. A more modern one is the prohibition of lotteries. The liberty of the citizen to do as he likes so long as he does not interfere with the liberty of others to do the same, which has been a shibboleth for some well-known writers, is interfered with by school laws, by the Post Office, by every state or municipal institution which takes his money for purposes thought desirable, whether he likes it or not. The Fourteenth Amendment does not enact Mr. Herbert Spencer's Social Statics. The other day we sustained the Massachusetts vaccination law. . . . United States and state statutes and decisions cutting down the liberty to contract by way of combination are familiar to this court. . . . Two years ago we upheld the prohibition of sales of stock on margins or for future delivery in the constitution of California. . . . The decision sustaining an eight hour law for miners is still recent. . . . Some of these laws embody convictions or prejudices which judges are likely to share. Some may not. But a constitution is not intended to embody a particular economic theory, whether of paternalism and the organic relation of the citizen to the State or of *laissez faire*. It is made for people of fundamentally differing views, and the accident of our finding certain opinions natural and familiar or novel and even shocking ought not to conclude our judgment upon the question whether statutes embodying them conflict with the Constitution of the United States.

General propositions do not decide concrete cases. The decision will depend on a judgment or intuition more subtle than any articulate major premise. But I think that the proposition just stated, if it is accepted, will carry us far toward the end. Every opinion tends to become a law. I think that the word liberty in the Fourteenth Amendment is perverted when it is held to prevent the natural outcome of a dominant opinion, unless it can be said that a rational and fair man necessarily would admit that the statute proposed would infringe fundamental principles as they have been understood by the traditions of our people and our law. It does not need research to show that no such sweeping condemnation can be passed upon the statute before us. A reasonable man might think it a proper measure on the score of health. Men whom I certainly could not pronounce unreasonable would uphold it as a first instalment of a general regulation of the hours of work. Whether in the latter aspect it would be open to the charge of inequality I think it unnecessary to discuss.

From *Lochner v. New York* (1905), pp. 46, 52–55, 57, 59–60, 74–76.

---

2. Eugenics

Try to identify the author of the following:

> Some day we will realize that the prime duty, the inescapable duty of the good citizens of the right type is to leave his or her blood behind him in the world; and that we have no business to permit the perpetuation of citizens of the wrong type. The great problem of civilization is to secure a relative increase of the valuable as compared with the less valuable or obnoxious elements in the population. . . . The problem cannot be met unless we give full consideration to the immense influence of heredity. . . . I wish very much that the wrong people could be prevented entirely from breeding; and when the evil nature of these people is sufficiently flagrant, this should be done. Criminals should be sterilized and feebleminded persons forbidden to leave offspring behind. . . . The emphasis should be laid on getting desirable people to breed.

It would appear that this quotation might come from *Mein Kampf* by Adolf Hitler. Instead, the words are those of Theodore Roosevelt (1913 as quoted in Howard and Rifkin 1977, p. 47). This should give some context to Holmes's rejection of Social Darwinian economic theory and the acceptance of its public policy. Justice Holmes criticized the majority in Lochner for reading a particular economic theory into the Constitution. In the case presented in Reading 3-13 that upholds a sterilization law, did Holmes read a particular social theory into the Constitution? Commentators seldom quote Holmes's famous passage on realism in full: "The life of the law has not been logic: it has been experience. The felt necessities of the time, the prevalent moral and political theories, intuitions of public policy, avowed or unconscious, even the prejudices which judges share with their fellow-men, have had a good deal more to do than the syllogism in determining the rules by which men should be governed" (Holmes 1881 in 1991, p. 1). Is realism purely descriptive?

By 1931, thirty states had laws permitting the sterilization of the "least fit." These laws reflected the influence of **eugenics,** the study of methods to improve the human race by controlling reproduction. In 1883, the British scientist Francis Galton, a cousin of Charles Darwin, coined the word *eugenics,* from the Greek, "good in birth" or "noble in heredity." The eugenics movement had a powerful following and a strong influence. For example, along with IQ testing, it played a critical role in U.S. immigration policy (Rose et al. 1984). Eugenics reached its most barbarous state when the Nazi Eugenic Sterilization Law (1933) mandated sterilization "with respect to all people, institutionalized or not, who suffered from allegedly hereditary disabilities, including feeblemindedness, schizophrenia, epilepsy, blindness, severe drug or alcohol addiction and physical deformities that seriously interfered with locomotion or were grossly offensive" (Kevles 1985, p. 116). In 1939, Nazi eugenic and anti-Semitic policies merged and included euthanizing the mentally ill and Jews. Does this historical perspective take undue advantage of hindsight? Is there a universal principle or natural law at stake in the debate over sterilization laws?

READING 3-13
Sterilizing Imbeciles
Buck v. Bell (1927)

JUSTICE OLIVER WENDELL HOLMES, Opinion of the Court

This is a writ of error to review a judgment of the Supreme Court of Appeals of the State of Virginia, affirming a judgment of the Circuit Court of Amherst County, by which the defendant in error, the superintendent of the State Colony for Epileptics and Feeble Minded, was ordered to perform the operation of salpingectomy upon Carrie Buck, the plaintiff in error, for the purpose of making her sterile. . . . The case comes here upon the contention that the statute authorizing the judgment is void under the Fourteenth Amendment as denying to the plaintiff in error due process of law and the equal protection of the laws.

Carrie Buck is a feeble minded white woman who was committed to the State Colony above mentioned in due form. She is the daughter of a feeble minded mother in the same institution, and the mother of an illegitimate feeble minded child. She was eighteen years old at the time of the trial of her case in the Circuit Court, in the latter part of 1924. An Act of Virginia, approved March 20, 1924, recites that the health of the patient and the welfare of society may be promoted in certain cases by the sterilization of mental defectives, under careful safeguard, &c.; that the sterilization may be effected in males by vasectomy and in females by salpingectomy, without serious pain or substantial danger to life; that the Commonwealth is supporting in various institutions many defective persons who if now discharged would become a menace but if incapable of procreating might be discharged with safety and become self-supporting with benefit to themselves and to society; and that experience has shown that heredity plays an important part in the transmission of insanity, imbecility, &c. The statute then enacts that whenever the superintendent of certain institutions including the above named State Colony shall be of opinion that it is for the best interests of the patients and of society that an inmate under his care should be sexually sterilized, he may have the operation performed upon any patient afflicted with hereditary forms of insanity, imbecility, &c., on complying with the very careful provisions by which the act protects the patients from possible abuse. . . .

The attack is not upon the procedure but upon the substantive law. It seems to be contended that in no circumstances could such an order be justified. It certainly is contended that the order cannot be justified upon the existing grounds. The judgment finds the facts that have been recited and that Carrie Buck "is the probable potential parent of socially inadequate offspring, likewise afflicted, that she may be sexually sterilized without detriment to her general health and that her welfare and that of society will be promoted by her sterilization," and thereupon makes the order. In view of the general declarations of the legislature and the specific findings of the Court, obviously we cannot say as matter of law that the grounds do not exist, and if they exist they justify the result. We have seen more than once that the public welfare may call upon the best citizens for their lives. It would be strange if it could not call upon those who already sap the strength of the State for these lesser sacrifices, often not felt to be such by those concerned, in order to prevent our being swamped with incompetence. It is better for all the world, if instead of waiting to execute degenerate offspring for crime, or to let them starve for their imbecility, society can prevent those who are manifestly unfit from continuing their kind. The principle that sustains compulsory vaccination is broad enough to cover cutting the Fallopian tubes. . . . Three generations of imbeciles are enough.

From *Buck v. Bell* (1927) 274 US 205, pp. 205–207.

DISCUSSION ISSUES

1. *The Realism of Sterilization Laws.* Richard Posner praised Holmes's rhetoric in Buck v. Bell, even though he criticized the reasoning and result (Posner 1992a, p. xxvii). Peter Read Treach countered that rhetoric is intrinsically moral, making it a contradiction to characterize an opinion as good rhetoric but bad law and morals (Treach 1989, p. 1259). Does Holmes's *Buck* opinion provide a good example of realism gone amuck? Consider the following "facts":

Carrie Buck's illegitimate daughter was conceived when she was raped by the nephew of her guardian; Carrie Buck might not have been mentally retarded at all under current definitions of that term; and Carrie's daughter, the third generation of "imbeciles," died at seven of an infectious disease, but attended regular public schools and made the honor roll in the last years of her life. (Hayman and Levit 1994, p. 186, note 6)

War crimes' prosecutors, headed by an American team, accused Nazi doctors of performing forced sterilizations. Defense lawyers for the Nazi medical practitioners countered that American doctors also performed forced sterilizations, as illustrated by Holmes's opinion in *Buck*. Logic textbooks cite *tu quoque* ("you too") as a type of bad reasoning (informal fallacy). Prosecutors argued that support of sterilization from American doctors and lawyers does not excuse Nazi practices. Should an accuser's practices ever have any bearing on the moral assessment of a subject's acts? (The film *Judgment at Nuremberg* offers a dramatic representation of the sterilization issue.)

2. *Fundamental Values Against Sterilization.* In 1942, the Supreme Court invalidated Oklahoma's Habitual Criminal Sterilization Act *(Skinner v. Oklahoma)*. Justice William O. Douglas grounded the opinion on one of the "basic civil rights of man," the fundamental interest in procreation and marriage. Douglas's references to fundamental (universal?) values seem out of step with the judicial thinking of the time. Twenty-three years after the Skinner decision, Douglas revived appeals to fundamental values in *Griswold v. Connecticut* (1965), which soon took on a new life in the famous abortion decision, *Roe v. Wade* (1973, see chapter 6, page 326). Does sterilization "forever deprive a person of a basic liberty"? Does the *Skinner* decision reflect a judge's individual consciousness becoming the consciousness of the nation (White 1988, p. 410)?

3. *Bias For and Against Racism?* A tension exists between the pulls of neat formulations and the pushes for more realistic appraisals. In 1886, California became the first state to uphold a zoning ordinance that required laundries to be located in brick or stone buildings. Legal Realist Jerome Frank claimed that racial prejudice was the true basis of the opinion and said it should have read, "Chinese are obnoxious yellow aliens who should stay where they belong and not come into white neighborhoods" (Frank 1931, p. 37). The Board of Supervisors refused to issue a permit to Yick Wo and imprisoned him for illegally operating his laundry. Can judges mold the law to suit biased interests? The U.S. Supreme Court (*Yick Wo v. Hopkins* (1886)118 US 351) found the ordinance unconstitutional as a violation of equal protection. The Court found proof of prejudice because the Board of Supervisors denied permits to 200 Chinese nationals and granted them to all but one non-Chinese applicant. Thus, the Court inferred purposeful, hostile discrimination from data regarding the administration of a seemingly neutral law. Is this use of statistical and other empirical data the type of social science promoted by realists? Is a decision in favor of Yick Wo also biased? Does the Constitution protect groups from prejudice (see chapter 7, page 365)?

E. MORAL CONSTRUCTIVISM: JUDGES AS ETHICISTS

Neither formalists nor realists said very much about ethics, however moral questions continue to arise concerning their approaches. **Ronald Dworkin** (1931–), who ranks as one of the foremost philosophers of law today, has made an explicit attempt to bring moral philosophy to the forefront of legal theory. His work has also redirected the focus of legal theory. Previously, theorists concentrated on general questions about the nature of law but, since Dworkin, they have attended more to particular studies of judicial decision making. Dworkin received graduate degrees from Harvard University and Oxford University before obtaining a law degree at Harvard. He clerked for Judge Learned Hand, practiced law briefly, and then began teaching law and philosophy at Yale University. In 1969, he succeeded H.L.A. Hart as Professor of Jurisprudence at Oxford. He continues to teach at Oxford while holding a Professor of Law position at New York University. His works include *Taking Rights Seriously* (1977) and *Law's Empire* (1986). In some sense, Dworkin returns the debate to natural law. Although his work is difficult to classify, at one point he welcomed the label "natural law," while defending his theory against the dismissive charge that it was nothing more than natural law dressed in modern clothes (see Reading 3-14).

Dworkin criticized legal positivist Hart for leaving principles out of his account of law. According to Dworkin, Hart's primary and secondary rules tell only part of the story. Dworkin sees judges as making decisions using **rules, policies,** and **principles** (see Reading 3-15). The use of rules in judicial decision making seems relatively noncontroversial. Judges apply rules in clear and determinative cases, but they encounter problems in borderline cases where rules do not fit exactly. According to Hart, judges should act as deputy legislators in these difficult cases. They should make new laws based on policies that advance a collective goal, such as the general welfare. While Hart allows for judicial discretion and does not place moral limits on it, Dworkin challenges the use of policy to make these decisions. In its place, he proposes a constructivist interpretation of legal practice. Dworkin's judges use moral principles to decide hard cases such as *Everson,* a religious establishment case (see chapter 5, page 277). He believes that moral judges justify their decisions in principles.

Dworkin used *Riggs et al. v. Palmer* (1889) to demonstrate a court's use of principles. A legislature cannot anticipate every consequence, so the judiciary may have to step in and interpret what the legislature might not have intended. For example, the rules governing the formation of a will are typically straightforward and specific. On the thirteenth day of August, 1880, Francis B. Palmer made his last will and testament, giving a small amount to his two daughters, Mrs. Riggs and Mrs. Preston. He also gave a substantial portion of the remainder to his grandson, Elmer Palmer. During probate (the court procedure to determine whether a will is valid), the court found that the will followed the letter of the law. According to the will and following the plain meaning of the statute, Elmer should have received his inheritance, but he did not. The dissent adopted a formalist approach, contending that he would have found in favor of Elmer. Justice Gray stated: "[I]f I believed that the decision of the question could be affected by considerations of an equitable nature, I should not hesitate to assent to views which commend themselves to the conscience. But the matter does not lie within the domain of conscience. We are bound by the rigid rules of law."

One element arose that was outside the bounds of conscience according to Justice Gray. After making the will, Francis remarried and began to have second thoughts about giving so much of his estate to Elmer. Elmer, then, willfully murdered his grandfather. The majority court found that the legislature never intended that "a donee [recipient of gift] who murdered the testator [person who dies and leaves a will] to make the will operative should have any benefit from it." In other words, according to the court, the legislature could not have intended for a murderer to benefit from the murder. Elmer's act as a murderer deprived him of any interest in the estate.

According to Dworkin, the court majority in *Riggs* did not use typical formalist methods. Dworkin cited the following as examples of formalist methods: finding a statute's plain meaning, discovering a legislative purpose, reconstructing legislative intent, or employing any other method within the context of rules (see chapter 4 for a description of these approaches). Rather, the *Riggs* court invoked a principle, namely, "no person may profit from her or his wrong." Dworkin defines a principle as "a standard that is to be observed, not because it will advance or secure an economic, political, or social situation deemed desirable, but because it is a requirement of justice or fairness or some other dimension of morality." The *Riggs'* court explicitly stated the moral principle: "No one shall be permitted to profit by his fraud, or to take advantage of his own wrong, or to found any claim upon his own iniquity, or to acquire property by his own crime." Judges, allegedly, use moral principles to fill in the gaps in law. As the majority in *Riggs* noted,

> "There was a statute in Bologna that whoever drew blood in the streets should be severely punished and yet it was not held to apply to the case of a barber who opened a vein in the street. It is commanded in the Decalogue that no work shall be done on the Sabbath, and yet, giving the command a rational interpretation founded upon its design, the Infallible Judge held that it did not prohibit works of necessity, charity or benevolence on that day."

According to Dworkin, judges do not, as legal positivists suggest, simply resort to discretion. Rather, judges try to discover the best interpretation by asking which moral principle best fits and best justifies the relevant rules and the past decisions. When judges interpret in this way, they are not free to make up law. The past constrains, but it does not completely limit interpretation. Dworkin draws an analogy between judicial decision making and writing the next chapter to a chain novel. A new chapter to a novel must roughly fit the old for the story to have continuity. Judges, similarly, continue the previous legal story by portraying law in the best light. Beyond that, however, the judicial novelist needs to propose principles of political morality that best advance legal practice. Judges, in Dworkin's view, become like contributors to a chain novel, trying to find the best interpretation. The law, then, has an integrity, a moral force.

Dworkin further claims that **law as integrity** provides **right answers** to questions of law. Realists see judges as going outside the law to their moral and political values to make decisions when the law does not provide a clear answer. Dworkin, on the other hand, sees judges in these hard cases as digging deeper into the law to find the strongest moral and political principles that could justify an authoritative decision. **Hercules,** Dworkin's concept of an ideal judge, resorts to political morality in making decisions. When it comes to difficult cases, Hercules looks outside the positive law to find the right answer—not to religion, but to political morality. He shares the realists disdain for metaphysics. He does not find the right answer in some transcendent reality, but internally, within the integrity of legal practice. While judges can and do disagree about proposed right answers within their community of practice, they treat and experience the proposed right answer as having moral authority.

READING 3-14

Moral Principles in Law
"'Natural' Law Revisited" (1982)

Ronald Dworkin

Everyone likes categories, and legal philosophers like them very much. So we spend a good deal of time, not all of it profitably, labeling ourselves and the theories of law we defend. One label, however, is particularly dreaded: no one wants to be called a natural lawyer. Natural law insists that what the law is depends in some way on what the law should be. This seems metaphysical or at least vaguely religious. In any case it seems plainly wrong. If some theory of law is shown to be a natural law theory, therefore, people can be excused if they do not attend to it much further.

In the past several years, I have tried to defend a theory about how judges should decide cases that some critics (though not all) say is a natural law theory and should be rejected for that reason. I have of course made the pious and familiar objection to this charge, that it is better to look at theories than labels. But since labels are so much a part of our common intellectual life it is almost as silly to flee as to hurl them. If the crude description of natural law I just gave is correct, that any theory which makes the content of law sometimes depend on the correct answer to some moral question is a natural law theory, then I am guilty of natural law. I am not now interested, I should add, in whether this crude characterization is historically correct, or whether it succeeds in distinguishing natural law from positivist theories of law. My present concern is rather this. Suppose this *is* natural law. What in the world is wrong with it?

A. Naturalism

I shall start by giving the picture of adjudication I want to defend a name, and it is a name which accepts the crude characterization. I shall call this picture naturalism. According to naturalism, judges should decide hard cases by interpreting the political structure of their community in the following, perhaps special way: by trying to find the best *justification* they can find, in principles of political morality, for the structure as a whole, from the most profound constitutional rules and arrangements to the details of, for example, the private law of tort or contract. Suppose the question arises for the first time, for example, whether and in what circumstances careless drivers are liable, not only for physical injuries to those whom they run down, but also for any emotional damage suffered by relatives of the victim who are watching. According to naturalism, judges should then ask the following questions of the history (including the contemporary history) of their political structure. Does the best possible justification of that history suppose a principle according to which people who are injured emotionally in this way have a right to recover damages in court? If so, what, more precisely, is that principle? Does it entail, for example, that only immediate relatives of the person physically injured have that right? Or only relatives on the scene of the accident, who might themselves have suffered physical damage?

Of course a judge who is faced with these questions in an actual case cannot undertake anything like a full justification of all parts of the constitutional arrangement, statutory system and judicial precedents that make up his "law." I had to invent a mythical judge, called Hercules, with superhuman powers in order even to contemplate what a full justification of the entire system would be like. Real judges can attempt only what we might call a partial justification of the law. They can try to justify, under some set of principles, those parts of the legal background which seem to them immediately relevant, like, for example, the prior judicial decisions about recovery for various sorts of damage in automobile accidents. Nevertheless it is useful to describe this as a partial justification—as a part of what Hercules himself would do—in order to emphasize that, according to this picture, a judge should regard the law he mines and studies as embedded in a much larger system, so that it is always relevant for him to expand his investigation by asking whether the conclusions he reaches are consistent with what he would have discovered had his study been wider.

It is obvious why this theory of adjudication invites the charge of natural law. It makes each judge's decision about the burden of past law depend on his judgment about the best political justification of that law, and this is of course a matter of political morality. Before I consider whether this provides a fatal defect in the theory, however, I must try to show how the theory might work in practice. It may help to look beyond law to other enterprises in which participants extend a discipline into the future by re-examining its past. This process is in fact characteristic of the general activity we call interpretation, which has a large place in literary criticism, history, philosophy and many other activities. Indeed, the picture of adjudication I have just sketched draws on a sense of what interpretation is like in these various activities, and I shall try to explicate the picture through an analogy to literary interpretation. I shall, however, pursue that analogy in a special context designed to minimize some of the evident differences between law and literature, and so make the comparison more illuminating.

B. The Chain Novel

Imagine, then, that a group of novelists is engaged for a particular project. They draw lots to determine the order of play. The lowest number writes the opening chapter of a novel, which he then sends to the next number who is given the following assignment. He must add a chapter to that novel, which he must write so as to make the novel being constructed the best novel it can be. When he completes his chapter, he then sends the two chapters to the next novelist, who has the same assignment, and so forth. Now every novelist but the first has the responsibility of interpreting what has gone before in the sense of interpretation I described for a naturalist judge. Each novelist must decide what the characters are "really" like; what motives in fact guide them; what the point or theme of the developing novel is; how far some literary device or figure consciously or unconsciously used can be said to contribute to these, and therefore should be extended, refined, trimmed or dropped. He must decide all this in order to send the novel further in one direction rather than another. But all these decisions must be made, in accordance with the directions given, by asking which decisions make the continuing novel better as a novel. . . .

C. The Chain of Law

Naturalism is a theory of adjudication not of the interpretation of novels. But naturalism supposes that common law adjudication is a chain enterprise sharing many of the features of the story we invented. According to naturalism, a judge should decide fresh cases in the spirit of a novelist in the chain writing a fresh chapter. The judge must make creative decisions, but must try to make these decisions "going on as before" rather than by starting in a new direction as if writing on a clean slate. He must read through (or have some good idea through his legal training and experience) what other judges in the past have written, not simply to discover what these other judges have said, or their state of mind when they said it, but to reach an opinion about what they have collectively *done,* in the way that each of our novelists formed an opinion about the collective novel so far written. Of course, the best interpretation of past judicial decisions is the interpretation that shows these in the best light, not aesthetically but politically, as coming as close to the correct ideals of a just legal system as possible. Judges in the chain of law share with the chain novelists the imperative of interpretation, but they bring different standards of success—political rather than aesthetic—to bear on that enterprise.

The analogy shows, I hope, how far naturalism allows a judge's beliefs about the personal and political rights people have "naturally"—that is, apart from the law—to enter his judgments about what the law requires. It does not instruct him to regard these beliefs as the only test of law. A judge's background and moral convictions will influence his decisions about what legal rights people have under the law. But the brute facts of legal history will nevertheless limit the role these convictions can play in those decisions. The same distinction we found in literary interpretation, between interpretation and ideal, holds here as well. An Agatha Christie mystery thriller cannot be interpreted as a philosophical novel about the meaning of death even by someone who believes that a successful philosophical novel would be a greater literary achievement than a successful mystery. It cannot be interpreted that way because, if it is, too much of the book must be seen as accidental, and too little as integrated, in plot, style and trope, with its alleged genre or point. Interpreted that way it becomes a shambles and so a failure rather than a success at anything at all. In the same way, a judge cannot plausibly discover, in a long and unbroken string of prior judicial decisions in favor of the manufacturers of defective products, any principle establishing strong consumers' rights. For that discovery would not show the history of judicial practice in a better light; on the contrary it would show it as the history of cynicism and inconsistency, perhaps of incoherence. A naturalist judge must show the facts of history in the best light he can, and this means that he must not show that history as unprincipled chaos.

Of course this responsibility, for judges as well as novelists, may best be fulfilled by a dramatic reinterpretation that both unifies what has gone before and gives it new meaning or point. This explains why a naturalist decision, though it is in this way tied to the past, may yet seem radical. A naturalist judge might find, in some principle that has not yet been recognized in judicial argument, a brilliantly unifying account of past decisions that shows them in a better light than ever before. American legal education celebrates dozens of such events in our own history. In the most famous single common law decision in American jurisprudence, for example, Cardozo reinterpreted a variety of cases to find, in these cases, the principle on which the modern law of negligence was built.

Nevertheless the constraint, that a judge must continue the past and not invent a better past, will often have the consequence that a naturalist judge cannot reach decisions that he would otherwise, given his own political theory, want to reach. A judge who, as a matter of political conviction, believes in consumers' rights may nevertheless have to concede that the law of his jurisdiction has rejected this idea. It is in one way misleading to say, however, that he will be then forced to make decisions *at variance with* his political convictions. The principle that judges should decide consistently with principle, and that law should be coherent, is part of his convictions, and it is this principle that makes the decision he otherwise opposes necessary. . . .

READING 3-15

Rules, Policies, Principles, and Rights

"Taking Rights Seriously" (1977)

Ronald Dworkin

THE MODEL OF RULES

Rules, Principles, and Policies

I want to make a general attack on positivism, and I shall use H. L. A. Hart's version as a target, when a particular target is needed. My strategy will be organized around the fact that when lawyers reason or dispute about legal rights and obligations, particularly in those hard cases when our problems with these concepts seem most acute, they make use of standards that do not function as rules, but operate differently as principles, policies, and other sorts of standards. Positivism, I shall argue, is a model of and for a system of rules, and its central notion of a single fundamental test for law forces us to miss the important roles of these standards that are not rules.

I just spoke of 'principles, policies, and other sorts of standards'. Most often I shall use the term 'principle' generically, to refer to the whole set of these standards other than rules; occasionally, however, I shall be more precise, and distinguish between principles and policies. Although nothing in the present argument will turn on the distinction, I should state how I draw it. I call a 'policy' that kind of standard that sets out a goal to be reached, generally an improvement in some economic, political, or social feature of the community (though some goals are negative, in that they stipulate that some present feature is to be protected from adverse change). I call a 'principle' a standard that is to be observed, not because it will advance or secure an economic, political, or social situation deemed desirable, but because it is a requirement of justice or fairness or some other dimension of morality. Thus the standard that automobile accidents are to be decreased is a policy, and the standard that no man may profit by his own wrong a principle. The distinction can be collapsed by construing a principle as stating a social goal (*i.e.,* the goal of a society in which no man profits by his own wrong), or by construing a policy as stating a principle (*i.e.,* the principle that the goal the policy embraces is a worthy one) or by adopting the utilitarian thesis that principles of justice are disguised statements of goals (securing the greatest happiness of the greatest number). In some contexts the distinction has uses which are lost if it is thus collapsed.

The difference between legal principles and legal rules is a logical distinction. Both sets of standards point to particular decisions about legal obligation in particular circumstances, but they differ in the character of the direction they give. Rules are applicable in an all-or-nothing fashion. If the facts a rule stipulates are given, then either the rule is valid, in which case the answer it supplies must be accepted, or it is not, in which case it contributes nothing to the decision. . . .

This first difference between rules and principles entails another. Principles have a dimension that rules do not—the dimension of weight or importance. When principles intersect (the policy of protecting automobile consumers intersecting with principles of freedom of contract, for example), one who must resolve the conflict has to take into account the relative weight of each. This cannot be, of course, an exact measurement, and the judgment that a particular principle or policy is more important than another will often be a controversial one. Nevertheless, it is an integral part of the concept of a principle that it has this dimension, that it makes sense to ask how important or how weighty it is.

Rules do not have this dimension. We can speak of rules as being *functionally* important or unimportant (the baseball rule that three strikes are out is more important than the rule that runners may advance on a balk, because the game would be much more changed with the first rule altered than the second). In this sense, one legal rule may be more important than another because it has a greater or more important role in regulating behavior. But we cannot say that one rule is more important than another within the system of rules, so that when two rules conflict one supersedes the other by virtue of its greater weight.

If two rules conflict, one of them cannot be a valid rule. The decision as to which is valid, and which must be abandoned or recast, must be made by appealing to considerations beyond the rules themselves. A legal system might regulate such conflicts by other rules, which prefer the rule enacted by the higher authority, or the rule enacted later, or the more specific rule, or something of that sort. A legal system may also prefer the rule supported by the more important principles. (Our own legal system uses both of these techniques.) . . .

HARD CASES

. . . Legal positivism provides a theory of hard cases. When a particular lawsuit cannot be brought under a clear rule of law, laid down by some institution in advance, then the judge has, according to that theory, a 'discretion' to decide the case either way. His opinion is written in language that seems to assume that one or the other party had a preexisting right to win the suit, but that idea is only a fiction. In reality he has legislated new legal rights, and then applied them retrospectively to the case at hand. In the last [section] I argued that this theory of adjudication is wholly inadequate; [here] I shall describe and defend a better theory.

I shall argue that even when no settled rule disposes of the case, one party may nevertheless have a right to win. It remains the judge's duty, even in hard cases, to discover what the rights of the parties are, not to invent new rights retrospectively. I should say at once, however, that it is no part of this theory that any mechanical procedure exists for demonstrating what the rights of parties are in hard cases. On the contrary, the argument supposes that reasonable lawyers and judges will often disagree about legal rights, just as citizens and statesmen disagree about political rights. . . .

The Rights Thesis

Principles and Policies

. . . Theories of adjudication have become more sophisticated, but the most popular theories still put judging in the shade of legislation. The main outlines of this story are familiar. Judges should apply the law that other institutions have made; they should not make new law. That is the ideal, but for different reasons it cannot be realized fully in practice. Statutes and common law rules are often vague and must be interpreted before they can be applied to novel cases. Some cases, moreover, raise issues so novel that they cannot be decided even by stretching or reinterpreting existing rules. So judges must sometimes make new law, either covertly or explicitly. But when they do, they should act as deputy to the appropriate legislature, enacting the law that they suppose the legislature would enact if seized of the problem.

That is perfectly familiar, but there is buried in this common story a further level of subordination not always noticed. When judges make law, so the expectation runs, they will act not only as deputy to the legislature but as a deputy legislature. They will make law in response to evidence and arguments of the same character as would move the superior institution if it were acting on its own. This is a deeper level of subordination, because it makes any understanding of what judges do in hard cases parasitic on a prior understanding of what legislators do all the time. This deeper subordination is thus conceptual as well as political.

In fact, however, judges neither should be nor are deputy legislators, and the familiar assumption, that when they go beyond political decisions already made by someone else they are legislating, is misleading. It misses the importance of a fundamental distinction within political theory, which I shall now introduce in a crude form. This is the distinction between arguments of principle on the one hand and arguments of policy on the other.

Arguments of policy justify a political decision by showing that the decision advances or protects some collective goal of the community as a whole. The argument in favor of a subsidy for aircraft manufacturers, that the subsidy will protect national defense, is an argument of policy. Arguments of principle justify a political decision by showing that the decision respects or secures some individual or group right. The argument in favor of anti-discrimination statutes, that a minority has a right to equal respect and concern, is an argument of principle. . . .

Legal Rights

Legislation

Legal argument, in hard cases, turns on contested concepts whose nature and function are very much like the concept of the character of a game. These include several of the substantive concepts through which the law is stated, like the concepts of a contract and of property. But they also include two concepts of much greater relevance to the present argument. The first is the idea of the 'intention' or 'purpose' of a particular statute or statutory clause. This concept provides a bridge between the political justification of the general idea that statutes create rights and those hard cases that ask what rights a particular statute has created. The second is the concept of principles that 'underlie' or are 'embedded in' the positive rules of law. This concept provides a bridge between the political justification of the doctrine that like cases should be decided alike and those hard cases in which it is unclear what that general doctrine requires. These concepts together define legal rights as a function, though a very special function, of political rights. If a judge accepts the settled practices of his legal system—if he accepts, that is, the autonomy provided by its distinct constitutive and regulative rules—then he must, according to the doctrine of political responsibility, accept some general political theory that justifies these practices. The concepts of legislative purpose and common law principles are devices for applying that general political theory to controversial issues about legal rights.

We might therefore do well to consider how a philosophical judge might develop, in appropriate cases, theories of what legislative purpose and legal principles require. We shall find that he would construct these theories in the same manner as a philosophical referee would construct the character of a game. I have invented, for this purpose, a lawyer of superhuman skill, learning, patience and acumen, whom I shall call Hercules. I suppose that Hercules is a judge in some representative American jurisdiction. I assume that he accepts the main uncontroversial constitutive and regulative rules of the law in his jurisdiction. He accepts, that is, that statutes have the general power to create and extinguish legal rights, and that judges have the general duty to follow earlier decisions of their court or higher courts whose rationale, as lawyers say, extends to the case at bar.

I. The constitution. Suppose there is a written constitution in Hercules' jurisdiction which provides that no law shall be valid if it establishes a religion. The legislature passes a law purporting to grant free busing to children in parochial schools. Does the grant establish a religion? The words of the constitutional provision might support either view. Hercules must nevertheless decide whether the child who appears before him has a right to her bus ride.

He might begin by asking why the constitution has any power at all to create or destroy rights. If citizens have a background right to salvation through an established church, as many believe they do, then this must be an important right. Why does the fact that a group of men voted otherwise several centuries ago prevent this background right from being made a legal right as well? His answer must take some form such as this. The constitution sets out a general political scheme that is sufficiently just to be taken as settled for reasons of fairness. Citizens take the benefit of living in a society whose institutions are arranged and governed in accordance with that scheme, and they must take the burdens as well, at least until a new scheme is put into force either by discrete amendment or general revolution. But Hercules must then ask just what scheme of principles has been settled. He must construct, that is, a constitutional theory; since he is Hercules we may suppose that he can develop a full political theory that justifies the constitution as a whole. It must be a scheme that fits the particular rules of this constitution, of course. It cannot include a powerful background right to an established church. But more than one fully specified theory may fit the specific provision about religion sufficiently well. One theory might provide, for example, that it is wrong for the government to enact any legislation that will cause great social tension or disorder; so that since the establishment of a church will have that effect, it is wrong to empower the legislature to establish one. Another theory will provide a background right to religious liberty, and therefore argue that an established church is wrong, not because it will be socially disruptive, but because it violates that background right. In that case Hercules must turn to the remaining constitutional rules and settled practices under these rules to see which of these two theories provides a smoother fit with the constitutional scheme as a whole.

F. CONTROVERSIES: SLAVERY AND APARTHEID

Slavery in the United States and apartheid in South Africa posed dilemmas for moral judges. Should judges confine themselves to the positive law? What if the positive law violated a higher moral principle or natural law? Should judges enforce unjust laws? In the context of an unjust law or an immoral legal system, consider the following questions: What discretion should judges have? Should they insert value judgments into vague or ambiguous statutory language to further the cause of justice? Should they act as policy makers? Should they appeal to moral principles consistent with the legal system and its history? Consider the following issues in light of these questions.

1. Slave Trade

The U.S. Congress prohibited slave trade in 1809 and passed laws punishing those engaged in slave trade. When the U.S. government later claimed title to a French slave-trading vessel it captured, Supreme Court Justice Story, sitting as a Circuit Court Judge, appealed to violations of natural law and upheld the title.

> Now in respect to the African slave trade . . . it cannot admit of serious question, that it is founded in a violation of some first principles, which ought to govern nations. It is repugnant to the great principles of Christian duty, the dictates of natural religion, the obligations of good faith and morality, and the external maxims of social justice. When any trade can be truly said to have these ingredients, it is impossible, that it can be consistent with any system of law, that purports to rest on the authority of reason or revelation. And it is sufficient to stamp any trade as interdicted by public law, when it can be justly affirmed, that it is repugnant to the general principles of justice and humanity." (*United States v. La Jeune* 1822)

In 1821, pirates captured *The Antelope,* a ship carrying 281 slaves, off the coast of Georgia (see Reading 3-15). U.S. Chief Justice John Marshall upheld a Spanish claim to have some of its property, the African slaves seized by an American vessel, returned to it. Does it make sense to hold that, while slavery is contrary to the law of nature, the judiciary should uphold the laws of nations that allow slavery?

The fugitive slave clause in the U.S. Constitution reads:

> No person held to service or labor in one state, under the laws thereof, escaping into another, shall, in consequence of any law or regulation therein, be discharged from such service or labor, but shall be delivered up on claim of any party to whom such service or labor may be due. (U.S. Constitution. Art IV, para 2, cl. 3)

However, some judges and justices expressed their personal misgivings about the law. Supreme Court Justice Joseph Story wrote to a friend that "[y]ou know full well that I have ever been opposed to slavery. But I take my standard of duty as a judge from the Constitution" (Cover 1975, p. 119). Justice Story made that statement after he authored the Supreme Court decision upholding, in dictum (nonbinding remarks made by judges), the Fugitive Slave Act (*Prigg v. Pennsylvania* 1842). The Supreme Court upheld the constitutionality of the law (*Jones v. Van Zandt* 1847) and, since the Supreme Court upheld the constitutionality of the act, it stood as a valid law. Some southern judges also had difficulty reconciling their personal opposition to slavery with their obligation to uphold slavery laws. In *State v. Mann* (see Reading 3-16), Judge Ruffin overturned the conviction of a defendant who shot and wounded his slave when she tried to run off.

Northern abolitionists placed great hope in a decision by Lemuel Shaw, Chief Justice of the Supreme Judicial Court of Massachusetts. Shaw had ruled that "an owner of a slave in another State where slavery is warranted by law, voluntarily bringing such a slave into this State, has no authority to detain him against his will, or to carry him out of the State against his consent, for the purpose of being held in slavery" (*Commonwealth v. Aves* 1836). However, their hopes turned to despair when Justice Shaw ruled on the Fugitive Slave Act (1793, 1850), which enacted procedures by which a fugitive slave in a free state could be returned to her or his master. Northern judges felt duty bound to uphold the law despite their personal misgivings. In the Thomas Sims case (1851), Justice Shaw enforced the Fugitive Slave Act by having Sims, who had escaped, returned to his master, a rice planter in Georgia. Robert M. Cover (see Reading 3-18) hypothesized that Herman Melville modeled Captain Vere in *Billy Budd* after Judge Shaw, who was Melville's father-in-law. Although Vere regarded Billy as innocent, he ordered him hung for killing under extreme provocation. How should judges resolve these clashes between justice and law, if that correctly describes their dilemma? On returning to Georgia, Sims received a public whipping and became a laborer (Finkelman 1985). Shaw's decision provoked a heated debate among abolitionists. In an attempt to attain more control over the judiciary, many abolitionists demanded that judges be elected; others argued for an independent judiciary despite its flaws. In Reading 3-19, John Mackie questions Dworkin's analysis of cases that arose under the Fugitive Slave Act.

READING 3-16

Slavery, Not Contrary to the Law of Nations
United States v. The Antelope (1825)

CHIEF JUSTICE JOHN MARSHALL

The question, whether the slave trade is prohibited by the law of nations has been seriously propounded, and both the affirmative and negative of the proposition have been maintained with equal earnestness.

That it is contrary to the law of nature will scarcely be denied. That every man has a natural right to the fruits of his own labour, is generally admitted; and that no other person can rightfully deprive him of those fruits, and appropriate them against his will, seems to be the necessary result of this admission. But from the earliest times war has existed, and war confers rights in which all have acquiesced. Among the most enlightened nations of antiquity, one of these was, that the victor might enslave the vanquished. This, which was the usage of all, could not be pronounced repugnant to the law of nations, which is certainly to be tried by the test of neral usage. That which has received the assent of all, must be the law of all.

Slavery, then, has its origin in force; but as the world has agreed that it is a legitimate result of force, the state of things which is thus produced by general consent, cannot be pronounced unlawful. . . .

No principle of general law is more universally acknowledged, than the perfect equality of nations. Russia and Geneva have equal rights. It results from this equality, that no one can rightfully impose a rule on another. Each legislates for itself, but its legislation can operate on itself alone. A right, then, which is vested in all by the consent of all, can be devested only by consent; and this trade, in which all have participated, must remain lawful to those who cannot be induced to relinquish it. As no nation can prescribe a rule for others, none can make a law of nations; and this traffic remains lawful to those whose governments have not forbidden it. . . .

The Courts of no country execute the penal laws of another; and the course of the American government on the subject of visitation and search, would decide any case in which that right had been exercised by an American cruiser, on the vessel of a foreign nation, not violating our municipal laws, against the captors.

It follows, that a foreign vessel engaged in the African slave trade, captured on the high-seas in time of peace, by an American cruiser, and brought in for adjudication, would be restored. . . .

From *The Antelope* (1825) 23 US 66, pp. 120–123.

An Attractive and Repulsive Judicial Opinion
State v. Mann (1829)

JUDGE RUFFIN

A Judge cannot but lament when such cases as the present are brought into judgment. It is impossible that the reasons on which they go can be appreciated, but where institutions similar to our own, exist and are thoroughly understood. The struggle, too, in the Judge's own breast between the feelings of the man, and the duty of the magistrate is a severe one, presenting strong temptation to put aside such questions, if it be possible. It is useless however, to complain of things inherent in our political state. And it is criminal in a Court to avoid any responsibility which the laws impose. With whatever reluctance therefore it is done the Court is compelled to express an opinion upon the extent of the dominion of the master over the slave in North Carolina.

The indictment charges a battery [unlawful use of force] on *Lydia,* a slave of Elizabeth Jones. . . . Here the slave had been hired by the Defendant, and was in his possession and the battery was committed during the period of hiring. . . . The enquiry here is, whether a cruel and unreasonable battery on a slave, by the hirer, is indictable. The Judge below instructed the Jury, that it is. He seems to have put it on the ground, that the Defendant had but a special property. Our laws uniformly treat the master or other person having the possession and command of the slave, as entitled to the same extent of authority. The object is the same—the services of the slave; and the same powers must be confided. In a criminal proceeding, and indeed in reference to all other persons but the general owner, the hirer and possessor of a slave, in relation to both rights and duties, is, for the time being, the owner. . . .

[U]pon the general question, whether the owner is answerable *criminaliter,* for a battery upon his own slave, or other exercise of authority or force, not forbidden by statute, the Court entertains but little doubt.—That he is so liable, has never yet been decided; nor, as far as is known, been hitherto contended. There have been no prosecutions of the sort. The established habits and uniform practice of the country in this respect, is the best evidence of the portion of power, deemed by the whole community, requisite to the preservation of the master's dominion. If we thought differently, we could not set our notions in array against the judgment of everybody else, and say that this, or that authority, may be safely lopped off. This has indeed been assimilated at the bar to the other domestic relations; and arguments drawn from the well established principles, which confer and restrain the authority of the parent over the child, the tutor over the pupil, the master over the apprentice, have been pressed on us. The Court does not recognize their application. There is no likeness between the cases. They are in opposition to each other, and there is an impassable gulf between them. The difference is that which exists between freedom and slavery—and a greater cannot be imagined. In the one, the end in view is the happiness of the youth, born to equal rights with that governor, on whom the duty devolves of training the young to usefulness, in a station which he is afterwards to assume among freemen. To such an end, and with such a subject, moral and intellectual instruction seem the natural means; and for the most part, they are found to suffice. Moderate force is superadded, only to make the others effectual. If that fails, it is better to leave the party to his own headstrong passions, and the ultimate correction of the law, than to allow it to be immoderately inflicted by a private person. With slavery it is far otherwise. The end is the profit of the master, his security and the public safety; the subject, one doomed in his own person, and his posterity, to live without knowledge, and without the capacity to make any thing his own, and to toil that another may reap the fruits. What moral considerations shall be addressed to such a being, to convince him what, it is impossible but that the most stupid must feel and know can never be true—that he is thus to labor upon a principle of natural duty, or for the sake of his own personal happiness, such services can only be expected from one who has no will of his own; who surrenders his will in implicit obedience to that of another. Such obedience is the consequence only of uncontrolled authority over the body. There is nothing else which can operate to produce the effect. The power of the master must be absolute, to render the submission of the slave perfect. I most freely confess my sense of the harshness of this proposition, I feel it as deeply as any man can. And as a principle of moral right, every person in his retirement must repudiate it. But in the actual condition of things, it must be so.—There is no remedy. This discipline belongs to the state of slavery. They cannot be disunited, without abrogating at once the rights of the master, and absolving the slave from his subjection. It constitutes the curse of slavery to both the bond and free portions of our population. But it is inherent in the relation of master and slave.

That there may be particular instances of cruelty and deliberate barbarity, where, in conscience the law might properly interfere, is most probable. The difficulty is to determine, where *a Court* may properly begin. Merely in the abstract it may well be asked, which power of the master accords with right. The answer will probably sweep away all of them. But we cannot look at the matter in that light. The truth is, that we are forbidden to enter upon a train of general reasoning on the subject. We cannot allow the right of the master to be brought into discussion in the Courts of Justice. The slave, to remain a slave, must be made sensible, that there is no appeal from his master; that his power is in no instance, usurped; but is conferred by the laws of man at least, if not by the law of God. The danger would be great indeed, if the tribunals of justice should be called on to graduate the punishment appropriate to every temper, and every dereliction of menial duty. No man can anticipate the many and aggravated provocations of the master, which the slave would be constantly stimulated by his own passions, or the instigation of others to give; or the consequent wrath of the master, prompting him to bloody vengeance, upon the turbulent traitor—a vengeance generally practised with impunity, by reason of its privacy. The Court therefore disclaims the power of changing the relation, in which these parts of our people stand to each other.

We are happy to see, that there is daily less and less occasion for the interposition of the Courts. The protection already afforded by several statutes, that all powerful motive, the private interest of the owner, the benevolences towards each other, seated in the hearts of those who have been born and bred together, the frowns and deep execrations of the community upon the barbarian, who is guilty of excessive and brutal cruelty to his unprotected slave, all combined, have produced a mildness of treatment, and attention to the comforts of the unfortunate class of slaves, greatly mitigating the rigors of servitude, and ameliorating the condition of the slaves. The same causes are operating, and will continue to operate with increased action, until the disparity in numbers between the whites and blacks, shall have rendered the latter in no degree dangerous to the former, when the police now existing may be further relaxed. This result, greatly to be desired, may be much more rationally expected from the events above alluded to, and now in progress, than from any rash expositions of abstract truths, by a Judiciary tainted with a false and fanatical philanthropy, seeking to redress an acknowledged evil, by means still more wicked and appalling than even that evil.

I repeat, that I would gladly have avoided this ungrateful question. But being brought to it, the Court is compelled to declare, that while slavery exists amongst us in its present state, or until it shall seem fit to the Legislature to interpose express enactments to the contrary, it will be the imperative duty of the Judges to recognize the full dominion of the owner over the slave, except where the exercise of it is forbidden by statute. And this we do upon the ground, that this dominion is essential to the value of slaves as property, to the security of the master, and the public tranquility, greatly dependent upon their subordination; and in fine, as most effectually securing the general protection and comfort of the slaves themselves.

Per Curiam. Let the judgment below be reversed and judgment entered for the Defendant.

From *State v. Mann* (1829) 13 NC 263.

READING 3-18

Judges Collaborating in Slavery
"Of Creon and Captain Vere" (1971)

Robert Cover

The judicial conscience is an artful dodger and rightfully so. Before it will concede that a case is one that presents a moral dilemma, it will hide in the nooks and crannies of the professional ethics, run to the caves of role limits, seek the shelter of separation of powers. And, indeed, it is right and fitting that such insulation exists. As Professor Herbert Wechsler has written:

> ... one of the ways in which a rich society avoids what might otherwise prove
> to be insoluble dilemmas of choice is to recognize a separation of functions,
> a distribution of responsibilities, with respect to problems of that kind, and
> this is particularly recurrent in the legal profession.

But with all its resources for avoiding definition of judicial problems as moral ones, it is yet possible to trap the elusive creature. There must be a doctrinal situation that leaves the judge sufficiently little room for maneuver and a dialectical situation that forces the judge to move beyond the pat and normally sufficient answer of reiteration of role expectations. . . .

Melville's Captain Vere in *Billy Budd* is one of the few examples of an attempt to portray the conflict patterns of Creon or Creon's minions in a context more nearly resembling the choice situations of judges in modern legal systems. Billy Budd, radical innocence personified, is overwhelmed by a charge of fomenting mutiny, falsely levied against him by the first mate Claggart. Claggart seems to personify dark and evil forces. Struck dumb by the slanderous charges, Billy strikes out and kills the mate with a single blow. Captain Vere must instruct a drumhead court on the law of the Mutiny Act as it is to be applied to Billy Budd—in some most fundamental sense "innocent," though perpetrator of the act of killing the first mate. In what must be, for the legal scholar, the high point of the novella, Vere articulates the "scruples" of the three officers (and his own) and rejects them.

> How can we adjudge to summary and shameful death a fellow creature innocent before God, and whom we feel to be so?—Does that state it aright? You sign sad assent. Well, I too feel that, the full force of that. It is Nature. But do these buttons that we wear attest that our allegiance is to Nature? No, to the King.

And, but a few paragraphs farther on, Vere asks the three whether "occupying the position we do, private conscience should not yield to that imperial one formulated in the code under which alone we officially proceed."

In Vere's words we have a positivist's condensation of a legal system's formal character. Five aspects of that formalism may be discerned and specified: First, there is explicit recognition of the role character of the judges—a consciousness of the formal element. It is a uniform, not nature, that defines obligation. Second, law is distinguished from both the transcendent and the personal sources of obligation. The law is neither nature nor conscience. Third, the law is embodied in a readily identifiable source which governs transactions and occurrences of the sort under consideration: here an imperial code of which the Mutiny Act is a part. Fourth, the will behind the law is vague, uncertain, but *clearly not* that of the judges. It is here "imperial will" which, in (either eighteenth- or) nineteenth-century terms as applied to England, is not very easy to describe except through a constitutional law treatise. But, in any event, it is not the will of Vere and his three officers. Fifth, a corollary of the fourth point, the judge is not responsible for the content of the law but for its straightforward application.

> For that law and the rigor of it, we are not responsible. Our vowed responsibility is in this: That however pitilessly that law may operate in any instances, we nevertheless adhere to it and administer it.

. . . I venture to suggest that Melville had a model for Captain Vere that may bring us very close to our main story. Melville's father-in-law was Chief Justice Lemuel Shaw of the Massachusetts Supreme Judicial Court. A firm, unbending man of stern integrity, Shaw dominated the Massachusetts judicial system very much as Captain Vere ran his ship. The Chief Justice was a noted, strong opponent to slavery and expressed his opposition privately, in print, and in appropriate judicial opinions. Yet, in the great causes célèbres involving fugitive slaves, Shaw came down hard for an unflinching application of the harsh and summary law. The effort cost Shaw untold personal agony. He was villified by abolitionists. I cannot claim that Vere is Lemuel Shaw (though he might be), for there is no direct evidence. I can only say that it would be remarkable that in portraying a man caught in the horrible conflict between duty and conscience, between role and morality, between nature and positive law, Melville would be untouched by the figure of his father-in-law in the *Sims Case,* the Latimer affair, or the Burns controversy. We know Melville's predilection to the ship as microcosm for the social order. He used the device quite plainly with respect to slavery in *Benito Cereno.*

The fugitive slave was very Budd-like, though he was as black as Billy was blonde. The Mutiny Act admitted of none of the usual defenses, extenuations, or mitigations. If the physical act was that of the defendant, he was guilty. The Fugitive Slave Act similarly excluded most customary sorts of defenses. The alleged fugitive could not even plead that he was not legally a slave so long as he was the person *alleged* to be a fugitive. The drumhead court was a special and summary proceeding; so was the fugitive rendition process. In both proceedings the fatal judgment was carried out immediately. There was no appeal.

More important, Billy's fatal flaw was his innocent dumbness. He struck because he could not speak. So, under the Fugitive Slave Acts, the alleged fugitive had no right to speak. And, as a rule, slaves had no capacity to testify against their masters or whites, generally. Billy Budd partakes of the slave, generalized. He was seized, impressed, from the ship *Rights of Man* and taken aboard the *Bellipotent.* Aboard the *Bellipotent* the Mutiny Act and Captain Vere held sway. The Mutiny Act was justified because of its necessity for the order demanded on a ship in time of war. So the laws of slavery, often equally harsh and unbending, were justified as necessary for the social order in antebellum America. Moreover, the institution itself was said to have its origin in war.

But most persuasive is Vere and his dilemma—the subject matter of this book. For, if there was a single sort of case in which judges during Melville's lifetime struggled with the moral-formal dilemma, it was slave cases. In these cases, time and again, the judiciary paraded its helplessness before the law; lamented harsh results; intimated that in a more perfect world, or at the end of days, a better law would emerge, but almost uniformly, marched to the music, steeled themselves, and hung Billy Budd.

Of course, *Billy Budd,* like any great work of literature, exists on many levels. I would not deny the theology in the work, nor the clash of elemental good and elemental evil in Budd and Claggart. But the novella is also about a judgment, within a social system, and about the man who, dimly perceiving the great and abstract forces at work, bears responsibility for that judgment. It is about starry-eyed Vere and Lemuel Shaw.

2

The rest of this book is not about literature, but about Lemuel Shaw and many judges like him. It is the story of earnest, well-meaning pillars of legal respectability and of their collaboration in a system of oppression—Negro slavery. I have chosen to analyze at length only the dilemma of the antislavery judge—the man who would, in some sense, have agreed with my characterization of slavery as oppression. It was he who confronted Vere's dilemma, the choice between the demands of role and the voice of conscience. And it was he who contributed so much to the force of legitimacy that law may provide, for he plainly acted out of impersonal duty.

In a static and simplistic model of law, the judge caught between law and morality has only four choices. He may apply the law against his conscience. He may apply conscience and be faithless to the law. He may resign. Or he may cheat: He may state that the law is not what he believes it to be and, thus preserve an appearance (to others) of conformity of law and morality. Once we assume a more realistic model of law and of the judicial process, these four positions become only poles setting limits to a complex field of action and motive. For in a dynamic model, law is always becoming. And the judge has a legitimate role in determining what it is that the law will become. The flux in law means also that the law's content is frequently unclear. We must speak of direction and of weight as well as of position. Moreover, this frequent lack of clarity makes possible "ameliorist" solutions. The judge may introduce his own sense of what "ought to be" interstitially, where no "hard" law yet exists. And, he may do so without committing the law to broad doctrinal advances (or retreats).

READING 3-19
Taking Rights Seriously But Playing Fast and Loose with the Law
"The Third Theory of Law" (1977)

J. L. Mackie

. . . I now want to . . . consider the merits of the third theory as a recommendation. I can do this best by going straight to a concrete example, taken from the legal history of the United States. Professor Dworkin, in a review of Robert M. Cover's book *Justice Accused,* applies his theory to cases which arose before the American Civil War under the Fugitive Slave Acts.

He finds it puzzling that such judges as Joseph Story and Lemuel Shaw, though themselves strongly opposed to slavery, enforced these acts, sending alleged runaway slaves back from states in which slavery was not permitted to states where it still existed and from which they were alleged to have escaped. But why is there a puzzle? Were these judges not, as they themselves said, simply doing their legal duty of enforcing what was then the law of the land, despite the fact that it conflicted with their own moral views? Professor Dworkin argues that it is not so simple. The relevant law was not settled: these cases were controversial. Though the judges in question explicitly denied this, in their deeper thinking they admitted it. But then, being legal positivists, they concluded that they had to legislate, to make new law by their findings. But why, then, did they not make the law in accordance with their moral convictions and their sense of justice? Because, says Professor Dworkin, following Cover, they saw themselves as subordinate legislators only, bound to make the law in harmony with the discoverable intentions of the superior legislators in Congress and, earlier, in the Constitutional Convention. These legislators had, in their several enactments, created and maintained a compromise between the slave states and the nonslave states; therefore, sending an alleged slave back to the state from which he had come was the natural fulfilment of that compromise.

According to Professor Dworkin, the reasoning of these judges was a "failure of jurisprudence." If they had been adherents, not of positivism, but of the third theory, they could have found in the general structure of the American Constitution "a conception of individual freedom antagonistic to slavery, a conception of procedural justice that condemned the procedures established by the Fugitive Slave Acts, and a conception of federalism inconsistent with the idea that the State of Massachusetts had no power to supervise the capture of men and women within its territory." These principles were "more central to the law than were the particular and transitory policies of the slavery compromise."

It is not in dispute that if these judges had been adherents of the natural law doctrine—as evidently they were not—they might have refused to enforce the Fugitive Slave Acts. Then the judges would have held that even if the Acts were settled law in the sense of being unambiguous and regularly enacted statutes, they were not genuine law because they violated principles of justice and natural right which were prior to any man-made system of law. The problem is whether the third theory would have yielded the same result.

First, was the law really not settled? Professor Dworkin says that the (federal) Fugitive Slave Acts "left open many questions of procedure, particularly about the power of the free states themselves to impose restrictions on the process in the interests of the alleged slave." And Massachusetts had enacted such restrictions. However, the judges held that these restrictions were overruled by the federal laws, and this seems to follow from a straightforward interpretation of Article VI of the United States Constitution: "This Constitution, and the laws of the United States which shall be made in pursuance thereof, . . . shall be the supreme law of the land; and the judges in every State shall be bound thereby, anything in the constitution or laws of any State notwithstanding." Professor Dworkin refers also to "narrowly legalistic and verbal arguments" on behalf of the alleged slaves, but arguments of that description, too easily produced, will not show that the law was not, for all that, settled. The only ground on which he can claim, in a way that is even initially plausible, that the law was not settled, is that the procedures laid down in these acts "offended ordinary notions of due process." The federal official who returned the alleged slave to his purported master was "a mere commissioner who received a higher fee if the alleged slave was sent back than if he was not, there was no question of a jury trial, and the defendant was not allowed to contest whether he was in fact a slave, that issue being left to be decided in the slave state after his return."

But it is far from clear that these provisions offend against due process. They would be defended on the ground that these proceedings were only preliminary: the legal issue about the fugitive's status was still to be decided in the state from which he had come, and that, surely, was where witnesses to his identity and status would be available. He was not being deprived of liberty without due process of law; the due process would take place in, say, Virginia. This argument could be rebutted only by casting doubt on the legal respectability of the Virginia courts, and whatever private doubts the Massachusetts judges may have had about this, it was an essential part of the federal compromise that they should not be guided by such doubts in their legal decisions. Article IV, Section I, of the Constitution says that "full faith and credit shall be given in each State to the public acts, records, and judicial proceedings of any other State." The Virginian slave-owner could have argued that if he were not allowed to get his slave back without bringing a large number of witnesses five hundred miles so as to have his claim heard before a Massachusetts jury which was likely to be hostile to the very institution of slavery on which his claim was based, he would be, in effect, being deprived of his property, namely the slave, without due process of law. Article IV, Section 2, of the Constitution is quite explicit: "No person held to service or labor in one State, under the laws thereof, escaping into another, shall, in consequence of any law or regulation therein, be discharged from such service or labor, but shall be delivered up on claim of the party to whom such service or labor may be due."

That, in the face of all this, Professor Dworkin can hold that the law was not settled brings out an important characteristic of his theory, highly relevant to the assessment of its merits as a recommendation: the third theory often takes as unsettled issues which on a legal positivist view belong clearly to the realm of settled law.

But suppose that the law was not settled, and that a judge at the time had tried to decide these cases by Professor Dworkin's method. What conclusion would he have reached? Hercules, being a product of Professor Dworkin's imagination, would no doubt have argued as Professor Dworkin does. But let us invent another mythical judge, say Rhadamanthus.[1] He might have argued as follows:

> What principles that are relevant to this case are implicit in the settled law? The fundamental fact is the Union itself, which arose out of an alliance, against Britain, of thirteen separate and very different colonies. It was recognized from the start that these colonies, and the states which they have become, have diverse institutions and ways of life. The Union exists and can survive only through compromises on issues where these differing institutions and ways of life come into conflict. One salient principle, then, enshrined as clearly as anything could be in the federal Constitution and in various statutes, is that the rights which individuals have by virtue of the institutions of the states in which they live are to be protected throughout the Union. A Virginian slave-owner's property in his slaves is one of these

---

[1] Cf. Plato, *The Apology of Socrates* 40–41: "Would it be such a bad journey if one arrived in Hades, having got rid of the self-styled judges here, and found the true judges who are said to have jurisdiction there, Minos and Rhadamanthus and Aeacus and Triptolemus and such other demigods as were just during their lives?"

rights; the clear intention of Article IV, Section 2, of the Constitution and of the Fugitive Slave Acts is to protect this right. Therefore, whatever merely technical defects may be found in them the law of the land, as determined by the third theory of law which I hold, is that the alleged slave should be returned from Massachusetts to Virginia, where it can be properly decided, by the evidence of many witnesses, whether he is in fact the slave of the man who claims him.

The contrary view, that the Constitution presupposes a conception of freedom antagonistic to slavery, cannot be upheld. Jefferson, who actually wrote the Declaration of Independence, and who later was mainly responsible for the amendments which most strongly assert individual rights, was himself a slave-owner. The individual freedom which the Constitution presupposes was never intended to apply to slaves. Nor will the requirements of procedural justice, which can indeed be seen as principles enshrined in the settled law, support a finding in favor of the alleged slave. On the presumption that slave-owners have legally valid property rights in their slaves, procedural justice will best be secured by sending the alleged slave back. The conception of federalism does no doubt give the state of Massachusetts the power to supervise the capture of men and women in its territory, but this power must be exercised in ways that respect the institutions of Virginia and the rights of citizens of Virginia, especially as these are further protected by federal law.

Even if Joseph Story and Lemuel Shaw had shared Professor Dworkin's theory of jurisprudence, they might still have followed Rhadamanthus rather than Hercules and, without for a moment abandoning their reliance on principles or their concern for rights, might have reached just those decisions they did reach by a more positivistic route. . . .

3. Apartheid

South Africans lived under a system of apartheid that resembled the slavery and racism found in the United States. Apartheid laws sought to segregate whites, coloureds, Asians, and blacks from each other in all areas of life. The "pass laws" regulated the movements of blacks, while the Group Areas Act resulted in the forced removal of blacks and coloureds from their homes. What actions should a moral judge take when confronted with enforcing an immoral law in an immoral system?

A trial court convicted Ms. Govender, a South African of Indian descent, of living in a "White group area" in violation of the Group Areas Act. She sought to have the automatic eviction order overturned by the Supreme Court's Transvaal Provincial Division. The appeals judge personally regarded the Group Areas Act and apartheid as morally wrong. The judge had three courses of action from which to choose. First, he could have disregarded his moral convictions and applied the letter of the law, thereby fulfilling his legal duties. Does a judge who stays within the letter of law fit the following stereotype? "Men who become judges are all of one type: they do not seriously question the status quo; their ambition is to serve the law and not be its master"

(Lord Devlin 1976, as quoted in Freeman 1994, p. 1284, fn. 7). Thus, the judge in the *Govender* case could have mechanically applied the statutory rules, since the relatively clear and unambiguous statute favored eviction. Second, after asking "How can a person of integrity judge those cases at all?" the judge could have resigned. Wendell Phillips, a practitioner and strong advocate of the resignation position, found that only a few American judges, such as Francis Jackson, even posed the possibility of resignation when asked to rule on the Fugitive Slave Laws (Cover 1975, p. 158). In a pragmatic vein, Joel Feinberg (in Feinberg and Coleman 2000, p. 119) pointed out that the resignation position might uphold the judge's integrity but that it does little for the hapless victims of the law. Third, through varying degrees of interpretation, the judge could have tried to find ways to bring the law closer to his moral stand. The judge could have taken the middle road and tried to ameliorate the injustice through various strategies. He might have maneuvered within the statutory language at the level of rules, invoked policy rationales to go outside the rules, or appealed to internal or external moral principles.

In the *Govender* case, compare what the judge could have done and what the judge did. First, the judge could have manipulated the statutory language to push the result in a certain direction. Indeed, the judge in the case rejected a previously near-unanimous practice of automatically issuing an eviction after finding a violation under the act. However, his interpretation stuck closely to the language of the statute. He found that the latest statutory authorization of the act (1966) stated that the court "may" order an eviction. He emphasized that the most recent interpretation did not use the mandatory "shall" that occurred in previous versions of the act. On that basis, the judge ordered the trial court to determine the appropriateness of the eviction. Second, the judge could have made a policy ruling that went beyond the statutory rules, and indeed, he did go beyond the statutory authority. He declared that the magistrates needed to consider "the personal hardship which such an order may cause and the availability of alternative accommodations" (at *Govender* 971). The decision established a new policy—namely, that eviction orders could not be made without a showing of available alternative accommodations (Ellmann 1997). Third, the judge could have followed the path of Dworkin's Hercules and issued a ruling based on moral principles. However, some commentators have charged that Dworkin's high road is not necessarily a morally higher road (Freeman 1994, pp. 88–90). Hercules does not appeal to external, objective ethical standards. Instead, he must always keep his analysis within the confines of a nation's legal practice. His decision must fit the institutional history, and he must constrain his moral stance to fit the institutional practices. Should Hercules lie in certain hard cases? Does lying violate the tests for Kantian universal ethical principles?

> If the judge decides that the reasons supplied by background moral rights are so strong that he has a moral duty to do what he can to support these rights, then it may be that he must lie, because he cannot be of any help unless he is understood as saying, in his official role, that the legal rights are different from what he believes they are. He could, of course, avoid lying by resigning, which will ordinarily be of very little help, or by staying in office

and hoping, against odds, that his appeal based on moral grounds will have
the same practical effect as a lie would. (Dworkin 1977, pp. 326–327)

161

CHAPTER 3
Legal Reasoning

The judge in *Govender* did not resign or lie. Instead, he adopted a middle
course. Judge Richard Goldstone decided the case of *S v. Govender* (1986),
then continued to make valuable contributions to South Africa's overthrow
of apartheid (Ellmann 1997). Later, he served as the chief prosecutor for the
Ad Hoc War Crimes Tribunals of the former Yugoslavia and Rwanda. He now
sits on South Africa's new post-apartheid Constitutional Court.

Justice Joseph Story's "Goldstone type" decision in the *Amistad* case
(which was made into a movie) brings together natural law, positivism, formalism, and realism. Howard Jones (1987) provides the following account. In
April 1839, a Portuguese ship left Sierra Leone loaded with its human cargo
of 500 slaves. Treaties, including the 1817 treaty between Spain and England,
had outlawed the slave trade, but slavery remained legal within most countries, including Cuba. In Havana, two Spanish merchants bought fifty-three
of the newly arrived slaves, including four children. In June 1839, they chartered the *Amistad* to take the cargo to another part of Cuba. The slaves, led
by Joseph Cinqué, mutinied and took over the ship, killing the captain and
the cook. The merchants fooled the slaves into thinking that they had headed
the ship back to Africa. An American revenue ship captured the *Amistad* near
Long Island in August 1839. The Americans took the *Amistad* in tow to Connecticut, which, unlike nearby New York, still had legalized slavery. The merchants sued in admiralty court for salvage of their property. Spain demanded
that the United States return the captives to Cuba to stand trial for mutiny
and murder. The Van Buren administration tried to comply and interfered
with the judicial process by arranging for the transfer of the captives to Cuba
before the legal proceedings were completed. These instances of political realism were never adequately addressed. In his arguments before the
Supreme Court, former President John Quincy Adams argued for the natural
law principles in the Declaration of Independence to prevail over a Constitution that protected slavery. In his 1841 opinion, Justice Story, however, appealed to the positive law. He agreed with Adams that, in the absence of positive law, the natural law should prevail, yet, when positive law addressed a
subject, Story gave it precedence over natural law principles. By law, the illegally enslaved captives had a right to revolt and to kill their kidnappers.
Story, in a constructivist mode, declared that, according to the "eternal principles of justice," the "kidnapped Africans" had the inherent right of self-
defense and could kill their captors to win freedom. For Story, who personally
disdained slavery, the positive law determined the status of blacks as free or
as slaves. In 1842, after eighteen months in prison, the remaining thirty-six
blacks, now free, returned to Africa. Story's approach offers a fascinating comparison to those of the Speluncean judges (see chapter 2, page 49), Judge
Shaw, and Justice Goldstone.

CHAPTER 4

Legal Institutions

CONSTITUTIONAL LAW

*Hobbes would send a sovereign lion to keep the polecats and foxes from de-
vouring one another; but who then will protect us from the sovereign lion?*
—PATRICK WATSON AND BENJAMIN BARBER (1988),
The Struggle for Democracy

The 1990s witnessed an unprecedented number of constitutions being made
throughout the world, yet for centuries, nations were formed without constitutions. Why do so many nations now find it necessary to develop written
constitutions? What philosophical principles should guide the writing of a
constitution? In the United States, the Constitution frames some of the most
controversial moral debates. Moral issues have become constitutionalized
and turn on who has what constitutional right. Three philosophical concepts
have emerged concerning the Constitution and its relationship to moral issues: **freedom** (used interchangeably with liberty), **rights,** and **equality.**
This chapter launches an analysis of constitutional law that continues in the
next three chapters. Chapter 5 covers freedom, chapter 6 discusses rights,
and chapter 7 talks about equality. The following discussion shows how liberalism, freedom, rights, and equality relate to one another.

American constitutional law has developed a distinctive sense of freedom, catalogue of rights, and concept of equality. While the three overlap considerably, American discussions often place them in separate categories. Individuals demonstrate that they have freedoms and rights by pointing to the
Constitution. For example, Americans pride themselves on the constitutional guarantees of freedom of speech. Does free speech have limits? Should
the Constitution allow governments to ban speech that targets the overthrow of the government (sedition)? Should the Constitution permit others
to forbid speech that instills hatred against minorities (hate speech)? What
rights does the Constitution grant? Does it guarantee a right of privacy?
Should the Constitution grant welfare rights? Debates over equality have
also taken place within the context of the Constitution. Does equality mean
a colorblind constitution? Should the Constitution promote a sense of equality that involves leveling the playing field for disadvantaged groups? The answers to these questions become more understandable within the context of
liberalism.

Because the Constitution establishes a legal and a political structure, constitutionalized moral questions also have a political dimension. While the Constitution provides the frame for debating many moral issues, liberalism provides the foundation of political philosophy for the debates. The term *liberalism* is used here in its broad philosophical sense, not as a label for any one political party. Classical liberalism has provided a legacy that remains strong today—for example, jurists still talk of natural rights, an idea that stems from liberalism. The idea of designing political institutions that protect individuals against the interference of government remains as forceful today as it was in the days of John Locke, considered the founder of classical liberalism, and the English Glorious Revolution (1688). Classical liberals drew a line between government and religion that set the tone for constitutional debate over freedom of religion and its counterpart, the nonestablishment of a religion. Modern liberals raised a different but related set of issues. Unlike classical liberals, modern ones denied the idea of a uniform human nature. Modern liberals believed that humans came in many diverse forms. They retained the classical liberals' fear that government would become too powerful and threaten individual freedom, but they also promoted an active role for government. They believed government should help individuals develop in diverse ways. Contemporary liberals have sought to reconcile freedom and equality. Classical, modern, and contemporary versions of liberalism have developed distinct senses of freedom, rights, and equality. Although each of these topics will occupy a separate chapter, a short overview here will place them within the context of liberalism.

B. FREEDOM

Freedom of speech and freedom of religion play essential roles in liberal constitutional orders. The First Amendment of the U.S. Constitution proclaims freedom of expression and conscience. Subversive, symbolic, and offensive speech pose important challenges to liberal free speech doctrines. Political freedom has a counterpart in economic freedom. Under liberal constitutional regimes, individuals have the freedom to contract and the freedom to own and accumulate property. Should political or economic freedom have priority over political freedom?

C. RIGHTS

Rights protect freedoms. The Bill of Rights of the U.S. Constitution primarily protects freedom of speech and freedom of religion. The Constitution guarantees individuals a right to free speech and a right to religious freedom, but there are other rights to consider. Moral, political, and legal disputes often appear in the form of competing rights. Rights protect individual freedoms from governmental interference, but they might also protect fundamental personal interests. For example, should a constitution protect fundamental personal interests by assuring a woman's right to an abortion, a person's right to die, or an individual's right to a particular sexual orientation? The right of individual choice serves as a pivotal point of contention between classical and modern liberalism. Proponents of the right to an abortion describe the right in classical liberal terms—that is, pregnant women have a privacy right, a right to make a choice about abortion without government interference. A competing focus in the abortion issue marks a shift, in a modern liberal direction, toward a concern to protect fundamental personal interests. Some commentators, such as Catherine MacKinnon (see chapter 6), interpret the abortion issue in terms of equality. The U.S. Supreme Court, however, has not accepted the modern liberal equality approach to the abortion issue. For example, in *Maher v. Roe* (1977), the Court rejected the claim that a state must give equal treatment to abortion and to childbirth. The Court found that the state may exercise its preferences by funding only the medical expenses incident to childbirth. Nevertheless, modern liberal concern for equality has come to occupy a more prominent place in constitutional debates.

D. EQUALITY

Liberalism, in its many forms, has tried to address the conflict between freedom and equality, with the Constitution serving as the battleground for these disputes over equality. Beginning in 1954, as the Supreme Court increasingly focused on problems of discrimination, it had to choose whether freedoms, rights, or equality has priority. The Court's recent decisions have indicated a turn against equality and toward freedoms and rights. The Court, overall, views affirmative action, designed as an equality measure for some, as a threat to the rights and freedoms of others. In addition, equality itself has become contested. How should courts interpret equality? Does equality, in a more abstract, formal sense, mean an equal measure of concern, respect, and opportunity for all individuals? Does "equal protection" mean making substantive value judgments (policy judgments) about the disadvantaged status of certain groups? The Supreme Court has most often opted for a formal sense of equality. It has occasionally considered, but rarely adopted, a substantive sense of equality. The hesitancy and failure of the legal system to address and solve social problems has led to an attack on its liberal foundations. The attacks on liberalism, particularly by legal scholars in the 1970s and 1980s, stimulated the formation of new legal theories, including critical legal studies, feminist jurisprudence, and critical race theory. In the 1990s, the critiques of liberalism began to lose their sting; liberalism has experienced a revival.

The state of nature has a law of nature to govern it, . . . that being all equal and independent, no one ought to harm another in his life, health, liberty, or possession. . . . And that men may be restrained from invading the others' rights. . . .

—JOHN LOCKE (1690)
Second Treatise on Civil Government, Ch. II, Sects. 6–7.

A theorist's conception of human nature (or state of nature) often plays a critical role in what the theorist believes the state should be and what its law should look like. The philosophy of **Thomas Hobbes** illustrates the relationship between a conception of a state of nature and a political theory (see chapter 1, page 6). His belief in a natural state of warring humans led Hobbes to justify an authoritarian civil state as the only one capable of keeping the ruthless forces, natural to all humans, in check. Hobbes's bleak vision of human nature paved the way for the tradeoff of liberty for security. Alternative views of human nature lead to alternative recommendations for political structures. Locke had a more benign view of human nature than Hobbes did. Freedom and equality prevailed in Locke's state of nature, which allowed humans to modify their conflicts of interests. Unlike Hobbes, Locke did not pose a state of war as a natural condition. Rather, according to Locke, a state of war arose from attempts of some to dominate others. To avoid this state of war, individuals voluntarily consented to form a civil society. Individuals formed a social contract establishing a government that would protect their natural rights better than they were able to do themselves in the state of nature. If the government violated the natural rights of those who consented to be governed, then the citizens could legitimately dissolve that government.

John Locke (1632–1704) wrote *Two Treaties on Government* (1689) in defense of the parliamentary monarchy. Locke did not only philosophize from his armchair at Oxford University—he also engaged in politics. He held the position of secretary (a prestigious position held by males) to an important political figure, the Earl of Shaftesbury. In his role as Shaftesbury's advisor, he had many opportunities to put political philosophy into practice, such as helping Shaftesbury, a proprietor of the colony, draft the Fundamental Constitution of Carolina (1669). He also had a major influence on the development of the U.S. Constitution, which incorporated Lockean principles, especially the idea of government formed by voluntary agreement and the concept of natural rights. Locke based the legitimacy of government on the idea of a voluntary agreement for the protection of its members (covenant) (see Reading 4-1). Humans had rights and duties even in a state of nature, so natural rights did not depend totally on the state for their existence. Rights existed in the state of nature. When natural rights carried over to civil society, they protected individuals from government. The ideas of a covenant and natural rights did not begin with Locke, however. Benjamin Franklin, among others, praised the Iroquois confederation as a model for colonialists to follow (see Johansen 1982). Moreover, recent scholarship has challenged Locke's preeminence in American political thought (see Bailyn 1967; Wood 1969). These scholars have uncovered an alternative influential paradigm that has competed with liberalism since the formation of the United States. This alternative political philosophy goes under various names—**civic humanism, republicanism,** and **communitarianism.** Since the differences among them need not concern us, for simplicity's sake, we will use the term "communitarian" to cover all of them. Communitarians differ from Hobbes and Locke over human nature; they see humans as essentially social beings who find fulfillment in community. According to communitarians, the role of government is not to protect natural rights (to property), but rather to create conditions for achieving the public good. Throughout this chapter and the next three chapters on constitutional law, consider whether a communitarian analysis would provide a better view than a liberal one on constitutional issues. In the meantime, the following selection provides a good introduction to the ways in which many political philosophers begin their inquiry with the initial formation of civil society.

READING 4-1

Liberal Foundations of American Law

"Of the State of Nature" and "Of the Beginnings of Political Societies" (1690)

John Locke

CHAPTER TWO: OF THE STATE OF NATURE

4. To understand political power right, and derive it from its original, we must consider what state all men are naturally in, and that is a state of perfect freedom to order their actions and dispose of their possessions and persons as they think fit, within the bounds of the law of nature, without asking leave, or depending upon the will of any other man.

A state also of equality, wherein all the power and jurisdiction is reciprocal, no one having more than another: there being nothing more evident than that creatures of the same species and rank promiscuously born to all the same advantages of nature, and the use of the same faculties, should also be equal one amongst another without subordination or subjection, unless the lord and master of them all should by any manifest declaration of his will set one above another, and confer on him by an evident and clear appointment an undoubted right to dominion and sovereignty. . . .

6. But though this be a state of liberty, yet it is not a state of licence, though man in that state have an uncontrollable liberty to dispose of his person or possessions, yet he has not liberty to destroy himself, or so much as any creature in his possession, but where some nobler use than its bare preservation calls for it. The state of nature has a law of nature to govern it, which obliges everyone. And reason, which is that law, teaches all mankind

who will but consult it that, being all equal and independent, no one ought to harm another in his life, health, liberty, or possessions. For men being all the workmanship of one omnipotent and infinitely wise maker, all the servants of one sovereign master, sent into the world by his order and about his business, they are his property whose workmanship they are, made to last during his, not one another's, pleasure. And being furnished with like faculties, sharing all in one community of nature, there cannot be supposed any such subordination among us that may authorize us to destroy one another, as if we were made for one another's uses, as the inferior ranks of creatures are for ours. Everyone, as he is bound to preserve himself, and not to quit his station wilfully, so by the like reason, when his own preservation comes not in competition, ought he, as much as he can, to preserve the rest of mankind, and may not, unless it be to do justice on an offender, take away or impair the life, or what tends to the preservation of the life, liberty, health, limb, or goods of another.

7. And that all men may be restrained from invading others' rights, and from doing hurt to one another, and the law of nature be observed, which willeth the peace and preservation of all mankind, the execution of the law of nature is in that state put into every man's hands, whereby everyone has a right to punish the transgressors of that law to such a degree as may hinder its violation. For the law of nature would, as all other laws that concern men in this world, be in vain, if there were nobody that in the state of nature had a power to execute that law, and thereby preserve the innocent and restrain offenders, and if anyone in the state of nature may punish another, for any evil he has done, everyone may do so. For in that state of perfect equality, where naturally there is no superiority or jurisdiction of one over another, what any may do in prosecution of that law, everyone must needs have a right to do.

8. And thus in the state of nature, one man comes by a power over another; but yet no absolute or arbitrary power to use a criminal, when he has got him in his hands, according to the passionate heats, or boundless extravagancy of his own will, but only to retribute to him, so far as calm reason and conscience dictates, what is proportionate to his transgression, which is so much as may serve for reparation and restraint. For these two are the only reasons why one man may lawfully do harm to another, which is what we call *punishment*. In transgressing the law of nature the offender declares himself to live by another rule than that of reason and common equity, which is that measure God has set to the actions of men for their mutual security; and so he becomes dangerous to mankind, the tie which is to secure them from injury and violence being slighted and broken by him. Which, being a trespass against the whole species, and the peace and safety of it provided for by the law of nature, every man upon this score, by the right he hath to preserve mankind in general, may restrain, or, where it is necessary, destroy things noxious to them, and so may bring such evil on anyone who hath transgressed that law as may make him repent the doing of it, and thereby deter him, and by his example others, from doing the like mischief. And, in this case and upon this ground, every man hath a right to punish the offender, and be executioner of the law of nature. . . .

12. By the same reason may a man in the state of nature punish the lesser breaches of that law. It will perhaps be demanded: With death? I answer: Each transgression may be punished to that degree, and with so much severity, as will suffice to make it an ill bargain to the offender, give him cause to repent, and terrify others from doing the like. Every offence that can be committed in the state of nature may in the state of nature be also punished, equally and as far forth as it may in a commonwealth; for though it would be besides my present purpose to enter here into the particulars of the law of nature, or its measures of punishment, yet it is certain there is such a law, and that too as intelligible and plain to a rational creature, and a studier of that law, as the positive laws of commonwealths; nay possibly plainer, as much as reason is easier to be understood than the fancies and intricate contrivances of men following contrary and hidden interests put into words. For so, truly, are a great part of the municipal laws of countries, which are only so far right as they are founded on the law of nature, by which they are to be regulated and interpreted.

13. To this strange doctrine, viz. that in the state of nature everyone has the executive power of the law of nature, I doubt not but it will be objected that it is unreasonable for men to be judges in their own cases, that self-love will make men partial to themselves and their friends. And, on the other side, that ill-nature, passion, and revenge will carry them too far in punishing others. And hence nothing but confusion and disorder will follow, and that therefore God hath certainly appointed government to restrain the partiality and violence of men. I easily grant that civil government is the proper remedy for the inconveniences of the state of nature, which must certainly be great where men may be judges in their own case, since 'tis easily to be imagined that he who was so unjust as to do his brother an injury will scarce be so just as to condemn himself for it. But I shall desire those who make this objection to remember that absolute monarchs are but men, and if government is to be the remedy of those evils which necessarily follow from men's being judges in their own cases, and the state of nature is therefore not [to] be endured, I desire to know what kind of government that is, and how much better it is than the state of nature, where one man commanding a multitude has the liberty to be judge in his own case, and may do to all his subjects whatever he pleases, without the least liberty to anyone to question or control those who execute his pleasure? And in whatsoever he doth, whether led by reason, mistake, or passion, must be submitted to? Much better it is in the state of nature, wherein men are not bound to submit to the unjust will of another, and if he that judges judges amiss in his own or any other case, he is answerable for it to the rest of mankind. . . .

CHAPTER EIGHT: OF THE BEGINNINGS OF POLITICAL SOCIETIES

95. Men being, as has been said, by nature all free, equal and independent, no man can be put out of this estate and subjected to the political power of another without his own consent. The only way whereby anyone divests himself of his natural liberty and puts on the bonds of civil society is by agree-

ing with other men to join and unite into a community for their comfortable, safe, and peaceable living one amongst another in a secure enjoyment of their properties, and a greater security against any that are not of it. This any number of men may do, because it injures not the freedom of the rest; they are left as they were, in the liberty of the state of nature. When any number of men have so consented to make one community or government, they are thereby presently incorporated, and make one body politic, wherein the majority have a right to act and conclude the rest.

96. For when any number of men have, by the consent of every individual, made a community, they have thereby made that community one body, with a power to act as one body, which is only by the will and determination of the majority. For that which acts any community being only the consent of the individuals of it, and it being necessary to that which is one body to move one way, it is necessary the body should move that way whither the greater force carries it, which is the consent of the majority; or else it is impossible it should act or continue one body, one community, which the consent of every individual that united into it agreed that it should; and so everyone is bound by that consent to be concluded by the majority. And therefore we see that in assemblies empowered to act by positive laws where no number is set by that positive law which empowers them, the act of the majority passes for the act of the whole, and of course determines, as having by the law of nature and reason the power of the whole.

97. And thus every man, by consenting with others to make one body politic under one government, puts himself under an obligation to everyone of that society to submit to the determination of the majority, and to be concluded by it; or else this original compact, whereby he with others incorporates into one society, would signify nothing, and be no compact, if he be left free, and under no other ties than he was in before, in the state of nature. For what appearance would there be of any compact? What new engagement if he were no further tied by any decrees of the society than he himself thought fit and did actually consent to? This would still be as great a liberty as he himself had before his compact, or anyone else in the state of nature hath, who may submit himself and consent to any acts of it if he thinks fit. . . .

99. Whosoever, therefore, out of a state of nature unite into a community, must be understood to give up all the power necessary to the ends for which they unite into society to the majority of the community, unless they expressly agreed in any number greater than the majority. And this is done by barely agreeing to unite into one political society, which is all the compact that is, or needs be, between the individuals that enter into or make up a commonwealth. And thus that which begins and actually constitutes any political society is nothing but the consent of any number of freemen capable of a majority to unite and incorporate into such a society. And this is that, and that only, which did or could give beginning to any lawful government in the world. . . .

From Locke (1690), "Of the State of Nature," Chapter 2, sections 3, 4, 6, 7, 8, 12, 13; "Of the Beginnings of Political Societies," Chapter 8, sections 95–97, 99, *The Second Treatise of Government.* In (1993) *John Locke, Political Writings.* David Wootton, editor. New York: Penguin Books, pp. 262–268, 309–311.

F. GOVERNMENT, THE CONSTITUTION, AND THE JUDICIARY

"To constitute means to make up, order, or form; thus, a nation's constitution should pattern a political system" (Greenberg 1993, p. 7). One way to address the nature of law is to examine the role played by constitutions in establishing and maintaining governments. Not all legal systems depend on constitutions. Constitutional law makes up only a small part of the laws of countries governed by a constitution. Most laws, when applied, do not raise constitutional questions, yet all laws must meet constitutional standards. In the United States, the Constitution has the status of being "the highest law in the land" (**Supremacy Clause,** Article VI, Section 2) giving federal constitutional law superiority over all other laws. The Constitution sets the standards that all other laws must meet. **Natural law theorists** and **legal positivists** would criticize this form of constitutionalism as not going far enough, since constitutionalism fails to specify and justify its standards. While a constitution forms a basis for a higher authority in law, natural law theorists push the analysis one step further, to an even higher level of law. They demand a justification for the constitutional standard (see page 58). However, positivists, such as **H.L.A. Hart,** believe the Constitution provides the framework, not the ultimate authority, for providing the rules of recognition—that is, the criteria for identifying valid law (see page 71).

Within a sympathetic reading of constitutionalism, some commentators note that the Constitution plays a similar role to the Bible in the American civic (see Bellah et al. 1985). However, the Constitution, unlike the Bible and perhaps certain versions of natural law, does not rely on an unquestioned higher authority. A constitution helps resolve a problem of political accountability, since all political officials must be accountable to an authority outside of themselves. A constitution, then, does not play some largely unspecified role within a vague rule of recognition, as Hart would contend. Instead, a constitution serves as the master legal document, as the final arbiter of authority over and above any individuals who are exercising power. What, then, is a constitution and why is it considered so important? Does a constitution set forth the fundamental principles that limit the activities of government?

1. Federalism Versus Antifederalism

After deciding to have a constitution, two difficult questions arise. First, what kind of constitution is needed? Second, who should interpret the constitution? In the *Federalist Papers,* Alexander Hamilton, James Madison, and John Jay set out to convince the voters of New York to ratify the proposed Constitution. The *Federalist Papers* did not convince everyone, however, since some politicians saw the Constitution as a device for concentrating power in the hands of the few. The antifederalists launched an attack on the proposed Constitution, which they thought would grant too much power to the president, the congress, and the judiciary. The **antifederalists** wanted a decentralized society, in which small groups could develop their own sense of community. They envisioned "a homogenous community with members who are united by their common interests and work together to achieve the public good" (Davis 1996, p. 47). Brutus, an anonymous antifederalist writer, attacked the ideas contained in the *Federalist Papers*. He rejected, in particular, the wide powers and life tenure of the federal judges. Mercy Otis Warren, a poet, playwright, and historian, wrote that "[t]here are no well defined limits of the Judiciary Powers, they seem to be left to the boundless ocean, that has broken over the chart of the Supreme Lawgiver *'thus far shalt thou go and no further'* " (Davis 1996, p. 125). Elbridge Gerry, a Massachusetts delegate to the Constitutional Convention, characterized the choice as ratifying the Constitution and placing liberties in jeopardy or rejecting it altogether and facing anarchy. However, the federalist view prevailed.

What is the relationship between a state's adopting a constitution as its fundamental law and democracy (see Preuss 1995)? According to philosopher **Jean Jacques Rousseau,** constitutionalism and democracy stand in tension since the people, through the popular will and not through some document, are the supreme law: "If a people promises simply and solely to obey, it dissolves itself by that very pledge; it ceases to be a people; for once there is a master, there is no longer a sovereign, and the body politic is therefore annihilated" (Rousseau 1762, *The Social Contract,* bk. 2, ch. 1, section 70). **James Madison** (1751–1836) defended constitutionalism against proponents of popular democracy:

> If men were angels no government would be necessary. If angels were to govern men, neither external nor internal controls of government would be necessary. In framing a government which is to be administered by men over men, the great difficulty lies in this; you must first enable the government to control the governed; and in the next place oblige it to control itself. A dependence on people is, no doubt, the primary control of the government; but experience has taught mankind the necessity of auxiliary precautions. (*Federalist Papers* 51, p. 322)

The history of the U.S. Constitution seems to have proven Rousseau wrong and Madison right. Constitutional history has demonstrated the compatibility between constitutionalism and democracy, yet some critics have persisted in questioning whose account of history has prevailed. Since most accounts assume the compatibility of the American Constitution and democracy, an alternative view requires at least an introduction to stimulate philosophical thinking about fundamental issues. One historical interpretation, which stands in sharp contrast to mainstream accounts, finds that the 1789 U.S. Constitution marked a turn away from democracy, at least in the populist sense of that word. Support for this thesis comes from various considerations. While the 1776 revolution removed British rule, it brought on a tame reaction to the British:

> No heads rolled in America; loyalists were tarred and feathered but not hung. Patriotic leaders permitted them to flee with their lives and they confiscated their lands only after proper legislative and judicial proceedings. (Hall 1989, p. 50)

In addition, the revolution did not bring about a break with English law or with an English sense of order. The **Articles of Confederation** decentralized power, leaving power contested, as symbolized by **Shays' Rebellion** (1786). Revolutionary soldiers demanded some fruits of the revolution. Those returning to fallow farms, wanted the debt that had accumulated while they fought for independence to be abolished. While Shays' Rebellion failed, it stimulated a fear that, in some eyes, only a stronger, more centralized order could quiet. The 1787 Constitutional Convention marked a movement to centralize power, but it had no legitimacy, since it exceeded its authority to amend the Articles of Confederation. Further, it could hardly have claimed to represent the people. Its fifty-five delegates had erratic attendance records and only thirty-nine signed the document. During the convention, the Federalists proposed a system designed to quell factions—that is, democratic upheavals *(Federalist 10)*. Some historians see the Constitution, widely regarded as an exemplar of protecting rights, as an economic document designed to stifle populist sentiment and influence. They point out that the body of the Constitution contains a number of references to debt and that the Bill of Rights (the first ten amendments), which were adopted in 1791, had strong opposition. According to this view, the protections for individual political rights came because of long, protracted political struggles. Sometimes, the struggles succeeded in refashioning the Constitution; at other times, the Constitution stifled progressive struggles. The history of the Constitution shows some victories for political rights, such as free speech, but the protection of social and economic rights seldom had an entry on the Constitution's agenda. The Constitution's record on equality proves even more mixed than its record on individual freedoms. For example, it contains ten provisions upholding the institution of slavery. One "alternative historian," Charles Beard, in *An Economic Interpretation of the Constitution* (1913), claimed that the delegates to the Constitutional Convention reflected the interests of their economic class. Political scientist Michael Parenti extends Beard's analysis in Reading 4-2. According to Parenti, the Constitution was and is an elitist document that champions the rights of property over the rights and liberties of persons. However, even if the Beard-Parenti analysis holds, does the elitist origins of the Constitution mean something different today because the Constitution has become a different document?

READING 4-2

The Constitution as an Elitist Document
"A Constitution for the Few" (1988)

Michael Parenti

During the period between the Revolution and the Constitutional Convention, the "rich and the wellborn" played a dominant role in public affairs.

> Their power was born of place, position, and fortune. They were located at or near the seats of government and they were in direct contact with legislatures and government officers. They influenced and often dominated the local newspapers which voiced the ideas and interests of commerce and identified them with the good of the whole people, the state, and the nation. The published writings of the leaders of the period are almost without exception those of merchants, of their lawyers, or of politicians sympathetic with them.

The United States of 1787 has been described as an "egalitarian" society free from the extremes of want and wealth that characterized the Old World, but there were landed estates and colonial mansions that bespoke an impressive munificence [sic. lavish wealth]. From the earliest English settlements, men of influence had received vast land grants from the crown. By 1700, three-fourths of the acreage in New York belonged to fewer than a dozen persons. In the interior of Virginia, seven persons owned a total of 1,732,000 acres. By 1760, fewer than 500 men in five colonial cities controlled most of the commerce, banking, mining, and manufacturing on the eastern seaboard and owned much of the land.

As of 1787, property qualifications left perhaps more than a third of the White male population disfranchised. Property qualifications for holding office were so steep as to prevent most voters from qualifying as candidates. Thus, a member of the New Jersey legislature had to be worth at least 1,000 pounds, while state senators in South Carolina were required to possess estates worth at least 7,000 pounds, clear of debt. In addition, the practice of oral voting, rather than use of a secret ballot, and an "absence of a real choice among candidates and programs" led to "widespread apathy." As a result, men of substance monopolized the important offices. Not long before the Constitutional Convention, the French *chargé d'affaires* wrote to his Foreign Minister:

> Although there are no nobles in America, there is a class of men denominated "gentlemen." . . . Almost all of them dread the efforts of the people to despoil them of their possessions, and, moreover, they are creditors, and therefore interested in strengthening the government, and watching over the execution of the law. . . . The majority of them being merchants, it is for their interest to establish the credit of the United States in Europe on a solid foundation by the exact payment of debts, and to grant to Congress powers extensive enough to compel the people to contribute for this purpose.

The Constitution was framed by financially successful planters, merchants, and creditors, many linked by kinship and marriage and by years of service in Congress, the military, or diplomatic service. They congregated in Philadelphia in 1787 for the professed purpose of revising the Articles of Confederation and strengthening the powers of the central government. They were aware of the weaknesses of the United States in its commercial and diplomatic dealings with other nations. There were also problems among the thirteen states involving trade, customs duties, and currency differences, but these have been exaggerated and in fact, some reforms were being instituted under the Articles.

Most troublesome to the framers of the Constitution was the increasingly insurgent spirit evidenced among the people. Fearing the popular takeover of state governments, the wealthy class looked to a national government as a means of protecting their interests. Even in states where they were inclined to avoid strong federation, the rich, once faced with the threat of popular rule "and realizing that a political alliance with conservatives from other states would be a safeguard if the radicals should capture the state government . . . gave up 'state rights' for 'nationalism' without hesitation."

The nationalist conviction that arose so swiftly among men of wealth during the 1780s was not the product of inspiration; it was not a "dream of nation-building" that suddenly possessed them. (If so, they kept it a secret in their public and private communications.) Rather, their newly acquired nationalism was a practical response to material conditions affecting them in a most immediate way. Their like-minded commitment to federalism was born of a common class interest that transcended state boundaries.

The populace of that day has been portrayed as irresponsible and parochial spendthrifts who never paid their debts and who believed in nothing more than timid state governments and inflated paper money. Most scholars say little about the actual plight of the common people, the great bulk of whom lived at a subsistence level. Most of the agrarian population consisted of poor freeholders, tenants, and indentured hands (the latter lived in conditions of servitude). Small farmers were burdened by heavy rents, ruinous taxes, and low incomes. To survive, they frequently had to borrow money at high interest rates. To meet their debts, they mortgaged their future crops and went still deeper into debt. Large numbers were caught in that cycle of rural indebtedness which is today still the common fate of agrarian peoples in many countries. . . .

The framers believed the states acted with insufficient force against popular uprisings, so Congress was given the task of "organizing, arming, and disciplining the Militia" and calling it forth, among other reasons, to "suppress Insurrections." The federal government was empowered to protect the states "against domestic Violence." Provision was made for "the Erection of Forts, Magazines, Arsenals, dock-Yards and other needful Buildings" and for the maintenance of an army and navy for both national defense and to establish an armed federal presence within the potentially insurrectionary states—a provision that was to prove a godsend to the industrial barons a century later when the army was used repeatedly to break strikes by miners and railroad and factory workers.

In keeping with their desire to contain the majority, the founders inserted "auxiliary precautions" *designed to fragment power without democratizing it.* By separating the executive, legislative, and judicial functions and then providing a system of checks and balances among the various branches, including staggered elections, executive veto, Senate confirmation of appointments and ratification of treaties, and a bicameral legislature, they hoped to dilute the impact of popular sentiments. They contrived an elaborate and difficult process for amending the Constitution, requiring proposal by two-thirds of both the Senate and the House, and ratification by three-fourths of the state legislatures. (Such strictures operate with anti-majoritarian effect to this day. Thus, although national polls show a substantial majority of Americans supports the Equal Rights Amendment, the proposal failed to make its way through the constitutional labyrinth.) To the extent that it existed at all, the majoritarian principle was tightly locked into a system of minority vetoes, making swift and sweeping popular action less likely.

The propertyless majority, as Madison pointed out in *Federalist* No. 10, must not be allowed to concert in common cause against the established social order. First, it was necessary to prevent a unity of public sentiment by enlarging the polity and then compartmentalizing it into geographically insulated political communities. The larger the nation, the greater the "variety of parties and interests" and the more difficult it would be for a majority to find itself and act in unison. As Madison argued, "A rage for paper money, for an abolition of debts, for an equal division of property, or for any other wicked project will be less apt to pervade the whole body of the Union than a particular member of it." An uprising of impoverished farmers may threaten Massachusetts at one time and Rhode Island at another, but a national government will be large and varied enough to contain each of these and insulate the rest of the nation from the contamination of rebellion.

Second, not only must the majority be prevented from finding horizontal cohesion, but its vertical force—that is, its upward thrust upon government—should be blunted by interjecting indirect forms of representation. Thus, the senators from each state were to be elected by their respective state legislatures. The chief executive was to be selected by an electoral college voted by the people but, as anticipated by the framers, composed of political leaders and men of substance who would gather in their various states and choose a president of their own liking. It was believed that they would usually be unable to muster a majority for any one candidate, and that the final selection would be left to the House, with each state delegation therein having only one vote. The Supreme Court was to be elected by no one, its justices being appointed to life tenure by the president and confirmed by the Senate. In time, of course, the electoral college proved to be something of a rubber stamp, and the Seventeenth Amendment, adopted in 1913, provided for popular election of the Senate—demonstrating that the Constitution is modifiable in democratic directions, but only with great difficulty.

The only portion of government directly elected by the people was the House of Representatives. Many of the delegates would have preferred excluding the public entirely from direct representation: John Mercer observed that he found nothing in the proposed Constitution more objectionable than "the mode of election by the people. The people cannot know and judge of the characters of Candidates. The worst possible choice will be made." Others were concerned that demagogues would ride into office on a populist tide only to pillage the treasury and wreak havoc on all. "The time is not distant," warned Gouverneur Morris, "when this Country will abound with mechanics [artisans] and manufacturers [industrial workers] who will receive their bread from their employers. Will such men be the secure and faithful Guardians of liberty? . . . Children do not vote. Why? Because they want prudence, because they have no will of their own. The ignorant and dependent can be as little trusted with the public interest."

When the delegates finally agreed to having "the people" elect the lower house, they were referring to a select portion of the population. Property qualifications disfranchised the poorest White males in various states. Half the adult population was denied suffrage because they were women. American Indians had no access to the ballot. About one-fourth, both men and women, had no vote because they were held in bondage, and even of the Blacks who had gained their legal freedom, in both the North and the South, none was allowed to vote until the passage of the Fourteenth Amendment, after the Civil War. . . .

Parenti, Michael. "A Constitution for the Few," c (1988) by Bedford/St. Martin's Press, Inc. from *Democracy for the Few,* 5E by Parenti. Reprinted with permission of Bedford/St. Martin's Press, Inc.

2. Separation of Powers: Montesquieu

Given a federal system that grants states considerable autonomy and power, how should the federal power be structured? The founders generally agreed to divide the federal government into three separate branches—namely, the executive, the legislative, and the judicial. Debates continue to this day over how much power the Constitution should and did grant to each competing branch. Montesquieu (1689–1755) offered the classical defense of separation-of-powers and checks and balances as a superior form of government. According to Montesquieu, there could be no liberty without separate executive, legislative, and judicial powers. "To prevent the abuse of power, 'tis necessary that by the very disposition of things power should be a check to power" (*Spirit of the Laws* [1748], chapter 4, section 2). If any of three branches become joined into one, "there can be no liberty"—that is "doing what the law permits":

> Again, there is no liberty, if the power of judging be not separated from the legislative and executive powers. Were it joined with the legislative, the life and liberty of the subject would be exposed to arbitrary control; for the judge would be then the legislator. Were it joined to the executive power, the judge might behave with all the violence of an oppressor. (Montesquieu, *Spirit of the Laws* [1748], Bk. XI, Chapter VI, section 5 in 1977)

3. Judicial Review

Alexander Hamilton (1757–1804) presented, in a *Federalist Paper* (see Reading 4-3) one of the earliest developed defenses of the judiciary as the interpreter of the Constitution. In keeping with Montesquieu's influential philosophy, Hamilton thought that the judiciary must remain a distinct and separate power in order to preserve liberty. He regarded the Constitution as the fundamental law that reflected the will of the people. He offered the following argument for judicial review: Only judges should give the final interpretation to the Constitution, since only the judiciary can express the will of the people as embodied in the Constitution. The judiciary should have power over the other branches of government, because even the president is not above the law.

In general, however, the founders held a different view than Hamilton and opted for a weak judiciary. The Constitutional Convention "rejected proposals for a Council of Revision to scrutinize congressional legislation and another to allow Congress to veto state legislation" (Hall 1989, p. 73). However, history, an obscure case, and a clever jurist undermined the founders' consensus on a weak judiciary. In the final days of his administration, President John Adams, a Federalist, made many last-minute judicial appointments, including one for William Marbury. The appointments followed the proper procedure and included the signature and seal of **John Marshall** (1755–1835), Adams' secretary of state, but Marshall's brother failed to deliver all of them in time. Marbury appealed to the U.S. Supreme Court to issue an order (a *writ of mandamus,* meaning "we command," a court order compelling a government official to do something) to James Madison, secretary of state under the new president, Thomas Jefferson, to deliver his judicial appointment. Outgoing President Adams had appointed Marshall chief justice to save the Constitution from the radicals led by Jefferson. Only three of six justices heard arguments in *Marbury v. Madison* (see Reading 4-4). Marshall found that Congress could not extend the Court's jurisdiction when it was fixed by the Constitution. He, therefore, ruled the congressional act (a section of the 1789 Judiciary Act) unconstitutional that extended the Court's jurisdiction. Ironically, Marshall's ruling gave the Court more power by arguing that Congress had given the Court too much power. Marshall's opinion, reprinted in Reading 4-4, provides the basis for all subsequent debates over judicial review.

READING 4-3

A Defense of Judicial Review
"Federalist Number 78" (1961)

Alexander Hamilton

. . . It proves incontestably, that the judiciary is beyond comparison the weakest of the three departments of power; that it can never attack with success either of the other two; and that all possible care is requisite to enable it to defend itself against their attacks. It equally proves, that though individual oppression may now and then proceed from the courts of justice, the general liberty of the people can never be endangered from that quarter; I mean so long as the judiciary remains truly distinct from both the legislature and the Executive. For I agree, that "there is no liberty, if the power of judging be not separated from the legislative and executive powers." And it proves, in the last place, that as liberty can have nothing to fear from the judiciary alone, but would have every thing to fear from its union with either of the other departments; that as all the effects of such a union must ensue from a dependence of the former on the latter, notwithstanding a nominal and apparent separation; that as, from the natural feebleness of the judiciary, it is in continual jeopardy of being overpowered, awed, or influenced by its coördinate branches; and that as nothing can contribute so much to its firmness and independence as permanency in office, this quality may therefore be justly regarded as an indispensable ingredient in its constitution, and, in a great measure, as the citadel of the public justice and the public security.

The complete independence of the courts of justice is peculiarly essential in a limited Constitution. By a limited Constitution, I understand one which contains certain specified exceptions to the legislative authority; such, for instance, as that it shall pass no bills of attainder [legislation to punish specific individuals], no *ex-post-facto* laws, and the like. Limitations of this kind can be preserved in practice no other way than through the medium of courts of justice, whose duty it must be to declare all acts contrary to the manifest tenor of the Constitution void. Without this, all the reservations of particular rights or privileges would amount to nothing.

Some perplexity respecting the rights of the courts to pronounce legislative acts void, because contrary to the constitution, has arisen from an imagination that the doctrine would imply a superiority of the judiciary to the legislative power. It is urged that the authority which can declare the acts of another void, must necessarily be superior to the one whose acts may be declared void. As this doctrine is of great importance in all the American constitutions, a brief discussion of the ground on which it rests cannot be unacceptable.

There is no position which depends on clearer principles, than that every act of a delegated authority, contrary to the tenor of the commission under which it is exercised, is void. No legislative act, therefore, contrary to the Constitution, can be valid. To deny this, would be to affirm, that the deputy is greater than his principal; that the servant is above his master; that the representatives of the people are superior to the people themselves; that men acting by virtue of powers, may do not only what their powers do not authorize, but what they forbid.

If it be said that the legislative body are themselves the constitutional judges of their own powers, and that the construction they put upon them is conclusive upon the other departments, it may be answered, that this cannot be the natural presumption, where it is not to be collected from any particular provisions in the Constitution. It is not otherwise to be supposed, that the Constitution could intend to enable the representatives of the people to substitute their *will* to that of their constituents. It is far more rational to suppose, that the courts were designed to be an intermediate body between the people and the legislature, in order, among other things, to keep the latter within the limits assigned to their authority. The interpretation of the laws is the proper and peculiar province of the courts. A constitution is, in fact, and must be regarded by the judges, as a fundamental law. It therefore belongs to them to ascertain its meaning, as well as the meaning of any particular act proceeding from the legislative body. If there should happen to be an irreconcilable variance between the two, that which has the superior obligation and validity ought, of course, to be preferred; or, in other words, the Constitution ought to be preferred to the statute, the intention of the people to the intention of their agents.

Nor does this conclusion by any means suppose a superiority of the judicial to the legislative power. It only supposes that the power of the people is superior to both; and that where the will of the legislature, declared in its statutes, stands in opposition to that of the people, declared in the Constitution, the judges ought to be governed by the latter rather than the former. They ought to regulate their decisions by the fundamental laws, rather than by those which are not fundamental. . . .

It can be of no weight to say that the courts, on the pretence of a repugnancy, may substitute their own pleasure to the constitutional intentions of the legislature. This might as well happen in the case of two contradictory statutes; or it might as well happen in every adjudication upon any single statute. The courts must declare the sense of the law; and if they should be disposed to exercise WILL instead of JUDGMENT, the consequence would equally be the substitution of their pleasure to that of the legislative body. The observation, if it prove any thing, would prove that there ought to be no judges distinct from that body.

From Hamilton "Federalist Number 78" in (1961), *The Federalist*, Benjamin Fletcher Wright, editor. New York: Barnes & Noble, pp. 491–495.

Judicial Review Established
Marbury v. Madison (1803)

CHIEF JUSTICE JOHN MARSHALL

The act to establish the judicial courts of the United States authorizes the supreme court 'to issue writs of mandamus, in cases warranted by the principles and usages of law, to any courts appointed, or persons holding office, under the authority of the United States.' [The] constitution vests the whole judicial power of the United States in one supreme court, and such inferior courts as congress shall, from time to time, ordain and establish. This power is expressly extended to all cases arising under the laws of the United States; and consequently, in some form, may be exercised over the present case; because the right claimed is given by a law of the United States.

In the distribution of this power it is declared that 'the supreme court shall have original jurisdiction in all cases affecting ambassadors, other public ministers and consuls, and those in which a state shall be a party. In all other cases, the supreme court shall have appellate jurisdiction.'

It has been insisted at the bar, that as the original grant of jurisdiction to the supreme and inferior courts is general, and the clause, assigning original jurisdiction to the supreme court, contains no negative or restrictive words; the power remains to the legislature to assign original jurisdiction to that court in other cases than those specified in the article which has been recited; provided those cases belong to the judicial power of the United States.

If it had been intended to leave it in the discretion of the legislature to apportion the judicial power between the supreme and inferior courts according to the will of that body, it would certainly have been useless to have proceeded further than to have defined the judicial power, and the tribunals in which it should be vested. The subsequent part of the section is mere surplusage [unnecessary words], is entirely without meaning, if such is to be the construction. If congress remains at liberty to give this court appellate jurisdiction, where the constitution has declared their jurisdiction shall be original; and original jurisdiction where the constitution has declared it shall be appellate; the distribution of jurisdiction made in the constitution, is form without substance.

Affirmative words are often, in their operation, negative of other objects than those affirmed; and in this case, a negative or exclusive sense must be given to them or they have no operation at all. [It] cannot be presumed that any clause in the constitution is intended to be without effect; and therefore such construction is inadmissible, unless the words require it.

When an instrument organizing fundamentally a judicial system, divides it into one supreme, and so many inferior courts as the legislature may ordain and establish; then enumerates its powers, and proceeds so far to distribute them, as to define the jurisdiction of the supreme court by declaring the cases in which it shall take original jurisdiction, and that in others it shall take appellate jurisdiction, the plain import of the words seems to be, that in one class of cases its jurisdiction is original, and not appellate; in the other it is appellate, and not original. If any other construction would render the clause inoperative, that is an additional reason for rejecting such other construction, and for adhering to the obvious meaning.

To enable this court then to issue a mandamus, it must be shown to be an exercise of appellate jurisdiction, or to be necessary to enable them to exercise appellate jurisdiction.

It has been stated at the bar that the appellate jurisdiction may be exercised in a variety of forms, and that if it be the will of the legislature that a mandamus should be used for that purpose, that will must be obeyed. This is true; yet the jurisdiction must be appellate, not original.

It is the essential criterion of appellate jurisdiction, that it revises and corrects the proceedings in a cause already instituted, and does not create that case. Although, therefore, a mandamus may be directed to courts, yet to issue such a writ to an officer for the delivery of a paper, is in effect the same as to sustain an original action for that paper, and therefore seems not to belong to appellate, but to original jurisdiction. Neither is it necessary in such a case as this, to enable the court to exercise its appellate jurisdiction.

The authority, therefore, given to the supreme court, by the act establishing the judicial courts of the United States, to issue writs of mandamus to public officers, appears not to be warranted by the constitution; and it becomes necessary to inquire whether a jurisdiction, so conferred, can be exercised.

The question, whether an act, repugnant to the constitution, can become the law of the land, is a question deeply interesting to the United States; but, happily, not of an intricacy proportioned to its interest. It seems only necessary to recognize certain principles, supposed to have been long and well established, to decide it.

That the people have an original right to establish, for their future government, such principles as, in their opinion, shall most conduce to their own happiness, is the basis on which the whole American fabric has been erected. The exercise of this original right is a very great exertion; nor can it nor ought it to be frequently repeated. The principles, therefore, so established are deemed fundamental. And as the authority, from which they proceed, is supreme, and can seldom act, they are designed to be permanent.

This original and supreme will organizes the government, and assigns to different departments their respective powers. It may either stop here; or establish certain limits not to be transcended by those departments.

The government of the United States is of the latter description. The powers of the legislature are defined and limited; and that those limits may not be mistaken or forgotten, the constitution is written. To what purpose are powers limited, and to what purpose is that limitation committed to writing; if these limits may, at any time, be passed by those intended to be restrained? The distinction between a government with limited and unlimited powers is abolished, if those limits do not confine the persons on whom they are imposed, and if acts prohibited and acts allowed are of equal obligation. It is a proposition too plain to be contested, that the constitution controls any legislative act repugnant to it; or, that the legislature may alter the constitution by an ordinary act.

Between these alternatives there is no middle ground. The constitution is either a superior, paramount law, unchangeable by ordinary means, or it is on a level with ordinary legislative acts, and like other acts, is alterable when the legislature shall please to alter it.

If the former part of the alternative be true, then a legislative act contrary to the constitution is not law: if the latter part be true, then written constitutions are absurd attempts, on the part of the people, to limit a power in its own nature illimitable.

Certainly all those who have framed written constitutions contemplate them as forming the fundamental and paramount law of the nation, and consequently the theory of every such government must be, that an act of the legislature repugnant to the constitution is void.

This theory is essentially attached to a written constitution, and is consequently to be considered by this court as one of the fundamental principles of our society. It is not therefore to be lost sight of in the further consideration of this subject.

If an act of the legislature, repugnant to the constitution, is void, does it, notwithstanding its invalidity, bind the courts and oblige them to give it effect? Or, in other words, though it be not law, does it constitute a rule as operative as if it was a law? This would be to overthrow in fact what was established in theory; and would seem, at first view, an absurdity too gross to be insisted on. It shall, however, receive a more attentive consideration.

It is emphatically the province and duty of the judicial department to say what the law is. Those who apply the rule to particular cases, must of necessity expound and interpret that rule. If two laws conflict with each other, the courts must decide on the operation of each.

So if a law be in opposition to the constitution: if both the law and the constitution apply to a particular case, so that the court must either decide that case conformably to the law, disregarding the constitution; or conformably to the constitution, disregarding the law: the court must determine which of these conflicting rules governs the case. This is of the very essence of judicial duty.

If then the courts are to regard the constitution; and the constitution is superior to any ordinary act of the legislature; the constitution, and not such ordinary act, must govern the case to which they both apply.

Those then who controvert the principle that the constitution is to be considered, in court, as a paramount law, are reduced to the necessity of maintaining that courts must close their eyes on the constitution, and see only the law.

This doctrine would subvert the very foundation of all written constitutions. [That] it thus reduces to nothing what we have deemed the greatest improvement on political institutions—a written constitution, would of itself be sufficient, in America where written constitutions have been viewed with so much reverence, for rejecting the construction. But the peculiar expressions of the Constitution of the United States furnish additional arguments in favour of its rejection.

The judicial power of the United States is extended to all cases arising under the constitution. [In] some cases then, the constitution must be looked into by the judges. And if they can open it at all, what part of it are they forbidden to read, or to obey?

[It] is apparent, that the framers of the constitution contemplated that instrument as a rule for the government of courts, as well as of the legislature. [It] is also not entirely unworthy of observation, that in declaring what shall be the supreme law of the land, the constitution itself is first mentioned; and not the laws of the United States generally, but those only which shall be made in pursuance of the constitution, have that rank.

Thus, the particular phraseology of the constitution of the United States confirms and strengthens the principle, supposed to be essential to all written constitutions, that a law repugnant to the constitution is void, and that courts, as well as other departments, are bound by that instrument. [The] rule must be discharged.

From *Marbury v. Madison* (1803) 5 US, 137.

F. CASES AND CONTROVERSIES

Did Hamilton's picture and Marshall's practice give too much authority to a single document and to the courts? What issues qualify as constitutional issues and on what grounds? Should abortion and physician-assisted suicide rise to the level of constitutional issues? Many commentators criticize the power of judicial review as, for example, undermining democratic principles of majority rule. With judicial review, appointed judges act in a counter-majoritarian manner. They make law and thereby take away legislative power. Other commentators have defended judicial review as a way to protect the minority from the tyranny of the majority. Alexander Bickel (see Reading 4-5) addressed the charge that judicial review, by exercising control against the prevailing majority, qualifies as undemocratic. Bickel found a unique role for the judiciary distinct from the legislature and the executive in its capacity to protect enduring values through its appeal to principles (see selections by Dworkin in chapter 3, pages 140–145).

If we associate liberalism with representative democracy, then John Hart Ely's process model of judicial review is particularly salient (see Reading 4-6). Ely disagreed with Bickel's thesis that judges qualify as the best candidates to sort out the enduring values of society because of their insulation from politics. No matter how well intentioned and well reasoned the argument, Ely believed that attempts to give the judiciary a role in forming substantive values was doomed. However, Ely still found a critical role for the courts—namely, policing the process of democratic representative government. Representative democracy has one critical drawback—the "Ins" try to keep out the "Outs." Courts must police this process. "We must let the courts police inhibitions on expression and other political activity because we cannot trust elected officials to do so" (Ely 1980, p. 106). Unblocking voting stoppages "is what judicial review ought preeminently to be about" (Ely 1980, p. 117). Courts need to police states like Alabama that redrew the boundary lines of the City of Tuskegee to create an "uncouth twenty-eight-sided figure," designed to dilute minority votes (Ely 1980, p. 140). "Courts should protect those who can't protect themselves" (Ely 1980, p. 152). Should, as Ely suggests, courts act as referees who intervene when the political process malfunctions?

The power of judicial review raises further issues in relation to the separation-of-powers doctrine. The question of the relative powers of the separate branches remains an open one. Does the separation-of-powers doctrine bar the Supreme Court from determining whether the President acted within the law (see Reading 4-7)? Paula Jones brought a sexual harassment suit against President William Clinton based on acts that allegedly occurred before he took office. The Court held that separation of powers does not bar the Court's jurisdiction over the executive and does not require a delay of Jones's private action against the president on grounds that it would unduly burden the president while in office. Given the subsequent impeachment proceedings against President Clinton, does the Court's analysis in *Clinton v. Jones* still hold? (Also see chapter 2, page 38 on impeachment and the morality of lying.)

READING 4-5

A Principled Although Non Democratic Judiciary
"The Counter-Majoritarian Difficulty" (1962)

Alexander Bickel

The root difficulty is that judicial review is a counter-majoritarian force in our system. There are various ways of sliding over this ineluctable [inevitable] reality. Marshall did so when he spoke of enforcing, in behalf of "the people," the limits that they have ordained for the institutions of a limited government. And it has been done ever since in much the same fashion by all too many commentators. Marshall himself followed Hamilton, who in the 78th *Federalist* denied that judicial review implied a superiority of the judicial over the legislative power—denied, in other words, that judicial review constituted control by an unrepresentative minority of an elected majority. "It only supposes," Hamilton went on, "that the power of the people is superior to both; and that where the will of the legislature, declared in its statutes, stands in opposition to that of the people, declared in the Constitution, the judges ought to be governed by the latter rather than the former." But the word "people" so used is an abstraction. Not necessarily a meaningless or a pernicious one by any means; always charged with emotion, but nonrepresentational—an abstraction obscuring the reality that when the Supreme Court declares unconstitutional a legislative act or the action of an elected executive, it thwarts the will of representatives of the actual people of the here and now; it exercises control, not in behalf of the prevailing majority, but against it. That, without mystic overtones, is what actually happens. It is an altogether different kettle of fish, and it is the reason the charge can be made that judicial review is undemocratic. . . .

I am aware that this timid assault on the complexities of the American democratic system has yet left us with a highly simplistic statement, and I shall briefly rehearse some of the reasons. But nothing in the further complexities and perplexities of the system, which modern political science has explored with admirable and ingenious industry, and some of which it has tended to multiply with a fertility that passes the mere zeal of the discoverer—nothing in these complexities can alter the essential reality that judicial review is a deviant institution in the American democracy. . . .

But nothing can finally depreciate the central function that is assigned in democratic theory and practice to the electoral process; nor can it be denied that the policy-making power of representative institutions, born of the electoral process, is the distinguishing characteristic of the system. Judicial review works counter to this characteristic. . . .

A further, crucial difficulty must also be faced. Besides being a counter-majoritarian check on the legislature and the executive, judicial review may, in a larger sense, have a tendency over time seriously to weaken the democratic process. Judicial review expresses, of course, a form of distrust of the legislature. . . . [W]rote James Bradley Thayer at the turn of the century,

> . . . [I]t should be remembered that the exercise of it [the power of judicial review], even when unavoidable, is always attended with a serious evil, namely, that the correction of legislative mistakes comes from the outside, and the people thus lose the political experience, and the moral education and stimulus that comes from fighting the question out in the ordinary way, and correcting their own errors. The tendency of a common and easy resort to this great function, now lamentably too common, is to dwarf the political capacity of the people, and to deaden its sense of moral responsibility. It is no light thing to do that.

To this day, in how many hundreds of occasions does Congress enact a measure that it deems expedient, having essayed consideration of its constitutionality (that is to say, of its acceptability on principle), only to abandon the attempt in the declared confidence that the Court will correct errors of principle, if any? It may well be, as has been suggested, that any lowering of the level of legislative performance is attributable to many factors other than judicial review. Yet there is no doubt that what Thayer observed remains observable. . . .

THE MORAL APPROVAL OF THE LINES: PRINCIPLE

Such, in outline, are the chief doubts that must be met if the doctrine of judicial review is to be justified on principle. Of course, these doubts will apply with lesser or greater force to various forms of the exercise of the power. For the moment the discussion is at wholesale, and we are seeking a justification on principle, quite aside from supports in history and the continuity of practice. The search must be for a function which might (indeed, must) involve the making of policy, yet which differs from the legislative and executive functions; which is peculiarly suited to the capabilities of the courts; which will not likely be performed elsewhere if the courts do not assume it; which can be so exercised as to be acceptable in a society that generally shares Judge Hand's satisfaction in a "sense of common venture"; which will be effective when needed; and whose discharge by the courts will not lower the quality of the other departments' performance by denuding them of the dignity and burden of their own responsibility. It will not be possible fully to meet all that is said against judicial review. Such is not the way with questions of government. We can only fill the other side of the scales with countervailing judgments on the real needs and the actual workings of our society and, of course, with our own portions of faith and hope. Then we may estimate how far the needle has moved.

The point of departure is a truism; perhaps it even rises to the unassailability of a platitude [commonplace saying]. It is that many actions of government have two aspects: their immediate, necessarily intended, practical effects, and their perhaps unintended or unappreciated bearing on values we hold to have more general and permanent interest. It is a premise we deduce not merely from the fact of a written constitution but from the history of the race, and ultimately as a moral judgment of the good society, that government should serve not only what we conceive from time to time to be our immediate material needs but also certain enduring values. This in part is what is meant by government under law. But such values do not present themselves ready-made. They have a past always, to be sure, but they must be continually derived, enunciated, and seen in relevant application. And it remains to ask which institution of our government—if any single one in particular—should be the pronouncer and guardian of such values.

Men in all walks of public life are able occasionally to perceive this second aspect of public questions. Sometimes they are also able to base their decisions on it; that is one of the things we like to call acting on principle. Often they do not do so, however, particularly when they sit in legislative assemblies. There, when the pressure for immediate results is strong enough and emotions ride high enough, men will ordinarily prefer to act on expediency rather than take the long view. Possibly legislators—everything else being equal—are as capable as other men of following the path of principle, where the path is clear or at any rate discernible. Our system, however, like all secular systems, calls for the evolution of principle in novel circumstances, rather than only for its mechanical application. Not merely respect for the rule of established principles but the creative establishment and renewal of a coherent body of principled rules—that is what our legislatures have proven themselves ill equipped to give us. . . .

Moreover, and more importantly, courts have certain capacities for dealing with matters of principle that legislatures and executives do not possess. Judges have, or should have, the leisure, the training, and the insulation to follow the ways of the scholar in pursuing the ends of government. This is crucial in sorting out the enduring values of a society, and it is not something that institutions can do well occasionally, while operating for the most part with a different set of gears. It calls for a habit of mind, and for undeviating institutional customs. Another advantage that courts have is that questions of principle never carry the same aspect for them as they did for the legislature or the executive. Statutes, after all, deal typically with abstract or dimly foreseen problems. The courts are concerned with the flesh and blood of an actual case. This tends to modify, perhaps to lengthen, everyone's view. It also provides an extremely salutary proving ground for all abstractions; it is conducive, in a phrase of Holmes, to thinking things, not words, and thus to the evolution of principle by a process that tests as it creates.

Their insulation and the marvelous mystery of time give courts the capacity to appeal to men's better natures, to call forth their aspirations, which may have been forgotten in the moment's hue and cry. This is what Justice Stone called the opportunity for "the sober second thought." Hence it is that the courts, although they may somewhat dampen the people's and the legislatures' efforts to educate themselves, are also a great and highly effective educational institution. . . . No other branch of the American government is nearly so well equipped to conduct [a vital national seminar]. And such a seminar can do a great deal to keep our society from becoming so riven that no court will be able to save it. Of course, we have never quite been that society in which the spirit of moderation is so richly in flower that no court need save it.

READING 4-6

The Courts as Process Police
"Policing the Process of Representation" (1980)

John Ely

The final point worth serious mention is that (again unlike a fundamental-values approach) a representation-reinforcing approach assigns judges a role they are conspicuously well situated to fill. My reference here is not principally to expertise. Lawyers *are* experts on process writ small, the processes by which facts are found and contending parties are allowed to present their claims. And to a degree they are experts on process writ larger, the processes by which issues of public policy are fairly determined: lawyers do seem genuinely to have a feel, indeed it is hard to see what other special value they have, for ways of insuring that everyone gets his or her fair say. But too much shouldn't be made of this. Others, particularly the full-time participants, can also claim expertise on how the political process allocates voice and power. And of course many legislators are lawyers themselves. So the point isn't so much one of expertise as it is one of perspective.

The approach to constitutional adjudication recommended here is akin to what might be called an "antitrust" as opposed to a "regulatory" orientation to economic affairs—rather than dictate substantive results it intervenes only when the "market," in our case the political market, is systemically malfunctioning. (A referee analogy is also not far off: the referee is to intervene only when one team is gaining unfair advantage, not because the "wrong" team has scored.) Our government cannot fairly be said to be "malfunctioning" simply because it sometimes generates outcomes with which we disagree, however strongly (and claims that it is reaching results with which "the people" really disagree—or would "if they understood"—are likely to be little more than self-deluding projections). In a representative democracy value determinations are to be made by our elected representatives, and if in fact most of us disapprove we can vote them out of office. Malfunction occurs when the *process* is undeserving of trust, when (1) the ins are choking off the channels of political change to ensure that they will stay in and the outs will stay out, or (2) though no one is actually denied a voice or a vote, representatives beholden to an effective majority are systematically disadvantaging some minority out of simple hostility or a prejudiced refusal to recognize commonalities of interest, and thereby denying that minority the protection afforded other groups by a representative system.

Obviously our elected representatives are the last persons we should trust with identification of either of these situations. Appointed judges, however, are comparative outsiders in our governmental system, and need worry about continuance in office only very obliquely. This does not give them some special pipeline to the genuine values of the American people: in fact it goes far to ensure that they won't have one. It does, however, put them in a position objectively to assess claims—though no one could suppose the evaluation won't be full of judgment calls—that either by clogging the channels of change or by acting as accessories to majority tyranny, our elected representatives in fact are not representing the interests of those whom the system presupposes they are. . . .

READING 4-7

The Judiciary's Power Over the Executive
Clinton v. Jones (1997)

JUSTICE JOHN PAUL STEVENS

This case raises a constitutional and a prudential question concerning the Office of the President of the United States. Respondent, a private citizen, seeks to recover damages from the current occupant of that office based on actions allegedly taken before his term began. The President submits that in all but the most exceptional cases the Constitution requires federal courts to defer such litigation until his term ends and that, in any event, respect for the office warrants such a stay. Despite the force of the arguments supporting the President's submissions, we conclude that they must be rejected. . . .

Petitioner's principal submission—that "in all but the most exceptional cases,". . . the Constitution affords the President temporary immunity from civil damages litigation arising out of events that occurred before he took office—cannot be sustained on the basis of precedent. . . .

The principal rationale for affording certain public servants immunity from suits for money damages arising out of their official acts is inapplicable to unofficial conduct. In cases involving prosecutors, legislators, and judges we have repeatedly explained that the immunity serves the public interest in enabling such officials to perform their designated functions effectively without fear that a particular decision may give rise to personal liability. . . . That rationale provided the principal basis for our holding that a former President of the United States was "entitled to absolute immunity from damages liability predicated on his official acts," . . . . Our central concern was to avoid rendering the President "unduly cautious in the discharge of his official duties." . . .

This reasoning provides no support for an immunity for *unofficial* conduct. . . .

Rather than arguing that the decision of the case will produce either an aggrandizement of judicial power or a narrowing of executive power, petitioner contends that—as a byproduct of an otherwise traditional exercise of judicial power—burdens will be placed on the President that will hamper the performance of his official duties. We have recognized that "[e]ven when a branch does not arrogate power to itself . . . the separation-of-powers doctrine requires that a branch not impair another in the performance of its constitutional duties." . . . As a factual matter, petitioner contends that this particular case—as well as the potential additional litigation that an affirmance of the Court of Appeals judgment might spawn—may impose an unacceptable burden on the President's time and energy, and thereby impair the effective performance of his office.

Petitioner's predictive judgment finds little support in either history or the relatively narrow compass of the issues raised in this particular case. As we have already noted, in the more than 200-year history of the Republic, only three sitting Presidents have been subjected to suits for their private actions. . . . If the past is any indicator, it seems unlikely that a deluge of such litigation will ever engulf the Presidency. As for the case at hand, if properly managed by the District Court, it appears to us highly unlikely to occupy any substantial amount of petitioner's time. . . .

From *Clinton v. Jones* (1997) 520 US 681, pp. 681, 684, 692–694, 701–702, 708–710.

G. CONTROVERSIES: CONSTITUTIONAL INTERPRETATION

Disputes over the power of the judiciary have taken the form of differences concerning how to interpret the Constitution. Today, advocates of broad discretion often favor a strong judiciary, while those who support judicial constraint want a limited judiciary. However, granting judges wide interpretative latitude does not always coincide with promoting greater freedom and equality. Likewise, limiting judges to the text or to the original intent of the Constitution's framers does not always match with wanting to maintain the status quo.

1. Textual Meaning

Despite the vague language found in the Constitution, some jurists prescribe sticking to the text as much as possible. William Howard Taft, president of the United States (1909–1913) and chief justice of the Supreme Court (1921–1930) relied on a textual interpretation of the Constitution when he held that the Fourth Amendment ("the right of people to be secure in their persons, houses, papers, and effects, against unreasonable searches and seizures") did not explicitly cover wiretapping by the government:

> The Amendment itself shows that the search is to be of material things—the person, the house, his papers or his effects. . . . The Amendment does not forbid what was done here. There was no searching. There was no seizure. The evidence was secured by the use of the sense of hearing and that only. There was no entry of the houses or offices of the defendants. . . . The language of the Amendment cannot be extended and expanded. (*Olmstead v. United States* 1928)

Does an appeal to the literal textual meaning of Constitutional language stifle attempts to keep pace with the changing times? Should judges give a literal reading to the categorical statements found in the Constitution? Justice Hugo Black also took a textual approach, giving a literal reading to the First Amendment—"Congress shall make no law . . . abridging the freedom of speech." Black insisted that "no law" meant "absolutely no law," but he had a narrow interpretation of what constituted speech. For example, he regarded bans on flag burning as constitutional since they prohibited conduct, not speech (*Street v. New York* 1969) (see chapter 5, page 252).

2. Original Intent

Some jurists contend that judges should abide by the framers' original intent (Berger 1987). Historically, different reactions to problems of debt repayment have provided an interesting context in which to explore original intent. Following the American Revolution, debt-ridden farmers in Rhode Island took over their legislature and issued paper money after the state refused to relieve their plight. In 1786, Daniel Shays led a similar rebellion in Massachusetts (see page 171). Thomas Jefferson, then ambassador to France, welcomed the rebellion: "The tree of liberty must be refreshed from time to time with the blood of patriots and tyrants. It is its natural manure." However, the rebellion sent a warning message to those attempting to establish a strong central government. According to some interpreters, the Constitutional Convention passed the contracts clause ("No state shall . . . pass any . . . Law impairing the Obligation of Contracts") to assure repayment of the debts. Therefore, the literal language forbids states to interfere in creditor-debtor contracts. However, during the depression in the 1930s, Minnesota passed legislation that authorized emergency relief against mortgage foreclosures. Justice George Sutherland (1922–1938), in dissent, appealed to original intent:

> The whole aim of construction . . . is to discover the meaning, to ascertain and give effect to the intent of its framers and the people who adopted it. As nearly as possible we should place ourselves in the condition of those who framed and adopted it. . . . (*Home Building and Loan Association v. Blaisdell* 1934).

Sutherland found that Minnesota's enactment ("to foreclose state action impairing the obligation of contracts *primarily and especially* in respect of such action aimed at giving relief to debtors *in time of emergency*") violated the original intent of the Contract Clause. He did not find any difference between Minnesota's debtors during the depression and those during the revolution. Charles Evans Hughes, chief justice from 1930 to 1941, writing for the majority, rejected Sutherland's original intent method: "It is no answer to say that this public need was not apprehended a century ago, or to insist that what the provision of the Constitution meant to the vision of that day it must mean to the vision of our time." Does the original intent method ignore the fact that times change? Roger Taney, chief justice from 1836 to 1864, wrote the most infamous original intent decision:

> It becomes necessary to determine who were the citizens of the several states when the constitution was adopted. And to do this we must recur to the governments and institutions of the colonies. We must inquire who at the time were recognized as citizens of the states, whose rights and liberties had been outraged by the English government and who declared their independence and assumed the powers of government to defend their rights by force of arms. We refer to these historical facts for the purpose of showing the fixed opinions concerning the Negro race upon which the statesmen of the day spoke and acted. (*Dred Scott v. Sandford* 1856 at p. 407)

Taney's interpretation led him to conclude that slaves could not bring a diversity suit (between parties of diverse jurisdiction, such as citizens of different states) in a federal court, since the framers did not intend to consider slaves as citizens. Does an appeal to "original understanding" avoid the *Dred Scott* outcome?

3. Original Understanding

Robert Bork proposed to interpret the Constitution, not on the basis of the framers' intent but according to the common understanding at the time of enactment (see Reading 4-8). Bork showed how original understanding provided a different analysis of the issues at stake in *Dred Scott*. The Due Process Clause of the Fifth Amendment prohibits the government from taking "life, liberty or property without due process of law." The Court in *Dred Scott* found that Congress had violated this clause by prohibiting the ownership of slaves. However, on Bork's analysis, the Court mistakenly gave a substantive reading of the Due Process clause instead of a procedural reading. Based on the common understanding at the time, the Due Process clause prohibited the government from taking property without some fair procedure.

4. Ethical/Normative Interpretation

Recently, some judges have imposed sentences that constrict the convicted person's reproductive freedom, such as drug-induced castration and wearing Norplant patches. A constitutional challenge to these might invoke the deeply rooted ethical notion of **autonomy.** While these sentencing programs do not violate any express constitutional provision, they do violate this underlying constitutional norm or value—namely, autonomy. Justice William O. Douglas put forth this type of argument in *Griswold v. Connecticut* (1965) when he argued that a number of cases suggested that "specific guarantees in the Bill of Rights have penumbras [indefinite shadows], formed by emanations [illuminations] from the guarantees that help give them life and substance." Douglas brought these strands together under the **right of privacy.** In this vein, Ronald Dworkin calls for a moral reading of the Constitution that would be the best conception of constitutional moral principles that fits the broad story of America's historical record (see chapter 3, page 140 and Dworkin 1996). Does Douglas's "discovery" of a right to privacy provide a good illustration of what Dworkin means by judges constructing moral principles? Dworkin defends judges who uphold substantive values through their interpretation of the Constitution. Do Justice William Brennan's views (Reading 4-9) echo Dworkin's?

READING 4-8

Value Neutral Judicial Interpretation
"The Original Understanding" (1990)

Robert Bork

[W]hat is or is not property would seem, at least as an original matter, a question for legislatures.

How, then, can there be a constitutional right to own slaves where a statute forbids it? Taney [in *Dred Scott*] created such a right by changing the plain meaning of the due process clause of the fifth amendment. He wrote: "[T]he rights of property are united with the rights of person, and placed on the same ground by the fifth amendment to the Constitution, which provides that no person shall be deprived of life, liberty, and property, without due process of law. And an act of Congress which deprives a citizen of the United States of his liberty or property, merely because he came himself or brought his property into a particular Territory of the United States, and who had committed no offence against the laws, could hardly be dignified with the name of due process of law."

The first sentence quotes the guarantee of due process, which is simply a requirement that the substance of any law be applied to a person through fair procedures by any tribunal hearing a case. The clause says nothing whatever about what the substance of the law must be. But Taney's second sentence transforms this requirement of fair procedures into a rule about the allowable substance of a statute. The substance Taney poured into the clause was that Congress cannot prevent slavery in a territory because a man must be allowed to bring slaves there. The second sentence is additionally dishonest because it postulates a man who had "committed no offence against the laws," but a man who brings slaves and keeps them in a jurisdiction where slavery is prohibited does commit an offense against the laws. Taney was saying that there can be no valid law against slaveholding anywhere in the United States.

How did Taney know that slave ownership was a constitutional right? Such a right is nowhere to be found in the Constitution. He knew it because he was passionately convinced that it *must* be a constitutional right. Though his transformation of the due process clause from a procedural to a substantive requirement was an obvious sham, it was a momentous sham, for this was the first appearance in American constitutional law of the concept of "substantive due process," and that concept has been used countless times since by judges who want to write their personal beliefs into a document that, most inconveniently, does not contain those beliefs. . . .

From Bork (1990), *The Tempting of America: The Political Seduction of Law.* New York: Free Press, p. 31.

READING 4-9

Substantive Judicial Interpretation
"The Constitution of the United States: Contemporary Ratification" (1986)

William J. Brennan, Jr.

It will perhaps not surprise you that the text I have chosen for exploration is the amended Constitution of the United States, which, of course, entrenches the Bill of Rights and the Civil War amendments, and draws sustenance from the bedrock principles of another great text, the Magna Carta. So fashioned, the Constitution embodies the aspiration to social justice, brotherhood, and human dignity that brought this nation into being. The Declaration of Independence, the Constitution, and the Bill of Rights solemnly committed the United States to be a country where the dignity and rights of all persons were equal before all authority. In all candor we must concede that part of this egalitarianism in America has been more pretension than realized fact. But we are an aspiring people, a people with faith in progress. Our amended Constitution is the lodestar [guiding light] for our aspirations. Like every text worth reading, it is not crystalline. The phrasing is broad and the limitations of its provisions are not clearly marked. Its majestic generalities and ennobling pronouncements are both luminous and obscure. This ambiguity of course calls forth interpretation, the interaction of reader and text. The encounter with the constitutional text has been, in many senses, my life's work. . . .

The Constitution is fundamentally a public text—the monumental charter of a government and a people—and a justice of the Supreme Court must apply it to resolve public controversies. For, from our beginnings, a most important consequence of the constitutionally created separation of powers has been the American habit, extraordinary to other democracies, of casting social, economic, philosophical, and political questions in the form of law suits, in an attempt to secure ultimate resolution by the Supreme Court. In this way, important aspects of the most fundamental issues confronting our democracy may finally arrive in the Supreme Court for judicial determination. Not infrequently, these are the issues upon which contemporary society is most deeply divided. They arouse our deepest emotions. The main burden of my twenty-nine terms on the Supreme Court has thus been to wrestle with the Constitution in this heightened public context, to draw meaning from the text in order to resolve public controversies. . . .

The view that all matters of substantive policy should be resolved through the majoritarian process has appeal under some circumstances, but I think it ultimately will not do. Unabashed enshrinement of majority will would permit the imposition of a social caste system or wholesale confiscation of property so long as a majority of the authorized legislative body, fairly elected, approved. Our Constitution could not abide such a situation. It is the very purpose of a Constitution—and particularly of the Bill of Rights—to declare certain values transcendent, beyond the reach of temporary political majorities. The majoritarian process cannot be expected to rectify claims of minority right that arise as a response to the outcomes of that very majoritarian process. As James Madison put it: "The prescriptions in favor of liberty ought to be levelled against that quarter where the greatest danger lies, namely, that which possesses the highest prerogative of power. But this is not found in either the Executive or Legislative departments of Government, but in the body of the people, operating by the majority against the minority" (I *Annals* 437). Faith in democracy is one thing, blind faith quite another. Those who drafted our Constitution understood the difference. One cannot read the text without admitting that it embodies substantive value choices; it places certain values beyond the power of any legislature. Obvious are the separation of powers; the privilege of the writ of habeas corpus; prohibition of bills of attainder and ex post facto laws; prohibition of cruel and unusual punishments; the requirement of just compensation for official taking of property; the prohibition of laws tending to establish religion or enjoining the free exercise of religion; and, since the Civil War, the banishment of slavery and official race discrimination. With respect to at least such principles, we simply have not constituted ourselves as strict utilitarians. While the Constitution may be amended, such amendments require an immense effort by the people as a whole.

To remain faithful to the content of the Constitution, therefore, an approach to interpreting the text must account for the existence of these substantive value choices, and must accept the ambiguity inherent in the effort to apply them to modern circumstances. The Framers discerned fundamental principles through struggles against particular malefactions of the crown; the struggle shapes the particular contours of the articulated principles. But our acceptance of the fundamental principles has not and should not bind us to those precise, at times anachronistic, contours. Successive generations of Americans have continued to respect these fundamental choices and adopt them as their own guide to evaluating quite different historical practices. Each generation has the choice to overrule or add to the fundamental principles enunciated by the Framers; the Constitution can be amended or it can be ignored. Yet with respect to its fundamental principles, the text has suffered neither fate. Thus, if I may borrow the words of an esteemed predecessor, Justice Robert Jackson, the burden of judicial interpretation is to translate "the majestic generalities of the Bill of Rights, conceived as part of the pattern of liberal government in the eighteenth century, into concrete restraints on officials dealing with the problems of the twentieth century".

We current justices read the Constitution in the only way that we can: as twentieth-century Americans. We look to the history of the time of framing and to the intervening history of interpretation. But the ultimate question must be, What do the words of the text mean in our time? For the genius of the Constitution rests not in any static meaning it might have had in a world that is dead and gone, but in the adaptability of its great principles to cope with current problems and current needs. What the constitutional fundamentals meant to the wisdom of other times cannot be their measure to the vision of our time. Similarly, what those fundamentals mean for us, our descendants will learn, cannot be the measure to the vision of their time. This realization is not, I assure you, a novel one of my own creation. Permit me to quote from one of the opinions of our Court, *Weems v. United States,* 217 U.S. 349, written nearly a century ago:

> Time works changes, brings into existence new conditions and purposes. Therefore, a principle to be vital must be capable of wider application than the mischief which gave it birth. This is peculiarly true of constitutions. They are not ephemeral enactments, designed to meet passing occasions. They are, to use the words of Chief Justice John Marshall, "designed to approach immortality as nearly as human institutions can approach it." The future is their care and provision for events of good and bad tendencies of which no prophesy can be made. In the application of a constitution, therefore, our contemplation cannot be only of what has been, but of what may be.

Interpretation must account for the transformative purpose of the text. Our Constitution was not intended to preserve a preexisting society but to make a new one, to put in place new principles that the prior political community had not sufficiently recognized. Thus, for example, when we interpret the Civil War amendments to the charter—abolishing slavery, guaranteeing blacks equality under law, and guaranteeing blacks the right to vote—we must remember that those who put them in place had no desire to enshrine the status quo. Their goal was to make over their world, to eliminate all vestige of slave caste. . . .

Brennan, William J., Jr. "The Constitution of the United States: Contemporary Ratification," from *The Great Debate: Interpreting Our Written Constitution.* Reprinted by permission of The Federalist Society.

H. LIBERALISM

Political labels seldom fit precisely. In politics, British liberals have more in common with American libertarians than with the liberals represented in the Democratic Party. To confuse matters more, British liberals, American libertarians, and members of the Democratic and Republican parties in the United States all come under the common philosophical umbrella of "liberalism." Some critics have quit searching for a common cloth with which to fashion an umbrella that will shade all liberals. Instead, they speak only of "liberalisms." Whatever definitional challenges the word poses, liberalism's changing character has helped it endure. Its strength lies in its ability to retain tensions among conflicting notions. Three main strands of liberalism—classical, modern, and contemporary—still remain identifiable.

1. Classical Liberalism

Classical liberal theorists include John Locke, Adam Smith, Alexis de Tocqueville, and Friedrich von Hayek. Classical liberalism focuses on "the idea of limited government, the maintenance of the rule of law, the avoidance of arbitrary and discretionary power, the sanctity of private property and freely made contracts, and the responsibility of individuals for their own fates" (Good and Pettil 1993, p. 293). Despite its commitment to individualism and its orientation to the secular, classical liberalism (in its Lockean form) retains unresolved tensions between the individual and the government, and between the secular and the religious. Classical liberalism makes a sharp divide between the individual and the government. Liberals focus on an individual's freedom from government interference. However, while classical liberalism sets out to form political structures that make governments the protector of individual thought and action, it has not always looked kindly on individuals who express radical thoughts and perform radical deeds. A concern for protecting the government from the individual lurks behind classical liberalism's more visible protection of the individual from the government. Throughout American history, cases concerning free speech and press have shown a deepseated concern for the security of the state and the preservation of the public peace. The free speech cases examined in the next chapter highlight the tension between protecting individuals and protecting the government.

A tension also exists between classical liberalism's professed secularism and its actual religious practices. Classical liberals proclaim a profound antipathy to religion as a means of providing the foundation for secular authority. Nevertheless, in spite of its overall secular orientation, classical liberalism retains religious elements. Locke, for example, mixed the sacred and the secular in his version of the state of nature. His concept of natural rights, preserved in the transition from a state of nature to a civil society, had a religious foundation. Further, Locke's principle of religious toleration did not extend to all religions. He had little toleration for Catholicism, which he viewed as a threat to the state. Given the liberal foundation of the U.S. Constitution, an analysis of constitutional law reveals similar favoritism toward certain religions (see Reading 4-10). A government, including the judiciary, will have a difficult time maintaining neutrality toward all religious practices in any society that is dominated by one religion. Does protection of religious freedom extend to all types of religion, including the spiritual practices of Native Americans (see page 283)? Does the First Amendment prohibition of a state religion bar the state from sanctioning all types of religious beliefs and practices, including Christian ones (see Discussion Issues page 287)? An understanding of classical liberalism sheds light on constitutional debates over religious freedom.

Locke's writings have become classics in liberal thought. He believed that the state of nature could not provide effective enforcement of natural rights or impartial adjudication of disputes. He claimed that only a political structure founded on voluntary consent could provide the impartial rule of law for its citizens. It seems intuitively obvious that law and impartiality should go together. What, then, justifies the admonition that the law should not favor, for example, certain types of speech or certain kinds of religious practices? Even if it is desirable, what prospects of success does an impartial judiciary have within a society partial to certain values and beliefs?

READING 4-10

Classical Liberalism
"Of the Ends of Political Society and Government" (1690)

John Locke

123. If man in the state of nature be so free as has been said; if he be absolute lord of his own person and possessions, equal to the greatest, and subject to nobody, why will he part with his freedom? Why will he give up this empire, and subject himself to the dominion and control of any other power? To which 'tis obvious to answer that, though in the state of nature he hath such a right, yet the enjoyment of it is very uncertain, and constantly exposed to the invasion of others. For all being kings as much as he, every man his equal, and the greater part no strict observers of equity and justice, the enjoyment of the property he has in this state is very unsafe, very insecure. This makes him willing to quit this condition which, however free, is full of fears and continual dangers. And 'tis not without reason that he seeks out, and is willing to join in society with others who are already united, or have a mind to unite, for the mutual preservation of their lives, liberties, and estates, which I call by the general name *property*.

124. The great and chief end, therefore, of men's uniting into commonwealths, and putting themselves under government, is the preservation of their property, to which in the state of nature there are many things wanting.

First, there wants an established, settled, known law, received and allowed by common consent to be the standard of right and wrong, and the common measure to decide all controversies between them. For though the law of nature be plain and intelligible to all rational creatures; yet men being biased by their interest, as well as ignorant for want of study of it, are not apt to allow of it as a law binding to them in the application of it to their particular cases.

125. Secondly, in the state of nature there wants a known and indifferent judge, with authority to determine all differences according to the established law. For everyone in that state being both judge and executioner of the law of nature, men being partial to themselves, passion and revenge is very apt to carry them too far, and with too much heat, in their own cases; as well as negligence and unconcernedness to make them too remiss in other men's.

126. Thirdly, in the state of nature there often wants power to back and support the sentence when right, and to give it due execution. They who by any injustice offended, will seldom fail, where they are able, by force to make good their injustice. Such resistance many times makes the punishment dangerous, and frequently destructive, to those who attempt it.

127. Thus mankind, notwithstanding all the privileges of the state of nature, being but in an ill condition while they remain in it, are quickly driven into society. Hence it comes to pass that we seldom find any number of men live any time together in this state. The inconveniences that they are therein exposed to, by the irregular and uncertain exercise of the power every man has of punishing the transgressions of others, make them take sanctuary under the established laws of government, and therein seek the preservation of their property. 'Tis this makes them so willingly give up every one his single power of punishing to be exercised by such alone as shall be appointed to it amongst them; and by such rules as the community, or those authorized by them to that purpose, shall agree on. And in this we have the original right and rise of both the legislative and executive power, as well as of the governments and societies themselves.

128. For in the state of nature, to omit the liberty he has of innocent delights, a man has two powers:

The first is to do whatsoever he thinks fit for the preservation of himself and others within the permission of the law of nature; by which law, common to them all, he and all the rest of mankind are one community, make up one society distinct from all other creatures. And were it not for the corruption and viciousness of degenerate men, there would be no need of any other; no necessity that men should separate from this great and natural community, and by positive agreements combine into smaller and divided associations.

The other power a man has in the state of nature is the power to punish the crimes committed against that law. Both these he gives up when he joins in a private, if I may so call it, or particular political society, and incorporates into any commonwealth, separate from the rest of mankind.

129. The first power, viz. of doing whatsoever he thought fit for the preservation of himself, and the rest of mankind, he gives up to be regulated by laws made by the society, so far forth as the preservation of himself and the rest of that society shall require. Which laws of the society in many things confine the liberty he had by the law of nature.

130. Secondly, the power of punishing he wholly gives up, and engages his natural force (which he might before employ in the execution of the law of nature, by his own single authority, as he thought fit) to assist the executive power of the society, as the law thereof shall require. For being now in a new state, wherein he is to enjoy many conveniences from the labour, assistance, and society of others in the same community, as well as protection from its whole strength, he is to part also with as much of his natural liberty in providing for himself as the good, prosperity, and safety of the society shall require: which is not only necessary, but just, since the other members of the society do the like.

131. But though men when they enter into society give up the equality, liberty, and executive power they had in the state of nature into the hands of the society, to be so far disposed of by the legislative as the good of the

society shall require; yet it being only with an intention in everyone the better to preserve himself his liberty and property (for no rational creature can be supposed to change his condition with an intention to be worse), the power of the society, or legislative constituted by them, can never be supposed to extend further than the common good; but is obliged to secure everyone's property by providing against those three defects above-mentioned that made the state of nature so unsafe and uneasy. And so whoever has the legislative or supreme power of any commonwealth is bound to govern by established standing laws, promulgated and known to the people, and not by extempory decrees; by indifferent and upright judges, who are to decide controversies by those laws; and to employ the force of the community at home only in the execution of such laws, or abroad to prevent or redress foreign injuries, and secure the community from inroads and invasion. And all this to be directed to no other end, but the peace, safety, and public good of the people.

From Locke (1690), "Of the Ends of Political Society and Government," Chapter 9, sections 123–131, *The Second Treatise of Government*. In (1993) *John Locke, Political Writings*. David Wootton, editor. New York: Penguin, pp. 322–327.

2. Modern Liberalism

Modern liberalism traces its philosophical roots to nineteenth-century British philosopher **John Stuart Mill** (1808–1873), who also became the foremost exponent of utilitarianism. Mill did not see human nature as having a uniform quality—rather he stressed human diversity. He saw humans as "progressive beings," constantly developing themselves. Mill believed (see Reading 4-11) that the best political system should go beyond the protective functions granted by classical liberals, such as Locke and should contribute to human development. Concern for human welfare underlies modern liberalism.

READING 4-11

Modern Liberalism
"Criterion of a Good Form" (1861)

John Stuart Mill

If we ask ourselves on what causes and conditions good government in all its senses, from the humblest to the most exalted, depends, we find that the principal of them, the one which transcends all others, is the qualities of the human beings composing the society over which the government is exercised.

We may take, as a first instance, the administration of justice; with the more propriety, since there is no part of public business in which the mere machinery, the rules and contrivances for conducting the details of the operation, are of such vital consequence. Yet even these yield in importance to the qualities of the human agents employed. Of what efficacy are rules of procedure in securing the ends of justice, if the moral condition of the people is such that the witnesses generally lie, and the judges and their subordinates take bribes? Again, how can institutions provide a good municipal administration, if there exists such indifference to the subject, that those who would administer honestly and capably cannot be induced to serve, and the duties are left to those who undertake them because they have some private interest to be promoted? Of what avail is the most broadly popular representative system, if the electors do not care to choose the best member of parliament, but choose him who will spend most money to be elected? How can a representative assembly work for good, if its members can be bought, or if their excitability of temperament, uncorrected by public discipline or private self-control, makes them incapable of calm deliberation, and they resort to manual violence on the floor of the House, or shoot at one another with rifles? How, again, can government, or any joint concern, be carried on in a tolerable manner by people so envious, that if one among them seems likely to succeed in anything, those who ought to co-operate with him form a tacit combination to make him fail? Whenever the general disposition of the people is such, that each individual regards those only of his interests which are selfish, and does not dwell on, or concern himself for, his share of the general interest, in such a state of things good government is impossible. The influence of defects of intelligence in obstructing all the elements of good government requires no illustration. Government consists of acts done by human beings; and if the agents, or those who choose the agents, or those to whom the agents are responsible, or the lookers-on whose opinion ought to influence and check all these, are mere masses of ignorance, stupidity, and baleful prejudice, every operation of government will go wrong: while, in proportion as the men rise above this standard, so will the government improve in quality; up to the point of excellence, attainable but nowhere attained, where the officers of government, themselves persons of superior virtue and intellect, are surrounded by the atmosphere of a virtuous and enlightened public opinion.

The first element of good government, therefore, being the virtue and intelligence of the human beings composing the community, the most important point of excellence which any form of government can possess is to promote the virtue and intelligence of the people themselves. The first question in respect to any political institutions is, how far they tend to foster in the members of the community the various desirable qualities, moral and intellectual; or rather (following Bentham's more complete classification) moral, intellectual, and active. The government which does this the best, has every likelihood of being the best in all other respects, since it is on these qualities, so far as they exist in the people, that all possibility of goodness in the practical operations of the government depends.

We may consider, then, as one criterion of the goodness of a government, the degree in which it tends to increase the sum of good qualities in the governed, collectively and individually; since, besides that their well-being is the sole object of government, their good qualities supply the moving force which works the machinery. This leaves, as the other constituent element of the merit of a government, the quality of the machinery itself; that is, the degree in which it is adapted to take advantage of the amount of good qualities which may at any time exist, and make them instrumental to the right purposes. Let us again take the subject of judicature as an example and illustration. The judicial system being given, the goodness of the administration of justice is in the compound ratio of the worth of the men composing the tribunals, and the worth of the public opinion which influences or controls them. But all the difference between a good and a bad system of judicature lies in the contrivances adopted for bringing whatever moral and intellectual worth exists in the community to bear upon the administration of justice, and making it duly operative on the result. . . .

From Mill (1861), *Representative Government,* Chapter II, in (1975) *John Stuart Mill, Three Essays.* New York: Oxford University Press, pp. 166–168.

3. Contemporary Liberalism

Contemporary liberals have had to grapple with a tension between classical and modern versions of liberalism. Freedom, a primary value for classical liberals, and equality, a priority for modern liberals, seem at odds. With freedom as a primary value, inequalities appear inevitable. Alternatively, a focus on equality seems to threaten freedom by requiring government intervention. Contemporary American philosopher John Rawls (1921–) has tried to reconcile freedom and equality. In keeping with classical liberalism, he proposes principles of justice that give priority to the protection of fundamental rights and liberties (right to vote, freedom of speech and conscience). Rawls does not permit sacrificing any fundamental rights and liberties for the general welfare. However, in adopting a qualified egalitarianism, he also presents a second principle of justice that accepts some social and economic inequalities but places limits on them. His principles do not permit unfair inequalities of opportunity or inequalities that do not benefit those who are the worst off. Rawls, like Hobbes and Locke, is a social contract theorist, but he does not use the social contract as a device to justify government. According to Rawls, the social contract, in the form of what he calls the **original position,** provides a fair procedure for rational individuals to choose binding moral principles ("justice as fairness"). He claims that if individuals were to make their choice of principles under a **veil of ignorance** (without particular knowledge of their own conditions), they would choose the principles of justice that he has proposed.

In later works, culminating in *Political Liberalism,* Rawls emphasizes the political doctrines, as distinguished from his previously comprehensive moral doctrines (see Reading 4-12). He rejects the idea of an essential human nature (see chapter 1, page 6) and acknowledges opposing comprehensive moral doctrines, each with its own account of the good. He believes that citizens differ over what they think is the good for society, and he fully accepts the irreconcilable nature of these conflicts. Rawls refuses to propose a philosophical system—above all the other systems—for choosing one of the competing comprehensive systems over the others. Even without a dominant "philosophy of life," Rawls argues that citizens with irreconcilable views can live together within a constitutional democracy, if they accept a political conception of justice. A political conception of justice provides the basis for forming reasonable political agreements through an **"overlapping consensus."** For example, a political conception of justice enables people of widely different ethnic groups and religions to thrive within the same political structure. Rawls, thus, proposes a political liberalism that accommodates a wide diversity of conceptions of the good through an overlapping consensus.

Rawls first proposed a theory of justice with universal elements that applied to all societies and then narrowed the theory's application to established liberal societies. More recently, however, he has explored ways to bring the same principles of the law of peoples to outlaw societies (see Reading 4-13). The law of peoples provides "the concepts and principles to use to judge the law of nations or international law" (Shute and Hurley 1993, p. 51). Hierarchical societies are well ordered but not liberal. Outlaw societies refuse to acknowledge the law of peoples. Were nations that legally allowed slavery or apartheid hierarchical (see chapter 3, page 148 Controversies)? Was the Nazi regime an outlaw society (see chapter 2, page 80 Controversies)? How adequate are Rawls's proposals for dealing with these nonliberal societies?

READING 4-12

Contemporary Liberalism
"Justice as Fairness: Political Not Metaphysical" (1985)

John Rawls

I now take up a point essential to thinking of justice as fairness as a liberal view. Although this conception is a moral conception, it is not, as I have said, intended as a comprehensive moral doctrine. The conception of the citizen as a free and equal person is not a moral ideal to govern all of life, but is rather an ideal belonging to a conception of political justice which is to apply to the basic structure. I emphasize this point because to think otherwise would be incompatible with liberalism as a political doctrine. Recall that as such a doctrine, liberalism assumes that in a constitutional democratic state under modern conditions there are bound to exist conflicting and incommensurable conceptions of the good. This feature characterizes modern culture since the Reformation. Any viable political conception of justice that is not to rely on the autocratic use of state power must recognize this fundamental social fact. This does not mean, of course, that such a conception cannot impose constraints on individuals and associations, but that when it does so, these constraints are accounted for, directly or indirectly, by the requirements of political justice for the basic structure.

Given this fact, we adopt a conception of the person framed as part of, and restricted to, an explicitly political conception of justice. In this sense, the conception of the person is a political one. As I stressed in the previous section, persons can accept this conception of themselves as citizens and use it when discussing questions of political justice without being committed in other parts of their life to comprehensive moral ideals often associated with liberalism, for example, the ideals of autonomy and individuality. The absence of commitment to these ideals, and indeed to any particular comprehensive ideal, is essential to liberalism as a political doctrine. The reason is that any such ideal, when pursued as a comprehensive ideal, is incompatible with other conceptions of the good, with forms of personal, moral, and religious life consistent with justice and which, therefore, have a proper place in a democratic society. As comprehensive moral ideals, autonomy and individuality are unsuited for a political conception of justice. As found in Kant and J. S. Mill, these comprehensive ideals, despite their very great importance in liberal thought, are extended too far when presented as the only appropriate foundation for a constitutional regime. So understood, liberalism becomes but another sectarian doctrine.

This conclusion requires comment: it does not mean, of course, that the liberalisms of Kant and Mill are not appropriate moral conceptions from which we can be led to affirm democratic institutions. But they are only two such conceptions among others, and so but two of the philosophical doctrines likely to persist and gain adherents in a reasonably just democratic regime. In such a regime the comprehensive moral views which support its basic institutions may include the liberalisms of individuality and autonomy; and possibly these liberalisms are among the more prominent doctrines in an overlapping consensus, that is, in a consensus in which, as noted earlier, different and even conflicting doctrines affirm the publicly shared basis of political arrangements. The liberalisms of Kant and Mill have a certain historical preeminence as among the first and most important philosophical views to espouse modern constitutional democracy and to develop its underlying ideas in an influential way; and it may even turn out that societies in which the ideals of autonomy and individuality are widely accepted are among the most well-governed and harmonious.

By contrast with liberalism as a comprehensive moral doctrine, justice as fairness tries to present a conception of political justice rooted in the basic intuitive ideas found in the public culture of a constitutional democracy. We conjecture that these ideas are likely to be affirmed by each of the opposing comprehensive moral doctrines influential in a reasonably just democratic society. Thus justice as fairness seeks to identify the kernel of an overlapping consensus, that is, the shared intuitive ideas which when worked up into a political conception of justice turn out to be sufficient to underwrite a just constitutional regime. This is the most we can expect, nor do we need more. We must note, however, that when justice as fairness is fully realized in a well-ordered society, the value of full autonomy is likewise realized. In this way justice as fairness is indeed similar to the liberalisms of Kant and Mill; but in contrast with them, the value of full autonomy is here specified by a political conception of justice, and not by a comprehensive moral doctrine. . . .

One of the deepest distinctions between political conceptions of justice is between those that allow for a plurality of opposing and even incommensurable conceptions of the good and those that hold that there is but one conception of the good which is to be recognized by all persons, so far as they are fully rational. Conceptions of justice which fall on opposite sides of this divide are distinct in many fundamental ways. Plato and Aristotle, and the Christian tradition as represented by Augustine and Aquinas, fall on the side of the one rational good. Such views tend to be teleological and to hold that institutions are just to the extent that they effectively promote this good. Indeed, since classical times the dominant tradition seems to have been that there is but one rational conception of the good, and that the aim of moral philosophy, together with theology and metaphysics, is to determine its nature. Classical utilitarianism belongs to this dominant tradition. By contrast, liberalism as a political doctrine supposes that there are many conflicting and incommensurable conceptions of the good, each compatible with the full rationality of human persons, so far as we can ascertain within a workable political conception of justice. As a consequence of this supposition, liberalism assumes that it is a characteristic feature of a free democratic culture that a plurality of conflicting and incommensurable conceptions of the good are affirmed by its citizens. Liberalism as a political doctrine holds that the question the dominant tradition has tried to answer has no practicable answer; that is, it has no answer suitable for a political conception of justice for a democratic society. In such a society a teleological political conception is out of the question: public agreement on the requisite conception of the good cannot be obtained. . . .

In justice as fairness, social unity is understood by starting with the conception of society as a system of cooperation between free and equal persons. Social unity and the allegiance of citizens to their common institutions are not founded on their all affirming the same conception of the good, but on their publicly accepting a political conception of justice to regulate the basic structure of society. The concept of justice is independent from and prior to the concept of goodness in the sense that its principles limit the conceptions of the good which are permissible. A just basic structure and its background institutions establish a framework within which permissible conceptions can be advanced. Elsewhere I have called this relation between a conception of justice and conceptions of the good the priority of right (since the just falls under the right). I believe this priority is characteristic of liberalism as a political doctrine and something like it seems essential to any conception of justice reasonable for a democratic state. Thus to understand how social unity is possible given the historical conditions of a democratic society, we start with our basic intuitive idea of social cooperation, an idea present in the public culture of a democratic society, and proceed from there to a public conception of justice as the basis of social unity in the way I have sketched. . . .

READING 4-13
Liberalism Goes Global
"The Law of Peoples" (1993)

John Rawls

I assume that working out the law of peoples for liberal democratic societies only will result in the adoption of certain familiar principles of justice, and will also allow for various forms of cooperative association among democratic peoples and not for a world state. Here I follow Kant's lead in *Perpetual Peace* (1795) in thinking that a world government—by which I mean a unified political regime with the legal powers normally exercised by central governments—would be either a global despotism or else a fragile empire torn by frequent civil strife as various regions and peoples try to gain political autonomy. On the other hand, it may turn out, as I sketch below, that there will be many different kinds of organizations subject to the judgment of the law of democratic peoples, charged with regulating cooperation between them, and having certain recognized duties. Some of these organizations (like the United Nations) may have the authority to condemn domestic institutions that violate human rights, and in certain severe cases to punish them by imposing economic sanctions, or even by military intervention. The scope of these powers is all peoples' and covers their domestic affairs.

If all this is sound, I believe the principles of justice between free and democratic peoples will include certain familiar principles long recognized as belonging to the law of peoples, among them the following:

1. Peoples (as organized by their governments) are free and independent and their freedom and independence is to be respected by other peoples.
2. Peoples are equal and parties to their own agreements.
3. Peoples have the right of self-defense but no right to war.
4. Peoples are to observe a duty of nonintervention.
5. Peoples are to observe treaties and undertakings.
6. Peoples are to observe certain specified restrictions on the conduct of war (assumed to be in self-defense).
7. Peoples are to honor human rights. . . .

The three necessary conditions for a well-ordered regime—that it respect the principles of peace and not be expansionist, that its system of law meet the essentials of legitimacy in the eyes of its own people, and that it honor basic human rights—are proposed as an answer as to where those limits lie. These conditions indicate the bedrock beyond which we cannot go.

We have discussed how far many societies of the world have always been, and are today, from meeting these three conditions for being a member in good standing of a reasonable society of peoples. The law of peoples provides the basis for judging the conduct of any existing regime, liberal as well as nonliberal. And since our account of the law of peoples was developed out of a liberal conception of justice, we must address the question whether the liberal law of peoples is ethnocentric and merely Western.

To address this question, recall that in working out the law of peoples we assumed that liberal societies conduct themselves toward other societies from the point of view of their own liberal political conception. Regarding this conception as sound, and as meeting all the criteria they are now able to apply, how else are they to proceed? To the objection that to proceed thus is ethnocentric or merely Western, the reply is: no, not necessarily. Whether it is so turns on the content of the political conception that liberal societies embrace once it is worked up to provide at least an outline of the law of peoples.

Looking at the outline of that law, we should note the difference between it and the law of peoples as it might be understood by religious and expansionist states that reject the liberal conception. The liberal conception asks of other societies only what they can reasonably grant without submitting to a position of inferiority, much less to domination. It is crucial that a liberal conception of the law of peoples not ask well-ordered hierarchical societies to abandon their religious institutions and adopt liberal ones. True, in our sketch we supposed that traditional societies would affirm the law of peoples that would hold among just liberal societies. That law is therefore universal in its reach: It asks of other societies only what they can accept once they are prepared to stand in a relation of equality with all other societies and once their regimes accept the criterion of legitimacy in the eyes of their own people. In what other relations can a society and its regime reasonably expect to stand?

Moreover, the liberal law of peoples does not justify economic sanctions or military pressure on well-ordered hierarchical societies to change their ways, provided they respect the rules of peace and their political institutions satisfy the essential conditions we have reviewed. If, however, these conditions are violated, external pressure of one kind or another may be justified depending on the severity and the circumstances of the case. A concern for human rights should be a fixed part of the foreign policy of liberal and hierarchical societies.

Looking back at our discussion, let's recall that besides sketching how the law of peoples might be developed from liberal conceptions of right and justice, a further aim was to set out the bearing of political liberalism for a wider world society once a liberal political conception of justice is extended to the law of peoples. In particular, we asked: What form does the toleration of nonliberal societies take in this case? Although tyrannical and dictatorial regimes cannot be accepted as members in good standing of a reasonable society of peoples, not all regimes can reasonably be required to be liberal. If so, the law of peoples would not express liberalism's own principle of toleration for other reasonable ways of ordering society. A liberal society must respect other societies organized by comprehensive doctrines, provided their political and social institutions meet certain conditions that lead the society to adhere to a reasonable law of peoples.

I did not try to present an argument to this conclusion. I took it as clear that if other nonliberal societies honored certain conditions, such as the three requirements . . ., they would be accepted by liberal societies as members in good standing of a society of peoples. There would be no political case to attack these nonliberal societies militarily, or to bring economic or other sanctions against them to revise their institutions. Critical commentary in liberal societies would be fully consistent with the civic liberties and integrity of those societies.

What conception of toleration of other societies does the law of peoples express? How is it connected with political liberalism? If it should be asked whether liberal societies are, morally speaking, better than hierarchical societies, and therefore whether the world would be a better place if all societies were liberal, those holding a comprehensive liberal view could think it would be. But that opinion would not support a claim to rid the world of nonliberal regimes. It could have no operative force in what, as a matter of right, they could do politically. The situation is parallel to the toleration of other conceptions of the good in the domestic case. Someone holding a comprehensive liberal view can say that their society would be a better place if every one held such a view. They might be wrong in this judgment even by their own lights, as other doctrines may play a moderating and balancing role given the larger background of belief and conviction, and give society's culture a certain depth and richness. The point is that to affirm the superiority of a particular comprehensive view is fully compatible with affirming a political conception of justice that does not impose it, and thus with political liberalism itself.

Political liberalism holds that comprehensive doctrines have but a restricted place in liberal democratic politics in this sense: Fundamental constitutional questions and matters concerning basic rights and liberties are to be settled by a public political conception of justice, exemplified by the liberal political conceptions, and not by those wider doctrines. For given the pluralism of democratic societies—a pluralism best seen as the outcome of the exercise of human reason under free institutions, and which can only be undone by the oppressive use of state power—affirming such a public conception and the basic political institutions that realize it, is the most reasonable basis of social unity available to us.

The law of peoples, as I have sketched it, is simply the extension of these same ideas to the political society of well-ordered peoples. That law, which settles fundamental constitutional questions and matters of basic justice as they arise for the society of peoples, must also be based on a public political conception of justice and not on a comprehensive religious, philosophical, or moral doctrine. I have sketched the content of such a political conception and tried to explain how it could be endorsed by well-ordered societies, both liberal and hierarchical. Except as a basis of a modus vivendi, expansionist societies of whatever kind could not endorse it; but in principle there is no peaceful solution in their case except the domination of one side or the peace of exhaustion.

---

4. Critiques of Liberalism

Communitarianism

Liberalism, particularly its Rawlsian version, has faced a flurry of criticism, particularly from communitarians. Contemporary communitarians follow a long line of advocates of community based politics and morality. Communitarianism has affinities with the civic humanism of the antifederalists (see page 166). Liberalism, according to communitarian **Michael Sandel** (see Reading 4-14), treats individuals as isolated atoms, making people strangers in a world in which community plays a critical role in determining who they are. The liberal view that individuals should choose their own values and goals ignores the reality and the value of community in shaping those values and goals. Communitarians, following Aristotle, argue that we cannot justify political structures without reference to common purposes and ends, just as we cannot identify ourselves without reference to the communities we inhabit.

Communitarians criticize all versions of liberalism as having unwarranted preoccupation with individual freedoms and rights. Sandel, for example, criticizes the priority that liberals give to individual rights over conceptions of the good. A liberal political framework protects and nourishes individual rights and freedoms, and allows individuals to pursue their own conceptions of the good without the state's imposing its sense of goods on them. Liberals cherish freedom of speech because it enables individuals to choose their own goods and not because the state promotes some values, such as rational deliberation and civic participation. Communitarians, in contrast, object to laws that, while supposedly promoting individual freedom, break down civil discourse and community. Pornography, hate speech, and plant closings can, in the name of freedom, destroy the valuable fabric of community (see chapter 5, page 246). Liberals, at least according to Sandel, do not want the state to affirm any one sense of the good life. They believe the state should guarantee a right to free speech, so that individuals can choose their own goods, their own life goals. Alternatively, a communitarian might defend free speech because "a life of political discussion is inherently worthier than a life unconcerned with public affairs" (Sandel 1984, p. 4).

Critical Legal Studies

Liberals of many varieties embrace the rule of law as a critical means for maintaining liberty. Hobbhouse provided the classical formulation of this:

> [T]he first condition of free government is government not by the arbitrary determination of the ruler, but by fixed rules of law, to which the ruler himself is subject. (Hobbhouse 1964, p. 17)

A contemporary version of legal realism, critical legal studies (CLS), launched an attack on liberalism and its undying faith in the rule of law during the early phase of the movement. Andrew Altman, one of the first philosophers to take CLS seriously, gave an overview of the CLS critique of liberalism before undertaking his defense of liberalism (see Reading 4-15). The next chapter focuses on liberty or freedom, the primary liberal value. To what extent do alternative visions such as communitarianism and critical legal studies undermine liberalism and freedom?

READING 4-14

Communitarian Critique of Liberalism
"Morality and the Liberal Ideal" (1984)

Michael J. Sandel

Liberals often take pride in defending what they oppose—pornography, for example, or unpopular views. They say the state should not impose on its citizens a preferred way of life, but should leave them as free as possible to choose their own values and ends, consistent with a similar liberty for others.

This commitment to freedom of choice requires liberals constantly to distinguish between permission and praise, between allowing a practice and endorsing it. It is one thing to allow pornography, they argue, something else to affirm it.

Conservatives sometimes exploit this distinction by ignoring it. They charge that those who would allow abortions favor abortion, that opponents of school prayer oppose prayer, that those who defend the rights of Communists sympathize with their cause. And in a pattern of argument familiar in our politics, liberals reply by invoking higher principles; it is not that they dislike pornography less, but rather that they value toleration, or freedom of choice, or fair procedures more.

But in contemporary debate, the liberal rejoinder seems increasingly fragile, its moral basis increasingly unclear. Why should toleration and freedom of choice prevail when other important values are also at stake? Too often the answer implies some version of moral relativism, the idea that it is wrong to "legislate morality" because all morality is merely subjective. "Who is to say what is literature and what is filth? That is a value judgment, and whose values should decide?"

Relativism usually appears less as a claim than as a question. "Who is to judge?" But it is a question that can also be asked of the values that liberals defend. Toleration and freedom and fairness are values too, and they can hardly be defended by the claim that no values can be defended. So it is a mistake to affirm liberal values by arguing that all values are merely subjective. The relativist defense of liberalism is no defense at all.

What, then, can be the moral basis of the higher principles the liberal invokes? Recent political philosophy has offered two main alternatives—one utilitarian, the other Kantian. The utilitarian view, following John Stuart Mill, defends liberal principles in the name of maximizing the general welfare. The state should not impose on its citizens a preferred way of life, even for their own good, because doing so will reduce the sum of human happiness, at least in the long run; better that people choose for themselves, even if, on occasion, they get it wrong. "The only freedom which deserves the name," writes Mill in *On Liberty,* "is that of pursuing our own good in our own way, so long as we do not attempt to deprive others of theirs, or impede their efforts to obtain it." He adds that his argument does not depend on any notion of abstract right, only on the principle of the greatest good for the greatest number. "I regard utility as the ultimate appeal on all ethical questions; but it must be utility in the largest sense, grounded on the permanent interests of man as a progressive being."

Many objections have been raised against utilitarianism as a general doctrine of moral philosophy. Some have questioned the concept of utility, and the assumption that all human goods are in principle commensurable. Others have objected that by reducing all values to preferences and desires, utilitarians are unable to admit qualitative distinctions of worth, unable to distinguish noble desires from base ones. But most recent debate has focused on whether utilitarianism offers a convincing basis for liberal principles, including respect for individual rights.

In one respect, utilitarianism would seem well suited to liberal purposes. Seeking to maximize overall happiness does not require judging people's values, only aggregating them. And the willingness to aggregate preferences without judging them suggests a tolerant spirit, even a democratic one. When people go to the polls we count their votes, whatever they are.

But the utilitarian calculus is not always as liberal as it first appears. If enough cheering Romans pack the Coliseum to watch the lion devour the Christian, the collective pleasure of the Romans will surely outweigh the pain of the Christian, intense though it be. Or if a big majority abhors a small religion and wants it banned, the balance of preferences will favor suppression, not toleration. Utilitarians sometimes defend individual rights on the grounds that respecting them now will serve utility in the long run. But this calculation is precarious and contingent. It hardly secures the liberal promise not to impose on some the values of others. As the majority will is an inadequate instrument of liberal politics—by itself it fails to secure individual rights—so the utilitarian philosophy is an inadequate foundation for liberal principles.

The case against utilitarianism was made most powerfully by Immanuel Kant. He argued that empirical principles, such as utility, were unfit to serve as basis for the moral law. A wholly instrumental defense of freedom and rights not only leaves rights vulnerable, but fails to respect the inherent dignity of persons. The utilitarian calculus treats people as means to the happiness of others, not as ends in themselves, worthy of respect.

Contemporary liberals extend Kant's argument with the claim that utilitarianism fails to take seriously the distinction between persons. In seeking above all to maximize the general welfare, the utilitarian treats society as a whole as if it were a single person; it conflates our many, diverse desires into a single system of desires. It is indifferent to the distribution of satisfactions among persons, except insofar as this may affect the overall sum. But this fails to respect our plurality and distinctness. It uses some as means to the happiness of all, and so fails to respect each as an end in himself.

In the view of modern-day Kantians, certain rights are so fundamental that even the general welfare cannot override them. As John Rawls writes in his important work, *A Theory of Justice,* "Each person possesses an inviolability founded on justice that even the welfare of society as a whole cannot override. . . . The rights secured by justice are not subject to political bargaining or to the calculus of social interests."

So Kantian liberals need an account of rights that does not depend on utilitarian considerations. More than this, they need an account that does not depend on any particular conception of the good, that does not presuppose the superiority of one way of life over others. Only a justification neutral about ends could preserve the liberal resolve not to favor any particular ends, or to impose on its citizens a preferred way of life. But what sort of justification could this be? How is it possible to affirm certain liberties and rights as fundamental without embracing some vision of the good life, without endorsing some ends over others? It would seem we are back to the relativist predicament—to affirm liberal principles without embracing any particular ends.

The solution proposed by Kantian liberals is to draw a distinction between the "right" and the "good"—between a framework of basic rights and liberties, and the conceptions of the good that people may choose to pursue within the framework. It is one thing for the state to support a fair framework, they argue, something else to affirm some particular ends. For example, it is one thing to defend the right to free speech so that people may be free to form their own opinions and choose their own ends, but something else to support it on the grounds that a life of political discussion is inherently worthier than a life unconcerned with public affairs, or on the grounds that free speech will increase the general welfare. Only the first defense is available in the Kantian view, resting as it does on the ideal of a neutral framework.

Now, the commitment to a framework neutral with respect to ends can be seen as a kind of value—in this sense the Kantian liberal is no relativist—but its value consists precisely in its refusal to affirm a preferred way of life or conception of the good. For Kantian liberals, then, the right is prior to the good, and in two senses. First, individual rights cannot be sacrificed for the sake of the general good; and second, the principles of justice that specify these rights cannot be premised on any particular vision of the good life. What justifies the rights is not that they maximize the general welfare or otherwise promote the good, but rather that they comprise a fair framework within which individuals and groups can choose their own values and ends, consistent with a similar liberty for others.

Of course, proponents of the rights-based ethic notoriously disagree about what rights are fundamental, and about what political arrangements the ideal of the neutral framework requires. Egalitarian liberals support the welfare state, and favor a scheme of civil liberties together with certain social and economic rights—rights to welfare, education, health care, and so on. Libertarian liberals defend the market economy, and claim that redistributive policies violate peoples' rights; they favor a scheme of civil liberties combined with a strict regime of private property rights. But whether egalitarian or libertarian, rights-based liberalism begins with the claim that we are separate, individual persons, each with our own aims, interests, and conceptions of the good; it seeks a framework of rights that will enable us to realize our capacity as free moral agents, consistent with a similar liberty for others.

Within academic philosophy, the last decade or so has seen the ascendance of the rights-based ethic over the utilitarian one, due in large part to the influence of Rawls's *A Theory of Justice*. The legal philosopher H. L. A. Hart recently described the shift from "the old faith that some form of utilitarianism must capture the essence of political morality" to the new faith that "the truth must lie with a doctrine of basic human rights, protecting specific basic liberties and interests of individuals. . . . Whereas not so long ago great energy and much ingenuity of many philosophers were devoted to making some form of utilitarianism work, latterly such energies and ingenuity have been devoted to the articulation of theories of basic rights."

But in philosophy as in life, the new faith becomes the old orthodoxy before long. Even as it has come to prevail over its utilitarian rival, the rights-based ethic has recently faced a growing challenge from a different direction, from a view that gives fuller expression to the claims of citizenship and community than the liberal vision allows. The communitarian critics, unlike modern liberals, make the case for a politics of the common good. Recalling the arguments of Hegel against Kant, they question the liberal claim for the priority of the right over the good, and the picture of the freely choosing individual it embodies. Following Aristotle, they argue that we cannot justify political arrangements without reference to common purposes and ends, and that we cannot conceive of ourselves without reference to our role as citizens, as participants in a common life.

This debate reflects two contrasting pictures of the self. The rights-based ethic, and the conception of the person it embodies, were shaped in large part in the encounter with utilitarianism. Where utilitarians conflate our many desires into a single system of desire, Kantians insist on the separateness of persons. Where the utilitarian self is simply defined as the sum of its desires, the Kantian self is a choosing self, independent of the desires and ends it may have at any moment. As Rawls writes, "The self is prior to the ends which are affirmed by it; even a dominant end must be chosen from among numerous possibilities."

The priority of the self over its ends means I am never defined by my aims and attachments, but always capable of standing back to survey and assess and possibly to revise them. This is what it means to be a free and independent self, capable of choice. And this is the vision of the self that finds expression in the ideal of the state as a neutral framework. On the rights-based ethic, it is precisely because we are essentially separate, independent selves that we need a neutral framework, a framework of rights that refuses to choose among competing purposes and ends. If the self is prior to its ends, then the right must be prior to the good.

Communitarian critics of rights-based liberalism say we cannot conceive ourselves as independent in this way, as bearers of selves wholly detached from our aims and attachments. They say that certain of our roles are partly constitutive of the persons we are—as citizens of a country, or members of a movement, or partisans of a cause. But if we are partly defined by the communities we inhabit, then we must also be implicated in the purposes and ends characteristic of those communities. As Alasdair MacIntyre writes in his book, *After Virtue,* "What is good for me has to be the good for one who inhabits these roles." Open-ended though it be, the story of my life is always embedded in the story of those communities from which I derive my identity—whether family or city, tribe or nation, party or cause. In the communitarian view, these stories make a moral difference, not only a psychological one. They situate us in the world and give our lives their moral particularity.

What is at stake for politics in the debate between unencumbered selves and situated ones? What are the practical differences between a politics of rights and a politics of the common good? On some issues, the two theories may produce different arguments for similar policies. For example, the civil rights movement of the 1960s might be justified by liberals in the name of human dignity and respect for persons, and by communitarians in the name of recognizing the full membership of fellow citizens wrongly excluded from the common life of the nation. And where liberals might support public education in hopes of equipping students to become autonomous individuals, capable of choosing their own ends and pursuing them effectively, communitarians might support public education in hopes of equipping students to become good citizens, capable of contributing meaningfully to public deliberations and pursuits.

On other issues, the two ethics might lead to different policies. Communitarians would be more likely than liberals to allow a town to ban pornographic bookstores, on the grounds that pornography offends its way of life and the values that sustain it. But a politics of civic virtue does not always part company with liberalism in favor of conservative policies. For example, communitarians would be more willing than some rights-oriented liberals to see states enact laws regulating plant closings, to protect their communities from the disruptive effects of capital mobility and sudden industrial change. More generally, where the liberal regards the expansion of individual rights and entitlements as unqualified moral and political progress, the communitarian is troubled by the tendency of liberal programs to displace politics from smaller forms of association to more comprehensive ones. Where libertarian liberals defend the private economy and egalitarian liberals defend the welfare state, communitarians worry about the concentration of power in both the corporate economy and the bureaucratic state, and the erosion of those intermediate forms of community that have at times sustained a more vital public life.

Liberals often argue that a politics of the common good, drawing as it must on particular loyalties, obligations, and traditions, opens the way to prejudice and intolerance. The modern nation-state is not the Athenian polls, they point out; the scale and diversity of modern life have rendered the Aristotelian political ethic nostalgic at best and dangerous at worst. Any attempt to govern by a vision of the good is likely to lead to a slippery slope of totalitarian temptations.

Communitarians reply, rightly in my view, that intolerance flourishes most where forms of life are dislocated, roots unsettled, traditions undone. In our day, the totalitarian impulse has sprung less from the convictions of confidently situated selves than from the confusions of atomized, dislocated, frustrated selves, at sea in a world where common meanings have lost their force. As Hannah Arendt has written, "What makes mass society so difficult to bear is not the number of people involved, or at least not primarily, but the fact that the world between them has lost its power to gather them together, to relate and to separate them." Insofar as our public life has withered, our sense of common involvement diminished, we lie vulnerable to the mass politics of totalitarian solutions. So responds the party of the common good to the party of rights. If the party of the common good is right, our most pressing moral and political project is to revitalize those civic republican possibilities implicit in our tradition but fading in our time.

Contemporary Realist Critique
of Liberalism
The CLS Attack (1993)

Andrew Altman

There are three main prongs to the CLS attack on the liberal embrace of the rule of law, three main elements to the CLS charge that the rule of law, as liberal theory conceptualizes it, is a myth. . . .

The first prong hinges on the claim that the rule of law is not possible in a social situation where the kind of individual freedom endorsed by the liberal view reigns. Such a situation would be characterized by a pluralism of fundamentally incompatible moral and political viewpoints. The establishment of the rule of law under the conditions of pluralism would require some mode of legal reasoning that could be sharply distinguished from moral and political deliberation and choice. There would have to be a sharp distinction, so the argument goes, between law, on one side, and both morals and politics, on the other. Without such a distinction, judges and other individuals who wield public power could impose their own views of the moral or political good on others under the cover of law. Such impositions, however, would destroy the rule of law and the liberal freedom it is meant to protect.

Thus, the liberal view requires that legal reasoning—that is, reasoning about what rights persons have under the law and why—be clearly distinguished from reasoning about political or ethical values. Legal reasoning is not to be confused with deciding which party to a case has the best moral or political argument. Yet it is precisely this kind of legal reasoning that is impossible in a setting of moral and political pluralism, according to CLS. The law-politics distinction collapses, and legal reasoning becomes tantamount to deciding which party has the best moral or political argument. Karl Klare puts the CLS position concisely: "This [liberal] claim about legal reasoning— that it is autonomous from political and ethical choice—is a falsehood."

Duncan Kennedy is even more blunt, but the essential point is the same:

> Teachers teach nonsense when they persuade students that legal reasoning is distinct, *as a method for reaching correct results,* from ethical or political discourse in general. . . . There is never a "correct legal solution" that is other than the correct ethical or political solution to that legal problem.

The second prong of the CLS attack on the rule of law revolves around the claim that the legal doctrines of contemporary liberal states are riddled by contradictions. The contradictions consist of the presence of pairs of fundamentally incompatible norms serving as authoritative elements of legal doctrine in virtually all departments of law. These contradictions are thought to defeat the notion that the rule of law actually reigns in those societies that most contemporary liberal philosophers regard as leading examples of political societies operating under the rule of law. Kennedy contends that the contradictions are tied to the fact that legal doctrine does not give us a coherent way to talk about the rights of individuals under the law:

"Rights discourse is internally inconsistent, vacuous, or circular. Legal thought can generate plausible rights justifications for almost any result." Klare echoes Kennedy's claim: "Legal reasoning is a texture of openness, indeterminacy, and contradiction."

As Klare and Kennedy suggest, the CLS view is that the consequence of these doctrinal contradictions is pervasive legal indeterminacy—that is, the widespread inability of the authoritative rules and doctrines to dictate a determinate outcome to legal cases. The contradictions enable lawyers and judges to argue equally well for either side of most legal cases, depending on which of two contradictory legal norms they choose to rely upon. Moreover, the existence of indeterminacy is tied to the collapse of the distinction between law and politics. Judges can and do covertly rely on moral and political considerations in deciding which of two incompatible legal norms they will base their decisions upon. In existing liberal states, we have not the rule of law but the rule of politics. Joseph Singer sums up this phase of the CLS attack on the rule of law nicely:

> While traditional legal theorists acknowledge the inevitability and desirability of some indeterminacy, traditional legal theory requires a relatively large amount of determinacy as a fundamental premise of the rule of law. Our legal system, however, has never satisfied this goal.

Closely associated with the first two prongs of the CLS attack on the rule of law is the thesis that the very idea of the rule of law serves as an instrument of oppression and domination. David Kairys expresses the general idea in a manner characteristic of much CLS writing:

> The law is a major vehicle for the maintenance of existing social and power relations. . . . The law's perceived legitimacy confers a broader legitimacy on a social system . . . characterized by domination. This perceived legitimacy of the law is primarily based . . . on the distorted notion of government by law, not people.

In the CLS view, then, the idea that our political society operates under the rule of law serves to perpetuate illegitimate relations of power. Exposing the rule of law as a myth is thought of in the CLS movement as an essential part of a strategy designed to undermine those relations of power. . . .

The third prong of the CLS attack focuses on the idea that law is capable of constraining the exercise of social and political power. The contention is made that to think of law as capable of such constraint is to adopt a form of fetishism—to be guilty of regarding a human creation as though it were an independent power capable of controlling those who in fact have created and sustained it. This form of fetishism disempowers human beings; it places them in thrall to forces over which they can and should be the masters. In this CLS view, then, the idea of the rule of law must be criticized as part of a general attack on ideas that disempower humans. . . .

Altman, Andrew. "Critical Legal Studies," *A Liberal Critique.* © 1993 by Princeton University Press. Reprinted by permission of Princeton University Press.

CHAPTER 5

Freedom

THE BILL OF RIGHTS

The only freedom which deserves the name is that of pursuing our own good in our own way, so long as we do not attempt to deprive others of theirs, or impede their efforts to obtain it.
—JOHN STUART MILL, *On Liberty,* 1975

Freedom of speech and freedom of religion rank among the most cherished liberties, but debates surrounding these constitutional guarantees often turn on differing philosophies of freedom. Pages 433–457 contain an examination of negative and positive conceptions of freedom. Classical liberals, such as John Locke, saw freedom negatively from a perspective of potential governmental interference. Other philosophers, such as Jean Jacques Rousseau, proposed a more positive concept of freedom that involves self-development. Whatever approach to freedom one takes, free speech has played a prominent role in political and legal thought. Pages 458–557 look at several philosophers' proposals for justifying free speech and then presents a variety of free speech cases. The balance of the chapter discusses issues of religion as they are divided by the Constitution into two categories. Cases collected in pages 557–585 address problems of religious establishment by the state and pages 586–603 finish the chapter with a consideration of controversies surrounding the free exercise of religion.

A. TYPES OF FREEDOM

"Freedom!" Only tyrants oppose freedom, yet many questions hide beneath the freedom cry, such as: Whose freedom? Freedom from what? Freedom to do what? What or who should protect freedom? What exactly should the law protect? Does law protect freedom or does it threaten freedom?

Freedom involves three elements: agents, constraints, and end states (MacCallum 1991). Freedom is (1) of someone (individual or collective agents); (2) from something (a constraint, impediment, or condition); (3) to do or not do, become or not become, something (end state, a goal). Freedom involves the possibility, although always with limits, of someone's doing or having something. Agents work toward goals under constraints, but what types of agents, constraints, and goals make up freedom? Does freedom apply to only certain types of agents? Does freedom apply to individuals, or is freedom something individuals realize together? Are the constraints on freedom external (environmental) or internal (within the person)? What types of goals does freedom seek? Do people value freedom because it enables them to do something or because it helps them become something or somebody? Does freedom have a negative quality? We seem to know what freedom is not. Freedom stands opposite to coercion, but is freedom the absence of constraint? Does freedom entail the prevention of outside interference? Does the demand, "leave me alone," capture the essence of freedom? Does freedom have a positive aspect? Does freedom enable individuals to do things to develop themselves? First, let us consider **negative freedom**—that is, "freedom from outside intervention."

1. Negative Freedom: Freedom From

In *Leviathan,* Thomas Hobbes defined freedom as freedom from external constraints or interference. In the *Second Treatise of Government,* John Locke also saw freedom as the freedom to do what one wants without interference. Freedom, however, does not mean lawlessness. Locke cautioned that freedom does not stand for "a liberty for every one to do what he wishes, to live as he pleases, and not be tied by any laws" (*Second Treatise of Government,* chapter IV, section 22). Negative liberty does not stand in opposition to the limits imposed by the "rule of law," but rather, goes hand in hand with law. In the words of twentieth-century British economist F. A. Hayek:

> While every law restricts individual freedom to some extent by altering the means which people may use in the pursuit of their aims, under the Rule of Law, the government is prevented from stultifying individual efforts by *ad hoc* action. Within the known rules of the game the individual is free to pursue his personal ends and desires, certain that the powers of government will not be used deliberately to frustrate his efforts. (Hayek 1944, p. 54)

Thus, the law, when obeyed, does not coerce, nor does it limit freedom. Hayek saw the rule of law as organized around the classical liberal idea of negative freedom. Philosopher John Hospers (see Reading 5-1), who ran for president of the United States on the Libertarian Party ticket, represents a philosophical movement that puts freedom at the forefront of political and legal thought. According to Hospers, "Government is the most dangerous institution known to man" (1974 in Sterba 1992, p. 47). **Libertarianism** takes liberty, or being unconstrained by others, as the ultimate moral and political ideal.

Isaiah Berlin (see Reading 5-2) offers a cautionary note to temper the libertarian praise for negative liberty, or freedom from external constraints. Frithjof Bergmann's imaginative account of negative liberty provides an even more critical assessment of negative liberty (see Reading 5-3). Whatever its allure, a negative conception of freedom also confronts difficulties. According to Bergmann, does seeing freedom as the absence of restraint distort our vision of freedom? Is there something more to freedom than this negative sense? What external conditions must be met before individuals can realize their freedoms? Free speech means little unless there are ways to ensure open avenues for speaking opportunities. Wealth provides access to free speech for a few; poverty prevents the exercise of free speech for many others. Bergmann exposes the dangers of thinking about freedom only in negative terms—that is, as a barrier that keeps government away from the individual. Problems in defending negative freedom have led some theorists to develop a positive developmental sense of freedom.

READING 5-1

Libertarian Praise of Liberty
"What Libertarianism Is" (1974)

John Hospers

Government is the most dangerous institution known to man. Throughout history it has violated the rights of men more than any individual or group of individuals could do: it has killed people, enslaved them, sent them to forced labor and concentration camps, and regularly robbed and pillaged them of the fruits of their expended labor. Unlike individual criminals, government has the power to arrest and try; unlike individual criminals, it can surround and encompass a person totally, dominating every aspect of one's life, so that one has no recourse from it but to leave the country (and in totalitarian nations even that is prohibited). Government throughout history has a much sorrier record than any individual, even that of a ruthless mass murderer. The signs we see on bumper stickers are chillingly accurate: "Beware: the Government Is Armed and Dangerous."

The only proper role of government, according to libertarians, is that of the protector of the citizen against aggression by other individuals. The government, of course, should never initiate aggression; its proper role is as the embodiment of the *retaliatory* use of force against anyone who initiates its use. . . .

Government, then, undertakes to be the individual's protector; but historically governments have gone far beyond this function. Since they already have the physical power, they have not hesitated to use it for purposes far beyond that which was entrusted to them in the first place. Undertaking initially to protect its citizens against aggression, it has often itself become an aggressor—a far greater aggressor, indeed, than the criminals against whom it was supposed to protect its citizens. . . .

Laws may be classified into three types: (1) laws protecting individuals against themselves, such as laws against fornication and other sexual behavior, alcohol, and drugs; (2) laws protecting individuals against aggressions by other individuals, such as laws against murder, robbery, and fraud; (3) laws requiring people to help one another; for example, all laws which rob Peter to pay Paul, such as welfare.

Libertarians reject the first class of laws totally. Behavior which harms no one else is strictly the individual's own affair. Thus, there should be no laws against becoming intoxicated, since whether or not to become intoxicated is the individual's own decision: but there should be laws against driving while intoxicated, since the drunken driver is a threat to every other motorist on the highway (drunken driving falls into type 2). Similarly, there should be no laws against drugs (except the prohibition of sale of drugs to minors) as long as the taking of these drugs poses no threat to anyone else. Drug addiction is a psychological problem to which no present solution exists. Most of the social harm caused by addicts, other than to themselves, is the result of thefts which they perform in order to continue their habit—and then the *legal* crime is the theft, not the addiction. The actual cost of heroin is about ten cents a shot; if it were legalized, the enormous traffic in illegal sale and purchase of it would stop, as well as the accompanying proselytization to get new addicts (to make more money for the pusher) and the thefts performed by addicts who often require eighty dollars a day just to keep up the habit. Addiction would not stop, but the crimes would: it is estimated that 75 percent of the burglaries in New York City today are performed by addicts, and all these crimes could be wiped out at one stroke though the legalization of drugs. (Only when the taking of drugs could be shown to constitute a threat to *others,* should it be prohibited by law. It is only laws protecting people against *themselves* that libertarians oppose.)

Laws should be limited to the second class only: aggression by individuals against other individuals. These are laws whose function is to protect human beings against encroachment by others; and this, as we have seen, is (according to libertarianism) the sole function of government.

Libertarians also reject the third class of laws totally: no one should be forced by law to help others, not even to tell them the time of day if requested, and certainly not to give them a portion of one's weekly paycheck. Governments, in the guise of humanitarianism, have given to some by taking from others (charging a "handling fee" in the process, which, because of the government's waste and inefficiency, sometimes is several hundred percent). And in so doing they have decreased incentive, violated the rights of individuals and lowered the standard of living of almost everyone.

All such laws constitute what libertarians call *moral cannibalism.* A cannibal in the physical sense is a person who lives off the flesh of other human beings. A *moral* cannibal is one who believes he has a right to live off the "spirit" of other human beings—who believes that he has a moral claim on the productive capacity, time, and effort expended by others. . . .

From Hospers (1974), *What Libertarianism Is.* In (1992) *Justice.* James Sterba, editor. Belmont, CA: Wadsworth, pp. 47–48, 51–52.

Cautionary Notes on Negative Liberty
"Two Concepts of Liberty" Part I (1969)

Isaiah Berlin

I am normally said to be free to the degree to which no man or body of men interferes with my activity. Political liberty in this sense is simply the area within which a man can act unobstructed by others. If I am prevented by others from doing what I could otherwise do, I am to that degree unfree; and if this area is contracted by other men beyond a certain minimum, I can be described as being coerced, or, it may be, enslaved. Coercion is not, however, a term that covers every form of inability. If I say that I am unable to jump more than ten feet in the air, or cannot read because I am blind, or cannot understand the darker pages of Hegel, it would be eccentric to say that I am to that degree enslaved or coerced. Coercion implies the deliberate interference of other human beings within the area in which I could otherwise act. You lack political liberty or freedom only if you are prevented from attaining a goal by human beings. Mere incapacity to attain a goal is not lack of political freedom. This is brought out by the use of such modern expressions as 'economic freedom' and its counterpart, 'economic slavery'. It is argued, very plausibly, that if a man is too poor to afford something on which there is no legal ban—a loaf of bread, a journey round the world, recourse to the law courts—he is as little free to have it as he would be if it were forbidden him by law. If my poverty were a kind of disease, which prevented me from buying bread, or paying for the journey round the world or getting my case heard, as lameness prevents me from running, this inability would not naturally be described as a lack of freedom, least of all political freedom. It is only because I believe that my inability to get a given thing is due to the fact that other human beings have made arrangements whereby I am, whereas others are not, prevented from having enough money with which to pay for it, that I think myself a victim of coercion or slavery. In other words, this use of the term depends on a particular social and economic theory about the causes of my poverty or weakness. If my lack of material means is due to my lack of mental or physical capacity, then I begin to speak of being deprived of freedom (and not simply about poverty) only if I accept the theory. If, in addition, I believe that I am being kept in want by a specific arrangement which I consider unjust or unfair, I speak of economic slavery or oppression. 'The nature of things does not madden us, only ill will does', said Rousseau. The criterion of oppression is the part that I believe to be played by other human beings, directly or indirectly, with or without the intention of doing so, in frustrating my wishes. By being free in this sense I mean not being interfered with by others. The wider the area of non-interference the wider my freedom.

This is what the classical English political philosophers meant when they used this word. They disagreed about how wide the area could or should be. They supposed that it could not, as things were, be unlimited, because if it were, it would entail a state in which all men could boundlessly interfere with all other men; and this kind of 'natural' freedom would lead to social chaos in which men's minimum needs would not be satisfied; or else the liberties of the weak would be suppressed by the strong. Because they perceived that human purposes and activities do not automatically harmonize with one another, and because (whatever their official doctrines) they put high value on other goals, such as justice, or happiness, or culture, or security, or varying degrees of equality, they were prepared to curtail freedom in the interests of other values and, indeed, of freedom itself. For, without this, it was impossible to create the kind of association that they thought desirable. Consequently, it is assumed by these thinkers that the area of men's free action must be limited by law. But equally it is assumed, especially by such libertarians as Locke and Mill in England, and Constant and Tocqueville in France, that there ought to exist a certain minimum area of personal freedom which must on no account be violated; for if it is overstepped, the individual will find himself in an area too narrow for even that minimum development of his natural faculties which alone makes it possible to pursue, and even to conceive, the various ends which men hold good or right or sacred. It follows that a frontier must be drawn between the area of private life and that of public authority. Where it is to be drawn is a matter of argument, indeed of haggling. Men are largely interdependent, and no man's activity is so completely private as never to obstruct the lives of others in any way. 'Freedom for the pike is death for the minnows'; the liberty of some must depend on the restraint of others. 'Freedom for an Oxford don', others have been known to add, 'is a very different thing from freedom for an Egyptian peasant.'

This proposition derives its force from something that is both true and important, but the phrase itself remains a piece of political claptrap. It is true that to offer political rights, or safeguards against intervention by the State, to men who are half-naked, illiterate, underfed, and diseased is to mock their condition; they need medical help or education before they can understand, or make use of, an increase in their freedom. What is freedom to those who cannot make use of it? Without adequate conditions for the use of freedom, what is the value of freedom? First things come first: there are situations in which—to use a saying satirically attributed to the nihilists by Dostoevsky—boots are superior to the works of Pushkin; individual freedom is not everyone's primary need. For freedom is not the mere absence of frustration of whatever kind; this would inflate the meaning of the word until it meant too much or too little. The Egyptian peasant needs clothes or medicine before, and more than, personal liberty, but the minimum freedom that he needs today, and the greater degree of freedom that he may need tomorrow, is not some species of freedom peculiar to him, but identical with that of professors, artists, and millionaires.

What troubles the consciences of Western liberals is, I think, the belief that the freedom that men seek differs according to their social or economic conditions, but that the minority who possess it have gained it by exploiting, or, at least, averting their gaze from, the vast majority who do not. They believe, with good reason, that if individual liberty is an ultimate end for human beings, none should be deprived of it by others; least of all that some should enjoy it at the expense of others. Equality of liberty; not to treat others as I should not wish them to treat me; repayment of my debt to those

who alone have made possible my liberty or prosperity or enlightenment; justice, in its simplest and most universal sense—these are the foundations of liberal morality. Liberty is not the only goal of men. I can, like the Russian critic Belinsky, say that if others are to be deprived of it—if my brothers are to remain in poverty, squalor, and chains—then I do not want it for myself, I reject it with both hands and infinitely prefer to share their fate. But nothing is gained by a confusion of terms. To avoid glaring inequality or widespread misery I am ready to sacrifice some, or all, of my freedom: I may do so willingly and freely: but it is freedom that I am giving up for the sake of justice or equality or the love of my fellow men. I should be guilt-stricken, and rightly so, if I were not, in some circumstances, ready to make this sacrifice. But a sacrifice is not an increase in what is being sacrificed, namely freedom, however great the moral need or the compensation for it. Everything is what it is: liberty is liberty, not equality or fairness or justice or culture, or human happiness or a quiet conscience. If the liberty of myself or my class or nation depends on the misery of a number of other human beings, the system which promotes this is unjust and immoral. But if I curtail or lose my freedom, in order to lessen the shame of such inequality, and do not thereby materially increase the individual liberty of others, an absolute loss of liberty occurs. This may be compensated for by a gain in justice or in happiness or in peace, but the loss remains, and it is a confusion of values to say that although my 'liberal', individual freedom may go by the board, some other kind of freedom—'social' or 'economic'—is increased. Yet it remains true that the freedom of some must at times be curtailed to secure the freedom of others. Upon what principle should this be done? If freedom is a sacred, untouchable value, there can be no such principle. One or other of these conflicting rules or principles must, at any rate in practice, yield: not always for reasons which can be clearly stated, let alone generalized into rules or universal maxims. Still, a practical compromise has to be found. . . .

From Berlin (1969), "Two Concepts of Liberty," *Four Essays on Liberty.* New York: Oxford University Press, pp. 121–126.

READING 5-3

Negative Liberty's Negative Side
"Freedom and Society" (1977)

Frithjof Bergmann

Imagine that late at night you are walking through the deserted streets of a small town, and suddenly a man, dressed somewhat like a peddler, accosts you and waves you on to follow. In the spirit of one who has only recently arrived and wants to explore, you turn after him into an alley, climb up a staircase, and moments later you are in a large, bare and whitewalled room. A yoga class seems to be in progress. A number of young people lie on the floor, their bodies in a pose of relaxation. Their teacher, wearing a black leotard, appears to be in the middle of an explanation. You notice that everybody's eyes are not closed but extraordinarily wide open and alive; then you begin to listen. . . .

"So let us take this sentence—the government that governs least is best—and look at it up close. What does it say? Imagine you told it to someone who never heard it, who had grown up in a completely different culture. What would be his reaction? Is it not likely that a traveler from far off might stare at you with bafflement and consternation; that he might blink and then burst into the response: 'What an unheard-of and weird thing to say! You would not say this of a doctor, would you? You would not think that a doctor who cured least was the best? Or that a gardener who gardened very little was the one to hire? Or that a worker who hardly worked was better than all others? So why do you hold such bizarre opinions when it comes to government? Maybe if a government barely governs, it only means that it does not perform its function, that it is a failure, a mistake?'

"And such a stranger might continue: 'If you really believe in this inverse proportion, why do you have any government at all? Surely, if the state marks the borderline of freedom, you would have still more freedom if there were no government whatever? Only the absence of government would be really least, and consequently best of all. So why do you not draw the logical conclusion and get rid of the state—or at least make sure it withers away gradually?'

"How would we reply," the yoga teacher asks, "if someone said this? Would we not respond that the results of such an abolition would be very different; that some few ruthless men perhaps would be still freer than under the most minimal of governments, but that the vast majority would be under the oppression of those few? But then, would you or I, mild as we are, not be among the latter? Would we not end up nearer to the bottom, with a much harsher life? Might not our existence be very like that of a dog, complete with bones from the table and a chain around our necks? So we owe a great deal to the interference of the state. Many of us would fall to a much lower level if it did not intercede.

"And this acknowledgment is important, for it implies that much of our picture-thinking has to be revised. Not all of us would be completely free in the 'natural condition' prior to the state. Some of us might be far more constrained than we are now, and the story that we have traded in some part of our freedom for security is therefore just a myth. But if this is true, if we never possessed this incommensurately precious good to barter it away, then our resisting and begrudging attitude also is not so obviously justified. Then at least some kinds of government—though certainly not all—give us not just material safety for a spiritual sacrifice, but do much more and should get their reward.

"Of course we know this. To our concrete thinking all this is very evident. If you work as a nurse's aide, you understand that your paycheck would be less if it were not for the minimum wage guarantees enforced by the state. The point is that from the clouds of our theoretical opinions our feet no longer touch this obvious ground. On that level a Pavlovian reflex jerks us back: authority, the state, makes us less free.

"Yet our traveler, recovered from his initial shock, might speak to us a second time. 'Why do you say that limiting the state makes people free? That word has such a grand and bell-like ring. But what real purpose does it serve when the facts are so very plain? A state imposes penalties and fines, and these are obstacles that hinder you in certain actions. But there are other obstacles besides those represented by the state—they surround you on all sides. Limiting the state reduces only some very few of all the obstacles you face. What of the remnant? How can the lowering of one kind of obstacle make you free? Why do you think of yourself in an open space when only one wall of your cage has been moved backwards by three feet?

" 'But in reality not even this occurred. You did not simply gain more space, for that ignores another and still more crucial fact: you cannot remove one obstacle in isolation. There is no fixed and stable sum from which you can subtract. A change in one place makes a difference in all others. The elements of the system interact. If you diminish hindrances in one sphere, those in other areas will go up. So your weakening of the state changed only one weight in a complicated clockwork mechanism. And what were the effects of this in other places?

" 'Consider the hindrances of poverty for instance. Go through a supermarket: not the asparagus because it costs too much. Not fresh bread but a loaf that is four days old. Where is the basket with the damaged cans? That's when the obstacles close in on you, and every step is up against a wall. Or take the barriers linked to work. You may not have the license to do the one thing which you could do best, and that can stop you cold—for then you cannot be insured; and there is the continuous control imposed on you within the work you do. Is it not as if your hands were strapped to a machine? Now put this block on top of the other, and now, like it or not, the next. Does not this grind you down more than all other pressures? Again, are you not impeded by ill health that could have been avoided; by a schooling that covers spontaneity with gravel, perhaps most of all by an indifference that spreads like a gas? But is it not likely that many of these obstacles grew larger as the direct result of the diminishment of others? You took the rocks that had pinned down someone's legs and lifted them from off his feet. But you piled them back on—and this time on his head!

" 'The one force in your culture on which most people have some influence you weakened. The state whose leaders are at least selected by elections you limited till it did least. But all the other powers you allowed to grow. Yet in their affairs you do not have a vote, and who their leaders are you hardly know. Is this not downright mad? To tie down and hold back the one force which in spite of all its flaws is somewhat open and accountable to you, and to give the advantage of this debility to elements which are inaccessible and closed? Is it not evident that this is upside-down; that you should have strengthened the one force over which you have some hold, so that through it you might have kept the rest in check? But this still misses the main point; for your state in actuality is not weak or limited at all! Your dictum that "least is best" must be a kind of game, like that with scissors, paper and a rock. For you accept compulsory education, do you not? But that allows the state to meddle with the raising of your children. And you apply for a license to get married. And it is the state that grants you a divorce; and there are even laws against homosexuality and fornication. So how large is your private territory? You can be arrested for having a too noisy party—that disturbs the peace, even if the country is at war. Sitting on a park bench can be a criminal offense. The government can tell you how big your bathroom has to be if you are building your own home. You even need a permit to bring your garbage to the dump! Just how far back have you pushed the state?

" 'Think of the slogan: the means of violence belong to the government. Spelled out this means that if your government betrays you, you can only sign petitions and write letters to your congressman. If you break a single window it is still a crime. But if the state decides that you were traitorous to it, then it can execute you. So whose hands are still tied, and who still throws the switches?

" 'Or take the measure of your deference to the law. From the time you watch Western movies: "He took the law into his own hands" is made to sound as if divinity had been defiled. The film cannot end, the sunset has to wait, till the law has been restored to the state. Your own beliefs count here for very little: if you disagree on a specific issue—on school busing or integrated housing, for example—you are wrong if you act on your own convictions. It is the law that has to be obeyed. You are more submissive than a child, for even parents say to their growing children: "These are my reasons. Weigh my arguments and then make your decision," but relative to laws your culture does just the reverse: this is right, because it is the law; no further questions—but laws are the voice of the state!

" 'No, you did not build a fence against the government so you could grow your own small garden. Your story has a very different plot. On the whole you were a very humble servant, but you did choose a single place—there you dug in your heels and drew a line: trade you made free; the economic you marked off; property became inviolable. The foundations for this predilection, for this one barricade against the state, were laid right from the start. They can be found in Hobbes and in Rousseau, and most especially in Locke. Their theories prepared the ground on which your institutions were erected. And that is still the single enclave you defend: What do you call it when the government stands helpless and has no control? In any area except for the economic this is Anarchy, and you associate it with pandemonium and slaughter. But in the economic the same condition has a different name: there it is Free Enterprise. And vice versa: if the state is vigilant in any other area, then that is Law and Order, but in the economic area the word for that is Socialism.

" 'Your double standard stretches one's imagination. On one side you protest a total tax on incomes in excess of 80,000 dollars. That is an abridgement of your rights. You think the state has no claim on that money, and no prerogative to redistribute it. Here you forget that no one produces the value represented by 80,000 dollars quite by himself, that others must have lent a hand, and that all kinds of chance conventions and arbitrary social customs need to be observed for such a paycheck to materialize. You isolate a single fact: that someone has possession of that money, that it is his property, and then you wonder how anyone but him could have a right to it.

" 'Yet, on the other side, you hardly question the right of governments to declare wars. Most of you condone the institution of conscription, and even the selection by lottery—a bingo game—of those the government will send to war. You refuse the government the right to property which is not even unambiguously yours. But to stake your life on the turning up of the right number, on a throw of dice, to that you give the state the right!

" 'And with that we come to the real issue. The hindrances of poverty, of mindless labor and of disease you did not choose to fight. You only wanted to curtail the state, and that by no means generally but only in one segment, that of the economic, of Free Enterprise—on that short front you took your stand. But this one spot which you finally selected was the worst and most calamitous place you could possibly have picked. How great a toll in sacrifices would have been exacted if the state had intervened more in the sphere of property or business? What real loss in freedom—in genuine self-expression—would be imposed by regulating mergers and other similar transactions? How many actions vital to the self would that stop? Would the affected notice it in their own personal lives, or would the difference be known only to their accountants? So how much freedom is gained? But what a price is paid! For by putting that very small restraint on a mere handful (who could still have had their private yachts—just slightly shorter ones) you could turn around the lives of millions. A minimal increase in some obstacles faced by a very few would empower you to take down hindrances which daunt the great majority far more than abstract governmental regulations—obstacles so insurmountable and close that their will to be themselves capitulates in desperation.

" 'Do not imagine therefore that your culture has granted you a high degree of freedom. The question of genuine freedom, of self-expression, has so far hardly ever been raised. That was not the measure by which your politics were judged. Your failures and successes, your long-range strategies and daily tactics can be assessed in the much plainer language of obstacles that either were removed or left to mount. Seen in that way, and coldly, your advances up to date are unimpressive and your retreats are very great. You have reduced some few hindrances, but only in that one most unintelligently chosen place, and other barriers grew higher than they were before. It is the waste of it, the crevasse between what you might have done and what you did, that seems most baffling and appalling. For no fundamental change, no total reconstruction was required. Minor adjustments might have sufficed. But you balked. You did not end that terrible imbalance. You watched its tilt grow steeper, but stood by and did not move.' ". . .

From Bergmann (1977), *On Being Free*. Notre Dame, IN: University of Notre Dame Press, pp. 177–183.

---

2. Positive Freedom: Freedom To

Does freedom involve only external constraints or are there also internal constraints on freedom? Are there internal obstacles that block self-development and human growth? **Jean Jacques Rousseau** agreed with Locke that giving in to our impulses does not constitute freedom. Rousseau spoke of one's "moral liberty, which alone makes him truly master of himself; for the mere impulse of appetite is slavery, while the obedience to a law which we prescribe for ourselves is liberty" (*Social Contract,* book 1, chapter VIII). According to Rousseau, individuals do not attain positive liberty by placing themselves under an authoritarian rule as Hobbes believed, or by consenting to limited government as Locke thought. Rather, individuals attain Rousseauean freedom by placing themselves under the general will, the common good. The state does not, as libertarians believe, continually threaten freedom, but instead the state promotes positive freedom. Some contemporary proponents of a positive sense of freedom, such as Charles Taylor (1979), claim that the state and law should facilitate, not hinder, self-development. The task of evaluating the content of speech becomes critical for a developmental sense of free speech. If, through education, individuals learn only to speak about trivial things and never to address important moral and political issues, then internal constraints have successfully prevented them from being free. They will never attain mastery over themselves. An internal voice of politeness that says "never speak of politics and religion among company" stifles individual growth. Critics of the developmental approach, such as Isaiah Berlin in his classic essay, "Two Concepts of Liberty," issue a caution about positive freedom (see Reading 5-4). They warn that positive freedom invites the state to determine what is best for individuals. Since the government, through its control of education, determines the type of self-development it wants to promote, the state, thereby, molds and controls individuals. Critics predict that policies informed by positive freedom will deteriorate into government control over the individual.

Must freedom have limits? Can freedom thrive if limited by law? Can freedom thrive without law? A case for the compatibility of law and freedom runs as follows. Unlimited freedom seems to lead to a Hobbesian state of nature—a state of chaos in which the strong trample on the freedoms of the weak. The law rescues individuals from the Hobbesian world, but paradoxically, it protects freedom by limiting it. The law must restrict an individual's freedom in order to enable everyone's freedom to flourish. Within the classical liberal tradition, law protects speech and religion from governmental interference; therefore, when the law restricts particular freedoms, it sets the stage for overall freedom (see Hayek 1960). Intuitively, however, law and freedom appear to be at loggerheads. After all, as some communitarians note (see chapter 4, page 207), individuals sometimes enjoy freedom in spite of law (Skinner 1991). Is law, then, an obstacle to freedom? In the battle waged between liberty and authority, does law always take authority's side? Do the limits placed on freedom depend on the type of freedom? Should economic freedoms, such as the freedom of contract upheld in the *Lochner* case (see chapter 3, page 132), have fewer limits than political freedoms, such as free speech? Should courts enforce constitutional guarantees against regulation of speech more rigorously than they block governmental regulation of economic markets? Limits on free speech will be examined on page 229.

READING 5-4

Positive Liberty's Negative Side
"Two Concepts of Liberty" Part II (1969)

Isaiah Berlin

THE NOTION OF POSITIVE FREEDOM

The 'positive' sense of the word 'liberty' derives from the wish on the part of the individual to be his own master. I wish my life and decisions to depend on myself, not on external forces of whatever kind. I wish to be the instrument of my own, not of other men's, acts of will. I wish to be a subject, not an object; to be moved by reasons, by conscious purposes, which are my own, not by causes which affect me, as it were, from outside. I wish to be somebody, not nobody; a doer—deciding, not being decided for, self-directed and not acted upon by external nature or by other men as if I were a thing, or an animal, or a slave incapable of playing a human role, that is, of conceiving goals and policies of my own and realizing them. This is at least part of what I mean when I say that I am rational, and that it is my reason that distinguishes me as a human being from the rest of the world. I wish, above all, to be conscious of myself as a thinking, willing, active being, bearing responsibility for my choices and able to explain them by references to my own ideas and purposes. I feel free to the degree that I believe this to be true, and enslaved to the degree that I am made to realize that it is not.

The freedom which consists in being one's own master, and the freedom which consists in not being prevented from choosing as I do by other men, may, on the face of it, seem concepts at no great logical distance from each other—no more than negative and positive ways of saying much the same thing. Yet the 'positive' and 'negative' notions of freedom historically developed in divergent directions not always by logically reputable steps, until, in the end, they came into direct conflict with each other.

One way of making this clear is in terms of the independent momentum which the, initially perhaps quite harmless, metaphor of self-mastery acquired. 'I am my own master'; 'I am slave to no man'; but may I not (as Platonists or Hegelians tend to say) be a slave to nature? Or to my own 'unbridled' passions? Are these not so many species of the identical genus 'slave'—some political or legal, others moral or spiritual? Have not men had the experience of liberating themselves from spiritual slavery, or slavery to nature, and do they not in the course of it become aware, on the one hand, of a self which dominates, and, on the other, of something in them which is brought to heel? This dominant self is then variously identified with reason, with my 'higher nature', with the self which calculates and aims at what will satisfy it in the long run, with my 'real', or 'ideal', or 'autonomous' self, or with my self 'at its best'; which is then contrasted with irrational impulse, uncontrolled desires, my 'lower' nature, the pursuit of immediate pleasures, my 'empirical' or 'heteronomous' self, swept by every gust of desire and passion, needing to be rigidly disciplined if it is ever to rise to the full height of its 'real' nature. Presently the two selves may be represented as divided by an even larger gap: the real self may be conceived as something wider than the individual (as the term is normally understood), as a social 'whole' of which the individual is an element or aspect: a tribe, a race, a church, a state, the great society of the living and the dead and the yet unborn. This entity is then identified as being the 'true' self which, by imposing its collective, or 'organic', single will upon its recalcitrant 'members', achieves its own, and therefore their, 'higher' freedom. The perils of using organic metaphors to justify the coercion of some men by others in order to raise them to a 'higher' level of freedom have often been pointed out. But what gives such plausibility as it has to this kind of language is that we recognize that it is possible, and at times justifiable, to coerce men in the name of some goal (let us say, justice or public health) which they would, if they were more enlightened, themselves pursue, but do not, because they are blind or ignorant or corrupt. This renders it easy for me to conceive of myself as coercing others for their own sake, in their, not my, interest. I am then claiming that I know what they truly need better than they know it themselves. What, at most, this entails is that they would not resist me if they were rational and as wise as I and understood their interests as I do. But I may go on to claim a good deal more than this. I may declare that they are actually aiming at what in their benighted state they consciously resist, because there exists within them an occult entity—their latent rational will, or their 'true' purpose—and that this entity, although it is belied by all that they overtly feel and do and say, is their 'real' self, of which the poor empirical self in space and time may know nothing or little; and that this inner spirit is the only self that deserves to have its wishes taken into account. Once I take this view, I am in a position to ignore the actual wishes of men or societies, to bully, oppress, torture them in the name, and on behalf, of their 'real' selves, in the secure knowledge that whatever is the true goal of man (happiness, performance of duty, wisdom, a just society, self-fulfillment) must be identical with his freedom—the free choice of his 'true', albeit often submerged and inarticulate, self.

This paradox has been often exposed. It is one thing to say that I know what is good for X, while he himself does not; and even to ignore his wishes for its—and his—sake; and a very different one to say that he has *eo ipso* [by that very fact] chosen it, not indeed consciously, not as he seems in everyday life, but in his role as a rational self which his empirical self may not know—the 'real' self which discerns the good, and cannot help choosing it once it is revealed. This monstrous impersonation, which consists in equating what X would choose if he were something he is not, or at least not yet, with what X actually seeks and chooses, is at the heart of all political theories of self-realization. It is one thing to say that I may be coerced for my own good which I am too blind to see: this may, on occasion, be for my benefit; indeed it may enlarge the scope of my liberty. It is another to say that if it is my good, then I am not being coerced, for I have willed it, whether I know this or not, and am free (or 'truly' free) even while my poor earthly body and foolish mind bitterly reject it, and struggle against those who seek however benevolently to impose it, with the greatest desperation.

This magical transformation, or sleight of hand, can no doubt be perpetrated just as easily with the 'negative' concept of freedom, where the self that should not be interfered with is no longer the individual with his actual wishes and needs as they are normally conceived, but the 'real' man within, identified with the pursuit of some ideal purpose not dreamed of by his empirical self. And, as in the case of the 'positively' free self, this entity may be inflated into some super-personal entity—a state, a class, a nation, or the march of history itself, regarded as a more 'real' subject of attributes than the empirical self. But the 'positive' conception of freedom as self-mastery, with its suggestion of a man divided against himself, has, in fact, and as a matter of history, of doctrine and of practice, lent itself more easily to this splitting of personality into two: the transcendent, dominant controller, and the empirical bundle of desires and passions to be disciplined and brought to heel. It is this historical fact that has been influential. This demonstrates (if demonstration of so obvious a truth is needed) that conceptions of freedom directly derive from views of what constitutes a self, a person, a man. Enough manipulation with the definition of man, and freedom can be made to mean whatever the manipulator wishes. Recent history has made it only too clear that the issue is not merely academic.

The consequences of distinguishing between two selves will become even clearer if one considers the two major forms which the desire to be self-directed—directed by one's 'true' self—has historically taken: the first, that of self-abnegation in order to attain independence; the second, that of self-realization, or total self-identification with a specific principle or ideal in order to attain the selfsame end.

From Berlin (1969), "Two Concepts of Liberty," *Four Essays on Liberty*. New York: Oxford University Press, pp. 131–134.

B. FREE SPEECH

Congress shall make no law abridging the freedom of speech or of the press.
—FIRST AMENDMENT, U.S. CONSTITUTION

And though all the winds of doctrine were let loose to play upon the earth, so Truth be in the field, we do injuriously, by licensing and prohibiting, to misdoubt her strength. Let her and Falsehood grapple; whoever knew Truth put to the worst, in a free and open encounter?
—JOHN MILTON (1644)
Areopagitica—a Speech for the Liberty of Unlicensed Printing
(protesting a licensing scheme for books)

The history of cases under the First Amendment's freedom of speech clause reflects the high value placed on speech. Why should the protection of speech have such a high value in the constitutional scheme? What value does free speech have? Free speech might have an extrinsic, or **instrumental value**—a means to an end. The importance of free speech would, then, lie in its value as a means to another value, such as truth or democracy. Alternatively, free speech might have an **intrinsic value**—its own value. Because speech makes humans, individually and collectively, human, it has a value, not as a means to something else (instrumental), but in its own right (intrinsic). However, the values associated with free speech might be more relative than the emphasis on truth and autonomy suggests. Some theorists take a pragmatic (see page 109) approach to free speech, while others take a more skeptical approach (see page 107). For **pragmatists** (Hand in Reading 5-7 and Posner in Reading 5-8), placing a value on free speech involves calculating the risks of protecting or not protecting different kinds of speech. For **skeptics** (Kairys in Reading 5-9), free speech doctrines serve political, ideological purposes rather than noble pursuits such as truth and autonomy.

1. Truth: The Free Exchange of All Ideas

Instrumental defenses of free speech focus on one of two values promoted by free speech—truth or democracy. Utilitarian **John Stuart Mill** (1806–1873) took up the case for truth, and his *On Liberty* (1859) has become its classic defense. Although he wrote it with Harriet Taylor, whom he later married, Mill alone has become identified with the classical case for a marketplace-of-ideas justification for free speech (see Reading 5-5). Mill drew a protective cover over private activities that did not directly harm the interests of others. According to Mill, speech competes in a marketplace of ideas, where truth and falsehood try to outbid one another. Society has no reason to think that it has enough knowledge to prejudge whether a claim is true or false. If society suppresses a truth, it denies itself a valuable piece of knowledge; if it suppresses a falsehood, then it denies the fuller understanding that comes from contrasting truth with error. The argument, of course, assumes that truth will prevail in the long run under conditions of open discussion.

Free speech may serve another value—that of democratic self-government (Mekilejohn 1948). Democratic politics depends on the vibrant free flow of ideas through speech. Deliberation helps citizens achieve compromise, resolve conflicts, and criticize officials; therefore political speech, holds a higher value than other forms, such as commercial speech. Like variants of the truth model, the democracy model allows for governmental interference in the marketplace of ideas to improve the quality of deliberation.

READING 5-5

Truth as a Value of Free Speech
"Of the Liberty of Thought and Discussion" (1859)

John Stuart Mill

The time, it is to be hoped, is gone by when any defense would be necessary of the "liberty of the press" as one of the securities against corrupt or tyrannical government. No argument, we may suppose, can now be needed against permitting a legislature or an executive, not identified in interest with the people, to prescribe opinions to them and determine what doctrines or what arguments they shall be allowed to hear. This aspect of the question, besides, has been so often and so triumphantly enforced by preceding writers that it needs not be specially insisted on in this place. Though the law of England, on the subject of the press, is as servile to this day as it was in the time of the Tudors, there is little danger of its being actually put in force against political discussion except during some temporary panic when fear of insurrection drives ministers and judges from their propriety; and, speaking generally, it is not, in constitutional countries, to be apprehended that the government, whether completely responsible to the people or not, will often attempt to control the expression of opinion, except when in doing so it makes itself the organ of the general intolerance of the public. Let us suppose, therefore, that the government is entirely at one with the people, and never thinks of exerting any power of coercion unless in agreement with what it conceives to be their voice. But I deny the right of the people to exercise such coercion, either by themselves or by their government. The power itself is illegitimate. The best government has no more title to it than the worst. It is as noxious, or more noxious, when exerted in accordance with public opinion than when in opposition to it. *If all mankind minus one were of one opinion, mankind would be no more justified in silencing that one person than he, if he had the power, would be justified in silencing mankind.* Were an opinion a personal possession of no value except to the owner, if to be obstructed in the enjoyment of it were simply a private injury, it would make some difference whether the injury was inflicted only on a few persons or on many. But the peculiar evil of silencing the expression of an opinion is that it is robbing the human race, posterity as well as the existing generation—those who dissent from the opinion, still more than those who hold it. If the opinion is right, they are deprived of the opportunity of exchanging error for truth; if wrong, they lose, what is almost as great a benefit, the clearer perception and livelier impression of truth produced by its collision with error.

It is necessary to consider separately these two hypotheses, each of which has a distinct branch of the argument corresponding to it. We can never be sure that the opinion we are endeavoring to stifle is a false opinion; and if we were sure, stifling it would be an evil still.

First, the opinion which it is attempted to suppress by authority may possibly be true. Those who desire to suppress it, of course, deny its truth; but they are not infallible. They have no authority to decide the question for all mankind and exclude every other person from the means of judging. To refuse a hearing to an opinion because they are sure that it is false is to assume that *their* certainty is the same thing as *absolute* certainty. All silencing of discussion is an assumption of infallibility. Its condemnation may be allowed to rest on this common argument, not the worse for being common. . . .

Let us now pass to the second division of the argument, and dismissing the supposition that any of the received opinions may be false, let us assume them to be true and examine into the worth of the manner in which they are likely to be held when their truth is not freely and openly canvassed. However unwilling a person who has a strong opinion may admit the possibility that his opinion may be false, he ought to be moved by the consideration that, however true it may be, if it is not fully, frequently, and fearlessly discussed, it will be held as a dead dogma, not a living truth. . . .

It still remains to speak of one of the principal causes which make diversity of opinion advantageous, and will continue to do so until mankind shall have entered a stage of intellectual advancement which at present seems at an incalculable distance. We have hitherto considered only two possibilities: that the received opinion may be false, and some other opinion, consequently, true; or that, the received opinion being true, a conflict with the opposite error is essential to a clear apprehension and deep feeling of its truth. But there is a commoner case than either of these: when the conflicting doctrines, instead of being one true and the other false, share the truth between them, and the nonconforming opinion is needed to supply the remainder of the truth of which the received doctrine embodies only a part. . . . [E]ven in revolutions of opinion, one part of the truth usually sets while another rises. Even progress, which ought to superadd, for the most part only substitutes one partial and incomplete truth for another; improvement consisting chiefly in this, that the new fragment of truth is more wanted, more adapted to the needs of the time than that which it displaces. Such being the partial character of prevailing opinions, even when resting on a true foundation, *every opinion which embodies somewhat of the portion of truth which the common opinion omits ought to be considered precious, with whatever amount of error and confusion that truth may be blended*. No sober judge of human affairs will feel bound to be indignant because those who force on our notice truths which we should otherwise have overlooked, overlook some of those which we see. Rather, he will think that so long as popular truth is one-sided, it is more desirable than otherwise that unpopular truth should have one-sided assertors, too, such being usually the most energetic and the most likely to compel reluctant attention to the fragment of wisdom which they proclaim as if it were the whole. . . .

We have now recognized the necessity to the mental well-being of mankind (on which all their other well-being depends) of freedom of opinion, and freedom of the expression of opinion, on four distinct grounds, which we will now briefly recapitulate:

First, if any opinion is compelled to silence, that opinion may, for ought we can certainly know, be true. To deny this is to assume our own infallibility.

Secondly, though the silenced opinion be an error, it may, and very commonly does, contain a portion of truth; and since the general or prevailing opinion on any subject is rarely or never the whole truth, it is only by the collision of adverse opinions that the remainder of the truth has any chance of being supplied.

Thirdly, even if the received opinion be not only true, but the whole truth; unless it is suffered to be, and actually is, vigorously and earnestly contested, it will, by most of those who receive it, be held in the manner of a prejudice, with little comprehension or feeling of its rational grounds. And not only this, but, fourthly, the meaning of the doctrine itself will be in danger of being lost or enfeebled, and deprived of its vital effect on the character and conduct: the dogma becoming a mere formal profession, inefficacious for good, but cumbering the ground and preventing the growth of any real and heartfelt conviction from reason or personal experience.

From Mill (1859), *On Liberty,* In (1956). Indianapolis: Bobbs-Merrill, pp. 16, 26–27.

Whatever the value of free speech, should it be completely free? Should speech have some limits? As former U.S. Supreme Court Justice Oliver Wendell Holmes remarked, "The most stringent protection of free speech would not protect a man falsely shouting fire in a theater and causing panic" (*Schenck v. United States,* see Discussion Issues, question 5, page 267). What limits can law impose on free speech? Within Supreme Court First Amendment analysis, for example, some types of speech (e.g., fighting words, libel, obscenity) do not receive any protection. What justifies placing these limits on speech? The marketplace-of-ideas justification, which says that presenting ideas through speech is like selling goods of various quality, seems to permit speech even if it harms some individuals or groups and to promote free speech even if the speech stifles further deliberation. Consider, then, two plausible cases for limiting speech while still placing a premium on truth. Each case attempts to show that truth is best served by placing limitations on speech. Returning to Reading 5-5 for the first case, Mill justifies limiting speech with his harm principle, which states that actual or potential harm to others provides the only justification for limiting speech. If a person's thought or action would harm another, then the government is justified in imposing limitations. This formulation depends on what constitutes harm and on an ability to predict the likelihood of harm, and is subject to a charge of **paternalism**—the view that someone knows what is in the best interest of someone else. It places government in the role of a fatherly protector against harmful speech. After reading Mill, keep the issues of defining and predicting harm, as well as those of paternalism, in mind when assessing the constitutional cases on free speech.

> No one pretends that actions should be as free as opinions. On the contrary, even opinions lose their immunity when the circumstances in which they are expressed are such as to constitute their expression a positive instigation to some mischievous act. An opinion that con-dealers are starvers of the poor, or that private property is robbery, ought to be unmolested when simply circulated through the press, but may justly incur punishment when delivered orally to an excited mob in the form of a placard [protest sign]. Acts of whatever kind, which without justifiable cause do harm to others may be, and in more important cases absolutely require to be, controlled by the unfavorable sentiments, and, when needful, by the active interference of mankind. (Mill 1859 in 1956, p. 67)

Harmful speech, then, undermines the prospects for truth to emerge through open discussion and deliberation.

The second case for limits on speech rejects the unqualified marketplace-of-ideas position that treats all harmless forms of speech as equal. Instead, it gives some forms of speech a higher value than others. For example, speech that promotes deliberation has a higher value than speech that discourages debate. The Supreme Court has generally agreed with this position, treating some speech as more free than other speech. Political speech receives more protection than commercial speech that is false, deceptive, or misleading. Historically, however, the Court has not given full protection to political speech, especially when it finds the speech subversive. The Court often balances the protection of political speech with concerns about public peace and national security. Is speech that might harm the government the sense of harm that Mill had in mind?

Thomas Scanlon, who teaches philosophy at Harvard University, rejects arguments for limiting harmful speech. If speech has an intrinsic value (a value in itself and not relative to other values), then it would seem to be more difficult to make a case for limiting speech even when it is harmful. The intrinsic-value defense of free speech is part of a more general theory of developmental freedom, which was examined in the previous section. Free speech helps develop rational, autonomous individuals. Therefore, to censor speech is to deny individuals their **autonomy**—their ability to make rational, independent judgments. Scanlon makes this argument in Reading 5-6. Free speech has an intrinsic value to the individual and aids in the development of rational human capacities. While being able to speak freely does not lead to a goal called autonomy, it is part of what it means to be an autonomous, independent thinker. Protecting individuals from some forms of speech is an objectionable form of internal control (see positive freedom, page 225). This paternalism prevents individuals from forming their own opinions and realizing their capacities.

READING 5-6

Autonomy as a Value of Free Speech
"A Theory of Freedom of Expression" (1972)

Thomas Scanlon

I

The doctrine of freedom of expression is generally thought to single out a class of "protected acts" which it holds to be immune from restrictions to which other acts are subject. In particular, on any very strong version of the doctrine there will be cases where protected acts are held to be immune from restriction despite the fact that they have as consequences harms which would normally be sufficient to justify the imposition of legal sanctions. It is the existence of such cases which makes freedom of expression a significant doctrine and which makes it appear, from a certain point of view, an irrational one. . . .

I want to consider a number of different ways in which acts of expression can bring about harms, concentrating on cases where these harms clearly can be counted as reasons for restricting the acts that give rise to them. I will then try to formulate the principle in a way which accommodates these cases. . . .

I. Like other acts, acts of expression can bring about injury or damage as a direct physical consequence. [Consider that] . . . the sound of my voice can break glass, wake the sleeping, trigger an avalanche, or keep you from paying attention to something else you would rather hear. . . .

2. [A]n assault (as distinct from a battery [an actual touching]) is committed when one person intentionally places another in apprehension of imminent bodily harm. . . . [A]ssaults and related acts can also be part of larger acts of expression, as for example when a guerrilla theater production takes the form of a mock bank robbery which starts off looking like the real thing, or when a bomb scare is used to gain attention for a political cause. . . .

3. Another way in which an act of expression can harm a person is by causing others to form an adverse opinion of him or by making him an object of public ridicule. Obvious examples of this are defamation and interference with the right to a fair trial.

4. As Justice Holmes said, "The most stringent protection of free speech would not protect a man in falsely shouting fire in a theater and causing a panic."

5. One person may through an act of expression contribute to the production of a harmful act by someone else, [for example] when the act of expression is the issuance of an order or the making of a threat or when it is a signal or other communication between confederates.

6. Suppose some misanthropic inventor were to discover a simple method whereby anyone could make nerve gas in his kitchen out of gasoline, table salt, and urine. It seems just as clear to me that he could be prohibited by law from passing out his recipe on handbills or broadcasting it on television as that he could be prohibited from passing out free samples of his product in aerosol cans or putting it on sale at Abercrombie & Fitch. In either case his action would bring about a drastic decrease in the general level of personal safety by radically increasing the capacity of most citizens to inflict harm on each other. The fact that he does this in one case through an act of expression and in the other through some other form of action seems to me not to matter. . . .

I will now state the principle of freedom of expression. . . . The principle, which seems to me to be a natural extension of the thesis Mill defends in Chapter II of *On Liberty,* and which I will therefore call the Millian Principle, is the following:

> There are certain harms which, although they would not occur but for certain acts of expression, nonetheless cannot be taken as part of a justification for legal restrictions on these acts. These harms are: (a) harms to certain individuals which consist in their coming to have false beliefs as a result of those acts of expression; (b) harmful consequences of acts performed as a result of those acts of expression, where the connection between the acts of expression and the subsequent harmful acts consists merely in the fact that the act of expression led the agents to believe (or increased their tendency to believe) these acts to be worth performing.

I hope it is obvious that this principle is compatible with the examples of acceptable reasons for restricting expression presented in I through 6 above. . . .

I would like to believe that the general observance of the Millian Principle by governments would, in the long run, have more good consequences than bad. But my defense of the principle does not rest on this optimistic outlook. I will argue . . . that the Millian Principle, as a general principle about how governmental restrictions on the liberty of citizens may be justified, is a consequence of the view, coming down to us from Kant and others, that a legitimate government is one whose authority citizens can recognize while still regarding themselves as equal, autonomous, rational agents. Thus, while it is not a principle about legal responsibility, the Millian Principle has its origins in a certain view of human agency from which many of our ideas about responsibility also derive. . . .

To regard himself as autonomous in the sense I have in mind a person must see himself as sovereign in deciding what to believe and in weighing competing reasons for action. He must apply to these tasks his own canons of rationality, and must recognize the need to defend his beliefs and decisions in accordance with these canons. This does not mean, of course, that he must be perfectly rational, even by his own standard of rationality, or that his standard of rationality must be exactly ours. Obviously the content of this notion of autonomy will vary according to the range of variation we are willing to allow in canons of rational decision. If just anything counts as such a canon then the requirements I have mentioned will become mere tautologies: an autonomous man believes what he believes and decides to do what he decides to do. I am sure I could not describe a set of limits on what can count as canons of rationality which would secure general agreement, and I will not try, since I am sure that the area of agreement on this question extends far beyond anything which will be relevant to the applications of the notion of autonomy that I intend to make. For present purposes what will be important is this. *An autonomous person cannot accept without independent consideration the judgment of others as to what he should believe or what he should do.* He may rely on the judgment of others, but when he does so he must be prepared to advance independent reasons for thinking their judgment likely to be correct, and to weigh the evidential value of their opinion against contrary evidence. . . .

The Millian Principle specifies two ways in which this prerogative must be limited if the state is to be acceptable to autonomous subjects. The argument for the first part of the principle is as follows.

The harm of coming to have false beliefs is not one that an autonomous man could allow the state to protect him against through restrictions on expression. . . .

The argument for the second half of the Millian Principle is parallel to this one. What must be argued against is the view that the state, once it has declared certain conduct to be illegal, may when necessary move to prevent that conduct by outlawing its advocacy. The conflict between this thesis and the autonomy of citizens is, just as in the previous case, slightly oblique. Conceding to the state the right to use this means to secure compliance with its laws does not immediately involve conceding to it the right to require citizens to believe that what the law says ought not to be done ought not to be done. Nonetheless, it is a concession that autonomous citizens could not make, since it gives the state the right to deprive citizens of the grounds for arriving at an independent judgment as to whether the law should be obeyed.

These arguments both depend on the thesis that to defend a certain belief as reasonable a person must be prepared to defend the grounds of his belief as not obviously skewed or otherwise suspect. There is a clear parallel between this thesis and Mill's famous argument that if we are interested in having truth prevail we should allow all available arguments to be heard. But the present argument does not depend, as Mill's may appear to, on an empirical claim that the truth is in fact more likely to win out if free discussion is allowed. Nor does it depend on the perhaps more plausible claim that, given the nature of people and governments, to concede to governments the power in question would be an outstandingly poor strategy for bringing about a situation in which true opinions prevail. . . .

3. Efficiency: Calculating the Risks

Free speech issues look quite different within conservative economics as opposed to radical politics. These positions seem far removed from the classical liberal (Mill, Scanlon) doctrine of free speech and as far removed from each other as they could get. The law and economics movement has been labeled "conservative" and critical legal studies "radical" (see chapter 1, page 27). A sampling of each here will provide fresh insights and give a further glimpse into contemporary forms of **legal realism** (see chapter 3, page 107). **Richard Posner,** an advocate of law and economics, takes Mill's marketplace-of-ideas metaphor seriously. He presents an economic reformulation of a constitutional test for free speech, the **clear-and-present-danger test** promoted by Judge Learned Hand in *The United States v. Dennis* (Reading 5-7). The case involved the indictment of top leaders of the Communist Party under the Smith Act (1940) for conspiring to advocate the overthrow of the U.S. government. Hand, in the lower court opinion, proposed the following test: "In each case, the courts must ask whether the gravity of the 'evil,' discounted by its improbability, justifies such invasion of free speech as is necessary to avoid the danger." Under the Hand formula, courts must weigh and balance competing concerns and values, while Posner would uphold a restriction on speech if the benefits of suppressing the speech were to outweigh the costs (see Reading 5-8). How should judges measure the costs and benefits? Is free speech a value that resists quantitative treatment in a formula? Does this balancing, in the words of Justice Hugo Black, turn " '[g]overnment of the people, by the people, and for the people' into a 'government over the people' " (*Konigsberg v. State Bar,* dissenting)?

4. Ideology: Promoting Political Agendas

David Kairys, a critical legal studies activist, cautions against being swept up by the rhetoric of free speech protection (see Reading 5-9). Historically, free speech protection has increased when it was least needed. If courts balance free speech concerns against other interests, they have space to give undue weight to the interests of the powerful and privileged. The delusion of free speech helps to keep ordinary citizens in their place but in reality, free speech law has done little to enhance the ability of ordinary citizens to engage in meaningful political debate.

READING 5-7

Costs and Benefits of Free Speech
United States v. Dennis (1950)

Judge Learned Hand

... [T]he phrase, "clear and present danger," is not a slogan or a shibboleth [watchword] to be applied as though it carried its own meaning; but ... it involves in every case a comparison between interests which are to be appraised qualitatively. ...

In each case they must ask whether the gravity of the "evil," discounted by its improbability, justifies such invasion of free speech as is necessary to avoid the danger. We have purposely substituted "improbability" for "remoteness," because that must be the right interpretation. Given the same probability, it would be wholly irrational to condone future evils which we should prevent if they were immediate; that could be reconciled only by an indifference to those who come after us. It is only because a substantial intervening period between the utterance and its realization may check its effect and change its importance, that its immediacy is important. ...

In the case at bar the defence seems to us to kick the beam. One may reasonably think it wiser in the long run to let an unhappy, bitter outcast vent his venom before any crowds he can muster and in any terms that he wishes, be they as ferocious as he will; one may trust that his patent [obvious] impotence will be a foil [shield] to anything he may propose. Indeed, it is a measure of the confidence of a society in its own stability that it suffers such fustian to go unchecked. Here we are faced with something very different. The American Communist Party, of which the defendants are the controlling spirits, is a highly articulated, well contrived, far spread organization, numbering thousands of adherents, rigidly and ruthlessly disciplined, many of whom are infused with a passionate Utopian faith that is to redeem mankind. It has its Founder, its apostles, its sacred texts—perhaps even its martyrs. It seeks converts far and wide by an extensive system of schooling, demanding of all an inflexible doctrinal orthodoxy. The violent capture of all existing governments is one article of the creed of that faith, which abjures [solemnly denies] the possibility of success by lawful means. That article, which is a commonplace among initiates, is a part of the homiletics [sermons] for novitiates [new converts], although, so far as conveniently it can be, it is covered by an innocent terminology, designed to prevent its disclosure. Our democracy, like any other, must meet that faith and that creed on the merits, or it will perish; and we must not flinch at the challenge. Nevertheless, we may insist that the rules of the game be observed, and the rules confine the conflict to weapons drawn from the universe of discourse. The advocacy of violence may, or may not, fail; but in neither case can there be any "right" to use it. Revolutions are often "right," but a "right of revolution" is a contradiction in terms, for a society which acknowledged it, could not stop at tolerating conspiracies to overthrow it, but must include their execution. The question before us, and the only one, is how long a government, having discovered such a conspiracy, must wait. When does the conspiracy become a "present danger"? The jury has found that the conspirators will strike as soon as success seems possible, and obviously, no one in his senses would strike sooner. Meanwhile they claim the constitutional privilege of going on indoctrinating their pupils, preparing increasing numbers to pledge themselves to the crusade, and awaiting the moment when we may be so far extended by foreign engagements, so far divided in counsel, or so far in industrial or financial straits, that the chance seems worth trying. That position presupposes that the [First] Amendment assures them freedom for all preparatory steps and in the end the choice of initiative, dependent upon that moment when they believe us, who must await the blow, to be worst prepared to receive it. . . .

As we have said, "clear and present danger" depends upon whether the mischief of the repression is greater than the gravity of the evil, discounted by its improbability; and it is of course true that the degree of probability that the utterance will bring about the evil is a question of fact. On the other hand, to compare the repression with the evil, when discounted, is not a question of fact at all; for it depends upon a choice between conflicting interests. . . .

From *United States v. Dennis* (1950) 183 F. 2d 201 (2d Cir.), pp. 212, 213, 215, 216.

READING 5-8

The Economic Basis of Freedom of Speech
"The Marketplace of Ideas and the Primacy of Political Over Economic Rights" (1986)

Richard Posner

Ideas are a useful good produced in enormous quantity in a highly competitive market. The marketplace of ideas of which Holmes wrote is a fact, not merely a figure of speech. This marketplace determines the "truth" of ideas, other than of purely deductive propositions such as the Pythagorean theorem. When we say that an idea (the earth revolves around the sun) is correct, we mean that all or most of the knowledgeable consumers have accepted ("bought") it. Even in science—the traditional domain of objective validity—ideas are discarded not because they are demonstrated to be false but because competing ideas give better answers to the questions with which the scientists of the day are most concerned.

If competition among ideas is the method by which truth is established, the suppression of an idea on the ground that it is false is irrational, barring some market failure. An idea is false only if rejected in the marketplace, and if it is rejected, there is no occasion to suppress it. To declare an idea true when the competing ideas have been suppressed would be like declaring a brand of beer to be the most popular brand when the sale of the other brands had been suppressed.

But this does not explain why constitutional protection has been thought necessary for this particular marketplace and not for others. Two possible explanations are congenial to economic thinking. The first is that regulation of the marketplace of ideas creates a danger of subverting the democratic process, thus conducing to that most dangerous of monopolies—the monopoly of government power. . . The second and broader explanation (the first is limited to political speech) emphasizes the fragility of markets in information. . . . [I]t is not feasible to create property rights in pure ideas. Hence they are likely to be underproduced. The problem is particularly serious if popular ideas are a good substitute in the marketplace—as in fact they are—for valuable but unpopular ideas. Then any costs that government imposes on unpopular ideas may cause massive substitution away from them. Indeed, the conjunction of "valuable" and "unpopular" suggests that there is a class of ideas the benefits of which are almost entirely external. So there is an economic reason to worry about "chilling" the exercise of freedom of expression. . . .

THE SCOPE OF THE PROTECTED ACTIVITY: INCITEMENT, THREATS, DEFAMATION, OBSCENITY

Not all statements communicate ideas in a sense to which the concept of marketplace is relevant; and some statements, whether true or false, have another attribute—dangerousness—that may justify public regulation if the market in ideas fails (in the economic sense of market failure) to regulate them. For example, if I say "I am going for a walk now," or "I am going to rob a bank," or "I am organizing an armed insurrection," I am not appealing to the marketplace of ideas but merely stating an intention, and my statement may be evidence of an attempt to commit a crime that may have nothing to do with ideas, a crime such as robbery. To punish the attempt does not impede the marketplace in ideas. Statements of intention are not intended to compete with other views, as a statement that the world is flat is intended to compete with other views; and there is no risk of underproduction, because there is no investment in producing the idea behind the statement. . . .

Now suppose I say, "armed insurrection tomorrow would be a good thing," or (if I am a producer of widgets) "the industry would be better off if the price of widgets were 10 percent higher," or "I intend to vote for X." These statements express genuine ideas, because they make a bid to displace competing ideas in the marketplace of ideas. The problem is that the first two may also be invitations to commit illegal acts (treason and price fixing, respectively). As invitations, they would seem punishable on the same principle that makes attempts and conspiracies punishable. But punishment will have the collateral effect of suppressing an idea.

An economic formula to deal with these mixed cases of idea and incitement was proposed by Judge Learned Hand (of course) in *United States v. Dennis*. The courts, he wrote, must in each case "ask whether the gravity of the 'evil' [i.e., if the instigation succeeds], discounted by its improbability, justifies such invasion of free speech as is necessary to avoid the danger." This is equivalent to Hand's negligence formula $(B < PL)$ if B is defined as the cost of the reduction in the stock of ideas as a result of the government's action, P as the probability that the crimes urged by the speaker will come to pass, and L as the social cost if they do come to pass. If B is less than PL, it is efficient for the government to take steps against the speaker. Query: Should there also be a discount for remoteness in the sense of futurity as distinct from unlikelihood, by analogy to discounting future lost earnings to present value in personal-injury cases. . . ?

The application of the *Dennis* formula depends on just what steps the government means to take. If it proposes to punish the speaker criminally, B will be substantial and will therefore require a substantial PL to offset it. But if the government just proposes to monitor the speaker's activity, so that it can take action if and when the danger of a criminal violation becomes imminent, B will be less (because the deterrence of free speech will be less), and therefore a lesser PL than in the first case will suffice to outweigh it and justify the government's action.

The formula, impossible though it is to quantify, is helpful in explaining why, for example, the advocacy of very great evils—genocide or revolution or whatever—is more likely to be tolerated than urging a lynching, which is a lesser evil, or even committing the trivial "evil" created by a blaring soundtruck. If the circumstances make the probability that genocidal advocacy will succeed remote, the discounted cost of the utterance may be smaller than that of a threat to lynch. In the case of the soundtruck, while the harms caused by its blare (L in the formula) are small, so is the cost in forgone benefits, since the speaker can propagate his message by less offensive means. The soundtruck case, like other cases involving restrictions on the time, place, and manner, rather than the substance, of the speech, is analytically similar to our case of the government's merely investigating, rather than punishing, the speaker. Notice that both the soundtruck and the incitement to crime impose external costs, a traditional rationale of regulation.

The *Dennis* formula may seem paternalistic and therefore not truly efficient. Suppose a group is trying to persuade people that a violent revolution would make them better off, and the circumstances make the probability of success sufficiently high to trigger the test even though no *immediate* revolutionary action is being urged. Since there is time for competing groups to persuade the people that a revolution would not make them better off, why interfere with the market in ideas? One answer is that, given the interval for counterpersuasion, P is really quite small, so that the formula would not justify repression. The case for repression is stronger where, as in the usual incitement case, the interval between speech and action is too short to permit competing views to be presented; in such a case punishing speech is like punishing monopoly—there is a similar kind of market failure. In the soundtruck case, too, the market in ideas cannot be relied upon to protect the victims of the harm (this is a general characteristic of time, place, and manner restrictions), because, as we have seen, the costs are external to the marketplace of ideas. A second soundtruck would make matters worse rather than better.

There is a similar economic argument for suppressing the advocacy of violent revolution even in the distant future. Although such advocacy may contain ideas (e.g., that capitalists make greater profits than they should, or that the gap between rich and poor is widening), it is also an invitation to engage in activities that are contrary to the criminal law. The invitation might be attractive even if the marketplace of ideas convincingly showed up the falsity of the advocate's ideas. Suppose the speaker urges the poor to rise up and take away the money of the rich because the rich are exploiting them. Even if counteradvocacy shows convincingly that the rich are not exploiting the poor, it is still the case that the poor might decide to rise up and despoil the rich, as invited to do by the speaker. To the extent that advocacy depends on the truth of certain ideas, the marketplace of ideas may weaken the advocacy by exposing the falsity of those ideas, but that merely reduces P in our free speech Hand formula—not necessarily to zero. . . .

READING 5-9

The Ideological Value of Free Speech
"Freedom of Speech" (1990)

David Kairys

THE REALITY AND IDEOLOGY OF FREE SPEECH

The basic principle that individuals and groups have the ability to express different and unpopular views without prior restraint or punishment is a necessary element of any democratic society. To the extent that we have enforced this principle in the roughly fifty years since the transformation—which we have, to an unprecedented degree, since the early 1960s—we can and should be proud. I do not question the principle or its importance and validity under any system of social relations.

However, free speech means much more than this in American politics and culture. Free speech is discussed as if it defined an economic or political system, or even a religion, rather than a series of rules prohibiting governmental limits on individual expression. It is what makes us good, and better (than other countries and people). Freedom of speech is at the core of our national identity.

Yet, the American celebration of free speech is unsettling, contradictory, and quite complex. The invocation of free speech gains wide acceptance when formulated generally and abstracted from current controversies, or when aimed at specific repressive practices in other countries. But specific applications in the United States are regularly greeted with contempt, evident in the recurring controversies over flag burning and demonstrations by Nazis. There is considerably less than a consensus about or a widespread understanding of the basic aspects of American speech law that truly distinguish it from more restrictive laws and practices prevalent almost everywhere else in the world. The rejection of seditious libel and other limits on unfettered dissent and criticism, the content barrier, expression in a variety of places and a variety of ways, the primacy of expression over competing concerns—all are controversial on the home field of free speech and may not command a majority of the population or, more certainly these days, the Supreme Court.

Simultaneously, the shortcomings of American speech law are generally ignored, even by some of its ardent advocates. The ideal is often assumed to be—or confused with—the reality. In fact, not only has the history of free speech been regularly misrepresented; the ability of our people to communicate meaningfully based even on the most libertarian version of free speech accepted by our courts has been greatly exaggerated. Moreover, the courts failed to provide an effective barrier in the most repressive period since the transformation (the 1950s); and in the last fifteen years, the central insights and distinguishing rules of American speech law have been substantially undercut by the Supreme Court without noticeable public debate or interest.

Since the Transformation

Throughout the posttransformation period, the basic approach set out in *Hague* and other cases of that era has been more or less followed depending mostly on the historical context. Thus, in the 1950s, Senator Joe McCarthy, the House Un-American Activities Committee, and many others resurrected the pretransformation tradition, and the judiciary essentially collapsed. Unpopular ideas and associations again became illegal; dissenters were jailed and lost jobs. The courts abdicated in the face of a reactionary media blitz, leading Justice Hugo Black to say:

> It has been only a few years since there was a practically unanimous feeling throughout the country and in our courts that this could not be done in our free land. . . . [The ultimate question is] whether we as a people will try fearfully and futilely to preserve democracy by adopting totalitarian methods, or whether in accordance with our traditions and our Constitution we will have the confidence and courage to be free.

On the other hand, during the 1960s, the civil rights movement demanded and obtained stringent enforcement and enlargement of speech rights. This is best exemplified by the Supreme Court decisions expanding the right to picket, protecting the press, and protecting even a demonstration with signs inside a public library.

However, even in the most libertarian periods, freedom of speech has been exclusively defined by the historically and culturally specific set of speech rights developed in the transformation period (mainly the 1930s), whose scope and importance in contemporary society are regularly exaggerated. First, the speaker, demonstrator, and writer must cope with the clear-and-present-danger standard and First Amendment balancing tests (in which the interest in speech is "balanced" against competing concerns). The clear-and-present-danger standard can easily be used, as it was in the opinions that first articulated it, to justify repression and punishment of dissent—to allow the bad-tendency doctrine in by the back door. Since the scope of the dangers referred to has never been meaningfully defined (or even limited to unlawful activities), the clear-and-present-danger formulation amounts to the notion that speech loses its protection when it becomes persuasive or effective concerning something a judge views as dangerous. First Amendment balancing tests, while purporting to require particular, legally determined results, provide, in the words of Professor Thomas Emerson, only "various considerations [that can] be enumerated but not weighted. There [is] no standard of reference upon which to base a reasoned, functional determination." This often reduces to a question of whether the speech at issue, given all the circumstances, will likely or potentially cause disruption, which means "harmless" and "futile" speech is protected while speech that is effective, persuasive, or apt to provoke a response is not. These rules tend to allow expression only if it is abstract and ineffective.

The effectiveness and usefulness of our speech rights are also diminished by the reality that effective communication in modern society is expensive. People of ordinary means must rely on the Constitution for a means of communication and organization. People with power and money do not need to picket, demonstrate, or distribute leaflets on the street. The mass media continuously express their perspectives, both explicitly and implicitly, by "more respectable"—and more effective—means.

But most basically, freedom of speech as we know it simply does not provide people of ordinary means entrée to society's dialogue on the issues of the day. Rather, they—we—are allowed to demonstrate, picket, hand out literature, gather in the streets, sing, chant, yell, and scream—all of which effectively amounts to a *display of displeasure or discontent,* without the means to explain why we are displeased much less to actually participate in any social dialogue. This display often will not even gain a spot on the local news unless some violation of the law, injury, destruction of property, or stunt accompanies it. If it does appear, it will usually be unexplained, without description of its context, and frequently misrepresented. Our ability to communicate is haphazard, burdensome, lacking an effective means to explain or persuade; and our messages are filtered, edited, and censured by media organizations mostly interested in pleasing the public and making profits rather than communication, education, or social dialogue. It should not be surprising that so many Americans—across the political spectrum—perceive themselves and their views as excluded from public discourse.

Essentially, the law and society have frozen the scope and nature of our speech rights at levels appropriate to the 1930s, when specific audiences, like factory workers, were geographically centered, and speaking, gathering, and distributing literature in public places were the primary means of communication. The speech rights conceived in that period do not provide access to our current means of communication. Technological, social, and cultural changes have rendered the fruits of the free-speech struggle somewhat obsolete. Television, radio, newspapers (increasingly concentrated and limited in number and diversity), and direct mail now constitute the battleground, and the marketplace of ideas. In the absence of mass-based demands, we have allowed no meaningful inroads into these media for people or groups without substantial money or power.

The scope and reality of our speech rights as a means of communication and persuasion are thus limited by these legal, economic, and practical barriers. I would not relinquish these rights—with considerable patience and persistence, they can and have been meaningful, and often they are all we have. But the ordinary person or group of ordinary persons has no means, based in the Constitution or elsewhere, to engage meaningfully in that dialogue on the issues of the day that the First Amendment is so often heralded as promoting and guaranteeing. . . .

THE IDEOLOGY OF FREE SPEECH

As we stray further from the ideal of free speech we celebrate, it becomes easier to see the ideological aspects of free speech in the United States. The struggle for free speech up to the transformation, waged largely by progressives and finally realized by the labor, civil rights, and other progressive movements, has been falsely redefined as a set of preexisting natural rights whose essence and history are legal rather than political. A false pride in the legal system has displaced a source for genuine pride in the people, who fought business interests and the government—including the courts—to achieve recognition of free speech.

This recast version of freedom of speech serves in our society to validate and legitimize existing social and power relations and to mask a lack of real participation and democracy. In all capitalist countries, a sharp distinction is drawn between a person's "private" and "public" life. In the public sphere, which includes selection of government officials and political expression, basic concepts of freedom, democracy, and equality are applicable. However, in the private sphere, which encompasses almost all economic activity, we allow no democracy or equality and only the freedom to buy and sell. Fundamental social issues, such as the use of our resources, investment, the environment, the work of our people, and the distribution of our goods and services, are all left to "private"—mainly corporate—decision makers.

The ideology of free speech is basic to widespread acceptance of this public/private split. Whatever the state of our economy and people, this ideology tells us that we are free and our society is democratic because we can vote and we have free speech. Like all effective ideology, this reflects as well as distorts reality. Thus, while freedom of speech is essential to any free and democratic society, so is the ability to participate meaningfully in the formulation of social policies and priorities and the provision of basic needs for shelter, health care, nutrition, education, and meaningful work.

But voting in elections increasingly dominated by fleeting, contentless media images and free speech that allows no meaningful entrée into the social dialogue are presently the only ways to participate in societal decisions that affect our lives. We have drawn the line defining the "private" sphere with a uniquely broad brush. Wider participation, on issues like workplace governance, plant closings, and environmental protection, already exists in a variety of forms in many countries. After two hundred years—and with democracy fueling revolts around the world—American democracy must mean more than voting every four years in elections devoid of content or context and the right to picket when you're really upset.

The ideological development and use of free speech in the United States have rendered this hard-won principle of liberation also an instrument of delusion: its reality is far less impressive than its rhetoric; its attainment and continued vitality depend more on popular movements than judges or courts; and its seeming embodiment of individual power and democracy masks powerlessness and society's refusal to allow real participation in the decisions that affect our lives. Our celebration of free speech should be tempered by the realization that its continued vitality even here is not at all assured, and channeled into efforts to protect transformation-era speech rights and to expand public access to the media and participation and democracy regarding the decisions that affect our lives.

C. CONTROVERSIES: SUBVERSIVE, SYMBOLIC, AND OFFENSIVE SPEECH

1. Subversive Speech

The U.S. Supreme Court did not develop a doctrine of free speech until it faced cases arising during World War I and its aftermath. When concern about disloyalty began to play a prominent role in politics after the United States entered the war, Congress passed the Espionage Act (1917), which made it a crime to "woefully obstruct the recruiting or enlistment service." The courts used three tests to rule on convictions under this act: bad tendency, clear and present danger, and incitement. Under the **bad tendency test,** the court determines whether a speech has a natural tendency to harm. Courts have interpreted harm to include the weakening of patriotism. The **clear-and-present danger test,** proposed by Justice Holmes, seems to be similar to Mill's harm principle (see Reading 5-10). "The question in every case is whether the words used are used in such circumstances and are of such a nature to create a clear and present danger that they will bring about the substantial evils that Congress has a right to prevent" (*Schenck v. United States* 1919). According to this test, the government cannot curtail speech that has only a remote tendency to cause danger, but only if there is an immediate risk of evil. Courts must forecast the likelihood that speech will produce danger, just as Mill's harm principle requires a prediction about harm. Notice that it does not require actual harm but only likely or imminent harm. The third test, the **incitement test,** looks only to the words and not to the circumstances (see *Masses, Publishing Co. v. Patten* 1917, in which Judge Learned Hand proposed (see chapter 1, page 19) an incitement test). Under this test, courts would examine the words and determine whether they contained a direct incitement of illegal acts. Abstract advocacy would not be punishable under the incitement test, however speech that advocated violation of the law, such as **civil disobedience,** would remain unprotected. Which test makes the best sense?

When confronted with a battery of tests, the law often opts for a combination of the proposals. The leading constitutional case, *Brandenburg v. Ohio* 1969 (see Reading 5-11), combined elements of the clear-and-present-danger and the incitement tests. Under *Brandenburg,* the incitement language of the speaker (Hand's "objective" focus on the words), not the probability of harm, became the central standard for limiting speech. In this test, the speech being restricted must be likely to incite imminent unlawful action, and it must directly advocate incitement—that is, action. The first requirement protects abstract advocacy of unlawful conduct, but it does not address the seriousness of the unlawful action. The second requirement protects speech that might later, and remotely, result in unlawful action.

2. Symbolic Speech

According to Supreme Court jurisprudence, burning draft cards and wearing armbands do not qualify as speech. Does the First Amendment protect symbolic expressions? Do these acts qualify as protected speech or as unprotected acts? Symbolic expressions lie at the heart of political disputes, but the nature of symbols changes over time. Today, the U.S. flag has a high symbolic value, but before the Civil War, it did not. In 1896, presidential candidate William McKinley used the flag and symbolic patriotism as a campaign theme. Flag statutes at the turn of the twentieth century targeted commercial defacement—that is, using the flag as an everyday object. For example, the Supreme Court upheld a Nebraska conviction of a brewery for placing a picture of the flag on its label (*Halter v. Nebraska* 1907). The flag took on such meaning in American culture that, by 1932, all forty-eight states had flag desecration statutes. However, beginning in the 1950s, the flag statutes gradually phased out commercial defacement and focused on contemptuous defilement (Fletcher 1993, chapter 7). In the early part of the 1900s, using the flag as clothing would have qualified as commercial desecration, but recently a Slovene member of Seton Hall's basketball team received hostile reactions when he refused to wear the U.S. flag on his uniform. Prosecuting for flag desecration waxed and waned, but the wave reached its crest with the case of Gregory Lee Johnson (Goldstein 1996). Johnson burned a flag while protesting outside the Republican National Convention in Dallas. In *Texas v. Johnson* (1989) the Court held that Texas, in violation of the First Amendment, had prosecuted Johnson for the content of his message (see Reading 5-12). After the *Johnson* decision, Congress passed the Flag Protection Act (1989): "Whoever knowingly mutilates, defaces, physically defiles, burns, maintains on the floor or ground, or tramples upon any flag of the United States shall be fined under this title or imprisoned for not more than one year, or both." The Court, in response, found the act to be unconstitutional (*United States v. Eichmann* 1990), and attempts to amend the Constitution to permit punishment for flag desecration failed. If it had been successful, the amendment would have been the fifth to overrule a Supreme Court decision but the first to modify a provision of the original Bill of Rights.

3. Offensive Speech

Pornography

Should the law regulate sexual representations in books, photographs, and films? Sexual materials remained largely unregulated by the criminal law in England and in the United States until the nineteenth century. In 1873, Congress passed "An Act for the Suppression of Trade in, and Circulation of Obscene Literature and Articles of Immoral Use," the so-called Comstock Act. The act's namesake, Anthony Comstock, with financial backing from board members of the Young Men's Christian Association (YMCA), had tirelessly campaigned against "bad books" and against the dissemination of contraceptive literature and devices. The states vigorously enforced the Comstock Act and passed similar legislation until the 1930s, when an era of more selective enforcement began. While the Supreme Court assumed that the First Amendment did not protect obscenity, a majority of justices could not agree on a definition of obscenity. Justice Stewart frankly admitted that he could not provide a definition of obscenity, "but I know it when I see it." Finally, the Court adopted the "Miller test" for identifying obscene materials: (1) "the average person, applying contemporary community standards" would find that "the work, taken as a whole, appeals to the prurient interest" (Roth 1957); (2) the work "depicts or describes, in a patently offensive way, sexual conduct specifically defined by the applicable state law"; and (3) the work, taken as a whole, lacks "serious literary, artistic, political, or scientific value" (*Miller v. California* 1973). However, the Court held that the private possession of pornographic material by an adult could not be criminalized (*Stanley v. Georgia* 1969). It also developed special protective measures for children both as an audience and as subjects.

Presumably, the restrictions on pornography protect society, but what do they protect society from? Do they protect society from indecency and filth? In *Miller,* the Court took note of the "lewd exhibition of the genitals." Is there a puritanical, anti-erotic assumption underlying the protection (Tribe 1988, p. 921)? How does obscenity, which involves offensive sexual conduct, differ from pornography? Is pornography morally objectionable because it harms women? Is pornography about the showing of genitalia, or is it more about violence against women? Some feminists, while accepting First Amendment protection of erotica, see pornography as creating a gender-specific set of injuries to women. The anti-obscenity position focuses on commercial depiction of offensive sex, while the feminist antipornography position focuses on the subjugation-of-women message in the material. Some feminists argue that pornography does not eroticizes sex, but rather eroticizes subjugation and violence against women. In other words, obscenity offends community values; pornography harms women.

Catherine MacKinnon, a law professor, and Andrea Dworkin, a feminist author, drafted an antipornography ordinance that was passed by the Minneapolis City Council (1983) but was then vetoed by the mayor. Indianapolis, led by its mayor, William Hudnut, passed a revised form of a similar ordinance in 1984 that did not provide for any public, criminal enforcement mechanisms, but did give women a private, civil cause of action. The debate over regulating pornography has divided feminists. Judge Frank Easterbrook, a staunch defender of the economic approach to legal questions, wrote the opinion for *American Booksellers v. Hudnut* (see Reading 5-13). As the Internet gains in popularity, another question arises. Can the government regulate indecent speech communicated over the Internet (see Reading 5-14)?

Are there some forms of speech that are so hateful against certain groups that they have no social utility and should not receive constitutional protection? Should principles of equality take priority over freedom of speech? Is hate speech a source of group harm? A distinguished sociologist, David Riesman, tries to persuade us that words hurt vulnerable groups, and even not-so-vulnerable groups, such as lawyers:

> Even [the lawyer's] day-to-day experience in practice bears out the contention that statements such as . . . "all lawyers are dishonest" cause harm to lawyers as a group, and a derivative harm to every individual lawyer. The legal profession has suffered in esteem and influence from such reiterated remarks. . . . And the devastating harm caused to racial or cultural minorities—to Negroes, to Jews, to American Indians, to Poles—as a result of systematic defamation needs no underscoring here; no member of these groups escapes some psychic or material hurt as a consequence of the attacks upon the groups with which he is voluntarily or involuntarily identified. (Riesman 1942, pp. 770–771)

The U.S. Supreme Court seemed to agree with Riesman's assessment as expressed in Justice Murphy's opinion in *Chaplinsky v. New Hampshire* (1942):

> [I]t is well understood that the right of free speech is not absolute at all times and under all circumstances. There are certain well-defined and narrowly limited classes of speech, the prevention and punishment of which have never been thought to raise any Constitutional problem. These include the lewd and obscene, the profane, the libelous, and the insulting or "fighting" words—those which by their very utterance inflict injury or tend to incite an immediate breach of the peace. It has been well observed that such utterances are not essential of any exposition of ideas, and are of such slight social value as a step to truth that any benefit that may be derived from them is clearly outweighed by the social interest in order and morality.

The State of Illinois put Riesman's sentiments concerning group libel into action. In January 1950, Beauharnais, president of the White League of America, distributed a leaflet designed to keep Negroes (as African Americans were commonly called at the time) from moving into Chicago's white neighborhoods. The leaflet proclaimed that, if "persuasion and the need to prevent the white race from being mongrelized by the negro will not unite us, then the rapes, robberies, knaves, guns and marijuana of the negro surely will." He was convicted of violating the Illinois criminal group libel law prohibiting the public display of any publication that "portrays depravity, criminality, unchastity, or lack of virtue of a class of citizens, of any race, color, creed, or religion to contempt, derision, or obloquy, or which is productive of breach of the peace or riots." The Supreme Court of the United States upheld his conviction (*Beauharnais v. Illinois* 1952). Justice Frankfurter, speaking for the majority, noted that Illinois had a long history of "exacerbated tension between races, often flaring into violence and destruction." He reasoned that since the Court would not protect the same speech directed against individuals, *(Chaplinsky),* then the judiciary should not second guess the Illinois legislature when it prohibited these words from being directed against groups. Frankfurter took

Chaplinsky's fighting words doctrine, which applied to individuals, and extended it to groups.

In the 1980s, a new set of free speech curbs emerged in response to reports of an increasing number of racial incidents, particularly on northern university campuses. Some universities responded to an increased incidence of hate speech by instituting hate speech codes (see Reading 5-15). The Supreme Court struck down a St. Paul ordinance because it "imposes special prohibitions on those speakers who express views on disfavored subjects" (see Reading 5-16). Should targeted groups just ignore hate speech? From an international and comparative law perspective, how effective are bans on hate speech (see Reading 5-17)?

READING 5-10

Advocating Illegal Action
Schenck v. United States (1919)

Justice Oliver Wendell Holmes

This is an indictment in three counts. The first charges a conspiracy to violate the Espionage Act of . . . 1917 . . . by causing and attempting to cause insubordination, &c., in the military and naval forces of the United States, and to obstruct the recruiting and enlistment service of the United States, when the United States was at war with the German Empire, to-wit, that the defendants wilfully conspired to have printed and circulated to men who had been called and accepted for military service under the Act of May 18, 1917, a document set forth and alleged to be calculated to cause such insubordination and obstruction. The count alleges overt acts in pursuance of the conspiracy, ending in the distribution of the document set forth. . . .

The document in question upon its first printed side recited the first section of the Thirteenth Amendment [abolishing slavery], said that the idea embodied in it was violated by the Conscription Act and that a conscript is little better than a convict. In impassioned language it intimated that conscription was despotism in its worst form and a monstrous wrong against humanity in the interest of Wall Street's chosen few. It said "Do not submit to intimidation," but in form at least confined itself to peaceful measures such as a petition for the repeal of the act. . . .

We admit that in many places and in ordinary times the defendants in saying all that was said in the circular would have been within their constitutional rights. But the character of every act depends upon the circumstances in which it is done. . . . The most stringent protection of free speech would not protect a man in falsely shouting fire in a theatre and causing a panic. It does not even protect a man from an injunction against uttering words that may have all the effect of force. . . . The question in every case is whether the words used are used in such circumstances and are of such a nature as to create a clear and present danger that they will bring about the substantive evils that Congress has a right to prevent. It is a question of proximity and degree. When a nation is at war many things that might be said in time of peace are such a hindrance to its effort that their utterance will not be endured so long as men fight and that no Court could regard them as protected by any constitutional right. It seems to be admitted that if an actual obstruction of the recruiting service were proved, liability for words that produced that effect might be enforced. . . .

Schenk v. United States (1919) 249 US 47, pp. 48–49, 50–51, 52.

READING 5-11

The Ku Klux Klan and Incitement
Brandenburg v. Ohio (1969)

PER CURIAM, Opinion of Whole Court

The appellant, a leader of a Ku Klux Klan group, was convicted under the Ohio Criminal Syndicalism statute for "advocat[ing] . . . the duty, necessity, or propriety of crime, sabotage, violence, or unlawful methods of terrorism as a means of accomplishing industrial or political reform" and for "voluntarily assembl[ing] with any society, group, or assemblage of persons formed to teach or advocate the doctrines of criminal syndicalism.". . .

The prosecution's case rested on the films and on testimony identifying the appellant as the person who communicated with the reporter and who spoke at the rally. The State also introduced into evidence several articles appearing in the film, including a pistol, a rifle, a shotgun, ammunition, a Bible, and a red hood worn by the speaker in the films.

One film showed 12 hooded figures, some of whom carried firearms. They were gathered around a large wooden cross, which they burned. No one was present other than the participants and the newsmen who made the film. Most of the words uttered during the scene were incomprehensible when the film was projected, but scattered phrases could be understood that were derogatory of Negroes and, in one instance, of Jews. . . .

"[T]he mere abstract teaching . . . of the moral propriety or even moral necessity for a resort to force and violence, is not the same as preparing a group for violent action and steeling it to such action." . . . A statute which fails to draw this distinction impermissibly intrudes upon the freedoms guaranteed by the First and Fourteenth Amendments. It sweeps within its condemnation speech which our Constitution has immunized from governmental control. . . .

Accordingly, we are here confronted with a statute which, by its own words and as applied, purports to punish mere advocacy and to forbid, on pain of criminal punishment, assembly with others merely to advocate the described type of action. Such a statute falls within the condemnation of the First and Fourteenth Amendments. . . .

Brandenburg v. Ohio (1969) 395 US 444, pp. 444–447, 448–449; 450, 452, 454–455.

READING 5-12

Flag Burning as Political Expression
Texas v. Johnson (1989)

JUSTICE WILLIAM BRENNAN, Opinion of the Court

After publicly burning an American flag as a means of political protest, Gregory Lee Johnson was convicted of desecrating a flag in violation of Texas law. This case presents the question whether his conviction is consistent with the First Amendment. We hold that it is not. . . .

While the Republican National Convention was taking place in Dallas in 1984, respondent Johnson participated in a political demonstration dubbed the "Republican War Chest Tour." As explained in literature distributed by the demonstrators and in speeches made by them, the purpose of this event was to protest the policies of the Reagan administration and of certain Dallas-based corporations. The demonstrators marched through the Dallas streets, chanting political slogans and stopping at several corporate locations to stage "die-ins" intended to dramatize the consequences of nuclear war. On several occasions they spray-painted the walls of buildings and overturned potted plants, but Johnson himself took no part in such activities. He did, however, accept an American flag handed to him by a fellow protestor who had taken it from a flagpole outside one of the targeted buildings.

The demonstration ended in front of Dallas City Hall, where Johnson unfurled the American flag, doused it with kerosene, and set it on fire. While the flag burned, the protestors chanted: "America, the red, white, and blue, we spit on you." After the demonstrators dispersed, a witness to the flag burning collected the flag's remains and buried them in his backyard. No one was physically injured or threatened with injury, though several witnesses testified that they had been seriously offended by the flag burning.

If there is a bedrock principle underlying the First Amendment, it is that the government may not prohibit the expression of an idea simply because society finds the idea itself offensive or disagreeable. . . .

We have not recognized an exception to this principle even where our flag has been involved. . . .

We are fortified in today's conclusion by our conviction that forbidding criminal punishment for conduct such as Johnson's will not endanger the special role played by our flag or the feelings it inspires. To paraphrase Justice Holmes, we submit that nobody can suppose that this one gesture of an unknown man will change our Nation's attitude towards its flag. . . . Indeed, Texas' argument that the burning of an American flag " 'is an act having a high likelihood to cause a breach of the peace,' ". . . and its statute's implicit assumption that physical mistreatment of the flag will lead to "serious offense," tend to confirm that the flag's special role is not in danger; if it were, no one would riot or take offense because a flag had been burned.

We are tempted to say, in fact, that the flag's deservedly cherished place in our community will be strengthened, not weakened, by our holding today. Our decision is a reaffirmation of the principles of freedom and inclusiveness that the flag best reflects, and of the conviction that our toleration of criticism such as Johnson's is a sign and source of our strength. . . . It is the Nation's resilience, not its rigidity, that Texas sees reflected in the flag—and it is that resilience that we reassert today.

The way to preserve the flag's special role is not to punish those who feel differently about these matters. It is to persuade them that they are wrong. "To courageous, self-reliant men, with confidence in the power of free and fearless reasoning applied through the processes of popular government, no danger flowing from speech can be deemed clear and present, unless the incidence of the evil apprehended is so imminent that it may befall before there is opportunity for full discussion. If there be time to expose through discussion the falsehood and fallacies, to avert the evil by the processes of education, the remedy to be applied is more speech, not enforced silence." . . .

Johnson was convicted for engaging in expressive conduct. The State's interest in preventing breaches of the peace does not support his conviction because Johnson's conduct did not threaten to disturb the peace. Nor does the State's interest in preserving the flag as a symbol of nationhood and national unity justify his criminal conviction for engaging in political expression. . . .

JUSTICE WILLIAM REHNQUIST, dissenting

In holding this Texas statute unconstitutional, the Court ignores Justice Holmes' familiar aphorism that "a page of history is worth a volume of logic." . . . For more than 200 years, the American flag has occupied a unique position as the symbol of our Nation, a uniqueness that justifies a governmental prohibition against flag burning in the way respondent Johnson did here. . . .

Here it may equally well be said that the public burning of the American flag by Johnson was no essential part of any exposition of ideas, and at the same time it had a tendency to incite a breach of the peace. Johnson was free to make any verbal denunciation of the flag that he wished; indeed, he was free to burn the flag in private. He could publicly burn other symbols of the Government or effigies of political leaders. He did lead a march through the streets of Dallas, and conducted a rally in front of the Dallas City Hall. He engaged in a "die-in" to protest nuclear weapons. He shouted out various slogans during the march, including: "Reagan, Mondale which will it be? Either one means World War III"; "Ronald Reagan, killer of the hour, Perfect example of U.S. power"; and "red, white and blue, we spit on you, you stand for plunder, you will go under." . . . For none of these acts was he arrested or prosecuted; it was only when he proceeded to burn publicly an American flag stolen from its rightful owner that he violated the Texas statute. . . .

The result of the Texas statute is obviously to deny one in Johnson's frame of mind one of many means of "symbolic speech." Far from being a case of "one picture being worth a thousand words," flag burning is the equivalent of an inarticulate grunt or roar that, it seems fair to say, is most likely to be indulged in not to express any particular idea, but to antagonize others. . . .

Texas v. Johnson (1989) 491 US 397, pp. 399, 413–414, 418–420; 421–422, 429–432, 434–435 (Rehnquist, J. dissenting).

READING 5-13

Pornography Harms
American Booksellers v. Hudnut (1985)

JUDGE FRANK EASTERBROOK

Indianapolis enacted an ordinance defining "pornography" as a practice that discriminates against women. "Pornography" is to be redressed through the administrative and judicial methods used for other discrimination. The City's definition of "pornography" is considerably different from "obscenity," which the Supreme Court has held is not protected by the First Amendment.

To be "obscene" under *Miller v. California,* . . . "a publication must, taken as a whole, appeal to the prurient interest, must contain patently offensive depictions or descriptions of specified sexual conduct, and on the whole have no serious literary, artistic, political, or scientific value." . . . Offensiveness must be assessed under the standards of the community. Both offensiveness and an appeal to something other than "normal, healthy sexual desires" . . . are essential elements of "obscenity."

"Pornography" under the ordinance is "the graphic sexually explicit subordination of women, whether in pictures or in words, that also includes one or more of the following:

(1) Women are presented as sexual objects who enjoy pain or humiliation; or
(2) Women are presented as sexual objects who experience sexual pleasure in being raped; or
(3) Women are presented as sexual objects tied up or cut up or mutilated or bruised or physically hurt, or as dismembered or truncated or fragmented or severed into body parts; or
(4) Women are presented as being penetrated by objects or animals; or
(5) Women are presented in scenarios of degradation, injury, abasement, torture, shown as filthy or inferior, bleeding, bruised, or hurt in a context that makes these conditions sexual; or
(6) Women are presented as sexual objects for domination, conquest, violation, exploitation, possession, or use, or through postures or positions of servility or submission or display." . . .

The Indianapolis ordinance does not refer to the prurient interest, to offensiveness, or to the standards of the community. It demands attention to particular depictions, not to the work judged as a whole. It is irrelevant under the ordinance whether the work has literary, artistic, political, or scientific value. The City and many amici [friends-of-the-court briefs] point to these omissions as virtues. They maintain that pornography influences attitudes, and the statute is a way to alter the socialization of men and women rather than to vindicate community standards of offensiveness. . . .

Civil rights groups and feminists have entered this case as amici on both sides. Those supporting the ordinance say that it will play an important role in reducing the tendency of men to view women as sexual objects, a tendency that leads to both unacceptable attitudes and discrimination in the workplace and violence away from it. Those opposing the ordinance point out that much radical feminist literature is explicit and depicts women in ways forbidden by the ordinance and that the ordinance would reopen old battles. It is unclear how Indianapolis would treat works from James Joyce's *Ulysses* to Homer's *Iliad;* both depict women as submissive objects for conquest and domination.

We do not try to balance the arguments for and against an ordinance such as this. The ordinance discriminates on the ground of the content of the speech. Speech treating women in the approved way—in sexual encounters "premised on equality" . . . is lawful no matter how sexually explicit. Speech treating women in the disapproved way—as submissive in matters sexual or as enjoying humiliation—is unlawful no matter how significant the literary, artistic, or political qualities of the work taken as a whole. The state may not ordain preferred viewpoints in this way. The Constitution forbids the state to declare one perspective right and silence opponents. . . .

III

[5] Under the First Amendment the government must leave to the people the evaluation of ideas. Bald or subtle, an idea is as powerful as the audience allows it to be. A belief may be pernicious—the beliefs of Nazis led to the death of millions, those of the Klan to the repression of millions. A pernicious belief may prevail. Totalitarian governments today rule much of the planet, practicing suppression of billions and spreading dogma that may enslave others. One of the things that separates our society from theirs is our absolute right to propagate opinions that the government finds wrong or even hateful.

The ideas of the Klan may be propagated. . . . Communists may speak freely and run for office. . . . The Nazi Party may march through a city with a large Jewish population. . . . People may criticize the President by misrepresenting his positions, and they have a right to post their misrepresentations on public property. . . . People may teach religions that others despise. People may seek to repeal laws guaranteeing equal opportunity in employment or to revoke the constitutional amendments granting the vote to blacks and women. They may do this because "above all else, the First Amendment means that government has no power to restrict expression because of its message [or] its ideas . . . ."

Under the ordinance graphic sexually explicit speech is "pornography" or not depending on the perspective the author adopts. Speech that "subordinates" women and also, for example, presents women as enjoying pain, humiliation, or rape, or even simply presents women in "positions of servility or submission or display" is forbidden, no matter how great the literary or political value of the work taken as a whole. Speech that portrays women in positions of equality is lawful, no matter how graphic the sexual content. This is thought control. It establishes an "approved" view of women, of how they may react to sexual encounters, of how the sexes may relate to each other. Those who espouse the approved view may use sexual images; those who do not, may not.

Indianapolis justifies the ordinance on the ground that pornography affects thoughts. Men who see women depicted as subordinate are more likely to treat them so. Pornography is an aspect of dominance. It does not persuade people so much as change them. It works by socializing, by establishing the expected and the permissible. In this view pornography is not an idea; pornography is the injury.

There is much to this perspective. Beliefs are also facts. People often act in accordance with the images and patterns they find around them. People raised in a religion tend to accept the tenets of that religion, often without independent examination. People taught from birth that black people are fit only for slavery rarely rebelled against that creed; beliefs coupled with the self-interest of the masters established a social structure that inflicted great harm while enduring for centuries. Words and images act at the level of the subconscious before they persuade at the level of the conscious. Even the truth has little chance unless a statement fits within the framework of beliefs that may never have been subjected to rational study.

Therefore we accept the premises of this legislation. Depictions of subordination tend to perpetuate subordination. The subordinate status of women in turn leads to affront and lower pay at work, insult and injury at home, battery and rape on the streets. In the language of the legislature, "[p]ornography is central in creating and maintaining sex as a basis of discrimination. Pornography is a systematic practice of exploitation and subordination based on sex which differentially harms women. The bigotry and contempt it produces, with the acts of aggression it fosters, harm women's opportunities for equality and rights [of all kinds]." Indianapolis Code § 16-1(a)(2).

Yet this simply demonstrates the power of pornography as speech. All of these unhappy effects depend on mental intermediation. Pornography affects how people see the world, their fellows, and social relations. If pornography is what pornography does, so is other speech. Hitler's orations affected how some Germans saw Jews. Communism is a world view, not simply a *Manifesto* by Marx and Engels or a set of speeches. Efforts to suppress communist speech in the United States were based on the belief that the public acceptability of such ideas would increase the likelihood of totalitarian government. Religions affect socialization in the most pervasive way. The opinion in *Wisconsin v. Yoder* [granting a free exercise exemption for Amish children to a state law requiring school attendance until age 16] . . . shows how a religion can dominate an entire approach to life, governing much more than the relation between the sexes. Many people believe that the existence of television, apart from the content of specific programs, leads to intellectual laziness, to a penchant for violence, to many other ills. The Alien and Sedition Acts passed during the administration of John Adams rested on a sincerely held belief that disrespect for the government leads to social collapse and revolution—a belief with support in the history of many nations. Most governments of the world act on this empirical regularity, suppressing critical speech. In the United States, however, the strength of the support for this belief is irrelevant. Seditious libel is protected speech unless the danger is not only grave but also imminent. . . .

Racial bigotry, anti-semitism, violence on television, reporters' biases—these and many more influence the culture and shape our socialization.

None is directly answerable by more speech, unless that speech too finds its place in the popular culture. Yet all is protected as speech, however insidious. Any other answer leaves the government in control of all of the institutions of culture, the great censor and director of which thoughts are good for us.

Sexual responses often are unthinking responses, and the association of sexual arousal with the subordination of women therefore may have a substantial effect. But almost all cultural stimuli provoke unconscious responses. Religious ceremonies condition their participants. Teachers convey messages by selecting what not to cover; the implicit message about what is off limits or unthinkable may be more powerful than the messages for which they present rational argument. Television scripts contain unarticulated assumptions. People may be conditioned in subtle ways. If the fact that speech plays a role in a process of conditioning were enough to permit governmental regulation, that would be the end of freedom of speech.

It is possible to interpret the claim that the pornography is the harm in a different way. Indianapolis emphasizes the injury that models in pornographic films and pictures may suffer. The record contains materials depicting sexual torture, penetration of women by red-hot irons and the like. These concerns have nothing to do with written materials subject to the statute, and physical injury can occur with or without the "subordination" of women. . . . [A] state may make injury in the course of producing a film unlawful independent of the viewpoint expressed in the film.

The more immediate point, however, is that the image of pain is not necessarily pain. In *Body Double,* a suspense film directed by Brian DePalma, a woman who has disrobed and presented a sexually explicit display is murdered by an intruder with a drill. The drill runs through the woman's body. The film is sexually explicit and a murder occurs—yet no one believes that the actress suffered pain or died. In *Barbarella* a character played by Jane Fonda is at times displayed in sexually explicit ways and at times shown "bleeding, bruised, [and] hurt in a context that makes these conditions sexual"—and again no one believes that Fonda was actually tortured to make the film. In *Carnal Knowledge* a woman grovels to please the sexual whims of a character played by Jack Nicholson; no one believes that there was a real sexual submission, and the Supreme Court held the film protected by the First Amendment. . . . And this works both ways. The description of women's sexual domination of men in *Lysistrata* was not real dominance. Depictions may affect slavery, war, or sexual roles, but a book about slavery is not itself slavery, or a book about death by poison a murder.

Much of Indianapolis's argument rests on the belief that when speech is "unanswerable," and the metaphor that there is a "marketplace of ideas" does not apply, the First Amendment does not apply either. The metaphor is honored; Milton's *Aeropagitica* and John Stewart Mill's *On Liberty* defend freedom of speech on the ground that the truth will prevail, and many of the most important cases under the First Amendment recite this position. The Framers undoubtedly believed it. As a general matter it is true. But the Constitution does not make the dominance of truth a necessary condition of freedom of speech. To say that it does would be to confuse an outcome of free speech with a necessary condition for the application of the amendment.

A power to limit speech on the ground that truth has not yet prevailed and is not likely to prevail implies the power to declare truth. At some point the government must be able to say (as Indianapolis has said): "We know what the truth is, yet a free exchange of speech has not driven out falsity, so that we must now prohibit falsity." If the government may declare the truth, why wait for the failure of speech? Under the First Amendment, however, there is no such thing as a false idea, . . . so the government may not restrict speech on the ground that in a free exchange truth is not yet dominant.

At any time, some speech is ahead in the game; the more numerous speakers prevail. Supporters of minority candidates may be forever "excluded" from the political process because their candidates never win, because few people believe their positions. This does not mean that freedom of speech has failed. . . .

American Booksellers v. Hudnut (1985) 771 F. 2d 323 (7th Cir.), pp. 324–325, 327–331.

READING 5-14

Indecency on the Internet
Reno v. American Civil Liberties Union (1997)

JUSTICE JOHN PAUL STEVENS

At issue is the constitutionality of two statutory provisions enacted to protect minors from "indecent" and "patently offensive" communications on the Internet. Notwithstanding the legitimacy and importance of the congressional goal of protecting children from harmful materials, we agree with the three-judge District Court that the statute abridges "the freedom of speech" protected by the First Amendment. . . .

. . . [T]he many ambiguities concerning the scope of its coverage render it problematic for purposes of the First Amendment. For instance, each of the two parts of the CDA uses a different linguistic form. The first uses the word "indecent," while the second speaks of material that "in context, depicts or describes, in terms patently offensive as measured by contemporary community standards, sexual or excretory activities or organs." Given the absence of a definition of either term, this difference in language will provoke uncertainty among speakers about how the two standards relate to each other and just what they mean. Could a speaker confidently assume that a serious discussion about birth control practices, homosexuality, the First Amendment issues raised by the Appendix to our *Pacifica* opinion, or the consequences of prison rape would not violate the CDA? This uncertainty undermines the likelihood that the CDA has been carefully tailored to the congressional goal of protecting minors from potentially harmful materials.

The vagueness of the CDA is a matter of special concern for two reasons. First, the CDA is a content-based regulation of speech. The vagueness of such a regulation raises special First Amendment concerns because of its obvious chilling effect on free speech. . . . Second, the CDA is a criminal statute.

In addition to the opprobrium [disgrace, shame] and stigma of a criminal conviction, the CDA threatens violators with penalties including up to two years in prison for each act of violation. The severity of criminal sanctions may well cause speakers to remain silent rather than communicate even arguably unlawful words, ideas, and images. . . .

We are persuaded that the CDA lacks the precision that the First Amendment requires when a statute regulates the content of speech. In order to deny minors access to potentially harmful speech, the CDA suppresses a large amount of speech that adults have a constitutional right to receive and to address to one another. That burden on adult speech is unacceptable if less restrictive alternatives would be at least as effective in achieving the legitimate purpose that the statute was enacted to serve. . . .

Reno v. American Civil Liberties Union (1997) 521 US 844, pp. 849, 853–857, 864–868, 870–872, 874, 877–879.

READING 5-15
Regulating Hate Speech on Campus
Doe v. University of Michigan (1989)

JUDGE COHN

It is an unfortunate fact of our constitutional system that the ideals of freedom and equality are often in conflict. The difficult and sometimes painful task of our political and legal institutions is to mediate the appropriate balance between these two competing values. Recently, the University of Michigan at Ann Arbor (the University), a state-chartered university, adopted a Policy on Discrimination and Discriminatory Harassment of Students in the University Environment (the Policy) in an attempt to curb what the University's governing Board of Regents (Regents) viewed as a rising tide of racial intolerance and harassment on campus. The Policy prohibited individuals, under the penalty of sanctions, from "stigmatizing or victimizing" individuals or groups on the basis of race, ethnicity, religion, sex, sexual orientation, creed, national origin, ancestry, age, marital status, handicap or Vietnam-era veteran status. . . .

Looking at the plain language of the Policy, it was simply impossible to discern any limitation on its scope or any conceptual distinction between protected and unprotected conduct. The structure of the Policy was in two parts; one relates to cause and the other to effect. Both cause and effect must be present to state a *prima facie* violation of the Policy. The operative words in the cause section required that language must "stigmatize" or "victimize" an individual. However, both of these terms are general and elude precise definition. Moreover, it is clear that the fact that a statement may victimize or stigmatize an individual does not, in and of itself, strip it of protection under the accepted First Amendment tests. . . .

The foregoing constitutes the Court's findings of fact and conclusions of law. . . . However, at this juncture, a few additional observations of a general nature would seem to be in order. As the Court noted at the hearing on August 25, 1989, there is nothing in the record to suggest that the University looked at the experience of any other university in developing its approach to the problem of discriminatory harassment. Had it done so, it might have discovered that Yale University, a private institution not subject to the strictures of the First Amendment, faced a similar dilemma pitting its efforts to promote equality against its commitment to free speech. In 1986, a sophomore at Yale was put on probation for two years by a University discipline board for disseminating a malicious flier intended to ridicule the homosexual community. The board eventually reversed the sanction, but only after a second hearing was held at which the student was represented by historian C. Vann Woodward, author of the University's 1975 report on free speech. . . . That report concluded that "freedom of expression is a paramount value, more important than civility or rationality." . . .

While the Court is sympathetic to the University's obligation to ensure equal educational opportunities for all of its students, such efforts must not be at the expense of free speech. . . .

Doe v. University of Michigan (1989) 721 F. Supp. 852 (E.D. Mich.) pp. 853, 867–868, 869.

READING 5-16

Regulating Hate Speech off Campus
R.A.V. v. City of St. Paul (1992)

JUSTICE ANTONIN SCALIA

In the predawn hours of June 21, 1990, petitioner and several other teenagers allegedly assembled a crudely made cross by taping together broken chair legs. They then allegedly burned the cross inside the fenced yard of a black family that lived across the street from the house where petitioner was staying. Although this conduct could have been punished under any of a number of laws,[1] one of the two provisions under which respondent city of St. Paul chose to charge petitioner (then a juvenile) was the St. Paul Bias-Motivated Crime Ordinance, St. Paul, Minn., Legis. Code, which provides:

> "Whoever places on public or private property a symbol, object, appellation, characterization or graffiti, including, but not limited to, a burning cross or Nazi swastika, which one knows or has reasonable grounds to know arouses anger, alarm or resentment in others on the basis of race, color, creed, religion or gender commits disorderly conduct and shall be guilty of a misdemeanor." . . .

[1] The conduct might have violated Minnesota statutes carrying significant penalties. See, *e.g.,* Minn. Stat. (1987) (providing for up to five years in prison for terroristic threats); (arson) (providing for up to five years and a $10,000 fine, depending on the value of the property intended to be damaged); (Supp. 1992) (criminal damage to property) (providing for up to one year and a $3,000 fine, depending upon the extent of the damage to the property).

Applying these principles to the St. Paul ordinance, we conclude that, even as narrowly construed by the Minnesota Supreme Court, the ordinance is facially unconstitutional. Although the phrase in the ordinance, "arouses anger, alarm or resentment in others," has been limited by the Minnesota Supreme Court's construction to reach only those symbols or displays that amount to "fighting words," the remaining, unmodified terms make clear that the ordinance applies only to "fighting words" that insult, or provoke violence, "on the basis of race, color, creed, religion or gender." Displays containing abusive invective, no matter how vicious or severe, are permissible unless they are addressed to one of the specified disfavored topics. Those who wish to use "fighting words" in connection with other ideas—to express hostility, for example on the basis of political affiliation, union membership, or homosexuality—are not covered. The First Amendment does not permit St. Paul to impose special prohibitions on those speakers who express views on disfavored subjects. . . .

In its practical operation, moreover, the ordinance goes even beyond mere content discrimination, to actual viewpoint discrimination. Displays containing some words—odious racial epithets, for example—would be prohibited to proponents of all views. But "fighting words" that do not themselves invoke race, color, creed, religion, or gender—aspersions upon a person's mother, for example—would seemingly be usable *ad libitum* [at one's pleasure] in the placards of those arguing *in favor* of racial, color, etc., tolerance and equality, but could not be used by those speakers' opponents. One could hold up a sign saying, for example, that all "anti-Catholic bigots" are misbegotten; but not that all "papists" are, for that would insult and provoke violence "on the basis of religion." St. Paul has no such authority to license one side of a debate to fight freestyle, while requiring the other to follow Marquis of Queensberry rules. . . .

Let there be no mistake about our belief that burning a cross in someone's front yard is reprehensible. But St. Paul has sufficient means at its disposal to prevent such behavior without adding the First Amendment to the fire. . . .

R.A.V. v. City of St. Paul (1992) 550 US 377, pp.379–380, 391–92, 396.

READING 5-17

Regulating Hate Speech Internationally
"The View from Abroad" (1999)

Phillipa Strum

Another major issue has to do with the efficacy or lack thereof of hate speech laws.

Whatever international conventions they have or have not signed, most of the world's nations view speech as a right at least theoretically inherent in human beings and basic to democracies. The Universal Declaration of Human Rights declares that "the advent of a world in which human beings shall enjoy freedom of speech and belief and freedom from fear and want has been proclaimed as the highest aspiration of the common people." The first session of the United Nations General Assembly in 1946 adopted a resolution saying, "Freedom of information is a fundamental human right and . . . the touchstone of all of the freedoms to which the United Nations is consecrated." As the various nations' constitutions and basic laws indicate, the only acceptable reason for limitations on speech is the prevention of serious harm, whether the harm is to the state (breach of peace, endangerment of national security) or to the individual (the psychological harms caused by hate speech). The argument for abridgment of speech is tied to the efficacy of abridgment: it is valid only if it achieves a substantial societal value. The laws of many nations indicate that abridgment of speech is permissible only when there is no other way in which to avoid the harms potentially done by it. This means that if hate speech laws don't work, there is no legitimate reason for their existence in a democratic society.

Great Britain and the United States have legal systems that are rooted in similar if not identical doctrines and values. Early American law was based largely upon English law, although the two systems have followed different paths since then. Britain now has had some years of experience with hate speech laws and can be examined for an indication of their effectiveness.

The Public Order Act enacted in 1986 modified already existing English law designed to minimize hate speech. In voting for it, some members of Parliament referred to the law as a reaction against the fear, alarm, and distress that had been caused to members of minority groups and as an attempt to deal with the racial discrimination that might be linked to racist speech. They were concerned about the damage done by hate speech to the reputations of target groups and about possible consequent economic damage, such as loss of business and loss of employment. . . .

Some of the impetus for laws against hate speech in Britain in the 1970s came from Jewish students on university campuses who were concerned about anti-Semitic speech. They and other students persuaded the National Union of Students to adopt a 1974 regulation against speech on campuses by "racist and fascist organizations." After the United Nations General Assembly passed a 1975 resolution equating Zionism with racism, however, the regulation was used to keep Zionist speakers—including the Israeli ambassador to Great Britain—off campuses. Among the first people prosecuted under the British Race Relations Act of 1965 were Black Power leaders. It is doubtful that the proponents of the National Union of Students' regulation or of the Race Relations Act intended either of those effects. In fact, the National Union of Students, disgusted with the results of its resolution, repealed it in 1977.

Canada is another nation whose legal system resembles that of the United States. The Canadian Supreme Court adopted a statutory definition of pornography that originally was part of a law proposed by Andrea Dworkin and Catharine MacKinnon (who referred to pornography as "our Skokie") for the city of Minneapolis. It embodied the idea that pornography violates women's civil rights and defined its production, sale, exhibition, or distribution as discrimination against women. Passed by the Minneapolis city council in 1984 but vetoed by the mayor, the ordinance was somewhat revised and then enacted by the city of Indianapolis. (It was invalidated by federal courts as a violation of the First Amendment.) The first prosecution under the Canadian version, which allowed the government to prosecute sexually explicit expression it believed to be "degrading" or "dehumanizing" to women, was against a gay and lesbian bookstore and the lesbian magazine it carried. Canadian authorities also used the law to prosecute Bell Hooks, the American black feminist author, and seize 1,500 copies of her *Black Looks: Race and Representation.* Ironically enough, Canadian customs officials, relying on the Supreme Court decision, confiscated two of Andrea Dworkin's books that bookstores were attempting to import from the United States. They did not, however, find sexually explicit art in *Penthouse* magazine to fall under the act.

The lesson is that hate speech laws are as discretionary as any other laws: they may be used against people whose speech we like or those whose speech we hate, depending upon who is in power and making the decision about which forms of speech fall under the laws. It is rarely the speech of the powerful that is banned by such laws. When the University of Michigan speech code was adopted, it was heralded as a blow against bigotry, but not a single white student who used racist language was held to account under it. White students used it about twenty times to charge black students, however, and one black student was punished for using the term "white trash." (The speech code was struck down by a federal court in 1989.) In discussing the issue of enforcement, African-American civil libertarian Henry Louis Gates Jr. tells of an exchange of epithets between a white police officer in Louisiana and the mother of a black suspect.

> Police officer: Get your black ass in the goddamned car.
> Mother: You god damn mother fucking police—I am going to [the Superintendent of Police] about this.

Only the mother, who later denied having used any profanity, was prosecuted for using "fighting words" (*Lewis v. City of New Orleans,* 1974).

The logical answer to the question raised by these examples of selective enforcement might seem to be a call for fairer enforcement. Civil libertarians would reply that ideas are so dangerous in their ability to convince that the people against whom speech is spoken are those most likely to find the speech threatening to society, morality, and so on. . . .

Some American civil libertarians have asked whether laws against hate speech do not lead people to ignore the deeper societal problems that underlie such speech. ACLU executive director Ira Glasser points to the fact that 80 percent of the poor in New York City are black and Latino; the unemployment rate for young black men hovers around 40 percent; a large number of black Americans who use or deal in drugs are arrested while the same activities by white Americans are largely ignored; 80 percent of the Americans who die from curable diseases such as bronchitis, asthma, pneumonia, and gallbladder disease are black; and few white Americans advocate spending money on the kind of programs that would eliminate many of these phenomena. Can those who advocate hate speech laws be serious, he asks, "when they suggest that if only we could repress college students and skinheads from *voicing* bigotry, we could reduce bigotry itself?"

This raises the question of exactly what hate speech laws are designed to do. If the goal is to drive hate speech underground, the laws may have some success. If the object is to eliminate the prejudices that produce hate speech, success is unlikely. Critical Race Theorists would reply that the articulation of hate stereotypes reinforces them and that while the society is dealing—or failing to deal—with the problems of subordination, it is unnecessary for people already victimized by racism to be further injured by words that wound. These opposing positions were inherent in the Skokie situation.

A last consideration that arises when considering the difference between speech jurisprudence and speech laws elsewhere has to do with the conditions of democracy. What elements must be present in a society if it is to accept the dangers of democracy, including the danger of unregulated speech? For democracy, with its assumption that the people are free to decide even if they make very wrong decisions, *is* dangerous. And speech, which affects the beliefs that people hold, has as much potential for harm as it does for good.

The American approach emphasizes the need for speech in a democracy and the great damage to the free flow of ideas that can be done when governments are allowed to decide who shall be permitted to say what. Other nations look at human history and argue that unfettered speech has caused a level of misery and injustice that cannot be allowed to be repeated. Germany and France, for example, both forbid the utterance of some Nazi speech. Both have based such laws on a desire to prevent injury to individuals but also to safeguard the two societies from the kinds of horrors that occurred during the Nazi period. They are uncertain of how well their countries would survive unregulated fascist speech. The German minister of the interior noted in 1982 that half of that country's population had grown up after World War II and had no firsthand experience of Nazi rule. Those Germans might be more open to persuasion by Nazi propaganda than people who had lived through the war years. He and other legislators were concerned about a rash of neo-Nazi incidents centering around a claim that reports of the murders of European Jews in the concentration camps were lies. The result was enactment of a 1985 addition to the criminal code, facilitating prosecution of those who espoused the "Auschwitz lie" in public. Just as some Americans speaking of the Holocaust are convinced that "it can't happen here," so many Europeans remember that it did happen there and are frightened at the possibility of history repeating itself.

The problem of whether it *could* happen here—that is, whether the United States enjoys a system so stable that it is unlikely to be threatened by a system of free speech—is central to the discussion. (The question also could be framed as one about whether a democratic society can afford *not* to have a system of free speech: whether the kind of informed decisions "we the people" are called upon to make in a democracy are possible in the absence of a free flow of ideas.) Some of the preconditions would seem to be the rule of law and a written constitution, an independent judiciary, and the existence of private groups devoted to maintaining the system of free speech. . . .

The American experience, coupled with the limits on the existence of organizations protective of speech that seem to accompany severe abridgments of speech elsewhere, suggests that such groups may be as important to a democratic polis as is a popularly elected government or the enumeration of rights in a nation's basic legal documents. That certainly was the assumption of the ACLU when it decided to oppose the village of Skokie [see Discussion Issues, question 2, page 266].

But, critics of American speech jurisprudence ask, can we "afford" it here? The questions remain: has the United States made a reasoned decision, based on American history and political culture, that we can weather even the most undemocratic speech and that it is best for us to absorb whatever hurts come from words that wound? Or is American free speech jurisprudence no more than an accident of the wording of the First Amendment and the role of the Supreme Court in interpreting it? If so, is it the wisest policy for a country with a history of religious bigotry, racism, and sexism?

Strum, Phillippa. "The View from Abroad," *When the Nazis Came to Skokie.* Copyright © (1999) Lawrence, KS: University Press of Kansas. Reprinted by permission from the University of Kansas.

DISCUSSION ISSUES

1. *Speech and Sedition.* Are there natural rights to think, speak, and publish? Why should the First Amendment protect individuals who, if they had the power, would deny free speech freedoms to others? Robert Bork would not protect speech that advocates the violent overthrow of the government, and refuses even to categorize it as political speech. He writes, "that term must be defined by a Madisonian system of government [because] it violates constitutional truths about processes and because it is not aimed at a new definition of political truth by a legislative majority. Violent overthrow of the government breaks down our system concerning the ways in which truth is defined. . . ." (Bork 1971, p. 31). In contrast, Thomas Emerson argues:

   > Yet popular participation in the governing process implies that social and political movements aimed at basic changes in society must be allowed to exist and have their say. For both theoretical and practical reasons this remains true even when the opposition goes to the length of advocating change by force and violence if necessary. The answer to such a challenge, in a democratic community, is to

punish overt action if and when it occurs, and to maintain the social and economic conditions necessary for a viable society. Suppression of political groups, apart from any use of violence, cannot be reconciled with constitutional government. (Emerson 1970, p. 160)

Which position is correct?

2. *Speech and War Crimes.* Compare the following cases:

a. *The Holocaust.* The Nuremberg Tribunal convicted and gave the death sentence to Julius Streicher, editor of an extremely anti-Semitic newspaper, for incitement to murder and extermination (crimes against humanity). After 1940, Streicher did not hold any government position, and his newspaper circulation dwindled.

b. *The Rwandan Genocide.* Radio Television Mille Collines (RTML), owned by members of President Habyarimana's inner political circle, openly fomented Hutu hatred of Tutsis. RTML began broadcasting nine months before the genocide in which Hutus slaughtered about 800,000 Tutsi and Hutu sympathizers. The government denied licenses to those with contrary views, and after the genocide began, RTML identified targets and their locations to those engaged in the genocide.

c. *Holocaust Survivors in Skokie Compared.* Aryeh Neier, as director of the American Civil Liberties Union, defended "freedom of speech for American Nazis seeking to hold a demonstration" in the Illinois town of Skokie, which had a large population of Jews and survivors of the Holocaust (Neier 1998, p. 207, see Discussion Issues, question 9, page 268). Later, as director of Human Rights Watch, he rejected defenses of media propagandists in Rwanda:

> The concept of freedom of speech requires freedom for a broad range of views—even Nazi views—provided that all other views, including those of anti-Nazis, may be expressed; it is not a license for government to disseminate an official view to the exclusion of others. When that exclusive official view incites crimes against humanity, it does not warrant a defense as freedom of expression. . . . Also, when incitement is so closely intertwined with the actual commission of the crime that they cannot be separated, it does not warrant the protection accorded to freedom of speech. Such an intertwined connection between expression and criminality may occur in circumstances in which only one point of view may be heard. The connection is severed when many voices compete. (Neier 1998, p. 270)

Does it make sense to defend freedom of speech where that freedom already operates but not in cases of incitement to mass murder where it does not exist?

3. *Speech and Paternalism.* In later writings, Scanlon found his defense of the intrinsic value of speech unrealistic. The view that autonomy underlies a liberal defense of free speech assumes that individuals have relatively equal and reasonable access to information. This assumption underestimates the powerfully effective ways of distorting and manipulating information. Do these situations justify government regulation in areas such as deceptive advertising (Scanlon 1979, pp. 532–533)? Do these limits on speech and communication amount to treating individuals as children?

4. *Speech and Emotions.* Do Mill, Emerson, Posner, and the later Scanlon, who was covered in Discussion Issue 3, have an excessively intellectual view of speech, modeled on rational persuasion? Posner, for example, claims that the probability of harm resulting from speech increases if the speech is emotive and likewise increases with the lowering of the educational level of the audience. Does highly

emotional speech have less value than highly intellectual speech? Should the courts protect the emotive content of speech? In *Cohen v. California,* the U.S. Supreme Court upheld Cohen's freedom to express himself by wearing a jacket bearing the words "Fuck the Draft" into a courthouse corridor. Justice Harlan recognized that expression "conveys not only ideas capable of relatively precise, detached explication, but otherwise inexpressible emotions as well" (*Cohen v. California* 1971). Harlan found that the Constitution's protections should extend to the speaker's emotions, while the dissent classified Cohen's expression as mainly conduct and not as speech.

5. *Restrictions on Speech.* Proponents of restricting speech often use Justice Holmes's analogy, in *Schenck,* to shouting fire in a crowded theater. Does the analogy hold—even in the *Schenck* case? A member of the Socialist Party, Schenck circulated leaflets during World War I that tried to persuade draftees to refuse conscription into the army. Does shouting fire have the same elements as Schenck's political speech (Derschowitz, 1989)? How does a judge decide whether these situations are analogous? The Court held in *Reno* that Internet prohibitions differ from the following prohibitions that were upheld by the Court: (1) "a New York statute that prohibited selling to minors under 17 years of age material that was considered obscene as to them even if not obscene to adults" (*Ginsberg*, New York 1968); (2) banning a radio "broadcast of a recording of a 12 minute monologue entitled 'Filthy Words' that had previously been delivered to a live audience" (*FCC v. Pacifica,* 1978); (3) "a zoning ordinance that kept adult movie theaters out of residential neighborhoods" (*Renton v. Playtime Theatres, Inc.* 1986). What are the arguments for and against using these cases as precedents in *Reno?*

6. *Offensive Speech.* Should speech that offends others, as opposed to speech that harms others, also be restricted (Feinberg 1985)? Should the government restrict speech that damages a reputation? Should the government forbid nude dancing if it offends sensibilities and causes psychological distress?

7. *Patriotism and Loyalty.* Do symbolic speech cases amount to "much ado about nothing"? Do flag desecration cases involve values other than free speech? Do cases involving national symbols turn on how much Congress and the country value patriotism and loyalty (see Fletcher 1993)? Is flag burning inherently inflammatory (see MacIntyre, 1984)? Is patriotism dangerous? Should we strive to become "citizens of the world" instead of lovers of a single country (see Nussbaum in Cohen 1996)?

8. *Loathsome Expression.* The American public reacted negatively to the Court's protection of flag desecration (*Texas v. Johnson,* see Reading 5-12), but they rushed to defend writer Salman Rushdie's right to free speech. The Ayatollah condemned Rushdie's *The Satanic Verses* as a blasphemy against Islam and put out a death warrant for Rushdie. Does this indicate that Americans have greater tolerance for unpopular views abroad than for unpatriotic ones at home? Is the real test of free speech, as Justice Holmes claimed, whether we tolerate speech that we loathe? (See chapter 6, page 314 on the issue of cultural relativism and religious rights.)

9. *Good Versus Bad Symbols.* The swastika is an abhorrent political symbol to many, and was especially so to the many Jewish survivors of the Holocaust living in Skokie, Illinois, during the late 1970s. When the American Nazi party wanted to hold a parade and display the swastika in Skokie, the village obtained an injunction to prohibit them, but the Supreme Court of Illinois considered the swastika to be a form of protected symbolic expression *(Skokie v. NSPA 1977).* Are there good and bad symbols? Is the symbolic speech in this case so "taunting and overwhelmingly offensive to the citizens of Skokie that it is like crying fire in a crowded theater"? Is this an example of hate speech? In its haste to take action, the Skokie City

Council had banned public demonstrations by members of political parties wearing military-style uniforms. The Nazis challenged Skokie's ordinance and were represented by Aryeh Neier, a Jewish attorney for the American Civil Liberties Union. Should the case hinge on the probability of violence? As it happened, three days before the march was to take place, the Nazis canceled it. They had requested permission to march in Skokie and other communities only after the city of Chicago had made it impossible for them to march there by requiring them to pay a high liability insurance premium. A federal court set aside the insurance requirement and the Nazis held a rally in a city park without any serious violence.

D. FREEDOM OF RELIGION: ESTABLISHMENT

*Congress shall make no law respecting an establishment of religion,
or prohibiting the free exercise thereof.*
— First Amendment, U.S. Constitution

1. Religious Establishment: Theory

John Locke's *Essay on Toleration* (1667), which influenced the American framers of the Constitution, has become a classical defense of religious freedom. However, Locke's relatively unknown earlier works conflict with his better known advocacy of religious toleration. In addition to their historical value, his earlier views also raise important questions about the relationships between opinion and action and between religion and politics. In *Two Tracts* (written while at Oxford but never published), Locke exposed religious toleration as a disguise for the promotion of rebellion and anarchy. He suspected those preaching religious toleration of pushing a political agenda, citing their selective support of religious positions that threatened government. While religion may most commonly involve individual expressions of belief, it also has a public, political dimension that may overshadow the private realm. Private opinion becomes something different when it is transformed into public action. Do some circumstances warrant the government's treatment of religion as a form of politics? Are governmental restrictions on religion justified when religious politics threaten the public order? Perhaps these questions have the issues reversed. Does religion threaten the public order or does government, by imposing its brand of religion, threaten that order? In *Essay on Toleration*, Locke argued against government's imposing uniformity of religious belief (see Reading 5-18). The government, according to Locke, should not engage in a policy of intolerance by, for example, penalizing those who refuse to worship in the Church of England. Since no one group, including the government, has a monopoly on religious truth, the marketplace of ideas seems to apply as much to religious expression as it does to any other form of opinion.

How should philosophical theories about religion translate into a constitutional framework? What should be the relationship between government and religion? First Amendment analysis divides into two parts—questions concerning the state establishment of religion and questions regarding the free exercise of religious opinion. Before the adoption of the First Amendment, however, some states did not separate government from religion. The religion clauses of the constitutions of Delaware and Maryland, for example, demanded Christianity while the constitutions of Pennsylvania and South Carolina imposed a belief in heaven and hell. Until 1833, Congregationalism was Massachusetts' established religion. Only Rhode Island and Virginia allowed full freedom of religion (see Pfeffer 1953). Some nations (for example, Iran, Israel, and the United Kingdom) do not separate government from religion (see Reading 5-19). Why should the United States build a wall completely separating government from religion? Does freedom of religion only prevent the establishment of a national church or religion? The readings address each of these questions.

READING 5-18

Toleration, Liberal Style
"A Letter Concerning Toleration" (1685)

John Locke

In the last place, let us now consider what is the magistrate's duty in the business of toleration: which certainly is very considerable.

We have already proved that the care of souls does not belong to the magistrate: not a magisterial care, I mean, (if I may so call it) which consists in prescribing by laws, and compelling by punishments. But a charitable care, which consists in teaching, admonishing, and persuading, cannot be denied unto any man. The care, therefore, of every man's soul belongs unto himself, and is to be left unto himself. But what if he neglect the care of his soul? I answer: What if he neglect the care of his health, or of his estate, which things are nearlier related to the government of the magistrate than the other? Will the magistrate provide by an express law, that such a one shall not become poor or sick? Laws provide, as much as is possible, that the goods and health of subjects be not injured by the fraud or violence of others; they do not guard them from the negligence or ill-husbandry of the possessors themselves. No man can be forced to be rich or healthful, whether he will or no. Nay, God himself will not save men against their wills. Let us suppose, however, that some prince were desirous to force his subjects to accumulate riches, or to preserve the health and strength of their bodies. Shall it be provided by law, that they must consult none but Roman physicians, and shall everyone be bound to live according to their prescriptions? What, shall no potion, no broth, be taken, but what is prepared either in the Vatican, suppose, or in a Geneva shop? Or, to make these subjects rich, shall they all be obliged by law to become merchants, or musicians? Or, shall everyone turn victualler [suppliers of provisions], or smith, because there are some that maintain their families plentifully, and grow rich in those professions?

But it may be said, there are a thousand ways to wealth, but only one way to heaven. 'Tis well said indeed, especially by those that plead for compelling men into this or the other way. For if there were several ways that lead thither, there would not be so much as a pretence left for compulsion. But now if I be marching on with my utmost vigour, in that way which, according to the sacred geography, leads straight to Jerusalem, why am I beaten and ill-used by others; because, perhaps, I wear not buskins; because my hair is not of the right cut; because perhaps I have not been dipped [i.e. baptized] in the right fashion; because I eat flesh upon the road, or some other food which agrees with my stomach; because I avoid certain byways, which seem unto me to lead into briars or precipices; because amongst the several paths that are in the same road, I choose that to walk in which seems to be the straightest and cleanest; because I avoid to keep company with some travellers that are less grave, and others that are more sour than they ought to be; or, in fine, because I follow a guide that either is, or is not, clothed in white, and crowned with a mitre [a bishop's headdress]? Certainly, if we consider right, we shall find that for the most part they are such frivolous things as these that (without any prejudice to religion or the salvation of souls, if not accompanied with superstition or hypocrisy) might either be observed or omitted; I say they are such like things as these, which breed implacable [not pacified] enmities [hatreds] amongst Christian brethren, who are all agreed in the substantial and truly fundamental part of religion.

But let us grant unto these zealots, who condemn all things that are not of their mode, that from these circumstances arise different ends. What shall we conclude from thence? There is only one of these which is the true way to eternal happiness. But in this great variety of ways that men follow, it is still doubted which is this right one. Now neither the care of the commonwealth, nor the right of enacting laws, does discover this way that leads to heaven more certainly to the magistrate, than every private man's search and study discovers it unto himself. I have a weak body, sunk under a languishing disease, for which (I suppose) there is one only remedy, but that unknown. Does it therefore belong unto the magistrate to prescribe me a remedy, because there is but one, and because it is unknown? Because there is but one way for me to escape death, will it therefore be safe for me to do whatsoever the magistrate ordains? Those things that every man ought sincerely to inquire into himself, and by meditation, study, search, and his own endeavours, attain the knowledge of, cannot be looked upon as the peculiar possession of any one sort of men. Princes indeed are born superior unto other men in power, but in nature equal. Neither the right nor the art of ruling does necessarily carry along with it the certain knowledge of other things; and least of all of the true religion. For if it were so, how could it come to pass that the lords of the earth should differ so vastly as they do in religious matters? But let us grant that it is probable the way to eternal life may be better known by a prince than by his subjects; or at least, that in this incertitude of things, the safest and most commodious [comfortable] way for private persons is to follow his dictates. You will say, what then? If he should bid you follow merchandise for your livelihood, would you decline that course for fear it should not succeed? I answer: I would turn merchant upon the prince's command, because in case I should have ill-success in trade, he is abundantly able to make up my loss some other way. If it be true, as he pretends, that he desires I should thrive and grow rich, he can set me up again when unsuccessful voyages have broke me. But this is not the case, in the things that regard the life to come. If there I take a wrong course, if in that respect I am once undone, it is not in the magistrate's power to repair my loss, to ease my suffering, or to restore me in any measure, much less entirely, to a good estate. What security can be given for the Kingdom of Heaven? ...

In the next place: as the magistrate has no power to impose by his laws the use of any rites and ceremonies in any Church, so neither has he any power to forbid the use of such rites and ceremonies as are already received, approved, and practised by any Church, because if he did so, he would destroy the Church itself, the end of whose institution is only to worship God with freedom, after its own manner.

You will say, by this rule, if some congregations should have a mind to sacrifice infants, or (as the primitive Christians were falsely accused) lustfully pollute themselves in promiscuous uncleanness, or practise any other such heinous enormities, is the magistrate obliged to tolerate them, because they are committed in a religious assembly? I answer, No. These things are not lawful in the ordinary course of life, nor in any private house; and therefore neither are they so in the worship of God, or in any religious meeting. But indeed if any people congregated upon account of religion should be desirous to sacrifice a calf, I deny that that ought to be prohibited by a law. Meliboeus, whose calf it is, may lawfully kill his own calf at home, and burn any part of it that he thinks fit, for no injury is thereby done to anyone, no prejudice to another man's goods. And for the same reason he may kill his calf also in a religious meeting. Whether the doing so be well-pleasing to God or no, it is their part to consider that do it. The part of the magistrate is only to take care that the commonwealth receive no prejudice, and that there be no injury done to any man, either in life or estate. And thus what may be spent on a feast, may be spent on a sacrifice. But if peradventure such were the state of things, that the interest of the commonwealth required all slaughter of beasts should be forborne for some while, in order to the increasing of the stock of cattle, that had been destroyed by some extraordinary murrain, who sees not that the magistrate, in such a case, may forbid all his subjects to kill any calves for any use whatsoever? Only 'tis to be observed that in this case the law is not made about a religious but a political matter; nor is the sacrifice but the slaughter of calves thereby prohibited.

By this we see what difference there is between the Church and the commonwealth. Whatsoever is lawful in the commonwealth cannot be prohibited by the magistrate in the Church. Whatsoever is permitted unto any of his subjects for their ordinary use, neither can nor ought to be forbidden by him to any sect of people for their religious uses. If any man may lawfully take bread or wine, either sitting or kneeling, in his own house, the law ought not to abridge him of the same liberty in his religious worship; though in the Church the use of bread and wine be very different, and be there applied to the mysteries of faith, and rites of divine worship. But those things that are prejudicial to the commonweal of a people in their ordinary use, and are therefore forbidden by laws, those things ought not to be permitted to Churches in their sacred rites. Only the magistrate ought always to be very careful that he do not misuse his authority, to the oppression of any Church, under pretence of public good.

From Locke (1685), "A Letter Concerning Toleration," in (1993) *Political Writings of John Locke*, David Wooton, editor. New York: Penguin, pp. 405–408, 414–415.

READING 5-19

A Wall of Separation
"Reply to the Danbury Baptist Association" (January 1, 1802)

Thomas Jefferson

GENTLEMEN,

The affectionate sentiments of esteem and approbation which you are so good as to express towards me, on behalf of the Danbury Baptist Association, give me the highest satisfaction. My duties dictate a faithful and zealous pursuit of the interests of my constituents, and in proportion as they are persuaded of my fidelity to those duties, the discharge of them becomes more and more pleasing.

Believing with you that religion is a matter which lies solely between man and his God, that he owes account to none other for his faith or his worship, that the legislative powers of government reach actions only, and not opinions, I contemplate with sovereign reverence that act of the whole American people which declared that their legislature should "make no law respecting an establishment of religion, or prohibiting the free exercise thereof," *thus building a wall of separation between church and State.* Adhering to this expression of the supreme will of the nation in behalf of the rights of conscience, I shall see with sincere satisfaction the progress of those sentiments which tend to restore to man all his natural rights, convinced he has no natural right in opposition to his social duties.

I reciprocate your kind prayers for the protection and blessing of the common Father and Creator of man, and tender you for yourselves and your religious association, assurances of my high respect and esteem.

From Jefferson (January 1, 1802), "Reply to the Danbury Baptist Association" reprinted in (1998) *Wall of Separation?* Mary C. Segars and Ted G. Jelen, editors. Lanham, MD: Rowman & Littlefield, p. 125.

---

2. Religious Establishment: Practice

Did the founders want to keep religion in the private sphere? Should the constitution be godless (see Reading 5-20)? The Constitution contains an establishment clause and a free exercise clause. In the next readings, consider two ways of thinking about the establishment of religion. In *Everson v. Board of Education* (see Reading 5-21), Justice Black uses Jefferson's "wall of separation" metaphor to mark the constitutional separation of church and state. On the other hand, Philip Kurland proposes a strict neutrality view as an alternative to the strict separation one in *Everson* (see Reading 5-22). The neutrality approach gives government more leeway to deal with religions. Should government be strictly neutral toward religion? On neutrality but not on the separation view, if the government gives aid to all nonpublic schools, and parochial schools happen to be among them, the government is not using religion as a standard for action or inaction.

Constitutionally, beyond prohibiting a state church, what other activities does the establishment clause forbid? In *Lemon v. Kurtzman* (1971), the Court set down a three-part test that governmental restrictions on religion must pass:

> First, the statute must have a secular legislative purpose; second, its principal or primary effect must be one that neither advances nor inhibits religion; finally, the statute must not foster an excessive government entanglement with religion. (*Lemon v. Kurtzman,* 1971)

With the *Lemon* test, the Court examines the purpose, effect, and entanglement of the proposed action. The Court has used the test to invalidate the official reading of prayers and Bible passages in public schools, even when the state composed a nondenominational prayer or when participation in the Bible reading was not required. Further, the Court has declined to allow even a voluntary moment of silence, on grounds that the practice sends a message of endorsement (see Reading 5-23). Justice Stevens relied on the first part of the *Lemon* test finding that an Alabama law had no secular purpose. Would every "moment of silence" statute fail the *Lemon* test?

The establishment clause forbids public schools from teaching religious doctrine, but what happens when the curriculum involves religious doctrine? Should the motive or purpose of a statute prove decisive? Should courts try to determine the statute's "real" purpose? Tennessee's Butler Act (1925) forbade the teaching of evolution theory in the public schools. At the largely staged Scopes Monkey Trial, Clarence Darrow, a foremost criminal defense attorney, defended John Scopes, who taught biology—and evolution—in a small town. William Jennings Bryan, frequent presidential candidate and secretary of state under Woodrow Wilson, prosecuted the highly publicized case. The Tennessee Supreme Court overturned Scopes' conviction on a, perhaps intentional, technicality but upheld the act, which was not repealed until 1967. After adopting a version of the Butler Act in 1929, Arkansas followed a similar history. In 1968, the U.S. Supreme Court found Arkansas' act unconstitutional because of a religious motive underlying the legislation (*Epperson v. Arkansas* 1968). Wendell Bird wrote an influential student note in the *Yale Law Journal* advocating an equal time case for scientific creationism. After graduation, he joined the Institute for Creation Research and helped to draft a number of state statutes (see Irons 1988, pp. 215–216). Louisiana's statute required public school teachers to balance the teaching of evolutionary theory with creation science, but in *Edwards v. Aquillard,* the Court failed to find a secular purpose for the statute (see Reading 5-24). The Kansas State Board of Education recently adopted science standards in which local school boards may decide not to focus or even discuss evolution in science courses. Will the board's action pass constitutional challenges?

READING 5-20

God and the Constitution
"Is the U.S. Constitution Godless?" (1996)

Isaac Kramnick and R. Laurence Moore

People always fall back on the opinions of the Founding Fathers of the United States as a trump card in any debate about public policy, regardless of how different our world is from that of the late 18th century. Whatever the hot issue—balanced budgets, gun control, welfare policy—at some point someone inevitably trots out his or her interpretation of what the framers of American government originally intended. Nowhere is this more ritualized than in discussions of relations between church and state.

Most recently, politicians such as Newt Gingrich and Pat Buchanan and Christian Right activists such as the Rev. Pat Robertson and Ralph Reed have insisted that the framers wanted to establish a Christian government, and would therefore have been foursquare in favor of prayers in the public schools. Opponents of school prayer angrily reply that the framers meant to construct a high wall separating church and state.

Efforts to determine the appropriate relationship between church and state usually have focused on interpreting the religion clauses of the First Amendment of the Bill of Rights, which state: "Congress shall make no law respecting an establishment of religion, or prohibiting the free exercise thereof." The problem is that little agreement exists on the meaning of those words, especially the establishment clause. Two opposing camps face off. One reads the establishment clause broadly, arguing that it removes the national government from any support of or involvement with religion. The other reads it narrowly, arguing that it prohibits only a state-supported church. The second group goes on to claim that, because the founders were themselves Christians, they may not have specified the role of religion in the new national government, but instead wanted to leave it open to individual states to decide how to support religion.

Another way of inferring the framers' intention, however, which we describe more fully in a recent book, *The Godless Constitution: The Case Against Religious Correctness,* relies on recent research that provides a more definitive picture of the founders' design. Rather than relying on the Bill of Rights, this approach focuses on the widespread debates in 1787 and 1788 over the clause in Article VI of the Constitution stating that "no religious test shall ever be required as a qualification to any office or public trust under the United States." These debates, not mentioned in the celebrated *Federalist* papers of Madison, Hamilton, and Jay, focused on the very issue of whether the new national government was Christian.

Scholars have had easy access to this debate only for the last decade and a half, since preparations for the celebration of the Constitution's bicentennial in 1987 produced a treasure trove of new publications. They include the University of Wisconsin's multivolume edition of all of the debates at the state conventions held in 1787 and 1788 to ratify the Constitution, and the University of Chicago's *Complete Anti-Federalist,* a collection of all the tracts written in 1787 and 1788 by critics of the proposed Constitution.

Looking at the ratification debates, we can see that the framers wanted to maintain a godly nation, but that their experience with the divisiveness of established churches during the colonial period had convinced them that the best way to do so was to keep religion in the private sphere, not subject to government dictates and interference. The fact that the framers did not view the separation of church and state as a threat to religion ought to make us skeptical of the Christian right's claim that to be a moral nation, the United States must incorporate religious views into its public schools and government policies.

In the debates over Article VI, many delegates to the state conventions angrily denounced the proposed new Constitution as ungodly, because nowhere did it mention either God or Christianity, and because Article VI prohibited religious tests for officeholders. One Massachusetts delegate was upset that the Constitution did not require men in power to be religious. He said that while he wanted to see "Christians" in office, under the Constitution "a papist, or an infidel was as eligible as they." The Rev. David Caldwell, a Presbyterian minister and a delegate at North Carolina's convention, worried that the Constitution's failure to require a religious test of officeholders was an invitation to "Jews and pagans of every kind" to govern the country. Disputants around America complained of the framers' "silence" and "indifference about religion."

The epithet given to the document by these opponents, "the godless Constitution," correctly recognized that the framers acted deliberately. Opponents offered a spate of proposals in 1787 and 1788 to remedy the perceived defect. In Connecticut, a delegate formally moved that the Constitution's one-sentence preamble be enlarged to include a Christian conception of politics. After the words "We the people of the United States," he proposed inserting "in a firm belief of the being and perfection of the one living God, the creator and supreme governor of the World, in His universal providence and the authority of His laws." All such proposals were rejected, although efforts to write similar amendments into the Constitution have continued throughout our history.

To be sure, critics have won a few minor victories. "In God we trust" is stamped on our money. Chaplains invoke God's name before sessions of Congress and the Supreme Court. Schoolchildren place the nation "under God" in the Pledge of Allegiance to the U.S. flag, a phrase inserted in 1952, early in the Cold War. But the Constitution remains what its enemies at the ratifying conventions said it was—a godless document.

The Bicentennial publications do not, of course, settle the many controversies that linger regarding applications or interpretations of the First Amendment. What exemptions to prevailing laws may people claim in the name of their religious practice? Is it fair for a state-supported university to provide aid for all student publications and clubs except religious ones? Those broad questions will continue to generate disagreement that no appeal to the founders' intentions can settle. Nonetheless, the 18th-century debates do allow us to discredit—thoroughly—the most outrageous claims of leaders of the Christian Coalition, the political extension of Pat Robertson's media empire. When those leaders call the separation of church and state "a lie of the left," they are wrong. Such assertions are historical nonsense, and the reticence [tendency to keep silent] shown by politicians of both political parties to refute them should cause us national shame.

However, we should not overlook the fact that the recently expanded historical record also underscores that, in writing a godless Constitution, the founders were not taking a stand against religion or turning their backs on the important role that they expected religion to play in democratic states. Most of them were religious, and even those who had little use for the Christianity that was preached in the churches of the time believed that a moral citizenry was necessary to democracy, and that morality often rested on religious conviction.

The framers placed religion in the private sphere without at all intending that religion would play no part in informing public debate. Their hope was that religion, while remaining above the struggles of political factions, would provide a moral foundation for American public life. Alexis de Tocqueville echoed Thomas Jefferson's views in his reflections on American democracy in the early 1830s: "In the United States religion exercises but little influence upon the laws and upon the details of public opinion; but it directs the customs of the community, and, by regulating domestic life, it regulates the state."

Recently, leaders of the religious right in this country have gotten considerable political mileage from the charge that many liberal academics, in particular, ignore religion in condescending ways. We believe that religious instruction has no place in college curricula. At the same time, the secular nature of the university does not require institutions to ignore Christian ideals in students' core educational courses.

Yet if anyone has brought disrespect to the place of religion in American life, it is those who have sought relentlessly to use religion to serve the partisan agenda of one wing of the Republican Party. We are now witnessing religion's playing the divisive role in politics that the founders most feared. What are we to make of a Roman Catholic candidate for President who urges his followers to mount a culture war, without the slightest recognition of how that historically ugly term was used against Catholics in 19th-century America? . . .

The Christian Coalition and the politicians who court its undeniable political clout seek to assign government the task of making Americans moral, forgetting the long struggles of most churches in this country to keep the business of churches free from the hypocrisy of politics. Religion in the United States is a vast cultural resource that, because of its strength, will always tempt some to misuse it in the political arena. That danger, however, does not make religion the enemy. We join the founders in suggesting that disrespect for religion is something this nation can ill afford. Those in the university who are declared secularists should champion the separation of church and state, while always remembering that the original purpose of that separation was, in large part, to promote respect for religion, whose health the founders deemed vital to democracy.

Church and State, Strict Separation
Everson v. Board of Education (1946)

JUSTICE HUGO BLACK

The "establishment of religion" clause of the First Amendment means at least this: Neither a state nor the Federal Government can set up a church. Neither can pass laws which aid one religion, aid all religions, or prefer one religion over another. Neither can force nor influence a person to go to or to remain away from church against his will or force him to profess a belief or disbelief in any religion. No person can be punished for entertaining or professing religious beliefs or disbeliefs, for church attendance or non-attendance. No tax in any amount, large or small, can be levied to support any religious activities or institutions, whatever they may be called, or whatever form they may adopt to teach or practice religion. Neither a state nor the Federal Government can, openly or secretly, participate in the affairs of any religious organizations or groups and *vice versa*. In the words of Jefferson, the clause against establishment of religion by law was intended to erect "a wall of separation between church and State." . . .

. . . Of course, cutting off church schools from these services, so separate and so indisputably marked off from the religious function, would make it far more difficult for the schools to operate. But such is obviously not the purpose of the First Amendment. That Amendment requires the state to be a neutral in its relations with groups of religious believers and non-believers; it does not require the state to be their adversary. State power is no more to be used so as to handicap religions than it is to favor them.

This Court has said that parents may, in the discharge of their duty under state compulsory education laws, send their children to a religious rather than a public school if the school meets the secular educational requirements which the state has power to impose. . . . It appears that these parochial schools meet New Jersey's requirements. The State contributes no money to the schools. It does not support them. Its legislation, as applied, does no more than provide a general program to help parents get their children, regardless of their religion, safely and expeditiously to and from accredited schools.

The First Amendment has erected a wall between church and state. That wall must be kept high and impregnable. We could not approve the slightest breach. New Jersey has not breached it here.

From *Everson v. Board of Education* (1946) 330 US 1, pp. 15–16, 18.

READING 5-22

Church and State, Strict Neutrality
"Of Church and State and the Supreme Court" (1961)

Philip B. Kurland

Like most commands of our Constitution, the religion clauses of the first amendment are not statements of abstract principles. History, not logic, explains their inclusion in the Bill of Rights; necessity, not merely morality, justifies their presence there. . . .

Religious toleration, summed up in the second of the two clauses, was . . . necessary to preserve the peace. Separation, represented by the first of the two clauses, was necessary to make such religious freedom a reality. But the separation clause had a greater function than the assurance of toleration of dissenting religious beliefs and practices. To suggest but two lessons of the evils resulting from the alliance of church and state, there was abundant evidence of the contributions of the churches to the warfare among nations as well as the conflict within them and equally obvious was the inhibition on scientific endeavor that followed from the acceptance by the state of church dogma. . . . But admittedly separation was a new concept in practice. Toleration had a long English history; separation—conceived in the English writings of Roger Williams—had its beginnings as an historical fact only on the shores of this continent. It is justified in Williams' terms by the necessity for keeping the state out of the affairs of the church, lest the church be subordinated to the state; in Jeffersonian terms its function is to keep the church out of the business of government, lest the government be subordinated to the church. Limited powers of government were not instituted to expand the realm of power of religious organizations, but rather in favor of freedom of action and thought by the people.

Nor were these two concepts closed systems at the time of the adoption of the first amendment. The objectives of the provisions were clear, but the means of their attainment were still to be developed and, indeed, are still in the course of development. Thus, like the other great clauses of the Constitution, the religion clauses cannot now be confined to the application they might have received in 1789.

The utilization or application of these clauses in conjunction is difficult. For if the command is that inhibitions not be placed by the state on religious activity, it is equally forbidden the state to confer favors upon religious activity. These commands would be impossible of effectuation unless they are read . . . to mean that religion may not be used as a basis for classification for purposes of governmental action, whether that action be the conferring of rights or privileges or the imposition of duties or obligations. . . . It must be recognized, however, that this statement of the "neutral" principle of equality, that religion cannot supply a basis for classification of governmental action, still leaves many problems unanswered. Not the least of them flows from the fact that the actions of the state must be carefully scrutinized to assure that classifications that purport to relate to other matters are not really classifications in terms of religion. "[C]lassification in abstract terms can always be carried to the point at which, in fact, the class singled out consists only of particular known persons or even a single individual. It must be admitted that, in spite of many ingenious attempts to solve this problem, no entirely satisfactory criterion has been found that would always tell us what kind of classification is compatible with equality before the law."

. . . [I]t might be desirable to repeat two propositions. First, the thesis proposed here as the proper construction of the religion clauses of the first amendment is that the freedom and separation clauses should be read as a single precept that government cannot utilize religion as a standard for action or inaction because these clauses prohibit classification in terms of religion either to confer a benefit or to impose a burden. Second, the principle offered is meant to provide a starting point for solutions to problems brought before the Court, not a mechanical answer to them.

Kurland, Philip B. "Of Church and State and the Supreme Court," *University of Chicago Law Review* 29 © (1961). Reprinted by permission of the University of Chicago Law Review.

READING 5-23
School Prayer
Wallace v. Jaffree (1985)

JUSTICE JOHN PAUL STEVENS

Appellee Ishmael Jaffree is a resident of Mobile County, Alabama. On May 28, 1982, he filed a complaint on behalf of three of his minor children; two of them were second-grade students and the third was then in kindergarten. The complaint named members of the Mobile County School Board, various school officials, and the minor plaintiffs' three teachers as defendants. The complaint alleged that the appellees brought the action "seeking principally a declaratory judgment and an injunction restraining the Defendants and each of them from maintaining or allowing the maintenance of regular religious prayer services or other forms of religious observances in the Mobile County Public Schools in violation of the First Amendment as made applicable to states by the Fourteenth Amendment to the United States Constitution." The complaint further alleged that two of the children had been subjected to various acts of religious indoctrination "from the beginning of the school year in September, 1981"; that the defendant teachers had "on a daily basis" led their classes in saying certain prayers in unison; that the minor children were exposed to ostracism from their peer group class members if they did not participate; and that Ishmael Jaffree had repeatedly but unsuccessfully requested that the devotional services be stopped. The original complaint made no reference to any Alabama statute. . . .

Just as the right to speak and the right to refrain from speaking are complementary components of a broader concept of individual freedom of mind, so also the individual's freedom to choose his own creed is the counterpart of his right to refrain from accepting the creed established by the majority. At one time it was thought that this right merely proscribed the preference of one Christian sect over another, but would not require equal respect for the conscience of the infidel, the atheist, or the adherent of a non-Christian faith such as Islam or Judaism. But when the underlying principle has been examined in the crucible of litigation, the Court has unambiguously concluded that the individual freedom of conscience protected by the First Amendment embraces the right to select any religious faith or none at all. This conclusion derives support not only from the interest in respecting the individual's freedom of conscience, but also from the conviction that religious beliefs worthy of respect are the product of free and voluntary choice by the faithful, and from recognition of the fact that the political interest in forestalling intolerance extends beyond intolerance among Christian sects—or even intolerance among "religions"—to encompass intolerance of the disbeliever and the uncertain. . . .

JUSTICE WILLIAM REHNQUIST, dissenting

It is impossible to build sound constitutional doctrine upon a mistaken understanding of constitutional history, but unfortunately the Establishment Clause has been expressly freighted with Jefferson's misleading metaphor for nearly 40 years. Thomas Jefferson was of course in France at the time the constitutional Amendments known as the Bill of Rights were passed by Congress and ratified by the States. His letter to the Danbury Baptist Association was a short note of courtesy, written 14 years after the Amendments were passed by Congress. He would seem to any detached observer as a less than ideal source of contemporary history as to the meaning of the Religion Clauses of the First Amendment.

Jefferson's fellow Virginian, James Madison, with whom he was joined in the battle for the enactment of the Virginia Statute of Religious Liberty of 1786, did play as large a part as anyone in the drafting of the Bill of Rights. He had two advantages over Jefferson in this regard: he was present in the United States, and he was a leading Member of the First Congress. But when we turn to the record of the proceedings in the First Congress leading up to the adoption of the Establishment Clause of the Constitution, including Madison's significant contributions thereto, we see a far different picture of its purpose than the highly simplified "wall of separation between church and State." . . .

. . . During the ratification debate in the Virginia Convention, Madison had actually opposed the idea of any Bill of Rights. His sponsorship of the Amendments in the House was obviously not that of a zealous believer in the necessity of the Religion Clauses, but of one who felt it might do some good, could do no harm, and would satisfy those who had ratified the Constitution on the condition that Congress propose a Bill of Rights. His original language "nor shall any national religion be established" obviously does not conform to the "wall of separation" between church and State idea which latter-day commentators have ascribed to him. His explanation on the floor of the meaning of his language—"that Congress should not establish a religion, and enforce the legal observation of it by law" is of the same ilk [kind]. When he replied to Huntington in the debate over the proposal which came from the Select Committee of the House, he urged that the language "no religion shall be established by law" should be amended by inserting the word "national" in front of the word "religion."

It seems indisputable from these glimpses of Madison's thinking, as reflected by actions on the floor of the House in 1789, that he saw the Amendment as designed to prohibit the establishment of a national religion, and perhaps to prevent discrimination among sects. He did not see it as requiring neutrality on the part of government between religion and irreligion. . . .

From *Wallace v. Jaffree* (1985) 472 US 38, pp. 42, 52–54, 57, 92, 98 (Rehnquist, dissenting).

READING 5-24
Creationism in the Schools
Edwards v. Aquillard (1987)

JUSTICE WILLIAM BRENNAN

The legislation . . . sought to alter the science curriculum to reflect endorsement of a religious view that is antagonistic to the theory of evolution.

In this case, the purpose of the Creationism Act was to restructure the science curriculum to conform with a particular religious viewpoint. Out of many possible science subjects taught in the public schools, the legislature chose to affect the teaching of the one scientific theory that historically has been opposed by certain religious sects. As in *Epperson,* the legislature passed the Act to give preference to those religious groups which have as one of their tenets the creation of humankind by a divine creator. The "overriding fact" that confronted the Court in *Epperson* was "that Arkansas' law selects from the body of knowledge a particular segment which it proscribes for the sole reason that it is deemed to conflict with . . . a particular interpretation of the Book of Genesis by a particular religious group." . . . Similarly, the Creationism Act is designed *either* to promote the theory of creation science which embodies a particular religious tenet by requiring that creation science be taught whenever evolution is taught *or* to prohibit the teaching of a scientific theory disfavored by certain religious sects by forbidding the teaching of evolution when creation science is not also taught. The Establishment Clause, however, "forbids *alike* the preference of a religious doctrine *or* the prohibition of theory which is deemed antagonistic to a particular dogma." . . . Because the primary purpose of the Creationism Act is to advance a particular religious belief, the Act endorses religion in violation of the First Amendment.

We do not imply that a legislature could never require that scientific critiques of prevailing scientific theories be taught. Indeed, the Court acknowledged in *Stone* that its decision forbidding the posting of the Ten Commandments did not mean that no use could ever be made of the Ten Commandments, or that the Ten Commandments played an exclusively religious role in the history of Western Civilization. . . . In a similar way, teaching a variety of scientific theories about the origins of humankind to schoolchildren might be validly done with the clear secular intent of enhancing the effectiveness of science instruction. But because the primary purpose of the Creationism Act is to endorse a particular religious doctrine, the Act furthers religion in violation of the Establishment Clause. . . .

From *Edwards v. Aquillard* (1987) 482 US 578, pp. 591–594.

E. FREEDOM OF RELIGION: FREE EXERCISE

Interpreting the free exercise clause in freedom of religion raises important problems. Controversies stem not from the exercise of pure religious belief but from the conduct stemming from the belief. Just as Locke discovered, religious belief is more than an internal conviction; it involves public conduct as well (see page 268). What if some religious conduct violates the morals of the larger liberal society? Consider the viability of a strict division between opinion and practice. Does the free exercise clause allow the government to restrict religious practices such as engaging in polygamy, refusing to send children to public schools, and using illegal drugs? In the 1870s, George Reynolds, a citizen of what was then the Utah territory, claimed that his Mormonism required polygamy as a religious duty. He, thereby, argued that Congress could not deny his free exercise of religion by making polygamy a crime. However, the U.S. Supreme Court drew a sharp distinction between beliefs and practices. On one hand, the Constitution forbids governmental interference with religious beliefs or opinions, but on the other hand, it permits restrictions on certain religious practices (*Reynolds v. United States* 1878).

Has the Court recently developed a trend toward less toleration of different religious practices? In *Employment Div. of Oregon Dept. of Human Res. v. Smith* (see Reading 5-25), the state dismissed employees who worked in drug rehabilitation programs because of a religious practice. The employees, members of the Native American Church, had ingested peyote for sacramental purposes at a church ceremony. The Court found that the state has no special burden to justify infringement on religious practices as long as the law is neutral. The Court seems to have taken the position that any criminal restriction and perhaps any civil regulation automatically applies even if it burdens an individual's religious beliefs and practices. Stephen Carter, a Yale law professor, thinks that recognition of religion's public character should lead to greater accommodation and recommends going beyond treating religion only as a matter of individual conscience (see Reading 5-26).

Peyote and Religion

Employment Division of Oregon
Department of Human Resources v. Smith (1990)
494 US 872, 878, 890

JUSTICE ANTONIN SCALIA

Respondents Alfred Smith and Galen Black were fired from their jobs with a private drug rehabilitation organization because they ingested peyote for sacramental purposes at a ceremony of the Native American Church, of which both are members. When respondents applied to petitioner Employment Division for unemployment compensation, they were determined to be ineligible for benefits because they had been discharged for work-related "misconduct"....

... The free exercise of religion means, first and foremost, the right to believe and profess whatever religious doctrine one desires. Thus, the First Amendment obviously excludes all "governmental regulation of religious *beliefs* as such."...

But the "exercise of religion" often involves not only belief and profession but the performance of (or abstention from) physical acts: assembling with others for a worship service, participating in sacramental use of bread and wine, proselytizing, abstaining from certain foods or certain modes of transportation. It would be true, we think (though no case of ours has involved the point), that a state would be "prohibiting the free exercise [of religion]" if it sought to ban such acts or abstentions only when they are engaged in for religious reasons, or only because of the religious belief that they display. It would doubtless be unconstitutional, for example, to ban the casting of "statues that are to be used for worship purposes," or to prohibit bowing down before a golden calf.

Respondents in the present case, however, seek to carry the meaning of "prohibiting the free exercise [of religion]" one large step further. They contend that their religious motivation for using peyote places them beyond the reach of a criminal law that is not specifically directed at their religious practice, and that is concededly constitutional as applied to those who use the drug for other reasons. They assert, in other words, that "prohibiting the free exercise [of religion]" includes requiring any individual to observe a generally applicable law that requires (or forbids) the performance of an act that his religious belief forbids (or requires). As a textual matter, we do not think the words must be given that meaning....

... We have never held that an individual's religious beliefs excuse him from compliance with an otherwise valid law prohibiting conduct that the State is free to regulate....

... The rule respondents favor would open the prospect of constitutionally required religious exemptions from civic obligations of almost every conceivable kind—ranging from compulsory military service, to the payment of taxes, to health and safety regulation such as manslaughter and child neglect laws, compulsory vaccination laws, drug laws, and traffic laws, to social welfare legislation such as minimum wage laws, child labor laws, animal cruelty laws, environmental protection laws, and laws providing for equality of opportunity for the races. The First Amendment's protection of religious liberty does not require this.

Values that are protected against government interference through enshrinement in the Bill of Rights are not thereby banished from the political process. . . . [A] society that believes in the negative protection accorded to religious belief can be expected to be solicitous of that value in its legislation. . . . It is therefore not surprising that a number of States have made an exception to their drug laws for sacramental peyote use. But to say that a nondiscriminatory religious-practice exemption is permitted, or even that it is desirable, is not to say that it is constitutionally required, and that the appropriate occasions for its creation can be discerned by the courts. It may fairly be said that leaving accommodation to the political process will place at a relative disadvantage those religious practices that are not widely engaged in; but that unavoidable consequence of democratic government must be preferred to a system in which each conscience is a law unto itself or in which judges weigh the social importance of all laws against the centrality of all religious beliefs.

Because respondents' ingestion of peyote was prohibited under Oregon law, and because that prohibition is constitutional, Oregon may, consistent with the Free Exercise Clause, deny respondents unemployment compensation when their dismissal results from use of the drug. The decision of the Oregon Supreme Court is accordingly reversed. . . .

From *Employment Div. of Oregon Dept. of Human Res. v. Smith* (1990) 494 US pp. 872, 878, 890.

READING 5-26

Trivializing Religious Devotion
"The Accommodation of Religion" (1993)

Stephen L. Carter

To be consistent with the Founders' vision and coherent in modern religiously pluralistic America, the religion clauses should be read to help avoid tyranny—that is, to sustain and nurture the religions as independent centers of power, the democratic intermediaries. . . . To do that, the clauses must be interpreted to do more than protect the religions against explicit discrimination. Nowadays, the government hardly ever adopts laws aimed at burdening particular religions. Consequently, the question of religious freedom arises most frequently when the religious ask for exemptions under the Free Exercise Clause from laws that apply to everybody else. And it must not be missed that those "laws that apply to everybody else" often reflect, albeit implicitly, the values and teachings of the nation's dominant religious traditions.

Consider an example: virtually unnoticed in the brouhaha surrounding George Bush's 1992 Christmas Eve pardons of Caspar Weinberger and other officials implicated in the Iran-Contra scandal were pardons for two Jehovah's Witnesses whose crime was refusing to register for military service in the 1940s and 1950s. The law has long allowed the Witnesses, and others with religious objections to combat, to register and then seek "conscientious objector" status; but it does not exempt from the registration requirement itself those with moral objections to war.

By seeking an exemption from a law that applies to everybody else, the war resisters are asking for what is called an "accommodation" of their religious belief. A few constitutional scholars—not many—believe that granting accommodations violates the Establishment Clause, because it provides to the religious something that others cannot have. President Bush's pardons of the Witnesses, then, might be seen as a version of religious preferment in which the government must not engage.

The Supreme Court, fortunately, has never accepted the idea that all accommodations are unconstitutional. So the government can generally allow religious exemptions, as the Congress did in the statute allowing the religious to wear unobtrusive religious apparel while on active military duty. . . . However, after a brief flowering of judicially created exemptions, the Court has looked increasingly askance at claims of a free exercise right to violate laws that everyone else must obey. The most notable recent example is the Court's 1990 decision in *Employment Division v. Smith,* which upheld the application of a state antidrug policy to state employees who, as members of the Native American Church, were required to use peyote during religious rituals.

. . . I argue for a broader understanding of religious freedom and, in consequence, a wider set of religious exemptions from laws of general application. In no other way can we enable the religions to stand as intermediaries between sovereign and citizen, thus limiting the prospect of majoritarian tyranny; and in no other way can we translate the Founders' ideal of religious freedom in a relatively simple society into a new ideal for a new era, one characterized by a regulatory regime far more intrusive than the Founders could possibly have contemplated.

WHAT ARE ACCOMMODATIONS?

The accommodation of a religious group's faith traditions in an otherwise applicable legal framework can best be envisioned as a form of affirmative action. Recognizing both the unique historical circumstances of the religions and the importance of nurturing their continued existence, the state chooses to grant them a form of differential treatment. When President Bush pardoned the Jehovah's Witnesses, he was not endorsing their religious claims, but he was seeking ways to accommodate them within a political structure that generally favors the adherents of the mainstream religions. . . .

Employment Division v. Smith is a much criticized—and justly criticized—decision, and it shows clearly just where the current Court's Free Exercise jurisprudence is heading: toward a clear separation of church and self, a world in which citizens who adopt religious practices at variance with official state policy are properly made subject to the coercive authority of the state, which can, without fear of judicial intervention, pressure them to change those practices. . . .

The judgment against the Native American Church, however, demonstrates that the political process will protect only the mainstream religions, not the many smaller groups that exist at the margins. It is as though the relevant legal principles have been designed in order to uphold state regulations infringing on faith traditions that lie far from the mainstream; perhaps the courts are unable to appreciate the concern about "incidental" infringements precisely because judges are not drawn from religious traditions likely to suffer them.

Justice Antonin Scalia, perhaps unknowingly, made this precise point at the conclusion of his opinion for the *Smith* majority:

> It may fairly be said that leaving accommodation to the political process will place at a relative disadvantage those religious practices that are not widely engaged in; but that unavoidable consequence of democratic government must be preferred to a system in which each conscience is a law unto itself or in which judges weigh the social importance of all laws against the centrality of all religious beliefs.

What Justice Scalia misses is that it was in order to avoid this "unavoidable consequence of democratic government" that the Free Exercise Clause was crafted in the first place. The fact that the defense of religious liberty burdens the courts is hardly a reason, as he implies it is, to forbear.

A more practical danger also lurks, one that the legal scholar Frederick Mark Gedicks has noted: "Without exemptions, some religious groups will likely be crushed by the weight of majoritarian law and culture. Such groups pose no threat to order. However, majoritarian dominance could radicalize some believers into destabilizing, antisocial activity, including violence." Of course, the dominant culture can do what it has always done in the face of threats to order, especially threats from people the nation itself has oppressed, such as Native Americans and slaves: it can declare the marginalized and violent dissenters to be criminals, and thus rid itself of them, their movements, and their religions all at once. . . .

THE CASE FOR SUBVERSIVE ANARCHY

. . . Justice Scalia's conception of a free exercise clause that only protects the religious against discrimination is an example of what is called "neutrality" in the legal literature, the idea that the state should not favor religion but also should not oppress it. The ideal of neutrality might provide useful protection for religious freedom in a society of relatively few laws, one in which most of the social order is privately determined. That was the society the Founders knew. In such a society, it is enough to say that the law leaves religion alone. It is difficult, however, to see how the law can protect religious freedom in the welfare state if it does not offer exemptions and special protection for religious devotion. To offer the religions the chance to win exemptions from laws that others must obey obviously carves out a special niche for religion, but that is hardly objectionable: carving out a special place for religion is the minimum it might be said that the Free Exercise Clause does.

Nowadays, the government rarely if ever enacts legislation intended to oppress a particular religion, which is why Michael McConnell has written that the difference between neutrality and accommodation "is the difference between a Free Exercise Clause that is a major restraining device on government action that affects religious practice and a Free Exercise Clause that will rarely have practical application."

That practical distinction is not, however, the important theoretical distinction. What matters more is the different attitudes that neutrality and accommodation evince toward the role of religious belief in a democratic polity. Neutrality treats religious belief as a matter of individual choice, an aspect of conscience, with which the government must not interfere but which it has no obligation to respect. This was the significance of Justice Scalia's almost snide closing reference in *Smith* to a land in which "every conscience is a law unto itself." In this sense, neutrality treats religious belief like any other belief, controlled by the same rules: the choice is free, but it is entitled to no special subsidy, and, indeed, it can be trampled by the state as long as it is trampled by accident.

Accommodation, however, can be crafted into a tool that accepts religion as a group rather than an individual activity. When accommodation is so understood, corporate worship, not individual conscience, becomes the obstacle around which state policy must make the widest possible berth. Accommodation is therefore closer to Tocqueville's (and the Founders') conception of religious groups as autonomous moral and political forces, intermediate institutions, separate heads of sovereignty vital to preventing majoritarian tyranny. Thus, the reason for accommodation becomes not the protection of individual conscience, but the preservation of the religions as independent power bases that exist in large part in order to resist the state. To allow the state, without very strong reason, to enforce policies that interfere with this corporate freedom would be antithetical to the understanding of religious purpose as resistance. . . .

From Carter (1993), *The Culture of Disbelief.* New York: Doubleday, pp. 124–129.

DISCUSSION ISSUES

1. *Selective Lockean Toleration.* As discussed earlier on pages 268–272, the Lockean roots for liberal religious toleration manifest an intolerance of certain religious beliefs. Did the Court in *Reynolds v. United States* (1878) reflect anti-Mormon sentiments in finding laws forbidding the practice of bigamy constitutional? How should the Court draw the line between permissible religious practices and those that are not permissible? In *Wisconsin v. Yoder* (1972), the Court allowed the Amish to refuse to abide by a "state requirement that all children be exposed to education with a minimum substantive content through the tenth grade" (Cohen and Danelski 1994, p. 587). Does religious toleration extend to only a select few? Does the Court have more toleration for the "idyllic agrarianism" of the

Amish (however false and mythological that view might be) than it does for the "criminal and anti-Christian" Mormons who practice polygamy?

2. *Intolerance of the Intolerant?* Does liberal toleration reflect an intoleration? Fundamentalist Christian parents in Tennessee objected to their children participating in a public school reading program (*Mozert v. Hawkins County Board of Education* 1987) that included the witches' chant from *MacBeth,* and excerpts from *The Wizard of Oz* and *Diary of Anne Frank.* They claimed that the program violated the constitutional guarantee of free exercise of religion because coerced exposure (indoctrination) to diversity, toleration, and rationality threatened their culture's survival. The parents showed how this indoctrination interfered with their ability to raise their children as fundamentalists. Is indoctrination a harm? Do those who preach tolerance rely on indoctrination? Is the indoctrination of tolerance necessary for democracy (see Stolzenberg 1993)?

3. *Definition of Religion.* Try to define religion. Is belief in a Supreme Being essential to all religion? In 1948, Congress defined religion as including "an individual's belief in relation to a Supreme Being involving duties superior to those arising from any human relation" and excluding "essentially political, sociological, or philosophical views or a merely personal moral code" (Selective Service Act, § 6[j] as quoted in Cohen and Danelski 1994, p. 623). During the Vietnam War, the U.S. Supreme Court faced the problem of defining religion in a series of cases on conscientious objection. The Supreme Court expanded the definition of religion to include nontheistic religious beliefs *(United States v. Seeger* 1965) and "sincere and central" moral beliefs (*Welsh v. United States* 1970). By interpreting religion so broadly, did the Court in *Welsh* contradict the provisions passed by Congress? How do religions differ from cults? Does the sincerity or truth of the religious belief matter? The Court held that a jury could address the sincerity of self-professed faith healers but not the truth of their beliefs (*United States v. Ballard* 1944).

4. *Religious Rituals.* In 1878, the Court in *Reynolds* asked, perhaps with some foresight: "Suppose one believed that human sacrifices were a part of religious worship, would it be seriously contended that the civil government under which he lived could not interfere to prevent a sacrifice?" The U.S. Supreme Court recently addressed the issue of religious animal sacrifices (*Church of the Lukumi Babalu Aye v. Hialeah* 1993). A Hialeah, Florida, ordinance made the religious sacrifice of animals unlawful. The Court found the ordinance unconstitutional, since it aimed to suppress the Santeria religion as practiced in Hialeah. Only Cuban Yurabas, who combine traditional African religion with Catholicism, practiced the rituals outlined in the ordinance. Further, the city passed the ordinance soon after it received an application from the Santeria religion to build a church in Hialeah. Does the state have an interest in preventing animal cruelty (see Locke's comments page 271)? What if Santeria had applied for an exemption to anticruelty laws on grounds of freedom of religion? Further, in the *Smith* case in Reading 5-25, if the government were to give the Native American Church an exemption from the federal control of peyote, could it then deny exemption to any other church claiming a similar use of peyote? In an earlier case, the government had argued that a group called the Church of the Awakening should not receive an exemption since it used peyote merely to expand consciousness and not primarily for religious purposes (see *Kennedy v. Bureau of Narcotics* 1972). Is the Church of the Awakening a cult and not a religion like the Native American Church? What differentiates a cult from a religion?

Rights

PRIVACY

We hold these truths to be self-evident, that all men are created equal,
that they are endowed by the Creator with certain inalienable Rights,
that among these are Life, Liberty and the Pursuit of Happiness.
— UNITED STATES DECLARATION OF INDEPENDENCE, 1776

Men are born and remain free and equal in rights; social distinctions
may be based only on general usefulness.
— THE FRENCH DECLARATION OF THE RIGHTS OF MAN AND CITIZEN, 1789

The Declaration of the Rights of Man (France, 1789), the Bill of Rights (United States, 1791), and the Universal Declaration of Human Rights (United Nations, 1948) represent the most notable human rights documents. The idea of rights, which plays an important role in many legal and political systems, seems commonplace today. However, the idea of natural rights came into prominence relatively recently, primarily during John Locke's time in the seventeenth century. Today, rights are central to political debate. In this chapter, pages 289–301 construct a framework to aid in an analysis of rights. Pages 301–314 explore the complex relationship between rights and obligations, taking on a stark reality in a case involving child abuse. Pages 314–356 trace the path taken by the Supreme Court beginning at the start of the twentieth century with economic rights, traveling through procedural rights, and concluding with fundamental privacy rights. Issues of abortion rights and the right to die make this discussion particularly important.

A. THEORIES OF RIGHTS

Individuals have rights and there are things no person or group may
do to them (without violating their rights).
— ROBERT NOZICK, *Anarchy, State, and Utopia*, 1974

Not everyone, past or present, has championed rights. Past societies, including that of ancient Athens, thrived without a modern sense of rights. Current political leaders, particularly those from nations in Africa and Asia, have spoken against the use of rights, objecting especially to the dominating Western concept of rights. Philosophers, past and present, have also disagreed about the viability of rights. Many political theorists have championed natural rights, but critics have questioned universality of natural rights, charging, for example, that Locke's natural rights protected only certain and not all interests. Nineteenth-century reformer Jeremy Bentham rejected natural rights as imaginary—"nonsense on stilts"—and promoted instead positive rights that originated in legislative laws. Even the conservative Edmund Burke largely agreed with the radical Bentham on natural rights.

The debate over rights continues among contemporary philosophers. Joel Feinberg calls rights "indispensably valuable possessions" (Feinberg 1966, p. 137), contrasting sharply with Alasdair MacIntyre's opinion that belief in human rights "is one with belief in witches and unicorns" (MacIntyre, 1984, p. 69). We have already had a chance to hear from such rights proponents as Ronald Dworkin (see Readings 3-14 and 3-15) and from their detractors, including Michael Sandel (see Reading 4-14). According to Dworkin, rights act as trumps (having higher priority) over policy goals and set limits to trade-offs made in policy debates. However, Sandel attacks liberals like Dworkin for giving priority to rights over goods. For Sandel, we must first articulate our community's values before we appeal to our rights. Perhaps, with all this disagreement, rights may seem too problematic to retain. However, imagine, as Joel Feinberg asks us to do in Reading 6-1, a world without rights. Some feminist critics associate Feinberg's rights world with a masculine world where men make claims against one another. Is a world without rights one in which (to paraphrase Feinberg) men could not stand up and look each other in the eye as equals? Does a world without rights mean a world without minimal self-respect? Would a "rightless" world be devoid of human dignity? Despite a lack of consensus about rights, they hold a prominent place in contemporary political and legal theory. Further, given the prominence of rights in politics and in law, it becomes imperative to understand them better. Rights, according to MacCallum (1991), have three components: agents, recipients, and objects. An analysis of rights requires asking questions about each element.

1. Agents of Rights

Who are the agents of rights or the rightholders? Some individuals and groups make their appeals for change by seeking to extend rights to different types of agents. At one time, the boundaries for those with rights did not extend to slaves or women, but now they do. Does it make sense to further extend the boundaries? People for the Ethical Treatment of Animals (PETA), for example, demands rights for animals, and pro-life groups, such as Operation Rescue, proclaim the rights of fetuses. According to these views, animals and fetuses qualify as rightholders, but do both agents qualify? On what grounds do some agents, like animals and fetuses, qualify as rightholders while others, such as children and machines, do not? Should rightholders have the capacity to demand their rights? Should only those with language qualify as rightholders?

2. Demands of Recipients

What do the agents who are demanding rights want? Recently, demands for the rights of people who are disabled have gained more prominence with the passage of the Americans with Disabilities Act. What demands do individuals with disabilities make? From whom do they demand rights? When someone claims that people with disabilities have the right to access public buildings, do they have a privilege or a claim? Do they have the privilege (or freedom) to enter public buildings without interference? Do they have a claim for others to take positive measures on their behalf? Do they have claims against private building owners to provide ramps and other devices for them? Rights-as-privileges place different demands on others than rights-as-claims do. In the former, rightholders demand noninterference by others; in the latter, the rightholders demand specific action. In either case, rightholders make demands on others. Are the demands of rightholders sufficiently strong to impose duties on others?

3. Content of Rights

What do rightholders demand? Since rights involve things of importance, does each valued activity require a right to protect it? In some cases, the content of a right might be clear but the application questionable. Glatung and Wirak proposed an unusual list of activities needing rights that included the right to sleep; the right not to be exposed to excessive and unnecessary heavy, degrading, dirty, and boring work; the right to identify with one's work product; and the right to belong to a primary (not necessarily the family) and secondary (not necessarily the nation) group (1978, p. 49). The content of some of these rights seems clear. However, because the idea of rights suffers from overuse, if too many rights become recognized, the power of using rights language to make demands is lost. Even when the rights in question have become commonplace, the content of the right might remain a mystery. Controversies over the right to an abortion and the right to a sexual orientation center on a right to privacy, but what does "privacy" mean? How does the Constitution support a right to privacy?

Discussions in international law use a general classification of rights (see page 34). Rights come in three types or "generations." **First-generation rights** include political and civil rights, such as the right to vote and the right of free speech. **Second-generation rights** address social and economic conditions, including the right to work, the right to education, and the right to health care. The first and second generation rights have resulted from international and multinational treaties. **Third-generation rights** consist largely of proposals to expand rights to global (peace), public (clean environment), and communal (group self-determination) goods. Do political and civil rights take priority over others? Liberals maintain that sacrificing or limiting political and civil rights in favor of social and economic rights can never be justified. Is it necessary to assure political and civil rights before moving on to questions of economic redistribution? Do political and civil rights become effective only when accompanied by assurances of social and economic rights? Contrary to the liberal thesis, should social and economic rights, which guarantee a basic subsistence, be considered fundamental?

The idea of rights relates to other political concepts, such as liberty and equality, as well. This relationship to other ideas can further an understanding of rights. For example, the idea of obligations stands as the closest kin to rights. Philosophical discussions of rights often use a framework created by Wesley

Hohfield, who clarified different interpretations of rights. The ambiguous use of the term *rights* accounts for some of the difficulty in resolving debates over rights, since it might mean any one of the following: freedom (liberty), power, immunity, or claim. For example, if a woman asserts a right to do something, she might mean that she has either the freedom to do something or the legal power to do it. She might claim that she has the right (freedom) to sunbathe topless in her back yard, or she might claim a right to legal protection or immunity. She might pursue her right to be free from stalking by a former boyfriend. Finally, she might be making a claim that involves someone else's associated duty, such as a claim that a right to work creates a duty of the government to find her a job. Rex Martin develops a weaker version of the rights-correlate-with-duties thesis (see Reading 6-2). He sees rights as giving normative direction to others, expanding the reach of rights beyond a focus on what the rightholder does. First, rights also extend to what others should not do to the rightholder—such as causing injury by torturing. Second, rights further extend to how others treat the rightholder—for example, the right to an education. Martin's analysis sets the stage for considering duties and obligations, not simply as the opposite of rights, but as alternative ways to construct a political and legal philosophy.

READING 6-1
A World Without Rights
"The Nature and Value of Rights" (1970)

Joel Feinberg

1

I would like to begin by conducting a thought experiment. Try to imagine Nowheresville—a world very much like our own except that no one, or hardly any one (the qualification is not important), has *rights*. If this flaw makes Nowheresville too ugly to hold very long in contemplation, we can make it as pretty as we wish in other moral respects. We can, for example, make the human beings in it as attractive and virtuous as possible without taxing our conceptions of the limits of human nature. In particular, let the virtues of moral sensibility flourish. Fill this imagined world with as much benevolence, compassion, sympathy, and pity as it will conveniently hold without strain. Now we can imagine men helping one another from compassionate motives merely, quite as much or even more than they do in our actual world from a variety of more complicated motives.

This picture, pleasant as it is in some respects, would hardly have satisfied Immanuel Kant [see Reading 2-2]. Benevolently motivated actions do good, Kant admitted, and therefore are better, *ceteris paribus* [all other things being equal], than malevolently motivated actions; but no action can have supreme kind of worth—what Kant called "moral worth"—unless its whole motivating power derives from the thought that it is *required by duty*. Accordingly, let us try to make Nowheresville more appealing to Kant by introducing the idea of duty into it, and letting the sense of duty be a sufficient motive for many beneficent and honorable actions. But doesn't this bring our original thought experiment to an abortive conclusion? If duties are permitted entry into Nowheresville, are not rights necessarily smuggled in along with them?

The question is well-asked, and requires here a brief digression so that we might consider the so-called **"doctrine of the logical correlativity of rights and duties."** This is the doctrine that (i) all duties entail other people's rights and (ii) all rights entail other people's duties. Only the first part of the doctrine, the alleged entailment from duties to rights, need concern us here. Is this part of the doctrine correct? It should not be surprising that my answer is: "In a sense yes and in a sense no." Etymologically, the word "duty" is associated with actions that are *due* someone else, the payments of debts *to* creditors, the keeping of agreements with promisees, the payment of club dues, or legal fees, or tariff levies to appropriate authorities or their representatives. In this original sense of "duty," all duties are correlated with the rights of those *to* whom the duty is owed. On the other hand, there seem to be numerous classes of duties, both of a legal and non-legal kind, that are *not* logically correlated with the rights of other persons. This seems to be a consequence of the fact that the word "duty" has come to be used for *any* action understood to be *required,* whether by the rights of others, or by law, or by higher authority, or by conscience, or whatever. When the notion of requirement is in clear focus it is likely to seem the only element in the idea of duty that is essential, and the other component notion—that a duty is something *due* someone else—drops off. Thus, in this widespread but derivative usage, "duty" tends to be used for any action we feel we *must* (for whatever reason) do. It comes, in short, to be a term of moral modality merely; and it is no wonder that the first thesis of the logical correlativity doctrine often fails.

Let us then introduce duties into Nowheresville, but only in the sense of actions that are, or are believed to be, morally mandatory, but not in the older sense of actions that are due others and can be claimed by others as their right. Nowheresville now can have duties of the sort imposed by positive law. A legal duty is not something we are implored or advised to do merely; it is something the law, or an authority under the law, *requires* us to do whether we want to or not, under pain of penalty. When traffic lights turn red, however, there is no determinate person who can plausibly be said to claim our stopping as his due, so that the motorist owes it to *him* to stop, in the way a debtor owes it to his creditor to pay. In our own actual world, of course, we sometimes owe it to our *fellow motorists* to stop; but that kind of right-correlated duty does not exist in Nowheresville. There, motorists "owe" obedience to the Law, but they owe nothing to one another. When they collide, no matter who is at fault, no one is morally accountable to anyone else, and no one has any sound grievance or "right to complain."

When we leave legal contexts to consider moral obligations and other extra-legal duties, a greater variety of duties-without-correlative-rights present themselves. Duties of charity, for example, require us to contribute to one or another of a large number of eligible recipients, no one of whom can claim our contribution from us as his due. Charitable contributions are more like gratuitous services, favors, and gifts than like repayments of debts or reparations;

and yet we do have duties to be charitable. Many persons, moreover, in our actual world believe that they are required by their own consciences to do more than that "duty" that *can* be demanded of them by their prospective beneficiaries. I have quoted elsewhere the citation from H. B. Acton of a character in a Malraux novel who "gave all his supply of poison to his fellow prisoners to enable them by suicide to escape the burning alive which was to be their fate and his." This man, Acton adds, "probably did not think that [the others] had more of a right to the poison than he had, though he thought it his duty to give it to them." I am sure that there are many actual examples, less dramatically heroic than this fictitious one, of persons who believe, rightly or wrongly, that they *must do* something (hence the word "duty") for another person in excess of what that person can appropriately demand of him (hence the absence of "right").

Now the digression is over and we can return to Nowheresville and summarize what we have put in it thus far. We now find spontaneous benevolence in somewhat larger degree than in our actual world, and also the acknowledged existence of duties of obedience, duties of charity, and duties imposed by exacting private consciences, and also, let us suppose, a degree of conscientiousness in respect to those duties somewhat in excess of what is to be found in our actual world. I doubt that Kant would be fully satisfied with Nowheresville even now that duty and respect for law and authority have been added to it; but I feel certain that he would regard their addition at least as an improvement. I will now introduce two further moral practices into Nowheresville that will make that world very little more appealing to Kant, but will make it appear more familiar to us. These are the practices connected with the notions of *personal desert* and what I call a *sovereign monopoly of rights*.

When a person is said to deserve something good from us what is meant in part is that there would be a certain propriety in our giving that good thing to him in virtue of the kind of person he is, perhaps, or more likely, in virtue of some specific thing he has done. The propriety involved here is a much weaker kind than that which derives from our having promised him the good thing or from his having qualified for it by satisfying the well-advertised conditions of some public rule. In the latter case he could be said not merely to deserve the good thing but also to have a *right* to it, that is to be in a position to demand it as his due; and of course we will not have that sort of thing in Nowheresville. That weaker kind of propriety which is mere desert is simply a kind of *fittingness* between one party's character or action and another party's favorable response, much like that between humor and laughter, or good performance and applause.

The following seems to be the origin of the idea of deserving good or bad treatment from others: A master or lord was under no obligation to reward his servant for especially good service; still a master might naturally feel that there would be a special fittingness in giving a gratuitous reward as a grateful response to the good service (or conversely imposing a penalty for bad service[see Reading 3-17]). Such an act while surely fitting and proper was entirely supererogatory [going beyond the call of duty]. The fitting response in turn from the rewarded servant should be gratitude. If the deserved reward had not been given him he should have had no complaint, since he only *deserved* the reward, as opposed to having a *right* to it, or a ground for claiming it as his due.

The idea of desert [what one deserves] has evolved a good bit away from its beginnings by now, but nevertheless, it seems clearly to be one of those words J. L. Austin said "never entirely forget their pasts." Today servants qualify for their wages by doing their agreed upon chores, no more and no less. If their wages are not forthcoming, their contractual rights have been violated and they can make legal claim to the money that is their due. If they do less than they agreed to do, however, their employers may "dock" them, by paying them proportionately less than the agreed upon fee. This is all a matter of right. But if the servant does a splendid job, above and beyond his minimal contractual duties, the employer is under no further obligation to reward him, for this was not agreed upon, even tacitly, in advance. The additional service was all the servant's idea and done entirely on his own. Nevertheless, the morally sensitive employer may feel that it would be exceptionally appropriate for him to respond, freely on *his* own, to the servant's meritorious service, with a reward. The employee cannot demand it as his due, but he will happily accept it, with gratitude, as a fitting response to his desert. . . .

In Nowheresville, nevertheless, we will have only the original weak kind of desert. Indeed, it will be impossible to keep this idea out if we allow such practices as teachers grading students, judges awarding prizes, and servants serving benevolent but class-conscious masters. Nowheresville is a reasonably good world in many ways, and its teachers, judges, and masters will generally try to give students, contestants, and servants the grades, prizes, and rewards they deserve. For this the recipients will be grateful; but they will never think to complain, or even feel aggrieved, when expected responses to desert fail. The masters, judges, and teachers don't *have* to do good things, after all, for *anyone*. One should be happy that they *ever* treat us well, and not grumble over their occasional lapses. Their hoped for responses, after all, are *gratuities,* and there is no wrong in the omission of what is merely gratuitous. Such is the response of persons who have no concept of *rights,* even persons who are proud of their own deserts.

Surely, one might ask, rights have to come in somewhere, if we are to have even moderately complex forms of social organization. Without rules that confer rights and impose obligations, how can we have ownership of property, bargains and deals, promises and contracts, appointments and loans, marriages and partnerships? Very well, let us introduce all of these social and economic practices into Nowheresville, but *with one big twist.* With them I should like to introduce the curious notion of a "sovereign right-monopoly." You will recall that the subjects in Hobbes's *Leviathan* had no rights whatever against their sovereign [Reading 1-2]. He could do as he liked with them, even gratuitously harm them, but this gave them no valid grievance against him. The sovereign, to be sure, had a certain duty to treat his subjects well, but this duty was owed not to the subjects directly, but to God, just as we might have a duty to a person to treat his property well, but of course no duty to the property itself but only to its owner. Thus, while the sovereign was quite capable of *harming* his subjects, he could commit no wrong against them that they could complain about, since they had no prior claims against his conduct. The only party *wronged* by the sovereign's mistreatment of his subjects was God, the supreme lawmaker. Thus, in repenting cruelty to his subjects, the sovereign might say to God, as David did after killing Uriah, "to

Thee only have I sinned" [second king of Israel, David, sent his general Uriah into battle defenseless].

Even in the *Leviathan,* however, ordinary people had ordinary rights *against one another.* They played roles, occupied offices, made agreements, and signed contracts. In a genuine "sovereign right-monopoly," as I shall be using that phrase, they will do all those things too, and thus incur genuine obligations toward one another; but the obligations (here is the twist) will not be owed directly *to* promisees, creditors, parents, and the like, but rather to God alone, or to the members of some elite, or to a single sovereign under God. Hence, the rights correlative to the obligations that derive from these transactions are all owned by some "outside" authority. . . .

There will, of course, be delegated authorities in the imaginary world, empowered to give commands to their underlings and to punish them for their disobedience. But the commands are all given in the name of the right-monopoly who in turn are the only persons to whom obligations are owed. Hence, even intermediate superiors do not have claim-rights against their subordinates but only legal *powers* to create obligations in the subordinates *to* the monopolistic rightholder, and also the legal *privilege* to impose penalties in the name of that monopoly.

2

So much for the imaginary "world without rights." If some of the moral concepts and practices I have allowed into that world do not sit well with one another, no matter. Imagine Nowheresville with all of these practices if you can, or with any harmonious subset of them, if you prefer. The important thing is not what I've let into it, but what I have kept out. The remainder of this paper will be devoted to an analysis of what precisely a world is missing when it does not contain rights and why that absence is morally important.

The most conspicuous difference, I think, between the Nowheresvillians and ourselves has something to do with the activity of *claiming.* Nowheresvillians, even when they are discriminated against invidiously [unjustly], or left without the things they need, or otherwise badly treated, do not think to leap to their feet and make righteous demands against one another, though they may not hesitate to resort to force and trickery to get what they want. They have no notion of rights, so they do not have a notion of what is their due; hence they do not claim before they take. . . .

In brief conclusion: To have a right is to have a claim against someone whose recognition as valid is called for by some set of governing rules or moral principles. To have a *claim* in turn, is to have a case meriting consideration, that is, to have reasons or grounds that put one in a position to engage in performative and propositional claiming. The activity of claiming, finally, as much as any other thing, makes for self-respect and respect for others, gives a sense to the notion of personal dignity, and distinguishes this otherwise morally flawed world from the even worse world of Nowheresville. . . .

From Feinberg, "The Nature and Value of Rights," *Journal of Value Inquiry,* © (1970) pp. 245–249. Reprinted with kind permission from Kluwer Academic Publishers.

A World of Rights
"The Concept of Rights" (1993)

Rex Martin

SOME MAIN FEATURES OF RIGHTS

To fix our thinking at the very outset on a specific matter, let us imagine the following scene. A group of people live in an out of the way place, a forest perhaps. In that place is a pond and the people there are used to going to the pond to fish. There are several well-worn paths by which they can go to the pond, depending on which part of the forest they are coming from. One day a fence is put across one of the paths and the people are told that the path is closed. One of them responds that this cannot be. They are going to the pond to fish and it is their right to do so and they have taken this path and it is their right to do so; the fence maker should remove the fence or, at the very least, the people should be able to climb over it and continue to the pond.

I presume the scenario is recognizable: the talk of rights seems natural and appropriate. There is, of course, much about the setting that we do not know and that would require filling in. We do not know, for example, what the political status of the people is: whether they are subjects of the same political jurisdiction or, for that matter, whether they are subjects of any political jurisdiction. For all we know these people might be bucolic [idyllically rural] inhabitants of a benign state of nature, of the sort imagined by Locke (at least in its very earliest stages) or by Rousseau. Nor do we know anything about the status of property among these people: whether they have private property or which persons, if any, can be said to have particular property interests. We do not even know what kind of right the fisher-to-be was asserting: whether it was a customary right or a legal one or a moral right of some sort. None of this is clear.

Yet the claim that there was a right here did not seem unintelligible and the suggestion that the fence maker should therefore give way seemed appropriate enough. Why should things be clear even to this extent, when so much else was indeterminate? I suppose, then, that we can tell something about the character of rights from this relatively uncluttered story and that, whatever this character is, it is independent of the many things we do not know from the story. What we might gather here, in particular, is the character rights would have regardless of whether they were customary or legal or moral in nature.

One conclusion we could draw from the story, once we assume that the way of acting in question is indeed a right, is that rights are fairly determinate things. The disputation seems to require such determinateness; for it matters, crucially, whether going to the pond *on this particular path* is a right. If simple access to the pond had been all that mattered, where other paths were available, the dispute would have reduced to issues merely of custom or convenience. I do not, of course, want to suggest that people never dispute about more abstract matters (the right to travel, for example). It's just that if we could not reach something fairly determinate from the abstract assertion of the right, then the assertion of a right here is irresolute; it would not tell people what they could or could not do and they would soon lose interest. So we can say that there is an appropriate determinateness to such disputes and that one of the points to an argument about rights is to settle on what that is: to decide what, specifically, the right is *to* in the context of the dispute.

A second conclusion we could draw is that whatever the right is to—considered determinately—it must be to something distributable, something that could (practicably speaking) be given to or provided for or engaged in by those who are relevantly said to be the rightholder(s). For any given right must define a class such that every member is assigned the thing in question. Thus, in the story, the people (presumably all those who live in the forest) are said to be the rightholders and all have the right of going to the pond on any of several paths, this one included. Going along on this particular path was something the relevant persons physically could do; in that way, clearly, it was distributable. But the sense in which we are interested is whether the capacity so to walk is itself parceled out to each of them in the defining rule, as it was presumably in the right we are discussing. When a distributable physical capacity is thus distributed to all the relevant individuals, the resulting arrangement is said to be "individuated." Following Dworkin (whose term it is) we can say, then, that all rights are individuated: they are rights to something which can be distributed to all the rightholders (be they natural individuals or collective bodies or what have you) and they assign the same capacity to each of them to enter into that distribution in the appropriate way. That thing can be said, in some relevant way, to be *due* to the rightholder, and due in the same way to each of the rightholders.

Yet another conclusion we could draw, coming close on the heels of the one just sketched, is that rights are—or involve—accredited ways of acting. This is, of course, the conclusion I most want to draw; it is, indeed, the hypothesis from which my argument . . . starts. And the question I will address is the character, in its main dimensions, of that accrediting.

We can readily imagine from the story that initially, before it is challenged, the way of acting is relatively unself-conscious—unreflective and routine. Here the right and the practice are virtually indistinguishable. Now, when a way of acting has been challenged or infringed, the practice in question may well be referred to by its proponent, explicitly, as a right. More important, the features in the practice that make for a right will be brought out or, at least, there will be an attempt to do so.

How, then, does the person whose action has been challenged make good a rights claim? Certainly that person could do so, for example, by drawing forth an acknowledgment that the action was indeed his or her practice, and the practice of others, if that was the case. More significantly, the claimant could elicit confirmation that this practice had been an accepted one, not merely by those who engaged in it but also by others whose judgment seemed relevant. The practice in question (going to the pond on this particular path) was accredited, then, by an appropriate social ratification—in the case at hand, it might be, by an unreflective and unspoken social acceptance. And, presumably, any practice can be said to be a right insofar as the way of acting involved is backed up—that is, endorsed and accredited—by some form of social recognition.

We say *social* here, for it is unlikely that a right could ever arise except in a social setting: it would be odd, and probably pointless (practically speaking), to talk of the rights of a wholly and permanently isolated individual. But my point is not simply about the setting of rights; I want, rather, to suggest that this factor of social recognition or ratification is actually a constituent of rights—that is, of our characterization of something as a right. Of course, the precise description of the social recognition involved would probably vary somewhat, even within the same society, depending on whether the right in question was said to be customary or legal or moral in nature. . . .

Thus, I would want to suggest that the central intuitions in my account would be preserved intact throughout the elaboration of a theory of rights. A right is *to* something which is both determinate and distributable. An identical or, at least, a similar capacity respecting that thing, as specified in the right, is assigned to every person who can relevantly be said to be a rightholder; in this regard, all rights are individuated. A right so understood is an accredited or established way of acting. The ground of this establishment, what accredits the way of acting and what principally qualifies it as a right, is something variously described as social recognition or acknowledgment or common acceptance (in a form appropriate to the kind of right involved, and with whatever reasons and argumentation that might be deemed necessary there). This acceptance would be supported as reasonable in the minimal sense given by the notion of explanatory reasonableness. And directives could be issued to others, to those who are not rightholders, and further initiatives taken on the basis of—or as part of—any such successful claim to rights status. . . .

WAYS OF ACTING AND WAYS OF BEING TREATED

I want to turn next to a further consideration, one that on reflection forces an expansion in my account. Up to now I have spoken of a right as if it specified, invariably, something that the rightholder as agent does or can do. True, many of the things typically captured in talk of rights would be so characterized—for example, the free exercise of religion, the liberty to travel, the right to vote or to own personal property. For each of them identifies a right to a specific way of acting, on the part of an agent, which way is secured or made fast—to a degree—for that agent by the relevant normative direction of the conduct of others. Thus, any one of these rights (as a right to a way of acting) could be given the now standard construal of a liberty or a freedom developed by MacCallum [see pages 290–291]: here someone (as an agent) is able to do A (for example, to make his or her own judgments in matters of religious or moral or scientific or philosophical belief) free from proscribed interferences with A (such as would be afforded by a state establishment of religion). These proscribed interferences give us, in effect, a clearer idea of the normative direction of the conduct of others insofar as that conduct is responsive to the endorsed way of acting, the liberty in question.

But not all rights identify ways of acting in precisely this sense. For not all of them identify things that agents (rightholders) do or can do. The right to life, for example, is construed by some theorists as the right not to be killed. And this says something about what *others* do or can do. Thus, if person 1 has a right to life then person 2 is to do something: person 2 is to forbear killing person 1 and even, perhaps, to prevent that person's being killed by person 3. And none of this is something the rightholder does or can do.

The crucial point I am making does not rest on a single example; others are at hand. The right not to be tortured, for instance, is fulfilled perhaps exclusively by what others do or can do. In short the way of acting is theirs, not the rightholder's. They forbear, they prevent, they set up alternatives. And someone has an effective right not to be tortured when these things are so. Indeed, one has this right even when one does and can do nothing.

A person has the right not to be tortured even when unconscious. It might be countered that a person has, even when asleep, the right to travel. That is so. But the way of acting is the rightholder's; it is, or essentially involves, something the rightholder does or can do. Or that others, acting on the rightholder's behalf, do or can do. Not so with the right not to be tortured.

The two rights we are discussing are classical in character; the right to life and the right not to be tortured clearly were contemplated by the philosophers and manifesto writers of an earlier time. And the rights themselves are enshrined in the great American documents of the eighteenth century: the right to life in the Declaration of Independence and the right not to be tortured in the Eighth Amendment (as part of the Bill of Rights) of the U.S. Constitution.

Thus, if we intended, when we talk of rights, that the specified way of acting is to be the rightholder's way of acting, we run afoul of the fact that some important rights are not captured by such an analysis. For they do not specify the rightholder's way of acting but, principally, the ways of acting of others toward the rightholder. Let us accept, then, that we must be able to classify rights as including both liberties of conduct *and* so-called freedoms from injury (that is, avoidance by others of causing such injuries to rightholders). And, since the latter are not ways of acting available to rightholders—something they do or can do—we would need to amend my formula to say that rights are established ways of acting *or* established ways of being acted toward, ways of being treated.

Now that I have made this accommodation, to include avoidances of injury among rights, it is much easier to address the problem posed by so-called social and economic rights: the right to a minimum wage, to an education, to disability or retirement benefits, to medical care and services, and so on. It is often said that the notion of rights as liberties represents the classical or earlier view of rights, characteristic of the seventeenth and eighteenth centuries; and that an enlarged view of rights, to include the positive services of others, is a later graft onto this earlier stock and represents the agitation for social reform in this century and the one previous. But this view, as we have seen, is too simple; the foundation of these social and economic rights already exists to an important degree in the classical rights to a certain kind of treatment by others (not to be killed, not to be tortured, etc.). For the economic and social rights have in common with rights to avoidance of injury a significant feature: all these rights concern, crucially, ways of being treated. Essentially then, they involve at their core, not ways of acting on the part of the rightholder, but ways of acting on the part of others towards the rightholder.

But the social and economic rights are not simply or even mainly rights to the forbearance and preventive actions of others; rather, they are principally rights to services on the part of others. Thus, one has an effective right to education when, on a basis available to all, schools are built, teachers are trained and certified, a general curriculum established, and an environment thus created for learning to read, write, do sums, and so on. The right to education, like the other social and economic rights, is not restricted to mere avoidances of injury. Indeed, the prevailing pattern for such rights is that a benefit is first provided generally and then the society follows through to assure its availability by (among other things) preventing people from denying it to eligible individuals. Here the preventive action *presupposes* the provision of the service and cannot be understood as independent of it.

Thus, we are able to distinguish this case from one where individuals act mainly to prevent someone from harming another person—while providing nothing but this prevention, or while providing principally only such prevention. And we need, accordingly, to identify a third major class of things one has a right *to:* not merely to liberties in the proper sense (as liberties of conduct or ways of acting for the rightholder) and to avoidances of injury but also to the provision of services (where this, like avoidance of injury, crucially involves ways of acting by others toward the rightholder).

These three classes are wide enough to cover the things typically regarded as rights. To accommodate these classes, then, we need only affirm our *amended* characterization of rights to say that rights are established ways of acting or of being acted toward, of being treated. For what is established in some cases is action by the rightholder but in others it is action toward the rightholder. . . .

"The Concept of Rights," copyright Rex Martin 1993. Reprinted from *A System of Rights* by Rex Martin (1993) by permission of Oxford University Press.

B. RIGHTS AND OBLIGATIONS

Political controversies quickly gravitate to conflicts over rights. When relationships between spouses or between parents and children go wrong, the continuing disputes often become battles over rights. Do parents have the right to punish their children? Do children have any rights? Do Amish parents violate their children's rights by forcing them to leave school after the eighth grade? (See Discussion Issues, question 1, page 287.) Although disputes often turn on rights, perhaps we could deal better with situations of alleged spousal and child abuse if we placed less emphasis on rights and paid more attention to obligations, duties, and responsibilities. Philosophers have developed criticisms of rights and have put forward new theories of obligations. One of the foremost critics, Richard Rorty, rejects the use of foundational reasoning about political morality and finds squabbles about human nature outmoded. He has little patience with debates about whether Hobbes or Locke had the most accurate picture of human nature. Instead, he sympathizes with controversial philosopher Friedrich Nietzsche's (1844–1900) views (see chapter 8, pages 414–415). Nietzsche found the very idea of "'inalienable human rights' a laughable attempt by the weaker members of the species to fend off the stronger" (Shute and Hurley 1993, p. 115). Rorty regards as hopeless the search for universal human rights based on conceptions of human nature and rationality (see Reading 6-3). In their place, he calls for sentimental education, thereby continuing his rejection of foundationalism begun in *Philosophy and Human Nature*.

DeShaney v. Winnebago County Department of Social Services (1989) dramatically illustrates the problems underlying the relationship between rights and obligations (see Reading 6-4). Joshua DeShaney survived beatings from his father, Randy, but sustained irreversible brain damage that will require lifelong institutionalization. A Wisconsin court sentenced Randy to two to four years in prison, but he was paroled after serving less than two years. Joshua's mother had divorced Randy in Wyoming when Joshua was one year old and had moved to Arizona after Randy moved to Wisconsin. She sued the state of Wisconsin for violating the Fourteenth Amendment of the U.S. Constitution, charging that the state had deprived Joshua of liberty without due process of law (see page 314). Does the government have a constitutional duty to protect children from abuse? Read the following chronology of the case and determine, after each stage, whether the state of Wisconsin assumed responsibility for Joshua at that time.

1. In January 1982, police investigated a charge of child abuse stemming from Randy's second divorce proceeding. Randy's second wife indicated during the court proceedings that Joshua was a prime candidate for child abuse. Although procedures called for the child protection unit of the Department of Social Services to see the child, Joshua was not seen. The Department of Social Services, after an interview with Randy, took no official action.

2. In January 1983, Joshua was hospitalized with severe injuries. He was taken there by Randy's live-in girlfriend, who was his brother's ex-wife. A child protection team in the hospital recommended that no action be taken due to insufficient evidence and Randy's agreeing to a treatment plan. After having taken temporary custody of Joshua, the juvenile court returned Joshua to his father.

3. In March 1983, Joshua was again in the hospital, but no action was taken. A caseworker visited the DeShaney's home on a monthly basis, recording signs of abuse, including what appeared to be a mark from a cigarette burn on Joshua's chin. The caseworker filed for a protective order.

4. On March 8, 1984, Joshua made another trip to the hospital. One day after the caseworker's last home visit, Randy beat Joshua so severely that he fell into a coma. Joshua survived, but with irreversible brain damage requiring lifelong institutionalization.

When, if ever, should Wisconsin have discharged its obligation to intervene? In delivering the opinion of the Court, Justice Rehnquist made three points. First, the Constitution protects individuals from the state, not individuals from each other. Second, the state does not have an affirmative duty to ensure life, liberty, or property. Third, the state did not have a special relationship with Joshua. The state had not restrained Joshua in a way to deprive him of liberty that would trigger the due process requirement. Therefore, Justice Rehnquist held that there was no point in the chronology at which the state took responsibility for Joshua's condition. In the lower court opinion of the case, Judge Richard Posner concluded: "The state does not have a duty enforceable by the federal courts to maintain a police force or a fire department, or to protect children from their parents." As Justice William Brennan noted in dissent, "Wisconsin . . . effectively confined Joshua DeShaney within the walls of Randy DeShaney's violent home until such time as DSS [Department of Social Services] took action to remove him." Through its family law provisions, Wisconsin took affirmative action by returning Joshua to his father's care with a state-promulgated treatment plan. In Brennan's opinion, it was at that point in January 1983 that the state brought its elaborate institutional structure into the DeShaney's lives, thereby triggering the state's obligation.

Legal theorists, such as Harvard law professor Mary Ann Glendon, have misgivings about rights (Reading 6-5). Glendon finds that the image of a rugged, lone, autonomous individual underlies the American preoccupation with talk about rights. Dependency becomes something to avoid in oneself and something to disdain in others, while rights rhetoric drowns out any talk of responsibility. According to philosopher Elizabeth Wolgast (Reading 6-6), rights talk, however valuable in some applications, does not effectively address certain injustices. When disputants formulate their differences using rights, they enter an adversarial relationship. For example, a patient's bill of rights places patients in an assertive role against medical doctors in situations where patients become highly dependent on and under the power of doctors. In the reading, Wolgast explores other situations in which rights talk fails us.

READING 6-3

Rights Are Wrong
"What's Wrong With Rights" (1996)

Richard Rorty

If one accepts the premise that the basic responsibility of the American left is to protect the poor against the rapacity [excessively possessive of their wealth] of the rich, it's difficult to argue that the postwar years have been particularly successful ones. As Karl Marx pointed out, the history of the modern age is the history of class warfare, and in America today, it is a war in which the rich are winning, the poor are losing, and the left, for the most part, is standing by.

Early American leftists, from William James to Walt Whitman to Eleanor Roosevelt, seeking to improve the standing of the country's poorest citizens, found their voice in a rhetoric of fraternity, arguing that Americans had a responsibility for the well-being of their fellow man. This argument has been replaced in current leftist discourse by a rhetoric of "rights." The shift has its roots in the fact that the left's one significant postwar triumph was the success of the civil-rights movement. The language of "rights" is the language of the documents that have sparked the most successful attempts to relieve human suffering in postwar America—the series of Supreme Court decisions that began with *Brown v. Board of Education* and continued through *Roe v. Wade.* The *Brown* decision launched the most successful appeal to the consciences of Americans since the Progressive Era.

Yet the trouble with rights talk, as the philosopher Mary Ann Glendon has suggested, is that it makes political morality not a result of political discourse—of reflection, compromise, and choice of the lesser evil—but rather an unconditional moral imperative: a matter of corresponding to something antecedently given, in the way that the will of God or the law of nature is purportedly given. Instead of saying, for example, that the absence of various legal protections makes the lives of homosexuals unbearably difficult, that it creates unnecessary human suffering for our fellow Americans, we have come to say that these protections must be instituted in order to protect homosexuals' rights.

The difference between an appeal to end suffering and an appeal to rights is the difference between an appeal to fraternity, to fellow-feeling, to sympathetic concern, and an appeal to something that exists quite independently from anybody's feelings about anything—something that issues unconditional commands. Debate about the existence of such commands, and discussion of which rights exist and which do not, seems to me a philosophical blind alley, a pointless importation of legal discourse into politics, and a distraction from what is really needed in this case: an attempt by the straights to put themselves in the shoes of the gays.

Consider Colin Powell's indignant reaction to the suggestion that the exclusion of gays from the military is analogous to the pre-1950s exclusion of African Americans from the military. Powell angrily insists that there is no analogy here—that gays simply do not have the rights claimed by blacks. As soon as the issue is phrased in rights talk, those who agree with Powell and oppose what they like to call "special rights for homosexuals" start citing the Supreme Court's decision in *Bowers v. Hardwick.* The Court looked into the matter and solemnly found that there is no constitutional protection for sodomy. So people arguing against Powell have to contend that *Bowers* was wrongly decided. This leads to an argumentative impasse, one that suggests that rights talk is the wrong approach.

The *Brown v. Board of Education* decision was not a discovery of a hitherto unnoticed constitutional right, or of the hitherto unnoticed intentions of the authors of constitutional amendments. Rather, it was the result of our society's long-delayed willingness to admit that the behavior of white Americans toward the descendants of black slaves was, and continued to be, incredibly cruel—that it was intolerable that American citizens should be subjected to the humiliation of segregation. If *Bowers v. Hardwick* is reversed, it will not be because a hitherto invisible right to sodomy has become manifest to the justices. It will be because the heterosexual majority has become more willing to concede that it has been tormenting homosexuals for no better reason than to give itself the sadistic pleasure of humiliating a group designated as inferior—designated as such for no better reason than to give another group a sense of superiority.

I may seem to be stretching the term "sadistic," but I do not think I am. It seems reasonable to define "sadism" as the use of persons weaker than ourselves as outlets for our resentments and frustrations, and especially for the infliction of humiliation on such people in order to bolster our own sense of self-worth. All of us have been guilty, at some time in our lives, of this sort of casual, socially accepted sadism. But the most conspicuous instances of sadism, and the only ones relevant to politics, involve groups rather than individuals. Thus Cossacks and the Nazi storm troopers used Jews, and the white races have traditionally used the colored races, in order to bolster their group self-esteem. Men have traditionally humiliated women and beaten up gays in order to exalt their own sense of masculine privilege. The central dynamic behind this kind of sadism is the simple fact that it keeps up the spirits of a lot of desperate, beaten-down people to be able to say to themselves, "At least I'm not a nigger!" or "At least I'm not a faggot!"

Sadism, however, is not the only cause of cruelty and needless suffering. There is also selfishness. Selfishness differs from sadism in being more realistic and more thoughtful. It is less a matter of a sense of one's own worth and more a matter of rational calculation. If I own a business and pay my workers more than the minimum necessary to keep them at work, there will be less for me. My paying them less is not sadistic, but it may well be selfish. If I prevent my slaves, or the descendants of my ancestors' slaves, from getting an education, there will be less chance for them to compete with me and my descendants for the good jobs. If suburbanites cast their votes in favor of financing public education through locally administered property taxes, there will be less chance for the children in the cities to be properly educated, and so to compete with suburban children for membership in a shrinking middle class. All these calculated actions are cruel and selfish, but it would be odd to call them sadistic.

Our knowledge of sadism is relatively new—it is something we have only begun to get a grip on with the help of Freud, and philosophers like Sartre and Derrida, who have capitalized on Freud's work. But it is as if the thrill of discovering something new has led us to forget other human impulses; on constant guard against sadism, we have allowed selfishness free reign.

Just as rights talk is the wrong approach to issues where appeals to human sympathy are needed, sadism is the wrong target when what is at hand is selfishness. But this is the way American leftists have learned to talk—and think—about the world.

You would not guess from listening to the cultural politicians of the academic left that the power of the rich over the poor remains the most obvious, and potentially explosive, example of injustice in contemporary America. For these academics offer ten brilliant unmaskings of unconscious sadism for every unmasking of the selfishness intrinsic to American political and economic institutions. Enormous ingenuity and learning are deployed in demonstrating the complicity of this or that institution, or of some rival cultural politician, with patriarchy or heterosexism or racism. But little gets said about how we might persuade Americans who make more than $50,000 a year to take more notice of the desperate situation of their fellow citizens who make less than $20,000.

Instead, we hear talk of "the dominant white patriarchal heterosexist culture." This idea isolates the most sadistic patterns of behavior from American history, weaves them together, and baptizes their cause "the dominant culture." It is as if I listed all the shameful things I have done in my life and then attributed them to the dark power of "my true, dominant self." This would be a good way to alienate myself from myself, and to induce schizophrenia, but it would not be a good way to improve my behavior. For it does not add anything to the nasty facts about my past to blame them on a specter. Nor does it add anything to the facts about the suffering endured by African Americans and other groups to invent a bogeyman called "the dominant culture."

The more we on the American left think that study of psychoanalytic or sociological or philosophical theory will give us a better grip on what is going on in our country, the less likely we are to speak a political language that will help bring about change in our society. The more we can speak a robust, concrete, and practical language—one that can be picked up and used by legislators and judges—the more use we will be.

From Rorty (June 1996), "What's Wrong With Rights," *Harper's Magazine,* pp. 15–18.

READING 6-4

Child Abuse: Rights and Obligations

DeShaney v. Winnebago County Department of Social Services (1989)

CHIEF JUSTICE WILLIAM REHNQUIST, Opinion of the Court

The Due Process Clause of the Fourteenth Amendment provides that "[n]o State shall . . . deprive any person of life, liberty, or property, without due process of law." Petitioners contend that the State deprived Joshua of his liberty interest in "free[dom] from . . . unjustified intrusions on personal security," . . . by failing to provide him with adequate protection against his father's violence. The claim is one invoking the substantive rather than the procedural component of the Due Process Clause; petitioners do not claim that the State denied Joshua protection without according him appropriate procedural safeguards, . . . but that it was categorically obligated to protect him in these circumstances. . . .

But nothing in the language of the Due Process Clause itself requires the State to protect the life, liberty, and property of its citizens against invasion by private actors. The Clause is phrased as a limitation on the State's power to act, not as a guarantee of certain minimal levels of safety and security. It forbids the State itself to deprive individuals of life, liberty, or property without "due process of law," but its language cannot fairly be extended to impose an affirmative obligation on the State to ensure that those interests do not come to harm through other means. Nor does history support such an expansive reading of the constitutional text. Like its counterpart in the Fifth Amendment, the Due Process Clause of the Fourteenth Amendment was intended to prevent government "from abusing [its] power, or employing it as an instrument of oppression". . . . Its purpose was to protect the people from the State, not to ensure that the State protected them from each other. The Framers were content to leave the extent of governmental obligation in the latter area to the democratic political processes.

Consistent with these principles, our cases have recognized that the Due Process Clauses generally confer no affirmative right to governmental aid, even where such aid may be necessary to secure life, liberty, or property interests of which the government itself may not deprive the individual. . . . If the Due Process Clause does not require the State to provide its citizens with particular protective services, it follows that the State cannot be held liable under the Clause for injuries that could have been averted had it chosen to provide them. As a general matter, then, we conclude that a State's failure to protect an individual against private violence simply does not constitute a violation of the Due Process Clause. . . .

JUSTICE WILLIAM BRENNAN, dissenting.

The Court's baseline is the absence of positive rights in the Constitution and a concomitant suspicion of any claim that seems to depend on such rights. From this perspective, the DeShaneys' claim is first and foremost about inaction (the failure, here, of respondents to take steps to protect Joshua), and only tangentially about action (the establishment of a state program specifically designed to help children like Joshua). And from this perspective, holding these Wisconsin officials liable—where the only difference between this case and one involving a general claim to protective services is Wisconsin's establishment and operation of a program to protect children— would seem to punish an effort that we should seek to promote.

I would begin from the opposite direction. I would focus first on the action that Wisconsin *has* taken with respect to Joshua and children like him, rather than on the actions that the State failed to take. . . .

As the Court today reminds us, "the Due Process Clause of the Fourteenth Amendment was intended to prevent government 'from abusing [its] power, or employing it as an instrument of oppression.' " My disagreement with the Court arises from its failure to see that inaction can be every bit as abusive of power as action, that oppression can result when a State undertakes a vital duty and then ignores it. Today's opinion construes the Due Process Clause to permit a State to displace private sources of protection and then, at the critical moment, to shrug its shoulders and turn away from the harm that it has promised to try to prevent. Because I cannot agree that our Constitution is indifferent to such indifference, I respectfully dissent.

JUSTICE HARRY BLACKMUN, dissenting.

Today, the Court purports to be the dispassionate oracle of the law, unmoved by "natural sympathy." . . . But, in this pretense, the Court itself retreats into a sterile formalism which prevents it from recognizing either the facts of the case before it or the legal norms that should apply to those facts. As JUSTICE BRENNAN demonstrates, the facts here involve not mere passivity, but active state intervention in the life of Joshua DeShaney—intervention that triggered a fundamental duty to aid the boy once the State learned of the severe danger to which he was exposed.

The Court fails to recognize this duty because it attempts to draw a sharp and rigid line between action and inaction. But such formalistic reasoning has no place in the interpretation of the broad and stirring Clauses of the Fourteenth Amendment. Indeed, I submit that these Clauses were designed, at least in part, to undo the formalistic legal reasoning that infected antebellum jurisprudence, which the late Professor Robert Cover analyzed so effectively in his significant work entitled *Justice Accused* (1975) [see chapter 3, Reading 3-8, page 153].

Like the antebellum judges who denied relief to fugitive slaves, . . . the Court today claims that its decision, however harsh, is compelled by existing legal doctrine. On the contrary, the question presented by this case is an open one, and our Fourteenth Amendment precedents may be read more broadly or narrowly depending upon how one chooses to read them. Faced with the choice, I would adopt a "sympathetic" reading, one which comports with dictates of fundamental justice and recognizes that compassion need not be exiled from the province of judging. Cf. A. Stone, Law, Psychiatry, and Morality 262 (1984) ("We will make mistakes if we go forward, but doing nothing can be the worst mistake. What is required of us is moral ambition. Until our composite sketch becomes a true portrait of humanity we must live with our uncertainty; we will grope, we will struggle, and our compassion may be our only guide and comfort").

Poor Joshua! Victim of repeated attacks by an irresponsible, bullying, cowardly, and intemperate father, and abandoned by respondents who placed him in a dangerous predicament and who knew or learned what was going on, and yet did essentially nothing except, as the Court revealingly observes, . . . "dutifully recorded these incidents in [their] files." It is a sad commentary upon American life, and constitutional principles—so full of late of patriotic fervor and proud proclamations about "liberty and justice for all"—that this child, Joshua DeShaney, now is assigned to live out the remainder of his life profoundly retarded. . . .

From *DeShaney v. Winnebago County Department of Social Services* (1989) 489 US 189, pp. 194–197, 204–205, 211–212 (Brennan, J. dissenting); 212–213 (Blackmun, J. dissenting).

READING 6-5
Responsibilities
"The Missing Language of Responsibility" (1991)

Mary Ann Glendon

[T]he . . . Chief Justice's statement in *DeShaney* could easily sound like an endorsement of an image of government that the United States decisively repudiated in the 1930s. Though we as a nation are committed in principle and in fact (if not to the same degree as other liberal democracies) to the education of the young, the protection of public health and safety, and assistance to the needy, the Court's language might suggest otherwise. The above passage all too readily lends itself to the interpretation that we are (in the Court's view) a nation of strangers—a nation that *in principle* leaves the helpless to their own devices. This potential for misunderstanding was compounded by the fact that Chief Justice Rehnquist described the events of the *DeShaney* case as having occurred in what he called the "free world": "While the State may have been aware of the dangers that Joshua faced in the free world, it played no part in their creation, nor did it do anything to render him any more vulnerable to them." The Chief Justice seems to have meant no more than to emphasize here the distinction between a "public" realm of governmental regulation, and a "private" realm where individuals are left free of state coercion. But "free world" was a most unfortunate choice of words to designate the hell of pain and terror from which a helpless little boy had no escape.

The United States long ago rejected a vision of the separation between public and private ordering that would leave the weak completely at the mercy of the strong. Like the shocking rescue cases in tort law, however, the *DeShaney* decision is apt to give the appearance of legitimating a failure to come to the aid of a fellow human being in distress. This aspect of the legal language that was used to refuse relief to Mr. Yania's widow [no duty to rescue drowning victim if not responsible for peril], to the survivors of the Joliet accident victims [a policeman has no duty to rescue accident victims], and to Joshua DeShaney, no doubt was unnoticed by the judges involved. Court opinions are, after all, primarily addressed to a specialized interpretive community, rather than to the litigants whose interests are directly affected, or to the broader public. Among lawyers, the denial of a civil damage remedy is regarded as neutral on the question of whether some obligation other than a legal one existed. Lawyers understand, too, that not every important problem can or should be "constitutionalized." Where the *DeShaney* opinion is to be faulted primarily is that it failed to take into consideration the increasing influence of legal discourse, especially the Supreme Court's constitutional discourse, on political discussion generally. . . .

As in the case of individual duties to rescue, it is instructive to cast a glance at how other countries to which we commonly compare ourselves conceive of governmental obligations to come to the aid of the needy. One factor that distinguishes the American welfare state from many others is the absence of a *constitutional* commitment to affirmatively protect the well-being of citizens. In most nations of Western Europe, programs such as old-age pensions, national health insurance, and unemployment compensation enjoy constitutional protection on a par with that accorded to such individual rights as property and free speech. The comparative constitutional law scholar Gerhard Casper, commenting on Chief Justice Rehnquist's statement in *DeShaney* that the Due Process Clauses confer no affirmative rights to government aid even where necessary to secure life, liberty, or property, has written: "It is very difficult to imagine any European Court possessed of the power of judicial review [making] a stark statement of this kind." The main reason this is so is that, when West European countries moved closer to the American concept of constitutionalism after World War II by adding

Bills of Rights to their constitutions, they also carried forward their own prior notions of the affirmative responsibilities of the state. Most of the newer European constitutions, unlike our eighteenth-century charter, expressly supplement "negative" rights (protections *against* government) with affirmative constitutional commitments to the protection of the health and welfare of citizens. These "positive rights" reflect the view that the state has a duty not only to refrain from violating the rights of its citizens, but affirmatively to promote their welfare through intervention in the economy and through insuring a minimum level of well-being to all.

At first glance, then, the gulf might seem great between European-style constitutional commitments to a social welfare state and the American constitutional regime of negative liberties. Chief Justice Rehnquist's opinion in the *DeShaney* case does contrast sharply with, say, the West German Constitutional Court's recent dictum that the state is obliged not only to offer minimum subsistence to those citizens who need it, but to create social conditions enabling or empowering individuals to pursue a dignified life. In practice, however, the opposition is less than the language used would suggest. For proclamations of social and economic rights in the constitutions of other nations do not give rise to directly enforceable rights of individuals. They are, rather, what European lawyers call "programmatic rights," statements of public goals and social aspirations whose implementation must await legislative or executive action, and budgetary appropriations. The European welfare states, like our own, are composed of complex statutory networks of social services, networks constructed through ordinary legislative politics. . . .

The principal virtue of the European constitutional formulations, however, does not lie in what is most obvious—their relatively greater attentiveness to the economic and social responsibilities of the state. After all, a mere commitment to social assistance from cradle to grave can lead to relaxed vigilance concerning who is eligible for the cradle and who is ready for the grave. It is, rather, that they keep responsibilities—of citizens and the state alike—prominently in view, along with rights. The place accorded to responsibilities by American and continental legal systems, respectively, seems related importantly to the shape of the welfare state in each country—its basic commitments, the spirit in which it is administered, the degree of support and approval it receives from taxpayers, and the extent to which it disables or empowers those who depend on it.

This comparative excursus [digression] is not intended to suggest that our Constitution needs amendment, or that European social welfare states could or should serve as models for law reform here. That is far from my intent. The point, once again, is to suggest that language does matter, and that, under modern American circumstances, legal language matters more than ever. This being so, we need to consider the likelihood that old legal language and old legal silences may be acquiring new and unfortunate meanings in a society whose rights talk is filled with uprooted law talk. . . .

Ineffective Rights
"Wrong Rights" (1987)

Elizabeth H. Wolgast

If the basic units of society are discrete and autonomous individuals, that fact must determine the way they should be treated. Thus it is a natural step from atomism to the concept of individual rights, rights that will attach to each individual regardless of his or her characteristics. As persons are independent, so their rights will be defined in a framework of independence. And as the indistinguishable atoms are equal, so their rights need to be equal. The concept of individual rights is a natural adjunct to atomism.

The language of rights is also a way of looking at wrongs, a conceptual grid, a schema. It both gives us a sense of *how* wrongs are wrong and points to the way to address them, that is, by establishing a right. Although it is a powerful and useful tool, still the schema of rights is sometimes unfit for the uses we make of it. It can bind us to a senseless stance, stereotype our reasoning, and lead to remedies that are grotesque. Our commitment to this language is deep, however; even in the face of bizarre consequences we hold it fast and view the consequent problems as demands for further rights. Thus our reasoning often goes on in an enclosed framework of rights, a framework from which counterexamples are excluded a priori. What does this commitment to rights mean to us, and how can it be sensibly limited? . . .

The language in which Feinberg [Reading 6-1] praises rights is recognizably atomistic. He thinks of individuals as independent units whose self-respect is of prime important to them *as* separate entities. Further, their capacity to claim rights is an important part of their active pursuit of their own interests. In such ways the language of rights both confirms the main features of the atomistic model and relies on its implicit values.

My claim is that such a conception of individuals and their rights may not be an effective means of addressing some injustices.

III

Consider the issue of the maltreatment of patients by doctors and medical staff in hospitals. In a hospital a patient is entirely at the mercy of medical people, whose expertise and positions give them great power, and so they are vulnerable to abuses of that power. The patient who is weak and frightened is by definition dependent on the staff; and they, in virtue of their practical knowledge and ability, are in the position of his rescuers—can instruct him and help him to survive. Abuse of such power and authority is, in view of the patient's helplessness, a frightening possibility. . . .

Here's the problem, then. The patient is weak, frightened, helpless, but needs to be treated in many ways as a normal person—needs to be respected, even in his wishes regarding treatment, and ultimately perhaps in his wish to die or to be sent home uncured. The issue may be addressed in various ways, but the most common way of dealing with it is to say that the patient has a *right* to respectful and considerate treatment, a right to have his wishes in regard to his treatment respected, a right to be informed about the character of his treatment, and so on. To force upon him decisions he might not accept if he weren't ill and dependent is then to subject him to a kind of domination. It is as if the patient could be mistreated *because he is ill,* and that thought recalls Samuel Butler's grotesque society Erewhon, where illness is a crime demanding punishment. There a judge trying a case of pulmonary congestion pronounces, "You may say that it is your misfortune to be criminal; I answer that it is your crime to be unfortunate."

In the wake of protests over mistreatment of patients, the American Hospital Association instituted a code of patients' rights which has been widely adopted in this country. . . .

Someone who presses a claim and demands respect for his rights does so from the stance of a peer vis-à-vis the one complained against, as Feinberg says; but the doctor-patient relationship is not one of peers. As one writer [H. Tristram Engelhardt] observes, "strong statements of patient rights imply a parity between physician and patient not usually possible in the situations under which . . . physician-patient relationships are developed." The patient needs the doctor; the doctor doesn't in the same way need him. Moreover, the patient "often enters into the arms of medicine as one might enter passionately into the arms of a lover—with great haste and need, but little forethought"; thus by definition a cool consideration of his situation is excluded. Once recovered and out of the hospital, *then* the patient can exercise his rights—take the doctor and hospital administrator to court and sue for damages. But this remedy is no remedy at all. What a sick and dependent person needs is responsible treatment from others *while he is unable to press claims against anyone.* . . .

IV

Another area where rights are spoken of commonly but, as I will claim, inappropriately is the matter of children. The idea that children have a set of rights that their parents ought to respect is prompted by the prevalence of child neglect and child abuse, wrongs that undeniably exist. It's not in doubt that something needs to be done about such wrongs; wrongs are no less wrong when the perpetrators are the victim's own parents. Nonetheless, parents who abuse children present a difficult problem for the community.

The difficulty is with the strategy of putting rights in the hands of dependent children, rights they must exercise if they can against *those on whom they depend.* As with patients' rights, the model applied here is that of two equal and independent peers in a voluntary relationship—like that of parties to a contract. But that model doesn't fit this case. The child doesn't enter into its relationship with its parents voluntarily and isn't independent or a peer in relation to its parents. The main features of atomism are absent in this relationship. . . .

A deeper question about the language of rights needs to be raised: Why, whenever we deal with a wrongful act or practice, do we feel impelled to refer to some right or other? Besides the influence of atomism, we think of a right as a justification for condemning something as wrong. Feinberg, for instance, says that claim rights are prior to and thus more basic than the duties with which they are correlated [Reading 6-1]. Thus they give a foundation for the demand that someone do or refrain from doing something and justify condemnation by showing the action as a violation of a (prior) right.

In practice the reasoning works like this. Burglary is wrong, everyone agrees; but what justifies us in calling it wrong? Some answer must exist, and one reasonable possibility is that it's wrong because a person has a right not to be burglarized, not to have his property invaded, abused, or stolen. Similarly we say that mugging is wrong, and then defend this judgment by arguing that it is wrong because a person has a right to walk down the street safely. Along these lines, murder is wrong because a person has a right to life; slander is wrong because a person has a right to be treated with respect; and so on. Rights proliferate as we seek justifications for every variety of things condemnable as wrong.

If justifications are needed, then the invocation of rights may make sense, but are such justifications necessary? Isn't murder simply wrong, wrong in itself? A common-sense answer might be yes—why should one need to justify such an obvious judgment? And if we reflect on the logical path that brought us here, we see that it is our conviction that we are justified in calling murder wrong that makes us sure that something must *justify* our judgment. We are of course justified; but does our justification imply that some separate justification lies behind it? What would happen if none did?

"Wrong Rights," *The Hypatia,* Winter '87. Copyright 1987 by Elizabeth Wolgast. Reprinted by permission of Indiana University Press.

DISCUSSION ISSUES

1. *Politics and Rights.* Legal scholars, primarily those associated with critical legal studies, have developed a radical critique of rights. Mark Tushnet (1984), for example, finds rights talk unstable and indeterminate. He says that given the abstract, vague nature of rights, slight changes in the social setting or modifications of judicial interpretation undermine a right's claim. Further, according to Tushnet, rights have a harmful side. The First Amendment protects the privileged's investments in politics and gives them control of politics. The Constitution opens streets and parks to the public to exercise free speech, but does not open the media to the public (see Reading 5-9). The streets and parks, used primarily by those with little political clout, have less political value than the media, which is controlled by those with power. Tushnet's attack on rights met stern resistance. Feminists and critical race theorists, in particular, accused him of throwing the proverbial baby out with the bath water (Williams 1991). His critics note that often those who are already privileged (for example, white males)

can afford to discard rights. Should those outside the political mainstream formulate their demands with rights language?

2. *Rights and Cultural Relativism.* Does it make sense to talk about rights that apply universally? Should individuals have different rights depending on their cultural attachments **(normative cultural relativism)?** The *Shari'a,* or divine law, derived from the *Qur'an* (a collection of sayings of the prophet, Mohammed), regulates Muslim life. The acceptance of the *Shari'a* makes a person a Muslim. Iran introduced many aspects of the *Shari'a* into its legal system. According to the *Shari'a,* a Muslim who repudiates Islam stands guilty of an offense (apostasy) that is punishable by death. Writer Salman Rushdie, in *The Satanic Verses,* ridiculed the *Qur'an* and described it as "a book 'sprouting' rules about how to 'fart', 'f——' and 'clean one's behind', and why only two sexual positions are legitimate, one of them being sodomy" (Parekh in Kymlicka 1995, p. 306). As a result, Iran's Iman Khomeini pronounced a death sentence *(fatawa)* on Rushdie. He responded that freedom of expression disappears without a writer's unrestrained right to offend. What justifications does Rushdie have for demanding a universal right to offend the holy books of another religion? (See also chapter 5, Discussion Issues, question 8, page 267 on Rushdie's free speech claim.)

3. *Group Rights.* Do groups, communities, and cultures have rights? In granting a partial exemption from compulsory schooling to the Amish, did the Supreme Court grant a right of certain groups to socialize their members (*Wisconsin v. Yoder* 1972 see pages 287–288)? How far do group rights extend? "David Thomas, a member of the Lyackson Indian Band in British Columbia, was forcibly and without consent captured and initiated into the ceremony of 'spirit dancing', in the course of which he was assaulted, battered, and wrongfully confined" (Green in Kymlicka 1995, p. 109). Should members of "internal minorities" have rights enforceable against their group?

C. TYPES OF RIGHTS

[N]or shall any State deprive any person of life, liberty, or property, without due process of law.
—Due Process Clause, Fourteenth Amendment, U.S. Constitution

1. Procedural Due Process

"Due process of law" gives process (procedures) that is due (fair). Read literally, the **due process clause** of the Fourteenth Amendment regulates procedures, thereby prohibiting the government from procedural irregularities in important matters. When a state initiates the process of taking someone's life in a capital punishment case, the due process clause requires the state to use fair procedures. Similarly, due process entitles a welfare recipient to an evidentiary hearing before benefits are terminated. These examples involve **procedural due process.** The due process clause, on the surface, says nothing about privacy rights, but rather, seems to cover only procedural rights. To understand the move from a clause that deals with procedural rights to one that grants privacy rights requires (depending on your viewpoint) a leap of faith or a historical understanding of the U.S. Supreme Court jurisprudence.

The Supreme Court has interpreted the due process clause not so much as a limitation on procedures but as a limitation on the state's substantive power to regulate its citizens' lives. The interpretation of due process beyond a concern for procedures is labeled **substantive due process.** Read literally, substantive due process gives substance to due process. During the so-called **Lochner Era** (1897–1937), the Court focused on the economic areas of life, reviewing the policy or substance (and not just the procedures) of state economic regulation (Reading 3-12). It has since abandoned its focus on economic interests and has turned to noneconomic ones. The Court has expanded the liberties found in the Bill of Rights (the first ten amendments to the Constitution), calling these **"fundamental rights."** It described these rights as "deeply rooted in this Nation's history and tradition" and "implicit in the concept of ordered liberty such that neither liberty nor justice would exist if they were sacrificed." Fundamental rights, then, have a historical and universal dimension. Thus, the Court gave substance to due process, so jurists now use the expression "substantive due process." The Court has fashioned privacy rights and abortion rights out of its substantive due process analysis, and it has entertained a similar analysis for a right to die.

D. CONTROVERSIES: PRIVACY, ABORTION, AND DEATH

1. Privacy Rights

The idea of fundamental rights provides a critical link to privacy rights. Building on a series of cases, the Court declared that fundamental rights include the **right to privacy.** The type of privacy addressed in this section should be distinguished from other types of privacy. First, a tort law sense of privacy emerged from an 1890 *Harvard Law Review* article by Samuel D. Warren and Louis D. Brandeis (later, a Supreme Court Justice). Warren, a wealthy paper manufacturer, was outraged by nosey newspaper reporters and gossip that followed a family wedding. As a result, in tort law, an individual can now sue other individuals for invasion of privacy. Second, a constitutional criminal law sense of privacy protects individuals from law enforcement, including unreasonable searches and seizures prohibited by the Fourth Amendment. Third, a constitutional noncriminal sense of privacy, addressed in this section, protects individuals in making certain important decisions about themselves.

Philosophers have struggled with whether a single theory unifies these different senses of privacy. Before analyzing privacy from philosophical and legal perspectives, consider why we should value privacy. Dystopian (the opposite of utopian) literature might provide some answers. **George Orwell's** *1984* describes a totalitarian society with no place to hide and no privacy (Reading 6-7). In Oceania, the fictional setting for *1984,* "war is peace," "freedom is slavery," and "ignorance is strength." The Thought Police see every move that is made and hear every sound that is whispered. Signs read, "BIG

BROTHER IS WATCHING YOU." The book symbolizes the complete loss of privacy. The government should not have control over everything an individual thinks or does, but should the government control some individual actions? If so, what actions should the government restrict? As discussed in chapter 5, John Stuart Mill's harm principle provided one modern liberal solution to the problem of justifying government interference. If what an individual does threatens to harm others, then the government has grounds for interference. Otherwise, the government should not interfere with self-regarding actions—that is, actions that affect only the individual involved. In other words, the government should leave individuals alone unless their conduct harms others. Protecting individual privacy protects autonomy. Again, let us turn to Mill:

> [T]he sole end for which mankind are warranted individually or collectively, in interfering with the liberty of action of any of their number is self-protection. *That the only purpose for which power can be rightfully exercised over any member of a civilized community, against his will, is to prevent harm to others.* His own good, either physical or moral, is not a sufficient warrant. He cannot rightfully be compelled to do or to forbear because it will be better for him to do so, because it will make him happier, because, in the opinions of others, to do so would be wise or even right. These are good reasons for remonstrating with him, or reasoning with him, or persuading him, or entreating him, but not for compelling him or visiting him with any evil in case he do otherwise. To justify that, the conduct from which it is desired to deter him must be calculated to produce evil to someone else. The only part of the conduct of anyone for which he is amenable to society is that which concerns others. In the part which merely concerns himself, his independence is, of right, absolute. Over himself over his own body and mind, the individual is sovereign. (1860 in 1956, p. 13)

Although the Court in *Skinner v. Oklahoma* (1942) does not mention the right of privacy, the case played an important role in developing the right to privacy (see Reading 6-8). The Court struck down Oklahoma's Habitual Sterilization Act that authorized sterilization of inmates convicted at least twice of felonies involving "moral turpitude." Skinner had the following convictions: stealing chickens (1926) and robbery with firearms (1929 and 1934). The Court found that the Habitual Sterilization Act led to unequal punishment for offenses that were basically the same. The act exempted embezzlement, so a clerk stealing from his employer's cashbox could never face sterilization, no matter how large or how frequent the embezzlement. An individual convicted three times for stealing chickens, however, could be sterilized. The Court found the nature of the punishment even more objectionable than the inequalities in application. Sterilization laws, according to the Court, affected something deeply personal—namely marriage and procreation. Compare *Skinner,* decided in 1942, with *Buck v. Bell,* decided in 1927, which upheld a sterilization law that targeted "mental defectives" (see Reading 3-13).

Griswold v. Connecticut (1965) brought the right of privacy into full bloom (see Reading 6-9). The state charged the medical director of Planned Parenthood of Connecticut with counseling married couples to use contraceptives. The Court invalidated a ban on the use of contraceptives by married couples and on counseling married couples concerning their use. Justice Douglas found a protected zone of privacy throughout the Constitution (right against unreasonable searches and seizures, freedom of association, etc.). The right of privacy, according to Douglas, protects the "intimate relation of husband and wife, and their physician's role in one aspect of that relationship." Privacy, then, seems to protect certain decisions about an individual's life, although some critics found Douglas creating a right out of thin air to justify his values.

When President Ronald Reagan appointed Robert Bork to the Supreme Court, Bork gained notoriety for his spirited attack on judicial activism during his unsuccessful Senate confirmation hearing. He contended that the Supreme Court failed to justify finding a right to privacy from an unbiased reading of the text of the Constitution (see Reading 6-10).

READING 6-7

Privacy and BIG BROTHER
1984 (1949)

George Orwell

It was a bright cold day in April, and the clocks were striking thirteen. Winston Smith, his chin nuzzled into his breast in an effort to escape the vile wind, slipped quickly through the glass doors of Victory Mansions, though not quickly enough to prevent a swirl of gritty dust from entering along with him.

The hallway smelt of boiled cabbage and old rag mats. At one end of it a colored poster, too large for indoor display, had been tacked to the wall. It depicted simply an enormous face, more than a meter wide: the face of a man of about forty-five, with a heavy black mustache and ruggedly handsome features. Winston made for the stairs. It was no use trying the lift. Even at the best of times it was seldom working, and at present the electric current was cut off during daylight hours. It was part of the economy drive in preparation for Hate Week. The flat was seven flights up, and Winston, who was thirty-nine, and had a varicose ulcer above his right ankle, went slowly, resting several times on the way. On each landing, opposite the lift shaft, the poster with the enormous face gazed from the wall. It was one of those pictures which are so contrived that the eyes follow you about when you move. BIG BROTHER IS WATCHING YOU, the caption beneath it ran.

Inside the flat a fruity voice was reading out a list of figures which had something to do with the production of pig iron. The voice came from an oblong metal plaque like a dulled mirror which formed part of the surface of the right-hand wall. Winston turned a switch and the voice sank somewhat, though the words were still distinguishable. The instrument (the telescreen, it was called) could be dimmed, but there was no way of shutting it off completely. He moved over to the window: a smallish, frail figure, the meagerness of his body merely emphasized by the blue overalls which were the uniform of the Party. His hair was very fair, his face naturally sanguine, his skin roughened by coarse soap and blunt razor blades and the cold of the winter that had just ended.

Outside, even through the shut window pane, the world looked cold. Down in the street little eddies of wind were whirling dust and torn paper into spirals, and though the sun was shining and the sky a harsh blue, there seemed to be no color in anything except the posters that were plastered everywhere. The black-mustachio'd face gazed down from every commanding corner. There was one on the house front immediately opposite. *Big Brother Is Watching You,* the caption said, while the dark eyes looked deep into Winston's own. Down at street level another poster, torn at one corner, flapped fitfully in the wind, alternately covering and uncovering the single word INGSOC. In the far distance a helicopter skimmed down between the roofs, hovered for an instant like a blue-bottle, and darted away again with a curving flight. It was the Police Patrol, snooping into people's windows. The patrols did not matter, however. Only the Thought Police mattered.

Behind Winston's back the voice from the telescreen was still babbling away about pig iron and the overfulfillment of the Ninth Three-Year Plan. The telescreen received and transmitted simultaneously. Any sound that Winston made, above the level of a very low whisper, would be picked up by it; moreover, so long as he remained within the field of vision which the metal plaque commanded, he could be seen as well as heard. There was of course no way of knowing whether you were being watched at any given moment. How often, or on what system, the Thought Police plugged in on any individual wire was guesswork. It was even conceivable that they watched everybody all the time. But at any rate they could plug in your wire whenever they wanted to. You had to live—did live, from habit that became instinct—in the assumption that every sound you made was overheard, and, except in darkness, every movement scrutinized.

Winston kept his back turned to the telescreen. It was safer; though, as he well knew, even a back can be revealing. A kilometer away the Ministry of Truth, his place of work, towered vast and white above the grimy landscape. This, he thought with a sort of vague distaste—this was London, chief city of Airstrip One, itself the third most populous of the provinces of Oceania. He tried to squeeze out some childhood memory that should tell him whether London had always been quite like this. Were there always these vistas of rotting nineteenth-century houses, their sides shored up with balks of timber, their windows patched with cardboard and their roofs with corrugated iron, their crazy garden walls sagging in all directions? And the bombed sites where the plaster dust swirled in the air and the willow herb straggled over the heaps of rubble; and the places where the bombs had cleared a larger path and there had sprung up sordid colonies of wooden dwellings like chicken houses? But it was no use, he could not remember: nothing remained of his childhood except a series of bright-lit tableaux, occurring against no background and mostly unintelligible.

The Ministry of Truth—Minitrue, in Newspeak [Oceania's official language]—was startlingly different from any other object in sight. It was an enormous pyramidal structure of glittering white concrete, soaring up, terrace after terrace, three hundred meters into the air. From where Winston stood it was just possible to read, picked out on its white face in elegant lettering, the three slogans of the Party:

WAR IS PEACE

FREEDOM IS SLAVERY

IGNORANCE IS STRENGTH.

319

CHAPTER 6
Rights

The Ministry of Truth contained, it was said, three thousand rooms above ground level, and corresponding ramifications below. . . .

READING 6-8

Privacy and Sterilization
Skinner v. Oklahoma (1942)

JUSTICE WILLIAM O. DOUGLAS

But the instant legislation runs afoul of the equal protection clause, though we give Oklahoma that large deference which the rule of the foregoing cases requires. We are dealing here with legislation which involves one of the basic civil rights of man. Marriage and procreation are fundamental to the very existence and survival of the race. The power to sterilize, if exercised, may have subtle, far-reaching and devastating effects. In evil or reckless hands it can cause races or types which are inimical to the dominant group to wither and disappear. There is no redemption for the individual whom the law touches. Any experiment which the State conducts is to his irreparable injury. He is forever deprived of a basic liberty. We mention these matters not to reëxamine the scope of the police power of the States. We advert to them merely in emphasis of our view that strict scrutiny of the classification [see page 371] which a State makes in a sterilization law is essential, lest unwittingly, or otherwise, invidious discriminations are made against groups or types of individuals in violation of the constitutional guaranty of just and equal laws. The guaranty of "equal protection of the laws is a pledge of the protection of equal laws." . . . When the law lays an unequal hand on those who have committed intrinsically the same quality of offense and sterilizes one and not the other, it has made as invidious a discrimination as if it had selected a particular race or nationality for oppressive treatment. . . . Sterilization of those who have thrice committed grand larceny [unlawful taking of something of high value], with immunity for those who are embezzlers [unlawful taking after lawful acquisition, e.g., from employer], is a clear, pointed, unmistakable discrimination. Oklahoma makes no attempt to say that he who commits larceny by trespass or trick or fraud has biologically inheritable traits which he who commits embezzlement lacks. Oklahoma's line between larceny by fraud and embezzlement is determined, as we have noted, "with reference to the time when the fraudulent intent to convert the property to the taker's own use" arises. . . . We have not the slightest basis for inferring that that line has any significance in eugenics [see page 135], nor that the inheritability of criminal traits follows the neat legal distinctions which the law has marked between those two offenses. In terms of fines and imprisonment, the crimes of larceny and embezzlement rate the same under the Oklahoma code. Only when it comes to sterilization are the pains and penalties of the law different. The equal protection clause would indeed be a formula of empty words if such conspicuously artificial lines could be drawn. . . . In *Buck v. Bell* [Reading 3-13], the Virginia statute was upheld though it applied only to feeble-minded persons in institutions of the State. But it was pointed out that "so far as the operations enable those who otherwise must be kept confined to be returned to the world, and thus open the asylum to others, the equality aimed at will be more nearly reached.". . . Here there is no such saving feature. Embezzlers are forever free. Those who steal or take in other ways are not. If such a classification were permitted, the technical common law concept of a "trespass" . . . based on distinctions which are "very largely dependent upon history for explanation" . . . could readily become a rule of human genetics. . . .

From *Skinner v. Oklahoma* (1942) 316 US 535, pp. 541–542.

READING 6-9

Privacy and Contraceptives
Griswold v. Connecticut (1965)

JUSTICE WILLIAM O. DOUGLAS

The foregoing cases suggest that specific guarantees in the Bill of Rights have penumbras [partial illuminations], formed by emanations [lights] from those guarantees that help give them life and substance. . . . Various guarantees create zones of privacy. The right of association contained in the penumbra of the First Amendment is one, as we have seen. The Third Amendment in its prohibition against the quartering of soldiers "in any house" in time of peace without the consent of the owner is another facet of that privacy. The Fourth Amendment explicitly affirms the "right of the people to be secure in their persons, houses, papers, and effects, against unreasonable searches and seizures." The Fifth Amendment in its Self-Incrimination Clause enables the citizen to create a zone of privacy which government may not force him to surrender to his detriment. The Ninth Amendment provides: "The enumeration in the Constitution, of certain rights, shall not be construed to deny or disparage others retained by the people."

The Fourth and Fifth Amendments were described in *Boyd* . . . as protection against all governmental invasions "of the sanctity of a man's home and the privacies of life." We recently referred in *Mapp v. Ohio* . . . to the Fourth Amendment as creating a "right to privacy, no less important than any other right carefully and particularly reserved to the people.". . .

We have had many controversies over these penumbral rights of "privacy and repose.". . . These cases bear witness that the right of privacy which presses for recognition here is a legitimate one.

The present case, then, concerns a relationship lying within the zone of privacy created by several fundamental constitutional guarantees. And it concerns a law which, in forbidding the *use* of contraceptives rather than regulating their manufacture or sale, seeks to achieve its goals by means having a maximum destructive impact upon that relationship. Such a law cannot stand in light of the familiar principle, so often applied by this Court, that a "governmental purpose to control or prevent activities constitutionally subject to state regulation may not be achieved by means which sweep unnecessarily broadly and thereby invade the area of protected freedoms." *(NAACP v. Alabama)*. . . . Would we allow the police to search the sacred precincts of marital bedrooms for telltale signs of the use of contraceptives? The very idea is repulsive to the notions of privacy surrounding the marriage relationship.

We deal with a right of privacy older than the Bill of Rights—older than our political parties, older than our school system. Marriage is a coming together for better or for worse, hopefully enduring, and intimate to the degree of being sacred. It is an association that promotes a way of life, not causes; a harmony in living, not political faiths; a bilateral loyalty, not commercial or social projects. Yet it is an association for as noble a purpose as any involved in our prior decisions. . . .

From *Griswold v. Connecticut* (1965) 381 US 479, pp. 484–486.

READING 6-10

Privacy Outside the Constitution
"Neutral Principles and Some First Amendment Problems" (1967)

Robert Bork

We have not carried the idea of neutrality far enough. We have been talking about neutrality in the *application* of principles. If judges are to avoid imposing their own values upon the rest of us, however, they must be neutral as well in the *definition* and the *derivation* of principles.

It is easy enough to meet the requirement of neutral application by stating a principle so narrowly that no embarrassment need arise in applying it to all cases it subsumes, a tactic often urged by proponents of "judicial restraint." But that solves very little. It certainly does not protect the judge from the intrusion of his own values. The problem may be illustrated by *Griswold v. Connecticut* [Reading 6-9], in many ways a typical decision of the Warren Court. *Griswold* struck down Connecticut's statute making it a crime, even for married couples, to use contraceptive devices. If we take the principle of the decision to be a statement that government may not interfere with any acts done in private, we need not even ask about the principle's dubious origin for we know at once that the Court will not apply it neutrally. The Court, we may confidently predict, is not going to throw constitutional protection around heroin use or sexual acts with a consenting minor. We can gain the possibility of neutral application by reframing the principle as a statement that government may not prohibit the use of contraceptives by married couples, but that is not enough. The question of neutral definition arises: Why does the principle extend only to married couples? Why, out of all forms of sexual behavior, only to the use of contraceptives? Why, out of all forms of behavior, only to sex? The question of neutral derivation also arises: What justifies any limitation upon legislatures in this area? What is the origin of any principle one may state?

To put the matter another way, if a neutral judge must demonstrate why principle *X* applies to cases *A* and *B* but not to case *C* (which is, I believe, the requirement laid down by Professors Wechsler [Reading 7-5] and Jaffe), he must, by the same token, also explain why the principle is defined as *X* rather than as *X minus,* which would cover *A* but not cases *B* and *C,* or as *X plus,* which would cover all cases, *A, B* and *C.* Similarly, he must explain why *X* is a proper principle of limitation on majority power at all. Why should he not choose *non-X?* If he may not choose lawlessly between cases in applying principle *X,* he may certainly not choose lawlessly in defining *X* or in choosing *X,* for principles are after all only organizations of cases into groups. To choose the principle and define it is to decide the cases.

It follows that the choice of "fundamental values" by the Court cannot be justified. Where constitutional materials do not clearly specify the value to be preferred, there is no principled way to prefer any claimed human value to any other. The judge must stick close to the text and the history, and their fair implications, and not construct new rights. The case just mentioned illustrates the point. The *Griswold* decision has been acclaimed by legal scholars as a major advance in constitutional law, a salutary [welcomed] demonstration of the Court's ability to protect fundamental human values. I regret to have to disagree, and my regret is all the more sincere because I once took the same position and did so in print. In extenuation I can only say that at the time I thought, quite erroneously, that new basic rights could be derived logically by finding and extrapolating a more general principle of individual autonomy underlying the particular guarantees of the Bill of Rights.

The Court's *Griswold* opinion, by Justice Douglas, and the array of concurring opinions, by Justices Goldberg, White and Harlan, all failed to justify the derivation of any principle used to strike down the Connecticut anti-contraceptive statute or to define the scope of the principle. Justice Douglas, to whose opinion I must confine myself, began by pointing out that "specific guarantees in the Bill of Rights have penumbras, formed by emanations from those guarantees that help give them life and substance." Nothing is exceptional there. In the case Justice Douglas cited, *NAACP v. Alabama,* the State was held unable to force disclosure of membership lists because of the chilling effect upon the rights of assembly and political action of the NAACP's members. The penumbra was created solely to preserve a value central to the first amendment, applied in this case through the fourteenth amendment. It had no life of its own as a right independent of the value specified by the first amendment.

But Justice Douglas then performed a miracle of transubstantiation [the actual change of bread and wine into the body and blood of Christ]. He called the first amendment's penumbra a protection of "privacy" and then asserted that other amendments create "zones of privacy." He had no better reason to use the word "privacy" than that the individual is free within these zones, free to act in public as well as in private. None of these penumbral zones—from the first, third, fourth or fifth amendments, all of which he cited, along with the ninth—covered the case before him. One more leap was required. Justice Douglas asserted that these various "zones of privacy" created an independent right of privacy, a right not lying within the penumbra of any specific amendment. He did not disclose, however, how a series of specified rights combined to create a new and unspecified right.

The *Griswold* opinion fails every test of neutrality. The derivation of the principle was utterly specious, and so was its definition. In fact, we are left with no idea of what the principle really forbids. Derivation and definition are interrelated here. Justice Douglas called the amendments and their penumbras "zones of privacy," though of course they are not that at all. They protect both private and public behavior and so would more properly be labelled "zones of freedom." If we follow Justice Douglas in his next step, these zones would then add up to an independent right of freedom, which is to say, a general constitutional right to be free of legal coercion, a manifest impossibility in any imaginable society.

Griswold, then, is an unprincipled decision, both in the way in which it derives a new constitutional right and in the way it defines that right, or rather fails to define it. We are left with no idea of the sweep of the right of privacy and hence no notion of the cases to which it may or may not be applied in the future. The truth is that the Court could not reach its result in *Griswold* through principle. The reason is obvious. Every clash between a minority claiming freedom and a majority claiming power to regulate involves a choice between the gratifications of the two groups. When the Constitution has not spoken, the Court will be able to find no scale, other than its own value preferences, upon which to weigh the respective claims to pleasure. Compare the facts in *Griswold* with a hypothetical suit by an electric utility company and one of its customers to void a smoke pollution ordinance as unconstitutional. The cases are identical.

In *Griswold* a husband and wife assert that they wish to have sexual relations without fear of unwanted children. The law impairs their sexual gratifications. The State can assert, and at one stage in that litigation did assert, that the majority finds the use of contraceptives immoral. Knowledge that it takes place and that the State makes no effort to inhibit it causes the majority anguish, impairs their gratifications.

The electrical company asserts that it wishes to produce electricity at low cost in order to reach a wide market and make profits. Its customer asserts that he wants a lower cost so that prices can be held low. The smoke pollution regulation impairs his and the company's stockholders' economic gratifications. The State can assert not only that the majority prefer clean air to lower prices, but also that the absence of the regulation impairs the majority's physical and aesthetic gratifications.

Neither case is covered specifically or by obvious implication in the Constitution. Unless we can distinguish forms of gratification, the only course for a principled Court is to let the majority have its way in both cases. It is clear that the Court cannot make the necessary distinction. There is no principled way to decide that one man's gratifications are more deserving of respect than another's or that one form of gratification is more worthy than another. Why is sexual gratification more worthy than moral gratification?

Why is sexual gratification nobler than economic gratification? There is no way of deciding these matters other than by reference to some system of moral or ethical values that has no objective or intrinsic validity of its own and about which men can and do differ. Where the Constitution does not embody the moral or ethical choice, the judge has no basis other than his own values upon which to set aside the community judgment embodied in the statute. That, by definition, is an inadequate basis for judicial supremacy. The issue of the community's moral and ethical values, the issue of the degree of pain an activity causes, are matters concluded by the passage and enforcement of the laws in question. The judiciary has no role to play other than that of applying the statutes in a fair and impartial manner.

One of my colleagues refers to this conclusion, not without sarcasm, as the "Equal Gratification Clause." The phrase is apt, and I accept it, though not the sarcasm. Equality of human gratifications, where the document does not impose a hierarchy, is an essential part of constitutional doctrine because of the necessity that judges be principled. To be perfectly clear on the subject, I repeat that the principle is not applicable to legislatures. Legislation requires value choice and cannot be principled in the sense under discussion. Courts must accept any value choice the legislature makes unless it clearly runs contrary to a choice made in the framing of the Constitution.

It follows, of course, that broad areas of constitutional law ought to be reformulated. Most obviously, it follows that substantive due process, revived by the *Griswold* case, is and always has been an improper doctrine. Substantive due process requires the Court to say, without guidance from the Constitution, which liberties or gratifications may be infringed by majorities and which may not. This means that *Griswold's* antecedents were also wrongly decided. . . . In *Lochner* [Reading 3-12], Justice Peckham, defending liberty from what he conceived as a mere meddlesome interference, asked, "[A]re we all . . . at the mercy of legislative majorities?" The correct answer, where the Constitution does not speak, must be "yes."

The argument so far also indicates that most of substantive equal protection is also improper. The modern Court, we need hardly be reminded, used the equal protection clause the way the old Court used the due process clause. The only change was in the values chosen for protection and the frequency with which the Court struck down laws.

The equal protection clause has two legitimate meanings. It can require formal procedural equality, and, because of its historical origins, it does require that government not discriminate along racial lines. But much more than that cannot properly be read into the clause. The bare concept of equality provides no guide for courts. All law discriminates and thereby creates inequality. The Supreme Court has no principled way of saying which non-racial inequalities are impermissible. What it has done, therefore, is to appeal to simplistic notions of "fairness" or to what it regards as "fundamental" interests in order to demand equality in some cases but not in others, thus choosing values and producing a line of cases as improper and as intellectually empty as *Griswold v. Connecticut*. . . .

1. *Paternalism.* Should the government interfere with a person's action for that person's benefit? Is "doing something for someone's own good" objectionable because the action treats an adult like a child? Consider the following laws that governments have used to protect individuals from themselves: (a) suicide as a criminal offense, (b) regulations that exclude women and children from certain dangerous jobs, and (c) prohibitions of buggery ("carnal copulation against nature; man or woman with a brute beast," *Black's Law Dictionary*) and felatio ("oral sex") (see G. Dworkin 1972). Individuals do not always act for their own benefit. What is wrong with doing something to other people for their own good? Are these laws paternalistic? What makes paternalism objectionable? Do paternalistic acts interfere with an individual's freedom and autonomy?

   Laws requiring motorcyclists to wear safety helmets while operating their machines raise questions concerning paternalism. The Oregon Supreme Court upheld a mandatory helmet law for motorcyclists (*State of Oregon v. Fetterly* 1969). The court used a **cost versus benefit** calculation (often associated with **utilitarianism,** which finds an action's value in its utility to produce pleasure or happiness). They argued that the rights of unhelmeted motorcyclists do not weigh heavily compared with the danger they pose to others. Does the government have a justified interest in protecting riders who refuse to wear helmets? Should the cost-benefit calculation include the medical expenses the state bears for serious injury in motorcycle accidents? Unlike the Oregon court, the Michigan Court of Appeals used a rights analysis. It invalidated a statute mandating that motorcyclists and their riders must wear helmets (*American Motorcycle Association v. Davids* 1968). An individual has a basic right to be left alone, and no amount of judicial fantasy should undermine that autonomy. Because the court refused to stretch its imagination, as other courts had, it could not find any public, health, safety, or welfare grounds with which to justify government interference. The court, quoting Mill, reasoned that individuals should be left alone unless they harmed others. Under what circumstances, if any, should individuals have to give up their autonomy rights?

2. *Scope of Privacy Protection.* The distinction between two distinct spheres of life—the public one and the private one—remains a mainstay of liberal philosophy. What specific activities fall under the heading of "private acts"? Do these activities fall into categories? Does domestic life qualify as a purely private affair? Either before or after *Griswold* (see Reading 6-9), could the government limit the size of a family? What did Carole Pateman mean when she said that "the dichotomy between the public and the private . . . is, ultimately, what the feminist movement is all about" (Phillips 1987, p. 103)? Do individuals have claims to privacy within a family, or does privacy attach to families as units and not to individuals (Kymlicka 1990, p. 259)?

3. *Privacy or Autonomy.* If privacy involves another person being acquainted with an individual's personal affairs, then *Griswold* (Reading 6-9) did not deal with privacy. Instead, the case addressed autonomy, which involves attempts by government to regulate personal affairs (Gross 1971). Does the argument in *Griswold* depend on one unifying sense of privacy?

4. *Privacy or Equality.* Assume the following facts are true: The enforcement of the ban on counseling and the use of birth control had its most pronounced, negative impact on the poor. Because Connecticut only enforced the bans against birth control clinics, and the clinics largely served the poor, therefore selective enforcement targeted the poor. Middle-class couples had ready access to birth control information and devices. Given these assumptions, does *Griswold* become a decision about equality and not about privacy (Shapiro, 1983) [see Reading 6-14]?

5. *Economic Versus Noneconomic Rights.* Should fundamental rights include economic (right to make contracts) and noneconomic ones (right to privacy)? Should greater protection be given to one than to the other? "[What] is it that makes my right to use contraceptives a right of Privacy, and fundamental, but my right to contract to work 16 hours a day . . . not a right of Privacy and not fundamental?" (Henkin 1974, p. 1427). For similar doubts as applied to abortion, see Ely (1973), p. 920.

2. Abortion Rights

The next step—to abortion rights—appears less mysterious, given the road from substantive due process through fundamental rights to privacy rights. The now-constitutionalized abortion debate remains heated. It not only involves complex moral considerations, but it also raises questions about the role of the judiciary in these moral debates. Are these matters best left to democratic decision makers? Should democratically elected state legislatures address controversial moral issues? What arguments favor an unelected judiciary's making moral decisions [see Reading 4-3]? Even given the judiciary's "jurisdiction" over moral matters, did it employ highly questionable concepts and reasoning in the abortion cases? The Supreme Court found that prohibitions against abortion threaten something it called privacy, yet, the things that are protected—privacy rights—seem to appear from nowhere [see Reading 6-10]. The Court in *Roe v. Wade* (1973), however, cites a progressive series of cases that establish privacy as a right (see Reading 6-11). In 1965, few people paid attention to the Court's "creation" and protection of privacy rights in *Griswold* (Reading 6-9). In a series of cases, the Court had found that fundamental personal rights include those regarding marriage, procreation, contraception, family relationships, child rearing, and education. Does the right to an abortion represent a logical extension of these? According to *Roe,* "The right of privacy . . . is broad enough to encompass a woman's decision whether or not to terminate her pregnancy." To the surprise of many, the Court upheld *Roe,* with some modifications, in *Planned Parenthood v. Casey* (1992) (see Reading 6-12).

John Noonan, formerly a law professor, now sits on the U.S. Court of Appeals, Ninth Circuit. He argues that the Court has dehumanized the unborn child in much the same way that nineteenth-century courts dehumanized slaves (see chapter 3, Controversies) by treating the idea of "person" as a legal fiction (Reading 6-13). Catherine MacKinnon has become one of the leading voices of **feminist jurisprudence,** which looks at law from a woman's perspective. She argues that abortion is an equality issue rather than a privacy issue (see Reading 6-14). The equality argument claims that laws discriminate against a group when they burden one vulnerable and underrepresented group more than another. Is there evidence that abortion laws were intended to discriminate against women or that they had a notable effect on women in particular? Are fetuses a vulnerable and under-represented group?

The Abortion Decision
Roe v. Wade (1973)

JUSTICE HARRY BLACKMUN

This right of privacy, whether it be founded in the Fourteenth Amendment's concept of personal liberty and restrictions upon state action, as we feel it is, or, as the District Court determined, in the Ninth Amendment's reservation of rights to the people, is broad enough to encompass a woman's decision whether or not to terminate her pregnancy. The detriment that the State would impose upon the pregnant woman by denying this choice altogether is apparent. Specific and direct harm medically diagnosable even in early pregnancy may be involved. Maternity, or additional offspring, may force upon the woman a distressful life and future. Psychological harm may be imminent. Mental and physical health may be taxed by child care. There is also the distress, for all concerned, associated with the unwanted child, and there is the problem of bringing a child into a family already unable, psychologically and otherwise, to care for it. In other cases, as in this one, the additional difficulties and continuing stigma of unwed motherhood may be involved. All these are factors the woman and her responsible physician necessarily will consider in consultation. . . .

The pregnant woman cannot be isolated in her privacy. She carries an embryo and, later, a fetus, if one accepts the medical definitions of the developing young in the human uterus. . . . The situation therefore is inherently different from marital intimacy, or bedroom possession of obscene material, or marriage, or procreation, or education, with which *Eisenstadt* and *Griswold, Stanley, Loving, Skinner,* and *Pierce* and *Meyer* were respectively concerned. As we have intimated above, it is reasonable and appropriate for a State to decide that at some point in time another interest, that of health of the mother or that of potential human life, becomes significantly involved. The woman's privacy is no longer sole and any right of privacy she possesses must be measured accordingly. . . .

XI

To summarize and to repeat:

1. A state criminal abortion statute of the current Texas type, that excepts from criminality only a *life-saving* procedure on behalf of the mother, without regard to pregnancy stage and without recognition of the other interests involved, is violative of the Due Process Clause of the Fourteenth Amendment.

(a) For the stage prior to approximately the end of the first trimester, the abortion decision and its effectuation must be left to the medical judgment of the pregnant woman's attending physician.

(b) For the stage subsequent to approximately the end of the first trimester, the State, in promoting its interest in the health of the mother, may, if it chooses, regulate the abortion procedure in ways that are reasonably related to maternal health.

(c) For the stage subsequent to viability, the State in promoting its interest in the potentiality of human life may, if it chooses, regulate, and even proscribe, abortion except where it is necessary, in appropriate medical judgment, for the preservation of the life or health of the mother. . . .

From *Roe v. Wade* (1973) 410 US 113, pp. 153, 159, 164–165, 172–173.

READING 6-12

The Abortion Precedent

Planned Parenthood of Southeastern Pennsylvania v. Casey (1992)

Justices O'Connor, Kennedy, and Souter

These considerations begin our analysis of the woman's interest in terminating her pregnancy but cannot end it, for this reason: though the abortion decision may originate within the zone of conscience and belief, it is more than a philosophic exercise. Abortion is a unique act. It is an act fraught with consequences for others: for the woman who must live with the implications of her decision; for the persons who perform and assist in the procedure; for the spouse, family, and society which must confront the knowledge that these procedures exist, procedures some deem nothing short of an act of violence against innocent human life; and, depending on one's beliefs, for the life or potential life that is aborted. Though abortion is conduct, it does not follow that the State is entitled to proscribe it in all instances. That is because the liberty of the woman is at stake in a sense unique to the human condition and so unique to the law. The mother who carries a child to full term is subject to anxieties, to physical constraints, to pain that only she must bear. That these sacrifices have from the beginning of the human race been endured by woman with a pride that ennobles her in the eyes of others and gives to the infant a bond of love cannot alone be grounds for the State to insist she make the sacrifice. Her suffering is too intimate and personal for the State to insist, without more, upon its own vision of the woman's role, however dominant that vision has been in the course of our history and our culture. The destiny of the woman must be shaped to a large extent on her own conception of her spiritual imperatives and her place in society.

It should be recognized, moreover, that in some critical respects the abortion decision is of the same character as the decision to use contraception, to which *Griswold v. Connecticut, Eisenstadt v. Baird,* and *Carey v. Population Services International* afford constitutional protection. We have no doubt as to the correctness of those decisions. They support the reasoning in *Roe* relating to the woman's liberty because they involve personal decisions concerning not only the meaning of procreation but also human responsibility and respect for it. As with abortion, reasonable people will have differences of opinion about these matters. One view is based on such reverence for the wonder of creation that any pregnancy ought to be welcomed and carried to full term no matter how difficult it will be to provide for the child and ensure its well-being. Another is that the inability to provide for the nurture and care of the infant is a cruelty to the child and an anguish to the parent. These are intimate views with infinite variations, and their deep, personal character underlay our decisions in *Griswold, Eisenstadt,* and *Carey.* The same concerns are present when the woman confronts the reality that, perhaps despite her attempts to avoid it, she has become pregnant.

It was this dimension of personal liberty that *Roe* sought to protect, and its holding invoked the reasoning and the tradition of the precedents we have discussed, granting protection to substantive liberties of the person. *Roe* was, of course, an extension of those cases and, as the decision itself indicated, the separate States could act in some degree to further their own legitimate interests in protecting prenatal life. The extent to which the legislatures of the States might act to outweigh the interests of the woman in choosing to terminate her pregnancy was a subject of debate both in *Roe* itself and in decisions following it.

While we appreciate the weight of the arguments made on behalf of the State in the cases before us, arguments which in their ultimate formulation conclude that *Roe* should be overruled, the reservations any of us may have in reaffirming the central holding of *Roe* are outweighed by the explication of individual liberty we have given combined with the force of *stare decisis* [to adhere to precedents, see page 28]. We turn now to that doctrine.

III

A.

The obligation to follow precedent begins with necessity, and a contrary necessity marks its outer limit. With Cardozo [see Reading 3-4], we recognize that no judicial system could do society's work if it eyed each issue afresh in every case that raised it. . . . Indeed, the very concept of the rule of law underlying our own Constitution requires such continuity over time that a respect for precedent is, by definition, indispensable. . . . At the other extreme, a different necessity would make itself felt if a prior judicial ruling should come to be seen so clearly as error that its enforcement was for that very reason doomed.

Even when the decision to overrule a prior case is not, as in the rare, latter instance, virtually foreordained, it is common wisdom that the rule of *stare decisis* is not an "inexorable command," and certainly it is not such in every constitutional case. . . . Rather, when this Court reexamines a prior holding, its judgment is customarily informed by a series of prudential and pragmatic considerations designed to test the consistency of overruling a prior decision with the ideal of the rule of law, and to gauge the respective costs of reaffirming and overruling a prior case. Thus, for example, we may ask whether the rule has proven to be intolerable simply in defying practical workability . . .; whether the rule is subject to a kind of reliance that would lend a special hardship to the consequences of overruling and add inequity to the cost of repudiation . . .;

whether related principles of law have so far developed as to have left the old rule no more than a remnant of abandoned doctrine . . .; or whether facts have so changed, or come to be seen so differently, as to have robbed the old rule of significant application or justification. . . .

1

A decision to overrule *Roe's* essential holding under the existing circumstances would address error, if error there was, at the cost of both profound and unnecessary damage to the Court's legitimacy, and to the Nation's commitment to the rule of law. It is therefore imperative to adhere to the essence of *Roe's* original decision, and we do so today. . . .

IV

We give this summary:

(a) To protect the central right recognized by *Roe* v. *Wade* while at the same time accommodating the State's profound interest in potential life, we will employ the undue burden analysis . . . . An undue burden exists, and therefore a provision of law is invalid, if its purpose or effect is to place a substantial obstacle in the path of a woman seeking an abortion before the fetus attains viability.

(b) We reject the rigid trimester framework of *Roe* v. *Wade.* To promote the State's profound interest in potential life, throughout pregnancy the State may take measures to ensure that the woman's choice is informed, and measures designed to advance this interest will not be invalidated as long as their purpose is to persuade the woman to choose childbirth over abortion. These measures must not be an undue burden on the right.

(c) As with any medical procedure, the State may enact regulations to further the health or safety of a woman seeking an abortion. Unnecessary health regulations that have the purpose or effect of presenting a substantial obstacle to a woman seeking an abortion impose an undue burden on the right.

(d) Our adoption of the undue burden analysis does not disturb the central holding of *Roe* v. *Wade,* and we reaffirm that holding. Regardless of whether exceptions are made for particular circumstances, a State may not prohibit any woman from making the ultimate decision to terminate her pregnancy before viability.

(e) We also reaffirm *Roe's* holding that "subsequent to viability, the State in promoting its interest in the potentiality of human life may, if it chooses, regulate, and even proscribe, abortion except where it is necessary, in appropriate medical judgment, for the preservation of the life or health of the mother." . . .

From *Planned Parenthood of Southeastern Pennsylvania v. Casey* (1992) 505 US 833, pp. 852–855, 869, 878–879.

Abortion and Slavery
"The Root and Branch of Roe v. Wade" (1984)

John T. Noonan

Whoever has the power to define the bearer of constitutional rights has a power that can make nonsense of any particular constitutional right. That this power belongs to the state itself is a point of view associated in jurisprudence with Hans Kelsen [see page 33]. According to Kelsen a person is simply a construct of the law. As he expresses it in *The Pure Theory of Law,* even the apparently natural physical person is a construction of juristic thinking. In this account it appears that just as we personify a corporation for legal purposes so we personify natural physical beings. There are no independent, ontological existences to which we respond as persons. Personhood depends on recognition by the law.

A corollary of that position appears to be what has always seemed to me one of the most terrifying of legal propositions: there is no kind of human behavior that, because of its nature, could not be made into a legal duty corresponding to a legal right [compare Reading 6-1]. When one thinks of the vast variety of human behavior it is at least startling to think that every variation could be converted into legal duties and legal rights. The proposition becomes terrifying when one thinks of Orwell's *1984* [Reading 6-7] or the actual conduct of the Nazi regime [chapter 2, Controversies: War Crimes] from which Hans Kelsen himself eventually had to flee.

There is one massive phenomenon in the history of our country that might be invoked to support Kelsen's point of view. That phenomenon is the way a very large class of human beings were treated prior to the enactment of the thirteenth and fourteenth amendments. When one looks back at the history of 200 years of slavery in the United States, and looks back at it as a lawyer observing that lawyers had a great deal to do with the classifications that made the phenomenon possible, one realizes that the law, in fact, has been used to create legal rights and legal duties in relation to human behavior that should never have been given a legal form and a legal blessing. To put it bluntly, law was the medium and lawyers were the agents responsible for turning one class of human beings into property. The result was that the property laws of the different states made it smooth and easy to transfer ownership of these human beings. The property laws resolved the questions that occurred at those critical junctions where humanity asserted itself either in the birth of a child to a slave or the death of the owner of a slave. The only question left open for argument was whether the human beings classified as property were realty or personalty. In the inheritance cases the slave child was treated like the issue of an animal, compared again and again in legal decisions to the issue of livestock.

Gross characterization of human beings in terms that reduced them to animals, or real estate, or even kitchen utensils now may seem so unbelievable that we all can profess shock and amazement that it was ever done. Eminently respectable lawyers were able to engage in this kind of characterization—

among them Thomas Jefferson, who co-authored the slave code of Virginia,
and Abraham Lincoln who argued on behalf of a slave owner seeking to recover as his property a woman and her four children who had escaped to the
free state of Illinois. Looking at such familiar examples and realizing how
commonplace it was for lawyers to engage in this kind of fiction, we learn, I
think, that law can operate as a kind of magic. All that is necessary is to permit legal legerdemain [tricks] to create a mask obliterating the human person being dealt with. Looking at the mask—that is looking at the abstract
category created by the law—is not to see the human reality on which the
mask is imposed. . . .

[Consider what happened in] *Scott v. Sanford.* Here the black plaintiff
attempted to assert his right to freedom in the federal court. The Supreme
Court held that the federal statute that should have made him free was an
interference with the property rights guaranteed by the Constitution to his
owner. The Court applied the due process clause of the fifth amendment—
gratuitously reading into this clause a concept of substantive due process—
and held the statute invalid. The property mask dropped over Dred Scott was
the means by which the Constitution was brought into play. As James
Buchanan, the President at the time, happily put it, the Court had achieved
"the final settlement" of the question of slavery in the Territories. It was a final settlement curiously like Adolph Hitler's "final solution" of "the Jewish
question" in Germany.

Buchanan's description, of course, was inaccurate. The Supreme Court
could not resolve an issue that so fundamentally divided the nation. The legal mask was shattered by the Civil War. The thirteenth and fourteenth
amendments were adopted. The legal profession forgot about its participation in molding the mask that made slavery possible. It is only in our time
that the analogy seems vital. . . .

Kelsen's jurisprudence makes . . . *Dred Scott* a defensible decision: according to it, there is nothing intrinsic in humanity requiring persons to be
legally recognized as persons. The relevance of Kelsen's reasoning was acknowledged in a modern case, *Byrn v. New York City Health and Hospital
Corporation,* decided a year before the Supreme Court decided *Roe v. Wade.*
In *Byrn,* Robert Byrn was appointed guardian *ad litem* [for the purpose of
the case] of an unborn child and asserted that child's constitutional right not
to be aborted. His position was rejected by the majority of the Court of Appeals of New York, speaking through Judge Charles Breitel. Breitel quoted
Kelsen explicitly to support his position that it was a policy determination of
the state whether legal personalty should be recognized or not. It was, Breitel stated, "not true that the legal order corresponds to the natural order."
Breitel did not go as far as Kelsen's statement that natural persons were juristic creations—Breitel seemed to assume that there might be natural persons—but he left the recognition of natural persons to the legislature. As
New York, at this time, had already enacted a fairly radical abortion law, he
held that the legislature had conclusively made the decision that left the unborn child outside the class of recognized humanity. . . .

To judge from the weight the [*Roe*] Court gave the being in the womb—
found to be protectable in any degree only in the last two months of preg-

nancy—the Court itself must have viewed the unborn as pure potentiality or a mere theory before viability. The Court's opinion appeared to rest on the assumption that the biological reality could be subordinated or ignored by the sovereign speaking through the Court. . . .

The progeny of *Roe* have confirmed the Kelsenite reading of *Roe* that there is no reality that the sovereign must recognize unless the sovereign, acting through the agency of the Court, decides to recognize it. This view would be psychologically incomprehensible if we did not have the history of the creation of the institution of slavery by judges and lawyers. With that history we can see that intelligent and humane lawyers have been able to apply a similar approach to a whole class of beings that they could see—that they were able to create a mask of legal concepts preventing humanity from being visible. A mask is a little easier to impose when the humanity concealed, being in the womb, is not even visible to the naked eye.

Kelsenite logic permits the judges at the apex of a system to dispense with correspondence to reality. The highest court is then free, within the limits that the society in which it functions will tolerate, to be inventive. It may, as the Supreme Court of the United States has sometimes thought, be constrained by the language of the Constitution and the purposes of its makers. Or, as has also sometimes happened, the Court, viewing itself as the final expounder of the Constitution's meaning, will exercise its inventiveness in creating new constitutional doctrine not dependent on text or purposes. Such doctrine—fantasy in the service of ideology—is "the branch" of *Roe v. Wade*. What then becomes possible was illustrated in 1983 by *Akron v. Akron Center for Reproductive Health*. In this case a whole set of constitutional requirements were created on behalf of the claims of an abortion clinic, named with Orwellian aptness, a center for "reproductive health." . . .

Most strikingly of all, *Akron* held that there could not be a legal requirement that a woman seeking an abortion be informed that the being she wished put to death was a child, that the child was alive, and that the child was human. The Court treated this information as prejudicing the choice of whether to abort or not—as a kind of unfair interference with free choice. The ordinance was bad because it was designed "to influence the woman's informed choice between abortion and childbirth." The holding went beyond the Kelsenite jurisprudential root and any mainline theory of constitutional interpretation. It was indeed, the invention of a kind of censorship by the Court itself. . . .

A final provision of the Akron ordinance was that "the remains of the unborn child" be "disposed of in a humane and sanitary manner." The Sixth Circuit Court of Appeals found the word "humane" impermissibly vague in a criminal statute. The ordinance could, the Court said, mean to "mandate some sort of 'decent burial' of an embryo at the earliest stages of formation . . . ." Justice Powell quoted this analysis and agreed; humane and sanitary burial was beyond the comprehension of a reasonable doctor.

In this conclusion one can observe in the most concrete way the Court's discomfort before reality. The Court cannot uphold a requirement of humane burial without conceding that the being who is to be buried is human. A mask has been placed over this being. Even death cannot remove the mask.

The Court's denial of reality stands in contrast with what Andre Gide has written on the humane burial of an unborn child:

> When morning came, "get rid of that," I said naively to the gardener's wife when she finally came to see how everything was. Could I have supposed that those formless fragments, to which I turning away in disgust was pointing, could I have supposed that in the eyes of the Church they already represented the sacred human being they were being readied to clothe? O mystery of incarnation! Imagine then my stupor when some hours later I saw "it" again. The thing which for me already had no name in any language, now cleaned, adorned, beribboned, laid in a little cradle, awaiting the ritual entombment. Fortunately no one had been aware of the sacrilege I had been about to commit; I had already committed it in thought when I had said get rid of "that." Yes, very happily that ill-considered order had been heard by no one. And, I remained a long time musing before "it." Before that little face with the crushed forehead on which they had carefully hidden the wound. Before this innocent flesh which I, if I had been alone, yielding to my first impulse, would have consigned to the manure heap along with the afterbirth and which religious attentions had just saved from the void. I told no one then of what I felt. Of what I tell here. Was I to think that for a few moments a soul had inhabited this body? It has its tomb in Couvreville in that cemetery to which I wish not to return. Half a century has passed. I cannot truthfully say that I recall in detail that little face. No. What I remember exactly is my surprise, my sudden emotion, when confronted by its extraordinary beauty.

If the Court could respond to Gide and understand what humane and sanitary burial is, it might also perceive the reality of the extraordinary beauty of each human being put to death in the name of the abortion liberty and concealed from legal recognition by a jurisprudence that substitutes a judge's fiat for the truth.

From Noonan (1984), "The Root and Branch of *Roe v. Wade*," 63 *Nebraska Law Review*, pp. 668–669, 671–673, 677–679.

READING 6-14

Abortion and Equality
"Privacy v. Equality" (1987)

Catherine A. MacKinnon

> *In a society where women entered sexual intercourse willingly, where adequate contraception was a genuine social priority, there would be no "abortion issue" . . . Abortion is violence . . . It is the offspring, and will continue to be the accuser of a more pervasive and prevalent violence, the violence of rapism.*
>
> —ADRIENNE RICH, *Of Woman Born* (1976)

Roe v. Wade guaranteed the right to choose abortion, subject to some countervailing considerations, by conceiving it as a private choice, included in the constitutional right to privacy. In this critique of that decision, I first situate abortion and the abortion right in the experience of women. The argument is that abortion is inextricable from sexuality, assuming that the feminist analysis of sexuality is our analysis of gender inequality. I then criticize the doctrinal choice to pursue the abortion right under the law of privacy. The argument is that privacy doctrine reaffirms and reinforces what the feminist critique of sexuality criticizes: the public/private split. The political and ideological meaning of privacy as a legal doctrine is connected with the concrete consequences of the public/private split for the lives of women. This analysis makes *Harris v. McRae,* in which public funding for abortions was held not to be required, appear consistent with the larger meaning of *Roe....*

The idea of privacy, if regarded as the outer edge of the limitations on government, embodies, I think, a tension between the preclusion of public exposure or governmental intrusion, on the one hand, and autonomy in the sense of protecting personal self-action on the other. This is a tension, not just two facets of one whole right. In the liberal state this tension is resolved by demarking the threshold of the state at its permissible extent of penetration into a domain that is considered free by definition: the private sphere. It is by this move that the state secures to individuals what has been termed "an inviolable personality" by ensuring what has been called "autonomy or control over the intimacies of personal identity." The state does this by centering its self-restraint on body and home, especially bedroom. By staying out of marriage and the family, prominently meaning sexuality—that is to say, heterosexuality—from contraception through pornography to the abortion decision, the law of privacy proposes to guarantee individual bodily integrity, personal exercise of moral intelligence, and freedom of intimacy. But if one asks whether *women's* rights to these values have been guaranteed, it appears that the law of privacy works to translate traditional social values into the rhetoric of individual rights as a means of subordinating those rights to specific social imperatives. In feminist terms, I am arguing that the logic of *Roe* consummated in *Harris* translates the ideology of the private sphere into the individual woman's legal right to privacy as a means of subordinating women's collective needs to the imperatives of male supremacy....

In the context of a sexual critique of gender inequality, abortion promises to women sex with men on the same reproductive terms as men have sex with women. So long as women do not control access to our sexuality, abortion facilitates women's heterosexual availability. In other words, under conditions of gender inequality, sexual liberation in this sense does not free women; it frees male sexual aggression. The availability of abortion removes the one remaining legitimized reason that women have had for refusing sex besides the headache. As Andrea Dworkin put it, analyzing male ideology on abortion, "Getting laid was at stake." The Playboy Foundation has supported abortion rights from day one; it continues to, even with shrinking disposable funds, on a level of priority comparable to that of its opposition to censorship.

Privacy doctrine is an ideal vehicle for this process. The liberal ideal of the private—and privacy as an ideal has been formulated in liberal terms— holds that, so long as the public does not interfere, autonomous individuals interact freely and equally. Conceptually, this private is hermetic [perfectly sealed]. It *means* that which is inaccessible to, unaccountable to, unconstructed by anything beyond itself. By definition, it is not part of or conditioned by anything systematic or outside of it. It is personal, intimate, autonomous, particular, individual, the original source and final outpost of the self, gender neutral. It is, in short, defined by everything that feminism reveals women have never been allowed to be or to have, and everything that women have been equated with and defined in terms of *men's* ability to have. To complain in public of inequality within it contradicts the liberal definition of the private. In this view, no act of the state contributes to—hence should properly participate in—shaping the internal alignments of the private or distributing its internal forces. Its inviolability by the state, framed as an individual right, presupposes that the private is not already an arm of the state. In this scheme, intimacy is implicitly thought to guarantee symmetry of power. Injuries arise in violating the private sphere, not within and by and because of it. . . .

Women with privileges get rights.

So women got abortion as a private privilege, not as a public right. We got control over reproduction that is controlled by "a man or The Man," an individual man or the doctors or the government. Abortion was not decriminalized; it was legalized. In *Roe* the government set the stage for the conditions under which women gain access to this right. Virtually every ounce of control that women won out of this legalization has gone directly into the hands of men—husbands, doctors, or fathers—or is now in the process of attempts to reclaim it through regulation. This, surely, must be what is meant by reform. . . .

When the law of privacy restricts intrusions into intimacy, it bars change in control over that intimacy. The existing distribution of power and resources within the private sphere will be precisely what the law of privacy exists to protect. It is probably not coincidence that the very things feminism regards as central to the subjection of women—the very place, the body; the very relations, heterosexual; the very activities, intercourse and reproduction; and the very feelings, intimate—form the core of what is covered by privacy doctrine. From this perspective, the legal concept of privacy can and has shielded the place of battery, marital rape, and women's exploited labor; has preserved the central institutions whereby women are *deprived* of identity, autonomy, control and self-definition; and has protected the primary activity through which male supremacy is expressed and enforced. Just as pornography is legally protected as individual freedom of expression—without questioning whose freedom and whose expression and at whose expense— abstract privacy protects abstract autonomy, without inquiring into whose freedom of action is being sanctioned at whose expense.

To fail to recognize the meaning of the private in the ideology and reality of women's subordination by seeking protection behind a right *to* that privacy is to cut women off from collective verification and state support in the same act. I think this has a lot to do with why we can't organize women on the abortion issue. When women are segregated in private, separated from each other, one at a time, a right to that privacy isolates us at once from each other and from public recourse. This right to privacy is a right of men "to be let alone" to oppress women one at a time. It embodies and reflects the private sphere's existing definition of womanhood. This is an instance of liberalism called feminism, liberalism applied to women as if we *are* persons, gender neutral. It reinforces the division between public and private that is *not* gender neutral. It is at once an ideological division that lies about women's shared experience and that mystifies the unity among the spheres of women's violation. It is a very material division that keeps the private beyond public redress and depoliticizes women's subjection within it. It keeps some men out of the bedrooms of other men.

DISCUSSION ISSUES

1. *Law and Morality.* Abortion remains a hotly contested issue. Should the judiciary intervene in disputes that lack moral consensus in order to permit a new moral consensus to evolve (Tribe 1988)? Should the judiciary refrain from intervention to avoid imposing its sense of morality? Where should the moral debate take place? Should the courts try to resolve moral controversies? Should state or federal legislatures decide moral issues?

2. *Substantive Due Process.* Justice Holmes criticized the Court for imposing its own economic philosophy in *Lochner v. New York* (1905) (see Reading 3-12). Is John Hart Ely correct when he charges the Court with imposing noneconomic rights in *Roe v. Wade* (Ely 1973)?

3. *Natural Rights.* Does the Court in *Roe* take a higher law–natural right's approach? Thomas Grey argues that, since the beginning, courts have enforced unwritten constitutional principles beyond the norms derived from the written Constitution (Grey 1975) (see chapter 3, page 138). Compare that with Bork who says, "[T]he choice of 'fundamental values' by the Court cannot be justified. The judge must stick close to the text and the history, and their implications, and not construct new rights" (Bork 1971, p. 8) (see Readings 4-8 and 6-10).

4. *Fetus as a Person.* The Court in *Roe* claimed that it did not have to "resolve the difficult question of when life begins." Many philosophers, however, assume that the abortion issue turns on whether the fetus is a person. In oral arguments, Sarah Weddington, counsel for the plaintiff Norma McCorvey ("Jane Doe"), and Robert Flowers, counsel for Texas, admitted that the issue of whether a fetus is a person would probably decide the case one way or another. If the fetus is a person (capable of having rights), then states must prohibit abortion. Judith Jarvis Thompson argued that, even if we grant that a fetus is a person, a woman still has a right to an abortion (Thompson 1971; see also Regan, 1979). Is the moral issue of personhood relevant to the legal issues of abortion? Thompson asks, "Is a person's right to life always stronger and more stringent than the mother's right to decide what happens in and to her body, and so outweighs it?" If another person's life were to depend on being plugged into your kidneys, would that stranger's right to life outweigh your decision to unplug that person?

5. *Viability.* The term *viability* has different definitions—a technological meaning and a developmental sense. It can signify the fetus's chances of survival, thereby making viability dependent on medical technology, which continues to push back the time when the fetus can be kept alive independent of the mother. However, viability can also mark the stage when the "brain begins to take on the cortical structure capable of higher mental functioning" (Rubenfield 1991, p. 623). Does

the fetus become a person (or more personlike) at that developmental stage? Does the fetus's capacity to be harmed depend on the development and functioning of its neural structures?

6. *Changing Conditions.* Do social, economic, and technological conditions radically alter a right? Suppose, for example, that the "nondestructive removal of a fetus would pose no greater threat to a woman than would a removal that destroyed the fetus" (Tushnet 1984, p. 1368). What if social and economic conditions change so that a woman giving birth to a child has no undue burden in raising the child? Would any of these conditions change the right to an abortion? If technological innovations can assure that a fertilized egg will thrive outside of a woman's womb, does that undermine a right to life position that sets the beginning of life at the time of fertilization?

7. *Chicken or Egg?* What legal status does a frozen fertilized egg have and who has custody over it? Is an egg an egg or an early chicken? The trial court, awarding custody to the female donor in *Davis v. Davis,* classified the disputed eight-cell frozen fertilized eggs not as pre-embryos, but as "children *in vitro.*" The Tennessee Supreme Court, however, found that a right to privacy includes a right not to procreate, upholding the male donor's right to block having the frozen embryos donated to a childless couple. The court found that, since the frozen embryos were in storage and not in the female donor's body, concerns over bodily integrity did not apply, as they would in an abortion case. Do husbands have a constitutional right to avoid procreation, or, as a New York trial judge stated in a similar case (*Kass v. Kass* 1995), do the "husband's rights and control of the procreative process end with ejaculation"? For more on these and other privacy cases, see Alderman and Kennedy (1997).

8. *Abortion and Sterilization.* The Constitutional Court of the Federal Republic of Germany (Judgment of Feb. 25, 1975, 39 BVerfG E 1) overturned a liberal federal law that permitted abortion on demand during the first three months of pregnancy. The West German Constitutional Court noted that its position stemmed in part from the "bitter experience" of Hitler's sterilization laws (compare Reading 3-13). The dissenters retorted that abortion was criminally prohibited in Nazi Germany (see Cohen and Danelski 1994, pp. 840–41). Do the same underlying values operate in sterilization and abortion cases?

9. *Abortion and Infanticide.* Illinois considers it murder for a third party to intentionally kill a fetus, but it exempts perpetrators from the death penalty (Homicide of an Unborn Child, Ill Rev Stat ch 38, sec 9-1.2[d][1989]). States can decide when life ends—for example, whether death means brain death or the point at which the heart stops. Do these examples show "that states are already in the business of defining when life begins" (Posner 1992, p. 444)? Are there constitutional limits to the states' power to define life? According to Ronald Dworkin, states cannot alter the constitutional rights of others with their definitions. For example, a state "cannot escape constitutional responsibilities to death-row inmates by declaring them already dead, or improve its congressional representation by declaring deceased citizens still alive" (Dworkin 1992, p. 402). Should a constitutional structure permit a legislative body to redefine or delete any constitutional rights under any circumstances?

10. *Abortion Funding.* Does *Roe* protect the rights of women who can afford to have an abortion but not the rights of those who cannot? Federal funds may be used for childbirth but not for abortion (see Reading 6-14). Does this have a negative effect on indigent (poor) women? Judge (now U.S. Supreme Court Justice) Ruth Bader Ginsburg argued that an Equal Protection basis for abortion would give stronger grounds for claiming that the government must provide public funding for abortions for poor women (Ginsburg 1985).

11. *Meaning of Privacy.* American courts have interpreted privacy as the right to be left alone. German courts have used a more positive sense of privacy—namely, the right to the free development of one's personality within a larger community. Would these different senses of privacy lead to different conclusions about abortion (Glendon 1987, pp. 37–39)?

3. Right to Die

Does privacy extend to a right to die (see Reading 6-15)? The American Medical Association (AMA) permits withholding treatment **(passive euthanasia)** but does not permit taking direct action designed to kill a patient **(active euthanasia** or mercy killing). The AMA does not regard passive euthanasia as intentional, mercy killing. James Rachels has said that there is no morally significant difference between the two, arguing that withholding treatment is as much an intentional act as pulling a plug (Rachels 1975, pp. 78–80). Physician-assisted suicide has become a highly visible issue largely because of the actions of Dr. Jack Kevorkian. In 1994, Oregon passed the Death With Dignity Act. This legislation allowed the terminally ill to obtain, after a fifteen-day waiting period, a physician's prescription for drugs to end life when two physicians had predicted that the patient would die within six months. The same year, the state of Washington passed legislation prohibiting physician-assisted suicide.

The Quinlin and Cruzan Cases

Is there a constitutional right to die? Karen Ann Quinlin suffered severe brain damage from anorexia, leaving her in a vegetative state. Her father sought to have her respirator disconnected. The New Jersey Supreme Court granted relief on grounds that Karen had a privacy right grounded in the federal Constitution (In re Quinlin [1976]). However, the U.S. Supreme Court has refused to find a constitutionally protected right to die.

Nancy Cruzan's car accident left her in a vegetative state. Her parents sought to have life-sustaining support discontinued, arguing that although she was clearly incompetent, she had previously and competently indicated her desire to die under such circumstances. The State of Missouri claimed that the evidence of Nancy's wishes to withdraw treatment did not meet its "clear and convincing" test. The case turned on this procedural issue, with the Supreme Court finding that Missouri's evidentiary requirement was not unconstitutional (*Cruzan v. Director, Missouri Department of Health* 1990). Nancy had virtually no chance of recovering her cognitive faculties, but neither was she "dying" nor "terminally ill" as those are defined by Missouri (and many other states). The State of Missouri withdrew from subsequent legal action by the Cruzans. A probate judge, after hearing new evidence, authorized disconnecting the feeding tubes. Nearly eight years after she lost consciousness and had feeding tubes implanted in her stomach, Nancy Cruzan died—twelve days after the cessation of nutrition and hydration. The Supreme Court upheld Washington's prohibition of assisted suicide in *Washington v. Glucksberg* (1997) (see Reading 6-16). The remaining Readings were written before the *Washington v. Glucksberg* decision, but they extend and enrich the debate outlined in the Court's opinion.

Six representatives of the modern liberal tradition in political philosophy filed an *amicus curiae* (friend-of-the-court) brief to the Supreme Court arguing in favor of a constitutional right to physician-assisted suicide (see Reading 6-17). The philosophers' case rests on the principles of individual autonomy and state neutrality. They believe that the state should respect the autonomy or independence of each individual and allow the individual to make decisions about her or his own death. That is, the state should remain neutral and allow citizens to write the scripts for the final act of life's drama (compare Reading 4-14). Are these principles neutral, or do they favor one moral viewpoint over others? Michael Sandel, a leading communitarian philosopher, takes issue with the "dream team of liberal political philosophy" (see Reading 6-18). He challenges the ethics of autonomy as being anything but neutral in that it devalues the life that is not independent. Is there a way of balancing the cries of compassion and the duty to preserve life? Will the "right to die" become a "duty to die" for persons with disabilities? An attorney and a psychologist answer, "Yes" (see Reading 6-19).

READING 6-15

Legalizing Euthanasia
"Should Active Euthanasia Be Legalized?" (1994)

Cheryl K. Smith and Yale Kamisar

In February, shortly before Dr. Jack Kevorkian completed his third assisted suicide in five days, New Hampshire legislators debated whether their state should become the first to legalize active euthanasia. The Michigan Legislature went in the opposite direction, issuing a temporary ban on active euthanasia that was set to go into effect on March 30.

And so, the debate continues. If patients can draft living wills that direct physicians not to prolong their lives through extraordinary treatment, then why not allow patients with terminal diseases the right to make their own choices as to the moment of death?

Yale Kamisar, the Henry K. Ransom Professor of Law at the University of Michigan, believes that legalizing active euthanasia will reduce the impetus to save lives. He fears that assisted suicide ultimately will be used against the poor and the incompetent.

Cheryl K. Smith, staff attorney for the Hemlock Society U.S.A. in Eugene, Ore., disagrees. She believes that the time has come to legalize active euthanasia so that the practice can be regulated and made more widely available to the terminally ill.

Yes: A Matter of Choice

Cheryl K. Smith

Americans have a common-law and constitutional right to refuse unwanted medical treatment. This right extends to the removal of life-sustaining equipment, including the administration of artificial nutrition and hydration. This "right-to-die" should extend to aid-in-dying, or active euthanasia, for the terminally ill, at their request.

Patient autonomy weighs heavily in favor of the legalization of voluntary active euthanasia. Respect for a person's autonomy requires that his or her considered value judgment must be taken seriously, even if that judgment is believed to be mistaken. Of course, the person desiring aid-in-dying must be both competent and fully informed. This implies voluntariness and disclosure of the risks, benefits, reasonable alternatives and probable results.

Relief of suffering, always a major goal of medicine, provides the best rationale for legal aid-in-dying for the terminally ill. The ethical principle of beneficence [active goodness] and the Hippocratic Oath support the physician's role in relieving suffering. An estimated 5 percent to 20 percent of terminal cancer patients experience uncontrollable pain at the end of life and dying patients sometimes experience other unbearable suffering.

Some argue that the Hippocratic Oath flatly prohibits physician participation in voluntary active euthanasia. The oath, however, contains an internal inconsistency that may make it impossible to adhere to in cases of intractable pain. The oath requires physicians to relieve pain, as well as giving no deadly medicine. In such cases, both courses—relieving pain and not giving a deadly drug—may not be possible.

Changing Values

In addition, as technology has progressed and values changed, other parts of the oath have been violated. These include not charging a fee for teaching the medical art and the edict not to perform certain surgery.

While historically valuable, the Hippocratic Oath should be relied upon as a guide, rather than strictly construed according to its meaning at the time it was written. After all, Hippocrates had no inkling of the state of the medical art in the 20th century.

Another reason for legalizing active euthanasia relates to regulation of the practice. It is currently occurring outside the law and without any reporting requirements. Few cases are discovered, fewer are prosecuted, and juries are hesitant to convict in those cases that are brought to trial, causing unnecessary expenditures and wasting judicial resources. Legalization, with medical record documentation and reporting requirements, will enable authorities to regulate the practice and guard against abuses, while punishing the real offenders.

Even with legalization, inadequate pain control and depression must be addressed. Some have argued that the physician-patient relationship is based on trust and that trust would be violated if doctors were allowed to participate in voluntary active euthanasia. In fact, the opposite may be true: Patients who are able to discuss sensitive issues such as this are more likely to trust their physicians.

Such open dialogue will enhance detection of treatable depression, which may decrease emotional suicides and resolution of other problems, such as pain. A study of euthanasia in the Netherlands showed that two-thirds of patients who asked their physicians for assurance that they would be assisted in dying when at the end stage of their disease did not need the assistance because other suitable alternatives were given.

The time has come to legalize active euthanasia as an option for patients who are suffering and dying despite, and sometimes because of medical intervention. A majority of Americans support this right, the practice is currently occurring unregulated, and the problem demands a compassionate response.

No: Preserve Traditional Restraints

Yale Kamisar

The distinction between letting people die and killing them by lethal injection is now an integral part of the medico-legal landscape. This is the compromise we have arrived at in the struggle to take a humane approach toward seriously ill patients while still preserving as many traditional restraints against killing as we possibly can. This may be neither the logician's or the philosopher's way to resolve the controversy, but it may nevertheless be a defensible pragmatic way to do so.

As eminent bioethicist Thomas Beauchamp of Georgetown University has written, rules against killing "are not isolated moral principles," but "pieces of a web of rules" that forms a moral code. "The more threads one removes," warned Beauchamp, "the weaker the fabric becomes."

For that reason, I think that the legalization of active euthanasia will have much greater impact than is generally realized on our society and on the dynamics of the sick room. Criminal penalties create unconscious as well as conscious inhibitions against committing certain acts.

But if active euthanasia were legal, these acts would not only be thinkable, but speakable—an acceptable alternative to treatment that could and would be discussed in polite conversation.

The first person to broach the subject might be the physician or a relative or close friend. Or the gravely ill person might ask advice of those close to her. What should relatives and friends tell her? How would a patient react to the suggestion that she end her life? How many patients would opt for euthanasia because they feel obliged or pressured to do so—to relieve their relatives of financial pressures or emotional strain? And how many severely ill patients will feel that to reject euthanasia, once it is a viable alternative and others are "doing it," would be selfish or cowardly?

Chilling Imperatives

I recall what a septuagenarian [seventy year old] said on the op ed pages of *The New York Times:* "There is a movement to limit use of medical technology to younger people. . . . A related movement thinks of us as leaves drying on trees, implying that we'd better drop off or be pulled. There is a children's book called 'Freddy the Leaf' that I have *not* bought for my tree-climbing machine."

In a recent article, University of Michigan philosophy professor David Velleman argues that legalizing active euthanasia may harm some patients by "denying them the possibility of staying alive by default:

"When someone shows impatience or displeasure with us, we jokingly say, 'Well, excuse me for living!' But imagine that it were no joke; imagine that living were something for which one might reasonably be thought to need an excuse."

We may be fairly sure of one thing. If we legalize active euthanasia for only the "terminally ill," it will not remain limited for very long. At first, living-will statutes provided that the directive only became operative when its maker became "terminally ill." But in response to strong criticism that such a restriction unduly limited the impact of such legislation, a growing number of states have removed the limitation either by statutory amendment or case law.

We may be fairly sure of another thing. If active euthanasia is legalized, it will not be confined to competent patients. As active euthanasia grows in acceptance, there will be a strong impetus to extend the same "benefit" to the incompetent patient who has a life-threatening illness but has never expressed any desire for euthanasia.

As SMU Law School's Thomas Mayo has observed, "the history of our activities and beliefs concerning the ethics of death and dying is a history of lost distinctions of former significance." If active euthanasia is legalized, there is little reason to think that that history will come to an end.

"Should Active Euthanasia be Legalized?" *ABA Journal* (September 1994). Reprinted by permission of the American Bar Association.

READING 6-16
Physician Assisted Suicide
Washington v. Glucksberg (1997)

CHIEF JUSTICE WILLIAM REHNQUIST

We begin, as we do in all due process cases, by examining our Nation's history, legal traditions, and practices. . . . In almost every State—indeed, in almost every western democracy—it is a crime to assist a suicide. The States' assisted-suicide bans are not innovations. Rather, they are longstanding expressions of the States' commitment to the protection and preservation of all human life. . . .

The Washington statute at issue in this case, Wash. Rev. Code § 9A.36.060 (1994), was enacted in 1975 as part of a revision of that State's criminal code. Four years later, Washington passed its Natural Death Act, which specifically stated that the "withholding or withdrawal of life-sustaining treatment . . . shall not, for any purpose, constitute a suicide" and that "[n]othing in this chapter shall be construed to condone, authorize, or approve mercy killing. . . ." In 1991, Washington voters rejected a ballot initiative which, had it passed, would have permitted a form of physician-assisted suicide. Washington then added a provision to the Natural Death Act expressly excluding physician-assisted suicide. . . .

The history of the law's treatment of assisted suicide in this country has been and continues to be one of the rejection of nearly all efforts to permit it. That being the case, our decisions lead us to conclude that the asserted "right" to assistance in committing suicide is not a fundamental liberty interest protected by the Due Process Clause. The Constitution also requires, however, that Washington's assisted-suicide ban be rationally related to legitimate government interests. . . . This requirement is unquestionably met here. . . . Washington's assisted-suicide ban implicates a number of state interests. . . .

First, Washington has an "unqualified interest in the preservation of human life.". . . The State's prohibition on assisted suicide, like all homicide laws, both reflects and advances its commitment to this interest. . . .

The State also has an interest in protecting the integrity and ethics of the medical profession. . . .

Next, the State has an interest in protecting vulnerable groups—including the poor, the elderly, and disabled persons—from abuse, neglect, and mistakes. . . .

Finally, the State may fear that permitting assisted suicide will start it down the path to voluntary and perhaps even involuntary euthanasia. . . .

From *Washington v. Glucksberg* (1997) 521 US 702, pp. 710–712, 716–717, 719, 728, 731–732, 735.

READING 6-17

A Philosophical Legal Brief
"Assisted Suicide: The Philosophers' Brief" (1997)

Ronald Dworkin with Thomas Nagel, Robert Nozick, John Rawls, Thomas Scanlon, and Judith Jarvis Thompson

INTRODUCTION

We cannot be sure, until the Supreme Court decides the assisted suicide cases and its decision is published, how far the justices might have accepted or rejected the arguments of the brief published below. In this introduction I [Ronald Dworkin] shall describe the oral argument before them last January, and offer some suggestions about how, if they decide against the brief's position, as many commentators now think they will, they might do the least damage to constitutional law.

The laws of all but one American state now forbid doctors to prescribe lethal pills for patients who want to kill themselves. These cases began when groups of dying patients and their doctors in Washington State and New York each sued asking that these prohibitions be declared unconstitutional so that the patients could be given, when and if they asked for it, medicine to hasten their death. The pleadings described the agony in which the patient plaintiffs were dying, and two federal Circuit Courts of Appeal—the Ninth Circuit in the Washington case and the Second Circuit in the New York case—agreed with the plaintiffs that the Constitution forbids the government from flatly prohibiting doctors to help end such desperate and pointless suffering.

Washington State and New York appealed these decisions to the Supreme Court, and a total of sixty amicus briefs were filed, including briefs on behalf of the American Medical Association and the United States Catholic Conference urging the Court to reverse the circuit court decisions, and on behalf of the American Medical Students Association and the Gay Men's Health Crisis urging it to affirm them. The justices' comments during oral argument persuaded many observers that the Court would reverse the decisions, probably by a lopsided majority. The justices repeatedly cited two versions—one theoretical, the other practical—of the "slippery slope" argument: that it would be impossible to limit a right to assisted suicide in an acceptable way, once that right was recognized.

The theoretical version of the argument denies that any principled line can be drawn between cases in which proponents say a right of assisted suicide is appropriate and those in which they concede that it is not. The circuit courts recognized only a right for competent patients already dying in great physical pain to have pills prescribed that they could take themselves. Several justices asked on what grounds the right once granted could be so severely limited. Why should it be denied to dying patients who are so feeble or paralyzed that they cannot take pills themselves and who beg a doctor to inject a lethal drug into them? Or to patients who are not dying but face years of intolerable physical or emotional pain, or crippling paralysis or dependence? But if the right were extended that far, on what ground could it be denied to anyone who had formed a desire to die—to a sixteen-year-old suffering from a severe case of unrequited love, for example?

The philosophers' brief answers these questions in two steps. First, it defines a very general moral and constitutional principle—that every competent person has the right to make momentous personal decisions which invoke fundamental religious or philosophical convictions about life's value for himself. Second, it recognizes that people may make such momentous decisions impulsively or out of emotional depression, when their act does not reflect their enduring convictions; and it therefore allows that in some circumstances a state has the constitutional power to override that right in order to protect citizens from mistaken but irrevocable acts of self-destruction. States may be allowed to prevent assisted suicide by people who—it is plausible to think—would later be grateful if they were prevented from dying.

That two-step argument would justify a state's protecting a disappointed adolescent from himself. It would equally plainly not justify forcing a competent dying patient to live in between these extremes, and if the Court adopted this argument, the federal courts would no doubt be faced with a succession of cases in years to come testing whether, for example, it is plausible to assume that a desperately crippled patient in constant pain but with years to live, who has formed a settled and repeatedly stated wish to die, would one day be glad he was forced to stay alive. But though two justices dwelled, during the oral argument, on the unappealing prospect of a series of such cases coming before the courts, it seems better that the courts do assume that burden, which they could perhaps mitigate through careful rulings, than that they be relieved of it at the cost of such terrible suffering.

The practical version of the slippery slope argument is more complex. If assisted suicide were permitted in principle, every state would presumably adopt regulations to insure that a patient's decision for suicide is informed, competent, and free. But many people fear that such regulations could not be adequately enforced, and that particularly vulnerable patients—poor patients dying in overcrowded hospitals that had scarce resources, for example—might be pressured or hustled into a decision for death they would not otherwise make. The evidence suggests, however, that such patients might be better rather than less well protected if assisted suicide were legalized with appropriate safeguards.

More of them could then benefit from relief that is already available—illegally—to more fortunate people who have established relationships with doctors willing to run the risks of helping them to die. The current two-tier system—a chosen death and an end of pain outside the law for those with connections and stony refusals for most other people—is one of the greatest scandals of contemporary medical practice. The sense many middle-class people have that if necessary their own doctor "will know what to do" helps to explain why the political pressure is not stronger for a fairer and more open system in which the law acknowledges for everyone what influential people now expect for themselves.

For example, in a recent study in the state of Washington, which guaranteed respondents anonymity, 26 percent of doctors surveyed said they had received explicit requests for help in dying, and had provided, overall, lethal prescriptions to 24 percent of patients requesting them. In other studies, 40 percent of Michigan oncologists surveyed reported that patients had initiated requests for death. 18 percent said they had participated in assisted suicide, and 4 percent in "active euthanasia"—injecting lethal drugs themselves. In San Francisco, 53 percent of the 1,995 responding physicians said they had granted an AIDS patient's request for suicide assistance at least once. These statistics approach the rates at which doctors help patients die in Holland, where assisted suicide is in effect legal.

The most important benefit of legalized assisted suicide for poor patients however, might be better care while they live. For though the medical experts cited in various briefs disagreed sharply about the percentage of terminal cases in which pain can be made tolerable through advanced and expensive palliative techniques, they did not disagree that a great many patients do not receive the relief they could have. The Solicitor General who urged the Court to reverse the lower court judgments conceded in the oral argument that 25 percent of terminally ill patients actually do die in pain. That appalling figure is the result of several factors, including medical ignorance and fear of liability, inadequate hospital funding, and (as the Solicitor General suggested) the failure of insurers and health care programs to cover the cost of special hospice care. Better training in palliative [caring without curing] medicine, and legislation requiring such coverage, would obviously improve the situation, but it seems perverse to argue that the patients who would be helped were better pain management available must die horribly because it is not; and, as Justice Breyer pointed out, the number of patients in that situation might well increase as medical costs continue to escalate.

According to several briefs, moreover, patients whose pain is either uncontrollable or uncontrolled are often "terminally sedated"—intravenous drugs (usually barbiturates or benzodiazepenes) are injected to induce a pharmacologic coma during which the patient is given neither water nor nutrition and dies sooner than he otherwise would. Terminal sedation is widely accepted as legal, though it advances death. But it is not subject to regulations nearly as stringent as those that a state forced to allow assisted suicide would enact. Because such regulations would presumably include a requirement that hospitals, before accepting any request for assistance in suicide, must demonstrate that effective medical care including state-of-the-art pain management had been offered. The guidelines recently published by a network of ethics committees in the Bay Area of California, for example, among other stringent safeguards, provide that a primary care physician who receives a request for suicide must make an initial referral to a hospice program or to a physician experienced in palliative care, and certify in a formal report filed in a state registry, signed by an independent second physician with expertise in such care, that the best available pain relief has been offered to the patient.

Doctors and hospitals anxious to avoid expense would have very little incentive to begin a process that would focus attention on their palliative care practices. They would be more likely to continue the widespread practice of relatively inexpensive terminal care which is supplemented, perhaps, with terminal sedation. It is at least possible, however, that patients' knowledge of the possibility of assisted suicide would make it more difficult for such doctors to continue as before. That is the view of the Coalition of Hospice Professionals, who said, in their own amicus brief, "Indeed, removing legal bans on suicide assistance will enhance the opportunity for advanced hospice care for all patients because regulation of physician-assisted suicide would mandate that all palliative measures be exhausted as a condition precedent to assisted suicide."

So neither version of the slippery slope argument seems very strong. It is nevertheless understandable that Supreme Court justices are reluctant, particularly given how little experience we have so far with legalized assisted suicide, to declare that all but one of the states must change their laws to allow a practice many citizens think abominable and sacrilegious. But as the philosophers' brief . . . emphasizes, the Court is in an unusually difficult position. If it closes the door to a constitutional right to assisted suicide it will do substantial damage to constitutional practice and precedent, as well as to thousands of people in great suffering. It would face a dilemma in justifying any such decision, because it would be forced to choose between the two unappealing strategies that the brief describes.

The first strategy—declaring that terminally ill patients in great pain do not have a constitutional right to control their own deaths, even in principle—seems alien to our constitutional system, as the Solicitor General himself insisted in the oral argument. It would also undermine a variety of the Court's own past decisions, including the carefully constructed position on abortion set out in its 1993 decision in *Casey* [Reading 6-12]. Indeed some amicus briefs took the occasion of the assisted suicide cases to criticize the abortion decisions—a brief filed on behalf of Senator Orrin Hatch of Utah and Representatives Henry Hyde of Illinois and Charles Canady of Florida, for example, declared that the abortion decisions were "of questionable legitimacy and even more questionable prudence." Protecting the abortion rulings was presumably one of the aims of the Clinton administration in arguing, through the Solicitor General, for the second strategy instead.

The first strategy would create an even more evident inconsistency within the practice of terminal medicine itself. Since the *Cruzan* decision discussed in the brief, lawyers have generally assumed that the Court would protect the right of any competent patient to have life sustaining equipment removed from his body even though he would then die. In the oral argument, several justices suggested a "common-sense" distinction between the moral significance of acts, on the one hand, and omissions, on the other. This distinction, they suggested, would justify a constitutional distinction between prescribing lethal pills and removing life support; for, in their view, removing support is only a matter of "letting nature take its course," while prescribing pills is an active intervention that brings death sooner than natural processes would."

The discussion of this issue in the philosophers' brief is therefore particularly significant. The brief insists that such suggestions wholly misunderstand the "common-sense" distinction, which is not between acts and omissions, but between acts or omissions that are designed to cause death and those that are not. One justice suggested that a patient who insists that life support be disconnected is not committing suicide. That is wrong: he is committing suicide if he aims at death, as most such patients do, just as someone whose wrist is cut in an accident is committing suicide if he refuses to try to stop the bleeding. The distinction between acts that aim at death and those that do not cannot justify a constitutional distinction between assisting in suicide and terminating life support. Some doctors, who stop life support only because the patient so demands, do not aim at death. But neither do doctors who prescribe lethal pills only for the same reason, and hope that the patient does not take them. And many doctors who terminate life support obviously do aim at death, including those who deny nutrition during terminal sedation, because denying nutrition is designed to hasten death, not to relieve pain.

There are equally serious objections, however, to the second strategy the philosophers' brief discusses. This strategy concedes a general right to assisted suicide but holds that states have the power to judge that the risks of allowing any exercise of that right are too great. It is obviously dangerous for the Court to allow a state to deny a constitutional right on the ground that the state lacks the will or resource to enforce safeguards if it is exercised, particularly when the case for the practical version of the "slippery slope" objection seems so weak and has been little examined. As Justice Rehnquist, who perhaps favors the first strategy, observed in the oral argument, "[I]f we assume a liberty interest but nevertheless say that, even assuming a liberty interest, a state can prohibit it entirely, that would be rather a conundrum."

If the justices believe that they cannot now accept the lower court decisions, in spite of the powerful defense offered by the respondents and the various briefs supporting them, then they should consider a third strategy—postponement. They might declare that both precedent and principle offer strong grounds for a constitutional right to manage one's own death, but that there is as yet too little experience with legally permitted assisted suicide for the Court to rule that states lack the constitutional power to follow their traditional practice of outlawing it.

That third strategy, unlike the first two, would in effect commit the Court to considering a new challenge in the future when a much more substantial record of experience is available—from Oregon and any other American state that follows its lead in permitting assisted suicide by legislation, and from the Netherlands, Switzerland, the Northern Territories of Australia, and any other jurisdiction whose legislature takes the same course. In the meantime, the public would have had an opportunity to participate more fully in the argument about principle; and, when circumstances make it possible, wide public discussion is a desirable and democratic preliminary to a final Supreme Court adjudication. Postponement is not what the philosophers' brief urges. But it would be the most statesmanlike way in which the Court could make the wrong decision. . . .

Ronald Dworkin, Thomas Nagel, Robert Nozick, Thomas Scanlon, Judith Jarvis Thompson (March 27, 1997) "Assisted Suicide: The Philosophers' Brief" *New York Review of Books.* Reprinted by permission from Ronald Dworkin.

READING 6-18

A Communitarian Debriefing
"Last Rights" (1997)

Michael Sandel

The Supreme Court will soon decide [*Washington v. Glucksberg,* Reading 6-16] whether terminally ill patients have a constitutional right to physician-assisted suicide. Most likely, the Court will say no. Almost every state prohibits suicide, and in oral arguments earlier this year the justices voiced doubts about striking down so many state laws on so wrenching a moral issue.

If the Court rules as expected, it will not simply be overruling the two federal courts that declared suicide a constitutional right. It will also be rejecting the advice of six distinguished moral philosophers who filed a friend of the court brief [Reading 6-17]. The authors of the brief comprise the Dream Team of liberal political philosophy—Ronald Dworkin (Oxford and NYU), Thomas Nagel (NYU), Robert Nozick (Harvard), John Rawls (Harvard), Thomas Scanlon (Harvard) and Judith Jarvis Thomson (MIT).

At the heart of the philosophers' argument is the attractive but mistaken principle that government should be neutral on controversial moral and religious questions. Since people disagree about what gives meaning and value to life, the philosophers argue, government should not impose through law any particular answer to such questions. Instead, it should respect a person's right to live (and die) according to his own convictions about what makes life worth living.

Mindful that judges are reluctant to venture onto morally contested terrain, the philosophers insist that the Court can affirm a right to assisted suicide without passing judgment on the moral status of suicide itself. "These cases do not invite or require the Court to make moral, ethical, or religious judgments about how people should approach or confront their death or about when it is ethically appropriate to hasten one's own death or to ask others for help in doing so," they write. Instead, say the philosophers, the Court should accord individuals the right to make these "grave judgments for themselves, free from the imposition of any religious or philosophical orthodoxy by court or legislature."

Despite their claim to neutrality, the philosophers' argument betrays a certain view of what makes life worth living. According to this view, the best way to live and die is to do so deliberately, autonomously, in a way that enables us to view our lives as our own creations. The best lives are led by those who see themselves not as participants in a drama larger than themselves but as authors of the drama itself. "Most of us see death . . . as the final act of life's drama," the brief states, "and we want that last act to reflect our own convictions. . . ." The philosophers speak for those who would end their lives upon concluding that living on "would disfigure rather than enhance the lives they had created." Citing the Court's language in a recent abortion case, *Planned Parenthood* v. *Casey* (1992) [Reading 6-12], the philosophers stress the individual's right to make "choices central to personal dignity and autonomy." Such freedom includes nothing less than "the right to define one's own concept of existence, of meaning, of the universe, and of the mystery of human life."

The philosophers' emphasis on autonomy and choice implies that life is the possession of the person who lives it. This ethic is at odds with a wide range of moral outlooks that view life as a gift, of which we are custodians with certain duties. Such outlooks reject the idea that a person's life is open to unlimited use, even by the person whose life it is. Far from being neutral, the ethic of autonomy invoked in the brief departs from many religious traditions and also from the views of the founders of liberal political philosophy, John Locke and Immanuel Kant. Both Locke and Kant opposed a right to suicide, and both rejected the notion that our lives are possessions to dispose of as we please.

Locke, the philosopher of consent, argued for limited government on the grounds that certain rights are so profoundly ours that we cannot give them up, even by an act of consent [Readings 4-1 and 4-10]. Since the right to life and liberty is unalienable, he maintained, we cannot sell ourselves into slavery or commit suicide: "No body can give more Power than he has himself; and he that cannot take away his own Life, cannot give another power over it."

For Kant, respect for autonomy entails duties to oneself as well as others, most notably the duty to treat humanity as an end in itself. This duty constrains the way a person can treat himself [Reading 2-2]. According to Kant, murder is wrong because it uses the victim as a means rather than respects him as an end. But the same can be true of suicide. If a person "does away with himself in order to escape from a painful situation," Kant writes, "he is making use of a person merely as a means to maintain a tolerable state of affairs till the end of his life. But man is not a thing—not something to be used as a means: he must always in his actions be regarded as an end in himself." Kant concludes that a person has no more right to kill himself than to kill someone else.

The philosophers' brief assumes, contrary to Kant, that the value of a person's life is the value he or she attributes to it, provided the person is competent and fully informed. "When a competent person does want to die," the philosophers write, "it makes no sense to appeal to the patient's right not to be killed as a reason why an act designed to cause his death is impermissible." Kant would have disagreed. The fact that a person wants to die does not make it morally permissible to kill him, even if his desire is uncoerced and well-informed.

The philosophers might reply that permitting assisted suicide does no harm to those who find it morally objectionable; those who prefer to view their lives as episodes in a larger drama rather than as autonomous creations would remain free to do so.

But this reply overlooks the way that changes in law can bring changes in the way we understand ourselves. The philosophers rightly observe that existing laws against assisted suicide reflect and entrench certain views about what gives life meaning. But the same would be true were the Court to declare, in the name of autonomy, a right to assisted suicide. The new regime would not simply expand the range of options, but would encourage the tendency to view life less as a gift and more as a possession. It might heighten the prestige we accord autonomous, independent lives and depreciate the claims of those seen to be dependent. How this shift would affect policy toward the elderly, the disabled, the poor and the infirm, or reshape the attitudes of doctors toward their ailing patients or children toward their aging parents, remains to be seen.

To reject the autonomy argument is not necessarily to oppose assisted suicide in all cases. Even those who regard life as a sacred trust can admit that the claims of compassion may sometimes override the duty to preserve life. The challenge is to find a way to honor these claims that preserves the moral burden of hastening death, and that retains the reverence for life as something we cherish, not something we choose.

READING 6-19

The Disabled's Duty to Die
"The Disability Rights Opposition to Physician Assisted Suicide" (1996)

Diane Coleman and Carol Gill

Most proponents of physician-assisted suicide would say that a representative of the disability community does not really belong on this panel today. They would say that physician-assisted suicide pertains to people who are terminally ill, not disabled.

The concerns of people with disabilities were similarly dismissed as irrelevant in the context of withdrawal of life-sustaining treatment or "passive euthanasia." Nevertheless, courts did not carefully protect non-terminal people with disabilities from a too hasty "final exit." Indeed, court after court declared that people with disabilities were essentially the same as people with terminal illnesses, stating that routine disability-related health care was artificially prolonging life, or that it did not matter how extended the individual's life-expectancy might be if their quality of life rendered their life "meaningless." This occurred in numerous appellate court cases involving people with quadriplegia, often locked away in nursing homes without hope of in-home support services, and it even occurred in a case involving a woman with cerebral palsy. . . .

1) People with disabilities do not have adequate protection from either the courts or disability organizations. The courts have consistently excused parents who have murdered children with disabilities. A woman in Wisconsin escaped sentencing after admittedly starving her son with cerebral palsy to death. She said she was responding to family pressure and the message of a T.V. show on euthanasia. A west coast mother recently killed her brain injured non-verbal teenaged daughter. The judge said her actions were understandable, that other parents could be expected to react in the same way. He sentenced her to community service. Meanwhile, disability watchdog organizations are losing funding. There have never been enough of these to serve people with disabilities adequately; now many are forced to shut down.

2) People with disabilities and incurable chronic diseases have experienced a long history of persecution and genocide. At the turn of the century, Chicago's Ugly Law ordered people with visible disabilities to hide themselves from public view. In the 1930's, 200,000 people with disabilities were put to death by Nazi physicians who were inspired by the contemporary euthanasia movements of England and the U.S [Reading 3-13]. Three years ago, a European judge ordered a hotel to refund money to a vacationing couple because they claimed their holiday was ruined by the presence of disabled people in the dining room. A physically disabled German man committed suicide after verbal and physical assaults by skinheads. There has been a rise in hate crimes against people with disabilities, internationally. A U.S. government report on child abuse recently found that children with disabilities are twice as likely to be abused as children who are nondisabled, simply because [of] their disabilities. Suffice it to say, contempt for life with disability is very much

around us. In this context, we should be extended more protections of our lives, as a minority group at risk, instead of fewer protections.

3) Assisted suicide will not remain confined to the imminently dying. Individuals and groups who have spearheaded this push for assisted suicide have clearly intended people with disabilities to be targeted once laws are relaxed for terminally ill people. In Final Exit, Hemlock Society founder Derek Humphrey writes: "What can those of us who sympathize with a justified suicide by a handicapped person do to help? . . . When we have statutes on the books permitting lawful physician aid-in-dying for the terminally ill, I believe that along with this reform there will come a more tolerant attitude to the other exceptional cases." Kevorkian has openly admitted that he designed his suicide device as an answer for quadriplegics. He has said that he perceives physical disability as a cause of extreme human suffering that can be addressed by "medicide." He also argued, as did the Nazis, that society will benefit from the deaths of incurably disabled people. Chillingly, he wrote: ". . . the voluntary self-elimination of individual and mortally diseased or crippled lives taken collectively can only enhance the preservation of public health and welfare." The courts have not prevented this man from following through on his intention to "enhance" society by eliminating people with disabilities who despair in the face of society's crushing oppression.

4) Assisted suicide enthusiasts have reinforced public prejudice and fear regarding disability. They describe our physical status or our simple need for human assistance, tools and technology as "pitiful," "helpless," "hopeless," "miserable," and inherently "undignified." This is an insult to our lifestyles. For example, many people with disabilities routinely manage incontinence through a variety of methods advertised in numerous disability magazines. These negative labels also promote myths about disability and "quality of life." Experienced people with disabilities have learned that there's more to life than toileting independently. Research consistently indicates that "quality of life" is determined by social supports and meaningful involvement in one's environment, not degree of disability. Most people with disabilities say that public misconceptions about disability trouble them far more than their physical limitations. If promoters of assisted suicide genuinely cared about people with disabilities, they would stop contributing to these negative public attitudes. Instead, they exploit disability prejudice in their public statements and expensive political advertisements to frighten the public into endorsing assisted suicide.

5) As long as people with disabilities are disenfranchised and treated as unwelcome and costly burdens on society, assisted suicide is forced "choice." Assisted suicide is not a free choice as long as people with disabilities are denied adequate healthcare, affordable personal assistance in our own homes, assistive technology, equal education, nondiscriminatory employment, and free access to our communities' structures and transportation systems. Based on recent developments in both public and private managed care, it is already possible in some states for impoverished disabled, elderly and chronically ill people to get assistance to die, but impossible for them to get shoes, eyeglasses, and tooth repair. Indeed, the 9th Circuit Court decision in effect recognizes assisted suicide as an acceptable solution to the economic burdens of healthcare. The so called "right to die" has become the "duty to die," with Court approval.

6) The great majority of problems that lead people with disabilities, chronic conditions, and even terminal illnesses to seek hastened deaths are remediable through other means, such as assisted independent living outside of nursing homes, sophisticated pain management, death counseling for individuals and families, augmentative communication technology, hospice support, etc. Unfortunately, our nation's health care system has not responded adequately or consistently to these important human needs. Most citizens, particularly poor citizens, must fight for access to health care every step of the way. Many physicians have limited knowledge or skills in pain management, and no knowledge of even the most simple and inexpensive disability-related technology and services. To legalize assisted suicide in a country that has been a pioneer in suicide prevention is a backward step into primitiveness.

7) Physicians must not be given the power to decide who lives and who is escorted to death. As disabled historian Hugh Gallagher warns, the Nazi experience demonstrates how easily compassionate and well-educated physicians can lose their moral compass. Furthermore, research shows that physicians learn very little about disabled people during medical training, they are poor at diagnosing treatable depression, they are often uninformed about options such as pain management and supported living for people with disabilities, and they have a high suicide rate, themselves. Moreover, research shows that physicians consistently and dramatically underestimate quality of life for people with disabilities compared to the assessments of people with disabilities themselves. In addition, most individuals with disabilities report longstanding problems with physicians, citing disability prejudice, ignorance about the disability lifestyle, and medical abuse as commonly issuing from physicians. It is unlikely that doctors will become more careful and accountable for our lives when current permissive attitudes about physician-assisted suicide are given the status of law.

8) The 2nd Circuit Court decision illustrates the logic that propels us down the slippery slope to endangerment. In numerous court cases since 1985 involving "passive euthanasia", "right to die" proponents have argued that passively withdrawing life supports was neither suicide nor mercy killing—it was just letting nature take its course. Now, the Court's decision articulates that there is no essential difference between assisted suicide and death from withdrawal of life supports. Will the next decision challenge the distinction between assisted suicide and mercy killing, or the distinction between voluntary requests to die and proxy requests or decisions made without consent at all? That is exactly what happened in the Netherlands—a country often cited by assisted suicide proponents as the model for the U.S. Specifically, according to a Dutch governmental report in 1990, 5,941 persons were given lethal injections without consent. Of those, 1,474 were fully competent, according to their physicians. In 8% of the cases, doctors admitted there were unexplored options. Regardless of options, they euthanized unconsenting patients because of such express reasons as "low quality of life," "no prospect of improvement," "the family could not take any more" (<u>Doctor Assisted Suicide and the Euthanasia Movement</u> ed. by Gary E. McCuen).

9) In fact, people with disabilities have already been endangered by relaxation of laws and policies protecting their lives. Medical rehabilitation

specialists report that quadriplegics and other significantly disabled people are dying wrongfully in increasing numbers because emergency room physicians judge their quality of life as low and, therefore, withhold aggressive treatment. Disabled people who need ventilators are often not offered assisted breathing as an option. Those who already use ventilators report that they are increasingly asked by medical personnel to consider "do not resuscitate" orders and withdrawal of life support. Children with non-terminal disabilities who never asked to die are killed "gently" by the denial of routine treatment. People with relatively mild disabilities are routinely denied life saving organ transplants. Many people with disabilities are terrified that managed care will further abridge their already limited options for life-extending treatments. Oregon's attempt to ration healthcare based on "quality of life" judgements (judgements made by nondisabled people) demonstrated how quickly the deck can be stacked against the lives of people with costly conditions. In the Netherlands, where disabled children, and adults with multiple sclerosis, quadriplegia, and depression are commonly assisted to die, disabled citizens express fear. Some carry wallet cards asking not to be euthanized. Dutch physicians follow a practice not to offer assisted ventilation to quadriplegics. Those who visit the U.S. have expressed surprise to see quadriplegics actively engaged in life with the use of costly portable ventilators and mouth-controlled power wheelchairs. Not surprisingly, the hospice movement is virtually non-existent in the Netherlands. When assisted death is a ready solution there is little incentive to develop life-enhancing supportive services for "incurables."

10) Many proponents of physician-assisted suicide have expressed the belief that adequate safeguards can be adopted to protect vulnerable people from various forms of pressure and abuse if the practice is legalized in conformance with the 2nd and 9th Circuit court opinions. This view is at best naive and at worst deliberately misleading. Similar statements were made during the last decade in the context of the withdrawal of life-sustaining treatment, but no meaningful safeguards have been established. In particular, people with disabilities are notably absent from hospital medical ethics committees. If, in fact, proponents of physician-assisted suicide believe that adequate safeguards against treatable suicidal feelings can be established, then they should be willing to allow physician-assisted for any citizen, regardless of their health status, after those safeguards have been observed. However, no one has proposed that physician-assisted suicide be made available to all citizens on a nondiscriminatory basis. Indeed, science fiction movies have been made depicting the atrocities of such a practice in futuristic society. But it appears that such practices are acceptable today if "only" applied to a loosely defined group of seriously ill or impaired individuals. The fact is that proponents of physician-assisted suicide are willing to risk the lives of hundreds of thousands of severely disabled people who are not terminally ill in order to secure a right to active euthanasia that would effectively shield them from legal scrutiny of their conduct. People with disabilities protest this cavalier devaluation of our lives.

11) Assisted suicide is discriminatory. As a policy, it singles out ill and disabled people as fitting subjects for dying. Meanwhile, neither the public nor health professionals endorse this so-called "autonomous" decision for

young, healthy Americans. If there is a constitutional right to control one's death through assistance, it should apply to all citizens, not just those judged (or misjudged) to have a deficient life.

12) Assisted suicide is classist. Those who are used to privilege, and the control over one's life that privilege affords, will benefit from having one more choice—the choice to die by their own schedule. Such individuals expect to control all aspects of their lives. Either they cannot truly fathom the experience of disenfranchised groups, or they are willing to risk the safety of many (society's poor and oppressed) to ensure their personal access to more options. On the other hand, those who lack privilege, who are socially devalued and feared, those who are denied meaningful options to live, will be endangered by legalization of assisted suicide. The historical reality of disabled people's experience is that society does not adequately support our lives unless pressured by strong legal sanctions. The Congress of the United States acknowledged that disabled people are a discrete and insular minority in its passage of the Americans with Disabilities Act in 1990. We are entitled to the equal protection of the laws under the 14th Amendment of the U.S. Constitution. The laws that protect our lives have often been the only buffer between us and annihilation. Now, under the guise of a 14th Amendment protection of an alleged liberty interest in assisted suicide, a certain class of people will be denied the 14th Amendment's equal protection of laws providing for suicide prevention when one poses a danger to oneself. . . .

From Coleman and Gill (April 29, 1996), "The Disability Rights Opposition to Physician Assisted Suicide," Testimony Before the Judiciary Committee of the U.S. House of Representatives, pp. 2–5.

CHAPTER 7

Equality

EQUAL PROTECTION

Man was born free, but is everywhere in bondage.
—Jean Jacque Rousseau *Social Contract,* 1962

All animals are equal, but some animals are more equal than others.
—George Orwell *Animal Farm,* 1946

The Declaration of Independence holds as a self-evident truth that "all men are created equal." The Declaration goes on to list self-evident truths other than equality, such as freedom (liberty). Does freedom take priority over equality? Does equality interfere with freedom? Are freedom and equality compatible? Does genuine freedom depend upon fulfillment of equality? The U.S. Constitution states: "No state shall . . . deny to any person within its jurisdiction the equal protection of the laws." What does equality mean? Although the readings on pages 357–364 do not provide an answer, they do present the complexities surrounding the seemingly simple term, *equality*. The conceptual debates over equality appear in a legal context on pages 364–372. When rights were examined in chapter 6, the due process clause of the Fourteenth Amendment served as the focus. Here, in discussing equality, we turn to another clause from the Fourteenth Amendment—namely, the equal protection clause. The distinction between formal and substantive equality serves as a base from which to explore the issues of discrimination and affirmative action (see Controversies, page 372).

A. THE NATURE OF EQUALITY

What does equality mean? The French Declaration of Rights states, "All men are born and remain equal" (Article I). Is that true? Is everyone born equal? Was nineteenth-century philosopher Jeremy Bentham correct when he claimed (in *Anarchical Fallacies*) that it would then follow that lunatics could lock up sane people, and idiots would have the right to govern? Does the French Declaration mean that it violates equality to treat individuals according to their luck or misfortune? Does it prohibit treating individuals according to their social and economic status? Does equality mean that we should treat similar cases similarly? Does equality mean "equality of opportunity" or "equality of results"? The idea of equality is so complex that Peter Westen finds it empty (see Reading 7-1). However, before we cast aside equality, let us first try to understand the different senses of equality that operate in daily life. In Reading 7-2, we will look at why, even if equality proves to be important in our daily lives, it should take priority in public policy.

READING 7-1

Equality, an Empty Idea
"Introduction to Speaking of Equality" (1990)

Peter Westen

One day, while on vacation in Guatemala, I go to a *campesino* [peasant or farmer's] market to buy food for dinner. I ask a vendor for one pound of black beans. He puts a brass weight marked "one pound" in one pan of a hand-held balance and pours beans into the other pan until the two come into balance. "Bueno," he says, "ya son iquales" ("Good, now they're equal").

What does the vendor mean when he says that the two pans of the scale are "equal"? Does he mean that they are absolutely identical in weight? Does he mean that they are highly similar in weight? Or does 'equal' mean something different from—something in between—'identical,' on the one hand, and 'similar,' on the other?

I try to buy a newspaper, but the vendor cannot make change for a $10 bill. I ask the pharmacist for change. She takes the $10 bill and gives me two $5 bills, while counting aloud, "5 + 5 = 10."

What does the pharmacist mean by saying "5 + 5 = 10"? Does 'equal' have the same meaning in arithmetic as it does for the *campesino?* If the pharmacist means something different, where does the difference lie—in the meaning of the word 'equal' or in something to which the 'equal' refers? Is there any core meaning of 'equality' that remains constant in both usages?

After buying snacks for my three children, I sit in a cafe and read the newspaper. I read that the people of Guatemala have recently adopted a new constitution, which states that "in Guatemala, all people are free and equal." What does it mean to say in law that all people are equal? Does the legal equality of one Guatemalan to another differ from the mathematical equality of "5 + 5 = 10" and the descriptive equality of the two pans of the balance scale? Is there any sense in which the meaning of equality remains the same in all three instances? Why does the concept of equality in the Guatemalan constitution seem more elusive, more complex, and more controversial than the equality of "5 + 5 = 10"? And if the former equality is more enigmatic than the latter, where does the enigma lie—in the concept of equality itself, or somewhere else?

I return home with the snacks for the children—chocolate for my son, gum for my daughters. "Because I want to treat you all equally," I say, "I have brought each of you your favorite treat." My son likes the chocolate but not my explanation. "I agree that you're treating us fairly," he says, "but you're not treating us equally because you're bringing us different things." Who is right? Am I right that I treated my children equally, or is my son right that I did not? Or is it possible that both of us are right?

My older daughter has a different problem with the gum. Like her younger sister she would rather have gum than chocolate, but unlike her sister, she does not care much for any kind of sweet. She would rather have the money than the gum. "I know you're trying to be fair," she says, "but it's not really equal to give the same thing to both of us if it's something she likes more than I do."

Am I right in thinking that I am treating my daughters equally by giving the same quantity of gum to each without further distinguishing between them? Or is the older child right when she says that no distribution is really equal which has a disparate impact on them by giving one more pleasure than the other? Are we both right? Or does the answer lie in the distinction some commentators draw between treating people "equally," on the one hand, and treating them "as equals," on the other? Have I succeeded in treating the girls equally and yet failed to treat them as equals? Or is it sophistic to distinguish between equal treatment and treatment as equals?

The older daughter's complaint also raises a question about the relationship between fair treatment and equal treatment. What is the connection between treating a person fairly and treating her equally? Why does she regard it as a form of moral criticism to call the treatment "unequal"? Is unequal treatment a moral concept, or is it a purely descriptive concept? Is it both?

I am still thinking about the relationship between equal treatment and fair treatment when my wife calls us to dinner. My wife serves the meal to the children by giving the largest portion to our son, who is a teenager and has the largest appetite, the next largest portion to the older daughter, who is going through a growth spurt, and the smallest portion to the youngest, who never eats much at dinner. She also gives everyone a glass of water. Everything goes smoothly until I suggest that we have treated the children equally by treating them in accordance with their needs. My son does not like my use of 'equal'.

"I don't get it," he says. "The more you talk about equality, the less I understand it. 'Equal' means giving us each the same amount: It means taking food and dividing it by the number of people at the table. What Mom did with the glasses of water was equal. What she did with the meal was proportional—dividing the meal in proportion to our needs. 'Equal' is equal; it's not proportional."

I resist the temptation to say that while some commentators agree with him, others (including Aristotle) disagree. Some agree that per-capita distributions are the only truly equal distributions. Others believe that, while per-capita distributions differ in substance from distributions in accord with needs (or in accord with merit, or effort, or wants), per capita distributions are no more inherently equal than other principled distributions.

Nor do I tell my son that some commentators would question the proposition he regards as self-evident, namely, that his mother treated him and his sisters equally by giving them each a glass of water. Whether it is truly equal, they would say, depends upon her *reason* for giving him a glass of water. If she gave him the glass of water because (and *only* because) she had already given water to his sisters, then she treated him equally. If, however, she gave him the glass of water because she believes every child is entitled to at least one glass of water per meal (and not because she had already given glasses of water to his sisters), then she did not treat him equally with his sisters. This is so, they say, because treatment is equal if and only if it is treatment to which a person is entitled only by virtue of its having already been given to others.

After dinner several children from the neighborhood come to the door soliciting contributions for their parish church's Lenten celebration. Each holds out a tin can asking that we favor him with our donation. Our girls both want to give a portion of their allowance, but they don't know how they should distribute it. My wife, not seeing any basis for distinguishing among the children, feels we should divide the donation among them equally. "Unless someone gives me a good reason for preferring one child over the others," she says, "I really think we have to treat them the same."

My son, who is embarrassed by the throng of children, doesn't feel presumptively obliged to treat them equally. "I don't see why it's up to us to find reasons for treating them differently; it's up to them to show us reasons for treating them the same. Why do we have to resolve doubts in their favor?"

The difference of opinion between my wife and son is the difference between competing normative propositions—competing maxims—regarding equality. My wife is proceeding in accord with what some call "the presumption of equality," that is, the normative proposition that "people ought to be treated equally unless there are good reasons for treating them differently." My son, feeling no presumption one way or the other, may be unconsciously proceeding in accord with what is sometimes called the "principle of equality," namely, the principle that "equals should be treated equally, and unequals should be treated unequally."

Which of the two propositions of equality is the more persuasive? Are they consistent with one another? What do they both mean in the context at hand? Who are the "people" who are to be treated equally within the meaning of the "presumption of equality"—only those children who are soliciting contributions at our door, or all the door-to-door solicitors in town? What would constitute a "good reason" for treating the children unequally within the meaning of the presumption? Is a personal preference for redheads a good reason? Who are the "equals" who are to be treated equally within the meaning of the "principle of equality"—the first child to approach us, or the one we wish most to please? And what is the meaning of "equal treatment" within both propositions of equality—to donate to the most courteous child, or to all the children per capita?

I turn on the evening news to hear about a controversial campaign by Guatemalan women in favor of affirmative action. Advocates on both sides of the controversy adopt the language of equality. I am reminded of other controversies in which both sides invoke 'equality' in support of their contrary positions—controversies over the use of sex tables in computing life insurance, the use of height and strength requirements for fire departments, and the maintenance of separate athletic events for men and women. How does the concept of equality accommodate such mutually exclusive positions, and what is the source of its compelling rhetorical force? Why is it easier to argue in favor of equality than against it? Why is inequality always on the defensive? Is it because equality is inherently desirable, or presumptively desirable? If either, how can equality also lend itself to the most controverted of social causes? How can equality be simultaneously both desirable and controversial?

In one sense, these questions regarding equality differ significantly. Some involve descriptive statements of equality; others involve prescriptive statements of equality. Some look to whether rules are equal on their face, others to whether rules are equal as applied. Some concern the meaning of 'equals,' others the meaning of 'equal treatment.' Some probe the relationship between equality and per-capita distribution, others the relationship between equality and rights of nondiscrimination. Some involve propositions of equality ("equals should be treated equally"), others the rhetorical force of equality. Yet in another sense the questions are also the same. They all call for an analysis of language—an inquiry into ordinary usages of the word 'equality.' Their answers turn not on contested moral propositions but on linguistic analysis of the concept of equality in moral and legal discourse.

It is fitting that these questions of equality should differ from one another and yet be the same, for equality is itself a relationship that uniquely straddles the gap between "different" and "same": things that are equal, being distinct things, are necessarily different; and yet, being equal, they are also the same. Moreover, the general concept of equality that underlies particular relationships of equality has both a fixed element, which remains the same in all its usages (at least regarding persons and things we perceive through the senses), and a variable term, which can differ greatly from one statement of equality to another. The key to understanding the meaning and rhetorical force of 'equality' in law and morals, I believe, lies in identifying the kinds of variable terms that enter into moral and legal statements of equality.

READING 7-2

Equality, a Public Goal
"Should Equality Be a Primary Social Policy Goal?" (1996)

Robert H. Bork and Mark Tushnet

DO THE CONCEPTS OF OUR LEGAL SYSTEM HINDER EFFORTS TO ACHIEVE A MERITOCRACY?

One of the standard arguments for rolling back affirmative action is that discrimination no longer exists to an extent necessary to require remedial action.

But Robert H. Bork, the former judge who is now a fellow at the American Enterprise Institute in Washington, D.C., calls into question the very notion of equality as desirable social policy. In an excerpt from his controversial new book, Slouching Towards Gomorrah: Modern Liberalism and American Decline *(Harper-Collins), Bork argues that modern attempts to achieve equality under the law have coalesced into the relentless pursuit of what he calls "radical egalitarianism."*

"The usual strategy for coping with the discomfort of knowing that others are superior in some way is to try to reduce the inequalities by bringing the more

*fortunate down or by preventing him from being more fortunate," Bork writes.
"This is the strategy of envy."*

*Mark Tushnet, a professor of constitutional law at Georgetown University
Law Center in Washington, D.C., rejects the argument that laws promoting
equality undermine advancement on the basis of merit. If anything, Tushnet
says, they open doors to the truly talented who would otherwise be shut out.*

Yes: The Passion for Equality Denigrates American Life

Robert H. Bork

Despite its rhetorical vagueness—or because of it—the Declaration of Independence profoundly moved Americans at the time of its inception, and it
does still. The proposition that all men are created equal said what the
colonists already believed; so, as historian Gordon Wood put it, equality became "the single most powerful and radical ideological force in all of American history." That is true and, though it verges on heresy to say so, it is also
profoundly unfortunate.

This pronouncement of equality was sweeping but sufficiently ambiguous so that even slaveholders, including Thomas Jefferson, subscribed to it.
The ambiguity was dangerous because it invited continual expansion of the
concept and its requirements.

The declaration was not, clearly, a document that was understood at the
time to promise equality of condition, not even among white male Americans.
The meaning of equality was heavily modified by the American idea of reward
according to individual achievement and reverence for private property.

But those modifications are hostile to the egalitarian impulse, which
constantly expands the areas in which equality is thought desirable or even
mandatory. Hence, they, like the constraints on the ideas of liberty and the
pursuit of happiness, gradually give way before the active principle of, in this
case, ever greater equality.

The apparent difficulty of requiring equality of wisdom and intelligence was solved in a satirical story by Kurt Vonnegut in 1961, even before the plethora of civil rights laws seeking equality by race, ethnicity,
sex, age, disability, and so on. Americans would achieve perfect equality by
forcing people of superior intelligence to wear mental handicap radios that
emit unsettling noises every 20 seconds to keep them from taking advantage of their brains, people of superior strength or grace to be burdened
with weights, and those of uncommon beauty to wear masks. Thus, social
reality can be made to conform with the envious man's and the law's
wishes.

The unwillingness to admit inherent individual differences is astounding.
Shortly after I became a federal judge, I spoke informally to a gathering of Yale
Law School alumni in Washington, D.C. Someone asked how I found the quality
of briefs and oral arguments, and I replied that some were quite good but a great
many were poor, some sadly so. The question was then put: Why should that be
so? I said many areas of law and procedure had become so complex that the gene
pool was inadequate to operate the system. Afterward, my clerks gathered

around and said, urgently: "Never say anything like that again." They did not deny that it was true, but they were adamant that it was not a politic thing to do.

This compassion born of the passion for equality leads to the power of claiming victim status. We have become what author Charles J. Sykes called "a nation of victims." The list of groups is virtually endless, once including everyone but ordinary white males. Now there is even a men's movement claiming victim status.

To quote Alexis de Tocqueville: "The nations of our time cannot prevent the conditions of men from becoming equal, but it depends upon themselves whether the principle of equality is to lead them to servitude or freedom, to knowledge or barbarism, to prosperity or wretchedness."

No: You Can't Have Excellence Without Equality

Mark Tushnet

Robert H. Bork doesn't share a passion for equality. He prefers a hierarchy of merit. He doesn't realize that the two are entirely compatible.

He is in the company of many defenders of natural inequality:

- Aristotle believed some people were slaves by nature and thought that natural differences between men and women justified male rule over women.
- John C. Calhoun likewise thought natural inequalities justified natural social hierarchies—a polite way of saying he believed in racial slavery.
- More recently, Allan Bloom prominently defended a natural hierarchy based on intellectual merit.

When it has been easy to identify who should be on top and who on bottom in these natural hierarchies—when they are defined by race and gender—the results have been unfortunate.

Let's take the idea of a hierarchy of merit seriously. How are we going to identify the people who deserve to be on top?

People don't come with visible markers—"Grade A" and the like—of intellectual or other kinds of merit. We don't have genetic tests that can help, and because there are lots of kinds of merit, I doubt that we ever will.

So we're going to be limited to indirect measures of merit. The one that's likely to seem most attractive is success: Cream rises to the top. At least successful people such as Bork and me may like to think so. By rooting the passion for equality in envy, Bork suggests that it comes from the resentment of those at the bottom toward the successes of those at the top.

Who knows whether that pop psychology is right? When I think about my life and background, Bork's psycho-diagnosis seems wrong.

My grandparents came to the United States from Eastern Europe early this century. They worked hard and managed to send most of their children to college. I grew up in suburban New Jersey and went to Ivy League schools.

I doubt that I benefited from "affirmative action" programs of any sort, and I feel the pull of the idea of a hierarchy of merit.

But, I have to say, I can't detect in myself any envy whatsoever at the successes of Michael Jordan and Bill Gates. I admire them because they are very good at what they do.

But so are thousands of single mothers in our inner cities, struggling as best they can to raise their children to be honest and hard-working. And so are thousands of production workers, going to hard jobs every day to try to make life better for their children.

Cream doesn't rise to the top when there's something in the way. The Americans With Disabilities Act shows that we understand how physical obstacles can interfere with a person's ability to achieve what he or she deserves. So can social obstacles—inadequate education, health services that do not allow people to deal with chronic difficulties due, in part, to unhealthy conditions in their neighborhoods and at their jobs.

The passion for equality may arise from a realistic appreciation that social obstacles to achievement are real. When such obstacles exist, we might be passionate about equality to make sure that merit really is rewarded.

Bork, Robert and Tushnet, Mark. "Equality" from *ABA Journal* (September 1994). Reprinted by permission of ABA Journal.

B. TYPES OF EQUALITY

No state shall . . . deny to any person within its jurisdiction the equal protection of the laws.

—Equal Protection Clause,
Fourteenth Amendment, U.S. Constitution

Constitutional equality usually involves an individual's complaint about an inequality, but a Fourteenth Amendment **equal protection** claim does not permit purely individual claims. These are dealt with by procedural due process (see chapter 6). The equal protection clause concerns itself with how public officials, including the legislature and executive, justify classifying individuals into groups and then making comparisons among the groups. Public officials must distinguish among different groups of individuals, and public policy often treats these groups unequally. For example, the tax code penalizes married couples. In addition, some classifications, such as race, raise more suspicions than others. Therefore, the courts give **strict scrutiny** to classifications (**suspect classes**) that appear to mask prejudices against groups.

Four issues arise regarding constitutional equality: who is involved, what the inequality is, what justification there is for the inequality, and what remedy fixes the inequality. Regarding the first issue of who is involved—not all groups are comparable. A children's rights advocate may claim an inequality because the government refuses driving privileges to six-year-olds, but this position stands open to the criticism that the advocate is comparing apples to oranges. Children and adults do not make up comparable groups, because six-year-olds do not have the abilities required to drive automobiles. Second, what are the inequalities? Are they tangible, quantifiable items, such as educational resources, measured in dollars? Are they privileges or benefits? Assume a plausible comparison between adult males and females. If only males qualify to vote, then an inequality emerges. Similarly, childbirth benefits such as a paid leave of absence that females qualify for, but not males, may indicate an inequality. Third, what justification does the state have for maintaining the inequality? Should courts require stronger justifications for treating groups differently in certain types of cases (for example, cases involving race) than in others (such as licensed and unlicensed optometrists)? Fourth, once an inequality has been established, what remedies are available to rectify it? Are remedies limited to removing formal obstacles to equality, or are more positive plans of action permitted?

An assessment of equality, therefore, requires four basic determinations. First, who made the claim, and what groups occupy each side of the equation or divide? Second, does the alleged inequality exist? Third, does the inequality have a viable justification? Fourth, what would remedy the inequality? Although this analysis oversimplifies, it serves as a framework for making sense of disputes concerning equality. Discussions often distinguish between two types of equality—formal and substantive.

1. Formal Equality

As the name implies, formal equality relies on thinking of equality in formal terms, somewhat like an equation where $A = B$ or $A \neq B$. The four issues outlined in the previous paragraph become matters of formal judgment (see chapter 3, p. 103 on formalism), the analysis of which involves four tasks. First, compare the individuals or groups on either side of the equation; second, determine whether an inequality exists on either side of the equation; third, assess the state's justification for the inequality; and fourth, remove government-sanctioned obstacles (formal or explicit) to the process for attaining equality. Thus, judges would formally analyze group comparability, type of inequality, justification for inequality, and obstacles to equality. Those making the judgments would, supposedly, make them on neutral grounds— meaning here two things. First, judges do not make any substantive judgments about one group over another. Second, they do not determine if any substantive values are at stake in retaining the classification.

Aristotle (384–322 B.C.), who studied at Plato's Academy; tutored Alexander the Great; and founded his own school, the Lyceum, provided a classical statement of formal equality (see Reading 7-3). He agreed with his teacher, Plato, that the state should play a critical role in education and that the state must direct the laws toward human good to create virtuous citizens (see chapter 8). The Greeks referred to the state of Athens not as "Athens" but as "the Athenians," which symbolized the state as a community of citizens who shared the tasks of government (see the discussion of Socrates' trial in chapter 1). An Athenian citizen was "a man who shares in the administration of justice and in the holding of office" (Aristotle *Politics,* 1275a). The administration of justice included developing rules that distributed goods and benefits according to proportional equality. Aristotle called this **distributive justice,** distinguishing it from **corrective justice,** which compensated or rectified unfair gains and losses. Compromise and proportion characterized Aristotle's thought. He believed that justice is a balance between one citizen's having too much and another too little, but equality does not mean that all individuals have identical goods and benefits. Judgments about equality take place against a background of ends pursued. **Proportional equality** treats all citizens in proportion to what they deserve, or to their demonstrated merits; the best flutes go to the best flute players. Equality requires making comparisons among similar kinds. According to Aristotle, equality does not mean giving equal shares to unequals. After making a qualitative judgment about kinds, the analysis becomes more formal, more like mathematics, where mathematicians draw lines to divide geometric shapes evenly or proportionately. Should judges draw similar lines when considering equality? Is equality a procedural matter that requires only a fair administration?

READING 7-3

Formal Equality
"How Equality is Determined"

Aristotle

5.34 But a Detailed Description of Special Justice is Needed

Special justice, however, and the corresponding way for something to be just [must be divided].

One species is found in the distribution of honours or wealth or anything else that can be divided among members of a community who share in a political system; for here it is possible for one member to have a share equal or unequal to another's.

Another species concerns rectification in transactions. This species has two parts, since one sort of transaction is voluntary, and one involuntary. Voluntary transactions include selling, buying, lending, pledging, renting, depositing, hiring out—these are called voluntary because the origin of these transactions is voluntary. Some involuntary ones are secret, e.g. theft, adultery, poisoning, pimping, slave-deception, murder by treachery, false witness; others are forcible, e.g. assault, imprisonment, murder, plunder, mutilation, slander, insult.

5.4 JUSTICE IN DISTRIBUTION

5.41 Justice, Fairness and Equality

Since the unjust person is unfair, and what is unjust is unfair, there is clearly an intermediate between the unfair [extremes], and this is what is fair; for in any action where too much and too little are possible, the fair [amount] is also possible. And so if what is unjust is unfair, what is just is fair (*ison*), as seems true to everyone even without argument.

And since what is equal (*ison*) [and fair] is intermediate, what is just is some sort of intermediate. And since what is equal involves at least two things [equal to each other], it follows that what is just must be intermediate and equal, and related to some people. In so far as it is intermediate, it must be between too much and too little; in so far as it is equal, it involves two things; and in so far as it is just, it is just for some people. Hence what is just requires four things at least; the people for whom it is just are two, and the [equal] things that are involved are two.

5.42 How Equality Is Determined

Equality for the people involved will be the same as for the things involved, since [in a just arrangement] the relation between the people will be the same as the relation between the things involved. For if the people involved are not equal, they will not [justly] receive equal shares; indeed, whenever equals receive unequal shares, or unequals equal shares, in a distribution, that is the source of quarrels and accusations.

This is also clear from considering what fits a person's worth. For everyone agrees that what is just in distributions must fit some sort of worth, but what they call worth is not the same; supporters of democracy say it is free citizenship, some supporters of oligarchy say it is wealth, others good birth, while supporters of aristocracy say it is virtue.

5.43 Justice Is Proportionate Equality

Hence what is just [since it requires equal shares for equal people] is in some way proportionate. For proportion is special to number as a whole, not only to numbers consisting of [abstract] units, since it is equality of ratios and requires at least four terms.

Now divided proportion clearly requires four terms. But so does continuous proportion, since here we use one term as two, and mention it twice. When, e.g., line A is to line B as B is to C, B is mentioned twice; and so if B is introduced twice, the terms in the proportion will be four.

What is just will also require at least four terms, with the same ratio [between the pairs], since the people [A and B] and the items [C and D] involved are divided in the same way. Term C, then, is to term D as A is to B, and, taking them alternately, B is to D as A is to C. Hence there will also be the same relation of whole [A and C] to whole [B and D]; this is the relation in which the distribution pairs them, and it pairs them justly if this is how they are combined.

Hence the combination of term A with C and of B with D is what is just in distribution, and this way of being just is intermediate, while what is unjust is contrary to what is proportionate. For what is proportionate is intermediate, and what is just is proportionate.

This is the sort of proportion that mathematicians call geometrical, since in geometrical proportion the relation of whole to whole is the same as the relation of each [part] to each [part]. But this proportion [involved in justice] is not continuous, since there is no single term for both the person and the item.

What is just, then, is what is proportionate, and what is unjust is what is counter-proportionate. Hence [in an unjust action] one term becomes more and the other less; and this is indeed how it turns out in practice, since the one doing injustice has more of the good, and the victim less. With an evil the ratio is reversed, since the lesser evil, compared to the greater, counts as a good; for the lesser evil is more choiceworthy than the greater, what is choiceworthy is good, and what is more choiceworthy is a greater good.

This, then, is the first species of what is just. . . .

DISCUSSION ISSUES

1. *Equally Bad Treatment.* Can individuals be treated equally but equally badly? "If a ruler were to boil his subjects in oil, jumping in afterwards himself, it would be an injustice, but it would be no inequality of treatment" (Frankena 1962, p. 17).

2. *Equally Bad Interracial Marriages.* A Virginia antimiscegenation statute (1924) prohibited interracial marriages. The Lovings married in the District of Columbia and later moved to Virginia. In 1959, they pled guilty to violating the Virginia statute, but the trial judge suspended their sentence on the condition that they not return to Virginia for twenty-five years. The state of Virginia argued before the Supreme Court of the United States that the statute did not violate equal protection, since it punished blacks and whites equally. The law contained the Pocahontas exception, permitting whites to marry "persons with one-sixteenth of the blood of the American Indian." Discounting the Pocahontas exception, the Virginia law, on its face, applied equally to blacks and whites, but the Court struck down the law (*Loving v. Virginia* 1967). Did the Court have to go beyond formal equality to a substantive equality analysis to reach its decision?

3. *Pregnant Men.* California's disability insurance excluded pregnant women from coverage. The Court, using a sense of formal equality, denied the charge of gender discrimination, arguing: "[T]he program divides potential recipients into two groups—pregnant women and non pregnant persons. While the first group is exclusively female, the second group includes members of both sexes. [T]here is no risk from which men are protected and women are not. Likewise, there is no risk from which women are protected and men are not" (*Gedulig v. Aiello* 1974). Apparently, the Court might have found it discriminatory to give benefits only to pregnant women and not to men, unless it had the possibility of pregnant men in mind. Congress overturned the decision. It passed the Pregnancy Discrimination Act, amending Title VII of the Civil Rights Act. The legislation prohibited discrimination based on pregnancy, childbirth, and related medical conditions. Is disadvantageous treatment of pregnant workers ever permissible? Is it paternalistic to treat pregnant workers differently than other workers?

4. *Topless Men.* A Texas federal appeals court struck down a regulation of female topless dancing, finding that the regulation made an invalid gender classification. "The regulation only regulates exposure of female breasts but not male breasts and, therefore, unconstitutionally discriminates against female topless dancers." The court refused judicial recognition of the "concept that the breasts of female topless dancers, unlike their male counterparts, are commonly associated with sexual arousal." One commentator nominated *Williams v. Fort Worth* (1989) as one of the ten worst non–supreme court decisions (Schwartz 1997). Compare Williams to *Plessy v. Ferguson* (1896), where the court took judicial notice of race as a scientific fact determined by the "one drop" rule (see chapter 3, Discussion Issue 6, page 130).

Substantive equality removes the appearance of neutrality in formal equality. Critics charge that formal equality, through its focus on neutrality and process, masks inequalities. Formal equality allows judges to appear to remove obstacles obstructing equality between groups while, in reality, making non-neutral value judgments about the groups. Formally, two groups may have an equal opportunity to take public transportation and to attend schools. Formal analysis would permit judges to ignore the difficult conditions under which one group must take public transportation to attend public school. Critics contend that debates over equality must face disputes over substantive values.

Substantive equality provides an alternative framework for judges. First, within a substantive framework, judges do not mechanically compare groups, but instead, they evaluate the actual status of groups claiming an inequality. Second, they do not simply move aspects from one side of the equation to the other side. Inequality involves more than individuals' not being similarly situated. Pregnant women in the workplace are in a particular social and economic situation that results from a special political history. A policy that gives pregnancy benefits, such as a paid leave of absence prior to and after the birth, equally to eligible male and female employees ignores critical gender differences. Judges, in the substantive view, must go beyond looking at the similarities among select individuals within each group and must assess the overall situation of the group. Third, judges must take positive action by either approving existing policies or proposing new ones. Therefore, substantively remedying an inequality involves more than formally removing obstacles. Substantive equality, in a sense, promotes inequality. It gives one group—women, for instance—a right to unequal treatment and resources. Some advocates further claim that equal opportunity provides little to groups most in need—that is, the disadvantaged—and that equality of resources constitutes true equality.

During the past century, the Supreme Court slowly adopted a substantive social (as opposed to economic) equality perspective. In *Lochner v. New York* (1905) (see Reading 3-12), the Court invalidated a New York statute setting maximum hours for bakers on the grounds that the statute violated the freedom of employers and employees to contract with each other. During the so-called Lochner Era, the Court invalidated many similar statutes and, as an activist judiciary, invalidated many pieces of social legislation to protect freedom of contract. The Court's protection of the value of freedom-of-contract came to an abrupt end in 1937. A seemingly innocuous case, *United States v. Carolene Products* (1938), ushered in radical changes in Supreme Court jurisprudence. *Carolene Products* concerned a congressional ban against the interstate shipment of skimmed milk mixed with nonmilk fats. The decision itself hardly qualified as historical, or even noteworthy. However, a footnote to the opinion, Footnote 4 by Justice Harlan Fiske Stone, took on a life of its own. It became, according to Justice Powell, "the most celebrated footnote in constitutional law" (1982, p. 1087):

> (1). There may be narrower scope for operation of the presumption of constitutionality when legislation appears on its face to be within a specific prohibition of the Constitution such as those of the first ten amendments, which are deemed equally specific when held to be embraced within the Fourteenth. . . .

(2). It is unnecessary to consider now whether legislation which restricts those political processes which can ordinarily be expected to bring about repeal of undesirable legislation, is to be subjected to more exacting judicial scrutiny under the general prohibition of the Fourteenth Amendment than are most other types of legislation.... (3). Nor need we enquire whether similar considerations enter into the review of statutes directed at particular religious or national, or racial minorities: whether prejudice against discrete and insular minorities may be a special condition, which tends seriously to curtail the operation of those political processes ordinarily to be relied upon to protect minorities, and which may call for a correspondingly more searching judicial inquiry.

Footnote 4 contains a very clear structure, with each of the three sentences containing a distinct jurisprudential doctrine. The first sentence summarizes the debate over incorporating the Bill of Rights. One side advocated complete incorporation, which would make the Bill of Rights binding on the states as well as the federal government. The other side, who eventually won the debate, proposed selective incorporation. Only a limited number of constitutional rights have become binding on the states. Furthermore, the Court almost immediately adopted the principles expressed in the second sentence, which proposed a more exacting form of scrutiny when legislation directly impeded the political process (see the discussion on Ely's representation reinforcement model in Reading 4-6). It took the Court many more years, culminating in *Brown v. Board of Education of Topeka,* to settle in on the theory set forth in the third sentence, which promotes the courts engaging in the strict scrutiny (demanding the most stringent form of justification) of legislation affecting "discrete and insular minorities."

Justice Frankfurter observed that "a footnote hardly seems to be an appropriate way of announcing a new constitutional doctrine. . . ." (*Kovacs v. Cooper,* 1941, pp. 90–91, concurring). While commentators may exaggerate the impact of the *Carolene Products* footnote, a great deal of contemporary constitutional jurisprudence stems from what appeared to be an innocuous footnote. Why has Footnote 4 generated such an intense interest among jurists? Professor Robert Cover (1982, pp. 1294–97) argued that the adoption of Footnote 4 brought the first full-fledged judicial recognition of a social sense of "minorities." Before that time, the judiciary did not consider that minorities had any qualitative status. Measured by numbers, minorities did not possess any qualities that would distinguish them as disadvantaged. Sometimes an individual is in the minority, and other times, in the majority. Therefore, a quantitative sense of "minorities" prevailed. According to Cover, Footnote 4 represented the first time that the Court turned its attention specifically to social or disadvantaged groups, the so-called "discrete and insular minorities." Minorities, then, became something more than numbers. Many jurists opposed Cover's sympathetic reading of Footnote 4 including Justice Rehnquist, who found the idea of "discrete and insular minorities" ("suspect classes") subject to arbitrary manipulation: "It would hardly take extraordinary ingenuity for lawyers to find 'discrete and insular' minorities at every turn in the road" (*Sugarman v. Dougall* 1973, dissenting). Rehnquist charged that the Court, without any standards, could freely create suspect classes. Given the contorted way in which the Court has drawn the boundaries around "discrete and insular minorities," Rehnquist's reservations may be on target. The Court has designated four distinct "suspect classes," including race, alienage (noncitizens), gender, and illegitimacy (children of unmarried couples). What factors could possibly unite these different groups? Bruce Ackerman (1985) gave a partial defense of the substantive equality approach contained in Footnote 4, applauding its past use in dealing with racial problems. However, he foresaw its limits in dealing with the most critical social problems of the future. Before examining substantive equality further, let us first look at the Court's substantive equality methodology.

Levels of Judicial Review

Substantive equality concerns seem to provide grounds for a more active judiciary that is more vigilant of inequalities. Some inequalities require greater judicial attention than others. These go to the Court as legislative classifications. The Court asks the legislature to justify treating classifications (or classes) differently. The degree of watchfulness or scrutiny set forth by the Court corresponds to different levels of judicial review. The Court has adopted three relatively clear tests for legislative classifications under its equal protection review: strict scrutiny test, intermediate level of review, and the rational relationship test. At one extreme, the **strict scrutiny test** virtually prohibits governmental use of some classifications, primarily race classifications. The test requires the government to prove that the statutory objective is compelling and that the classification is necessary. Few laws could pass this test. At the other end, the **rational relationship test** presumes the legitimacy of some classifications (economic and social welfare). The person challenging the classification must show that the government does not have a legitimate objective and that the classification does not bear a rational relationship to the objective. In the 1970s, the Court developed an **intermediate standard of review** requiring the government to show an important statutory objective and requiring the classification to be substantially related to the objective. The Court used intermediate review for gender and illegitimacy.

Constitutional Standard	Burden of Proof	Objective Required	Classification Required
Strict scrutiny	Government	Compelling	Necessary
Intermediate	Government	Important	Substantially related
Rational basis	Challenger	Legitimate	Rationally related

Suspect Classes (Disadvantaged Groups)

Notice the difference that a slight twist makes. The situation changes dramatically depending on whether courts focus on traits or emphasize groups. If a trait, such as race or gender, determines a classification, then any classification based on that trait becomes suspect, even those designed to help that group. Any classification based on race, then, is suspect. Discriminating against whites would prove as problematic as discriminating against blacks, since both classifications rely on the suspect trait of race. This line of reasoning fits a formal equality model, within which it is difficult to defend so-called benign classifications such as affirmative action. Even race classifications that help blacks prove problematic, since they depend on race as a means of classifying groups. The antidiscrimination principle exemplifies the trait-based approach (Reading 7-7).

Alternatively, courts could focus not so much on the trait as on the group. A substantive equality model regards discrimination as more than drawing lines unequally between groups. A substantive analysis proceeds along the following lines. Discriminatory treatment directs prejudice and harm at a particular group, which may be distinguished by a trait or traits. However, the problem lies not in the means of classification, but in the fact that some groups (blacks) within the overall classification (race) suffer disproportionately. If the government were to base medical benefits on the size of infants' ears, for example, the critical problem would not lie in using the trait "ear size" as a means of classification. Rather, judicial focus would fall on the denial of benefits to small-eared infants. Judges would then ask the following kinds of questions: Is this the first and only instance in which they have been denied a benefit that a comparable group has been given? Have they experienced a history of discriminatory treatment? Does this group qualify as a suspect class—that is, a disadvantaged group? Does the suspect class require an extremely vigilant judicial eye? Should the Court offer judicial protection by strictly scrutinizing the legislature's goals and objections? In other words, should the Court demand extremely strong justifications from the legislature? A judge employing a group disadvantaging principle would ask these questions (Reading 7-8).

When it has used groups instead of traits, the Court has considered a number of factors to determine whether a group has qualified as a suspect class. Although the Court has never clearly stated the criteria for suspect group status, it has given some indications. For example, the Court has stated that poverty had "none of the traditional indicia of suspectness: the class is not saddled with such disabilities, or subjected to such a history of purposeful unequal treatment, or relegated to such a position of political powerlessness as to command extraordinary protection from the majoritarian process" (*San Antonio Independent School District v. Rodriguez* 1973). Based on this finding, should poverty qualify as a suspect class? Consider the Court's analysis of government regulations that treat members of an immediate family differently from close relatives: "As a historical matter, [close relatives] have not been subjected to discrimination; they do not exhibit obvious immutable, or distinguishing characteristics that define them as a discrete group and they are not a minority or politically powerless" (*Lying v. Castillo* 1986). Should age qualify as a suspect class? The Court gave the following reasons for rejecting it: "While the treatment of the aged in this Nation has not been wholly free of discrimination, such persons, unlike, say, those who have been discriminated against on the basis of race or national origin, have not experienced a 'history of purposeful unequal treatment' or been subjected to unique disabilities on the basis of stereotyped characteristics not truly indicative of their abilities." (*Massachusetts Board of Retirement v. Murgia* 1976). Do the aged have a strong case for being considered a disadvantaged group? What groups have been victimized by discrimination?

1. Discrimination

Isaiah Berlin notes a common assumption that "equality needs no reasons, only inequality does so" (Olafson, 1961, page 130). Courts focus largely on inequalities, such as discrimination. Does inequality ever have a good reason? Do legislatures sometimes have good reasons for treating people differently? When does treating people differently become prejudicial discrimination? In 1892, the police arrested Homer Plessy for taking a seat in the white coach of a railway car. Plessy described himself as "seven-eights Caucasian and one-eighth African blood" (see chapter 3, Discussion Issue 6, page 130). The state charged Plessy with violation of a statute enforcing racial segregation in railway coaches. The U.S. Supreme Court upheld the constitutionality of the statute, claiming that separation did not constitute inequality under the Fourteenth Amendment as long as the facilities and opportunities were somewhat similar (*Plessy v. Ferguson* 1896). "Separate but equal" became the law of Jim Crow, which was "a derogatory term used for a black person that came from a song-and-dance routine depicting a comic, jumping, stupid rag doll" (Berman et al. 1996, p. 704, fn. 2). Southern states relied on the separate-but-equal doctrine to segregate everything from public toilets to courtroom Bibles.

In another case, an eight-year-old girl traveled twenty-one blocks to a black school every day. The Topeka, Kansas, Board of Education refused her entrance to a white school just five blocks from her home. Her father, Oliver Brown, sued the school board. A lower court found the black school and the white school basically equal. In *Brown v. Board of Education,* the U.S. Supreme Court refused to engage in a formal equality inquiry (see Reading 7-4). It did not focus on tangible and measurable factors, such as buildings, curricula, qualifications, and teachers' salaries, on each side of the equality equation. Instead, it turned to the effects of segregation politics on public education, finding separate educational facilities inherently unequal.

Brown has generated a great deal of controversy among constitutional scholars, as the readings illustrate. Herbert Wechsler (see Reading 7-5) finds the *Brown* decision unprincipled, since it rests on changeable social science evidence rather than on **neutral principles.** He faults the Court for not giving reasons that would go beyond the immediate case and that would apply to similar future cases. In addition, his analysis of *Brown* raises the following question: What if blacks had truly equal facilities and did better in segregated schools than they did in integrated ones? Paul Brest (see Reading 7-6) defends a nonneutral principle that relies on substantive values widely accepted in society. His **antidiscrimination principle** disfavors decisions and practices that depend on race-based classifications. Owen Fiss (see Reading 7-7) tries to show that the antidiscrimination principle does not go far enough. He proposes a stronger substantive equality principle—namely, the **group disadvantaging principle.** Fiss claims that the choice between Brest's antidiscrimination trait-based principle and his own group disadvantage principle makes a difference in two types of cases. His principle would reject innocent criteria such as test performances if they had a particularly negative effect on disadvantaged groups, while the antidiscrimination principle would reject affirmative action remedies. Further, the group disadvantage principle would require special treatment remedies. Reading 7-8 is a fictional tale that represents the skeptic (see section on skepticism in chapter 3, page 107). Its author, Derrick Bell, who has serious doubts about commitments to fight racism, thinks that a crisis will test the force of equal protection. Dr. Martin Luther King, Jr. believed that racial prejudice would disappear when Americans faced a common extraordinary crisis. In a metaphorical tale, Bell tests that belief. An amber cloud descends on white adolescents with wealthy parents, turning their skin a dull amber color. The nation seeks a cure for this illness they dub "Ghetto Disease." Would the courts use the equal protection clause to strike down legislation that limited a cure to whites and excluded blacks? Would Congress and the country manifest the same willingness to cure the Ghetto Disease in blacks? How deeply embedded in the American psyche is racial prejudice?

READING 7-4

Integration
Brown v. Board of Education (1954)

CHIEF JUSTICE EARL WARREN

Today, education is perhaps the most important function of state and local governments. Compulsory school attendance laws and the great expenditures for education both demonstrate our recognition of the importance of education to our democratic society. It is required in the performance of our most basic public responsibilities, even service in the armed forces. It is the very foundation of good citizenship. Today it is a principal instrument in awakening the child to cultural values, in preparing him for later professional training, and in helping him to adjust normally to his environment. In these days, it is doubtful that any child may reasonably be expected to succeed in life if he is denied the opportunity of an education. Such an opportunity, where the state has undertaken to provide it, is a right which must be made available to all on equal terms.

We come then to the question presented: Does segregation of children in public schools solely on the basis of race, even though the physical facilities and other "tangible" factors may be equal, deprive the children of the minority group of equal educational opportunities? We believe that it does.

In *Sweatt* v. *Painter* [see page 389] . . . in finding that a segregated law school for Negroes could not provide them equal educational opportunities, this Court relied in large part on "those qualities which are incapable of objective measurement but which make for greatness in a law school." In *McLaurin* v. *Oklahoma State Regents* . . . the Court, in requiring that a Negro admitted to a white graduate school be treated like all other students, again resorted to intangible considerations: ". . . his ability to study, to engage in discussions and exchange views with other students, and, in general, to learn his profession." Such considerations apply with added force to children in grade and high schools. To separate them from others of similar age and qualifications solely because of their race generates a feeling of inferiority as to their status in the community that may affect their hearts and minds in a way unlikely ever to be undone. The effect of this separation on their educational opportunities was well stated by a finding in the Kansas case by a court which nevertheless felt compelled to rule against the Negro plaintiffs:

> "Segregation of white and colored children in public schools has a detrimental effect upon the colored children. The impact is greater when it has the sanction of the law; for the policy of separating the races is usually interpreted as denoting the inferiority of the negro group. A sense of inferiority affects the motivation of a child to learn. Segregation with the sanction of law, therefore, has a tendency to [retard] the educational and mental development of negro children and to deprive them of some of the benefits they would receive in a racial[ly] integrated school system."

Whatever may have been the extent of psychological knowledge at the time of *Plessy* v. *Ferguson,* this finding is amply supported by modern authority. Any language in *Plessy* v. *Ferguson* contrary to this finding is rejected.

We conclude that in the field of public education the doctrine of "separate but equal" has no place. *Separate educational facilities are inherently unequal.* Therefore, we hold that the plaintiffs and others similarly situated for whom the actions have been brought are, by reason of the segregation complained of, deprived of the equal protection of the laws guaranteed by the Fourteenth Amendment. This disposition makes unnecessary any discussion whether such segregation also violates the Due Process Clause of the Fourteenth Amendment. . . .

From *Brown v. Board of Education* (1954) 347 US 483, pp. 493–95.

READING 7-5
Neutrality
"Toward Neutral Principles of Constitutional Law" (1959)

Herbert Wechsler

I. THE BASIS OF JUDICIAL REVIEW

. . . The courts have both the title and the duty when a case is properly before them to review the actions of the other branches in the light of constitutional provisions, even though the action involves value choices, as invariably action does. In doing so, however, they are bound to function otherwise than as a naked power organ; they participate as courts of law. This calls for facing how determinations of this kind can be asserted to have any legal quality. The answer, I suggest, inheres primarily in that they are—

or are obliged to be—entirely principled. A principled decision, in the sense I have in mind, is one that rests on reasons with respect to all the issues in the case, reasons that in their generality and their neutrality transcend any immediate result that is involved. When no sufficient reasons of this kind can be assigned for overturning value choices of the other branches of the Government or of a state, those choices must, of course, survive. Otherwise, as Holmes said in his first opinion for the Court, "a constitution, instead of embodying only relatively fundamental rules of right, as generally understood by all English-speaking communities, would become the partisan of a particular set of ethical or economical opinions. . . ."

The virtue or demerit of a judgment turns, therefore, entirely on the reasons that support it and their adequacy to maintain any choice of values it decrees, or, it is vital that we add, to maintain the rejection of a claim that any given choice should be decreed. . . .

I turn to the decisions that for me provide the hardest test of my belief in principled adjudication, those in which the Court in recent years has vindicated claims that deprivations based on race deny the equality before the law that the fourteenth amendment guarantees. The crucial cases are, of course, those involving the white primary [election], the enforcement of racially restrictive covenants [real estate sold only to whites], and the segregated schools. . . .

I come to the school decision, which for one of my persuasion stirs the deepest conflict I experience in testing the thesis I propose. Yet I would surely be engaged in playing Hamlet without Hamlet if I did not try to state the problems that appear to me to be involved.

The problem for me, I hardly need to say, is not that the Court departed from its earlier decisions holding or implying that the equality of public educational facilities demanded by the Constitution could be met by separate schools *[Plessy]*. I stand with the long tradition of the Court that previous decisions must be subject to reexamination when a case against their reasoning is made. Nor is the problem that the Court disturbed the settled patterns of a portion of the country; even that must be accepted as a lesser evil than nullification of the Constitution. Nor is it that history does not confirm that an agreed purpose of the fourteenth amendment was to forbid separate schools or that there is important evidence that many thought the contrary; the words are general and leave room for expanding content as time passes and conditions change. Nor is it that the Court may have miscalculated the extent to which its judgment would be honored or accepted; it is not a prophet of the strength of our national commitment to respect the judgments of the courts. Nor is it even that the Court did not remit the issue to the Congress, acting under the enforcement clause of the amendment. That was a possible solution, to be sure, but certainly Professor Freund is right that it would merely have evaded the claims made.

The problem inheres strictly in the reasoning of the opinion, an opinion which is often read with less fidelity by those who praise it than by those by whom it is condemned. The Court did not declare, as many wish it had, that the fourteenth amendment forbids all racial lines in legislation, though subsequent per curiam [by the whole court] decisions may, as I have said, now go that far. Rather, as Judge Hand observed, the separate-but-equal formula was not overruled "in form" but was held to have "no place" in public education on the ground that segregated schools are "inherently unequal," with deleterious effects upon the colored children in implying their inferiority, effects which retard their educational and mental development. So, indeed, the district court had found as a fact in the Kansas case, a finding which the Supreme Court embraced, citing some further "modern authority" in its support.

Does the validity of the decision turn then on the sufficiency of evidence or of judicial notice to sustain a finding that the separation harms the Negro children who may be involved (see chapter 3, Discussion Issue 6, page 130)? . . .

I find it hard to think the judgment really turned upon the facts. Rather, it seems to me, it must have rested on the view that racial *segregation* is, in principle, a denial of equality to the minority against whom it is directed; that is, the group that is not dominant politically and, therefore, does not make the choice involved. For many who support the Court's decision this assuredly is the decisive ground. But this position also presents problems. Does it not involve an inquiry into the motive of the legislature, which is generally foreclosed to the courts? Is it alternatively defensible to make the measure of validity of legislation the way it is interpreted by those who are affected by it? In the context of a charge that segregation *with equal facilities* is a denial of equality, is there not a point in *Plessy* in the statement that if "enforced separation stamps the colored race with a badge of inferiority" it is solely because its members choose "to put that construction upon it"? Does enforced separation of the sexes discriminate against females merely because it may be the females who resent it and it is imposed by judgments predominantly male? Is a prohibition of miscegenation [marriage between a man and a woman of different races] a discrimination against the colored member of the couple who would like to marry?

For me, assuming equal facilities, the question posed by state-enforced segregation is not one of discrimination at all. Its human and its constitutional dimensions lie entirely elsewhere, in the denial by the state of freedom to associate, a denial that impinges in the same way on any groups or races that may be involved. I think, and I hope not without foundation, that the Southern white also pays heavily for segregation, not only in the sense of guilt that he must carry but also in the benefits he is denied. In the days when I was joined with Charles H. Houston in a litigation in the Supreme Court, before the present building was constructed, he did not suffer more than I in knowing that we had to go to Union Station to lunch together during the recess. Does not the problem of miscegenation show most clearly that it is the freedom of association that at bottom is involved, the only case, I may add, where it is implicit in the situation that association is desired by the only individuals involved? . . .

Wechsler, Herbert. "Toward Neutral Principles of Constitutional Law," 73 *Harvard Law Review*. Copyright © (1959) by the Harvard Law Review Association.

READING 7-6

Antidiscrimination

"In Defense of the Antidiscrimination Principle" (1976)

Paul Brest

By the "antidiscrimination principle" I mean the general principle disfavoring classifications and other decisions and practices that depend on the race (or ethnic origin) of the parties affected. . . .

The heart of the antidiscrimination principle is its prohibitions of race-dependent decisions that disadvantage the members of minority groups. *Brown v. Board of Education* settled that the principle applies to racial segregation as well as to other forms of differential treatment, correcting the Court's earlier approval of the pernicious notion of "separate but equal." The first order of business in the era following *Brown* was to halt the ongoing, pervasive, and often overt practices of discriminatory exclusion of blacks from schools, voting booths, jobs, restaurants, housing, and the like. The Court expanded the concept of "state action" under the fourteenth amendment, and then in effect construed the thirteenth amendment to prohibit a broad range of private discrimination—just as Congress began to use its power over interstate commerce to achieve similar results. By the late 1960's, the civil rights enforcement effort had eliminated the most flagrant practices. Covert discrimination continued to flourish, however, and the very successes of the '60's dispelled any notions that blacks would quickly become integrated into the economic and social life of the nation. . . .

My "defense" of the antidiscrimination principle is that it prevents and rectifies racial injustices without subordinating other important values. At the risk of stating the obvious, the antidiscrimination principle is not the only principle of justice that should guide policymaking. For example, I believe that governments should assure that people are not denied fundamental needs because of their poverty and, more generally, should promote greater equalization in the distribution of wealth among individuals. To adopt the antidiscrimination principle as the exclusive principle of *racial* justice surely does not preclude adopting these or other principles concerned with *economic* justice. . . .

I. THE ANTIDISCRIMINATION PRINCIPLE

The antidiscrimination principle rests on fundamental moral values that are widely shared in our society. Although the text and legislative history of laws that incorporate this principle can inform our understanding of it, the principle itself is at least as likely to inform our interpretations of the laws. This is especially true with respect to the equal protection clause of the fourteenth amendment. The text and history of the clause are vague and ambiguous and cannot, in any event, infuse the antidiscrimination principle with moral force or justify its extension to novel circumstances and new beneficiaries. Therefore, the argument of this section does not ultimately turn on author-

Stated most simply, the antidiscrimination principle disfavors race dependent [trait based] decisions and conduct—at least when they selectively disadvantage the members of a minority group. By race-dependent, I mean decisions and conduct (hereafter, simply decisions) that would have been different but for the race of those benefited or disadvantaged by them. Race-dependent decisions may take several forms, including overt racial classifications on the face of statutes and covert decisions by officials.

A. Rationales for the Antidiscrimination Principle

The antidiscrimination principle guards against certain defects in the *process* by which race-dependent decisions are made and also against certain harmful *results* of race-dependent decisions. Restricting the principle to a unitary purpose vitiates its moral force and requires the use of sophisticated reasoning to explain applications that seem self-evident.

I. Defects of Process.—The antidiscrimination principle is designed to prevent both irrational and unfair infliction of injury.

Race-dependent decisions are irrational insofar as they reflect the assumption that members of one race are less worthy than other people. Not all such decisions are necessarily irrational, however. For example, if black laborers tend to be absent from work more often than their white counterparts—for whatever reason—it is not irrational for an employer to prefer white applicants for the job. If Americans of Japanese ancestry were more prone to disloyalty than Caucasians during World War II, it was not irrational for the United States government to take special precautions against sabotage and espionage by them. Regulations and decisions based on statistical generalizations are commonplace in all developed societies and essential to their functioning. And it is often rational for decisionmakers to rely on weak and even dubious generalizations. Consider, for example, a fire department's or airline's policy against employing overweight personnel, based on the rather slight probability that they will suffer a heart attack while on duty.

In short, the mere fact that most blacks are industrious and most Japanese-Americans loyal does not make the employer's or the Government's decision irrational. Indeed, if all race-dependent decisions were irrational, there would be no need for an antidiscrimination principle, for it would suffice to apply the widely held moral, constitutional, and practical principle that forbids treating persons irrationally. The antidiscrimination principle fills a special need because—as even a glance at history indicates—race-dependent decisions that are rational and purport to be based solely on legitimate considerations are likely in fact to rest on assumptions of the differential worth of racial groups or on the related phenomenon of racially selective sympathy and indifference. . . .

2. Harmful Results.—A second and independent rationale for the antidiscrimination principle is the prevention of the harms which may result from race-dependent decisions. Often, the most obvious harm is the denial of the opportunity to secure a desired benefit—a job, a night's lodging at a motel, a vote. But this does not completely describe the consequences of race-dependent decisionmaking. Decisions based on assumptions of intrinsic worth and selective indifference inflict psychological injury by stigmatizing their victims as inferior. Moreover, because acts of discrimination tend to occur in pervasive patterns, their victims suffer especially frustrating, cumulative and debilitating injuries. . . .

Recognition of the stigmatic injury inflicted by discrimination explains applications of the antidiscrimination principle where the material harm seems slight or problematic. For example, it fully explains the harmfulness of de jure [lawful] school segregation without the need to invoke controversial social science evidence concerning the effects of segregation on achievement, interracial attitudes, and the like, and thus explains the Supreme Court's casual extension of *Brown* to prohibit the segregation of public beaches, parks, golf courses and buses. It also explains how present practices that are racially neutral may nonetheless perpetuate the harms of past de jure segregation. . . .

The cumulative disadvantage caused by the use of race as a proxy even for legitimate characteristics provides an independent ground for disfavoring nonbenign race-dependent decisions regardless of the integrity of the process by which they were made. To the unprejudiced employer who would prefer white applicants to blacks solely for reasons of efficiency, the antidiscrimination principle says in effect: "If you were the only one to do this, we would permit you to make efficient generalizations based on race. But so many other firms might employ similar generalizations that black individuals would suffer great cumulative harms. And, in the absence of an overriding justification, this cannot be permitted."

I have argued that the prevention of stigmatic and cumulative harms, as well as concerns for process, support the antidiscrimination principle. Individuals may, however, be stigmatized by *non*-race-dependent practices that *appear* to be discriminatory, and may also suffer cumulative disabilities from various non-race-dependent practices. Whereas the process rationales for the antidiscrimination principle apply only to race-dependent decisions, the result-oriented rationales seem to disfavor all practices that produce these harms and thus to support a doctrine broader than the antidiscrimination principle. . . .

READING 7-7

Group Disadvantage
"Group Rights and the Equal Protection Clause" (1976)

Owen M. Fiss

The Equal Protection Clause has generally been viewed in this second way [a way that deemphasizes the actual language of the constitution]. The words—no state shall "deny to any person within its jurisdiction the equal protection of the laws"—do not state an intelligible rule of decision. In that sense the text has no meaning. The Clause contains the word "equal" and thereby gives constitutional status to the ideal of equality, but that ideal is capable of a wide range of meanings. This ambiguity has created the need for a mediating principle, and the one chosen by courts and commentators is the antidiscrimination principle. When asked what the Equal Protection Clause means, an informed lawyer—even one committed to Justice Black's textual approach to the First Amendment [see page 188]—does not repeat the words of the Clause—a denial of equal protection. Instead, he is likely to respond that the Clause prohibits discrimination.

One purpose of this essay is simply to underscore the fact that the antidiscrimination principle is not the Equal Protection Clause, that it is nothing more than a mediating principle. I want to bring to an end the identification of the Clause with the antidiscrimination principle. But I also have larger ambitions. I want to suggest that the antidiscrimination principle embodies a very limited conception of equality, one that is highly individualistic and confined to assessing the rationality of means. I also want to outline another mediating principle—the group-disadvantaging principle—one that has as good, if not better, claim to represent the ideal of equality, one that takes a fuller account of social reality, and one that more clearly focuses the issues that must be decided in equal protection cases. . . .

III. THE LIMITATIONS OF THE ANTIDISCRIMINATION PRINCIPLE

The appeal of the antidiscrimination principle may be unfounded. The ideals served by the principle may not have any intrinsic merit, or the connection between those ideals and the principle may be nothing more than an illusion. As we have seen, the antidiscrimination principle may be criticized on this level. But I believe the criticism runs deeper. The antidiscrimination principle has structural limitations that prevent it from adequately resolving or even addressing certain central claims of equality now being advanced. For these claims the antidiscrimination principle either provides no framework of analysis or, even worse, provides the wrong one. Conceivably, the principle might be adjusted by making certain structural modifications; and indeed, on occasion, over the last twenty-five years, that has occurred, though on an ad hoc and incremental basis, and at the expense of severing the principle from its theoretical foundations and widening the gap between the principle and the ideals it is supposed to serve.

The Permissibility of Preferential Treatment

One shortcoming of the antidiscrimination principle relates to the problem of preferential treatment for blacks. This is a difficult issue, but the antidiscrimination principle makes it more difficult than it is: the permissibility of preferential treatment is tied to the permissibility of hostile treatment against blacks. *The antidiscrimination principle does not formally acknowledge social groups, such as blacks; nor does it offer any special dispensation for conduct that benefits a disadvantaged group.* It only knows criteria or classifications; and the color black is as much a racial criterion as the color white. The regime it introduces is a symmetrical one of "color blindness," making the criterion of color, any color, presumptively impermissible. . . .

I use the term "group" to refer to a social group, and for me, a social group is more than a collection of individuals, all of whom, to use a polar example, happen to arrive at the same street corner at the same moment. A social group, as I use the term, has two other characteristics. (1) It is an *entity* (though not one that has a physical body). This means that the group has a distinct existence apart from its members, and also that it has an identity. It makes sense to talk about the group (at various points of time) and know that you are talking about the same group. You can talk about the group without reference to the particular individuals who happen to be its members at any one moment. (2) There is also a condition of *interdependence.* The identity and well-being of the members of the group and the identity and well-being of the group are linked. Members of the group identify themselves—explain who they are—by reference to their membership in the group; and their well-being or status is in part determined by the well-being or status of the group. That is why the free blacks of the antebellum period—the Dred Scotts—were not really free, and could never be so long as the institution of Negro slavery still existed. Similarly, the well-being and status of the group is determined by reference to the well-being and status of the members of the group. The emancipation of one slave—the presence of one Frederick Douglass—may not substantially alter the well-being or status of the group; but if there were enough Frederick Douglasses, or if most blacks had his status, then surely the status of blacks as a social group would be altered. That is why the free black posed such a threat to the institution of slavery. Moreover, the identity and existence of the group as a discrete entity is in part determined by whether individuals identify themselves by membership in the group. If enough individuals cease to identify themselves in terms of their membership in a particular group (as occurs in the process of assimilation), then the very identity and separate existence of the group—as a distinct entity—will come to an end.

I would be the first to admit that working with the concept of a group is problematic, much more so than working with the concept of an individual or criterion. It is "messy." For example, in some instances, it may be exceedingly difficult to determine whether particular individuals are members of the group; or whether a particular collection of persons constitutes a social group. I will also admit that my definition of a social group, and in particular the condition of interdependence, compounds rather than reduces, these classificatory disputes. But these disputes do not demonstrate the illegitimacy of this category of social entity nor deny the validity or importance of the idea. They only blur the edges. Similarly, the present reality of the social groups should not be obscured by a commitment to the ideal of a "classless society" or the individualistic ethic—the ideal of treating people as individuals rather than as members of groups. Even if the Equal Protection Clause is viewed as the means for furthering or achieving these individualistic ideals (and I am not sure why it should be), there is no reason why the Clause—as an instrument for bringing about the "good society"—must be construed as though it is itself governed by that ideal or why it should be assumed that the "good society" had been achieved in 1868, or is so now.

The conception of blacks as a social group is only the first step in constructing a mediating principle. We must also realize they are a very special type of social group. They have two other characteristics as a group that are critical in understanding the function and reach of the Equal Protection Clause. One is that blacks are very badly off, probably our worst-off class (in terms of material well-being second only to the American Indians), and in addition they have occupied the lowest rung for several centuries. In a sense, they are America's perpetual underclass. It is both of these characteristics—the relative position of the group and the duration of the position—that make efforts to improve the status of the group defensible. This redistribution may be rooted in a theory of compensation—blacks as a group were *put* in that position by others and the redistributive measures are *owed* to the group as a form of compensation. The debt would be viewed as owed by society, once again viewed as a collectivity. But a redistributive strategy need not rest on this idea of compensation, it need not be backward looking (though past discrimination might be relevant for *explaining* the identity and status of blacks as a social group). The redistributive strategy could give expression to an ethical view against caste, one that would make it undesirable for any social group to occupy a position of subordination for any extended period of time. What, it might be asked, is the justification for that vision? I am not certain whether it is appropriate to ask this question, to push the inquiry a step further and search for the justification of that ethic; visions about how society should be structured may be as irreducible as visions about how individuals should be treated—for example, with dignity. But if this second order inquiry is appropriate, a variety of justifications can be offered and they need not incorporate the notion of compensation. Changes in the hierarchical structure of society—the elimination of caste—might be justified as a means of (a) preserving social peace; (b) maintaining the community as a community, that is, as one cohesive whole; or (c) permitting the fullest development of the individual members of the subordinated group who otherwise might look upon the low status of the group as placing a ceiling on their aspirations and achievements. . . .

I would therefore argue that blacks should be viewed as having three characteristics that are relevant in the formulation of equal protection theory: (a) they are a social group; (b) the group has been in a position of perpetual subordination; and (c) the political power of the group is severely circumscribed. Blacks are what might be called a specially disadvantaged group, and I would view the Equal Protection Clause as a protection for such groups. Blacks are the prototype of the protected group, but they are not the only group entitled to protection. There are other social groups, even as I have used the term, and if these groups have the same characteristics as blacks—perpetual subordination and circumscribed political power—they should be considered specially disadvantaged and receive the same degree of protection. What the Equal Protection Clause protects is specially disadvantaged groups, not just blacks. A concern for equal treatment and the word "person" appearing in the Clause permit and probably require this generality of coverage.

Some of these specially disadvantaged groups can be defined in terms of characteristics that do not have biological roots and that are not immutable; the Clause might protect certain language groups and aliens. Moreover, in passing upon a claim to be considered a specially disadvantaged group, the court may treat one of the characteristics entitling blacks to that status as a sufficient but not a necessary condition; indeed the court may even develop variable standards of protection [see page 371]—it may tolerate disadvantaging practices that would not be tolerated if the group was a "pure" specially disadvantaged group. Jews or women might be entitled to less protection than American Indians, though nonetheless entitled to some protection. Finally, these judicial judgments may be time-bound. Through the process of assimilation the group may cease to exist, or even if the group continues to retain its identity, its socioeconomic and political positions may so improve so as to bring to an end its status as specially disadvantaged.

Fiss, Owen M. "Group Rights and the Equal Protection Clause," *Philosophy and Public Affairs.* © (1976) by Princeton University Press. Reprinted by permission of Princeton University Press.

READING 7-8

Racism's Future
"The Declining Importance of the Equal-Protection Clause" (1989)

Derrick Bell

THE CHRONICLE OF THE AMBER CLOUD

At midnight the Lord smote all the first-born in the land of Egypt, from the first-born of Pharaoh who sat on his throne to the first-born of the captive who was in the dungeon, and all the first-born of the cattle. And Pharaoh rose up in the night, he, and all his servants, and all the Egyptians; and there was a great cry in Egypt, for there was not a house where one was not dead.

—Exodus 12:29–30

THE AMBER CLOUD descended upon the land without warning, its heavy, chilling mist clearly visible throughout the long night it rolled across the nation. By morning, it was gone, leaving disaster in its wake. The most fortunate young people in the land—white adolescents with wealthy parents—were stricken with a debilitating affliction, unknown to medical science, but whose symptoms were all too familiar to parents whose children are both poor and black.

The media called it Ghetto Disease, a term that made up in accuracy what it lacked in elegance. Within days, the teen-age offspring of the nation's most prosperous families changed drastically in both appearance and behavior. Their skins turned a dull amber color. Those afflicted by the disease could not hide it. Because its cause and contagious potential were unknown, its victims, after an initial wave of sympathy, were shunned by everyone not so afflicted.

Perhaps the victims' bizarre personality changes were a direct result of the Amber Cloud itself; perhaps they simply reflected the youths' reaction to being

treated as lepers, both in public and in all but the most loving of homes. Whatever the cause, the personality changes were obvious and profound. Youngsters
who had been alert, personable, and confident became lethargic, suspicious,
withdrawn, and hopelessly insecure, their behavior like that of many children in
the most disadvantaged and poverty-ridden ghettos, barrios, and reservations.

The calamity dominated all discussion. The wealthy felt the effects directly and were distraught. Before the crisis ended, more than one parent had
publicly expressed envy for their ancient Egyptian counterparts whose first-
born were singled out and slain during the night of the Passover. Attendance
and achievement in the finest schools plummeted. Antisocial behavior rose
sharply as parents whose child-rearing credo had been "privileged permis-
siveness" lost the status-based foundation of their control. Apathy was the
principal symptom of the afflicted; but in many cases, undisciplined behavior
in the home escalated to gang warfare in suburban streets. Police had difficulty coping with serious crimes committed by those who earlier had committed only minor misdemeanors. Upper-income enclaves, which had long excluded blacks and the poor, now were devastated from within.

Working-class whites, although not directly affected by the cloud, sympathized deeply with the plight of the wealthy. Long accustomed to living the
lives of the well-to-do vicariously through television and tabloids, they reacted
with an outpouring of concern and support for the distressed upper class.

Private efforts raised large sums of money to further Ghetto Disease research. At the same time, governmental welfare programs extended their operations from the inner-city poor to the suburban rich. No one questioned the
role of government in the emergency. Even those far to the political right
sounded themes of the necessity of state involvement. The proffered public
aid was not "welfare," they said, for the nation's future—now in danger—
must of necessity be secured.

The young victims did not blame their plight on blacks. But many of their
well-to-do and powerful parents claimed that subversive black elements
were responsible for the disaster—an accusation they supported by noting
that no children of color were affected and by recalling that some civil rights
leaders recently had expressed bitterness at the government's failure to improve the conditions in which ghetto children were raised and educated. Police officials soon responded to political pressures to "do something" about
the crisis by rounding up civil rights leaders on a variety of charges. During
the next few months, a growing number of whites urged even greater retaliatory measures against black leaders and those whom they represented.

Racial hostility did not extend to a group of black social scientists, all experts on the destructive behavior of black ghetto life, who worked with government experts to develop an effective treatment plan. During the search
for a cure, hundreds of blacks volunteered for extensive psychiatric testing
designed to determine the precise nature of Ghetto Disease.

After a year of strenuous effort, the president announced the development of a psychological-conditioning process and a special synthesis of mind-
altering chemicals that appeared capable of curing Amber Cloud victims.
Both the treatment and the new medicine were very expensive; together
they would cost up to $100,000 per person. But a nation that had prayed for
a cure "at any cost" proved willing to assume the burden.

Civil rights leaders hailed the discovery and urged that the treatment be made available to nonwhite youths whose identical behavior symptoms were caused by poverty, disadvantage, and racial prejudice. They cited scientific appraisals predicting that the treatment would prove as effective in curing minority youths as Amber Cloud victims. They also argued that society owed minorities access to the cure, both because blacks had been instrumental in developing the cure and because the nation was responsible for ghetto pathology afflicting poor minorities.

The public responded negatively to this initiative, criticizing the attempt to "piggyback" onto the Amber Cloud crisis the longstanding problems of minority youth. Moderate critics felt that minority leaders were moving too fast; the vehement openly charged that the problem with ghetto youths was not disease but inherent sloth, inferior IQ, and a life-long commitment to the "black lifestyle."

A presidential task force recommended legislative action authorizing the billions needed to effectuate the cure. Congress budgeted the costs largely by cutting appropriations for defense systems. "Defense," it was argued, "must begin at home." The Amber Cloud Cure bill included a "targeting" provision that specifically limited treatment to the victims of the Amber Cloud. Over the furious objections of minority-group legislators, the Amber Cloud Cure bill was quickly enacted.

Civil rights litigants prepared and filed lawsuits challenging the exclusion of minority youths from coverage under the Amber Cloud Cure Act. The lower courts, however, dismissed the suits on a variety of procedural grounds. The treatment program was carried out with maximum efficiency and patriotic pride, as the nation faced and overcame yet another emergency. Following the cure of the last Amber Cloud victim, a national day of prayer and thanksgiving was proclaimed, and the nation and its privileged youth returned to normality. The supply of the cure was exhausted.

2. Affirmative Action

Malign (Invidious) Discrimination

After the landmark decision in *Brown v. Board of Education* (1954), courts began to take affirmative steps to remedy segregation. The Supreme Court left it to the lower courts to carry out desegregation policies, but after a decade of massive resistance from the states, it began to take a more active role in setting guidelines. The Court explicitly adopted color consciousness as a remedy for purposeful discrimination, striking down a North Carolina law that required colorblindness in student assignments. The Court, then, focused more on effects and results of discrimination and its disadvantaging impacts than on its purpose. However, despite this one period of highlighting discrimination's effects, the Court never abandoned the distinction between *de jure* ("by law") and *de facto* ("by fact") discrimination. It approved of busing as a way to end segregation, and it set guidelines for districtwide remedies to eliminate segregation in northern cities. However, in 1974, the Court set firmer limits on judicial remedies after a lower court ordered predominantly white suburban school districts to participate in a desegregation plan along with the predominantly black inner-city districts. The Supreme Court overturned Detroit's inter-district remedy for segregation (*Millikin v. Bradley* 1974). Intra-district remedies had pushed the limit; inter-district ones exceeded the limit.

Benign Discrimination

The affirmative action debate overlaps with disputes over desegregation, and yet affirmative action disputes have taken on a life of their own. During the 1960s, the federal government began to take steps to eliminate racial discrimination. President John F. Kennedy, in 1961, used the term *affirmative action* when he launched the Equal Employment Opportunity Commission (EEOC). His successor, Lyndon Baines Johnson, issued an executive order that required federal contractors to demonstrate that they had taken affirmative actions to ensure inclusion of racial minorities. The Civil Rights Act (1964) set the legislative framework for affirmative action and, finally, the 1972 amendments to the Civil Rights Act granted enforcement powers over purposeful and systemic discrimination.

In general, affirmative action cases differ from desegregation cases in three ways. First desegregation cases focused on harmful governmental laws and policies. The courts required evidence of purposeful discrimination or *de jure* discrimination. Affirmative action did not target harmful discrimination, but rather promoted so-called benign discrimination programs, voluntarily created by governmental and nongovernmental agencies. Second, in desegregation cases, the courts directed remedies at governmental officials, while in affirmative action cases, the courts examined nonjudicial remedies that affected individuals. Finally, color-conscious remedies became required for eliminating *de jure* discrimination, but color-conscious policies have become highly questionable in affirmative action cases. Arguments for affirmative action fall into two categories: backward looking **(corrective justice)** and forward looking **(distributive justice).**

Corrective Justice

Backward-looking arguments treat affirmative action as a corrective form of justice that gives restitution for an injury. Affirmative action proponents use tort law as one model. If a person suffers a civil wrong (a tort), the courts remedy the wrong by compensating the injured person. Blacks suffer because of past discrimination and thereby deserve compensation. Although similarities and dissimilarities emerge with any model, critics of affirmative action have focused on key dissimilarities. The disputes have revolved around three issues: (1) the nature of the victims, (2) the nature of the wrongdoers, and (3) the causes of social suffering. First, critics contend that tort victims have different characteristics than affirmative action recipients do. Unlike typical tort cases, parties in affirmative action cases may not have suffered directly from past discrimination. Further, affirmative action may not benefit the ones most deserving of compensation. Proponents admit that affirmative action compensates members of a group, not specific injured individuals, but they defend group compensation. As evidence, they cite the reparations paid primarily to the descendants of—not the direct victims of— Japanese-Americans interned during World War II. They argue that these "victims" deserve compensation, since they could have done better if their parents and grandparents had not suffered injuries at the hands of the U.S. government. Thus, defenders of affirmative action see nothing wrong with targeting better-off blacks since they would have also "done better but for racial discrimination" (Mosley and Capaldi 1996, p. 31).

Second, critics question not only the nature of affirmative action recipients but also the nature of the perpetrators. They raise concerns about those affected by affirmative action plans. That is, why should those who played no role in past discriminatory practices bear the burden of harm from affirmative action? Proponents of affirmative action defend the shift of the costs to those who did nothing unjust. They admit that individuals—such as young, poor white males—did not inflict the injuries, but they contend that they have benefited from the injuries (**unjust enrichment,** meaning that persons should not be permitted to enrich themselves at the expense of others). Finally, critics dispute the causes of the social and economic ills that are suffered disproportionately by blacks today. They acknowledge the harms of past racial discrimination, but they disagree about the cause of present injuries. They refuse to place the cause of the current plight of blacks on past discrimination, instead locating it in another realm, such as culture, innate characteristics, or class (see Reading 7-11).

Distributive Justice

Instead of correcting for a past wrong, proponents of forward-looking justifications of affirmative action base their claims on distributive justice. Their arguments project forward to a just society (or, at least, a more diverse society) based on a fair and equitable distribution of opportunities, benefits, or goods. Affirmative action provides the means to achieve these goals.

The means for affirmative action come in a wide variety of policies, ranging from weak ones that increase the applicant pool, to strong policies that cover a continuum from preferential treatment to quotas. Opponents of affirmative action reject both the ends and the means, citing the bad consequences of affirmative action. Some charge, for example, that affirmative action programs reinforce a stigma of victimization in blacks, while other opponents object to affirmative action because it undermines **meritocracy** (see Reading 7-13). In other words, policies should reward individuals for achievements, not for group membership. Affirmative action programs allegedly provide benefits for group status and not for individual accomplishments. Opponents also object to affirmative action as a means that, by its external interference, stifles individual freedom. Critics fault affirmative action for violating the rights of innocent nonminority individuals, who become victims of affirmative action. They advocate more justifiable alternative means, such as the free market economy.

When the University of California at Davis Medical School opened in 1968, it did not have any minority students. To remedy the situation, two years later, it implemented a special admissions program that reserved 16 of 100 slots for minorities. When Allan Bakke, a white man, received a rejection letter from the university, he claimed that the university's policy violated the Equal Protection Clause of the Fourteenth Amendment. He charged that the medical school had admitted minority students with lower test scores than his. In a mixed opinion, the U.S. Supreme Court ruled in favor of Bakke's admission (see Reading 7-9), however the Court gave affirmative action some breathing room. It allowed schools to use color consciousness as a factor in admissions to achieve diversity. Subsequent cases made it clear that benign racial classifications would be subject to the same strict scrutiny judicial review as invidious (malign) ones. Schools must demonstrate that their affirmative action programs qualify as a necessary means to a compelling end.

In 1992, the center of the affirmative action controversy shifted from California to Texas and from the Supreme Court to a circuit court. The University of Texas School of Law had a history of controversies over its admissions policies, dating back to 1946 when H. M. Sweatt, a postal worker, applied for admission to the racially segregated law school. During a continuance of the case, Texas had established an interim black law school in Austin. In 1950, the U.S. Supreme Court overturned a Texas law that allowed only whites to attend the University of Texas Law School (*Sweatt v. Painter* 1950). In 1992, Cheryl Hopwood, a white female, was denied admission even though her scores were significantly higher than those of some minority students who were admitted. She joined three other white plaintiffs to challenge the admissions policy. The U.S. Court of Appeals (Fifth Circuit) ruled that race may not be used as a factor in law school admissions (Reading 7-10). Further, it held that diversity can never be a sufficiently compelling reason for racial discrimination.

Justice Harlan, dissenting in *Plessy v. Ferguson,* set forth the classical formulation of a **principle of colorblindness:** "There is no caste here. Our Constitution is color blind, and neither knows nor tolerates classes among citizens." The readings provide a sampling of the controversy generated by affirmative action. T. Alexander Aleinikoff, a legal scholar, argues against colorblind principles and in favor of race-conscious policies (see Reading 7-11). Philosopher Nicholas Capaldi takes a bold and provocative stance against affirmative action, questioning the liberal paradigm underlying defenses of affirmative action (see Reading 7-12). Contrary to liberal defenders of affirmative action, Capaldi rejects their acceptance of the goodness of human nature. He further resists the liberal temptation to blame all bad behavior on environmental factors. He perceives newly arrived Africans in America as incomplete individuals, contending that they have remained socially dysfunctional. Finally, Laura Purdy, a philosopher, urges us to expand the debate over affirmative action to consider deeper social issues such as the viability of meritocracy (see Reading 7-13). For example, the disputants over affirmative action, pro and con, assume they know how to define qualifications, yet few commentators question the meaning of qualifications for medical school and medical practice. Do current criteria assure caring doctors? Purdy challenges us to rethink the notion of qualifications.

READING 7-9

Race as an Admissions Factor

Bakke v. Regents of University of California (1978)

JUSTICE LEWIS POWELL

The fourth goal asserted by petitioner is the attainment of a diverse student body. This clearly is a constitutionally permissible goal for an institution of higher education. Academic freedom, though not a specifically enumerated constitutional right, long has been viewed as a special concern of the First Amendment. The freedom of a university to make its own judgments as to education includes the selection of its student body. Mr. Justice Frankfurter summarized the "four essential freedoms" that constitute academic freedom:

> " 'It is the business of a university to provide that atmosphere which is most conducive to speculation, experiment and creation. It is an atmosphere in which there prevail "the four essential freedoms" of a university—to determine for itself on academic grounds who may teach, what may be taught, how it shall be taught, and who may be admitted to study.' " . . .

The atmosphere of "speculation, experiment and creation"—so essential to the quality of higher education—is widely believed to be promoted by a diverse student body. . . .

Ethnic diversity, however, is only one element in a range of factors a university properly may consider in attaining the goal of a heterogeneous student body. Although a university must have wide discretion in making the sensitive judgments as to who should be admitted, constitutional limitations protecting individual rights may not be disregarded. Respondent urges—and the courts below have held—that petitioner's dual admissions program is a racial classification that impermissibly infringes his rights under the Fourteenth Amendment. As the interest of diversity is compelling in the context of a university's admissions program, the question remains whether the program's racial classification is necessary to promote this interest. . . .

It may be assumed that the reservation of a specified number of seats in each class for individuals from the preferred ethnic groups would contribute to the attainment of considerable ethnic diversity in the student body. But petitioner's argument that this is the only effective means of serving the interest of diversity is seriously flawed. In a most fundamental sense the argument misconceives the nature of the state interest that would justify consideration of race or ethnic background. It is not an interest in simple ethnic diversity, in which a specified percentage of the student body is in effect guaranteed to be members of selected ethnic groups, with the remaining percentage an undifferentiated aggregation of students. The diversity that furthers a compelling state interest encompasses a far broader array of qualifications and characteristics of which racial or ethnic origin is but a single though important element. Petitioner's special admissions program, focused *solely* on ethnic diversity, would hinder rather than further attainment of genuine diversity. . . .

In summary, it is evident that the Davis special admissions program involves the use of an explicit racial classification never before countenanced by this Court. It tells applicants who are not Negro, Asian, or Chicano that they are totally excluded from a specific percentage of the seats in an entering class. No matter how strong their qualifications, quantitative and extracurricular, including their own potential for contribution to educational diversity, they are never afforded the chance to compete with applicants from the preferred groups for the special admissions seats. At the same time, the preferred applicants have the opportunity to compete for every seat in the class.

The fatal flaw in petitioner's preferential program is its disregard of individual rights as guaranteed by the Fourteenth Amendment. . . . Such rights are not absolute. But when a State's distribution of benefits or imposition of burdens hinges on ancestry or the color of a person's skin, that individual is entitled to a demonstration that the challenged classification is necessary to promote a substantial state interest [see page 371]. Petitioner has failed to carry this burden. For this reason, that portion of the California court's judgment holding petitioner's special admissions program invalid under the Fourteenth Amendment must be affirmed. . . .

In enjoining petitioner from ever considering the race of any applicant, however, the courts below failed to recognize that the State has a substantial interest that legitimately may be served by a properly devised admissions program involving the competitive consideration of race and ethnic origin. For this reason, so much of the California court's judgment as enjoins petitioner from any consideration of the race of any applicant must be reversed. . . .

From *Bakke v. Regents of University of California* (1978) 438 US 265, pp. 311–315, 319–320.

READING 7-10

Race, Not an Admissions Factor
Hopwood v. Texas (1996)

JUDGE JERRY E. SMITH, Fifth Circuit

Here, the plaintiffs argue that diversity is not a compelling governmental interest under superseding Supreme Court precedent. Instead, they believe that the Court finally has recognized that only the *remedial* use of race is compelling. In the alternative, the plaintiffs assert that the district court misapplied Justice Powell's *Bakke* standard, as the law school program here uses race as a strong determinant rather than a mere "plus" factor and, in any case, the preference is not narrowly applied. The law school maintains, on the other hand, that Justice Powell's formulation in *Bakke* is law and must be followed—at least in the context of higher education.

[6] We agree with the plaintiffs that any consideration of race or ethnicity by the law school for the purpose of achieving a diverse student body is not a compelling interest under the Fourteenth Amendment. Justice Powell's

argument in *Bakke* garnered only his own vote and has never represented the view of a majority of the Court in *Bakke* or any other case. Moreover, subsequent Supreme Court decisions regarding education state that non-remedial state interests will never justify racial classifications. Finally, the classification of persons on the basis of race for the purpose of diversity frustrates, rather than facilitates, the goals of equal protection. . . .

In short, there has been no indication from the Supreme Court, other than Justice Powell's lonely opinion in *Bakke,* that the state's interest in diversity constitutes a compelling justification for governmental race-based discrimination. Subsequent Supreme Court caselaw strongly suggests, in fact, that it is not.

Within the general principles of the Fourteenth Amendment, the use of race in admissions for diversity in higher education contradicts, rather than furthers, the aims of equal protection. Diversity fosters, rather than minimizes, the use of race. It treats minorities as a group, rather than as individuals. It may further remedial purposes but, just as likely, may promote improper racial stereotypes, thus fueling racial hostility.

The use of race, in and of itself, to choose students simply achieves a student body that looks different. Such a criterion is no more rational on its own terms than would be choices based upon the physical size or blood type of applicants. Thus, the Supreme Court has long held that governmental actors cannot justify their decisions solely because of race. . . .

Accordingly, we see the caselaw as sufficiently established that the use of ethnic diversity simply to achieve racial heterogeneity, even as part of the consideration of a number of factors, is unconstitutional. Were we to decide otherwise, we would contravene precedent that we are not authorized to challenge.

While the use of race *per se* is proscribed, state-supported schools may reasonably consider a host of factors—some of which may have some correlation with race—in making admissions decisions. The federal courts have no warrant to intrude on those executive and legislative judgments unless the distinctions intrude on specific provisions of federal law or the Constitution.

A university may properly favor one applicant over another because of his ability to play the cello, make a downfield tackle, or understand chaos theory. An admissions process may also consider an applicant's home state or relationship to school alumni. Law schools specifically may look at things such as unusual or substantial extracurricular activities in college, which may be atypical factors affecting undergraduate grades. Schools may even consider factors such as whether an applicant's parents attended college or the applicant's economic and social background.

For this reason, race often is said to be justified in the diversity context, not on its own terms, but as a proxy for other characteristics that institutions of higher education value but that do not raise similar constitutional concerns. Unfortunately, this approach simply replicates the very harm that the Fourteenth Amendment was designed to eliminate.

The assumption is that a certain individual possesses characteristics by virtue of being a member of a certain racial group. This assumption, however, does not withstand scrutiny. "[T]he use of a racial characteristic to establish a presumption that the individual also possesses other, and socially relevant, characteristics, exemplifies, encourages, and legitimizes the mode of thought and behavior that underlies most prejudice and bigotry in modern America." Richard A. Posner.

To believe that a person's race controls his point of view is to stereotype him. . . .

Instead, individuals, with their own conceptions of life, further diversity of viewpoint. Plaintiff Hopwood is a fair example of an applicant with a unique background. She is the now-thirty-two-year-old wife of a member of the Armed Forces stationed in San Antonio and, more significantly, is raising a severely handicapped child. Her circumstance would bring a different perspective to the law school. . . .

From *Hopwood v. Texas* (1996) 78 F.3d 932 (5th Cir.), pp. 944–948.

READING 7-11

Race Consciousness
"A Case for Race-Consciousness" (1991)

T. Alexander Aleinikoff

> I believe that [whites] today, raised white in a racist society, are often ridden with *white solipsism*—not the consciously held *belief* that one race is inherently superior to all others, but a tunnel-vision which simply does not see nonwhite experience or existence as precious or significant, unless in spasmodic, impotent guilt-reflexes, which have little or no long-term, continuing momentum or political usefulness.
>
> [W]hen a white man says he's white, . . . the impression that the nonwhite person gets is that *he means more than color.* . . .
>
> —*MALCOLM X (1964)*

A. COLORBLINDNESS AND ANTIDISCRIMINATION LAW

One response is that if past categorization based on race has created the problem, then the best solution might simply be to now forbid categorization altogether. Justice Scalia suggests this colorblind approach in his opinion in *Croson:* "The difficulty of overcoming the effects of past discrimination is as nothing compared with the difficulty of eradicating from our society the source of those effects, which is the tendency—fatal to a nation such as ours—to classify and judge men and women on the basis of . . . the color of their skin." . . .

The allure of colorblindness is strong. It is rooted in the dissenting opinion of the case that ratified American apartheid. And it fits with liberal, individualistic principles that each person should be assessed on individual merits, not upon the basis of group membership. Color-consciousness, under this account, is irrational and immoral because it is so rarely relevant to acceptable purposes.

Colorblindness also has powerful strategic appeal. In a world of white supremacy, most classifications based on race will have the intent or effect of harming blacks. Colorblindness sweeps these away. Furthermore, since whites are likely to look after their own, insisting that blacks get precisely what whites get will materially advance black interests. Colorblindness also keeps white guilt and anxiety at an acceptable level. As Alan Freeman has noted, colorblindness designates as "wrongdoers" only those "racists" who continue to take race into account; colorblind whites are absolved even if they continue to benefit from an unequal state of affairs. Finally, there is the risk that noticing race, even for a "benign" purpose, will only serve to affirm the view of racial differences that supported racial domination in the past. . . .

B. FROM COLORBLINDNESS TO RACE-CONSCIOUSNESS

Colorblindness may seem to be a sensible strategy in a world in which race has unjustly mattered for so long. Yet the claim that colorblindness today is the most efficacious route to colorblindness tomorrow has always been controversial. Justice Blackmun's paradoxical aphorism in *Bakke* reflects the usual counterclaim: "In order to get beyond racism, we must first take account of race. There is no other way. And in order to treat some persons equally, we must treat them differently." . . .

The claim I wish to press here is different from Blackmun's familiar stance in the affirmative action debate. I will argue in this section that a legal norm of colorblindness will not end race-consciousness; rather, it will simply make the unfortunate aspects and consequences of race-consciousness less accessible and thus less alterable. Furthermore, colorblind strategies are likely to deny or fail to appreciate the contribution that race-consciousness can make in creating new cultural narratives that would support serious efforts aimed at achieving racial justice.

Before these claims can be made, however, two varieties of colorblindness should be distinguished. The first, which I will call "strong colorblindness," argues that race should truly be an irrelevant, virtually unnoticed, human characteristic. Richard Wasserstrom has described this "assimilationist ideal":

> [A] nonracist society would be one in which the race of an individual would be the functional equivalent of the eye color of individuals in our society today. In our society no basic political rights and obligations are determined on the basis of eye color. No important institutional benefits and burdens are connected with eye color. Indeed, except for the mildest sort of aesthetic preferences, a person would be thought odd who even made private, social decisions by taking eye color into account.

The second type, "weak colorblindness," would not outlaw all recognition of race, but would condemn the use of race as a basis for the distribution of scarce resources or opportunities and the imposition of burdens. Under "weak colorblindness," race might function like ethnicity: an attribute that could have significance for group members, and one that society as a whole could recognize, but not one upon which legal distinctions could be based. Furthermore, individuals would be able to choose how important a role race would play in their associations and identifications, but their race would not be used by others to limit their opportunities or define their identities. Thus, college courses on "African-American literature" might well be permissible under a weak colorblindness regime, but such a regime would not tolerate allocating places in the class based on race or allowing race to be used as a factor in the choice of an instructor. In the sections that follow, I will argue that strong colorblindness is impossible and undesirable, and that weak [color-blindness]—although perhaps able to be implemented as a legal strategy—is an inadequate response to current manifestations of racial inequality.

1. *Masking Race-Consciousness.*—It is apparently important, as a matter of widespread cultural practice, for whites to assert that they are strongly colorblind, in the sense that they do not notice or act on the basis of race. One can see this at work in such statements as: "I judge each person as an individual." Of course, it cannot be that whites do not notice the race of others. Perhaps what is being said is that the speaker does not begin her evaluation with any preconceived notions. But this too is difficult to believe, given the deep and implicit ways in which our minds are color-coded. To be truly colorblind in this way, as David Strauss has shown, requires color-consciousness: one must notice race in order to tell oneself not to trigger the usual mental processes that take race into account. . . .

. . . Whites believe that they can act in a colorblind fashion merely by acting as they always have. Colorblindness puts the burden on blacks to change; to receive "equal" treatment, they must be seen by whites as "white." Hence, the "compliment" that some whites pay to blacks: "I don't think of you as black." Colorblindness is, in essence, not the absence of color, but rather monochromatism: whites can be colorblind when there is only one race—when blacks become white.

2. *Local Knowledge: Race-Consciousness as Cultural Critique.*—Strong colorblindness, I have argued, is unlikely to produce the result it promises—a world in which race does not matter. In this section, I want to make the case for race-consciousness more direct by focusing on the benefits of race-consciousness in undermining and shifting deep cultural assumptions and ultimately, perhaps, making progress in overcoming racism. In presenting these claims, I hope also to undermine the case for weak colorblindness. To be effective, strategies for attacking racism may well demand affirmative race-conscious governmental policies.

Clifford Geertz, in a collection of his essays entitled *Local Knowledge,* has stated that:

> To see ourselves as others see us can be eye-opening. To see others as sharing a nature with ourselves is the merest decency. But it is from the far more difficult achievement of seeing ourselves amongst others, as a local example of the forms human life has locally taken, a case among cases, a world among worlds, that the largeness of mind, without which objectivity is self-congratulation and tolerance a sham, comes.

Colorblindness operates at Geertz's level of "merest decency." It begins and ends with the observation that there is something, under the skin, common to all human beings. I do not want to discount the deep humanism underlying this perspective. Indeed, it is a significant improvement over the racist ideologies that have been prevalent throughout United States history and that have denied the "inner" equality of the races. But Geertz clearly seeks more than this; he would reorient the usual hierarchical relationship between dominant and subordinate cultures by rotating the axis through its center point, making the vertical horizontal. This shift requires two related transformations: the first is to appreciate the contingency, the nonuniversalism of one's own culture—to view it as an example of "local knowledge"; the second is to recognize and credit the "local knowledges" of other groups. Of course, these two efforts are related. By valorizing the dominated, one is likely to cast doubts on the dominant group's characterizations or definition of the dominated group, which, in turn, tells us something new about the dominant group as well. . . .

Recognizing the Dominated.—Finally, recognizing race validates the lives and experiences of those who have been burdened because of their race. White racism has made "blackness" a relevant category in our society. Yet colorblindness seeks to deny the continued social significance of the category, to tell blacks that they are no different from whites, even though blacks as blacks are persistently made to feel that difference. Color-consciousness allows for recognition of the distinct and difficult difference that race has made; it facilitates white awareness of the efforts of African-Americans to describe and examine that difference. This is not simply the telling of a story of oppression. Color-consciousness makes blacks subjects and not objects, undermining the durability of white definitions of "blackness." It permits recognition of the strength and adaptive power of a black community able to survive slavery and oppression; and it acknowledges the contributions of black culture—not simply as windows on "the race question" but as distinct (if varied) voices and traditions, worthy of study in their own right.

It is difficult to improve upon Adrienne Rich's insight:

> I used to envy the "colorblindness" which some liberal, enlightened, white people were supposed to possess; raised as I was, where I was, I am and will to the end of my life be acutely, sometimes bitterly, aware of color. Every adult around me in my childhood, white or black, was aware of it; it was a sovereign consciousness, a hushed and compelling secret. But I no longer believe that "colorblindness"—if it even exists—is the opposite of racism; I think it is, in this world, a form of naiveté and moral stupidity. It implies that I would look at a black woman and see her as white, thus engaging in white solipsism to the utter erasure of her particular reality.

Here is the turn of the axis, the recognition of others that helps one to see one's own culture as "a world among worlds."

3. *Weak Colorblindness and Its Costs.*—It is common for advocates of affirmative action to point out that a legal strategy dedicated to "equality of opportunity" is likely to replicate deeply imbedded inequalities. The familiar metaphor is of a race between two runners, one of whom starts many yards back from the starting line, or is encumbered by ankle weights. Color-conscious policies are said to remove the advantage that has for several centuries been granted to whites. The simplicity of this argument should not disguise its soundness or moral power. Unfortunately, however, affirmative

action programs based on the objective of overcoming past societal discrimination are deemed to run afoul of the Court's model of weak colorblindness. To the extent [race-conscious] policies help ameliorate material disadvantage due to societal discrimination, the negative injunction of weak colorblindness imposes heavy costs.

Beyond this familiar terrain in the affirmative action debate, there are other advantages to race-conscious programs that also call into question the adequacy of weak colorblindness. As Justice Stevens has noted, there are a number of situations in which it seems eminently reasonable for government decision makers to take race into account. For example:

> in a city with a recent history of racial unrest, the superintendent of police might reasonably conclude that an integrated police force could develop a better relationship with the community and thereby do a more effective job of maintaining law and order than a force composed only of white officers.

Similar claims could be made about integrated civil service and school administrations. That situations exist that could benefit from race-conscious policies should hardly be surprising, given the prominent role that race has played in allocating benefits and burdens throughout American history. Indeed, Justice Powell's famous "diversity" argument in *Bakke* implicitly acknowledges the reasonableness of some manner of color-conscious decision making in a world in which race has mattered and continues to matter. To the extent that weak colorblindness makes these forms of race-consciousness problematic, it is simply nearsighted social policy.

Most fundamentally, weak colorblindness sacrifices much of the cultural critique that race-consciousness can provide. If the task is to subject dominant views to scrutiny and challenge through the investigation and acceptance of nondominant perspectives, then it would appear sensible to permit decision makers to adopt facilitative programs that necessarily take notice of race. . . .

Aleinikoff, T. Alexander. "A Case for Race Consciousness." This article originally appeared in 91 *Columbia Law Review* 1060 (1991). Reprinted by permission of the author.

READING 7-12

Immorality of Affirmative Action
"Affirmative Action: Con" (1996)

Nicholas Capaldi

AFFIRMATIVE ACTION IS IMMORAL

As a society the United States is committed to six major normative premises:

1. We are committed to the belief in a *cosmic order* ("In God We Trust").
2. We are committed to the belief in the sanctity of the *individual*.

The *Declaration of Independence* declares:

> We hold these truths to be self-evident, that all men are created equal, that they are endowed by their Creator with certain unalienable Rights, that among these are Life, Liberty, and the pursuit of Happiness. That to secure these rights, Governments are instituted among Men, deriving their just powers from the consent of the governed.

In his dissent in the *Plessy v. Ferguson* case (1896), Justice Harlan enunciated the fundamental principle of individuality in a specific way, namely that the U.S. Constitution is and ought to be *color-blind*. This reiterates the point that it is the individual as such and not membership in a group that defines who we are. "Our constitution is color-blind, and neither knows nor tolerates classes among citizens. . . . The law regards man as man, and takes no account of his surroundings or of his color." . . .

Let us now turn to the preference argument. This argument maintains that because of the history of slavery and discrimination, African Americans have never been made to feel that they belong. This is especially problematic in a democratic society. Affirmative action is a way to help African Americans realize the basic values of the United States.

This argument rests upon a number of misconceptions. First of all, it is conceptualizing the problem in terms of the notion of a "democratic society." This is incorrect for two reasons. The United States is not a democracy but a republic. In a republic, government is limited to serving other interests because those interests reflect the basic rights of individuals. That is, political institutions are subordinate to moral preconceptions. James Madison argued that it was a utopian delusion to expect unanimity; factions were inevitable; the instrument for avoiding factional strife was checks and balances [see Reading 4-2]. Democracy is not an intrinsic end but a quite limited institutional arrangement that reflects more fundamental values. There is a serious confusion here of normative priority. Politicizing U.S. society and politicizing the issue of why African Americans do not participate as much as we would all wish is the wrong way to approach this issue.

Second, conceptualizing the problem from the point of view of groups (that is, African Americans conceived of as a voting block) is symptomatic of the failure to develop a sense of individuality [see Reading 7-7]. The question is not whether my group participates fully, the question is whether "I" or "you" participate fully.

Third, part of the reason that so many African Americans feel that they do not belong is that they have failed to embrace, much less understand, the fundamental values that animate our society. . . .

BEYOND AFFIRMATIVE ACTION: A NEW APPROACH

What really inhibits these people is *not* a lack of opportunity, *not* a lack of political rights, and *not* a lack of resources but a character defect, a *moral inadequacy*. Having little or no sense of individuality, they are incapable of loving what is best in themselves; unable to love themselves, they are incapable of loving others; incapable of loving others, they cannot sustain life within the family; in fact, they find family life stultifying. What they substitute for love of self, others, and family is loyalty to a mythical community. Instead of an umpire, they want a leader, and they conceive of such leaders as protectors who relieve them of all responsibility. This is what makes their sense of community pathological.

The leadership of pathological communalism inevitably exploits the group in the interests of itself. What such groups end up with are leaders who are their mirror image: leaders who are themselves incomplete individuals and who seek to control others because they cannot control themselves, who seek the emasculation of autonomous individuals, who prize equality and not competition. Of course, the relationship of the leadership to the rest of the community remains hierarchical in a feudal sense. In place of a market economy and limited government, we get economic and political tyranny. For example, "Willie Brown recently encouraged students to, 'basically, just terrorize' Professor Glynn Custred, co-author of the California Civil Rights Initiative, which would outlaw state-sponsored affirmative action."

Hate crimes can be explained using this same model. Hate crimes are crimes directed against an individual seen as a representative of a group. Such hate itself reflects pathological identification with one group and the conceptualization of the world as a conflict among groups. Racism, in this sense, is not the result of ignorance but reflects pathological group identification. It can be overcome only by promoting a sense of individual autonomy among all members of a society.

African Americans are not the only ones who exhibit the pathology of the incomplete individual, but they are the most visible. It is not slavery and discrimination that caused them to be incomplete individuals, for they were incomplete individuals before those events. . . . Many others exhibit the same forms of pathological behavior under a variety of circumstances.

What do I mean by saying that African Americans were "incomplete individuals" before arriving in the United States? To begin with, only those who developed within the modern Western European tradition of liberal culture could even become individuals, in the sense of being autonomous and inner directed. For most of history and in most parts of the world, anonymity prevailed because people identified themselves by membership in some group. In Africa, the relevant locus of identification was and is the tribe.

What happens when a nonindividualist culture comes into contact with liberal culture, as for example in the transition from feudalism to capitalism, the advent of colonialism, the transition of former "iron curtain" countries or Third World communities to a market economy, or the current detribalization in Africa? A frequent result, as detailed by Oscar Lewis, is the culture of poverty. The *culture of poverty* is marked by social, moral, and economic disintegration and perpetual dependence. So the second thing I mean by identifying African Americans as incomplete individuals is that given their background in Africa, it was to be expected that they would react to and adapt to their marginal position by developing a culture of poverty. It was not the slavery per se that led to the culture of poverty, but the meeting of two different worlds and the lack of resources within their prior world for adapting to the new world. This condition was perpetuated even after slavery was ended. The substitution of a new Afrocentrism to replace the emphasis of

Dr. Martin Luther King, Jr., on the Christian (therefore Western European) dignity of humans as moral agents is a replay of the clash of cultures. Affirmative action is another adaptation to resist the development of the individuality for which Dr. King was striving.

Finally, another thing that contributed to (but did not cause) the perpetuation of the culture of poverty [was] government policies of segregation, paternalism, and most especially the dominance of the liberal paradigm. All of these failed to promote the sense of personal responsibility. I hasten to add that this factor is not a particular social structure but the failure to promote or encourage a change in psychological makeup; wherever individualism was allowed to flourish, many African Americans were able to participate to a remarkable degree despite public policies.

The question is not whether any of us will experience hostility in our lives but how we respond to the hostility, and how we respond reflects in part our sense of self. Nathan Glazer says, "some groups—even those bearing the badge of discrimination—have achieved more than equality. . . . To label [discrimination] as the cause of the economic differences between groups, even when it is extensive and pervasive, is a gross oversimplification." I am not "blaming the victim" but calling attention to a different contextual explanation. But it is also true that the problem can never be solved by blaming the perpetrators of slavery or calling attention to conditions that no longer exist.

Consider the following analogy. Imagine an airplane with one hundred seats, fifty on each side of a center aisle. Imagine that forty of the passengers become violently ill on one flight. Imagine that of the ill passengers thirty are seated on the left side of the aisle and ten are seated on the right side of the aisle. Someone suggests that sitting on the left side of an airplane must cause a greater degree of motion sickness even though no engineering study can confirm this. On the other hand, someone else calls attention to the fact that the forty ill passengers chose the steak dinner while all of the other passengers chose the chicken dinner. Is it not more reasonable to suspect food poisoning than position on the aircraft? The proponents of affirmative action and supporters of the liberal paradigm are like those who keep calling attention to the fact that most of the sick people sat on the left side of the plane.

In an important sense, it no longer matters who is to blame. Blame is not the issue. The issue is how to solve the problem, and the problem can only be solved by promoting individuality. As Ralph Ellison reminds us: "Our task is that of making ourselves individuals. . . . We create the race by creating ourselves and then to our great astonishment we will have created a culture. Why waste time creating a conscience for something which doesn't exist? For you see, blood and skin do not think." . . .

Disqualifying Qualifications
"Why Do We Need Affirmative Action?" (1994)

Laura M. Purdy

Why is affirmative action sometimes morally required? Three general strategies for defending affirmative action have been suggested. One is that it appropriately compensates members of disadvantaged groups for past discrimination, another is that it counteracts current and ongoing discrimination, and a third is that it helps to secure more equality in society.

Affirmative action has been the subject of a great deal of controversy and confusion. Part of it has arisen because of conflicting definitions of affirmative action, and of the related notions of preferential treatment and reverse discrimination. A second problem has been that the populations for which it has been pressed vary in significant ways among themselves. Thus, for example, points which might be relevant to the situation of white middle class women might not be so for members of certain ethnic minorities. Hence, remedies that make sense for the one will not necessarily do so for the other. Thirdly, even for the same group, some proposals address the particular problem better than others and so, even where some action is well warranted, not every remedy will be equally justifiable. Accordingly, steps that would seem morally reasonable or even mandatory for one situation (admission to higher education, for instance) might be thoroughly inappropriate for another (such as tenuring a faculty member). These problems would create some obstacles to intelligent discussion, even if affirmative action were not such a deeply political issue. But it is such an issue, not only because it involves fundamental concepts in ethics and political philosophy (concepts that bear upon our most basic ways of looking at the world and about which there is substantial debate), but also because it appears to be a zero-sum game: any victory for members of one class appears to be a loss for another. That the debate is mostly conducted by those with something to lose, whether it be a job, or just the satisfaction of knowing they deserve their job, helps to keep tempers hot.

Whatever the reasons for controversy, many people seem to have reached the conclusion that little more can usefully be said about the issue: we shall simply have to agree to disagree, and attempt to find compromises—fighting it out in schools, workplaces, legislatures, and courts. Given the prevailing political winds, however, existing affirmative action programs are clearly in jeopardy. In any case, it is doubtful that anything worthwhile remains to be said about this issue; consequently, despite this pessimism about further reasoned debate here, I believe it is worth another look. This paper starts with definitions and moves on to questions about qualifications . . . .

WHAT IS AFFIRMATIVE ACTION?

Some people distinguish between the kind of procedural practices that increase the probability of finding qualified individuals in the relevant classes, and the substantive ones that advantage members of such classes. I take it for granted that such procedural practices are morally necessary, as do most people: the rancor [bitter disputes] here is focused on substantive rules that benefit individuals who are members of certain groups like white women, African-Americans, and the disabled.

Substantive affirmative action principles can take various forms. One ("weak" affirmative action), involves selecting members of disadvantaged groups (hereafter "D's") whenever their qualifications are as good as those of their competitors; another ("strong"), involves selecting them even when they are somewhat less qualified. Both of these practices may be known as **"preferential treatment."** Preferential treatment is used both by proponents and by opponents of affirmative action to describe what it requires in practice. **"Reverse discrimination,"** on the other hand, tends to be used by opponents of affirmative action, and seems generally intended to convey the idea that systematically preferring candidates in certain classes is as unjust as the kind of discrimination that spurred affirmative action policies in the first place.

These definitions immediately raise some questions. First and foremost, how do we judge "qualifications"?

QUALIFICATIONS

Opponents of affirmative action programs often assume that we know what the right qualifications are for any given enterprise, and that judgments about them are generally unproblematic. But there are good reasons for doubting whether these beliefs are as solid as they are taken to be: our conception of appropriate qualifications may be too high, too narrow, or just plain unwarranted.

There are surely enterprises for which we can be reasonably confident that we know what it takes to do a job well, since they require clearly definable and measurable skills. A good typist, for example, needs speed and accuracy and these abilities are easily and reliably measured by means of a typing test.

But requirements for many other ventures are a good deal less clear. In question may be both what it takes to achieve a given result, and what result is desirable. We like to think, for instance, that only the most literate students can think philosophically. Yet I have often been surprised at the acuity of otherwise quite savage students, as well as by untutored children. In fact, students at all levels are sometimes clearly capable of doing well in courses for which they lack prerequisites. This is not to say that having certain skills and knowledge is not desirable, but that we may sometimes overlook alternative ways to acquire them, judge them necessary when they are not, or mistakenly link them with others.

Another example of debatable standards of qualification comes from the heart of the affirmative action debate, admission to professional schools. One might reasonably infer from discussions of *Bakke,* for instance, that the standards for admission to medical school are valid and clear; at most, there seem to be a few questions about the relevance of social issues like the importance of role models for white women or the probability of practicing in under-served populations for minorities. Thus discussion centers on whether it is unjust to select traditionally less qualified students rather than more qual-ified ones in order to promote these non-traditional ends. But what about even the relatively prosaic [commonplace] decision-making difficulties that admissions committees face with several non-commensurable measures, like GPA [undergraduate grade point average], MCAT [standardized test for ad-mission to medical school], recommendations, prestige of school, and so forth? And, as I have argued elsewhere, it also fails to take account of bias embedded in those measures.

But that is just the tip of the iceberg. Do the MCATs really measure what an individual knows? More to the point, do their scales validly portray the relationship between someone's score and success in medical studies? Worse yet, what do we know about the relationship between success in medical school and good doctoring? The inadequacies of the contemporary medical establishment are becoming increasingly evident, and the education of physicians plays no small role in the crisis. For this and other reasons, med-ical education clearly needs fundamental rethinking, a process pursued more or less actively at any given time by those involved. Some changes would make quite a difference in our conception of who is most qualified for medical school. What, for example, about a requirement that aspiring doc-tors first work as nurses, in order to test and reinforce their capacity for con-scientious caring? Until such issues are better settled, why confine the de-bate to the narrow questions now so often regarded as central? Medicine is not the only field where this point is relevant.

Examples of the widespread tendency to set unnecessary and hence overly restrictive standards for opportunities and performance can easily be found in legal cases. For example, in the 1971 *Griggs v. Duke Power Com-pany,* the Supreme Court found that the company's employment standards (a high school diploma, and certain scores on an aptitude test) unreasonably excluded blacks from its better paying jobs, for those requirements hadn't been shown to be relevant to the jobs in question. Height and weight rules have similarly operated to exclude white women and members of small eth-nic groups from some occupations. They have been found unconstitutional under Title VII when potential employers could neither show why the re-quirement was relevant nor would let applicants attempt to prove that they could do the job anyway. Interestingly, as Judith Baer points out, in some sit-uations "the relevance of these requirements could not be proved even in in-stances where common sense might suggest that they were sound: height re-quirements for police officers, for example. The assertion that taller officers are more impressive authority figures than their shorter counterparts may seem plausible, but there is no evidence to support this hypothesis." Re-course to such notions as "authority figure" might also suggest unjustifiable assumptions about how to understand a given job, perhaps giving undue pri-ority to specific ways of dealing with people.

That in turn raises the more general point that what is considered im-portant or desirable is often a contestable moral or political issue. Examples that will be familiar to academics are the relative valuation of different areas of specialization within a discipline, or the ranking of different approaches to certain problems. For example, as Sheila Ruth has pointed out, the discipline of philosophy has had—and still has to a considerable extent—a hierarchy by which such "central" areas as metaphysics, epistemology, philosophy of language, and logic are considered the most prestigious, as well as a hierarchy of abstractness valuing more theoretical work above the more applied. These judgments create a network of effects, ranging from what gets published, to who and what wins the prestigious positions and prizes. Yet, it is hardly clear that the initial premises of this system are justified, and hence at least some judgments about who is better qualified will be seriously questionable.

This issue becomes especially pressing as we make decisions about the aims of enterprises for which individuals are being selected. Education, for example, is currently being torn by debate about whether it should be passing on "traditional wisdom" or helping to create a more just world. Yet that choice bears fundamentally on who is most qualified for many jobs. In particular, overtly "political" work, long anathema in academe, must now in some cases be taken seriously. Doing so is especially difficult for those who see the status quo as politically neutral since they are used to rejecting politically aware scholarship without having to distinguish good from bad.

The upshot of all this is that we should be much warier of the view that takes it for granted that we know how to evaluate qualifications. What follows is that there needs to be a great deal more to affirmative action decisions than whether it is ever defensible to prefer those with "worse" qualifications. . . .

Purdy, Laura M. "Why Do We Need Affirmative Action," *Journal of Social Philosphy* © (1994). Reprinted by permission of the Journal of Social Philosophy.

DISCUSSION ISSUES

1. *Perpetrator's Perspective.* Do the Supreme Court decisions on equal protection reflect a perpetrator's perspective? The analyses focus on the individual mind-set and responsibility of the perpetrator. For example, the Court asks, "Did the perpetrator intentionally discriminate?" A victim perspective centers on those who feel the brunt of harsh oppression, then and now. Would adopting the victim's viewpoint more directly address racial inequality? (see Freeman 1989, pp. 123–126.)

2. *Resentment and Victimization.* Do racially preferential policies "inevitably produce resentment in the better qualified," and do they generally lower the self-esteem of those who benefit from them (Nagel 1973)? Should decisions about racial preference policies depend on what effect the policies might have on different groups? Is it perverse and "dangerously gratuitous" to base decisions on social psychology predictions (O'Neil 1974, p. 925)?

3. *Bakke's Rejection Letter.* Did the admissions policy in *Bakke* sacrifice merit for a greater social good? Would it have been morally odd but defensible by liberals, as Michael Sandel claims, for Bakke to have received the following rejection letter?

Dear (Unsuccessful) Applicant,
   We regret to inform you that your application for admissions has been rejected. Please understand that we intend no offense by our decision. Your

rejection indicates neither that we hold you in contempt nor even that we regard you as less deserving of admission than those who were accepted.

It is not your fault that when you came along society happened not to need the qualities you had to offer. Those admitted instead of you were not themselves deserving of a place, not worthy of praise for the factors that led to their admission. We are in any case only using them—and you—as instruments of a wider social purpose.

You will likely find this news disappointing in the sense that your hopes of reaping the benefits given those whose qualities do coincide with society's needs at any given moment will not be realized. But this sort of disappointment occurs whenever an individual's preferences must give way to society's preferences, and should not be exaggerated by the thought that your rejection reflects in any way on your intrinsic moral worth; please be assured that those who were admitted are intrinsically as worthless as you. . . .

Sincerely yours. . . .

(Sandel 1982, pp. 141–42).

4. *Minority Facts.* Should any of the following facts affect judgments about affirmative action in the *Bakke v. Regents of the University of California* (1978) (Reading 7-9) decision (see O'Neil 1985, p. 71)? Bakke's admissions rating score was two points lower than any applicant accepted under the regular admissions plan. More than thirty unadmitted applicants had higher scores in both years that Bakke applied. Should any of the following facts affect judgments about affirmative action in the *Hopwood v. Texas* (1996) (see Reading 7-10) decision (Olivas, 1996)? (a) The number of white law students is at an all time high, representing 85% of total enrollment, whereas blacks constitute 6%. (b) Unknown to the admissions committee, plaintiff Cheryl Hopwood was a single mother who had a child born with cerebral palsy. (c) Another plaintiff in *Hopwood* had high test scores but poor letters of recommendation. (d) There is a direct correlation between parents' income levels and the Scholastic Aptitude Test (SAT). (e) Studies indicate that standardized test scores are less predictive of Hispanic students' than of Anglo students' first-year grade-point averages.

5. *Applicants' Rights.* Should rights trump equality? Do affirmative action policies violate applicants' rights? Do applicants have a constitutional right for the state to provide them with a medical or legal education? Do applicants have a right to be treated fairly in the admissions process? Do applicants have a right to be admitted on quantitative scores alone? (See Reading 3-15.)

6. *Other Special Advantages.* Are there other special advantage programs that we seldom question? By allowing mortgage interest and property tax deductions, does the tax code give a special advantage to nonpoor homeowners over poor renters? Is it unjust to give veterans preference in civil service jobs? Is it discriminatory for colleges and universities to give admissions preference to athletes? How do colleges and universities justify giving preferences to the daughters and sons of alumni?

7. *Discrimination and Symmetry.* If injustice is "discriminating for or against a group of citizens, favoring them with special immunities and privileges or depriving them of those guaranteed to others," is affirmative action the same injustice? Is it a contradiction "to assert that the ideal of equality justifies the violation of justice?" (Newton 1973).

Responsibility and Punishment

CRIMINAL LAW

There would seem to be testimony in favor of our views not only in what each of us does as a private citizen, but also in what legislators themselves do. For they impose corrective treatments and penalties on anyone who does vicious actions, unless his action is forced or caused by ignorance that he is not responsible for and they honor anyone who does fine actions.

—ARISTOTLE *Nichomachean Ethics,* Book iii, Ch 5, 3.42

Does criminal law symbolize humanity's progress or its shame? On pages 407–415, we ask whether criminal law should instill virtue or whether all the talk of virtue and vice simply hide our revenge? The examination of the nature of crime begins on page 416, with a focus on what acts should count as criminal (the *actus reus* element needed for crime). Beginning on page 427, criminal procedure highlights a debate over the fairness and justice of plea-bargaining. The conditions under which the criminal justice system should waive the *mens rea* elements or the mental requirements (the insanity defense), and when it should regard the mental element as irrelevant (strict liability) are also discussed. Pages 450–473 capture the disputes over the final phase of the criminal law process—namely, punishment. The last Controversies section, on page 473, details the ongoing disputes over the death penalty. The excursion into criminal law concludes on page 490 with a brief consideration of international criminal law, bringing the text full circle to the issue, addressed in chapter 1, of universal norms of conduct.

A. APPROACHES TO CRIME AND MORALITY: ARISTOTLE AND NIETZSCHE

Lead the people by edicts, keep them in line with penal law and they will avoid punishments but have no sense of shame. Lead them with virtue, keep them in line with rites, and they will not only have a sense of shame but will order themselves harmoniously.

—CONFUCIUS *Analects* (in 1979) 2:3

407

CHAPTER 8
*Responsibility and
Punishment*

1. Virtuous Persons

One view holds that criminal law shows the state at its best when it deals with its worst citizens and confronts the nastier aspects of human behavior. Without criminal law, madness and immorality would erupt. In *Lord of the Flies,* William Golding showed how Hobbesian brutality emerges when civilized individuals find themselves without the social cohesion provided by law and tradition (see chapter 1, page 12, Discussion Issue 1). Criminal behavior, within a law-and-order society, shows humans (not the state) at their worst. Supposedly, humans contracted out of an unpleasant, free-for-all called "state of nature" to form a secure order. They traded nature's chaos for government's security. However, criminal acts serve as reminders that today's civilization may not have completely shed its past primitiveness. Murder, mayhem, serial killings, and other atrocities, committed in advanced societies, raise doubts about law's protective function. Nevertheless, a world in which criminal acts are confronted by law seems preferable to a lawless world. Criminal law goes beyond maintaining order, however; it also reflects society's common morality.

Tort Law Compared with Criminal Law

Tort law covers largely private matters, while criminal law transforms some seemingly private matters among individuals into public ones. For example, the punishment of children within the privacy of the home becomes public when it turns into criminal abuse. Criminal law's public nature goes beyond collective concerns to concerns that reflect society's morals. A list of criminal acts represents a codification of what society regards as morally reprehensible. Tort law has moral elements, often expressed as "blameworthiness" that casts blame on a wrongdoer. Tortuous wrongs, however, pale in comparison with criminal ones. A **tortfeasor** (individual who commits a tort, civil wrong) deserves blame; a criminal stands guilty of immorality. When someone murders another person, obviously, the perpetrator has directed the wrong at an individual. However, the murderer also has committed a crime against the state, since murder constitutes a public wrong. Although a certain individual or individuals feel the direct effect of a criminal act, crime has a collective element—a group dimension. Criminal acts indirectly harm others and, thus, become matters of collective concern chipping away at collective security. Does a private criminal law make sense? In an extreme **libertarian** world without a state, or an **anarchist** society (without rulers), individuals would seek private revenge (see also the milder version of libertarianism represented by Hospers in chapter 5, Reading 5-1). Private police would provide protection for their employers (see Nozick 1974), but would not bring finality to disputes or guarantee enforcement of a settled dispute.

Since the private sector fails to protect individuals, a minimal state fills the gap. Within a minimal state, judges make common law, and legislators draft criminal statutes to determine the categories of crimes. The state has evolved far beyond a minimal stage, having attained almost exclusive control over criminal law. Private citizens play a far smaller role in the criminal justice system than they did in the past. For example, if a colonial shopkeeper wanted to prosecute a thief, the shopkeeper had to pay for the defendant's prosecution (Friedman 1993, p. 27). Before the Civil War, vigilante societies kept order in southern states. In South Carolina, for example, the "manorial authority of the planter was supported, not superseded, by the state" (Hindus 1980, p. 250). Today, the state has the primary responsibility for protecting its citizens, as well as the accused, and must abide by numerous procedural safeguards. The state gives the accused more than the benefit of the doubt; it must prove its case beyond a reasonable doubt.

The state uses criminal law to enforce public morality—but what kind of morality or ethics should criminal law reflect? A **virtue ethics** offers one way to ground morality by emphasizing the kind of person someone should become, rather than the acts the person should perform. **Aristotle** (384–322 B.C.) provided the first systematic presentation of a virtue ethics. He (and Confucius) believed that virtue, a state of character, stands as a mean between the extremes of "too little" and "too much" (see Reading 8-1). Courage lies between the deficit, of cowardice, and the excess, of foolhardiness. The law should instill virtues in its citizens, but this does not mean that the law serves only the *status quo.* Laws and virtue change over time. Martha Nussbaum, a contemporary Aristotelian, specializes in ancient philosophy and teaches in a law school. She interprets Aristotle as believing that a system of laws should allow citizens to make moral progress, to attain higher virtues (Reading 8-2).

2. Slave Morality

A study of criminality leads to images of an orderly society sinking into chaos. Czech novelist **Franz Kafka** pictured criminal law as the state acting at its worst (see Reading 8-3). Of all the branches of law, criminal law links most closely to **dystopia,** in which nightmares of a future hell clash sharply with utopian dreams of a future paradise. Authoritarian systems often show their most brutal sides when applying criminal law, which, along with its bureaucratic web, entangle citizens in a Kafkaesque nightmare. The state holds a monopoly on legitimate violence. The brutal force of the police, the militia, and the military are at its command, ready to crush its citizens. However, a clever state should seldom need to resort to direct force, relying instead on the disguised threats from its courts and bureaucrats. **Friedrich Nietzsche** (1844–1900) digs beneath the moral veneer of criminal law and questions the law's attempt to instill virtue in citizens (see Reading 8-4). According to Nietzsche, "enforcement of virtue morality" disguises a desire for revenge. Humans, by nature, do not only seek pleasure—they inflict pain. The weak invented morality to domesticate the strong.

Virtuous Persons
"Virtues of Character" (1985)

Aristotle

2. VIRTUES OF CHARACTER IN GENERAL

2.1 How a Virtue of Character Is Acquired

Virtue, then, is of two sorts, virtue of thought and virtue of character. Virtue of thought arises and grows mostly from teaching, and hence needs experience and time. Virtue of character [i.e. of *éthos*] results from habit [*ethos*]; hence its name 'ethical', slightly varied from '*ethos*'.

Virtue Comes About, Not By a Process of Nature, But By Habituation
Hence it is also clear that none of the virtues of character arises in us naturally.

(1) What Is Natural Cannot Be Changed by Habituation For if something is by nature [in one condition], habituation cannot bring it into another condition. A stone, e.g., by nature moves downwards, and habituation could not make it move upwards, not even if you threw it up ten thousand times to habituate it; nor could habituation make fire move downwards, or bring anything that is by nature in one condition into another condition.

Thus the virtues arise in us neither by nature nor against nature, but we are by nature able to acquire them, and reach our complete perfection through habit.

(2) Natural Capacities Are Not Acquired by Habituation Further, if something arises in us by nature, we first have the capacity for it, and later display the activity. This is clear in the case of the senses; for we did not acquire them by frequent seeing or hearing, but already had them when we exercised them, and did not get them by exercising them.

Virtues, by contrast, we acquire, just as we acquire crafts, by having previously activated them. For we learn a craft by producing the same product that we must produce when we have learned it, becoming builders, e.g., by building and harpists by playing the harp; so also, then, we become just by doing just actions, temperate by doing temperate actions, brave by doing brave actions.

(3) Legislators Concentrate on Habituation What goes on in cities is evidence for this also. For the legislator makes the citizens good by habituating them, and this is the wish of every legislator; if he fails to do it well he misses his goal. [The right] habituation is what makes the difference between a good political system and a bad one.

(4) Virtue and Vice Are Formed by Good and Bad Actions Further, just as in the case of a craft, the sources and means that develop each virtue also ruin it. For playing the harp makes both good and bad harpists, and it is analogous in the case of builders and all the rest; for building well makes good builders, building badly, bad ones. If it were not so, no teacher would be needed, but everyone would be born a good or a bad craftsman.

It is the same, then, with the virtues. For actions in dealings with [other] human beings make some people just, some unjust; actions in terrifying situations and the acquired habit of fear or confidence make some brave and others cowardly. The same is true of situations involving appetites and anger; for one or another sort of conduct in these situations makes some people temperate and gentle, others intemperate and irascible.

Conclusion: The Importance of Habituation   To sum up, then, in a single account: A state [of character] arises from [the repetition of] similar activities. Hence we must display the right activities, since differences in these imply corresponding differences in the states. It is not unimportant, then, to acquire one sort of habit or another, right from our youth; rather, it is very important, indeed all-important. . . .

Arguments from the Nature of Virtue of Character   By virtue I mean virtue of character; for this [pursues the mean because] it is concerned with feelings and actions, and these admit of excess, deficiency and an intermediate condition. We can be afraid, e.g., or be confident, or have appetites, or get angry, or feel pity, in general have pleasure or pain, both too much and too little, and in both ways not well; but [having these feelings] at the right times, about the right things, towards the right people, for the right end, and in the right way, is the intermediate and best condition, and this is proper to virtue. Similarly, actions also admit of excess, deficiency and the intermediate condition.

Now virtue is concerned with feelings and actions, in which excess and deficiency are in error and incur blame, while the intermediate condition is correct and wins praise, which are both proper features of virtue. Virtue, then, is a mean, in so far as it aims at what is intermediate.

Moreover, there are many ways to be in error, since badness is proper to what is unlimited, as the Pythagoreans pictured it, and good to what is limited; but there is only one way to be correct. That is why error is easy and correctness hard, since it is easy to miss the target and hard to hit it. And so for this reason also excess and deficiency are proper to vice, the mean to virtue; 'for we are noble in only one way, but bad in all sorts of ways.'

2.23 Definition of Virtue

Virtue, then, is (a) a state that decides, (b) [consisting] in a mean, (c) the mean relative to us, (d) which is defined by reference to reason, (e) i.e., to the reason by reference to which the intelligent person would define it. It is a mean between two vices, one of excess and one of deficiency.

It is a mean for this reason also: Some vices miss what is right because they are deficient, others because they are excessive, in feelings or in actions, while virtue finds and chooses what is intermediate.

Hence, as far as its substance and the account stating its essence are concerned, virtue is a mean; but as far as the best [condition] and the good [result] are concerned, it is an extremity. . . .

3.4 VIRTUE AND VICE ARE IN OUR POWER

3.41 The Relevant Actions Are in Our Power

We have found, then, that we wish for the end, and deliberate and decide about what promotes it; hence the actions concerned with what promotes the end will express a decision and will be voluntary. Now the activities of the virtues are concerned with [what promotes the end]; hence virtue is also up to us, and so is vice.

For when acting is up to us, so is not acting, and when No is up to us, so is Yes. Hence if acting, when it is fine, is up to us, then not acting, when it is shameful, is also up to us; and if not acting, when it is fine, is up to us, then acting, when it is shameful, is also up to us. Hence if doing, and likewise not doing, fine or shameful actions is up to us; and if, as we saw, [doing or not doing them] is [what it is] to be a good or bad person; then it follows that being decent or base is up to us.

The claim that no one is willingly bad or unwillingly blessed would seem to be partly true but partly false. For while certainly no one is unwillingly blessed, vice is voluntary. If it is not, we must dispute the conclusion just reached, that a human being originates and fathers his own actions as he fathers his children. But if our conclusion appears true, and we cannot refer [actions] back to other origins beyond those in ourselves, then it follows that whatever has its origin in us is itself up to us and voluntary.

3.42 Our Practices of Reward and Punishment Imply That Virtue and Vice Are Up to Us

There would seem to be testimony in favour of our views not only in what each of us does as a private citizen, but also in what legislators themselves do. For they impose corrective treatments and penalties on anyone who does vicious actions, unless his action is forced or is caused by ignorance that he is not responsible for; and they honour anyone who does fine actions; they assume that they will encourage the one and restrain the other. But no one encourages us to do anything that is not up to us and voluntary; people assume it is pointless to persuade us not to get hot or distressed or hungry or anything else of that sort, since persuasion will not stop it happening to us.

3.43 We Punish for Some Types of Ignorance, Assuming That They Are Up to Us

Indeed, legislators also impose corrective treatments for the ignorance itself, if the person seems to be responsible for the ignorance. A drunk, e.g., pays a double penalty; for the origin is in him, since he controls whether he gets drunk, and his getting drunk is responsible for his ignorance.

They also impose corrective treatment on someone who [does a vicious action] in ignorance of some provision of law that he is required to know and that is not hard [to know]. And they impose it in other cases likewise for any other ignorance that seems to be caused by the agent's inattention; they assume it is up to him not to be ignorant, since he controls whether he pays attention. . . .

READING 8-2

Improving Virtues
"Non-Relative Virtues: An Aristotelian Approach" (1988)

Martha Nussbaum

. . . Aristotle's ethical and political writings provide many examples of how such progress (or, more generally, such a rational debate) might go. We find argument against Platonic asceticism, as the proper specification of moderation (appropriate choice and response vis-à-vis the bodily appetites) and the consequent proneness to anger over slights, that was prevalent in Greek ideals of maleness and in Greek behavior, together with a defense of a more limited and controlled expression of anger, as the proper specification of the virtue that Aristotle calls "mildness of temper." (Here Aristotle evinces some discomfort with the virtue term he has chosen, and he is right to do so, since it certainly loads the dice heavily in favor of his concrete specification and against the traditional one.) And so on for all the virtues.

In an important section of *Politics* II, . . . Aristotle defends the proposition that laws should be revisable and not fixed, by pointing to evidence that there is progress toward greater correctness in our ethical conceptions, as also in the arts and sciences. Greeks used to think that courage was a matter of waving swords around; now they have (the *Ethics* informs us) a more inward and a more civic and communally attuned understanding of proper behavior toward the possibility of death. Women used to be regarded as property, bought and sold; now this would be thought barbaric. And in the case of justice as well we have, the *Politics* passage claims, advanced toward a more adequate understanding of what is fair and appropriate. Aristotle gives the example of an existing homicide law that convicts the defendant automatically on the evidence of the prosecutor's relatives (whether they actually witnessed anything or not, apparently). This, Aristotle says, is clearly a stupid and unjust law; and yet it once seemed appropriate—and, to a tradition-bound community, must still be so. To hold tradition fixed is then to prevent ethical progress. What human beings want and seek is not conformity with the past, it is the good. So our systems of law should make it possible for them to progress beyond the past, when they have agreed that a change is good. (They should not, however, make change too easy, since it is no easy matter to see one's way to the good, and tradition is frequently a sounder guide than current fashion.) . . . .

From Nussbaum (1988), "Non-Relative Virtues: An Aristotelian Approach," *Midwest Studies in Philosophy*. Peter A. French, Theodore E. Uehling, Jr., and Howard K. Wettstein, editors. Notre Dame, IN: University of Notre Dame Press, p. 32.

READING 8-3
Law as Bureaucratic Hell
"Before the Law" (1925)

Franz Kafka

Before the Law stands a doorkeeper. To this doorkeeper there comes a man from the country and prays for admittance to the Law. But the doorkeeper says that he cannot grant admittance at the moment. The man thinks it over and then asks if he will be allowed in later. "It is possible," says the doorkeeper, "but not at the moment." Since the gate stands open, as usual, and the doorkeeper steps to one side, the man stoops to peer through the gateway into the interior. Observing that, the doorkeeper laughs and says: "If you are so drawn to it, just try to go in despite my veto. But take note: I am powerful. And I am only the least of the doorkeepers. From hall to hall there is one doorkeeper after another, each more powerful than the last. The third doorkeeper is already so terrible that even I cannot bear to look at him." These are difficulties the man from the country has not expected; the Law, he thinks, should surely be accessible at all times and to everyone, but as he now takes a closer look at the doorkeeper in his fur coat, with his big sharp nose and long, thin, black Tartar beard, he decides that it is better to wait until he gets permission to enter. The doorkeeper gives him a stool and lets him sit down at one side of the door. There he sits for days and years. He makes many attempts to be admitted, and wearies the doorkeeper by his importunity. The doorkeeper frequently has little interviews with him, asking him questions about his home and many other things, but the questions are put indifferently, as great lords put them, and always finish with the statement that he cannot be let in yet. The man, who has furnished himself with many things for his journey, sacrifices all he has, however valuable, to bribe the doorkeeper. The doorkeeper accepts everything, but always with the remark: "I am only taking it to keep you from thinking you may have omitted anything." During these many years the man fixes his attention almost continuously on the doorkeeper. He forgets the other doorkeepers, and this first one seems to him the sole obstacle preventing access to the Law. He curses his bad luck, in his early years boldly and loudly; later, as he grows old, he only grumbles to himself. He becomes childish, and since in his yearlong contemplation of the doorkeeper he has come to know even the fleas in his fur collar, he begs the fleas as well to help him and to change the doorkeeper's mind. At length his eyesight begins to fail, and he does not know whether the world is really darker or whether his eyes are only deceiving him. Yet in his darkness he is now aware of a radiance that streams inextinguishably from the gateway of the Law. Now he has not very long to live. Before he dies, all his experiences in these long years gather themselves in his head to one point, a question he has not yet asked the doorkeeper. He waves him nearer, since he can no longer raise his stiffening body. The doorkeeper has to bend low toward him, for the difference in height between them has altered much to the man's disadvantage. "What do you want to know now?" asks the doorkeeper; "you are insatiable." "Everyone strives to reach the Law," says the man, "so how does it happen that for all these many years no one but myself has ever begged for admittance?" The doorkeeper recognizes that the man has reached his end, and, to let his failing senses catch the words, roars in his ear: "No one else could ever be admitted here, since this gate was made only for you. I am now going to shut it."

READING 8-4

Venomous Virtue Morality
"To the Teachers of Selfishness" (1882)

Friedrich Nietzsche

To the teachers of selfishness.—A man's virtues are called *good* depending on their probable consequences not for him but for us and society: the praise of virtues has always been far from "selfless," far from "unegoistic." Otherwise one would have had to notice that virtues (like industriousness, obedience, chastity, filial piety, and justice) are usually harmful for those who possess them, being instincts that dominate them too violently and covetously and resist the efforts of reason to keep them in balance with their other instincts. When you have a virtue, a real, whole virtue (and not merely a mini-instinct for some virtue), you are its *victim.* But your neighbor praises your virtue precisely on that account. One praises the industrious even though they harm their eyesight or the spontaneity and freshness of their spirit. One honors and feels sorry for the youth who has worked himself into the ground because one thinks: "For society as a whole the loss of even the best individual is merely a small sacrifice. Too bad that such sacrifices are needed! But it would be far worse if the individual would think otherwise and considered his preservation and development more important than his work in the service of society." Thus one feels sorry for the youth not for his own sake but because a devoted *instrument,* ruthless against itself—a so-called "good man"—has been lost to society by his death.

Perhaps one gives some thought to the question whether it would have been more useful for society if he had been less ruthless against himself and had preserved himself longer. One admits that there would have been some advantage in that, but one considers the other advantage—that a sacrifice has been made and that the attitude of the sacrificial animal has once again been confirmed for all to see—greater and of more lasting significance.

Thus what is really praised when virtues are praised is, first, their instrumental nature and, secondly, the instinct in every virtue that refuses to be held in check by the over-all advantage for the individual himself—in sum, the unreason in virtue that leads the individual to allow himself to be transformed into a mere function of the whole. The praise of virtue is the praise of something that is privately harmful—the praise of instincts that deprive a human being of his noblest selfishness and the strength for the highest autonomy. . . .

The praise of the selfless, the self-sacrificial, the virtuous—that is, of those who do not apply their whole strength and reason to their own preservation, development, elevation, promotion, and the expansion of their power, but rather live, in relation to themselves, modestly and thoughtlessly, perhaps even with indifference or irony—this praise certainly was not born from the spirit of selflessness. The "neighbor" praises selflessness *because it brings him advantages.* If the neighbor himself were "selfless" in his thinking, he would repudiate this diminution of strength, this mutilation for *his* benefit; he would work against the development of such inclinations, and above all he would manifest his selflessness by *not* calling it *good!*

This indicates the fundamental contradiction in the morality that is very prestigious nowadays: the *motives* of this morality stand opposed to its *principle.* What this morality considers its proof is refuted by its criterion of what is moral. In order not to contravene its own morality, the demand "You shall renounce yourself and sacrifice yourself" could be laid down only by those who thus renounced their own advantage and perhaps brought about their own destruction through the demanded sacrifice of individuals. But as soon as the neighbor (or society) recommends altruism *for the sake of its utility,* it applies the contradictory principle. "You shall seek your advantage even at the expense of everything else"—and thus one preaches, in the same breath, a "Thou shalt" and "Thou shalt not."

Nietzsche, Fredrich. "On the Virtuous" from *The Portable Nietzsche,* edited by Walter Kaufmann, translated by Walter Kaufmann, © (1954) by The Viking Press, renewed © (1982) by Viking Penguin Inc. Used by permission of Viking Penguin, a division of Penguin Putnam Inc.

B. CRIMINAL LAW

Oh, drive straight up the way and you'll hit Progress Road, then go till you can't anymore. Progress dead-ends at the Prison. [Directions to a maximum security prison in Waynesburg, Pennsylvania]

—PATRICIA J. WILLIAMS, 1998

1. Nature of Crime

About three and a half centuries ago, there was a stir in the colony of New Haven, Connecticut. A sow had given birth to a "monstrous" piglet. In the minds of the colonialists, this was no accident. Surely, the misbirth was some sort of omen. Specifically, it had to be a sign of sin, a sign of a revolting, deadly crime: carnal intercourse with the mother pig.

Who could have done such a horrendous act? The finger of suspicion pointed to Thomas Hogg (unfortunate name). Hogg insisted he was innocent. Was he telling the truth? The magistrates put him to the test: they took him to a pigsty, and forced him to scratch at two sows in enclosure. One sow, the mother of the monster-piglet, reacted with a show of "lust" when Hogg touched her. The other sow made no reaction at all. Hogg's guilt was now crystal clear. (Friedman 1993, p. 1)

Crime as a Social Judgment

What is a crime? What should a list of crimes include? Do lists differ from society to society? Does the idea of crime change over time? Colonial America linked crime with sin, while the nineteenth century took a more secular view and crime increasingly came under the watchful eyes of science. Cesare Lombrosco, regarded as the father of modern criminology, published *Criminal Man* (1876). (However, not until 1950 did a book appear with the title *The Criminality of Women* [Pollak 1950; see Pollock 1999]). Lombrosco outlined the science of anthropometry, which revealed correlations between physical characteristics and criminality.

Legislators do not always listen to ministers or scientists when they construct criminal codes. Despite a decreasing rate of serious crimes, nineteenth-century state lawmakers increased the number of criminal offenses. For example, Rhode Island went from 50 crimes in 1822 to 128 crimes in 1872 (see Hall et al. 1996, pp. 284–290). Legal historian Lawrence Friedman (Reading 8-5) finds no answer to the age-old question, "what is crime?" Instead, he tries to expose crimes as more than legal judgments. He believes that what society deems as criminal reflects its political and social judgments.

Crime as a Political Judgment

The law divides crimes into two categories, **misdemeanors** (petty or lesser crimes) and **felonies.** A felony is "as bad a word as you can give to a man or thing" (*Morisette v. United States* 1952). Before examining felonies such as larceny and murder, though, consider the image people have of crime. (For a discussion of images of law and lawyers, see chapter 1, page 2.) That may sound strange, but Friedman emphasizes that the social judgment about crimes may not fit reality. Do people visualize crime as "a stark, staring face that belongs to a frightening reality of our time—the face of a human predator, the face of the habitual criminal" (former-president Ronald Reagan as quoted in Reiman 1998, p. 54)? More specifically, do people see the typical criminal as male, black, and poor? Jeffrey Reiman, a philosopher involved with criminal justice studies, tries to debunk that image (Reading 8-6). He claims that the real danger to person and property does not come from the dominant image of crime as a one-on-one harm, but from the criminal justice system itself. Reiman accuses the criminal justice system of harming the poor, while refusing to criminalize harms by and for the rich.

Crime as a Legal Judgment

Friedman and Reiman emphasize problems with social and political judgments about crime, but problems also arise with legal judgments about what constitutes a crime. A crime is *"Actus non facit reum, nisi mens sit rea,"* which Jurist William Blackstone, translated as "An unwarrantable act, without a vicious will there is no crime at all." A crime (the ***corpus delecti,*** or body of the crime) must have a ***mens rea*** and an ***actus reus.*** It must include a particular mental state and a certain act. For example, with larceny, the accused must have intended to permanently take away property that he or she knew belonged to someone else (see Reading 8-6). If the state fails to prove the *mens rea* elements of larceny, the accused goes free. The *mens rea* and *actus reus* seldom operate in tandem. An emphasis on one produces a different legal and moral judgment about crime than does an emphasis on the other. If the judgment places a high value on culpability *(mens rea)* and low value on dangerousness *(actus reus)*, then attempting to commit a crime becomes as bad as completing the crime. In the culpability theory, therefore, a person who attempts a murder should face as severe a penalty as the person who completes the act (Schulhofer 1974). Alternatively, if the judgment places a low value on culpability and a high value on the resulting harm, then attempting a crime should not carry any criminal liability if no harm is done or if some good just happens to result from the completed act (Robinson 1975). This difference applies to torts and criminal law. Tort liability requires proof of harm, but criminal law punishes even harmless attempts.

Case of a New York Subway Shooting

George Fletcher highlights the difficulties involved in deciphering the nature and elements of a crime (Reading 8-7). Consider the following troubling case. Bernhard Goetz, a white male, entered a New York City subway car. When a passenger on the car said "give me five dollars," Goetz shot and wounded four unarmed black youths. According to Goetz's subsequent confession, he then walked over to Darrell Cabey, one of the youths, and said, "You seem to be [doing] all right; here's another." He then fired another shot, which severed Cabey's spinal cord (Fletcher 1988, p. 1). What crimes did Goetz commit (*People v. Goetz* 1986)? Which has greater importance in this case, *mens rea* or *actus reus?* Is intent to murder crucial to the case? If so, then should the state try Goetz for attempted murder? Alternatively, should the prosecution focus on the harm done? If the prosecution treats *actus reus* as the most important element, then should it charge Goetz with relatively indisputable acts he committed such as assault (threat to use force to injure another)? Does Goetz have a viable self-defense plea? Under common law, a person who is attacked and is in a life-threatening situation first has a duty to retreat before acting out of self-defense. According to the law, should Goetz have first retreated before he defended himself with a weapon? Did Goetz face a life-threatening situation? Should the law use a subjective or objective standard to assess perceived danger? What should the criminal law do with someone who uses unreasonable defensive force?

READING 8-5

Crime as a Social Judgment
"Introduction to Crime and Punishment in American History" (1993)

Lawrence Friedman

Crime definitions, then, are specific to specific societies. Social change is constantly at work on the criminal justice system, criminalizing, decriminalizing, recriminalizing. Heretics were burned at the stake in medieval Europe; there is no such crime today. Colonial Massachusetts put witches to death. In antebellum Virginia and Mississippi, two slave states, black runaways, and any whites who helped them, committed crimes. Selling liquor was a crime in the 1920s, during Prohibition. It was a crime during the Second World War to sell meat above the fixed, official price; or to rent an apartment at excessive rent. These are now extinct or obsolete crimes.

Every state, and the federal government, has a penal code: a list of crimes to be punished. In every state, too, and in the federal government, criminal provisions are scattered elsewhere among the statute books. This is particularly true of regulatory crimes. The modern criminal code, even after pruning, is still much bulkier than older codes. There were no such crimes as price-fixing, monopoly, insider trading, or false advertising in the Middle Ages. Many new crimes—wiretapping, for example—are specific to high-tech society. We live in a welfare and regulatory state. Such a state produces thousands of newfangled offenses: dumping toxic wastes, securities fraud, killing endangered species, making false Medicare claims, inserting a virus into computer programs, and so on.

Clearly, there are crimes and crimes. It is conventional to draw a line between property crimes, crimes against the person, morals offenses, offenses against public order, and regulatory crimes. Social reactions depend on the type of crime. Typologies are not very systematic; but they can be illuminating. For example, there are what we might call *predatory* crimes—committed for money and gain; usually, the victims are strangers. These are the robberies and muggings that plague the cities and inspire so much dread. There are also lesser and greater crimes of *gain:* shoplifting, minor embezzlements, confidence games, cheats, frauds, stock manipulations in infinite form. There are also what we might call *corollary* crimes, crimes that support or abet other crime—conspiracies, aiding and abetting, harboring criminals; also perjury, jail break, and the like. Much rarer are *political* crimes—treason, most notably; also, sedition, and, in a larger sense, all illegal acts motivated by hatred of the system, and which strike out against the constituted order. Then there are crimes of *desperation*—men or women who steal bread to keep from starving, addicts who steal or turn a trick to support their habit. Some crimes are *thrill* crimes—joyriding, shoplifting at times, acts of vandalism, and the like; some of these, too, can be little bursts of petty treason. There are crimes of *passion*—violence generated by thwarted love, jealousy, hatred that rises to the level of obsession. There are also crimes of addiction—crimes that arise from *failure of control;* crimes that stem from what some of us might consider flaws of character, or overwhelming temptation; this can be as minor as public drunkenness, or as horrific as rape. Lastly, there are what we might call *subcultural* crimes—acts that are defined as crimes by the big culture, yet validated in some smaller social grouping: Mormon polygamy in the nineteenth century, for example.

All crimes are acts that society, or at least some dominant elements in society, sees as threats. The threat may be physical (street crime) and affect the quality of life. Rape and sexual assault terrorize women and reinforce a rigid gender code. Morals crimes attack the way of life of "decent" people. Certain white-collar crimes—antitrust violations, securities fraud—strike a blow at the economy; regulatory crimes pollute the atmosphere, or the market. Traffic codes ration space on city streets and highways, and attempt to avoid strangulation; traffic crimes upset this public order. And so it goes. The sense of threat, and ideas about what to do about dangers, change prismatically from period to period, and are different in different social groupings. . . .

Friedman, Lawrence M. "Crime and Punishment in American History" © (1993). Reprinted by permission of Basic Books, a member of Perseus Books, L.L.C.

READING 8-6
Crime as a Political Judgment
"The Rich Get Richer and the Poor Get Prison: Ideology, Class, and Criminal Justice" (1998)

Jeffrey Reiman

In short, *asked to design a system that would maintain and encourage the existence of a stable and visible "class of criminals," we "constructed" the American criminal justice system!*

What is to be made of this? First, it is, of course, only part of the truth. Some steps have been taken to reduce sentencing discretion. And some prison officials do try to treat their inmates with dignity and to respect their privacy and self-determination to the greatest extent possible within an institution dedicated to involuntary confinement. Minimum security prisons and halfway houses are certainly moves in this direction. Some prisons do provide meaningful job training, and some parole officers are not only fair but go out of their way to help their "clients" find jobs and make it "legally." And plenty of people are arrested for doing things that no society ought to tolerate, such as rape, murder, assault, or armed robbery, and many are in prison who might be preying on their fellow citizens if they were not. *All of this is true.* Complex social practices are just that: *complex.* They are neither all good nor all bad. For all that, though, the "successes" of the system, the "good" prisons, the halfway houses that really help offenders make it, are still the exceptions. They are not even prevalent enough to be called the beginning of the trend of the future. *On the whole, most of the system's practices make more sense if we look at them as ingredients in an attempt to maintain rather than to reduce crime!*

This statement calls for an explanation. The one I will offer is that the practices of the criminal justice system keep before the public the *real* threat of crime and the *distorted* image that crime is primarily the work of the poor. The value of this *to those in positions of power* is that it deflects the discontent and potential hostility of Middle America away from the classes above them and toward the classes below them. If this explanation is hard to swallow, it should be noted in its favor that it not only explains our dismal failure to make a significant dent in crime but also explains why the criminal justice system functions in a way that is biased against the poor at every stage from arrest to conviction. Indeed, even at the earlier stage, when crimes are defined in law, the system primarily concentrates on the predatory acts of the poor and tends to exclude or deemphasize the equally or more dangerous predatory acts of those who are well off. In sum, I will argue that *the criminal justice system fails to reduce crime substantially while making it look as if crime is the work of the poor.* It does this in a way that conveys the image that the real danger to decent, law-abiding Americans comes from below them, rather than from above them, on the economic ladder. This image sanctifies the status quo with its disparities of wealth, privilege, and opportunity and thus serves the interests of the rich and powerful in America—the very ones who could change criminal justice policy if they were really unhappy with it.

Therefore, it seems appropriate to ask you to look at criminal justice "through the looking glass." On the one hand, this suggests a reversal of common expectations. Reverse your expectations about criminal justice and entertain the notion that the system's real goal is the very reverse of its announced goal. On the other hand, the figure of the looking glass suggests the prevalence of image over reality. My argument is that the system functions the way it does *because it maintains a particular image of crime: the image that it is a threat from the poor.* Of course, for this image to be believable there must be a reality to back it up. The system must actually fight crime— or at least some crime—but only enough to keep it from getting out of hand and to keep the struggle against crime vividly and dramatically in the public's view—never enough to substantially reduce or eliminate crime.

I call this outrageous way of looking at criminal justice policy the *Pyrrhic defeat* theory. A "Pyrrhic victory" is a military victory purchased at such a cost in troops and treasure that it amounts to a defeat. The Pyrrhic defeat theory argues that the failure of the criminal justice system yields such benefits to those in positions of power that it amounts to success. In what follows, I will try to explain the failure of the criminal justice system to reduce crime by showing the benefits that accrue to the powerful in America from this failure. I will argue that from the standpoint of those with the power to make criminal justice policy in America: *Nothing succeeds like failure.* I challenge you to keep an open mind and determine for yourself whether the Pyrrhic defeat theory does not make more sense out of criminal justice policy and practice than the old-fashioned idea that the goal of the system is to reduce crime.

The Pyrrhic defeat theory has several components. Above all, it must provide an explanation of *how* the failure to reduce crime substantially could benefit anyone—anyone other than criminals, that is. . . . I argue there that the failure to reduce crime substantially broadcasts a potent *ideological* message to the American people, a message that benefits and protects the powerful and privileged in our society by legitimating the present social order with its disparities of wealth and privilege and by diverting public discontent and opposition away from the rich and powerful and onto the poor and powerless. . . .

Of central importance is that the threat posed by the Typical Criminal is not the greatest threat to which we are exposed. The acts of the Typical Criminal are not the only acts that endanger us, nor are they the acts that endanger us the most. [W]e have as great or sometimes even a greater chance of being killed or disabled by an occupational injury or disease, by unnecessary surgery, or by shoddy emergency medical services than by aggravated assault or even homicide! Yet even though these threats to our well-being are graver than that posed by our poor young criminals, they do not show up in the FBI's Index of serious crimes. The individuals responsible for them do not turn up in arrest records or prison statistics. *They never become part of the reality reflected in the criminal justice mirror, although the danger they pose is at least as great and often greater than the danger posed by those who do!*

Similarly, the general public loses more money *by far* from price-fixing and monopolistic practices and from consumer deception and embezzlement than from all the property crimes in the FBI's Index combined. Yet these far more costly acts are either not criminal, or if technically criminal, not prosecuted, or if prosecuted, not punished, or if punished, only mildly. In any event, although the individuals responsible for these acts take more money out of the ordinary citizen's pocket than our Typical Criminal, they rarely show up in arrest statistics and almost never in prison populations. *Their faces rarely appear in the criminal justice mirror, although the danger they pose is at least as great and often greater than that of those who do. . . .*

The inescapable conclusion is that the criminal justice system does not simply *reflect* the reality of crime; it has a hand in *creating* the reality we see.

READING 8-7

Crime as a Legal Judgment
"A Crime of Self Defense" (1988)

George Fletcher

A SHOOTING IN THE SUBWAY

Goetz [accused of shooting four unarmed black youths on a New York subway] says, "Don't go passing [judgments] of morality. . . ." But the law cannot avoid judgments of morality. Goetz had given his lawyers materials from which they could craft a theory of self-defense based on his need to strike back with deadly force in order to save himself. If the jury agreed with him that his fear was sufficient to excuse him, that would be one moral judgment; if it imposed a rigorous standard of reasonableness and concluded that he overreacted in shooting, that would be another moral judgment. In either case, moral judgment was inescapable.

The distinctive feature of the law is not its rules and its commands, but the opportunity offered by legal debate and criminal trials to articulate and refine our views about the issues that divide us. It is not easy to think through and express our feelings about Goetz's shooting four black youths on the subway. It is not easy even to formulate the conflict between those who side with the victims and those who side with the gunman who thought himself in danger. We know that the conflict must be more profound than a conflict between black and white, between criminals and decent people, between the unemployed lower class and the established working and middle classes. The law helps us see what is at stake when a confrontation erupts into violence. It provides us with words and concepts for refining our reactions, expressing our judgments, and engaging in debate with those who disagree with us.

The law should be understood, therefore, as a stylized form of discourse. The boundaries of this discourse have been "fined and refined," as Thomas Hobbes wrote, by generations of learned lawyers. By the common understanding of the tradition, lawyers do not speak of love and friendship, of God or the angels, of salvation or the afterlife, of beauty and ultimate moral worth. These are the concerns that shape our lives, but it would be improper for an advocate to appeal to them in search of advantage for his client. Lawyers have agreed to argue not about what people are, but about what they do. The focus is not on why we do what we do, but on the moral qualities of our actions.

As poets have refined sensibilities about human yearning, lawyers have sharpened insights into the ways in which human actions disturb the social order. Their idiom speaks of harm and causation, obligation and responsibility, fault and excuse. These concepts and others like them are the filters that enable us to see what happened when Goetz pulled his gun and shot Canty, Allen, Ramseur, and Cabey. Of course, we may disagree about what we see. Some may see the red of aggression; others, the blue of fear; still others, the yellow of irrational overreaction. If we argue about these shades and hues, we can be certain, at least, that the picture is not simply black and white.

Legal argument is rooted in a shared faith in reason. The law moves forward by comparing one case with another, judging whether they are alike or different, whether the solution for one applies as well to the next. None of these judgments would be possible without the guidance of reason. Our passions divide us, but reason unites us in the quest for answers that all can accept. The clearest manifestation of reason in legal argument is the fact of argument itself. We know that appealing to another's reason differs from appealing to his or her prejudice or self-interest. An appeal to reason testifies to respect for the person to be persuaded. An appeal to prejudice or passion expresses contempt; it denigrates the other from a person to be persuaded by argument to an object to be manipulated by playing on emotional forces.

As Maimonides said about God, however, it is easier to postulate what reason is not than to conclude what it is. Reason is not passion, not prejudice, not the drive for pleasure. As God transcends the material world, reason transcends these impulses of the human condition. The analogy with the divine dignifies human reason, but as we can never be sure that we know whether God exists and in what form, we can readily slip into skepticism about both the existence and the dictates of our reason.

Doubts about the clarity of reason's call lead lawyers to take refuge in the authority of those who, by the conventions of the profession, provide the guideposts to decisions under the law. Rather than debate private visions of what is right and good, lawyers proceed by mustering on their side of the case authoritative legal materials that point to the result they advocate. In a criminal case, these materials include the text of our federal and state constitutions, the criminal code and the code of criminal procedure, and the voluminous body of judicial opinions that seek to justify decisions in specific appellate cases. This library of written materials is typically sufficient to indicate an answer to routine legal problems. But in an unusual case like the prosecution of Bernhard Goetz, the written law is but the beginning of the argument.

Lawyers begin their arguments with citations of statutes and cases and, if they are true advocates, quickly move beyond these anchors of authority with their own reasoned vision of justice in the particular case. Significantly, lawyers in the Anglo-American legal tradition prefer to invoke cases rather than to rely squarely on the words of a statute. Case law comes closer to the law of reason. When a decision departs from the received principles of the tradition, lawyers and judges tend to disregard it. Cases become influential precedents only when they capture the more refined sentiments of justice that have crystallized in our tradition.

The agony of Bernhard Goetz illustrates in one tangled life both the promise and the despair of the legal system. Unlike modern skeptics, Goetz has a strong vision of right and wrong. In his four-hour taped confession in New Hampshire, he repeatedly says that it is up to others to decide whether he was right or wrong. He does not want to be let off on grounds of mental illness. As he says:

> You decide. I became a vicious animal and if you think that is so terrible, I just wish anyone could have been there in my place. Anyone who is going to judge me, fine, I was vicious. My intent was to kill 'em, and, and you just decide what's right and wrong.

In his own moral vision, he had rightfully done everything possible to comply with the law, but it was clear that the law was wrongfully unresponsive to his fears of a repeat mugging. His contempt for the legal system generated a sense of justified self-reliance in carrying a loaded gun in public, whether he had bureaucratic approval or not. Yet his rebellion against the system went further than satisfying his immediate needs. Though never charged with gunrunning, he admits in his confession that he frequently bought guns and sold them to friends at cost.

Goetz's rage at the legal system, of course, does not control our judgment of what he did. His conception of right and wrong cannot displace the necessity of a community judgment about the rights and wrongs of carrying unlicensed weapons and shooting four youths on the subway. The problem of our judging Goetz is most acute in the tangle of passionate and reasoned arguments that run through the law of self-defense. If he is guilty of a crime of self-defense, it would be by virtue of our judgment that his beliefs do not prevail over the rule of reason in the law. Yet to have confidence in our judgment about whether Goetz acted criminally, though in perceived self-defense, we need to understand the complicated moral sentiments triggered by an argument of self-defense. . . .

PASSION AND REASON IN SELF-DEFENSE

Self-defense was always the central issue in the Goetz case—from the decision of the first grand jury not to indict on the shooting charges to the final verdict in June 1987. A legal system is possible only if the state enjoys a monopoly of force. When private individuals appeal to force and decide who shall enjoy the right to "life, liberty and the pursuit of happiness," there can be no pretense of the rule of law. Yet the state's monopoly also entails an obligation to secure its citizens against violence. When individuals are threatened with immediate aggression, when the police cannot protect them, the monopoly of the state gives way. The individual right of survival reasserts itself. No inquiry could be more important than probing this boundary between the state's obligation to protect us and the individual's right to use force, even deadly force, to repel and disarm an aggressor. There is no simple rule that traces this boundary between the authority of the state and the right of individuals to protect themselves. The inquiry itself generates an ongoing debate about the values that lie at the foundation of the legal system. . . .

The struggle between passion and reason in the law of self-defense is played out against a background of shared, albeit vague, assumptions about the contours of the defense. First, in order to be properly resisted, an attack must be *imminent*. Further, the defender's response must be both *necessary* and *proportional* to the feared attack. And finally, the defender must act with the *intention* not of hurting the victim per se, but of thwarting the attack. There is no statute or authoritative legal source that expresses this consensus, but lawyers all over the world would readily concur that these are the basic, structural elements of a valid claim of self-defense.

The requirement of *imminence* means that the time for defense is now! The defender cannot wait any longer. This requirement distinguishes self-defense from the illegal use of force in two temporally related ways. A preemptive strike against a feared aggressor is illegal force used too soon; and retaliation against a successful aggressor is illegal force used too late. Legitimate self-defense must be neither too soon nor too late.

In the case of a preemptive strike, the defender calculates that the enemy is planning an attack or surely is likely to attack in the future, and therefore it is wiser to strike first than to wait until the actual aggression. Preemptive strikes are illegal in international law as they are illegal internally in every legal system of the world. They are illegal because they are not based on a visible manifestation of aggression; they are grounded in a prediction of how the feared enemy is likely to behave in the future.

The line between lawful self-defense and an unlawful preemptive strike is not so easily staked out, but there are some clear instances of both categories. Because the general principles of international law are the same as those of domestic legal systems, we can ponder some dramatic examples among current international events.

Think about the various military moves that Israel has made against Arab forces in the last 20 years. The strike against the Iraqi nuclear reactor in 1981 was clearly preemptive, for the supposition that the Iraqis would use the reactor for military purposes was based on an inference from private Israeli military intelligence. Even if it is true that the Iraqis intended to manufacture a nuclear bomb, that activity hardly constitutes an attack against Israel. Israel has its own nuclear weapons, and its government would hotly contest the inference that this fact alone establishes its intention to bomb Arab territory.

Preemptive strikes are always based on assumptions, more or less rational, that the enemy is likely to engage in hostile behavior. Israel could well argue that it did not wish to take the chance that Iraq would use nuclear weapons against the Jewish state as well as against Iran and other opponents of the Baghdad regime. Be that as it may, there is no doubt that the air attacks on the reactor constituted a preemptive strike. The possible attack by Iraq was not sufficiently imminent to justify a response in self-defense.

More controversial is Israel's attack against Egypt in June 1967, initiating the spectacular Israeli victory in the Six-Day War. Egypt closed the Straits of Tiran to Israeli shipping, amassed its troops on Israel's border, and secured command control over the armies of Jordan and Iraq. In the two weeks preceding the Israeli response on June 5, Nasser had repeatedly made bellicose threats, including the total destruction of Israel. The question is whether Egypt's threat was sufficiently imminent to justify Israel's response under international law. Perhaps Egypt was merely bluffing; perhaps its leaders did not know whether they intended to attack or not. There is no doubt, however, that Egypt was attempting to intimidate Israel by behaving as though it were about to attack (unlike Iraq in the reactor incident). Israel took the Egyptians at face value; it responded to what appeared to be an attack in the offing. Could Israel have waited longer? Of course it could have. But the requirement of imminence does not require that guns actually fire, that bombs be in the air. And if anything short of letting the missiles fly constitutes an imminent attack, then that requirement was fulfilled in the June 1967 conflict between Egypt and Israel.

The distinction between a preemptive strike and a response to an imminent attack haunts our analysis of the Goetz case. We know that Canty asked Goetz for five dollars. But we don't know his tone of voice and his body language. The request for five dollars could be understood as panhandling, as harassment, as intimidation (hand it over or else!), or as a prelude to a violent assault whatever Goetz did. If Canty was merely begging, with no threat implicit in his request, there was no imminent attack. If the request was a veiled threat of violence, the circumstances are much closer to an imminent attack.

In cases of interpersonal as well as international violence, the outbreak might be neither defensive nor preemptive. It could be simply a passionate retaliation for past wrongs suffered by the person resorting to violence. Retaliatory acts seek to even the score—to inflict harm because harm has been suffered in the past.

Retaliation, as opposed to defense, is a common problem in cases arising from wife battering and domestic violence. The injured wife waits for the first possibility of striking against a distracted or unarmed husband. The man may even be asleep when the wife finally reacts. Goetz's response to the four young blacks was retaliatory so far as he perceived them as "four young muggers" rather than as individuals; he was striking back for having been mugged by the "same type of guys" in 1981 and suffering lasting injuries to his knee and chest.

Retaliation is the standard case of "taking the law into one's own hands." There is no way, under the law, to justify killing a wife batterer or a rapist as retaliation or revenge, however much sympathy there may be for the wife wreaking retaliation. Private citizens cannot function as judge and jury toward each other. They have no authority to pass judgment and to punish each other for past wrongs.

Those who defend the use of violence rarely admit that their purpose is retaliation for a past wrong. The argument typically is that the actor feared a recurrence of the past violence, thus the focus shifts from past to future violence, from retaliation to an argument of defending against an imminent attack. This is the standard maneuver in battered-wife cases. In view of her prior abuse, the wife arguably has reason to fear renewed violence. Killing the husband while he is asleep then comes into focus as an arguably legitimate defensive response rather than an illegitimate act of vengeance for past wrongs.

The New York statute on self-defense recognizes two distinct forms of imminent attack on which Goetz could and did ground his claim of self-defense. The first is that one is subject to the "imminent use of deadly physical force"; the second, making New York more favorable than many states to claims of self-defense, is that a robbery is about to be committed. In both cases, provided that other conditions of self-defense are satisfied, Goetz would be entitled to respond with deadly force. . . .

These four elements, then—imminence, necessity, proportionality, and intention—provide the general framework for the law of self-defense. The first three elements bear on the objective reality of the circumstances of using force; the fourth element of intention speaks to what the actor knows and his reasons for acting. The actor's subjective perceptions of reality introduce an additional element in the analysis that goes beyond his intention to repel the attack. If Goetz was mistaken about whether an attack was imminent and whether his defensive response was necessary and proportional, he might well be excused for acting under circumstances that do not meet the objective requirements of self-defense. In most legal systems of the world, the case of mistaken or putative self-defense is clearly distinguished, in terminology and legal consequences, from real self-defense based upon the criteria of imminence, necessity, and proportionality. The essential difference is that real self-defense justifies the use of force, while putative self-defense merely excuses it.

Under American law, and in particular New York law, there is no distinction between mistaken and real self-defense. Indeed the law is geared to the case of mistaken self-defense, the assumption being that whatever is true about the case of a subjective but mistaken perception of reality would be true about a correct perception of imminence, necessity, and proportionality. The New York statute applies, therefore, whenever the defendant "reasonably believes" that the conditions of self-defense are present. Of this phrase and its problematic meaning, there will be more to say later....

THE SIGNIFICANCE OF SUFFERING

The multiplicity of charges camouflages basic uncertainty in the legal system about why an act of shooting should be treated as a crime. Two conflicting schools of thought have emerged about the essential nature of criminal wrongdoing. A traditional approach emphasizes the victim's suffering and the actor's responsibility for bringing about irreversible damage. A modern approach to crime takes the act—the range of the actor's control over what happens—as the core of the crime. It is a matter of chance, the modernists say, whether a shot intended to kill actually hits its target. It is purely fortuitous, as the argument goes, that Goetz failed to kill one of his four intended victims. It is a matter of providence, as Gregory Waples later argued to the jury, that the volley of shots did not injure an innocent bystander on the train.

The traditionalists root their case in the way we feel about crime and suffering. Modernists hold to arguments of rational and meaningful punishment. Despite what we might feel, the modernist insists, reason demands that we limit the criminal law to those factors that are within the control of the actor. The occurrence of harm is beyond his control and therefore ought not to have weight in the definition of crime and fitting punishment. The tension between these conflicting schools infects virtually all of our decisions in designing a system of crime and punishment....

Reprinted with the permission of The Free Press, a Division of Simon and Schuster, Inc. from *A Crime Of Self Defense: Bernard Goetz and the Law on Trial* by George P. Fletcher. Copyright © 1988 by George P. Fletcher.

2. Criminal Procedure: Plea Bargaining

"How does the defendant plead, guilty or not guilty?" Defendants' guilty pleas occur with increasing frequency. This high rate of guilty pleas has a peculiarly contemporary sound, since common law courts discouraged and, therefore, rarely heard guilty pleas. For 700 years, the law treated guilty pleas and confessions as synonymous. The earliest reported American decision on a guilty plea was in 1804. Utilitarian philosopher and social reformer Jeremy Bentham advocated the abolition of the guilty plea (Bentham 1827, vol. 3, p. 127). Given the rarity of guilty pleas, prosecutors had little to bargain with, however plea bargaining became more common at the turn of the twentieth century. Corruption seemed responsible for increased plea bargaining with guilty pleas increasing along with confessions. The U.S. Supreme Court began to take a careful look at the admissibility of confessions in state trials (*Brown v. Mississippi* 1936), readily excluding confessions produced by means of physical coercion. The Court, for example, found that a confession obtained by whipping a helpless defendant was involuntary and a violation of due process. The Court also examined cases of nonphysical coercion. For example, in *Chambers v. Florida* (1940), the power imbalance between the police and the suspects undermined the voluntary nature of the confessions. Police had found an elderly white man murdered near Fort Lauderdale, Florida. Without any warrants, they arrested more than twenty black men, releasing all but four after six days of isolation. After police interrogated the remaining four men for fifteen hours straight, they confessed. The confessions led to their convictions and death sentences, but the Supreme Court reversed the convictions:

> Under our constitutional system, courts stand against any winds that blow as havens of refuge for those who might otherwise suffer because they are helpless, weak, outnumbered, or because they are nonconforming victims of prejudice and public excitement. . . . No higher duty, no more solemn responsibility, rests upon this Court than that of translating into living law and maintaining this constitutional shield deliberately planned and inscribed for the benefit of every human being subject to our Constitution—of whatever race, creed or persuasion. (*Chambers v. Florida* 1940, Justice Black)

In the 1960s, the Court, under Chief Justice Earl Warren, began to turn away from a case-by-case analysis of voluntariness. It first emphasized the Sixth Amendment **right to counsel** (the court must appoint an attorney if the defendant cannot afford one) (*Escobedo v. Illinois* 1964). It, then, settled on the Fifth Amendment **privilege against self-incrimination** (requiring the government to prove its case without using the defendant as a witness) as the focal point for determining the admissibility of confessions (*Miranda v. Arizona* 1966). In this case, a rape victim picked Ernesto Miranda from a lineup of four Hispanics. After two hours of questioning, Miranda signed a confession, later claiming that the police had promised to drop other charges if he confessed to the rape. The Court then issued directives for police to inform the accused of their right to remain silent, to consult a lawyer, and to have a lawyer present during interrogation. In 1976, when Miranda was murdered during a fight, Phoenix police read Miranda's accused killer his **Miranda rights** (warnings police must give to a person taken into custody) (Baker 1983, pp. 408–409). The Warren Court succeeded in constructing national standards for criminal procedure. States could no longer use defendants' silence against them (*Griffin v. California* 1965) and prosecutors could not use the fruits of illegal searches and seizures as incriminating evidence at trial (the **exclusionary rule**, *Mapp v. Ohio* 1961).

Procedural safeguards mandated by the Court stemmed the tide of guilty pleas obtained through confessions, however new pressures for self-incrimination came from an increased use of plea bargaining. A century ago, the Court stood steadfastly against plea bargaining:

> A man may not barter away his life or his freedom, or his substantial rights. . . . No sort of pressure can be permitted to bring the party to forgo any right or advantage however slight. The law will not suffer the least weight to be put in the scale against him.

According to one historian, "the history of plea negotiations is a history of mounting pressure for self-incrimination" (Alschuler 1979, p. 157). Alschuler claims that the Supreme Court has reversed its course in opposition to guilty pleas, which runs counter to 700 years of common law history. The 1960s "due process revolution increased the pressure for plea bargaining." According to Alschuler, "the more formal and elaborate the trial process, the more likely it is that this process will be subverted through pressures for self-incrimination." He says that pressures from plea bargaining yield injustices, and cites as evidence a case in which a defendant rejected the prosecutor's recommendation for a five-year sentence for forging a check (*Bordenkirker v. Hayes* 1978). Under the Kentucky Habitual Criminal Act, the defendant instead received a life sentence following a trial. Kenneth Kipnis advocates the abolition of plea bargaining (Reading 8-8). Would taking plea bargaining (prosecutorial discretion) away from prosecutors shift power to judges? Prosecutors take an administrative view of plea bargaining, pointing out that it helps them handle huge case loads. Should reformers turn their energies to reducing case loads? Since plea bargaining reduces the number of trials (or **transaction costs** in law and economic terms), narrows the range of options, and leaves less to chance than a trial, does its economic efficiency make plea bargaining justifiable?

READING 8-8

Bargaining Away Our Rights
"Criminal Justice and the Negotiated Plea"
(1976)

Kenneth Kipnis

I

As one goes through the literature on plea bargaining one gets the impression that market forces are at work in this unlikely context. The terms "bargain" and "negotiation" suggest this. One can see the law of supply and demand operating in that, other things being equal, if there are too many defendants who want to go to trial, prosecutors will have to concede more in order to get the guilty pleas that they need to clear their case load. And if the number of prosecutors and courts goes up, prosecutors will be able to concede less. Against this background it is not surprising to find one commentator noting: "In some places a 'going rate' is established under which a given charge will automatically be broken down to a given lesser offense with the recommendation of a given lesser sentence." Prosecutors, like retailers before them, have begun to appreciate the efficiency of the fixed-price approach.

The plea bargain in the economy of criminal justice has many of the important features of the contract in commercial transactions. In both institutions offers are made and accepted, entitlements are given up and obtained, and the notion of an exchange, ideally a fair one, is present to both parties. Indeed one detects something of the color of consumer protection law in a few of the decisions on plea bargaining. . . .

II

Not too long ago plea bargaining was an officially prohibited practice. Court procedures were followed to ensure that no concessions had been given to defendants in exchange for guilty pleas. But gradually it became widely known that these procedures had become charades of perjury, shysterism, and bad faith involving judges, prosecutors, defense attorneys and defendants. This was scandalous. But rather than cleaning up the practice in order to square it with the rules, the rules were changed in order to bring them in line with the practice. . . .

Without going deeply into detail, I believe that it can be asserted without controversy that the liberal-democratic approach to criminal justice—and in particular the American criminal justice system—is an institutionalization of two principles. The first principle refers to the intrinsic point of systems of criminal justice.

A.

Those (and only those) individuals who are clearly guilty of certain serious specified wrongdoings deserve an officially administered punishment which is proportional to their wrongdoing. . . .

A second principle makes reference to the limits placed upon the power of the state to identify and punish the guilty.

B.

Certain basic liberties shall not be violated in bringing the guilty to justice.

This second principle can be seen to underlie the constellation of constitutional checks on the activities of virtually every person playing a role in the administration of the criminal justice system.

Each of these principles is related to a distinctive type of injustice that can occur in the context of criminal law. An injustice can occur in the outcome of the criminal justice procedure. That is, an innocent defendant may be convicted and punished, or a guilty defendant may be acquitted or, if convicted, he or she may receive more or less punishment than is deserved. Because these injustices occur in the meting out of punishment to defendants who are being processed by the system, we can refer to them as internal injustices. They are violations of the first principle. On the other hand, there is a type of injustice which occurs when basic liberties are violated in the operation of the criminal justice system. It may be true that Star Chamber proceedings, torture, hostages, bills of attainder, dragnet arrests, unchecked searches, *ex post facto* laws, unlimited invasions of privacy, and an arsenal of other measures could be employed to bring more of the guilty to justice. But these steps lead to a dystopia where our most terrifying nightmares can come true. However we limit the activity of the criminal justice system in the interest of basic liberty, that limit can be overstepped. We can call such infringements upon basic liberties external injustices. They are violations of the second principle. If, for example, what I have suggested in the previous section is correct, then plea bargaining can bring about an external injustice with respect to a basic liberty secured by the Fifth Amendment. The remainder of this section will be concerned with internal injustice or violations of the first principle.

It is necessary to draw a further distinction between aberrational and systemic injustice. It may very well be that in the best criminal justice system that we are capable of devising human limitations will result in some aberrational injustice. Judges, jurors, lawyers, and legislators with the best of intentions may make errors in judgment that result in mistakes in the administration of punishment. But despite the knowledge that an unknown percentage of all dispositions of criminal cases are, to some extent, miscarriages of justice, it may still be reasonable to believe that a certain system of criminal justice is well calculated to avoid such results within the limits referred to by the second principle. We can refer to these incorrect outcomes of a sound system of criminal justice as instances of aberrational injustice. In contrast, instances of systemic injustice are those that result from structural flaws in the criminal justice system itself. Here incorrect outcomes in the operations of the system are not the result of human error. Rather, the system itself is not well calculated to avoid injustice. What would be instances of aberrational injustice in a sound system are not aberrations in an unsound system: they are a standard result. . . .

Systemic injustice in the context of criminal law is a much more serious matter than aberrational injustice. It should not be forgotten that the criminal sanction is the most severe imposition that the state can visit upon one of its citizens. While it is possible to tolerate occasional error in a sound system, systematic carelessness in the administration of punishment is negligence of the highest order. . . .

In contrast to plea bargaining, the disposition of criminal cases by jury trial seems well calculated to avoid internal injustices even if these may sometimes occur. Where participants take their responsibilities seriously we have good reason to believe that the outcome is just, even when this may not be so. In contrast, with plea bargaining we have no reason to believe that the outcome is just even when it is.

I think that the appeal that plea bargaining has is rooted in our attitude toward bargains in general. Where both parties are satisfied with the terms of an agreement, it is improper to interfere. Generally speaking, prosecutors and defendants are pleased with the advantages they gain by negotiating a plea. And courts, which gain as well, are reluctant to vacate negotiated pleas where only "proper" inducements have been applied and where promises have been understood and kept. Such judicial neutrality may be commendable where entitlements are being exchanged. But the criminal justice system is not such a context. Rather it is one in which persons are justly given, not what they have bargained for, but what they deserve, irrespective of their bargaining position.

To appreciate this, let us consider another context in which desert plays a familiar role; the assignment of grades in an academic setting. Imagine a "grade bargain" negotiated between a grade-conscious student and a harried instructor. A term paper has been submitted and, after glancing at the first page, the instructor says that if he were to read the paper carefully, applying his usually rigid standards, he would probably decide to give the paper a grade of D. But if the student were to waive his right to a careful reading and conscientious critique, the instructor would agree to a grade of B. The grade-point average being more important to him than either education or justice in grading, the student happily accepts the B, and the instructor enjoys a reduced workload.

One strains to imagine legislators and administrators commending the practice of grade bargaining because it permits more students to be processed by fewer instructors. Teachers can be freed from the burden of having to read and to criticize every paper. One struggles to envision academicians arguing for grade bargaining in the way that jurists have defended plea bargaining, suggesting that a quick assignment of a grade is a more effective influence on the behavior of students, urging that grade bargaining is necessary to the efficient functioning of the schools. There can be no doubt that students who have negotiated a grade are more likely to accept and to understand the verdict of the instructor. Moreover, in recognition of a student's help to the school (by waiving both the reading and the critique), it is proper for the instructor to be lenient. Finally, a quickly assigned grade enables the guidance personnel and the registrar to respond rapidly and appropriately to the student's situation.

What makes all of this laughable is what makes plea bargaining outrageous. For grades, like punishments, should be deserved. Justice in retribution, like justice in grading, does not require that the end result be acceptable to the parties. To reason that because the parties are satisfied the bargain should stand is to be seriously confused. For bargains are out of place in contexts where persons are to receive what they deserve. And the American courtroom, like the American classroom, should be such a context.

In this section, until now I have been attempting to show that plea bargaining is not well calculated to insure that those guilty of wrongdoing will receive the punishment they deserve. But a further point needs to be made. While the conviction of the innocent would be a problem in any system we might devise, it appears to be a greater problem under plea bargaining. With the jury system the guilt of the defendant must be established in an adversary proceeding and it must be established beyond a reasonable doubt to each of twelve jurors. This is very staunch protection against an aberrational conviction. But under plea bargaining the foundation for conviction need only include a factual basis for the plea (in the opinion of the judge) and the guilty plea itself. Considering the coercive nature of the circumstances surrounding the plea, it would be a mistake to attach much reliability to it. . . .

Plea bargaining substantially erodes the standards for guilt and it is reasonable to assume that the sloppier we are in establishing guilt, the more likely it is that innocent persons will be convicted. So apart from having no reason whatever to believe that the guilty are receiving the punishment they deserve, we have far less reason to believe that the convicted are guilty in the first place than we would after a trial.

In its coercion of criminal defendants, in its abandonment of desert as the measure of punishment, and in its relaxation of the standards for conviction, plea bargaining falls short of the justice we expect of our legal system. I have no doubt that substantial changes will have to be made if the institution of plea bargaining is to be obliterated or even removed from its central position in the criminal justice system. No doubt we need more courts and more prosecutors. Perhaps ways can be found to streamline the jury trial procedure without sacrificing its virtues. Certainly it would help to decriminalize the host of victimless crimes—drunkenness and other drug offenses, illicit sex, gambling, and so on—in order to free resources for dealing with more serious wrongdoings. And perhaps crime itself can be reduced if we begin to attack seriously those social and economic injustices that have for too long sent their victims to our prisons in disproportionate numbers. In any case, if we are to expect our citizenry to respect the law, we must take care to insure that our legal institutions are worthy of that respect. I have tried to show that plea bargaining is not worthy, that we must seek a better way. Bargain justice does not become us.

Kipnis, Kenneth. "Criminal Justice and the Negotiated Plea." 86 *Ethics.* © (1976) University of Chicago. Reprinted with the permission of the University of Chicago.

C. CONTROVERSIES: CRIMINAL RESPONSIBILITY AND THE INSANITY DEFENSE

1. Criminal Responsibility

"Even a dog distinguishes between being stumbled over and being kicked" (Holmes 1881, p. 3). Like dogs, the criminal justice system recognizes the difference between accidentally and intentionally causing harm. The *mens rea* element, which is necessary for a crime, captures the intent factor, but not every injury rises to the level of criminal harm. "[A]n injury can amount to a crime only when inflicted by intention" (*Morisette v. United States* 1952, Justice Jackson), yet *mens rea* conveys something more than simple intent. It has a variety of meanings, including a vicious will (Blackstone), felonious intent, criminal intent, malice aforethought, guilty knowledge, fraudulent intent, and evil knowledge. Since the phrase's connotations add blameworthiness to simple intent, intent qualifies as an element of a crime only if it is morally blameworthy.

The *mens rea* requirement has a number of controversial exceptions. Insanity is the most notable exception, although it would more accurately be considered an excuse rather than an exception. Insanity constitutes an affirmative defense to a criminal charge, and a successful insanity plea destroys *mens rea*. Since insane people do not act voluntarily, so the argument goes, they do not operate from a blameworthy or evil mind. A guilty verdict for murder, for example, should not apply to a man who believed he was squeezing lemons and not his wife's neck (an example from The Model Penal Code section 4.01 comment, p. 156).

A second exception to the *mens rea* requirement comes under the heading of "strict liability." According to one theory, some civil and criminal wrongs should not require a showing of fault or intent. The law has experienced a trend in favor of such liability without fault. The offenses proposed for inclusion under "strict liability" include statutory rape (intercourse with a minor), bigamy (marrying one person while still being married to another), public welfare matters (such as marketing impure food or drugs), and felony murder. Since this chapter deals with criminal law, we will focus on **felony murder** (an unintentional death that occurs during the commission of a felony). Hart (1968) has critiqued the idea of **criminal strict liability** (imposing a criminal sanction without requiring a showing of criminal intent) along the following lines. Does a strict liability standard undermine the basic ideas of individual freedom and responsibility? Society holds individuals accountable who act of their own free will, but strict liability discounts freely chosen acts. Does strict liability abandon the moral weight attached to criminal sanctions? Criminal punishment permits society to express its moral indignation and *mens rea* includes moral blame. Therefore, absent *mens rea,* strict liability lacks moral force.

Some critics have proposed abolishing the insanity defense, while others have gone a step further and called for the elimination of the *mens rea* requirement. Lady Barbara Wootton, a nonlawyer magistrate in England, maintained that the law ought to be preventive and not punitive. She advocated the abolition of *mens rea* from criminal law, condemning it as a way for moralists to impose their old-fashioned values on the law (Wootton 1963). She proposed having the concept of responsibility wither away in criminal law (see the reply by Hart 1968, and analysis in Reading 8-19). Would the elimination of *mens rea* result in the eradication of criminal law's moral component? Is criminal law, unlike tort law, inherently moral?

2. *Mens Rea* and the Insanity Tests

Plato painted a picture of reason and emotion that has had a lasting impact on Western thought *(Phaedrus)*. According to Plato, the charioteer, representing Reason, has two horses—a good one and a bad one. The good one represents Spirit or Volition, which allies with Reason. "The right-hand horse is upright and cleanly made; he has a lofty neck and an aquiline nose; his color is white, and his eyes dark; he is a lover of honor and modesty and temperance, and the follower of true glory; he needs no touch of the whip, but is guided by word and admonition only" (Jowett 1937, p. 253). The bad horse represents Emotion (appetite or passion): "The other is a crooked lumbering animal, put together anyhow; he has a short thick neck; he is flat-faced and of dark color, with gray eyes and blood-red complexion; the mate of insolence and pride, shaggered and deaf, hardly yielding to whip or spur" (Jowett 1937, p. 253). Reason must control Emotion; otherwise, Emotion will rule. In modern terms, insanity will prevail if the mind loses control. Consider the cases in Readings 8-9 and 8-10. In the first, a trial court convicted the defendant. After reading the second, refer back to the issue of cultural defenses in the *Kimura* case (chapter 2, page 78, Discussion Issue 4). What models of criminal responsibility should apply? What approaches to the insanity defense should prevail? Should an insanity test focus on reason, the emotions, or mental disease?

A Gruesome Murder
State v. Cameron (1983)

JUSTICE STAFFORD, Supreme Court of Washington

Petitioner, Gary Cameron, was charged with the premeditated first degree murder of his stepmother, Marie Cameron. His principal defense was that he was insane at the time he committed the offense. The Court of Appeals affirmed a guilty verdict and this court granted Cameron's petition for review. We reverse the trial court and the Court of Appeals. In doing so, we shall discuss only those issues on which reversal is granted.

At the outset it should be noted that petitioner does not challenge the charge that he stabbed Marie Cameron numerous times or that she died as a result of those wounds. Further, there does not seem to be any serious question that, except for the defense of insanity, the stabbing was done with an intent to kill. Rather, the challenge focuses on three errors alleged to have denied him a fair trial: (1) the definition of insanity in such a way as to prevent the jury's consideration of his insanity defense; (2) the admission of foreign pubic hairs found on the victim's body; and (3) the admission of hearsay evidence of an alleged statement made by the victim two months prior to her murder.

I.

Turning first to the insanity defense, it is clear there is evidence running counter to petitioner's contention. This, however, does not detract from petitioner's challenge to the trial court's insanity instruction. The question is whether there is evidence of insanity which the jury could have considered but for the court's instruction. We hold there is.

The basic facts reveal that on the morning of June 9, 1980, petitioner stabbed Marie Cameron in excess of 70 times, leaving the knife sticking in her heart. The body was left in the bathtub with no apparent attempt to conceal it. Later that day a police officer saw petitioner in downtown Shelton wearing only a pair of women's stretch pants, a woman's housecoat, a shirt and no shoes. He was stopped and questioned. After first giving a false name, he corrected it and explained he was dressed that way because "I just grabbed what I could . . . My mother-in-law turned vicious." He also stated he was headed for California. Having no known reason to detain petitioner, the officer released him to continue hitchhiking.

The next day petitioner was detained by the Oregon State Police as he wandered along the shoulder of Interstate 5 near Salem. Since he was wearing only the stretch pants and one shoe he was thought to be an escapee from a nearby mental hospital. A check revealed petitioner was wanted in Shelton for the death of Marie Cameron.

Petitioner was arrested and informed of his constitutional rights. He then gave two confessions, the first being a tape-recorded oral confession and the second a signed written confession. Neither is challenged by petitioner.

In the oral confession petitioner stated generally that he was living in or about the home of his father and stepmother. He left home dressed as he was because his stepmother had become violent. "[S]he's into different types of sorcery. She's just strictly a very evil person . . . and she became very violent with me, with a knife in her hand, and so, uh, I don't deny that I'm the one that did what went on out there." He indicated that when he walked into the bathroom he had not expected her. When he saw her, she had the knife which he was able to take from her easily by bending her wrist back. Then, as he stated: "I took the knife and really stabbed her."

In describing the stabbing, petitioner related: "I just kept stabbing her and stabbing her, because she wasn't feeling . . . it was as if she was laughing . . . as if she was up to something that morning, and I don't know . . . she plays around with witchcraft and that stuff . . ." The last place he saw her was in the bathtub about which he said "she kept moving and moving and moving, and kind of grabbed me like this, but laughing, as if she was enjoying . . . and it was kind of sickening, but it was really maddening to me, because of her offense towards me, it was like . . . you know, it was almost like she was mechanical . . . I mean, the thing was set up that, that's what she wanted to happen. . . . I feel that deep inside she was asking somebody to put her out of her misery . . . she was very symbolic with the 'Scarlet Whore Beast' she was very much into sorcery very, uh, anti-God, not really anti-God but takes the God's truth and twists it into her sorcery."

Concerning his feelings about the incident petitioner said: "I felt confused . . . I felt no different from the beginning than the end there was no difference. . . . legally I know, that it is against the law, but as far as right and wrong in the eye of God, I would say I felt no particular wrong."

When asked further about the incident petitioner responded: "I washed the blood off me, and I changed clothes, and then I looked back at her and she was, uh, she was still moving around, after being stabbed, what I thought was in the heart, and the throat . . . about seven or eight times, and she just . . . she kept moving. It was like, . . . there was a smile on her face, she kept lunging for me, while she was dead . . . I wasn't trying to be vicious . . . it would look that way, but that wasn't the intent, but she kept lunging at me, over and over again, and the nature of her attack, I was, ah, mad enough I wanted to kill her, I felt that I was justified in self defense at that point . . ." The last petitioner saw of the knife "I tried to stick it in her heart . . . she's some kind of an animal."

Petitioner explained further "she's into a very strong sorcery trip, and that's why so many stab wounds . . . I'm not a goring [sic] person . . . I've never been violent in my life, but for some reason . . . there was some evil spirit behind her that was . . . it was like, it was like there was something within her that, that wasn't really part of her body . . . she was smiling . . . she was almost like enjoying playing and it was disgusting."

When petitioner subsequently gave the written confession he added: "My attack wasn't a vicious attack the first time. I was trying to stop the spirit that was moving in her. She kept saying, 'Gary, Gary, Gary', as if she was enjoying it." When she stopped moving he washed himself, changed his clothes and then "My stepmother started moving again as if a spirit was in her. I took the knife and started stabbing her again. When I realized there was something in her that wouldn't stop moving, I started stabbing her in the head and heart. I wanted to kill the spirit that seemed to be attacking my spirit." Once again he changed his clothes but again found her moving and again stabbed her numerous times until all movement stopped. He then changed clothes once more and left.

As with the petitioner's testimony we note the testimony of the psychiatrists and psychologists is not without some disparity. Nevertheless, there is ample evidence which, under a proper insanity instruction, could have been considered by the jury as a matter of defense.

Prior to trial, petitioner made a motion to acquit on the ground of insanity pursuant to RCW 10.77.080. Three psychiatrists, Doctors Jarvis, Allison and Bremner and a psychologist, Dr. Trowbridge, were called to testify. They agreed petitioner suffered from paranoid schizophrenia both at the time of the killing and at the time of trial. Although stating it differently, all four appeared to agree that petitioner believed he was an agent of God, required to carry out God's directions. They also agreed that petitioner believed God commanded him to kill his stepmother and that he was therefore obligated to kill the "evil spirit". Consequently, all doctors concurred he was legally insane at the time of the murder.

The trial court denied the motion for acquittal and submitted the issue of insanity to the jury. At trial, the four doctors repeated their earlier testimony. All agreed that at the time of the killing, and at the time of trial, petitioner suffered from the mental disease of paranoid schizophrenia. While expressing their views in slightly different ways, they agreed petitioner understood that, as a mechanical thing, he was killing his stepmother and knew it was against the laws of man. They stressed, however, that at the time, he was preoccupied with the delusional belief that his stepmother was an agent of satan who was persecuting him, as were others like Yasser Arafat and the Ayatollah Khomeini. He believed he was being directed by God to kill satan's angel and that by so doing, he was obeying God's higher directive or law. At this time he believed himself to be a messiah and in fact compared himself with Jesus Christ.

The doctors pointed out, in different ways, that because of his delusional beliefs, petitioner felt God had directed him to send her from this life to another. He had no remorse over the killing. He felt it was justified by God and that he was merely doing a service. "He felt he would generally be protected from any difficulties . . . because 'God would not allow it to happen'."

Concerning the legal tests for insanity the mental health experts opined that while he understood it was against the law to kill, he believed he was responding to God's directive and thus had an obligation to rid the world of this "demon", "sorceress" or "evil spirit". Thus, while technically he understood the mechanical nature of the act, he did not have the capacity to discern between right and wrong with reference to the act. Some of the doctors expressed the clear view that at the time of the killing, he was unable to appreciate the nature and quality of his acts. No doctor contended otherwise. . . .

From *State v. Cameron* (1983) 674 P.2d 650, pp. 651–653.

READING 8-10

Reasons for Infanticide
People v. Sherwood (1936)

JUDGE CROUCH, Court of Appeals of New York

The defendant stands convicted of murder in the first degree. On the date of the homicide she was 27 years of age. The victim was her own infant son aged 2 years and 3 months. On August 20, 1935, under circumstances hereinafter to be stated, she put the child in his carriage, walked three and one-half miles from her lodging place to a secluded spot off the main highway, and, in a small pool of water eight inches deep, held his head under water until he was drowned.

The sole defense was that at the time of the crime she was laboring under such a defect of reason as not to know the nature and quality of the act or that the act was wrong. It is now urged that the verdict was against the weight of the evidence, and that it was rendered under misapprehension of the applicable law because of erroneous instructions. . . .

The serious question is whether the conclusion which was reached can or ought in justice to stand. Technical legal error there was in instructions to the jury, which may or may not have affected the result. Error also there was in an incident of the charge, which, whether it be called technical legal error or not, did almost beyond doubt affect the verdict. Under such circumstances we think the verdict should be set aside.

The claim of the defense was that the mother killed the child because she had become obsessed with a delusion that in death alone could there be safety and freedom from pain, suffering, and misery for her son. The time has gone by when such a claim could seem fantastic, either to judge or juror. While we still—and rightly—accept the validity of such claims with the utmost caution, we nevertheless know now that they may be valid. The claim here rests upon evidence which, on the one hand, neither discloses nor even suggests any rational motive for the tragic act; and, on the other hand, does build up a personality which might well crack and crumble under the hard blows which fate, within a brief period, dealt it. Born of indifferent stock in a small Western town, the defendant at 9 years of age had lost her mother. For a time she was in an orphanage, and then for a period served her itinerant father and his successive wives as a household drudge. There followed a period of a few years when she lived at various places in the Middle West with a succession of Salvation Army families, doing household and other work, and getting some scattered and interrupted schooling. Following that insecure and sorry young girlhood, she commenced when about 16 years old to earn her own independent way. Shortly she went on the stage as a chorus girl with traveling companies. When she was 19 years old she met and married her husband, a stage electrician, whose job, like her own, kept him moving from place to place. Within a year a baby girl was born. The couple finally came to rest in Newburgh on the Hudson, where the man secured a job with a moving picture house. After a period of comparative peace and security, what small prosperity had come to them was ended by the illness of the husband. Early in 1933 the boy baby was born. The evidence of the doctor who attended the defendant and of the nurse at a prenatal clinic shows clearly that the child was not an unwanted one. On the contrary, it was desired, welcomed, and after birth was lovingly and carefully attended to and looked after. The husband's illness developed into tuberculosis. The home, the only one the defendant had ever known, was broken up. He went to a sanitarium, the little daughter was taken by the mother-in-law, and the defendant with the infant son went to a lodging house, the landlady of which looked after the child while the defendant, as her sole means of support, worked as a waitress in a restaurant. In April, 1935, her husband died. Several months later the defendant met a man who, after a time, offered to provide a home for her and her son, to marry her and to educate the boy. On a day fixed they were to leave Newburgh for a new home in the West. She gave up her job. She made ready to go. The day came but not the man. She waited until she realized she had been deceived. She tried to get work and failed. Without a job, without means, she and her little son were evicted by the landlady—though the latter denied that—and thereupon was committed the act for which her life is forfeit. A laconic [brief] statement made to the police the same day tells the story: "My husband, Fred Sherwood, died about four months ago, and since that time I have found it very difficult to make a living for myself and my two children, Dorothy, aged seven, and James, aged two. This afternoon, August 20th, 1935, shortly before twelve o'clock noon I took my younger child, James Sherwood, in a stroller down to Caesar's Lane at New Windsor, New York. There is a very shallow brook there and I let him wade in the brook until he seemed to get tired of it, and then I picked him up in my arms and held him under water for about half an hour. During this period of time his head was completely covered with water. I picked him up then, put a clean suit on him and held him in my arms for some time. . . . Later I walked up to the state road and was given a ride to the City of Newburgh. After I got into the City I walked into Police headquarters and told the lieutenant at the desk what I had done."

During the ride back to town she carried the dead child in her arm. In that fashion she entered police headquarters. The lieutenant of police in charge testifies: "In a low monotone voice she came up alongside of my desk and said to me, 'Here he is.' . . . I said, 'You killed him?' She said, 'Yes, I drowned him.' I said, 'Where did you drown him?' She said, 'In Caesar's Lane.' I said, 'What did you do that for?' She said, 'I couldn't take care of him any longer and I thought he would be better off dead.' "

At no time was there the slightest evidence of emotion, except for a moment when, taken back to the scene of the crime, she was "teary-eyed" at the sight of the wet, discarded baby clothes; nor was there ever the least sign of regret or of doubt that she had acted for the best, as she regarded it. That the defendant knew what she was doing—the nature and quality of the act—although perhaps a matter of small doubt to the lay mind, was still an issue because both experts called as witnesses by the defendant denied that she had such knowledge. That she knew it was wrong was, when the case went to the jury, open to serious and substantial doubt. . . . It was of the utmost importance, therefore, that the law as respects criminal responsibility . . . should have been made clear to the jury.

In the main charge it was not made clear that a defect of reason which inhibited a knowledge *either* of the nature and quality of the act *or* that the act was wrong excused a person from criminal liability. At various points the two matters were referred to in the conjunctive, with the word "and" instead of the word "or." The error was called to the attention of the court at the close of the main charge, and the court said merely: "If I made that error, I so charge." Left in that way, the distinction might doubtfully be considered as having been made clear. But thereafter—and it was the court's last word before the jury retired—the court upon request charged that a mere false belief would not be sufficient to excuse her, "unless it was the result of some mental *disease* which prevented her from knowing the nature and quality of the act *and* that it was wrongful." Here was a repetition of the same error, complicated with a reference to "some mental disease," i.e., some pathological condition, instead of a "defect of reason," as the statute reads. No disease, no pathological condition, existed or was claimed to exist. It may be doubted whether the jury had a clear conception of when a person is or is not criminally liable. . . .

From *People v. Sherwood* (1936) 3 NE 2d 581, pp. 581–583.

The Knowledge Element: The M'Naghten Rule

The law did not have a settled doctrine on insanity until the 1840s, when science began to speak authoritatively on insanity. Developments in psychiatry, particularly Isaac Ray's *Medical Jurisprudence of Insanity* (1838), became influential. A case soon arose that put one definition of insanity into the limelight. Daniel M'Naghten murdered Edward Drummond, Prime Minister Robert Peel's private secretary, by mistake. He had intended to kill Peel because, in his words: "The tories in my native city have compelled me to do this. They follow and persecute me wherever I go, and have entirely destroyed my peace of mind." Expert witnesses cited Ray's scientific work and urged the court to adopt a liberal, general standard of insanity based on medical judgments. M'Naghten's personal history also became an issue at the trial. After contracting typhus in 1834, M'Naghten began to suffer chronic insomnia and headaches, which caused him to "run out to the running Clyde [River] and bathe his burning brow and even plunge into the river to obtain relief from the burning pain." The defense's final witness, a surgeon, declared M'Naghten insane, even though he had never examined M'Naghten but had only observed the trial. The jury quickly returned a verdict of "not guilty," but the jailer kept the prisoner in custody "till Her Majesty's pleasure be known."

The *M'Naghten* case provoked heated public debate between medical practitioners and politicians. Queen Victoria, who had survived a number of assassination attempts, expressed outrage at the use of a flimsy insanity defense to acquit political opponents. M'Naghten had associations with political radicals in his native Scotland. Members of the medical establishment, on the other hand, thought only they had the expertise to deal with the complexities of determining insanity. A prestigious committee of the House of Lords finally settled the matter. It refused to accept a medical or disease model. Instead, the Law Lords—the British equivalent of the U.S. Supreme Court—adopted the M'Naghten rule (*Regina v. M'Naghten* 1843). It formulated a more restrictive rule than the medical establishment wanted and opted for a cognitive approach that focused on the defendant's knowledge of right and wrong. The M'Naghten test asks whether the defendant, at the time of the crime, labored "under such a defect of reason, from disease of the mind, as not to know the nature and quality of the act he was doing; or if he did know it, that he did not know he was doing what was wrong." Did the defendant have the capacity to understand the nature of the act in a moral context? The test relies on three crucial elements: (1) a mental element (a diseased state of mind); (2) a knowledge or cognitive element (inability to know the nature and quality of the act); and (3) a moral element (inability to know the wrongfulness of the act). The M'Naghten rule treats insanity as an intellectual disease. Moral knowledge, symbolized by Plato's charioteer, should control the emotions and impulses, but when a diseased mind causes a depravity in moral knowledge, an individual loses control. The charioteer becomes defective, and criminal insanity takes hold. How would a court decide the M'Naghten case under the M'Naghten rule? Does the M'Naghten model lose touch with reality? The U.S. Supreme Court described it as "a separate little man in the top of one's head called reason whose function it is to guide another unreal little man called instinct, emotion or impulse in the way he should go" (*Holloway v. United States* 1945). As the title of one article asks, "Is the Insanity Test Insane?" (Gerber 1975).

The Emotion Element: The Irresistible Impulse Test

Does insanity consist of more than cognitive impairment? Can an otherwise insane person still know the difference between right and wrong? An alternative view to the M'Naghten test takes the emotions seriously. According to this model, reason does not simply lose control; rather, the emotions take over without impairing reason. The following case illustrates how this model operates (*State v. Felter* 1868). A farmer bludgeoned his wife to death, tried to burn the house down "so that she would not get anything," and then tried to commit suicide by cutting his throat from ear to ear. His daughter testified: "My mother is dead—my father killed her; he struck her—I don't know with what; he was mad at her before I left; it was because she poured buttermilk out; I left because he was going to kill me." The trial court used the M'Naghten rule to refuse the defendant's insanity plea, but the appeals court reversed the conviction, using a "wild beast" test. In using this alternative irresistible impulse test, a jury needs to determine "[w]hether passion or insanity was the ruling force and controlling agency which led to the homicide." The M'Naghten and irresistible impulse tests ask different questions. M'Naghten asks whether, to use Plato's metaphor, natural passion dismounted reason from the driver's seat. The irresistible impulse test asks whether an uncontrollable impulse, which arose from an insane condition of the mind, forced the loss of control. In short, did the defendant have the capacity to control her or his behavior? Under the irresistible impulse test, the charioteer no longer controls the bad horse.

The Medical or Disease Element: The Product or Durham Rule

Ray's medical or disease model lost at M'Naghten's trial, but it found one early supporter. In 1870, the New Hampshire Supreme Court adopted a medical test *(State v. Pike)*. It said that if a defendant's act resulted from a mental disease, then the law could refuse to find the defendant accountable. While the M'Naghten rule focused on cognitive incapacity and the irresistible impulse test concentrated on volitional incapacity, the New Hampshire court's product test shifted the focus from the effects to the cause—that is, the mental disease itself. In 1954, Judge Bazelon revived the product test *(Durham v. United States)* which gives the fullest possible range to expert psychiatric testimony. In this model, a mental disease either causes the charioteer's failure to understand, or it causes the impulse horse to run wild. The rule separates mental illness from moral responsibility. Should mental illness exempt all those who are afflicted from moral responsibility? Friedman cited *State v. Padilla* (1959) as an example of a particularly brutal murder for which the accused got off because of diminished capacity:

> Padilla drank beer in a bar in Roswell, New Mexico, from noon until midnight and smoked at least two marijuana cigarettes. He left the bar with a half case of beer, went to the home of the victim, a five-year-old child, and "took her into his car. He then drove approximately fourteen miles. . . . [Then] he raped the child and thereafter killed her by stabbing her with a screwdriver." He took a seat cover from the car, put it over her body, and covered it with sand. (1993, p. 405)

Padilla, a twenty-five-year old Mexican-American, had a second-grade education and an intelligence level of "dull normal." The Supreme Court of New Mexico overturned Padilla's conviction on grounds of "diminished capacity." Friedman (1993) concludes: "A crime so horrible evokes rage, not understanding; it is the kind of crime that gives the system its sorest, most difficult test" (p. 406). Is Friedman correct that the system did not pass the test in *Padilla?*

A Mixture of Elements: The Model Penal Code

The Model Penal Code (1962) proposed a test that used the best elements and rejected the worst of the previous three models: "A person is not responsible for criminal conduct if at the time of such conduct as a result of mental disease or defects he lacks substantial capacity either to appreciate the criminality of his conduct or to conform his conduct to the requirements of law." The test contains both M'Naghten cognitive elements and irresistible impulse volitional elements. It also softens those rules by not requiring complete cognitive or volitional incapacity. The test for the Model Penal Code proposal came in *United States v. Hinkley*. On March 30, 1981, John W. Hinkley shot and wounded President Ronald Reagan and three others as they left the Washington Hilton Hotel. His victims included James Brady, Reagan's press secretary, who later became a strong advocate of gun control. Hinkley had become obsessed with the movie *Taxi Driver,* which he had seen fifteen times. The film's central character, Travis Bickle, an alienated, violent taxi driver (played by Robert DeNiro), becomes infatuated with a woman who works for a presidential candidate. When Bickle's romantic efforts fail, he decides to take revenge by assassinating the presidential candidate. He fails there as well. Bickle then becomes involved with Iris, a prostitute (played by Jodi Foster), and, in the end, rescues her. Hinkley identified with the character of Bickle and fired six shots at President Reagan in an attempt to impress Jodi Foster. After an eight-week-long trial, the jury returned a verdict of "not guilty by reason of insanity," and came under harsh criticism for using the Model Penal Code test. The verdict in *Hinkley* caused a political uproar similar to the one that followed the M'Naghten ruling. In 1984, Congress responded with a proposal that closely resembled the M'Naghten Rule for federal crimes.

Abolishing the Insanity Defense

Dissatisfaction with the competing definitions has led some writers, such as Norval Morris, to call for abolishing the insanity defense (see Reading 8-11), which some states have already done. Defenders of the insanity defense, such as Sanford Kadish, remind the abolitionists of criminal law's moral foundations (see Reading 8-12), pointing out that the state uses punishment as a means of moral condemnation. If a person does not have free will, then that person has no moral responsibility for the act. The state punishes voluntary acts, but not involuntary ones. A final perspective opts for giving these moral judgments back to representatives of the people—the jury—charging that scientific and professional experts have too much influence over the insanity determination. They maintain that criminal law judgments primarily reflect society's moral judgment rather than science's value-free judgment. Daniel Robinson, in arguing for giving judgment about the insanity defense back to the jurors who represent the moral community, may have overlooked an institutional reality (see Reading 8-13). Legal issues have become increasingly complex, requiring greater reliance on experts, particularly scientific ones, such as geneticists, who testify before lay juries to explain DNA evidence. Proponents of scientific courts claim that expert testimony has reached a level of complexity beyond the capabilities of lay jurors. Should the criminal law base its judgments on science whenever feasible?

READING 8-11

Abolition of the Insanity Defense
"The Criminal Responsibility of the Mentally Ill" (1982)

Norval Morris

Hence we are brought to the central issue—the question of fairness, the sense that it is unjust and unfair to stigmatize the mentally ill as criminals and to punish them for their crimes. The criminal law exists to deter and to punish those who would or who do choose to do wrong. If they cannot exercise choice, they cannot be deterred and it is a moral outrage to punish them. The argument sounds powerful but its premise is weak.

Choice is neither present nor absent in the typical case where the insanity defense is currently pleaded; what is at issue is the degree of freedom of choice on a continuum from the hypothetically entirely rational to the hypothetically pathologically determined—in states of consciousness neither polar condition exists.

The moral issue sinks into the sands of reality. Certainly it is true that in a situation of total absence of choice it is outrageous to inflict punishment; but the frequency of such situations to the problems of criminal responsibility becomes an issue of fact in which tradition and clinical knowledge and practice are in conflict. . . .

And indeed I think that much of the discussion of the defense of insanity is the discussion of a myth rather than of a reality. It is no minor debating point that in fact we lack a defense of insanity as an operating tool of the criminal law other than in relation to a very few particularly heinous and heavily punished offenses. There is not an operating defense of insanity in relation to burglary or theft, or the broad sweep of index crimes generally; the plea of not guilty on the ground of insanity is rarely to be heard in city courts of first instance which handle the grist of the mill of the criminal law—though a great deal of pathology is to be seen in the parade of accused and convicted persons before these courts. As a practical matter we reserve this defense for a few sensational cases where it may be in the interest of the accused either to escape the possibility of capital punishment (though in cases where serious mental illness is present, the risk of execution is slight) or where the likely punishment is of a sufficient severity to make the indeterminate commitment of the accused a preferable alternative to a criminal conviction. Operationally the defense of insanity is a tribute, it seems to me, to our hypocrisy rather than to our morality.

To be less aggressive about the matter and to put aside anthropomorphic allegations of hypocrisy, the special defense of insanity may properly be indicted as producing a morally unsatisfactory classification on the continuum between guilt and innocence. It applies in practice to only a few mentally ill criminals, thus omitting many others with guilt-reducing relationships between their mental illness and their crime; it excludes other powerful pressures on human behavior, thus giving excessive weight to the psychological over the social. It is a false classification in the sense that if a team of the world's most sensitive and trained psychiatrists and moralists were to select from all those found guilty of felonies and those found not guilty by reason of insanity any given number who should not be stigmatized as criminals, very few of those found not guilty by reason of insanity would be selected. How to offer proof of this? The only proof, I regret, is to be found by personal contact with a flow of felony cases through the courts and into the prisons. No one of serious perception will fail to recognize both the extent of mental illness and retardation among the prison population and the overwhelming weight of adverse social circumstances on criminal behavior. This is, of course, not an argument that social adversities should lead to acquittals; they should be taken into account in sentencing. And the same is true of the guilt and sentencing of those pressed by psychological adversities. The special defense is thus a morally false classification. And it is a false classifica-

tion also in the sense that it does not select from the prison population those
most in need of psychiatric treatment. . . .

445

CHAPTER 8
Responsibility and
Punishment

Morris, Norval. "Madness and the Criminal Law." © (1982) University of Chicago Press.
Reprinted with the permission of the University of Chicago.

READING 8-12

The Insanity Defense's Moral Foundation
"The Decline of Innocence" (1968)

Sanford Kadish

The criminological positivists at the turn of the century started a good deal
of creative rethinking about the criminal law. Some of their proposals have
gained widespread acceptance in the criminal law as we know it today. Others made no headway at all. One particular proposal, and a very fundamental one indeed, began a controversy which has ebbed and flowed regularly
since. That is the proposal to eliminate from the criminal law the whole apparatus of substantive principles, or at least some of them, such as the legal
insanity defence, which owe their presence to the law's traditional concern
for distinguishing the guilty and the innocent in terms of their blameworthiness. The essence of the proposal is that innocence in this sense, moral innocence, if you will, should not disqualify a person from the consequences of
the penal law. Moral innocence should, it is urged, give way to social dangerousness as the basis for a criminal disposition.

In recent years there has been a resurgence of the controversy produced
by serious proposals to eliminate the defence of legal insanity and, more radical still, to eliminate across the board the requirements of *mens rea* from the
definition of criminal offences and defences. If I may raise my colours at the
outset, I am frankly a friend to neither proposal. In this brief paper I would
like to discuss the implications of these suggested reforms and to develop my
reasons for believing that the case has not been made. . . .

I turn now to what I referred to as the fundamental objection to this proposal. Essentially it is that it opens to the condemnation of a criminal conviction a class of persons who, on any commonsense notion of justice, are beyond blaming and ought not to be punished. The criminal law as we know
it today does associate a substantial condemnatory onus with conviction for
a crime. So long as this is so a just and humane legal system has an obligation to make a distinction between those who are eligible for this condemnation and those who are not. It is true, as has been argued, that a person
adjudicated not guilty but insane suffers a substantial social stigma. It is
also true that this is hurtful and unfortunate, and indeed, unjust. But it results from the misinterpretation placed upon the person's conduct by people in the community. It is not, like the conviction of the irresponsible, the

paradigmatic affront to the sense of justice in the law which consists in the deliberative act of convicting a morally innocent person of a crime, of imposing blame when there is no occasion for it.

This sentiment of justice has attained constitutional stature in decisions of the United States Supreme Court. Obviously I do not bring the Supreme Court into this for its legal authority in the U.K. What is relevant is that in these decisions the court was responding to a fundamental sense of justice, which, unlike the mandate of the court, does not stop at national boundaries. The animating principle in several recent decisions was that to convict a person of a crime in circumstances in which it was impossible for him to conform violates a fundamental principle of justice. It was this principle which led the court to hold that it constituted an unconstitutional imposition of cruel and unusual punishment to make it a crime for a person "to be" a narcotic addict. The same principle persuaded the court in another case to find a violation of due process of law in the conviction of a person for failing to register as a previously convicted offender upon arrival in Los Angeles in the absence of any circumstances calculated to give notice of her obligation to do so. As observed recently by Mr. Justice Fortas: "Our morality does not permit us to punish for illness. We do not impose punishment for involuntary conduct, whether the lack of volition results from 'insanity,' or addiction to narcotics, or from other illnesses."

Of course the spirit behind these proposals to abolish the insanity defence is humane rather than punitive: what is contemplated is that persons, once convicted, who are insane would then receive all the care and treatment appropriate to their condition, as indeed would all persons who commit crime. The answer was given by the Washington Supreme Court when it declared unconstitutional the abolition amendment . . . : "Yet the stern and awful fact still remains, and is patent to all men, that the status and condition in the eyes of the world, and under the law, of one convicted of crime is vastly different from that of one simply adjudged insane. We cannot shut our eyes to the fact that the element of punishment is still in our criminal laws." . . .

READING 8-13

Let Society and the Jury Decide Insanity
"Jural Science and Social Science" (1996)

Daniel N. Robinson

Jural science is not a species of natural science, nor for that matter (*pace* [with all due respect to] legal positivism) is it a "social science" in the current acceptation of the term [see chapter 2, page 68]. Whether a court is convened to determine criminal guilt or the settlement of property or the validity of contracts or the propriety of preserving a citizen in his liberties, it is the specific individual who is the subject of the judicial process. The question at law is not whether this defendant is, in some psychological or social or ethnic respect, "like" other defendants who were found guilty; or whether the testator was genetically related to persons who were certified to be insane; or whether others whose psychological profiles matched the prisoner's thereupon returned to a life of crime when paroled. . . .

There are, to be sure, instances in which this is the right, the best, and the only plausible explanation; instances in which profound retardation precludes the possibility of *mens rea,* or where the recorded life of the defendant or the deceased is so filled with the indisputable signs of derangement as to turn his or her actions into mere reactions or undeliberated responses. In a word, *furiosi* [wildly deranged individuals] exist, and it takes no expert to identify them, for there is no narrative into which their conduct can be coherently inserted. And, after all, jurors and judges are guided by narrative. The explanation they seek is in fact the narrative that succeeds in integrating the otherwise fragmented collection of persons, facts, motives, and actions. What is required for purposes of adjudication is not a causal explanation of the violent act—"because the bullet struck a vital organ"—but a narrative explanation: he committed the act "because, in his hatred for the victim, he resolved to track him down and to fire what became the fatal shot." If the quest for suspects fails, then a search for (physical, material) causes is most likely to produce answers; lacking both forms of explanation, the event tends to be regarded as accident. Instead of weighing or testing the claim that a defendant or testator was insane, courts might more properly determine whether the offenses and actions can be integrated into a coherent account which is rendered neither more coherent nor explicative by assuming mental disorder on the part of the actor. Note, then, that scientific or medical or "expert" evidence—if, in matters of the mind, there is such—comes to be needed only when all else fails. Even then, however, caution is needed. As Judge David Bazelon, one of psychiatry's most loyal defenders, observed, "Psychiatry . . . is the ultimate wizardry. My experience has shown that in no case is it more difficult to elicit productive and reliable expert testimony than in cases that call on the knowledge and practice of psychiatry." . . .

The issue is not the state's role as *parens patriae* [guardian of persons under legal disability] where a citizen's death or severe degradation is involved, but its role in cases such as *Jones v. United States* (463 U.S. 354; 1983) arising in the wake of *Hinckley.* Jones, arrested for a minor theft, was found not guilty by reason of insanity and proceeded to spend eight years in confinement in St. Elizabeth's Hospital in Washington, D.C. Eight years being far longer than the time he would have served had he been convicted of the crime rather than acquitted, Jones's lawyers argued that Jones had a right to a commitment hearing. The linchpin of the argument was that the state should not derive greater powers of incarceration through acquittals than it enjoys as a result of successful convictions. . . .

The imperfect solution is to adopt legal criteria of insanity that do not depend upon psychological or psychiatric theories or experts as to the nature or true sign or invariable element of "mental disease," for all such promised *stigmata* [marks of disgrace] have by now proved chimerical [illusional]. The judging community itself, if not misled or confused by presumed experts and their conflicting texts, must finally be counted on to recognize those who can be justly held to the same standards the community has adopted for itself. The punishments of law typically include a period of exile from this same community; in this way members not only protect themselves but lay down the conditions under which they are prepared to have their own liberties constrained. If ordinary citizens are forced to accept the authority of expert judgment in such matters, this does not mean that they abandon confidence in their own competence to make such judgments. Instead, they end up with lower regard for the jural and moral precepts that seem to be at the bottom of the confusion. In the circumstance, the real danger is that, as public impatience mounts and various ad hoc remedies are applied in response to popular enthusiasms, an important provision of the law will be muted. . . .

The point is that the psychological defects and eccentricities that would clearly raise questions of competence and intent are either drawn from the domain in which jurors can enter empathically or are drawn from a domain so foreign as to require a guide or expert if the relevant signs are to be read right. But the need for expert guidance does not create it. Where the mental health professionals are on firmest footing is in diagnosing conditions so severe as to leave no doubt in any observer's mind: the legendary "wild beast."

There is no reason to fear that the rejection of expertise in these areas will result in a cruel or barbarous disregard of the mentally disturbed. If history is a guide, the mentally wayward have suffered more at the hands of experts armed with theories than when entrusted to that tireless rider on the Clapham omnibus. Left to his own judgment and experience, and despite confusions and misapprehensions, he is likely to remain open to the possibility that witches sometimes cry.

D. CONTROVERSIES: CRIMINAL RESPONSIBILITY AND STRICT LIABILITY

1. Who Killed Whom?

The **felony murder rule** (holding an individual criminally liable for accidental deaths that occur, for example, during a robbery) provides an interesting challenge or exception to requiring proof of *mens rea*. A criminal must have a blameworthy state of mind—that is, if someone unintentionally and accidentally shoots another person, the person who fired the shot does not have the state of mind necessary for criminal conviction. However, the *mens rea* requirement may be waived if a murder occurs during the commission of a felony. Any individuals, armed or unarmed, who are involved in a felony, may face murder charges even if none of the suspects fired the fatal shot. Should any of the following factors make a critical difference in applying the felony murder rule: (1) the status of the victim (police officer or accomplice), (2) the defendant's degree of involvement in the crime (major or minor role),

(3) the seriousness of the crime (murder or robbery)? State courts have taken a variety of stances on felony murder. In one case, seventeen Joliet police officers staked out the Illinois Wine and Liquor Warehouse. Upon seeing the police, one suspect (Papes) fled in one direction and two others (Rock and Hickman) fled in another direction. A police sergeant apprehended Papes and found a weapon in his possession. Another police officer, pursuing Rock and Hickman, fired his shotgun and later discovered that he had mistakenly killed a fellow police detective. The police finally apprehended Rock and Hickman. Neither of the defendants had a weapon on his person. The trial court arrested (refused) the jury's finding that Rock and Hickman were guilty of the murder of the detective. An appellate court remanded (sent back) the case to the trial court for sentencing for the crime of murder under Illinois' felony murder rule (*People v. Hickman* 1973). Should unarmed defendants face murder charges when a police officer accidentally kills someone? Should the rule take the status of the victim into account? Should it matter whether the victim is a police officer, a bystander, or an accomplice to the crime?

Consider a case in which a robbery sparked a gun battle. The robbery victim was accidentally killed by his employee after the robbers opened fire. A court upheld the robbers' murder conviction under California's felony murder rule (*People v. Harrison* 1959) Compare a case in which a gas station owner killed a robber when the robber pointed a gun at him. The owner also wounded an accomplice, Washington, as he fled from the vault with a money bag, but no weapon, in hand. A jury convicted Washington of first degree murder. Thus, it found an unarmed accomplice guilty of murder for participating in a robbery in which his fellow robber was killed by the victim of the robbery. California's Supreme Court overturned Washington's murder conviction (*People v. Washington* 1965), refusing to give any weight to whether the person killed was an innocent victim or one of the felons. However, the Court found that it was important to know whether the felons initiated a gun battle *(Harrison)* and whether the felons or someone else killed the victims. The court could not see that any purpose was served by holding felons strictly responsible for killings committed by their victims.

2. Degrees of Murdering?

Should the application of the felony murder rule depend on the defendant's degree of participation in the crime? The U.S. Supreme Court gave an affirmative answer in *Tison v. Arizona* (1986). In that case, two brothers helped their father escape from jail and then hijacked a car into the Arizona desert. The father murdered the car's four occupants (a mother, father, two-year-old daughter, and fifteen-year-old niece) and later died of exposure. Evidence showed that the brothers had no intentions of killing any members of the family, but the Court upheld their murder convictions under the felony murder rule (*Tison v. Arizona* 1986). Justice O'Connor, who wrote the Tison opinion, distinguished it from a previous case, *Enmund v. Florida* (1982), in which the Court had reversed a death sentence on factual grounds under Florida's felony murder rule. She noted that Enmund had driven a getaway car and that, unlike the Tison brothers, he had played only a minor role in the felony. Did Justice O'Connor successfully distinguish Enmund?

3. The Case for Abolition

In 1957, the British abolished the felony murder rule. George Fletcher, who urges the United States to do the same, thinks that *People v. Fuller* (1970) gives strong support to the abolitionist position. Should the nature of the crime make a difference with the felony murder rule? A police officer observed two men rolling tires toward their parked car. When the suspects saw the patrol car, they dropped the tires, jumped into their vehicle, and drove away. A car chase ensued. The suspect's car ran a red light and crashed into another car (uninvolved in the incident), killing its driver. The driver and the passenger of the fleeing vehicle were charged with the murder of the driver, but the trial court rejected these charges. A California appeals court, however, upheld the murder charges against both men. The felony murder rule applies only to felonies and, while the defendants did steal tires, did they commit a felony? Under California law, burglary includes breaking into vehicles with locked doors, therefore Fletcher conjectures that burglary in California would include breaking into a locked car trunk. Presumably then a killing that occurred when the suspects stole tires from a locked car trunk would constitute murder, but it would not qualify as murder if the trunk had been unlocked. Should a murder charge turn on whether the killing occurred while the suspects stole tires from a locked or an unlocked car trunk? Should murder convictions hinge on these fine distinctions (see chapter 3, page 103, on formalism)? Fletcher (1981) finds that the rule undermines individual responsibility and proportionate punishment. "Punishment must be proportional to wrong doing. When the felony-murder rule converts an accidental death into first-degree murder, then the punishment is rendered disproportionately to the wrong for which the offender is personally responsible" (p. 428).

E. THEORIES OF PUNISHMENT

1. Types of Punishment

Punishment distinguishes criminal law from all other types of law. The nature of punishment seems easier to address than the justification for punishment, but what exactly is punishment? A nine-year old asks her parents to tell her what "being grounded" means. Then she asks them to ground her because she has just discovered that her best friend has been sentenced to being confined to her house over a weekend. Does grounding qualify as punishment? Are definitions of punishment culturally relative? For example, in Japan, parents punish their children by placing them outside the front door instead of restricting them to the house. Now consider more serious acts. Does simply telling murderers that they were wrong constitute an inadequate punishment, or is it no punishment at all? The Kapauku Papuans from West New Guinea do not take harsh action against a murderer (Pospisil 1970). Instead, to prevent war, the "authority" orders the defendant's relatives to pay blood money to the victim's brothers and to reprimand the defendant. Thus, the relatives, who had nothing to do with the murder, receive harsher treatment (a fine) than the murderer, who gets a scolding. H.L.A. Hart (1968) proposed that a punishment must include the following:

1. It must involve pain or other consequences normally considered unpleasant.
2. It must be for an offense against legal rules.
3. It must be of an actual or supposed offender for his offense.
4. It must be intentionally administered by human beings other than the offender.
5. It must be imposed and administered by an authority constituted by a legal system against which the offense is committed. (pp. 4–5).

Does parental grounding in the United States or the authority's orders in New Guinea contain any or all of Hart's five elements of punishment?

Ancient Punishments

Given an understanding of the nature of punishment, what justifies it? Hammurabi, who reigned over Babylon from 1792 to 1750 B.C., developed one of the oldest codifications of the law:

1. If a man accuse a man, and charge him with murder, but cannot convict him, the accuser shall be put to death.
2. If a man steals ox or sheep, ass or pig, or boat—if it belonged to god or palace, he shall pay thirty fold; if it belonged to a common man, he shall restore ten fold. If the thief has nothing wherewith to pay, he shall be put to death.
3. If a fire breaks out in a man's house and a man who goes to extinguish it cast his eye on the household property of the owner of the house, and take the household property of the owner of the house, that man shall be thrown into the fire.
4. If a priestess or a nun who is not a resident in a convent opens a wine shop or enters a wine shop for a drink, they shall burn that woman.
5. If the wife of a man be taken in lying with another man, they shall bind them and throw them into the water. If the husband of the woman spares the life of his wife, the king shall spare the life of his servants.
6. If a man destroys the eye of another man, they shall destroy his eye.
7. If he breaks a man's bone, they shall break his bone.
8. If a man knocks out the tooth of a man of his own rank, they shall knock out his tooth.
9. If a man knocks out a tooth of a common man, he shall pay one-third mana of silver. (Robbins 1990, pp. 21–22)

Do these punishments seem outlandish and bizarre? Do they have any conceivable justification?

Modern Punishments

Turning to a more contemporary debate over punishment, what, if anything, justifies castration as a punishment for sex offenses? The debate (see Reading 8-14) stems from a conviction for the rape of a thirteen-year-old girl. The defendant requested surgical castration. A Texas district court initially approved the request but later reneged, amidst considerable protest. What theories of punishment underlie this and other debates concerning forms of punishment?

READING 8-14

Castrating Punishment
"Sex Offenders: Is Castration an Acceptable Punishment?" (1992)

Douglas J. Besharov and Andrew Vachhs

YES: CONSIDER CHEMICAL TREATMENT

Douglas J. Besharov

Surgical castration has never been very popular in this country, although it has been used sporadically in a number of states for more than 100 years, and was a common remedy in Germany and Denmark as late as the 1960s.

Although many castrated men may be capable of intercourse, the limited research that exists suggests that the repeat-offense rate is low. On humanitarian and civil liberties grounds, however, most experts now oppose the procedure and it is unlikely that many courts will turn to it as an alternative to incarceration—especially since there is a better option.

First tried more than 25 years ago, the use of hormone suppressors—also known as "chemical castration"—has proven highly effective for certain sex offenders. The most common drug used is medroxyprogesterone acetate, a synthetic progesterone originally developed as a contraceptive marketed as Depo-Provera.

According to a 1990 article in the *American Journal of Criminal Law,* this treatment, when given to men, "reduces the production and effects of testosterone, thus diminishing the compulsive sexual fantasy. Formerly insistent and commanding urges can be voluntarily controlled." It creates what another writer called "erotic apathy." Fifty sex offender clinics in this country now use chemical therapy, and it is even more widely used in Europe.

Low Recidivism

Carefully conducted research indicates that hormone therapy works—when coupled with appropriate counseling—for most paraphiliacs (sex offenders driven by overwhelming sexual fantasies). Recidivism [repeat offender] rates are under 5 percent.

Just as in surgical castration, the subject can still have erections, and many successfully impregnate their wives. For this reason, hormone treatment does not work for antisocial personalities or for those whose sex offenses are motivated by feelings of anger, violence or power. The treatment does not reach the causes of their harmful behavior. Thus, proper diagnosis is essential.

Some may argue that hormone treatment as an alternative to incarceration is too lenient for serious sex crimes. First, it is possible to combine treatment with incarceration. But more importantly, we should remember how frequently serious offenders serve very short sentences. Nationally, convicted rapists serve less than 6 years in jail, and that does not include all those who plead guilty to a lesser offense. For too many offenders, the sexual abuse and violence in prisons merely heightens their propensity to commit further crime.

Recognizing the sexual side of some rapes in no way seeks to blame the victim, or denies the violent, hateful aspect of rape. Promoting an apparently effective therapy does not condone the behavior, but it does protect future victims.

Others will oppose using these drugs because, even though they work, they are an invasion of bodily integrity and reproductive freedom. (Side effects include weight gain, hot flashes and hypertension.) But it is more accurate to see them as equivalent to the psychotropic drugs, which include antidepressants, antipsychotics and tranquilizers, now routinely used to treat many mental disorders.

Some would even deny defendants the right to accept the treatment in lieu of imprisonment—because the choice is inherently coercive. Perhaps it is. But the question is this: When faced with the certainty of incarceration, wouldn't we all want to be able to make such a choice? To ask the question is to answer it.

After all the sensationalism, the use of hormone-suppressing drugs, in certain cases, holds great promise for reducing the level of sexual violence against women and children. As a voluntary alternative, it is in both the defendant's and society's interest.

NO: PRAGMATICALLY IMPOTENT

Andrew Vachhs

As a criminal justice response to the chronic, dangerous sexual psychopath, castration of any kind is morally pernicious and pragmatically impotent. Even if we could ignore the implications of mutilation-as-compensation for criminal offenses, castration must be rejected on the most essential of grounds: The "cure" will exacerbate the "disease."

Proponents of castration tell us: 1) It will heal the offender (and thus protect society), and 2) it would be the offender's own choice.

Violent sex offenders are not victims of their heightened sex drives. Rapists may be "expressing their rage." Predatory pedophiles may be "replaying their old scripts." But any sexual sadist, properly interviewed, will tell you the truth: They do what they do because they want to do it. Their behavior is not the product of sickness—it is volitional.

Castration will not remove the source of a violent sex offender's rage—only one single instrument of its expression. Rapes have been committed with broomsticks, coke bottles—any blunt object. Indeed, most criminal statutes now incorporate just such a possibility.

And imagine a violent rapist whose hatred of women occupies most of his waking thoughts. Imagine him agreeing to castration to avoid a lengthy prison sentence. Imagine his rage festering geometrically as he stews in the bile of what "they" have done to him. Does anyone actually believe such a creature has been rendered harmless?

An escalating pattern is characteristic of many predatory sex offenders—castration is likely to produce an internal demand for even higher levels of stimulation.

The castration remedy implies some biomedical cause for sexual offenses. Once fixed, the offender ceases to be a danger. This is nonsense—the motivation for sexual assault will not disappear with the severed genitalia or altered hormones.

In Germany, Klaus Grabowski avoided a life sentence by agreeing to castration. Released, he began covert hormone injections. In 1980, he strangled a 7-year-old girl and buried her body. At trial, his defense was that the castration had removed any sexual feelings, that he had lured the child to his apartment because he loved children and killed her in response to blackmail threats.

High Predatory Drive

Even the most liberal of Americans have become suspicious of a medical model to explain sex offenders. Such offenders may plot and plan, scheme and stalk for months, utilize the most elaborate devices to avoid detection, even network with others and commercially profit from their foul acts.

But some psycho-apologist can always be found to claim the poor soul was deep in the grip of irresistible impulse when he was compelled to attack. Imagine the field day the expert-witness fraternity will have explaining how the castrated child molester who later killed his new victims was rendered insane as a result of the castration itself.

Sex offender treatment is the growth industry of the 1990s. Chemical castration already looms as a Get-Out-of-Jail-Free Card.

Castration validates the sex offender's self-portrait: He is the victim; he can't help himself. It panders to our ugliest instincts, not the least of which is cowardice—the refusal to call evil by its name.

Nor can castration be defended because the perpetrator chooses it. Leaving aside the obvious issue of coercion, under what theory does a convicted criminal get to select his own (non-incarcerative) sentence?

America loves simple solutions to complex problems, especially solutions with political utility, like boot camp for youthful offenders. The last thing our cities need is muggers in better physical shape.

When it comes to our own self-interest (and self-defense), the greatest sickness is stupidity. Castration qualifies . . . on all counts.

Besharov, Douglas J. and Vachhs, Andrew. "Sex Offenders" from *ABA Journal* (July 1992). Reprinted by permission of ABA Journal.

2. Theories of Punishment: An Overview

A wide variety of theories attempt to justify some punishments and reject others. **Utilitarian** theories of punishment have a forward-looking view of punishment: "[A]ll punishment is a mischief. . . . If it ought to be admitted, it ought to be admitted in so far as it promises to exclude some greater evil" (Bentham 1789, p. 158). Utilitarians see punishment as a means to a future (forward) goal, primarily **deterrence** (punishing to stop future crime). In contrast, **retributivist** theorists (correcting past wrongs) look backward to the crime and ask what justice requires to correct the past wrong. **Rehabilitation** theorists (reforming the wrong-doer) retain the forward-looking quality of utilitarianism, but they shift the focus from society in general to the individual. Whereas utilitarians want a system of punishment that affects the behavior of future wrongdoers, rehabilitation theorists want to affect the current wrongdoer's future behavior. Another difference revolves around the two elements of a crime—utilitarians place their emphasis on the *actus reus,* while rehabilitation theorists focus on the *mens rea.* Representing another perspective, **restitution** theorists (restoring the victim) see utilitarians and rehabilitation theorists as misguided. They demand a reorientation away from the wrongdoer's *actus reus* and *mens rea.* Restitution theorists turn the spotlight away from the perpetrator and toward the victim.

Deterrence and Utilitarianism

Utilitarianism and deterrence often go together, although rehabilitation has some utilitarian promoters. According to utilitarians, punishment increases overall utility (the greatest good for the greatest number) through its deterrent (or other) effects (see Reading 5-8 for a cost/benefit analysis of free speech). Does punishment have deterrent effects? Punishment deters the criminal, and it reminds the public to obey the law, yet objectionable means might also have deterrent effects. A sheriff might frame an innocent African American to stop a series of lynchings (McCloskey 1965, p. 255), but how would the sheriff predict that the framing of an innocent person would stop the lynchings (Sprigge 1965)? Utilitarians respond to these challenges by pointing out how unrealistic they are, but are there realistic situations where immoral means achieve deterrent ends? Richard Brandt admits that immoral acts might achieve overall utility, but he does not think that this criticism applies to rules (see Reading 8-15).

Retributivism

The Golden Rule states, "Do unto others as you would have others do unto you." Law enforcement seems to have its own version of the Golden Rule, which translates as "Do unto others as they have not done to you" (Reiman 1998, pp. 88–89). Theorists often associate the *jus talionis* principle **(retaliation)** with the "eye for an eye" approach of Hammurabi's code. Immanuel Kant provided a classical defense of retributivism (see also chapter 2, on Kant's universalism, especially Reading 2-2):

> Judicial punishment can never be used merely as a means to promote some other good for the criminal himself or for civil society but instead it must in

all cases be imposed on him only on the ground that he has committed a crime; for a human being can never be manipulated merely as a means to the purposes of someone else and can never be confused with the objects of the Law of things. His innate personality [that is, his right as a person] protects him against such treatment, even though he may indeed be condemned to lose his civil personality. He must first be found to be deserving of punishment before any consideration is given to the utility of this punishment for himself or for his fellow citizens. The law concerning punishment is a categorical imperative, and woe to him who rummages around in the winding paths of a theory of happiness looking for some advantage to be gained by releasing the criminal from punishment or by reducing the amount of it—in keeping with the Pharisaic motto: "It is better that one man should die than that the whole people should perish." If legal justice perishes, then it is no longer worth while for men to remain alive on this earth. If this is so, what should one think of the proposal to permit a criminal who has been condemned to death to remain alive, if, after consenting to allow dangerous experiments to be made on him, he happily survives such experiments and if doctors thereby obtain new information that benefits the community? Any court of justice would repudiate such a proposal with scorn if it were suggested by a medical college, for [legal] justice ceases to be justice if it can be bought for a price.

What kind and what degree of punishment does public legal justice adopt as its principle and standard? None other than the principle of equality (illustrated by the pointer on the scales of justice), that is, the principle of not treating one side more favorably than the other. Accordingly, any undeserved evil that you inflict on someone else among the people is one that you do to yourself. If you vilify him, you vilify yourself; if you steal from him, you steal from yourself; if you kill him, you kill yourself. Only the Law of retribution (*jus talionis*) can determine exactly the kind and degree of punishment; it must be well understood, however, that this determination [must be made] in the chambers of a court of justice (and not in your private judgment). All other standards fluctuate back and forth and, because extraneous considerations are mixed with them, they cannot be compatible with the principle of pure and strict legal justice. (Kant 1985)

A number of commentators, such as Pincoffs (1966), have clarified and recast Kant's argument as follows. Punishment addresses not only the act but also the intention. According to Kant, who focuses on intentional acts, wrongful intentional acts merit punishment. He emphasizes intent because he regards all humans as **autonomous agents** (individuals capable of making independent, rational moral judgments) (see Reading 5-6 for a Kantian defense of free speech). Kant treats criminals as rational agents who must bear the full responsibility for their acts. When rational agents commit acts, they have, in a sense, consented to, agreed to, or authorized others to do the same to them (Reiman, 1985). It would be futile for criminals to question the justification for Kant's retribution theory, because if criminals were to dismiss Kant's theory of retribution, they would have to reject Kant's treatment of criminals, including themselves, as autonomous. Any theory of punishment should treat individuals as ends (as autonomous agents), not merely as a means of achieving a utilitarian goal, such as deterrence. Utilitarian goals always remain subject to criticism, including criticism from criminals, but Kantian ends do not fall under the same criticism. Only retribution theory treats criminals as autonomous agents, as **ends in themselves** (having an independent value). Kant also adopts an equal treatment version of retributivism, arguing that criminals deserve the same punishment as their victims (death for death, etc.). Thus, Kant justifies punishment by elevating criminals to the status of rational and free moral agents. Some critics who are more sociologically oriented have charged Kant with providing an abstract philosophical cover, a "transcendental sanction," for the rules of existing society (Murphy 1973 in Simmons et al. 1995). Kant's aloofness allows him to avoid a fundamental analysis of how to change a system that breeds crimes.

Friedrich Nietzsche's criticism takes a more psychological route (see Reading 8–4):

> Even if he turns to the law-courts, he desires revenge as a private individual; but also, as a thoughtful, prudent man of society, he desires the revenge of society upon one who does not respect it. Thus, by legal punishment private honor as well as that of society is restored—that is to say, punishment is revenge. Punishment undoubtedly contains the first . . . element of revenge, in so far as by its means society helps to preserve itself, and strikes a counter-blow in self-defense. Punishment desires to prevent further injury, to scare off other offenders. In this way the two elements of revenge, different as they are, are united in punishment. . . . (Nietzsche 1878, p. 212)

He sees retribution as a disguised form of revenge. Michael Moore rounds out the discussion with an elaborate rebuttal to Nietzsche's charges (see Reading 8-16).

Mixed System

Utilitarian and retributivist justifications of punishment have both positive and negative aspects. It makes sense to want a system of punishment that has a lasting positive effect by deterring future wrongdoers, which makes the forward-looking feature of utilitarianism attractive. The drawback to the utilitarian approach lies in what it fails to exclude as means to the ends, such as allowing for questionable steps to be taken toward the improved future. Future benefits may come about through unacceptable methods of punishment.

A similar analysis applies to retributivism. It makes sense to treat wrongdoers as responsible adults. Society should not forget past wrongs or simply let "bygones be bygones." This way of looking at retributivism makes its backward-looking feature attractive, but difficulties arise when it is applied to an entire system of punishment. A retributive penal system's purpose would be "to set up and preserve a correspondence between moral turpitude and suffering" (Rawls 1955).

John Rawls opts for a mixture of utilitarianism and retributivism (see Reading 8-17). He applies utilitarianism to the entire penal system and retributivism to specific cases of punishment. This enables him to retain the merits of both theories without their defects. Does Rawls avoid another problem, posed by Alan Goldman, of avoiding excessive punishment of the guilty to deter potential wrongdoers (see Reading 8-18)? Is there a fundamental conflict between the utilitarian goal of deterrence and the retributivist proportionality requirement (punishment must be proportional to the seriousness of the offense)?

The therapeutic model (to psychologically restore the offender) and the moral education model (to instill better values in the offender) provide two ways of shifting punishment away from its negative force and toward doing something positive for the criminals. Karl Menninger, a psychiatrist, explains the elements of the therapeutic model:

> [T]he convicted offender would be detained indefinitely, pending a decision as to whether and how and when to reintroduce him successfully into society. All the skill and knowledge of modern behavioral science would be used to examine his personality assets, liabilities and potentialities, the environment from which he came, its effects upon him, and his effects upon it. Having arrived at some diagnostic grasp of the offender's personality, those in charge can decide whether there is a chance that he can be redirected into a mutually satisfactory adaptation to the world. If so, the most suitable techniques in education, industrial training, group administration, and psychotherapy should be selectively applied (in Altman 1996, p. 125).

The book *A Clockwork Orange* by Anthony Burgess and the film version directed by Stanley Kubrick provide a classical antidote to the therapeutic model. In the story, the governor bemoans the change to the therapeutic program to turn bad into good. He longs for the days of an "eye for an eye," asking rhetorically why the state should not hit back at the brutal hooligans who severely hit it. The prison chaplain warns patient #6655321 that it may be more horrible to be good than to be bad. Richard Wasserstrom offers a theoretical critique of the rehabilitation approach (see Reading 8–19).

In *Laws,* Plato proposed that the Nocturnal Council (composed of men with the highest knowledge) visit those found guilty of heresy. The heretics believed that the gods were indifferent to humans or subject to bribes. While they served time in the House of Corrections, the Nocturnal Council would reason with the heretics about the error of their thinking. This indicates that Plato found a critical role for moral education in punishment—however, he recommended the death penalty after a second conviction. Jean Hampton, a contemporary political theorist, justifies punishment "as a way to prevent wrongdoing insofar as it can teach both wrongdoers and the public at large the moral reasons for choosing not to perform an offense" (Hampton 1984 in Simmons et al. 1995, p. 117). Unlike most versions of the rehabilitation theory, moral education does not regard the offender as sick. The moral approach does not socially condition wrongdoers, but rather it teaches them about the moral boundaries they have transgressed. Perhaps, as restitution advocates claim, rehabilitation theorists have focused wrongly on the perpetrator. Should punishment theory begin to address the victim?

Restitution

Criminal acts harm individuals, and criminal wrongdoings harm society, but at most, only secondarily. Punishment, then, should force the offender to make good (restitute) the loss suffered by the victim. Randy Barnett advocates a fundamental shift toward viewing punishment as restitution (see Reading 8-20). Should punishment still address the secondary effects of criminal wrongdoing on society?

Deterrence

"*A Utilitarian Theory of Criminal Punishment*" (1959)

Richard Brandt

Traditional utilitarian thinking about criminal justice has found the rationale of the practice, in the United States, for example, in three main facts. (Those who disagree think the first two of these "facts" happen not to be the case.) (1) People who are tempted to misbehave, to trample on the rights of others, to sacrifice public welfare for personal gain, can usually be deterred from misconduct by fear of punishment, such as death, imprisonment, or fine. (2) Imprisonment or fine will teach malefactors [convicted criminals] a lesson; their characters may be improved, and at any rate a personal experience of punishment will make them less likely to misbehave again. (3) Imprisonment will certainly have the result of physically preventing past malefactors from misbehaving, during the period of their incarceration.

In view of these suppositions, traditional utilitarian thinking has concluded that having laws forbidding certain kinds of behavior on pain of punishment, and having machinery for the fair enforcement of these laws, is justified by the fact that it maximizes expectable utility. Misconduct is not to be punished just for its own sake; malefactors must be punished for their past acts, according to law, as a way of maximizing expectable utility.

The utilitarian principle, of course, has implications for decisions about the severity of punishment to be administered. Punishment is itself an evil, and hence should be avoided where this is consistent with the public good. Punishment should have precisely such a degree of severity (not more or less) that the probable disutility of greater severity just balances the probable gain in utility (less crime because of the more serious threat). The cost, in other words, should be counted along with the value of what is bought; and we should buy protection up to the point where the cost is greater than the protection is worth. How severe will such punishment be? Jeremy Bentham had many sensible things to say about this. Punishment, he said, must be severe enough so that it is to no one's advantage to commit an offense even if he receives the punishment; a fine of $10 for bank robbery would give no security at all. Further, since many criminals will be undetected, we must make the penalty heavy enough in comparison with the prospective gain from crime, that a prospective criminal will consider the risk hardly worth it, even considering that it is not certain he will be punished at all. Again, the more serious offenses should carry the heavier penalties, not only because the greater disutility justifies the use of heavier penalties in order to prevent them, but also because criminals should be motivated to commit a less serious rather than a more serious offense. Bentham thought the prescribed penalties should allow for some variation at the discretion of the judge, so that the actual suffering caused should roughly be the same in all cases; thus, a heavier fine will be imposed on a rich man than on a poor man. . . .

How satisfactory is this theory of criminal justice? Does it have any implications that are far from being acceptable when compared with concrete justified convictions about what practices are morally right?

Many criminologists would argue that Bentham was mistaken in his facts: The deterrence value of threat of punishment, they say, is much less than he imagined, and criminals are seldom reformed by spending time in prison. If these contentions are correct, then the ideal rules for society's treatment of malefactors are very different from what Bentham thought, and from what actual practice is today in the United States. To say all this, however, is not to show that the utilitarian *principle* is incorrect. . . . Utilitarian theory might still be correct, but its implications would be different from what Bentham thought. . . .

[A] popular objection to the utilitarian theory is that the utilitarian must approve of prosecutors or judges occasionally withholding evidence known to them, for the sake of convicting an innocent man, if the public welfare really is served by so doing. Critics of the theory would not deny that there *can* be circumstances where the dangers are so severe that such action is called for; they only say that utilitarianism calls for it all too frequently. Is this criticism justified? Clearly, the utilitarian is not committed to advocating that a provision should be written into the *law* so as to permit punishment of persons for crimes they did not commit if to do so would serve the public good. Any such provision would be a shattering blow to public confidence and security. The question is only whether there should be an informal moral rule to the same effect, for the guidance of judges and prosecutors. Will the rule-utilitarian necessarily be committed to far too sweeping a moral rule on this point? We must recall that he is not in the position of the act-utilitarian, who must say that an innocent man must be punished if in *his particular case* the public welfare would be served by his punishment. The rule-utilitarian rather asserts only that an innocent man should be punished if he falls within a class of cases such that net expectable utility is maximized if *all* members of the class are punished, taking into account the possible disastrous effects on public confidence if it is generally known that judges and prosecutors are guided by such a rule. . . . When we take these considerations into account, it is *not* obvious that the rule-utilitarian is committed to action that we are justifiably convinced is immoral. . . .

Everything considered, the utilitarian theory seems to be in much less dire distress, in respect of its implications for criminal justice, than has sometimes been supposed. It does not seem possible to show that in any important way its implications are clearly in conflict with our valid convictions about what is right. The worst that can be said is that utilitarian theory does not in a clear-cut way definitely require us to espouse some practices we are inclined to espouse. But to this the utilitarian may make two replies. First, that there is reason to think our ordinary convictions about punishment for crime ought to be thoroughly re-examined in important respects. Second, the utilitarian may reply that if we consider our convictions about the punishments we should administer *as a parent*—and this is the point where our moral opinions are least likely to be affected by the sheer weight of tradition—we shall find that we think according to the principles of rule-utilitarianism. Parents do regard their punishment of their children as justified only in view of the future good of the child, and in order to make life in the home tolerable and in order to distribute jobs and sacrifices equally.

From Brandt (1959), *Ethical Theory*. Englewood Cliffs, NJ: Prentice Hall, pp. 490–491, 494–495, 496.

READING 8-16
Retributivism
"The Moral Worth of Retribution" (1987)

Michael Moore

RETRIBUTIVISM AND THE POSSIBLE MODES OF ITS JUSTIFICATION

. . . *Retributivism* is the view that punishment is justified by the moral culpability of those who receive it. A retributivist punishes because, and only because, the offender deserves it. Retributivism thus stands in stark contrast to utilitarian views that justify punishment of past offenses by the greater good of preventing future offenses. It also contrasts sharply with rehabilitative views, according to which punishment is justified by the reforming good it does the criminal. . . .

. . . [C]onstruct a thought experiment . . . of the kind Kant (1965, p. 102) originated [see Discussion Issue 2, page 488]. Imagine that [atrocious] crimes are being done, but that there is no utilitarian or rehabilitative reason to punish. The murderer has truly found Christ, for example, so that he or she does not need to be reformed; he or she is not dangerous for the same reason; and the crime can go undetected so that general deterrence does not demand punishment (alternatively, we can pretend to punish and pay the person the money the punishment would have cost us to keep his or her mouth shut, which will also serve the ends of general deterrence). In such a situation, should the criminal still be punished? My hypothesis is that most of us still feel some inclination, no matter how tentative, to punish. That is the particular judgment I wish to examine. (For those persons—saints or moral lepers, we shall see which—who do not have even a tentative inclination to punish, I argue that the reason for affirming such inclinations are also reasons to feel such inclinations.) . . .

THE CASE AGAINST RETRIBUTIVE JUDGMENTS

. . . I think that the most serious objection to retributivism as a theory of punishment lies in the emotional base of retributive judgments. If stated as an objection to there being an emotional base at all to judgments about deserved punishment, the objection is far too broad to be acceptable. All moral judgments would lose to such a charge if it were well founded. If stated as an objection to the unhinging quality of retributive emotions, the objection is psychologically implausible. Any emotion in pathological cases can unhinge reason, and there is nothing about retributive emotions that make it at all plausible that they always unhinge our reason when we experience them. The objection thus needs a third construction, which is this: The emotions that give rise to retributive judgments are always pathological—not in their intensity or their ability to unhinge our reason, but in their very nature. Some emotions, such as racial prejudice, have no moral worth even if typically experienced in a not very intense way. The true objection here is that the retributive urge is one such emotion.

In discussing this version of the objection to the emotional base of retributivism, I shall by and large rely on Nietzsche, who to my mind remains one of the most penetrating psychologists of the unsavory side of our emotional life [see Reading 8-4]. He is also one of the few thinkers to have delved deeply into the psychology of revenge. . . .

THE CORRECTNESS OF RETRIBUTIVE JUDGMENTS

The problem with the Nietzschean case against retributivism does not lie, . . . in its presupposition that generally there is a strong connection between virtuous emotions and true moral judgments, vices and false moral judgments. The real problem for the Nietzschean critic is to show that retributive judgments are *inevitably* motivated by the black emotions of *ressentiment*. For if the critic cannot show this, then much of the contamination of those particular judgments is lifted. It is lifted because the retributive judgment would then not arise out of the kind of moral hallucination nonvirtuous emotions typically represent; rather, the retributive judgment would be only the vehicle for the expression of the emotions of *ressentiment*— dangerous for that reason, but not lacking in epistemic import for that reason. . . .

Resentment, indifference to others, self-deception, fear, cowardice, and pity are not virtues [see Reading 8-1]. They do not perhaps add up to the witches' brew of a full batch of the *ressentiment* emotions, but to the extent they motivate antiretributive judgments, they make such judgments suspect. If one accepts, as Nietzsche did, that both retributive and antiretributive judgments are often motivated by, or at least expressions of, nonvirtuous emotions, where does that leave us? It should leave us asking whether we cannot make our judgments about punishment in such a way that they are not motivated by either set of unworthy emotions.

When we make a retributive judgment—such as that Stephen Judy deserved the death penalty for his rape-murder of a young mother and his murder of her three children—we need not be motivated by the *ressentiment* emotions. Nor is the alternative some abstract, Kantian concern for justice, derived by reason alone and unsullied by any strong emotional origin. Our concern for retributive justice might be motivated by very deep emotions that are nonetheless of a wholly virtuous nature. These are the feelings of guilt we would have if we did the kinds of acts that fill the criminal appellate reports of any state. . . .

To be sure, there is an entire tradition that regards guilt as a useless passion. For one thing, it is always backward-looking rather than allowing one to get on with life. For another, it betrays an indecision that Nietzsche among others found unattractive: "The bite of conscience is indecent," Nietzsche thought (*Twilight,* p. 467), because it betrays the earlier decision about which one feels guilty. Yet Nietzsche and his followers are simply wrong here. Guilt feelings are often a virtue precisely because they do look to the past. [M]orality itself—including the morality of good character—has to take the past seriously. The alternative, of not crying over spilt milk (or blood), is truly indecent. A moral being *feels* guilty when he or she *is* guilty of past wrongs.

The virtue of feeling guilty is not raised so that punishment can be justified by its capacity to induce guilt. That is a possible retributive theory of punishment—a kind of moral rehabilitative theory—but it is not mine. Rather, the virtue of our own imagined guilt is relevant because of the general connection between the virtue of an emotion and its epistemic [knowledge] import. We should trust what our imagined guilt feelings tell us; for acts like those of Richard Herrin [sentenced to an eight- to twenty-five-year prison term for "heat-of-passion" manslaughter of his girlfriend with a hammer], that if we did them we would be so guilty that some extraordinarily severe punishment would be deserved. We should trust the judgments such imagined guilt feelings spawn because nonneurotic guilt, unlike *ressentiment,* comes with good epistemic credentials.

Next, we need to be clear just what judgments . . . our guilt feelings validate in this way. First and foremost, to *feel* guilty causes the judgment that we *are* guilty, in the sense that we are morally culpable. Second, such guilt feelings typically engender the judgment that we deserve punishment. I mean this not only in the weak sense of desert—that it would not be unfair to be punished—but also and more important in the strong sense that we *ought* to be punished. . . .

Our feelings of guilt thus generate a judgment that we deserve the suffering that is punishment. If the feelings of guilt are virtuous to possess, we have reason to believe that this last judgment is correct, generated as it is by emotions whose epistemic import is not in question. . . .

It is admittedly not an easy task to separate the emotions one feels, and then in addition, discriminate which of them is the cause of one's retributive judgments. We can no more choose which emotion it will be that causes our judgments or actions than we can choose the reason for which we act. We can choose whether to act or not and whether to judge one way or another, but we cannot make it be true that some particular reason or emotion caused our action or our judgment. We must look inward as best we can to detect, but not to will, which emotions bring about our judgments; and here there is plenty of room for error and self-deception.

When we move from our judgments about the justice of retribution in the abstract, however, to the justice of a social institution that exists to exact retribution, perhaps we can gain some greater clarity. For if we recognize the dangers retributive punishment presents for the expression of resentment, sadism, and so on, we have every reason to design our punishment institutions to minimize the opportunity for such feelings to be expressed. There is no contradiction in attempting to make a retributive punishment system humane; doing so allows penitentiaries to be faithful to their names—places for penance, not excuses for sadism, prejudice, hatred, and the like.

Even the old biblical injunction—"Vengeance is mine, saith the Lord"—has something of this insight behind it. Retributive punishment is dangerous for individual persons to carry out, dangerous to their virtue and, because of that, unclear in its justification. But implicit in the biblical injunction is a promise that retribution will be exacted. For those like myself who are not theists, that cleansing function must be performed by the state, not God. If the state can perform such a function, it removes from retributive punishment, not the guilt, as Nietzsche [has] it, but the *ressentiment*.

READING 8-17

A Mixed System
"Two Concepts of Rules" (1955)

John Rawls

The subject of punishment, in the sense of attaching legal penalties to the violation of legal rules, has always been a troubling moral question. The trouble about it has not been that people disagree as to whether or not punishment is justifiable. Most people have held that, freed from certain abuses, it is an acceptable institution. Only a few have rejected punishment entirely, which is rather surprising when one considers all that can be said against it. The difficulty is with the justification of punishment: various arguments for it have been given by moral philosophers, but so far none of them has won any sort of general acceptance; no justification is without those who detest it. I hope . . . to state the utilitarian view in a way which allows for the sound points of its critics.

For our purposes we may say that there are two justifications of punishment. What we may call the retributive view is that punishment is justified on the grounds that wrongdoing merits punishment. It is morally fitting that a person who does wrong should suffer in proportion to his wrongdoing. That a criminal should be punished follows from his guilt, and the severity of the appropriate punishment depends on the depravity of his act. The state of affairs where a wrongdoer suffers punishment is morally better than the state of affairs where he does not; and it is better irrespective of any of the consequences of punishing him.

What we may call the utilitarian view holds that on the principle that bygones are bygones and that only future consequences are material to present decisions, punishment is justifiable only by reference to the probable consequences of maintaining it as one of the devices of the social order. Wrongs committed in the past are, as such, not relevant considerations for deciding what to do. If punishment can be shown to promote effectively the interest of society it is justifiable, otherwise it is not.

I have stated these two competing views very roughly to make one feel the conflict between them: one feels the force of *both* arguments and one wonders how they can be reconciled. . . . The resolution which I am going to propose is that in this case one must distinguish between justifying a practice as a system of rules to be applied and enforced, and justifying a particular action which falls under these rules; utilitarian arguments are appropriate with regard to questions about practices, while retributive arguments fit the application of particular rules to particular cases.

We might try to get clear about this distinction by imagining how a father might answer the question of his son. Suppose the son asks, "Why was *J* put in jail yesterday?" The father answers, "Because he robbed the bank at *B*. He was duly tried and found guilty. That's why he was put in jail yesterday." But suppose the son had asked a different question, namely, "Why do people put other people in jail?" Then the father might answer, "To protect good people from bad people," or "To stop people from doing things that would make it uneasy for all of us; for otherwise we wouldn't be able to go to bed at night and sleep in peace." There are two very different questions here. One question emphasizes the proper name: It asks why *J* was punished rather than someone else, or it asks what he was punished for. The other question asks why we have the institution of punishment: Why do people punish one another rather than, say, always forgiving one another?

Thus the father says in effect that a particular man is punished, rather than some other man, because he is guilty, and he is guilty because he broke the law (past tense). In his case the law looks back, the judge looks back, the jury looks back, and a penalty is visited upon him for something he did. That a man is to be punished, and what his punishment is to be, is settled by its being shown that he broke the law and that the law assigns that penalty for the violation of it.

On the other hand we have the institution of punishment itself, and recommend and accept various changes in it, because it is thought by the (ideal) legislator and by those to whom the law applies that, as a part of a system of law impartially applied from case to case arising under it, it will have the consequence, in the long run, of furthering the interests of society.

One can say, then, that the judge and the legislator stand in different positions and look in different directions: one to the past, the other to the future. The justification of what the judge does, qua judge, sounds like the retributive view; the justification of what the (ideal) legislator does, qua legislator, sounds like the utilitarian view. Thus both views have a point (this is as it should be since intelligent and sensitive persons have been on both sides of the argument); and one's initial confusion disappears once one sees that these views apply to persons holding different offices with different duties, and situated differently with respect to the system of rules that make up the criminal law.

One might say, however, that the utilitarian view is more fundamental since it applies to a more fundamental office, for the judge carries out the legislator's will so far as he can determine it. Once the legislator decides to have laws and to assign penalties for their violation (as things are there must be both the law and the penalty) an institution is set up which involves a re-tributive conception of particular cases. It is part of the concept of the criminal law as a system of rules that the application and enforcement of these rules in particular cases should be justifiable by arguments of a retributive character. The decision whether or not to use law rather than some other mechanism of social control, and the decision as to what laws to have and what penalties to assign, may be settled by utilitarian arguments, but if one decides to have laws then one has decided on something whose working in particular cases is retributive in form.

The answer, then, to the confusion engendered by the two views of punishment is quite simple: one distinguishes two offices, that of the judge and that of the legislator, and one distinguishes their different stations with respect to the system of rules which make up the law; and then one notes that the different sorts of considerations which would usually be offered as reasons for what is done under the cover of these offices can be paired off with the competing justifications of punishment. One reconciles the two views by the time-honored device of making them apply to different situations.

But can it really be this simple? Well, this answer allows for the apparent intent of each side. Does a person who advocates the retributive view necessarily advocate, as an *institution,* legal machinery whose essential purpose is to set up and preserve a correspondence between moral turpitude and suffering? Surely not. What retributionists have rightly insisted upon is that no man can be punished unless he is guilty, that is, unless he has broken the law. Their fundamental criticism of the utilitarian account is that, as they interpret it, it sanctions an innocent person's being punished (if one may call it that) for the benefit of society.

On the other hand, utilitarians agree that punishment is to be inflicted only for the violation of law. They regard this much as understood from the concept of punishment itself. The point of the utilitarian account concerns the institution as a system of rules: utilitarianism seeks to limit its use by declaring it justifiable only if it can be shown to foster effectively the good of society. Historically it is a protest against the indiscriminate and ineffective use of the criminal law. It seeks to dissuade us from assigning to penal institutions the improper, if not sacrilegious, task of matching suffering with moral turpitude. Like others, utilitarians want penal institutions designed so that, as far as humanly possible, only those who break the law run afoul of it. They hold that no official should have discretionary power to inflict penalties whenever he thinks it for the benefit of society; for on utilitarian grounds an institution granting such power could not be justified. . . .

Excessive Punishments in Mixed Systems
"The Paradox of Punishment" (1979)

Alan H. Goldman

The paradox of punishment is that a penal institution somewhat similar to that in use in our society seems from a moral point of view to be both required and unjustified. Usually such a statement would be a confused way of saying that the practice is a necessary evil, hence it *is* justified, all things considered. But in the case of punishment this reduction does not appear so simple.

The paradox results from the intuitive plausibility of two theses: one associated with a retributivist point of view and another associated with a utilitarian justification of the institution of punishment. Some philosophers have thought that objections to these two theories of punishment could be overcome by making both retributive and utilitarian criteria necessary for the justification of punishment. Utilitarian criteria could be used to justify the institution, and retributive to justify specific acts within it; or utilitarian to justify legislative decisions regarding punishment, and retributive to justify enforcement decisions. (These distinctions in levels of justification are matters of degree, since when justifying an institution, one must consider acts within it; and when justifying legislative decisions, one must consider their applications in the judicial system.) The compromise positions, according to which punishment must be both deserved and beneficial, have considerable plausibility. But if I am right about the two theses to be assessed here, these criteria may be ultimately inconsistent. If so, then the mixed theory of justification, initially attractive, is at least as problematic as its rivals....

The problem is that while the mixed theory can avoid punishment of the innocent, it is doubtful that it can avoid excessive punishment of the guilty if it is to have sufficient deterrent effect to make the social costs worthwhile. In our society the chances of apprehension and punishment for almost every class of crime are well under fifty percent. Given these odds a person pursuing what he considers his maximum prospective benefit may not be deterred by the threat of an imposition of punishment equivalent to the violation of the rights of the potential victim. If threats of sanctions are not sufficient to deter such people, they would probably fail to reduce crime to a tolerable enough level to make the social costs of the penal institution worthwhile. On the other hand, in order to deter crime at all effectively, given reasonable assumptions about police efficiency at bearable costs, sanctions must be threatened and applied which go far beyond the equivalence relation held to be just. The limitation stipulated in our first premise then, in effect, annuls just and effective pursuit of the social goal stipulated in our second premise. And yet pursuit of this goal seems morally required and impossible without effective punitive threats. Hence the paradox, or, more strictly, the dilemma.

Caught in this dilemma, our society does not limit punishment to deprivation of rights forfeited, that is, rights of others which have been violated by the criminal. Especially in regard to crimes against property, punishments by imprisonment are far more severe, on the average, than the harm caused to victims of these crimes. Probably because such punishment is administered by officials of the state, cloaked in appropriate ritual and vested with authority, most of us systematically ignore its relative severity. If, however, we imagine an apolitical context, in which there is money and property, but no penal institution, would theft of several thousand dollars justify the victim's taking the perpetrator and locking him away in some small room for five to ten years? In our society such deprivation of freedom is a small portion of the harms likely to be suffered in prison as punishment for a felonious crime against property. The disproportion between violated or deprived rights of the victims and those of the criminals in these crimes is obvious. . . .

READING 8-19

Rehabilitation, Debunked
"The Therapeutic Model" (1980)

Richard Wasserstrom

There is a view, held most prominently but by no means exclusively by persons in psychiatry, that we ought never punish persons who break the law and that we ought instead to do something much more like what we do when we treat someone who has a disease. According to this view, what we ought to do to all such persons is to do our best to bring it about that they can and will function in a satisfactory way within society. The functional equivalent to the treatment of a disease is the rehabilitation of an offender, and it is a rehabilitative system, not a punishment system, that we ought to have if we are to respond, even to criminals, in anything like a decent, morally defensible fashion. . . .

. . . [O]ne of the chief theoretical objections to a proposal of the sort just described is that it ignores the whole question of general deterrence. Were we to have a system such as that envisioned by Lady Wootton [see page 434] or Menninger [see page 458], we would ask one and only one question of each person who violated the law: What is the best, most efficacious thing to do to this individual to diminish substantially the likelihood that he or she will misbehave in this, or similar fashion, again? If there is nothing at all that need be done in order for us to be quite confident that he or she will not misbehave again (perhaps because the person is extremely contrite, or because we are convinced it was an impulsive, or otherwise unlikely-to-be-repeated act), then the logic of this system requires that the individual be released forthwith. For in this system it is the future conduct of the actor, and it alone, that is the only relevant consideration. There is simply no room within this way of thinking to take into account the achievement of general deterrence. H. L. A. Hart has put the matter this way in explaining why the *reform* (when any might be called for) of the prisoner cannot be the general justifying aim of a system of punishment.

The objection to assigning to Reform this place in punishment is not merely that punishment entails suffering and Reform does not: but that Reform is essentially a remedial step for which ex hypothesi there is an opportunity only at the point where the criminal law has failed in its primary task of securing society from the evil which breach of the law involves. Society is divisile at any moment into two classes: (i) those who have actually broken a given law and (ii) those who have not yet broken it but may. *To take Reform as the dominant objective would be to forego the hope of influencing the second—and in relation to the more serious offences—numerically much greater class. We should thus subordinate the prevention of the first offences to the prevention of recidivism.*

A system of punishment will on this view find its justification in the fact that the announcement of penalties and their infliction upon those who break the laws induces others to obey the laws. The question why punish anyone at all *is* answered by Hart. We punish because we thereby deter potential offenders from becoming actual offenders. For Hart, the case for punishment as a general social practice or institution rests on the prevention of crime; it is not to be found either in the inherent appropriateness of punishing offenders or in the contingently "corrective" or rehabilitative powers of fines or imprisonments on some criminals.

Yet, despite appearances, the appeal to general deterrence is not as different as might be supposed from the appeal to a rehabilitative ideal. In both cases, the justification for doing something (or nothing) to the offender rests upon the good consequences that will ensue. General deterrence just as much as rehabilitation views what should be done to offenders as a question of *social control.* It is a way of inducing those who can control their behavior to regulate it in such a way that it will conform to the dictates of the law. The disagreement with those who focus upon rehabilitation is only over the question of whose behavioral modification justifies the imposition of deprivations upon the criminals. Proponents of general deterrence say it is the modification of the behavior of the noncriminals that matters; proponents of rehabilitation say it is the modification of the behavior of the criminals that is decisive. Thus, a view such as Hart's is less a justification of punishment than of a system of threats of punishment. For if the rest of society could be convinced that offenders would be made to undergo deprivations that persons would not wish to undergo we would accomplish all that the deterrent theory would have us achieve through our somewhat more visible applications of these deprivations to offenders. This is so because it is the belief that punishment will follow the commission of an offense that deters potential offenders. The actual punishment of persons is necessary to keep the threat of punishment credible.

To put matters this way is to bring out the fact that the appeal to general deterrence, just as much as the appeal to rehabilitation, appears to justify a wholly forward-looking system of social control. . . .

From Wasserstrom (1980), "The Therapeutic Model," *Philosophy and Social Issues.* Notre Dame, IN: University of Notre Dame Press, pp. 122–130.

READING 8-20

Restitution

"Restitution: A New Paradigm of Criminal Justice" (1977)

Randy Barnett

OUTLINE OF A NEW PARADIGM

The idea of restitution is actually quite simple. It views crime as an offense by one individual against the rights of another. The victim has suffered a loss. Justice consists of the culpable offender making good the loss he has caused. It calls for a complete refocusing of our image of crime. Kuhn would call it a "shift of worldview." Where we once saw an offense against society, we now see an offense against an individual victim. In a way, it is a common-sense view of crime. *The armed robber did not rob society, he robbed the victim.* His debt, therefore, is not to society; it is to the victim. There are really two types of restitution proposals: a system of "punitive" restitution and a "pure" restitutional system. . . .

Pure Restitution. "Recompense or restitution is scarcely a punishment as long as it is merely a matter of returning stolen goods or money. . . . The point is not that the offender deserves to suffer; it is rather that the offended party desires compensation." This represents the complete overthrow of the paradigm of punishment. No longer would the deterrence, reformation, disablement, or rehabilitation of the criminal be the guiding principle of the judicial system. The attainment of these goals would be incidental to, and as a result of, reparations paid to the victim. No longer would the criminal deliberately be made to suffer for his mistake. Making good that mistake is all that would be required. What follows is a possible scenario of such a system.

When a crime occurred and a suspect was apprehended, a trial court would attempt to determine his guilt or innocence. If found guilty, the criminal would be sentenced to make restitution to the victim. If a criminal is able to make restitution immediately, he may do so. This would discharge his liability. If he were unable to make restitution, but were found by the court to be trustworthy, he would be permitted to remain at his job (or find a new one) while paying restitution out of his future wages. This would entail a legal claim against future wages. Failure to pay could result in garnishment or a new type of confinement.

If it is found that the criminal is not trustworthy, or that he is unable to gain employment, he would be confined to an employment project. This would be an industrial enterprise, preferably run by a private concern, which would produce actual goods or services. The level of security at each employment project would vary according to the behavior of the offenders. Since the costs would be lower, inmates at a lower-security project would receive higher wages. There is no reason why many workers could not be permitted to live with their families inside or outside the facility, depending, again, on the trustworthiness of the offender. Room and board would be deducted from the wages first, then a certain amount for restitution. Anything over that amount the worker could keep or apply toward further restitution, thus hastening his release. If a worker refused to work, he would be unable to pay for his maintenance, and therefore would not in principle be entitled to it. If he did not make restitution he could not be released. The exact arrangement which would best provide for high productivity, minimal security, and maximum incentive to work and repay the victim cannot be determined in advance. Experience is bound to yield some plans superior to others. In fact, the experimentation has already begun.

While this might be the basic system, all sorts of refinements are conceivable, and certainly many more will be invented as needs arise. A few examples might be illuminating. With such a system of repayment, victim *crime insurance* would be more economically feasible than at present and highly desirable. The cost of awards would be offset by the insurance company's right to restitution in place of the victim (right of subrogation). The insurance company would be better suited to supervise the offender and mark his progress than would the victim. To obtain an earlier recovery, it could be expected to innovate so as to enable the worker to repay more quickly (and, as a result, be released that much sooner). The insurance companies might even underwrite the employment projects themselves as well as related industries which would employ the skilled worker after his release. Any successful effort on their part to reduce crime and recidivism would result in fewer claims and lower premiums. The benefit of this insurance scheme for the victim is immediate compensation, conditional on the victim's continued cooperation with the authorities for the arrest and conviction of the suspect. In addition, the centralization of victim claims would, arguably, lead to efficiencies which would permit the pooling of small claims against a common offender.

Another highly useful refinement would be *direct arbitration* between victim and criminal. This would serve as a sort of healthy substitute for plea bargaining. By allowing the guilty criminal to negotiate a reduced payment in return for a guilty plea, the victim (or his insurance company) would be saved the risk of an adverse finding at trial and any possible additional expense that might result. This would also allow an indigent criminal to substitute personal services for monetary payments if all parties agreed. . . .

ADVANTAGES OF A RESTITUTIONAL SYSTEM

1. The first and most obvious advantage is the assistance provided to victims of crime. They may have suffered an emotional, physical, or financial loss. Restitution would not change the fact that a possibly traumatic crime has occurred (just as the award of damages does not undo tortious conduct). Restitution, however, would make the resulting loss easier to bear for both victims and their families. At the same time, restitution would avoid a major pitfall of victim compensation/welfare plans: Since it is the criminal who must pay, the possibility of collusion between victim and criminal to collect "damages" from the state would be all but eliminated.

2. The possibility of receiving compensation would encourage victims to report crimes and to appear at trial. This is particularly true if there were a

crime insurance scheme which contractually committed the policyholder to testify as a condition for payment, thus rendering unnecessary oppressive and potentially tyrannical subpoenas and contempt citations. Even the actual reporting of the crime to police is likely to be a prerequisite for compensation. Such a requirement in auto theft insurance policies has made car thefts the most fully reported crime in the United States. Furthermore, insurance companies which paid the claim would have a strong incentive to see that the criminal was apprehended and convicted. Their pressure and assistance would make the proper functioning of law enforcement officials all the more likely.

3. Psychologist Albert Eglash has long argued that restitution would aid in the rehabilitation of criminals. "Restitution is something an inmate does, not something done for or to him. . . . Being reparative, restitution can alleviate guilt and anxiety, which can otherwise precipitate further offenses." Restitution, says Eglash, is an active effortful role on the part of the offender. It is socially constructive, thereby contributing to the offender's self-esteem. It is related to the offense and may thereby redirect the thoughts which motivated the offense. It is reparative, restorative, and may actually leave the situation better than it was before the crime, both for the criminal and victim.

4. This is a genuinely "self-determinative" sentence. The worker would know that the length of his confinement was in his own hands. The harder he worked, the faster he would make restitution. He would be the master of his fate and would have to face that responsibility. This would encourage useful, productive activity and instill a conception of reward for good behavior and hard work. Compare this with the current probationary system and "indeterminate sentencing" where the decision for release is made by the prison bureaucracy, based only (if fairly administered) on "good behavior"; that is, passive acquiescence to prison discipline. Also, the fact that the worker would be acquiring *marketable* skills rather than more skillful methods of crime should help to reduce the shocking rate of recidivism.

5. The savings to taxpayers would be enormous. No longer would the innocent taxpayer pay for the apprehension and internment of the guilty. The cost of arrest, trial, and internment would be borne by the criminal himself. In addition, since now-idle inmates would become productive workers (able, perhaps, to support their families), the entire economy would benefit from the increase in overall production.

6. Crime would no longer pay. Criminals, particularly shrewd white-collar criminals, would know that they could not dispose of the proceeds of their crime and, if caught, simply serve time. They would have to make full restitution plus enforcement and legal costs, thereby greatly increasing the incentive to prosecute. While this would not eliminate such crime it would make it rougher on certain types of criminals, like bank and corporation officials, who harm many by their acts with a virtual assurance of lenient legal sanctions. It might also encourage such criminals to keep the money around for a while so that, if caught, they could repay more easily. This would make a full recovery more likely.

A restitutional system of justice would benefit the victim, the criminal, and the taxpayer. The humanitarian goals of proportionate punishment, rehabilitation, and victim compensation are dealt with on a *fundamental* level making their achievement more likely. In short, the paradigm of restitution would benefit all but the entrenched penal bureaucracy and enhance justice at the same time. What then is there to stop us from overthrowing the paradigm of punishment and its penal system and putting in its place this more efficient, more humane, and more just system? . . .

Barnett, Randy. "Restitution: A New Paradigm of Criminal Justice" 87 *Ethics,* © (1977) by the University of Chicago. Reprinted by permisson.

F. CONTROVERSIES: THE DEATH PENALTY

Excessive bail shall not be required, nor excessive fines imposed, nor cruel and unusual punishments inflicted.
—EIGHTH AMENDMENT, U.S. CONSTITUTION

The death penalty strikes a deep chord among advocates and opponents. The following two selections represent the opinions of two of the most eloquent writers on the topic, John Stuart Mill and Albert Camus.

1. Defending the Death Penalty

In England during the eighteenth century, even petty crimes such as pickpocketing were punishable by death. However, nineteenth-century reforms reserved the death penalty for only the most heinous crimes. John Stuart Mill, serving in Parliament from 1862 to 1865, argued against abolishing the death penalty, claiming that it was the most humane way to deter crime.

When there has been brought home to any one, by conclusive evidence, the greatest crime known to the law; and when the attendant circumstances suggest no palliation [lessening] of the guilt, no hope that the culprit may even yet not be unworthy to live among mankind, nothing to make it probable that the crime was an exception to his general character rather than a consequence of it, then I confess it appears to me that to deprive the criminal of the life of which he has proved himself to be unworthy—solemnly to blot him out from the fellowship of mankind and from the catalogue of the living—is the most appropriate, as it is certainly the most impressive, mode in which society can attach to so great a crime the penal consequences which for the security of life it is indispensable to annex to it. I defend this [death] penalty, when confined to atrocious cases, on the very ground on which it is commonly attacked—on that of humanity to the criminal; as beyond comparison the least cruel mode in which it is possible adequately to deter from the crime. If, in our horror of inflicting death, we endeavour to devise some punishment for the living criminal which shall act on the human mind with a deterrent force at all comparable to that of death, we are driven to inflictions less severe indeed in appearance, and therefore less efficacious, but far more cruel in reality. . . . What comparison can there really be, in point of severity, between consigning a man to the short pang of a rapid death, and immuring [confining] him in a living tomb, there to linger out what may be a long life in the hardest and most monstrous toil, without any of its alleviation's or rewards—debarred from all pleasant sights and sounds, and cut off from all earthly hope, except a slight mitigation of bodily restraint, or a small improvement in diet? . . .

There is not, I should think, any human infliction which makes an impression on the imagination so entirely out of proportion to the real severity of the punishment of death. The punishment must be mild indeed which does not add more to the sum of human misery than is necessarily or directly added by the execution of a criminal. . . . The most that human laws can do to anyone in the matter of death is to hasten it; the man would have died at any rate; not so very much later, and on the average, I fear, with a considerably greater amount of bodily suffering. Society is asked, then, to denude itself of an instrument of punishment which, in the grave cases to which alone it is suitable, effects it purposes at less cost of human suffering than any other; which, while it inspires more terror, is less cruel in actual fact than any punishment that we should think of substituting for it. . . .

For what else than effeminacy [excessive softness] is it to be so much more shocked by taking a man's life than by depriving him of all that makes life desirable or valuable? Is death, then, the greatest of all earthly ills? *Usque adeone mori miserum est?* [Is it, indeed, so dreadful a thing to die?] . . .

I cannot think that the cultivating of a peculiar sensitiveness of conscience on this one point, over and above what result from the general cultivation of the moral sentiments, is permanently consistent with assigning in our own minds to the fact of death no more than the degree of relative importance which belongs to it among the other incidents of our humanity. The men of old cared too little about death, and gave their own lives or took those of others with equal recklessness. Our danger is of the opposite kind, lest we should be so much shocked by death, in general and in the abstract, as to care too much about it in individual cases, both those of other people and our own, which call for its being risked. . . . (Mill 1868 reprinted in Bender 1997, pp. 28–29, 30, 31–32)

2. Rejecting the Death Penalty

Albert Camus (1913–1960), a French novelist and existential philosopher born and educated in Algeria, joined the resistance movement against the Nazi occupation of Paris. He saw World War II as marking a fundamental break in human experience. Camus sought to break the cycle of political violence whether in the form of Hitler's atrocities, Stalin's barbarisms, the Allies' fire bombings of Dresden, or the American obliteration of Hiroshima and Nagasaki. Camus shifted the way of thinking about violence from something beyond human control to a matter of individual responsibility. He believed that the downward spiral of violence breaks when potential murder victims refuse any association with the executioners. According to Camus, individuals also share responsibility for the bureaucratic murder called the death penalty.

Here again, when our official jurists speak of death without suffering, they do not know what they are talking about, and furthermore they betray a remarkable lack of imagination. The devastating, degrading fear imposed on the condemned man for months or even years is a punishment more terrible than death itself, and one that has not been imposed on his victim. A murdered man is generally rushed to his death, even at the height of his terror of the mortal violence being done to him, without knowing what is happening: the period of his horror is only that of his life itself, and his hope of escaping whatever madness has pounced upon him probably never deserts him. For the man condemned to death, on the other hand, the horror of his situation is served up to him at every moment for months on end. Torture by hope alternates only with the pangs of animal despair. His lawyer and his confessor, out of simple humility, and his guards, to keep him docile, unanimously assure him that he will be reprieved. He believes them with all his heart, yet he cannot believe them at all. He hopes by day, despairs by night. And as the weeks pass, his hope and despair increase proportionally, until they become equally insupportable. According to all accounts, the color of his skin changes; fear acts like an acid. "It's nothing to know you're going to die," one such man in the Fresnes prison said, "but to know if you're going to live is the real torture." (Camus 1961, p. 205)

3. The Supreme Court and the Death Penalty

In the 1960s, the National Association for the Advancement of Colored People's Legal and Educational Fund launched a major legal attack on the constitutionality of the death penalty. In 1972, its litigation efforts reached the U.S. Supreme Court with *Furman v. Georgia. Furman* combined three cases (a murderer and a rapist from Georgia and a rapist from Texas). All three black defendants had received death sentences after jury trials. In a five-to-four decision, the Court invalidated capital punishment laws as **"cruel and unusual punishment"** in violation of the Eighth and Fourteenth Amendments. The official decision totaled 230 pages, with all nine justices writing opinions. Justices Brennan and Marshall took strong moral and ethical stands, for which some commentators attacked them and others praised them.

Justice Brennan posed a test for whether a punishment is cruel and unusual:

> If a punishment is unusually severe, if there is a strong probability that it is inflicted arbitrarily, if it is substantially rejected by contemporary society, and if there is no reason to believe that it serves any penal purpose more effectively than some less severe punishment, then the continued infliction of that punishment violates the command of the [cruel and unusual punishment] Clause [of the Eighth Amendment] that the state may not inflict inhuman and uncivilized punishments upon those convicted of crimes. . . . The question, then, is whether the deliberate infliction of death is today consistent with the command of the Clause that the State may not inflict punishments that do not comport with human dignity.

Justice Marshall rejected the idea of punishment for retribution:

> [At] times a cry is heard that morality requires vengeance to evidence society's abhorrence of the act. But the Eighth Amendment is our insulation from our baser selves. The cruel and unusual language limits the avenues through which vengeance can be channeled.

Marshall found the death penalty "abhorrent to currently existing moral values":

> [W]hether or not punishment is cruel or unusual depends, not on whether its mere mention "shocks the conscience and sense of justice of the people," but

on whether people who were fully informed as to the purposes of the penalty and its liabilities would find the penalty shocking, unjust and unacceptable.

What should be the role of ethical thinking in Supreme Court decision making? (See chapter 4, page 176, on judicial review.) Should the Court reinforce public morality as it manifests itself in legislation? During the 1970s, opposition to the death penalty declined dramatically, as measured by public opinion polls. Should the Court reflect overall public opinion? Should the Court pay attention, as Marshall suggested, to *informed* public opinion?

After *Furman,* judges and juries did not have free discretion to impose the death penalty. Thirty-nine states had their capital punishment laws declared unconstitutional under *Furman,* and states began redrafting their laws. The Court examined a number of the new proposals, focusing on procedural and other safeguards in capital punishment cases (see following Discussion Issue 6, page 489, on "vile murderers"). On one hand, the Court found laws mandating the death penalty for certain crimes to be unconstitutional (*Woodson v. North Carolina* 1976). On the other hand, it upheld laws that provided standards with which to guide and limit judicial discretion in capital cases (*Gregg v. Georgia* 1976). *Gregg* paved the way for states to reinstate the death penalty (see Reading 8-21). Georgia had the death penalty, not only for murder, but also for "kidnapping for ransom or where the victim is harmed, armed robbery, rape, treason, and aircraft hijacking." After *Furman,* Georgia amended its capital punishment statute, requiring juries to find at least one of ten specified aggravating circumstances and authorizing juries to consider mitigating circumstances. The Court found that Georgia had provided sufficient safeguards against arbitrariness and caprice.

John Stuart Mill admitted that the possibility of error in carrying out a death sentence is the strongest argument against the death penalty. However, he countered by noting that the British criminal system guards against the possibility of errors with excessively protective procedures. Justice Blackmun issued a dramatic blanket rejection of efforts to provide procedural and other safeguards. Just before his retirement from the Court, Justice Blackmun bemoaned his active participation in promoting the death penalty and wrote a stinging condemnation of the Court's desires to "tinker with the machinery of death":

> Experience has taught us that the constitutional goal of eliminating arbitrariness and discrimination from the administration of death can never be achieved without compromising an equally essential component of fundamental fairness—individualized sentencing. It is tempting, when faced with conflicting constitutional commands, to sacrifice one for the other or to assume that an acceptable balance between them already has been struck. In the context of the death penalty, however, such jurisprudential maneuvers are wholly inappropriate. The death penalty must be imposed "fairly, and with reasonable consistency, or not at all. . . ."
>
> From this day forward, I no longer shall tinker with the machinery of death. For more than twenty years I have endeavored—indeed, I have struggled—along with a majority of this Court, to develop procedural and substantive rules that would lend more than just an appearance of fairness to the death penalty endeavor. Rather than continue to coddle the Court's delusion that the desired level of fairness has been achieved and the need

for regulation eviscerated, I feel morally and intellectually obligated simply to concede that the death penalty experiment has failed. It is virtually self-evident to me now that no combination of procedural rules or substantive regulations ever can save the death penalty from its inherent constitutional deficiencies. The basic question—does the system accurately and consistently determine which defendants "deserve" to die?—cannot be answered in the affirmative. [The] problem is that the inevitably factual, legal, and moral error gives us a system that we know must wrongly kill some defendants, a system that fails to deliver the fair, consistent, and reliable sentences of death required by the Constitution. . . .

[The] arbitrariness inherent in the sentencer's discretion to afford mercy is exacerbated by the problem of race. Even under the most sophisticated death penalty statutes, race continues to play a major role in determining who shall live and who shall die. Perhaps it should not be surprising that the biases and prejudices that infect society generally would influence the determination of who is sentenced to death, even within the narrow pool of death-eligible defendants selected according to objective standards. No matter how narrowly the pool of death-eligible defendants is drawn according to objective standards, *Furman's* promise will still go unfulfilled so long as the sentence is free to exercise unbridled discretion within the smaller group and thereby to discriminate. (*Collins v. Collins* 1994, Justice Blackmun)

Justice Scalia lashed out at Justice Blackmun for trying to impose his personal views on the Constitution and implored Blackmun to base his analysis on the Constitution's text. He noted that Justice Blackmun "did not select as the vehicle for his announcement that the death penalty is always unconstitutional [a case currently before the Court], for example, the case of the 11-year-old girl raped by four men and then killed by stuffing her panties down her throat." Is there a rational framework that could resolve the disputes among the justices? Debates about the death penalty often become emotionally charged, reflecting conflicting ethical and political perspectives. Does this emotional posturing accurately describe the Supreme Court justices' stances on the death penalty? Do judicial opinions on controversial topics create a veneer for emotional, subjective ethical opinions? Edward Lazarus (1998), a former clerk to Justice Blackmun, recently provided the public with a rare insider's view of the Court. He found the Court deeply divided, ethically and politically, over the death penalty. Justices Brennan and Marshall, as we have seen, stood on the left as fervent death penalty abolitionists, while Justice Rehnquist (now joined by Justice Scalia) stood firmly on the right with a consistent and adamant belief in the death penalty. The Court and the public seem equally charged, politically and emotionally, over the death penalty.

In 1987, the Court finally stopped its post-*Furman* tinkering (*McCleskey v. Kemp*). It would no longer make any attempts to smooth out the arbitrariness of administering the death penalty. In *McCleskey v. Kemp,* McCleskey, a black man, killed a police officer during a robbery attempt, and a Georgia court sentenced him to death. The Supreme Court ignored the procedural issues raised in McCleskey, and instead, latched onto a substantive discrimination claim. A statistical study by David Baldus had found a correlation between the race of defendants and the race of the victims that seemed to demonstrate racial discrimination in death penalty cases. The study showed that the state of Georgia imposed the death sentence on those convicted of killing whites more frequently than it did on those convicted of killing blacks. Georgia passed its current death penalty statute in 1973 and Mc-Cleskey received his death sentence in 1979. Baldus found that between 1973 and 1979, Georgia executed eleven murderers, nine of whom were black men. In ten of the cases, the victims were white (Amsterdam 1988, pp. 84–86). The Court, in a five-to-four decision, upheld McCleskey's death sentence and dismissed the discrimination claim.

Hugo Bedau, a philosopher and long-time opponent of the death penalty, outlines in Reading 8-22 how philosophical developments on theories of the person might have an impact on the death penalty debate. Reading 8-23 discusses the conclusions drawn by sociologist Michael Radelet and his colleagues from their study of innocent victims of the death penalty. Ernest Van den Haag, a former psychiatrist who teaches jurisprudence at Fordham University, is one of the most frequently cited defenders of the death penalty. His best-bet argument has become a classic in the literature, and he rejects opposition to the death penalty that is based on the theory that it is discriminatorily applied (see Reading 8-24). Jonathan Glover summarizes a response in Reading 8-25 put forward by Conway (1974) to Van den Haag's best-bet argument. The death penalty has obvious effects on the accused, but what broader repercussions does it have? Does the death penalty say something about civilization? Despite an increasing public acceptance of the death penalty in the United States, a worldwide trend against it has emerged. South Africa's Constitutional Court recently abolished the death penalty, and the Ad Hoc War Crimes Tribunals for the Former Yugoslavia and for Rwanda do not include the death penalty as a punishment option. International law does not sentence those responsible for genocide to death. Perhaps the death penalty's justification depends on whether the focus is on the murderer's moral status or the executioner's moral status. In Reading 8-26, Jeffrey Reiman tries to shift the terms of the debate to what the death penalty says about those who implement it. He believes that the less force a state uses against its people, the more civilized it is.

READING 8-21

A Justly Applied Death Penalty
Gregg v. Georgia (1976)

JUSTICES STEWART, POWELL, AND STEVENS

I

The petitioner, Troy Gregg, was charged with committing armed robbery and murder. In accordance with Georgia procedure in capital cases, the trial was in two stages, a guilt stage and a sentencing stage. The evidence at the guilt trial established that on November 21, 1973, the petitioner and a traveling companion, Floyd Allen, while hitchhiking north in Florida were picked up by Fred Simmons and Bob Moore. Their car broke down, but they continued north after Simmons purchased another vehicle with some of the cash he was carrying. While still in Florida, they picked up another hitchhiker, Dennis Weaver, who rode with them to Atlanta, where he was let out about 11 p.m. A short time later the four men interrupted their journey for a rest stop along the highway. The next morning the bodies of Simmons and Moore were discovered in a ditch nearby.

On November 23, after reading about the shootings in an Atlanta newspaper, Weaver communicated with the Gwinnett County police and related information concerning the journey with the victims, including a description of the car. The next afternoon, the petitioner and Allen, while in Simmons' car, were arrested in Asheville, N.C. In the search incident to the arrest a .25-caliber pistol, later shown to be that used to kill Simmons and Moore, was found in the petitioner's pocket. After receiving the warnings required by *Miranda* v. *Arizona*, . . . and signing a written waiver of his rights, the petitioner signed a statement in which he admitted shooting, then robbing Simmons and Moore. He justified the slayings on grounds of self-defense. The next day, while being transferred to Lawrenceville, Ga., the petitioner and Allen were taken to the scene of the shootings. Upon arriving there, Allen recounted the events leading to the slayings. His version of these events was as follows: After Simmons and Moore left the car, the petitioner stated that he intended to rob them. The petitioner then took his pistol in hand and positioned himself on the car to improve his aim. As Simmons and Moore came up an embankment toward the car, the petitioner fired three shots and the two men fell near a ditch. The petitioner, at close range, then fired a shot into the head of each. He robbed them of valuables and drove away with Allen.

A medical examiner testified that Simmons died from a bullet wound in the eye and that Moore died from bullet wounds in the cheek and in the back of the head. He further testified that both men had several bruises and abrasions about the face and head which probably were sustained either from the fall into the ditch or from being dragged or pushed along the embankment. Although Allen did not testify, a police detective recounted the substance of Allen's statements about the slayings and indicated that directly after Allen had made these statements the petitioner had admitted that Allen's account was accurate. The petitioner testified in his own defense. He confirmed that Allen had made the statements described by the detective, but denied their truth or ever having admitted to their accuracy. He indicated that he had shot Simmons and Moore because of fear and in self-defense, testifying they had attacked Allen and him, one wielding a pipe and the other a knife. . . .

The Supreme Court of Georgia affirmed the convictions and the imposition of the death sentences for murder. . . . After reviewing the trial transcript and the record, including the evidence, and comparing the evidence and sentence in similar cases in accordance with the requirements of Georgia law, the court concluded that, considering the nature of the crime and the defendant, the sentences of death had not resulted from prejudice or any other arbitrary factor and were not excessive or disproportionate to the penalty applied in similar cases. . . .

The death penalty is said to serve two principal social purposes: retribution and deterrence of capital crimes by prospective offenders.

In part, capital punishment is an expression of society's moral outrage at particularly offensive conduct. This function may be unappealing to many, but it is essential in an ordered society that asks its citizens to rely on legal processes rather than self-help to vindicate their wrongs. . . .

"Retribution is no longer the dominant objective of the criminal law," . . . but neither is it a forbidden objective nor one inconsistent with our respect for the dignity of men. . . . Indeed, the decision that capital punishment may be the appropriate sanction in extreme cases is an expression of the community's belief that certain crimes are themselves so grievous an affront to humanity that the only adequate response may be the penalty of death. . . .

In summary, the concerns expressed in *Furman* that the penalty of death not be imposed in an arbitrary or capricious manner can be met by a carefully drafted statute that ensures that the sentencing authority is given adequate information and guidance. As a general proposition these concerns are best met by a system that provides for a bifurcated proceeding at which the sentencing authority is apprised of the information relevant to the imposition of sentence and provided with standards to guide its use of the information. . . .

From *Gregg v. Georgia* (1976) 428 US 153, pp. 158–162, 182–184, 186–187, 195, 228–230 (Brennan, J. dissenting), pp. 238–241 (Marshall, J. dissenting).

READING 8-22

Moral Persons and the Death Penalty
"Why the Death Penalty Is a Cruel and Unusual Punishment" (1997)

Hugo Adam Bedau

The [fundamental or fixed rights] argument can be advanced from each of three directions. The first draws upon familiar constitutional principles. According to these principles, even the persons convicted of the gravest crimes retain their fundamental rights of "due process of law" and "equal protection of the laws." These rights are not forfeitable and cannot be waived. If government officials violate them, that is sufficient to nullify whatever legal burdens were placed on the person arising out of that violation and quite apart from whatever consequences may ensue. What this shows is that our society already has in place, and fully acknowledges, the principle that the individual *cannot* do anything that utterly nullifies his or her "moral worth" and standing as a person. The essence-relative argument against the death penalty thus does not aim to invent an unfamiliar type of reasoning and then inject it into constitutional thinking. It merely extends something that has long been done into the area of the substantive constitutional law of punishments.

The second line of reasoning draws upon quotidian [ordinary, customary] experience. This assures us that those persons actually condemned by law to die for their crimes are not merely living members of *homo sapiens* but are also persons capable of the full range of moral action and passion indigenous to moral creatures. However dangerous, irrational, self-centered, stupid, or beyond improvement such a person may in fact be, these deficiencies do not overwhelm all capacity for moral agency—for responsible action, thought, and judgment, in solitude and in relationship with other persons. In particular, none of these capacities vanishes as a result of the person's being at fault for causing wilful, deliberate homicide. The act of murder does not cause the varying moral capacities of murderers that experience amply reveals. No plausible empirical argument can support an alleged loss of moral agency in a convicted murderer as a result of the act of murder. Even more to the point, so far as moral agency is concerned, there is no evidence to show that convicted murderers are different from other convicts. So the doctrine that certain persons, who had basic human rights prior to any criminal acts, forfeit or relinquish all those rights by such acts and thereby cease to be moral persons, receives no support from experience.

The third direction in which to look for support is more obscure and controversial; it concerns moral theory and the nature of the person. Despite recent remarks from the federal bench expressing hostility to all such theories, they cannot be ignored. Human beings are not merely biological specimens of the species *homo sapiens;* nor are we merely self-motivating information-processing creatures. We are moral beings; the meaning of this proposition cannot be intuitively grasped or read off from any value-neutral set of descriptions about our behavioral capacities. It can be understood only as the product of reflective thought about our own capacities as agents and patients, and any remotely adequate account will embody or rely upon moral theory. As a consequence, the nature of the person (as well as any account of that nature) itself changes over time as a result of changes in our self-perceptions. History assures us that we are permanently engaged in our own progressive self-understanding as individuals and as societies. For several centuries—and in particular, since the Age of Enlightenment—philosophers have struggled to enunciate a conception of the person as fundamentally social, rational, and autonomous, and as immune to change in these respects by virtue of any contingencies of history or circumstance. Such personal traits and capacities are no guarantee against immorality in private or public conduct. Nor do they protect us from mortality; they decay with senescence [growing old] and can vanish prior to biological death. It is also true that in particular cases illness, abnormality, and other misfortunes can prevent their normal development in otherwise "normal" persons. Yet these capacities are not, and cannot be thought of as, vulnerable to destruction by the agent's own acts that are deliberate, intentional, responsible—the very qualities properly deemed necessary in a person's conduct before the criminal law subjects a person's harmful conduct to judgment, condemnation, and punishment. On such a theory, even the worst and most dangerous murderer is not a fit subject for annihilation by others. Not even the convicted criminal is a mere object, a thing, to be disposed of by the decision of others, as though there were no alternative. Society has no authority to create and sustain any institution whose nature and purpose is to destroy some of its own members. So cruelty, which does this, matters—because our own status as moral creatures matters. Accordingly, deliberate, institutionalized, lethally punitive cruelty matters, too. Bringing it to an end in all human affairs heads the list of desiderata for any society of persons who understand themselves as moral agents. . . .

READING 8-23

Mistaken Killings
"Executing the Innocent" (1992)

Michael L. Radelet, Hugo Adam Bedau, and Constance E. Putnam

Current capital punishment law already embodies several features that probably reduce the likelihood of executing the innocent. These include abolition of mandatory death penalties, bifurcation of the capital trial into two distinct phases (the first concerned solely with the guilt of the offender, and the second devoted to the issue of sentence), and the requirement of automatic appellate review of a capital conviction and sentence. All three developments have taken place within the past twenty years. Yet, as our Inventory of Cases shows, more than one hundred miscarriages of justice in homicide cases (including forty innocent defendants who were sent to death row) occurred during these same years—despite these protections. Like the procedural reforms urged by Borchard in the 1930s, the reforms actually adopted in the 1970s leave untouched the major causes of grave error. They also do not alter the fact that most of the errors caught in time are corrected not thanks to the system but in spite of the system—that is, in spite of the obstacles to re-investigating and re-opening a case, to persuading a higher court to reconsider, and to securing executive intervention to halt the march to the execution chamber.

Sixty years ago the German refugee scholar and lawyer Max Hirschberg, in his study of wrongful convictions, rightly observed, "Innocent men wrongfully convicted are countless. It is the duty of science to open our eyes to this terrible fact. It is the duty of ethics to rouse indolent and indifferent hearts." As for capital punishment, he added, "*Every* doubt, and not merely 'reasonable' doubt, should be over before a death sentence is imposed." But, as Hirschberg must have realized, it is impossible to operate a criminal justice system in which "every doubt" is resolved in favor of the accused. His demand, like Borchard's reforms, simply cannot be implemented in practice. Against the background of sixty years of studying the problem, from Borchard's day to our own, it is absurd to grope any further in the forlorn hope of eliminating the risk of executing the innocent by reforming criminal procedure.

If it is impossible, for diverse reasons, to introduce into the criminal justice system reforms that would appreciably reduce the likelihood of fatal error in capital cases, then we must live with a system essentially like the present one—and expect more errors in the decades ahead to be added to those documented in this book. Many Americans seem willing to accept such errors because they believe that the really brutal killers—a multiple murderer like Gary Gilmore or a serial murderer like Ted Bundy, for example—simply *must* be executed; they believe that justice for the victims requires no less. Isn't it worth it to be able to punish cunning and remorseless killers with a richly deserved death?

There are many replies to this rhetorical question, but [our position] parries it with a counter-question: What reason is there to believe that our criminal justice system can effectively distinguish between the Gilmores and Bundys who are guilty and arguably "deserve" to die, and the Zimmermans, Domers, and Brandleys who unarguably do not? The evidence is starkly against the capacity of police, prosecutors, witnesses, jurors, judges—the people on whom the system depends—to make this distinction with unfailing and consistent perfection, as the unimpeachable record shows.

The history of capital punishment in western civilization might well be said to have begun with the execution of the innocent—Socrates in Athens in 399 B.C. [see Reading 1-4] and Jesus in Jerusalem in A.D. 30. In the centuries from those days to the present, countless others who were innocent have been put to death. Most were not famous; their names, if remembered at all, are known but to a few. Just a century ago, Illinois executed three of the Haymarket anarchists—August Spies, Adolph Fischer, and George Engel—only to have them all later exonerated by Governor Altgeld (one of the rare instances in any century that such an error has been officially admitted). What errors of the same sort in our time will historians record a century from now?

Voltaire's naive Candide, despite the endless folly and horror he encounters, stoutly maintains that his mentor, Doctor Pangloss, is right—we *do* live in "the best of all possible worlds." But Candide's beloved, the no-nonsense Cunigunde, disagrees. We side with her; we believe our world could be made significantly better by ending the death penalty for every crime, once and for all. We agree also with Voltaire's younger contemporary, the Marquis de Lafayette, who uttered these oft-quoted words: "Till the infallibility of human judgment shall have been proved to me, I shall demand the abolition of the death penalty."

READING 8-24

Not Executing the Guilty
"Deterrence and Uncertainty" (1969)

Ernest Van den Haag

. . . [T]he abolitionist argument from capriciousness [unpredictable inconsistencies], or discretion, or discrimination, would be more persuasive if it were alleged that those selectively executed are not guilty. But the argument merely maintains that some other guilty, but more favored persons, or groups, escape the death penalty. This is hardly sufficient for letting anyone else found guilty escape the penalty. On the contrary, that some guilty persons or groups elude it argues for extending the death penalty to them.

. . . Justice requires punishing the guilty—as many of the guilty as possible, even if only some can be punished—and sparing the innocent—as many of the innocent as possible, even if not all are spared. It would surely be wrong to treat everybody with equal injustice in preference to meting out justice at least to some. . . . [I]f the death penalty is morally just, however discriminatory applied to only some of the guilty, it does remain just in each case in which it is applied.

From Van den Haag (1969), "Deterrence and Uncertainty," 60 *Journal of Criminal Law, Criminology and Police Science,* p. 397.

READING 8-25

Death Penalty as a Questionable Bet
"Execution and Assassination" (1977)

Jonathan Glover

[The Van den Haag argument] presupposes the [questionable] attitude . . . that a murder is a greater evil than the execution of a murderer. But since this attitude probably has overwhelming widespread support, it is worth noting that, even if it is accepted, the best-bet argument is unconvincing. This is because, as Conway has pointed out, it overlooks the fact that we are not choosing between the chance of a murderer dying and the chance of a victim dying. In leaving the death penalty, we are opting for the certainty of the murderer dying which we hope will give us a chance of a potential victim being saved. This would look like a good bet only if we thought an execution substantially preferable to a murder and either the statistical evidence or the intuitive (supported by history and common sense) arguments made the effectiveness of the death penalty as a deterrent look reasonably likely.

From Glover (1977), *Causing Death and Saving Lives.* New York: Penguin Books, pp. 228–240.

The Death Penalty as a Blight on Civilization

"Why the Death Penalty Should Be Abolished" (1998)

Jeffrey Reiman

IV. PAIN AND CIVILIZATION

. . . [T]hough the death penalty is a just punishment for murder, no injustice is done to actual or potential victims if we refrain from imposing the death penalty. In this section, I shall show that, in addition, there are good moral reasons for refraining.

[One] argument [retributivist] for the justice of the death penalty for murderers proves the justice of beating assaulters, raping rapists, and torturing torturers. Nonetheless, I take it that it would not be right for us to beat assaulters, rape rapists, or torture torturers, *even though it were their just deserts*—and even if this were the only way to make them suffer as much as they made their victims suffer. Calling for the abolition of the death penalty, though it be just, then, amounts to urging that we as a society place execution in the same category of sanction as beating, raping, and torturing and treat it as something it would also not be right for us to do to offenders, *even if it were their just deserts.*

To argue for placing execution in this category, I must show what would be gained therefrom. To show that, I shall indicate what we gain from placing torture in this category and argue that a similar gain is to be had from doing the same with execution. I select torture because I think the reasons for placing it in this category are, due to the extremity of torture, most easily seen—but what I say here applies with appropriate modification to other severe physical punishments, such as beating and raping. First, and most evident, placing torture in this category broadcasts the message that we as a society judge torturing so horrible a thing to do to a person that we refuse to do it even when it is deserved. Note that such a judgment does not commit us to an absolute prohibition on torturing. No matter how horrible we judge something to be, we may still be justified in doing it if it is necessary to prevent something even worse. Leaving this aside for the moment, what is gained by broadcasting the public judgment that torture is too horrible to inflict even if deserved?

1. The Advancement of Civilization and the Modern State

I think that the answer to the question just posed lies in what we understand as civilization. In *The Genealogy of Morals,* Friedrich Nietzsche says that in early times "pain did not hurt as much as it does today." The truth in this intriguing remark is that progress in civilization is characterized by a lower tolerance for one's own pain and that suffered by others. And this is appropriate, since, via growth in knowledge, civilization brings increased power to prevent or reduce pain, and, via growth in the ability to communicate and interact with more and more people, civilization extends the circle of people with whom we empathize. If civilization is characterized by lower tolerance for our own pain and that of others, then publicly refusing to do horrible things to our fellows both signals the level of our civilization *and, by our example, continues the work of civilizing*. This gesture is all the more powerful if we refuse to do horrible things to those who deserve them. I contend, then, that the more horrible things we are able to include in the category of what we will not do, the more civilized we are and the more civilizing. Thus we gain from including torture in this category, and, if execution is especially horrible, we gain still more by including it.

But notice, it is not just any refraining from horrible punishments that is likely to produce this gain. It is important to keep in mind that I am talking about modern states, with their extreme visibility, their moral authority (tattered of late but not destroyed), and their capacity to represent millions, even hundreds of millions, of citizens. It is when modern states refrain from imposing grave harms on those who deserve them that a powerful message about the repugnant nature of such harms is broadcast. It is this message that I contend contributes to civilization by increasing people's repugnance for such harmful acts generally. And, I believe that, because of modern states' unique position—their size, visibility, and moral authority, modern states have a duty to act in ways that advance civilization. . . .

Some evidence for the larger reach of my claim about civilization and punishment is found in what Émile Durkheim identified, nearly a century ago, as "two laws which seem . . . to prevail in the evolution of the apparatus of punishment." The first, the *law of quantitative change,* Durkheim formulates thusly:

> The intensity of punishment is the greater the more closely societies approximate to a less developed type—and the more the central power assumes an absolute character.

And the second, which Durkheim refers to as the *law of qualitative change,* is this:

> Deprivations of liberty, and of liberty alone, varying in time according to the seriousness of the crime, tend to become more and more the normal means of social control.

Several things should be noted about these laws. First of all, they are not two separate laws. As Durkheim understands them, the second exemplifies the trend toward moderation of punishment referred to in the first. Second, the first law really refers to two distinct trends, which usually coincide but do not always. Moderation of punishment accompanies both the movement from less to more advanced types of society and the movement from more to less absolute rule. Normally these go hand in hand, but where they do not, the effect of one trend may offset the effect of the other. Thus, a primitive society without absolute rule may have milder punishments than an equally primitive, but more absolutist, society. This complication need not trouble us, since the claim I am making refers to the first trend, namely, that punishments tend to become milder as societies become more advanced; and that this is a trend in history is not refuted by the fact that it is accompanied by other trends and even occasionally offset by them. Finally, and most important for our purposes, Durkheim's claim that punishment becomes less intense as societies become more advanced is a generalization that he supports with an impressive array of evidence from historical societies from pre-Christian times to the time in which he wrote—and this supports my claim that reduction in the horrible things we do to our fellows is in fact part of the advance of civilization. . . .

2. The Horribleness of the Death Penalty

To complete the argument, however, I must show that execution is horrible enough to warrant its inclusion alongside torture. Against this it will be said that execution is not especially horrible, since it only hastens a fate that is inevitable for all of us. I think that this view overlooks important differences in the manner in which people reach their inevitable ends. I contend that execution is especially horrible, and it is so in a way similar to (though not identical with) the way in which torture is especially horrible. I believe we view torture as especially awful because of two of its features, which also characterize execution: intense pain and the spectacle of one person being completely subject to the power of another. This latter is separate from the issue of pain, since it is something that offends us about unpainful things, such as slavery (even voluntarily entered) and prostitution (even voluntarily chosen as an occupation). Execution shares this separate feature, since killing a bound and defenseless human being enacts the total subjugation of that person to his fellows. . . .

In particular, I have suggested that the state, by the vivid example of its unwillingness to execute even those—*especially those*—who deserve it, would contribute to the process of civilizing humankind, which I take in part to include reducing our tolerance for pain imposed on our fellows. I have called this an advance in civilization for two reasons: first, because history shows that the harshness of punishments seems generally to decline over time, and second, because it seems good to reduce our willingness to impose pain on our fellows. The first condition here is empirical, a matter of what history actually records. And while I think that the elimination of ear cropping, branding, drawing and quartering, and boiling in oil, as well as the practice of throwing members of unpopular religions to the lions for public entertainment, all suggest that the taming that I have in mind is the general trend of history, there are exceptions, of course. The Nazis, for example, tortured their enemies with awful ferocity. But most would recognize Nazism as a step backward in civilization. So, my claim is a broad empirical claim, much in the vein of Richard Rorty's recent suggestion that, in the West, there has been a tendency to want to reduce or eliminate cruelty. But it is equally a moral claim. I have argued that even stable historical trends do not count as advances in civilization unless they are also, on independent grounds, good.

In sum, my argument is that, though the death penalty is just punishment for some murders, execution is a horrible thing to do to our fellows, and, if the state can avoid execution without thereby doing injustice to actual or potential victims of murder, then, in addition to whatever is good about causing less pain, the state would also, by its example, contribute to a general reduction in people's tolerance for doing painful things to one another, a reduction that I think is an advance in civilization. And I think that modern states are morally bound to promote the advance of civilization because they are uniquely positioned to do so and because of the goodness that must characterize a trend if it is to count as an advance in civilization. . . .

Reiman, Jeffrey. "Why the Death Penalty Should Be Abolished," *The Death Penalty: For and Against*. Copyright © (1998) Rowman and Littlefield. Reprinted by permission.

DISCUSSION ISSUES

1. *Absurd Murderers*. "[T]wo men rob a grocery store and flee in opposite directions. The owner of the store follows one of the robbers and kills him. Neither robber may have been armed with a deadly weapon. If the felony-murder doctrine applied, however, the surviving robber could be convicted of first degree murder even though he was captured by the policeman and placed under arrest at the time his accomplice was killed" (*People v. Washington* 1965, Justice Traynor). Does this hypothetical case prove the absurdity of the felony murder rule when taken to its extremes?

2. *Retribution Without Consequences*. "Even if a civil society resolved to dissolve itself with the consent of all its members—as might be supposed in the case of a people inhabiting an island resolving to separate and scatter themselves throughout the world—the last murderer lying in prison ought to be executed before the resolution was carried out. This ought to be done in order that every one may realize the desert of his deeds, and that bloodguiltiness may not remain upon the people; for otherwise they will all be regarded as participators in the murder as a public violation of justice" (Kant 1797 as quoted in Pincoffs 1966, p. 198). Should a criminal face punishment without any utilitarian reasons to punish? Should the state ever show mercy by not punishing a criminal? Assume that deterrence has had its full effect on the individual. For example, the murderer might have truly found Christ (Moore 1987, p. 184), or the Nazi war criminal might have been a model citizen for the past fifty years. Further, assume either that punishing these individuals would not have any general deterrent effect or that pretending to punish them would have the optimal deterrent effect. Given these assumptions, a person who still believes that the state should punish these individuals qualifies as a retributivist. Does Michael Moore's retributivist test stand up to close analysis (see Moore 1997)?

3. *Punishment Fitting the Crime*. How would a legislator match, in detail, specific crimes with specific punishments? "Whosoever shall be guilty of rape, polygamy, sodomy with man or woman, shall be punished, if a man, by castration, if a woman, shall be punished by cutting through the cartilage of her nose a hole of one half inch deep in diameter at the least. . . . [W]hosoever shall maim another, or shall disfigure him . . . shall be maimed, or disfigured in the like sort; or if that cannot be, for want of some part, then as nearly as may be, in some other part of at least equal value" (Thomas Jefferson, *Bill for Proportioning Crime and Punishment* [1779] as quoted in Reiman [1999], p. 19). Kant, who accepted the proportionality of punishment argument, exempted crimes against humanity, such

as rape, pederasty ("unnatural carnal copulation between males," *Black's Law Dictionary*), and bestiality ("a sexual connection between a human and an animal," *Black's Law Dictionary*), as ones that should not be inflicted on criminals (Reiman 1998, p. 71, n. 6). Yet, in some other cases, particularly those involving property rights, theorists accept that the punishment must exceed the crime in order to have a deterrent effect (Goldman 1979 in Simmons et al. 1995). Should punishment be adjusted according to the harm inflicted on the victim or the unfair advantage gained by the criminal (Davis in Simmons 1995)?

4. *Economics of Punishment.* Law and economics proponents Gary Becker, Richard Posner, and others have applied economic analysis to criminal law. Becker believes that fines are economically preferable to imprisonment, while criminal sanctions provide a way to price conduct, according to Posner (1986, p. 172). Since tort law does not provide enough deterrent, criminal law supplies additional "kickers" or disincentives to bypassing the market. Jules Coleman defends the following two objections to an economic analysis of criminal law: "[I]t is simply a mistake to think of the criminal law as an enforcer of resource transfers. Moreover, the key moral notions of criminal responsibility—of guilt and fault—are simply absent from the economic infrastructure" (Coleman 1988, pp. 161–162). Murder and rape have nothing to do with transferring resources. In addition, criminal law, unlike tort law, involves morality. Does this position hold? One case provides an illustration of noneconomic and economic judicial analyses of the rights of indigents to counsel (*Merritt v. Faulkner* 1983). Judge Swygert examined an indigent plaintiff's claim in terms of various factors, such as the plaintiff's ability to collect facts and the complexity of the legal issues in the case. Justice Richard Posner, in dissent, argued for a presumption against appointment of counsel in prisoner civil rights cases on economic grounds. Which analysis seems more plausible?

5. *State as Murderer?* If murder is wrong, how can the state murder someone to show that murder is wrong? Primoratz (1989) finds this argument invalid:

> In order to be able to talk of the state as "murdering" the person it executes, one has to use the "murder" in the very same sense—that is, in the usual sense, which implies the idea of *wrongful* taking the life of another—both when speaking of what the murderer has done to the victim and of what the state is doing to him by way of punishment. But this is precisely the question at issue: whether capital punishment *is* "murder," whether it is wrongful or morally justified and right.

Does it ever make sense to accuse a state of murder?

6. *Vile Murders.* The issue of Georgia's aggravating circumstances requirement to impose the penalty came before the U.S. Supreme Court in *Godfrey v. Georgia* 1980. A distraught husband facing a divorce murdered his wife and her mother in the presence of his eleven-year-old daughter before calling the police. A jury found, beyond a reasonable doubt, the following aggravating circumstances: "that the offense of murder was outrageous or wantonly vile, horrible and inhuman." The jury then imposed the death sentence. The Supreme Court reversed the death sentence, admitting that the husband's acts were heinous, but finding him no more depraved than any other person guilty of murder. The Court, therefore, claimed that the husband's acts did not distinguish this case from cases in which the death penalty was not imposed. Dissenting Justices White and Rehnquist found the husband's acts "so macabre and revolting that, if anything, 'vile,' 'horrible,' and 'inhuman' are descriptively inadequate." Does the decision in this case depend on whose sense of gore should serve as the standard? Perhaps another issue underlies the

majority's position. The relevant Georgia law required a finding that the offense "involved torture, depravity of mind, or an aggravated battery to the victim." The prosecutor and the trial judge both found these elements lacking in this case, but the jury apparently ignored the prosecutor and the judge. Does the majority's position more accurately reflect a concern for the discrepancy during the sentencing phase of the trial?

7. *Unsophisticated Science and Covert Racism.* According to some commentators, *McCleskey* (discussed earlier, see page 477) raised a subtle discrimination claim that required a sophisticated understanding of statistics and a willingness to uncover covert forms of racism. "Several clerks, even one of Rehnquist's, suggested that the Court appoint a special master—an independent expert—to give the mathematically challenged Justices a neutral assessment of Baldus's methods and findings" (Lazarus 1998, p. 202). Should the legal demonstration of racial discrimination depend on sophisticated scientific analyses? Does the proof of racial discrimination depend on a prior willingness to look? "[I]t is precisely the sense that racial discrimination is a terrible evil that inhibits the Justices from 'finding' it in all but the clearest circumstances" (Kennedy 1988, p. 1418).

G. INTERNATIONAL CRIMINAL LAW

After World War II, the completion of the Nuremberg trials marked what many thought would be the final international trial for grave crimes against humanity. However, genocides in the former Yugoslavia and in Rwanda in the 1990s led to the international community again constructing *ad hoc* war crimes tribunals. The Tadic trial (see Reading 8-27) revealed the hopes and concerns for establishing a regime of international criminal justice. On July 17, 1998, the world community took a step closer to creating a global justice structure when more than 100 nations signed the Rome Statute of the International Criminal Court. In the words of United Nations Secretary General Kofi Anan, "There can be no global justice unless the worst of crimes— crimes against humanity—are subject to the law." The United States, along with a handful of other nations, refused to sign the Rome Treaty. Discussions for and against a permanent international war crimes tribunal pose not only legal and political questions but also theoretical and moral ones. As a permanent International Criminal Court (ICC) comes closer to being a reality, the need to develop international normative criminal standards intensifies. Historically, political philosophers have had a difficult time trying to justify the state and its law (see chapter 2). Now they face the challenge of constructing theories of global justice by attending to the problem of justifying an international court and its laws. Do any of the philosophies we have surveyed provide the foundations for meeting the new challenges or should we start from scratch and develop an entirely new philosophy of law?

International Criminal Justice
Balkan Justice (1997)

Michael P. Scharf

*Civilization asks whether law is so laggard as to be utterly helpless
to deal with crimes of this magnitude by criminals of this order of importance. It does not expect that you can make war impossible. It does
expect that your juridical action will put the forces of International
Law, its precepts, its prohibitions and, most of all, its sanctions, on the
side of peace, so that men and women of good will, in all countries,
may have "leave to live by no man's leave, underneath the law."*

—ROBERT H. JACKSON
Opening Speech for the Prosecution at Nuremberg, November 21, 1945

. . . Dusko Tadic was found guilty of 11 of the 34 counts in the indictment, including the persecution charge, but was acquitted of the castration charge,
the fire extinguisher charge, and all of the specific murder charges. Perhaps
the biggest surprise was his acquittal of the charges relating to grave
breaches of the Geneva Conventions, based on the conclusion of two of the
three judges that Serbia had not been directly involved in these acts, and
therefore that they were not committed in an international armed conflict.
"Although this is the first trial conducted by the international tribunal and
thus has some historic dimension, the goal of the trial chamber was always
first and foremost to provide the accused with the fair trial to which he was
entitled," Judge McDonald said after pronouncing the verdict and summa-
rizing the Tribunal's 301-page decision. "This, we believe, has been done." . . .

Despite the mixed verdict, historians are likely to rank the trial of Dusko
Tadic among the most important trials of the century. Unlike other
renowned criminal trials such as the treason trials of Esther and Julius
Rosenberg, the Chicago Seven trial, the Watergate trials, the Rodney King
case, and the O.J. Simpson trial, the importance of the Tadic case lies not in
the status of the defendant or even the nature of his alleged crimes, but in
the fact that the proceedings constituted an historic turning point for the
world community. Just as the Nuremberg trials following World War II
launched the era of human rights promulgation fifty years ago, the Tadic
trial has inaugurated a new age of human rights enforcement.

As the Yugoslav Tribunal itself reflected in its first annual report: "The
United Nations, which over the years has accumulated an impressive corpus
of international standards enjoining States and individuals to conduct themselves humanely, has now set up an institution to put those standards to the
test, to transform them into living reality. A whole body of lofty, if remote,
United Nations ideals will be brought to bear upon human beings. Through
the Tribunal, those imperatives will be turned from abstract tenets into inescapable commands."

At the opening session of the Yugoslav Tribunal in November 1993, U.N.
Under-Secretary General for Legal Affairs Carl-August Fleischhauer said

that in setting up the Tribunal, the Security Council had demonstrated a determination to achieve three aims: "First, to put an end to the crimes being committed in the former Yugoslavia; second, to take effective measures to bring to justice the persons who are responsible for those crimes; and, third, to break the seemingly endless cycle of ethnic violence and retribution." It is no overstatement to suggest that the success or failure of the Yugoslav Tribunal in meeting these goals of deterrence, justice, and peace will decide the direction of human rights enforcement into the next century.

With respect to the first of these goals, the trial of Dusko Tadic should be seen as an effort not merely to bring an individual to justice but to understand the most barbarous butchery to blight Europe in fifty years—and perhaps prevent a repetition of recent history. The record of the trial provides an authoritative and impartial account to which future historians may turn for truth, and future leaders for warning. While there are various means to achieve an historic record of abuses after a war, the most authoritative rendering is possible only through the crucible of a trial that accords full due process.[1]

If, to paraphrase American writer and philosopher George Santayana, we are condemned to repeat our mistakes if we have not learned the lessons of the past, then we must establish a reliable record of those mistakes if we wish to prevent their recurrence. The chief prosecutor at Nuremberg, Robert Jackson, underscored the logic of this proposition when he reported to President Truman that one of the most important legacies of the Nuremberg trials was that they documented the Nazi atrocities "with such authenticity and in such detail that there can be no responsible denial of these crimes in the future and no tradition of martyrdom of the Nazi leaders can arise among informed people." Similarly, the Tadic trial has generated a comprehensive record of the nature and extent of international crimes in the Balkans, how they were planned and executed, the fate of individual victims, who gave the orders, and who carried them out. By carefully establishing these facts one witness at a time in the face of vigilant cross-examination by distinguished defense counsel, the Tadic trial produced a definitive account that can endure the test of time and resist the forces of revisionism.

A half century after Nuremberg, historians like Daniel Jonah Goldhagen continue to address the question of how so many ordinary people could be so readily enlisted to participate in atrocities. Goldhagen's recent work, *Hitler's Willing Executioners,* hypothesizes that the Holocaust was a product of the German people's unique cultural predisposition to "eliminationist anti-semitism." But the Tadic case suggests a different answer. Lead prosecutor Grant Niemann believes the trial proved that "human beings are universally capable of doing the things Tadic has done." The most extraordinary hall-

---

[1] One means of establishing an historic record of atrocities which is in vogue these days is through the establishment of a "Truth Commission." See generally, Priscilla B. Hayner, "Fifteen Truth Commissions—1974 to 1994: A Comparative Study," in N. Kritz, ed., *Transnational Justice: How Emerging Democracies Reckon with Former Regimes* 1, (1995), p. 223. Yet, truth commissions are a poor substitute for prosecutions. They do not have prosecutory powers such as the power to subpoena witnesses or punish perjury, and they are viewed as one-sided since they do not provide those accused of abuses with the panoply of rights available to a criminal defendant.

mark of the Yugoslav carnage was its intimacy. Torturers knew their victims and had often grown up alongside them as neighbors and friends. Perhaps the real lesson of the Tadic trial is that given the right set of circumstances, many of us can become willing executioners. It is what the American historian Hannah Arendt, in her classic account of the Eichmann trial, referred to as the "banality of evil."[2] Four centuries earlier, the philosopher Thomas Hobbes hypothesized that there is everywhere a thin line between civilization and barbarism.

What are the circumstances that can lure out this dark side of human nature and push us across that thin line? "That is one of the mysteries of the Yugoslav conflict," says deputy prosecutor Graham Blewitt. "What transforms ordinary people into savages? The Tadic case gave us a glimpse of how provocation, incitement, and propaganda can raise hatred and fear to such an extent that ordinary people turn on their neighbors in a bloodthirsty way," he added. Throw in official sanction, a bit of coercion by persons in authority, pressure from assenting comrades, and opportunities for personal gain. Then add a long history of ethnic tension and you have the active ingredients of ethnic cleansing—Bosnian style.

What is most shocking about the Balkan conflict is not that atrocities were committed, but that the rest of the world did so little to prevent them or bring them to an end. As the Court TV anchor, Terry Moran, observed during the trial, "The Tadic trial proved once again how very difficult it is for people to care about evil in countries and places that are far from their personal experiences. Whether we are humankind in fact as well as in name is an open question in light of what happened in Bosnia and the international community's continuing inadequate response." . . .

[2]Hannah Arendt, *Eichmann in Jerusalem: A Report on the Banality of Evil* (1964), p. 252. Arendt concluded that Adolf Eichman, who stood trial in Jerusalem in the summer of 1962 as "the engineer of Hitler's Final Solution," was no monster nor a "perverted sadist" as the prosecution had described him. Rather, Arendt believed that "the trouble with Eichman was precisely that so many were like him, and that the many were neither perverted nor sadistic, that they were, and still are, terribly and terrifyingly normal." (p. 276).

Table of Cases

495

Epperson v. Arkansas (1968) 393 US 97.

Escobedo v. Illinois (1964) 378 US 478.

Everson v. Board of Education (1946) 330 US 1.

FCC v. Pacifica Foundation (1978) 438 US 726.

Filartiga v. Pena-Irala (2d Cir. 1980) 630 F.2d 876.

Fletcher v. Peck (1810) 10 US 87.

Furman v. Georgia (1972) 408 US 238.

Gedulig v. Aiello (1974) 417 US 484.

Ginsberg v. New York (1968) 390 US 629.

Godfrey v. Georgia (1980) 446 US 420.

Griffin v. California (1965) 380 US 609.

Griswold v. Connecticut (1965) 381 US 479.

Halter v. Nebraska (1907) 205 US 34.

Henningsen v. Bloomfield Motors, Inc., and Chrysler Corporation (1960) 161 A.2d 69.

Holloway v. United States (1945) 326 US 687.

Home Building and Loan Association v. Blaisdell (1934) 290 US 398 448.

Hopwood v. Texas (1996) 78 F.3d 932.

Hynes v. New York Central R.R. (1921) 23 131 N.E. 898.

In re Quinlin (1976) 70 N.J. 10.

Jackson Municipal School District v. Evers (1966) 357 F.2d 653.

Jane Doe v. Louisiana (Phipps) (1986) 479 So. 2d 369.

Jones v. Van Zandt (1847) 46 US 215.

Kennedy v. Bureau of Narcotics (1972) 459 F.2d 415.

Konigsberg v. State Bar of California (1961) 366 US 36.

Kovacs v. Cooper (1941) 336 US 77.

Lemon v. Kurtzman (1971) 403 US 602.

Lochner v. New York (1905) 198 US 45.

Loving v. Virginia (1967) 388 US 1.

Lying v. Castillo (1986) 477 US 635.

Maher v. Roe (1977) 432 US 464.

Mapp v. Ohio (1961) 367 US 643.

Marbury v. Madison (1803) 5 US 137.

Massachusetts Board of Retirement v. Murgia (1976) 427 US 307.

Masses, Publishing Co. v. Patten (1917) 244 Fed. 535.

McCleskey v. Kemp (1987) 481 US 279.

Merritt v. Faulkner (1983) 697 F.2d 761.

Miller v. California (1973) 413 US 15.

Millikin v. Bradley (1974) 418 US 717.

Miranda v. Arizona (1966) 384 US 436.

Morisette v. United States (1952) 342 US 246.

Mozert v. Hawkins County Board of Education (1987) 827 F.2d 1058.

Muller v. Oregon (1908) 208 US 412.

Olmstead v. United States (1928) 277 US 438, 464.

Penry v. Lynaugh (1988) 847 US 1233.

People v. Fuller (1970) 86 Cal. App. 3d 618.

People v. Goetz (1986) 497 N.E.2d 41.

People v. Harrison (1959) 176 Cal. App. 2d 330.

People v. Hickman (1973) 297 N.E. 2d 582.

People v. Washington (1965) 402 P.2d 130.

Planned Parenthood of Southeastern Pennsylvania v. Casey (1992) 505 US 833.

Plessy v. Ferguson (1896) 163 US 537.

Prigg v. Pennsylvania (1842) 41 US 539.

Queen v. Dudley and Stephens (1884-85) 14 Q. B. 273. [England]

Bibliography

Abadinsky, Howard (1991). *Law & Justice,* second edition. Chicago: Nelson-Hall.

Abel, Richard L., editor (1995). *Law & Society.* New York: New York University Press.

Ackerman, Bruce (1985). "Beyond Carolene Products," 98 *Harvard Law Review* 713.

Alderman, Ellen and Caroline Kennedy, editors (1997). *The Right to Privacy.* New York: Vintage.

Alschuler, Albert W. (1979). "Plea Bargaining and Its History," 13 *Law & Society Review* 211.

Altman, Andrew (1990). *Critical Legal Studies.* Princeton, NJ: Princeton University Press.

_____ (1996). *Arguing About Law.* Belmont, CA: Wadsworth.

Amsterdam, Anthony G. (1988). "Race and the Death Penalty," 7 *Criminal Justice Ethics* 84.

An-Na'im, Abdullah Ahmend (1990). "The Muslim World," 3 *Harvard Human Rights Journal* 13.

Aristotle (1985). *Nichomachean Ethics.* Terence Irwin, translator. Indianapolis: Hackett.

Arthur, John and Amy Shapiro, editors (1995). *Campus Wars.* Boulder, CO: Westview.

Auerbach, Jerald S. (1976). *Unequal Justice.* New York: Oxford University Press.

Austin, John (1869). *Lectures on Jurisprudence,* Vol. II, third edition. London: Campbell.

Bailyn, Bernard (1967). *The Ideological Origins of the American Revolution.* Cambridge, MA: The Belknap Press of Harvard University Press.

Baker, Liva (1983). *Miranda.* New York: Basic Books.

Barton, John H. et al., editors (1983). *Law in Radically Different Cultures.* St. Paul, MN: West.

Beard, Charles (1935). *An Economic Interpretation of the Constitution.* New York: Macmillan.

Beck, Lewis, editor and translator (1949). *Kant's Critique of Practical Reasoning and Other Writings of Moral Philosophy.* Chicago: University of Chicago Press.

Becker, Gary S. (1968). "Crime and Punishment: An Economic Approach," 76 *Journal of Political Economy* 169.

Bellah, Robert N. et al. (1985). *Habits of the Heart.* New York: Harper & Row.

Belliotti, Raymond A. (1992). *Justifying Law.* Philadelphia, PA: Temple University Press.

Bender, David L., editor (1997). *The Death Penalty: Opposing Viewpoints.* San Diego, CA: Greenhaven.

Bentham, Jeremy (1789). *An Introduction to the Principles of Morals and Legislation.* In 1970, J. H. Burns and H. L. A. Hart, editors. New York: Methuen.

_____ (1827). *Rationale of Judicial Evidence.* London: John Bowring.

Berger, Raoul (1987). *Federalism: The Founders' Design.* Norman, OK: University of Oklahoma Press.

Bergmann, Frithjof (1977). *On Being Free.* Notre Dame, IN: University of Notre Dame Press.

Berlin, Isaiah (1969). *Four Essays on Liberty.* New York: Oxford University Press.

Berman, Harold J. and William R. Griener, editors (1980). The *Nature and Functions of Law,* third edition. New York: Foundation.

Berman, Harold J. et al., editors (1996). *The Nature and Functions of Law,* fifth edition. New York: Foundation.

Blasi, Vincent, editor (1983). *The Burger Court.* New Haven, CT: Yale University Press.

Bodin, Jean (1576). *Six Books of the Commonwealth.* In 1955 M. J. Tooley, translator. New York: Oxford University Press.

Bok, Sissela (1978). *Lying.* New York: Pantheon Books.

Bork, Robert (1971). "Neutral Principles and Some First Amendment Problems," 1 *Indiana Law Journal* 47.

Brewer, Scott (1996). "Exemplary Reasoning: Semantics, and Rational Force of Legal Arguments by Analogy," 109 *Harvard Law Review* 923.

Brint, Michael and William Weaver, editors (1991). *Pragmatism in Law and Society.* Boulder, CO: Westview Press.

Burton, S. J. (1985). *An Introduction to Law and Legal Reasoning.* Boston: Little, Brown.

Camus, Albert (1961). *Resistance, Rebellion, and Death.* New York: Knopf.

Chapman, John and J. Roland Pennock, editors (1971). *Nomos XIII, Privacy.* New York: Lieber-Atherton.

Christie, George C. and Patrick H. Martin, editors (1995). *Jurisprudence.* St. Paul, MN: West.

Christopher, Paul (1994). *The Ethics of War & Peace.* Englewood Cliffs, NJ: Prentice Hall.

Cicero (1928). *De Legibus.* C. W. Keyes, translator. Cambridge, MA: Harvard University Press.

Claude, Richard P. (1983). "The Case of Joelito Filartiga and the 'Clinic of Hope,'" 5 *Human Rights Quarterly* 275.

Claude, Richard Pierre and Burns H. Weston, editors (1992). *Human Rights in the World Community.* Philadelphia, PA: University of Pennsylvania Press.

Cohen, Joshua, editor (1996). *For Love of Country.* Boston: Beacon Press.

Cohen, William and David J. Danelski (1994). *Constitutional Law,* third edition. Westbury, NY: Foundations.

Coleman, Jules L. (1988). *Markets, Morals and the Law.* New York: Cambridge University Press.

Coleman, Jules, editor (1994). *Jurisprudence.* New York: Garland Publishing.

Confucius (1939). *Analects.* Arthur Waley, translator. New York: Macmillan.

Conway, David (1974). "Capital Punishment and Deterrence," 3 *Philosophy and Public Affairs* 431.

Cooper, Jeremy (1993). "Poverty and Constitutional Justice in India," 44 *Mercer Law Review.*

Copleston, Frederick (1962). *A History of Philosophy.* Garden City, NY: Doubleday & Company.

Cover, Robert (1975). *Justice Accused.* New Haven, CT: Yale University Press.

Cover, Robert (1982). "The Origins of Judicial Activism in the Protection of Minorities," 91 *Yale Law Journal* 1287.

D'Amato, Anthony (1976). "Obligation to Obey the Law: A Study of the Death of Socrates," 49 *Southern California Law Review* 1079.

_____ (1980). "The Speluncean Explorers—Further Proceedings," 32 *Stanford Law Review* 467.

_____ editor (1990). *International Law Anthology.* Cincinnati, OH: Anderson.

Dau-Schmidt, Kenneth G. and Thomas S. Ulen, editors (1998). *Law and Economics Anthology.* Cincinnati, OH: Anderson Publishing Company.

Davidson, Lance S. (1998). *Ludicrous Laws & Mindless Misdemeanors.* New York: John Wiley & Sons.

Davis, F. James (1991). *Who Is Black?* University Park, PA: The Pennsylvania State University Press.

Davis, Sue, editor (1996). *American Political Thought.* Englewood Cliffs, NJ: Prentice Hall.

Derschowitz, Alan M. (1989). "Shouting 'Fire,'" *Atlantic Monthly,* pp. 72–74.

Dixon, Martin (1993). *Textbook on International Law,* second edition. London: Blackstone Press.

Donner, Ruth (1994). *The Regulation of Nationality in International Law,* second edition. Irvington-on-Hudson, NY: Transnational.

Dworkin, Ronald (1972). "Paternalism," 56 *The Monist* 1.

_____ (1977). *Taking Rights Seriously.* Cambridge, MA: Harvard University Press.

_____ (1992). "Unremunerated Rights: Whether and How Roe Should Be Overruled," 59 *University of Chicago Law Review* 402.

_____ (1996). *Freedom's Law.* Cambridge, MA: Harvard University Press.

Ellmann, Stephen (1997). "Executioners, Jailers, Slave-Trappers and the Law: What Role Should Morality Play in Judging?" 19 *Cardozo Law Review* 1047.

Ely, John Hart (1973). "The Wages of Crying Wolf: A Comment on *Roe v. Wade,*" 82 *Yale Law Journal* 920.

_____ (1980). *Democracy and Distrust.* Cambridge, MA: Harvard University Press.

Emerson, Thomas (1970). *The System of Freedom of Expression.* New York: Vintage.

Feinberg, Joel (1966). "Duties, Rights and Claims," 3 *American Philosophical Quarterly* 137.

_____ (1985). *Offense to Others.* New York: Oxford University Press.

Feinberg, Joel and Hyman Gross, editors (1995). *Philosophy of Law,* fifth edition. Belmont, CA: Wadsworth.

Feinberg, Joel and Jules Coleman, editors (2000), *Philosophy of Law.* Belmont, CA: Wadsworth/Thompson Learning.

Finkelman, Paul (1985). *Slavery in the Courtroom.* Washington, DC: Library of Congress.

Finnis, John (1980). *Natural Law and Natural Rights.* Oxford, England: Clarendon Press.

Fletcher, George (1980). "Reflections on Felony-Murder," 12 *Southwestern University Law Review,* 413.

_____ (1988). *A Crime of Self-Defense.* New York: The Free Press.

_____ (1993). *Loyalty.* New York: Oxford University Press.

_____ (1978). *Rethinking Criminal Law.* Boston: Little, Brown.

_____ (1996). *Basic Concepts of Legal Thought.* New York: Oxford University Press.

Forde, Steven (1998). "Hugo Grotius on Ethics and War," 92 *American Political Science Review* 639.

Frank, Jerome (1931). "Are Judges Human?" 80 *University of Pennsylvania Law Review* 17.

Frank, Jerome (1932). "What Courts Do In Fact," 26 *Illinois Law Review* 645.

Freeman, Alan (1989). "Legitimizing Racial Discrimination Through Antidiscrimination Law: A Critical Review of Supreme Court Doctrine," 62 *Minnesota Law Review* 1049.

Freeman, M. D. A., editor (1994). *Lloyd's Introduction to Jurisprudence,* sixth edition. London: Sweet & Maxwell.

Friedman, Lawrence M. (1973). *A History of American Law.* New York: Simon & Schuster.

_____ (1993). *Crime and Punishment in American History.* New York: Basic Books.

_____ (1998). *American Law.* New York: W. W. Norton.

Friedman, Lawrence M. and Harry N. Scheiber, editors (1978). *American law and the Constitutional Order.* Cambridge, MA: Harvard University Press.

Fuller, Lon (1959). "Positivism and Fidelity to Law—A Reply to Professor Hart," 71 *Harvard Law Review* 630.

Fuller, Lon L. (1964). *The Morality of Law.* New Haven, CT: Yale University Press.

Galatung, Johan and Anders Helge Wirak (1978). "On the Relationship Between Human Rights and Human Needs," 8 *Bulletin of Peace Proposals* 251.

Geertz, Clifford (1973). *The Interpretation of Cultures.* New York: Basic Books.

Gerber, R. J. (1975). "Is the Insanity Test Insane?" 20 *The Journal of American Jurisprudence* 111.

Ginsburg, Ruth Bader (1985). "Some Thoughts on Autonomy and Equality in Relation to *Roe v. Wade,*" 63 *North Carolina Law Review* 375.

Glendon, Mary Ann (1987). *Abortion and Divorce in Western Law.* Cambridge, MA: Harvard University Press.

Glendon, Mary Ann et al., editors (1994). *Comparative Legal Traditions.* St. Paul, MN: West.

Godwin, Mike (1998). *Cyber Rights.* New York: Random House.

Golding, Martin P. (1986). "Jurisprudence and Legal Philosophy in Twentieth Century America: Major Themes and Developments," 36 *Journal of Legal Education* 441.

Golding, William (1954). *Lord of the Flies.* London: Farber and Farber.

Goldstein, Robert Justin (1996). *Burning the Flag.* Kent, OH: Kent State University Press.

Goodin, Robert E. and Philip Pettit, editors (1993). *A Companion to Contemporary Political Philosophy.* Cambridge, MA: Basil Blackwell.

Gorr, Michel J. and Sterling Harwood, editors (1995). *Crime and Punishment.* Boston: Jones and Bartlett.

Greenberg, Douglas et al., editors (1993). *Constitutionalism & Democracy.* New York: Oxford University Press.

Grey, Thomas (1975). "Do We Have an Unwritten Constitution," 27 *Stanford Law Review* 703.

_____ (1983). "Landell's Orthodoxy," 45 *University of Pittsburgh Law Review* 1.

Gross, Hyman (1971). "Privacy and Autonomy," *Nomos XIII, Privacy,* John Chapman and J. Roland Pennock, editors. New York: Leiber-Atherton, pp. 169–182.

Gutman, Amy (Summer 1989). "The Central Role of Rawls's Theory," *Dissent* 338.

Hall, Jerome, editor (1938). *Readings in Jurisprudence.* Indianapolis: Bobbs-Merrill.

Hall, Kermit L. (1989). *The Magic Mirror.* New York: Oxford University Press.

Hall, Kermit L. et al. (1996). *American Legal History.* New York: Oxford University Press.

Hamilton, Edith and Huntington Cairns, editors (1982). *The Collected Dialogues of Plato.* Princeton, NJ: Princeton University Press.

Harris, D. J., editor (1991). *Cases and Materials on International Law,* fourth edition. London: Sweet & Maxwell.

Hart, H. L. A. (1958). "Positivism and the Separation of Law and Morals," 71 *Harvard Law Review* 593.

_____ (1968). *Punishment and Responsibility: Essays in the Philosophy of Law.* New York: Oxford University Press.

_____ (1983). *Essays in Jurisprudence and Philosophy.* London: Clarendon.

_____ (1994). *The Concept of Law,* second edition. New York: Oxford University Press.

Hart, H. L. A. and Tony Honoré (1959, 1985). *Causation in the Law.* New York: Oxford University Press.

Harvey, Cameron, editor (1988). *Anthology of Legal Humour.* London: Carswell.

Hayek, F. A. (1944). "Planning and the Rule of Law," *The Road to Serfdom.* London: Routledge & Kegan Paul, 54.

Hayek, F. A. (1960). *The Constitution of Liberty.* London: Routledge & Kegan Paul.

Hayman, Robert L., Jr. and Nancy Levit, editors (1994). *Jurisprudence.* St. Paul, MN: West.

Henkin, Louis (1974). "Privacy and Autonomy," *Columbia Law Review* 74.

Hill, Christopher (1975). *The World Turned Upside Down.* New York: Penguin Books.

Hindus, Michael (1980). *Prison and Plantation: Crime, Justice, and Authority in Massachusetts and South Carolina.* Chapel Hill, NC: University of North Carolina Press.

Hobbes, Thomas (1668). *Leviathan.* In 1994, Edwin Curley, editor. Indianapolis: Hackett.

Hobbhouse, L. T. (1964). *Liberalism.* New York: Oxford University Press.

Hocart, A. M. (1970). *Kings and Councillors.* Chicago: University of Chicago Press.

Hoebel, E. Adamson (1954). *The Laws of Primitive Man.* Cambridge, MA: Harvard University Press.

Holmes, Oliver Wendell, Jr. (1881). *The Common Law.* Boston: Little, Brown. Reprinted in 1991. Mineola, NY: Dover.

_____ (1897). "The Paths of Law," 10 *Harvard Law Review* 457.

_____ (1899). "A Theory of Interpretation," 12 *Harvard Law Review* 417.

_____ (1918). "Natural Law," 32 *Harvard Law Review* 40.

Holt, Jim (February 1998). "Hypotheses: The Loophole, A Logician Challenges the Constitution," *Lingua Franca,* 92.

Honoré, Ted (1988). "Right to Rebel," 8 *Oxford Journal of Legal Studies* 34.

Howard, Ted and Jeremy Rifkin (1977). *Who Should Play God?* New York: Dell.

Irons, Peter (1988). *The Courage of Their Convictions.* New York: Free Press.

Jacobs, Herbert et al., editors (1996). *Courts, Laws, and Politics in Comparative Perspectives.* New Haven: Yale University Press.

James, William (1910). *Pragmatism.* New York: Longmanns, Green.

James, William (1925). *What Pragmatism Means.* New York: Longmanns, Green.

Jefferson, Thomas (1955). *The Papers of Thomas Jefferson.* Princeton, NJ: Princeton University Press.

Johansen, Bruce E. (1982). *Forgotten Fathers.* Boston: MA: Harvard Common Press.

Jones, Howard (1987). *Mutiny on the Amistad.* New York: Oxford.

Jowett, B., editor (1937). *The Dialogues of Plato.* New York: Random House.

Kant, Immanuel (1797). *The Metaphysical Elements of Justice.* In (1985) John Ladd, translator. New York: Macmillan.

_____ *Critique of Practical Reasoning and Other Writings of Moral Philosophy.* In 1949, Lewis White Beck, translator. Chicago: University of Chicago Press.

Kavanaugh, John P. (1983). "Ethical Issues in Plant Relocation," *Ethical Theory and Business,* second edition. Tom L. Beauchamp and Norman E. Bowie, editors. Englewood Cliffs, NJ: Prentice-Hall.

Kennedy, Duncan (1982). *Legal Education and the Reproduction of Hierarchy.* Cambridge, MA: Afar.

Kennedy, Randall (1988). *"McCleskey v. Kemp:* Race, Capital Punishment and the Supreme Court," 101 *Harvard Law Review* 1388.

Kevles, Daniel J. (1985). *In the Name of Eugenics.* Berkeley, CA: University of California Press.

King, Martin Luther, Jr. (1964). *Why We Can't Wait.* New York: Mentor.

Kornstein, Daniel J. (1994). *Kill All Them Lawyers?* Princeton, NJ: Princeton University Press.

Kritz, Neil J., editor (1995). *Transitional Justice.* Volume 1, Washington, DC: United States Institute of Peace.

Kronman, Anthony (1990). "Precedent and Tradition," 99 *Yale Law Journal* 1029.

Kymlicka, Will (1990). *Contemporary Political Philosophy.* Oxford, England: Clarendon Press.

Kymlicka, Will, editor (1995). *The Rights of Minority Cultures.* New York: Oxford University Press.

Lawson, MackRaneta (1999). *A Layperson's Guide to the Criminal Law.* Westport, CT: Greenwood Press.

Lazarus, Edward (1998). *Closed Chambers.* New York: Random House.

Leff, Arthur Allen (1974). "Economic Analysis of Law: Some Realism about Nominalism," 60 *Virginia Law Review* 451.

Leff, Arthur Allen (1979). "Unspeakable Ethics, Unnatural Law," *Duke Law Journal* 1229.

Levi, Edward. (1949). *An Introduction to Legal Reasoning.* Chicago: University of Chicago Press.

_____ (1965). "The Nature of Judicial Reasoning," 32 *University of Chicago Law Review* 395.

Levinson, Sanford (1985). "On Interpretation: The Adultery Clause of the Ten Commandments," 58 *Southern California Law Review* 719.

Llewellyn, K. N. (1930). *The Bramble Bush.* New York: Oceana.

Low, Peter W. et al. (1986). *The Trial of John W. Hinckley, Jr: A Case Study in the Insanity Defense.* Mineola, NY: Foundation Press.

Lyons, David (1984). *Ethics and the Rule of Law.* New York: Cambridge University Press.

MacCormick, Neil (1981). "Natural Law Reconsidered," 1 *Oxford Journal of Legal Studies* 99.

Machan, Tibor R., editor (1974). *The Libertarian Alternative.* Chicago: Nelson-Hall.

MacIntyre, Alisdair (1984). *Is Patriotism a Virtue? The Lindley Lecture.* Lawrence: Kansas University Press.

MacIntyre, Alasdair (1988). *After Virtue,* second edition. Notre Dame, IN: University of Notre Dame Press.

Marx, Karl (1882). *Rheinische Zeitung,* reprinted in *Karl Marx & Frederich Engels, Collected Works* (1975). New York: International Publishers.

Massey, Stephen J. (1986). "Individual Responsibility for Assisting Nazis in Persecuting Civilians," 71 *Minnesota Law Review* 136.

Matsuda, Mari J. et al., editors (1993). *Words That Wound.* Boulder, CO: Westview Press.

May, Larry and Stacey Hoffman, editors (1991). *Collective Responsibility.* Lanham, MD: Rowman & Littlefield.

McCloskey, H. J. (1965). "A Non-Utilitarian Approach to Punishment," 8 *Inquiry.*

McInnes, Mitchell (1990). "The Question of the Duty to Rescue in Canadian Tort Law," 13 *Dalhousie Law Journal* 85.

Meiklejohn, Alexander (1948). *Free Speech and Its Relation to Self-Government.* New York: Harper & Brothers.

Mill, John Stuart (1956). *On Liberty.* Indianapolis, IN: Bobbs-Merrill.

Miller, Barbara and Lynn Parisi (1992). *Individual Rights in International Perspective.* Boulder, CO: Social Science Education Consortium.

Miller, David, editor (1991). *Liberty.* Oxford, England: Oxford University Press.

Mitchell, E. T. (1937). "Social Ideals and the Law," 46 *The Philosophical Review.*

Montesquieu, Baron de (1748). *Spirit of the Laws* in 1977. Berkeley, CA: University of California Press.

Moore, Michael (1997). *Placing Blame: A General Theory of Criminal Law.* Oxford, England: Clarendon.

Mosley, Albert G. and Nicholas Capaldi (1996). *Affirmative Action.* Lanham, MD: Rowman & Littlefield.

Murphy, Jeffrey G., editor (1985). *Punishment and Rehabilitation.* Belmont, CA: Wadsworth.

Murphy, Jeffrey C. and Jules Coleman (1990). *Philosophy of Law.* Boulder, CO: Westview.

Nagel, Thomas (1973). "Equal Treatment and Compensatory Discrimination," 2 *Philosophy & Public Affairs* 348.

Neier, Aryeh (1998). *War Crimes.* New York: Random House.

Newton, Lisa (1973). "Reverse Discrimination as Unjustified," 83 *Ethics* 308.

Nielsen, Kai (1959). "An Examination of the Thomistic Theory of Natural Moral Law," 4 *Natural Law Forum* 1.

Nietzsche, Friedrich (1882). *The Gay Science.* Walter Kaufmann, translator. New York: Vintage.

_____ (1878) *Human, All-Too-Human.* In 1911, Paul V. Cohen, translator. London: T. N. Foulis.

Northrop, F. S. C. (1959). *The Complexity of Legal and Ethical Experience.* Boston: Little, Brown.

Nozick, Robert (1974). *Anarchy, State, and Utopia.* New York: Basic Books.

Nussbaum, Martha C. (1993). "The Use and Abuse of Philosophy in Legal Education," 45 *Stanford Law Review* 1627.

Oda, Hiroshi (1992). *Japanese Law.* London: Butterworths.

Olafson, Frederick A., editor (1961). *Justice and Social Policy.* Englewood Cliffs, NJ: Prentice Hall.

Olivas, Michael A. (March 29, 1996). "The Decision is Flatly, Unequivocally Wrong," *The Chronicle of Higher Education* B3.

O'Neil, Timothy J. (1974). "Racial Preferences and Higher Education," 60 *Virginia Law Review* 925.

_____ (1985). *Bakke & the Politics of Equality.* Middletown, CT: Wesleyan University Press.

Parenti, Michael (1988). *Democracy for the Few.* New York: St. Martin's Press.

Patterson, Dennis, editor (1996). *A Companion to Philosophy of Law and Legal Theory.* Cambridge, MA: Blackwell.

Pfeffer, Leo (1953). *Church, State, and Freedom.* Boston: Beacon.

Phillips, Anne, editor (1987). *Feminism and Equality.* Oxford, England: Blackwell.

Pincoffs, Edmund L. (1966). *The Rationale of Legal Punishment.* New York: Humanities.

Pitamic, Leonidas (1933). *A Treatise on the State.* Baltimore, MD: J. H. Furst.

Pojman, Louis P., editor (2000). *The Moral Life.* New York: Oxford University Press.

Pollack, J. (1950). *The Criminality of Woman.* Philadelphia, PA: University of Pennsylvania Press.

Pollock, Jocelyn M. (1999). *Criminal Women.* Cincinnati, OH: Anderson.

Popkin, Richard (1967). "Skepticism," *Encyclopedia of Philosophy.* New York: MacMillan, pp. 459–460.

Posner, Richard (1986). "Free Speech in an Economic Perspective," 20 *Suffolk University Law Review* 1.

_____ (1986). *Economic Analyses of Law,* third edition. Boston: Little, Brown.

_____ (1990). *The Problems of Jurisprudence.* Cambridge, MA: Harvard University Press.

_____ (1992a). "Legal Reasoning From the Bottom Up," 59 *University of Chicago Law Review* 444.

_____ editor (1992b). *The Essential Holmes.* Chicago: University of Chicago Press.

Pospisil, Leopold (1970). *Anthropology of Law.* New York: Harper & Row.

Pound, Roscoe (1906). "The Causes of Popular Dissatisfaction with the Administration of Justice," 40 *American Law Review.*

Powell, Lewis (1982). "Carolene Products Revisited," 82 *Columbia Law Review* 1087.

Presser, Stephen B. and Jamil S. Zainaldin, editors (1989). *Law and Jurisprudence in American History,* St. Paul, MN: West.

Preuss, Ulrich K. (1995). *Constitutional Revolution.* Deborah Lucas Schneider, translator. Atlantic Highlands, NJ: Humanities.

Primoratz, Igor (1989). *Justifying Legal Punishment.* Atlantic Highlands, NJ: Humanities.

Purcell, Edward A., Jr. (1973). *The Crisis of Democratic Theory.* Lexington, KY: The University Press of Kentucky.

Rachels, James (1975). "Active and Passive Euthanasia," 2 *The New England Journal of Medicine,* 78.

Rawls, John (1971). *A Theory of Justice.* Cambridge, MA: Belknap Press.

_____ (1985). "Justice as Fairness: Political Not Metaphysical," 14 *Philosophy and Public Affairs* 225.

Ray, Isaac (1838). *A Treatise on the Medical Jurisprudence of Insanity.* Boston: Little, Brown.

Regan, Donald (1979). "Rewriting *Roe v. Wade,*" 77 *Michigan Law Review* 1569.

Reiman, Jeffrey H. (1985). "Justice, Civilization, and the Death Penalty," 14 *Philosophy and Public Affairs* 115.

_____ (1998). *The Rich Get Richer and the Poor Get Prison,* fifth edition. Boston: Allyn and Bacon.

Reiss, Hans, editor (1991). *Kant, Political Writings.* New York: Cambridge University Press.

Rhodes, Robert E., Jr. and Howard Pospesel (1997). *Premises and Conclusions: Symbolic Logic for Legal Analysis.* Upper Saddle River, NJ: Prentice Hall.

Riesman, David (1942). "Democracy and Defamation: Control of Group Libel," 42 *Columbia Law Review.*

Robbins, Sara (1990). *Law: A Treasury of Art and Literature.* New York: Harkavy.

Robinson, Paul H. (1975). "A Theory of Justification: Societal Harm as a Prerequisite for Criminal Liability," 23 *UCLA Law Review* 266.

Rose, Steven, Leon J. Kamin, and R. C. Lewontin (1984). *Not In Our Genes.* New York: Penguin.

Rousseau, Jean Jacques (1762) *On the Social Contract.* In 1954, Willmoore Kendall, translator. Chicago: Henry Regnery.

Rubenfield, Jeb (1991). "On the Legal Status of the Proposition that 'Life Begins at Conception,'" 43 *Stanford Law Review* 623.

Russell, Bertrand (1959). *The Problems of Philosophy.* New York: Oxford University Press.

Ryan, Alan, editor (1979). *The Idea of Freedom.* New York: Oxford University Press.

Sandel, Michael J. (1982). *Liberalism and the Limits of Justice.* New York: Cambridge University Press.

_____ editor (1984). *Liberalism and Its Critics.* New York: New York University Press.

Scanlon, Thomas (1979). "Freedom of Expression and Categories of Expression," 40 *University of Pittsburgh Law Review* 519.

Schall, James V. (1998). *Jacques Maritain.* Lanham, MD: Rowman & Littlefield.

Schauer, Frederick (1982). *Free Speech: A Philosophical Inquiry.* New York: Cambridge University Press.

_____ (1987). "Precedent," 39 *Stanford Law Review* 571.

_____ (1989). "Formalism," 97 *Yale Law Journal* 509.

Schlessinger, Rudolf B. et al., editors (1998). *Comparative Law.* New York: Foundation.

Schulhofer (1974). "Harm and Punishment: A Critique on the Emphasis on the Results of Conduct in Criminal Law," 122 *University of Pennsylvania Law Review* 1497.

Schwartz, Bernard (1997). *Book of Legal Lists.* New York: Oxford University Press.

Sheffer, Martin S. (1999). *God versus Caesar.* Albany, NY: State University of New York Press.

Shiel, Timothy C. (1998). *Campus Hate Speech on Trial.* Lawrence, KS: University Press of Kansas.

Shute, Stephen and Susan Hurley, editors (1993). *On Human Rights.* New York: Basic Books.

Sigmund, Paul E., editor (1988). *St. Thomas Aquinas on Politics and Ethics.* New York: W. W. Norton.

Simmons, A. John, Marshall Cohen, Joshua Cohen, and Charles R. Beitz, editors (1995). *Punishment.* Princeton, NJ: Princeton University Press.

Soper, Philip (1992). "Some Natural Confusions about Natural Law," 90 *Michigan Law Review* 2393.

Sprigge, T. L. S. (1965). "A Utilitarian Reply to Dr. McCloskey," 8 *Inquiry.*

Sterba, James P., editor (1992). *Justice.* Belmont, CA: Wadsworth.

Stolzenberg, Boami Maya (1993). " 'He Drew a Circle That Shut Me Out': Assimilation, Indoctrination, and the Paradox of a Liberal Education," 106 *Harvard Law Review* 3.

Suber, Peter (1998). *The Case of the Speluncean Explorers.* New York: Routledge.

Tesón, Fernando R. (1998). *A Philosophy of International Law.* Boulder, CO: Westview.

Thompson, Judith Jarvis (1971). "A Defense of Abortion," 1 *Philosophy & Public Affairs* 47.

_____ (1986). *Rights, Restitution, and Risk.* Cambridge, MA: Harvard University Press.

Tocqueville, Alexis de (1956). *Democracy in America* (1835, 1840). Richard D. Hefner, editor. New York: Mentor.

Treach, Peter Read (1989). "Lapse of Judgment," 77 *California Law Review* 1259.

Tribe, Laurence (1988). *American Constitutional Law,* second edition. Mineola, NY: Foundation.

Tushnet, Mark (1984). "An Essay on Rights," 62 *Texas Law Review,* 1364.

Van den Haag, Ernest (March 31, 1978). "The Collapse of the Case Against the Death Penalty," *National Review* 31.

Walker, Samuel (1994). *Hate Speech.* Lincoln, NE: University of Nebraska Press.

Wasserstrom, Richard A. (1963). "The Obligation to Obey the Law," 10 *UCLA Law Review* 780.

Watson, Patrick and Benjamin Barber (1988). *The Struggle for Democracy.* Toronto: Lester & Orpen Dennys.

White, G. Edward (1988). *The American Judicial Tradition.* New York: Oxford University Press.

Wigmore, John H. (1935). *A Student's Textbook of the Law of Evidence.* Chicago: University of Chicago Press.

Williams, Patricia J. (1991). *Alchemy of Race and Rights.* Cambridge, MA: Harvard University Press.

_____ (March 9, 1998). "The Slough of Despond," *The Nation*, p. 10.

Woo, Deborah (1989). *"People v. Fumiko Kimura:* But Which People?" 17 *International Journal of the Sociology of Law.*

Wood, Gordon S. (1967). *The Creation of the American Republic, 1776–1787.* New York: W. W. Norton.

Wootton, Barbara (1963). *Crime and Criminal Law.* London: Sweet & Maxwell.

Wright, R. George, editor (1992). *Legal and Political Obligations.* Lanham, MD: University Press of America.

Wyzanski, Charles E., Jr. (April 1946). "Nuremberg: A Fair Trial?" 177 *Atlantic Monthly,* pp. 66–70.

Zinn, Howard (1995). *A People's History of the United States.* New York: Harper Collins.

Index

509